ABOUT TIME

THE UNAUTHORIZED GUIDE TO
DOCTOR WHO

2008-2009

SERIES 4, THE 2009 SPECIALS

TAT WOOD & DOROTHY AIL

Also available from Mad Norwegian Press...

AHistory: An Unauthorized History of the Doctor Who Universe [4th Edition, Volumes 1, 2 and 3]
by Lance Parkin and Lars Pearson

*Unhistory: Apocryphal Stories Too Strange for even AHistory: An Unauthorised History
of the Doctor Who Universe* (ebook-only supplement) by Lance Parkin and Lars Pearson

*Running Through Corridors: Rob and Toby's Marathon Watch
of Doctor Who* (Vol. 1: The 60s, Vol. 2: The 70s) by Robert Shearman and Toby Hadoke

Space Helmet for a Cow: An Unlikely 50-Year History of Doctor Who
by Paul Kirkley (Vol. 1: 1963-1989, Vol. 2: 1990-2013)

Wanting to Believe: A Critical Guide to The X-Files, Millennium and the Lone Gunmen
by Robert Shearman

The About Time Series by Tat Wood and Lawrence Miles
- *About Time 1: The Unauthorized Guide to Doctor Who* (Seasons 1 to 3)
- *About Time 2: The Unauthorized Guide to Doctor Who* (Seasons 4 to 6)
- *About Time 3: The Unauthorized Guide to Doctor Who* (Seasons 7 to 11) [2nd Ed]
- *About Time 4: The Unauthorized Guide to Doctor Who* (Seasons 12 to 17) [2nd Ed forthcoming]
- *About Time 5: The Unauthorized Guide to Doctor Who* (Seasons 18 to 21)
- *About Time 6: The Unauthorized Guide to Doctor Who* (Seasons 22 to 26)
- *About Time 7: The Unauthorized Guide to Doctor Who* (Series 1 to 2)
- *About Time 8: The Unauthorized Guide to Doctor Who* (Series 3)
- *About Time 9: The Unauthorized Guide to Doctor Who* (Series 4, the 2009 Specials)

Essay Collections
- *Chicks Dig Comics: A Celebration of Comic Books by the Women Who Love Them*
- *Chicks Dig Gaming: A Celebration of All Things Gaming by the Women Who Love It*
- *Chicks Dig Time Lords: A Celebration of Doctor Who by the Women Who Love It*,
2011 Hugo Award Winner, Best Related Work
- *Chicks Unravel Time: Women Journey Through Every Season of Doctor Who*
- *Companion Piece: Women Celebrate the Humans, Aliens and Tin Dogs of Doctor Who*
- *Queers Dig Time Lords: A Celebration of Doctor Who by the LGBTQ Fans Who Love It*
- *Whedonistas: A Celebration of the Worlds of Joss Whedon by the Women Who Love Them*

Guidebooks
- *I, Who: The Unauthorized Guide to the Doctor Who Novels and Audios*
by Lars Pearson (vols. 1-3, ebooks only)
- *Dusted: The Unauthorized Guide to Buffy the Vampire Slayer*
by Lawrence Miles, Pearson and Christa Dickson (ebook only)
- *Redeemed: The Unauthorized Guide to Angel* by Pearson and Christa Dickson

Published by Mad Norwegian Press (www.madnorwegian.com).
Copyright © 2019 Tat Wood and Dorothy Ail.
Content Editor: Lars Pearson.
Cover art: Jim Calafiore. Cover colors: Richard Martinez.
Jacket & interior design: Christa Dickson.
ISBN: 978-1935234203. Printed in Illinois. First Edition: March 2019

table of contents

Essays

how does this book work?

About Time prides itself on being the most comprehensive, wide-ranging and at times almost *unnervingly* detailed handbook to *Doctor Who* that you might ever conceivably need, so great pains have been taken to make sure there's a place for everything and everything's in its place. Here are the "rules"…

Every *Doctor Who* story (or, since 2005's relaunch, episode) gets its own entry, and every entry is divided up into four major sections. The first, which includes the headings **Which One is This?**, **Firsts and Lasts** and **Watch Out For…**, is designed to provide an overview of the story for newcomers to the series or relatively "lightweight" fans who aren't too clued-up on a particular era of the programme's history. We might like to *pretend* that all *Doctor Who* viewers know all parts of the series equally well, but there are an awful lot of people who – for example – know the 70s episodes by heart and don't have a clue about the 80s or 60s. This section also acts as an overall Spotters' Guide to the series, pointing out most of the memorable bits.

After that comes the **Continuity** section, which is where you'll find all the pedantic detail. Here there are notes on the Doctor (personality, props and cryptic mentions of his past), the supporting cast, the TARDIS and any major characters who might happen to wander into the story. Following these are **The Non-Humans**, which can best be described as "high geekery"… we're old enough to remember the *Doctor Who Monster Book*, but not too old to want a more grown-up version of our own, so expect full-length monster profiles.

Next is **History**, for stories set on Earth, and **Planet Notes** otherwise – or sometimes vice versa if it's a messed-up Earth or a planet we've seen before. Within these, *Dating* is our best-guess on available data for when a story happens. Also, given its prominence in the new series, we've added a section on *The Time War*.

To help us with the *Dating*, we may have recourse to **Additional Sources**: facts and factoids not in broadcast *Doctor Who* but nonetheless reliable, such as the DVD commentaries, *The Sarah Jane Adventures*, *Torchwood* or cut scenes.

Of crucial importance: note that throughout the **Continuity** section, *everything* you read is "true" – i.e. based on what's said or seen on-screen – except for sentences in square brackets [like this], where we cross-reference the data to other stories and make some suggestions as to how all of this is supposed to fit together. You can trust us absolutely on the non-bracketed material, but the bracketed sentences are often just speculation. (Another thing to notice here: anything written in single inverted commas – 'like this' – is a word-for-word quote from the script or something printed on screen, whereas anything in double-quote marks "like this" isn't.)

The third main section is **Analysis**, which comprises anything you might need to know to watch the episode the same way that anyone on the first night, sat in front of BBC1 on a Saturday teatime (or whenever), would have; the assumed background knowledge. Some of this is current issues or concerns – part of the "plucked from today's headlines" appeal of *Doctor Who* right from the power-politics over new technology in the very first story (1.1, "An Unearthly Child") – some of it is more nuanced. Overseas or younger viewers might not be aware of the significance of details that don't get flagged up overtly as worth knowing, such as the track-record of a particular performer and what that brings to the episode, or what a mention of a specific district of London would mean to UK viewers. These are your crib-notes.

The Big Picture handles the politics, social issues and suchlike occupying the minds of the authors. Many *Doctor Who* fans know that 15.4, "The Sun Makers" was supposed to be satirical, but even an apparently throwaway piece of fluff such as 17.1, "Destiny of the Daleks" has a weight of real-world concerns behind it. New for this volume, **English Lessons** (and sometimes **Welsh Lessons**) tackles the allusions and vocabulary that BBC1 viewers all have at their fingertips and all the nuances underlying apparently innocent remarks. More than ever before, the **Oh, Isn't That…?** listing will tell you why what might seem an innocuous piece of casting means more to us first-nighters than to anyone else.

Up next is **Things That Don't Make Sense**, which in this volume continues to cover plot-

how does this book work ?

logic, anachronisms, science-idiocy, characters' apparent amnesia about earlier stories or incidents and other stupid lapses, but rarely the production flaws or the naff effects and sets for which the series was hitherto notorious. Finally, for this section, **Critique** is as fair-minded a review as we can muster; when necessary, this has required a bipartisan approach with *Prosecution* and *Defence*.

The final section, **The Facts**, covers cast, transmission dates and ratings, overseas translations, edits and what we've now taken to calling **Production**: the behind-the-scenes details that are often so well-known by hardened fans as to have the status of family history. We try to include at least one detail never before made public, although these days finding anything nobody's said to any of the dozens of interviewers hanging around Cardiff is increasingly hard, unless you get into outright gossip or somehow manage to crack BBC Wales' occasionally impenetrable news-management arrangements.

A lot of "issues" relating to the series are so big that they need forums all to themselves, which is why most story entries are followed by mini-essays. Here we've tried to answer all the questions that seem to demand answers, although the logic of these essays changes from case to case. Some of them are actually trying to find *definitive* answers, unravelling what's said in the TV stories and making sense of what the programme-makers had in mind. Some have more to do with the real world than the *Doctor Who* universe, and aim to explain why certain things about the series were so important at the time. Some are purely speculative, some delve into scientific theory and some are just whims, but they're *good* whims and they all seem to have a place here. Occasionally we've included endnotes on the names and events we've cited, for those who aren't old enough or British enough to follow all the references.

We should also mention the idea of "canon" here. Anybody who knows *Doctor Who* well, who's been exposed to the TV series, the novels, the comic-strips, the audio adventures and the trading-cards you used to get with Sky Ray ice-lollies will know that there's always been some doubt about how much of *Doctor Who* counts as "real", as if the TV stories are in some way less made-up than the books or the short stories. We devoted a thumping great chunk of Volume 6 to

this topic, but for now it's enough to say that *About Time* has its own specific rules about what's canonical and what isn't. In this book, we accept everything that's shown in the TV series to be the "truth" about the *Doctor Who* universe (although obviously we have to gloss over the parts where the actors fluff their lines). Those non-TV stories which have made a serious attempt to become part of the canon, from Virgin Publishing's New Adventures to the audio adventures from Big Finish, aren't considered to be 100 percent "true", but do count as supporting evidence. Here they're treated as what historians call "secondary sources", not definitive enough to make us change our whole view of the way the *Doctor Who* universe works, but helpful pointers if we're trying to solve any particularly fiddly continuity problems.

It's worth remembering that unlike (say) the stories written for the old *Dalek* annuals, the early Virgin novels were an honest attempt to carry on the *Doctor Who* tradition in the absence of the TV series, so it seems fair to use them to fill the gaps in the programme's folklore even if they're not exactly – so to speak – "fact".

You'll also notice that we've divided up *About Time* according to "era", not according to Doctor. Since we're trying to tell the *story* of the series, both on- and off-screen, this makes sense. The actor playing the Main Man might be the only thing we care about when we're too young to know better, but anyone who's watched the episodes with hindsight will know that there's a vastly bigger stylistic leap between "The Horns of Nimon" and "The Leisure Hive" than there is between "Logopolis" and "Castrovalva". Volume 4 covers the producerships of Philip Hinchcliffe and Graham Williams, two very distinct stories in themselves, and everything changes again – when Williams leaves the series, not when Tom Baker does – at the start of the 1980s. With Volume 7, the amount of material has necessitated that the remainder of the Russell T Davies era was covered in Volume 8 and here in Volume 9.

There's a kind of logic here, just as there's a kind of logic to everything in this book. There's so much to *Doctor Who*, so much material to cover and so many ways to approach it, that there's a risk of our methods irritating our audience even if all the information's in the right places. So we need to be consistent, and we have been. As a

result, we're confident that this is as solid a reference guide / critical study / monster book as you'll
ever find. In the end, we hope you'll agree that the
only realistic criticism is: "Haven't you told us *too*
much here?"

series 4

X4.1: "Partners in Crime"

(5th April, 2008)

Which One is This? The French title for this is *Le Retour de Donna Noble*, the main point of the whole 48 minutes. The blobbly stress-ball-ish Adipose fill the streets of London (well, one street, and it's Cardiff really). They look like miniature Yeti (5.2, "The Abominable Snowmen" et seq.) and, appropriately, we first see one in someone's loo. For the benefit of anyone who didn't already know what the word "Adipose" means, the script rather spells it out.

Firsts and Lasts It's the start of the 21-month Series 4. Donna Noble becomes a full-time companion (See X3.0, "The Runaway Bride", if you haven't already.) She comes complete with more literal baggage than we've ever seen anyone bring on the Ship.

Talking of baggage, this is the start of companions coming with Deep Mysteries, meaning many plot-points hinge on the apparently-normal Earth-women having some kind of messed-up alien influence that will profoundly intertwine them into the Doctor's past and future. It was attempted with Ace (see Volume 6) and the BBC Books landed up ridiculing the cookie-cutter all-purpose companion Sam Jones as being part of an alien plot (see also X4.15, "Planet of the Dead"), but now it comes fitted-as-standard. We don't have the Doctor popping back into Donna's childhood (as Steven Moffat isn't in charge yet), but both she and her grandad will turn out to have manipulative super-beings stage-managing coincidences.

This story makes it clear that the Shadow Proclamation is an organisation, rather than just someone (Lamont Cranston? Hank Marvin?) proclaiming something. For this series, the BBC also completely rejigged their website, including adding pieces of concept art and storyboards, and changing the colour from a restful green-blue to hyperactive red and gold.

Watch Out For...
• This season's catch-all theme (well, one of them; it's a pile-up of Big Bad clues this year) is planets going missing, so pay attention to why the

Series 4 Cast/Crew

• David Tennant (the Doctor)
• Catherine Tate (Donna Noble)

• Russell T Davies (executive producer)

Adipose shape their children from human fat in the first place. There's also a running-gag about the bees going missing. This is a real-world concern, but *Doctor Who* uses a terrifying enviro-crisis as a plot-coupon.

• A poignant period detail: Sylvia tells Donna "It's not like the 80s. Nobody's unemployed these days." However, *real* poignancy comes when you see the DVD extras, and the scenes they recorded before it became obvious that actor Howard Attfield was too ill to continue as Donna's father.

• As we'll see in **The Big Picture**, the name of *The Observer* science correspondent (Penny Carter) is another piece of RTD name-recycling. The character's treatment – caught snooping, then repeatedly tied to a chair – is what most people in Britain would like to see happen to more journalists. (However, if the way she's tied up looks a bit odd, it's because Verona Joseph at the time was six months pregnant.)

• Donna, missing her deceased father, pops up to the allotment to see her grandad (he gets all of her dad's scripted dialogue). And... oh look! It's that cheerful newspaper-vendor from "Voyage of the Damned" (X4.0), again played by Bernard Cribbins. He doesn't bump into the Doctor this time, though (never fear, you'll have the gag later in the season).

• ... indeed, Donna doesn't either for half the episode, despite some cleverly-choreographed near-misses. The episode hinges on them finally stumbling across each other at the worst possible time and their attempted communication being interrupted. It's what the "I'll save you" scene from "42" (X3.7) would have been like in real life.

• The climax makes the alien menace endearing and individualised and is possibly the only time you will see visual references to *Close Encounters of the Third Kind*, the 1991 Milk Marketing Board adverts and *Evita* rubbing up against each other. The Mill's software, called "Massive", allowed each individual Adipose to move quasi-independently in the crowd-scenes. (If you rewatch the same few scenes over and over, you might spot a degree of doubling-up in small patches within the same shot.) One does a little dance, another jumps for joy when on board the Mothership. There's also a nasty squelch as a taxi drives over one. The taxis, if you look, each have a window-sticker saying "ATMOS", which will become significant in a few episodes from now.

• There's an unannounced cameo towards the end. This wasn't in the version shown to the press (see below for full details).

The Continuity

The Doctor He shows up to investigate the presence of alien technology and knows Adipose Industries is at the centre of it. He's embarrassed when a woman gives him her phone number. Companionless, he starts explaining a technical issue to himself in the TARDIS, then stops. Donna's reappearance boggles him, and apparently charades isn't this iteration's strong point. To Donna's eyes, he looks older than the last time they met ["The Runaway Bride"].

He accepts Donna as a travelling companion, but only after – following on from the Martha disaster ('it got complicated, and that was all my fault', he admits) – he lays the ground rule that he's just looking for a mate. He's so used to the "bigger on the inside" spiel, he starts saying it to someone who doesn't need it.

• *Background.* Until now, he apparently has no idea what happens when identical sonic devices are held against each other [see *Inventory*]. While examining a catflap, he can't resist a deadpan about not being a cat person [X2.1, "New Earth"; X3.3, "Gridlock" and also 26.4, "Survival"].

• *Ethics.* He's offended by the principle of using unwitting human beings to breed Adipose, regardless of whether they're harmful. He therefore issues Matron his now-standard this-is-your-one-chance formulation, but tries to save her after hearing the Adipose parents' plans to kill her.

• *Inventory: Sonic Screwdriver:* It can lock doors from ten feet away through glass, or activate a window cleaner's cradle. Somehow, it can generate a 'sonic cage' which limits access to anyone with another sonic device. While unlocking a fire door, it looks and sounds like a small blue firecracker going off. When the Doctor's sonic screwdriver

and Miss Foster's sonic pen are held against each other, the feedback loop creates an ungodly sound that half-paralyses everyone in the room. Miss Foster's sonic pen also gives off a blue light [um, perhaps that's characteristic of sonic devices].

• *Inventory: Psychic Paper.* It identifies the Doctor as a Health and Safety inspector, under the name John Smith [it gets sillier when he passes himself off as 'Health and Safety... film department']. It also convinces an Adipose client that he's a representative of the company.

• *Inventory: Other.* He's rigged up a device that alerts him to an Adipose birth – it looks like three kitchen utensils stuck together in a trefoil, with a light that goes on in the middle, rather like a restaurant beeper. [The BBC website notes it's been contrived out of a watch, safety pin, rubber band, and other bits and bobs.] As scripted, he has to plug the sonic screwdriver into this device to call the Shadow Proclamation [suggesting he had a good idea all along that the planetary quarantine had been transgressed]. He's disappointed that Adipose Industries don't have free pens.

Something resembling an ordinary stethoscope lets him eavesdrop through unbreakable plate glass [we'll see it several more times this season]. He throws Miss Foster's sonic pen into a bin.

The TARDIS The Doctor obligingly flies the Ship past the stargazing hill of Donna's grandfather, then holds it in mid-air while she waves to him, then it swoops upwards into space.

Donna thinks that the Ship's heating should be turned up a notch. [Those raised on the 70s Target books have come to half-accept that Time Lords have a lower body-temperature, as stated by the Master in *Doctor Who and the Sea Devils*. You can use this as supporting evidence if you really want – but shouldn't it be the other way around?]

The Supporting Cast
• *Donna Noble.* [X4.13, "Journey's End" will try to make sense of the notion that Dalek Caan manipulated events to bring the Doctor and Donna together, as part of his scheme to instigate a human-Time Lord metacrisis and overthrow the Daleks. Both here and there, though, it's hard to see exactly what he might have usefully changed and how he went about it. The Doctor and Donna meeting again *isn't* coincidence, since she's been deliberately investigating spots of alleged weirdness to find him (not a bad strategy). Even her

How Does This Play in Pyongyang?

The recent surge of interest in lost black and white episodes alerted non-fans to the fact that exporting *Doctor Who* didn't start with BBC Wales. Rumours of a South Korean link in the "bicycle chain" (film copies leaving one territory for another, like pass-the-parcel) were being investigated, sparked by BBC documentation which simply said "Korea". South Korea had the series from 1978 – part of the third major phase in the overseas export-drive for this and other BBC series. The Foreign and Commonwealth Office has recently been sending British media to North Korea, notably the seemingly-irresistible *Sherlock* (or "Curly Fu" as it's called in China). Nobody in North Korea, as far as we've been able to find out, has legally watched *Doctor Who*. Indeed, in line with Beijing's edicts on dramas about time travel being unwholesome and therefore not to be broadcast on Chinese state television (although this doesn't stop people showing *Doctor Who* and running conventions), plus North Korea's tendency to be more hardline than their neighbours when possible, it's unlikely that anyone would risk being caught streaming it.

Doctor Who was always available to be bought. Sydney Newman, the BBC mogul who caused the series (if not, effectively, its sole "creator"), ensured that all episodes were telerecorded (a laborious process of pointing a 16mm camera at a superior-grade PAL monitor; the US term is "kinescope"). BBC Enterprises, a subdivision of the corporation with responsibility for distributing programmes elsewhere, monitoring commercial exploitation and securing co-production money for big projects, took care to offer the programme to other broadcasters – within set terms. The six copies of each episode they usually run off were each sold for a finite number of showings (thus on 16mm film rather than any of the many video systems in use, as almost all services had telecine) and the contracts stipulated precisely what was to happen to the film copies afterwards (see **What were the BBC Thinking?** under 3.1, "Galaxy Four").

Anyone who's seen episode six of 2.5, "The Web Planet" dubbed into Spanish (and if you haven't you ought, although not while on medication) or 2.6, "The Crusades" in Arabic (!) will be dimly aware of this, but the extent is sometimes hard to get a handle on. The recent developments in the archive-quest have got armchair detectives and online commentators exercised, and it has emerged (not least through *Wiped!*, Richard Molesworth's comprehensive book on this topic)

that the Chinese national network was one of the first to express an interest in purchasing "Marco Polo" (1.4). The stories with spaceships and monsters sold slightly better (which is why more copies of them did the rounds) and were returned to London rather later (which is why the historical stories are less well-represented in the archives now).

The rediscovery of significant amounts of Troughton in Nigeria exercised some portions of the media to wonder why old episodes would be *there*, but even in this phase of the programme's relative youth, the distribution of BBC television worldwide was routine. It was one of a number of popular shows, alongside *It's Lulu!*, *The Forsyte Saga* and *Hancock's Half Hour* that were less trouble to buy ready-made, with production techniques, performers and costumes that local producers couldn't match, than remake from a copyrighted format. (That said, there was a Finnish remake of *Hancock's Half Hour* called *Kaverukset*. "What a diabolical liberty," to quote the original.) However stagey it may look *now*, 1960s-style *Doctor Who* was not readily amenable to being made by any television company lacking even rudimentary video-recording, not to mention a ready supply of appropriate period costumes and sets. While it's fun to imagine "what-if" scenarios of a 60s American attempt to purchase the series format, as they did for *Steptoe and Son, Man About the House* or *Till Death Us Do Part* among many others, nobody ever seems to have done so. (Unless you count Ireland's bizarre *Fortycoats*.)

New Zealand started the ball rolling in 1964, then Canada the following year (CBC then gave up after Season One and didn't pick it up until Eccleston, whereupon they chipped in to make the next couple of years but skipped the Specials after X3.13, "Last of the Time Lords"). Australia's loyal ABC began at roughly the same time and continued well into the 80s, even co-funding "The Five Doctors" (20.7). BBC Enterprises then began distributing the redubbed versions. South America got Spanish versions, starting with Venezuela in 1967, Mexico 68 (appropriately) and Chile in 69. Most of the voices are, on the strength of that one episode we have access to, fairly accurately copied, but the Doctor gets the same gravelly voice as announces *Doctorrrrr Mysterio!* as if Hartnell's Doctor were entering Lucha Libre. (Maybe he was – see 2.4, "The Romans" and his onesie in 2.7, "The

continued on Page 11...

9

ABOUT TIME 2008-2009

parking her car by the TARDIS isn't *so* unlikely, since they're both headed to the same building. Nor is her grandad being the guy who shook his fist at the *Titanic* in "Voyage of the Damned" anything worth raising an eyebrow over.]

She finally "gets" the Big Picture the Doctor mentioned when last they met, and so she's been looking for him for quite some time. She thinks the *Titanic* incident was a hoax, but she's otherwise been investigating everything from UFO sightings to crop circles to sea monsters, even disappearing bees.

In the meantime, she tried a trip to Egypt and was disappointed by her inability to break out of "tourist mode". It was 'all bus trips and guide books and don't drink the water'. [See X4.10, "Midnight"; X4.16, "The Waters of Mars". And let's be generous and assume that, as part of her plan to join the Doctor on his travels, Donna has been working out – her ability to hang on to the spar with no other support is impressive, even allowing for adrenalin.]

As a child, Donna vanished one day without telling anyone, panicking everyone in her family. It turned out she'd wandered to Strathclyde. She asks Wilf 'permission to board ship' as if he were an old sailor [he was in a parachute regiment: "Voyage of the Damned"].

Her employment has been irregular as of late and she's moved back to live with her mum. [Some of the language is a little confusing as to where Donna was living before "The Runaway Bride".] She shares a blue Toyota Yaris with Sylvia and can drive it reasonably well [see, of course, X4.11, "Turn Left"]. As part of her cover for infiltrating Adipose Industries, she landed a job with the Health and Safety Executive. She quit after two days, but somehow kept the ID. [Presuming, of course, that Donna hasn't faked the ID and given the Health and Safety story to her mum, but the Adipose receptionist seems convinced.] When Donna bluffs that she's gone to church, her mum is bewildered, Wilf is concerned.

While clinging onto a spar of metal several dozen stories above ground, she screams at the Doctor that it's all his fault and she should have stayed home. [We'll see this characterisation again. She seems to enjoy travelling with the Doctor, but gets stroppy if anything goes wrong.]

As part of her plan to rejoin the Doctor, Donna has packed up all the possessions she wants to bring in the boot of her mum's car: hot-weather clothing, cold-weather clothing, any number of bags and a hat box, in case they go to the Planet of the Hats.

She seems grossed out upon thinking the Doctor is using the word 'mate' as verb rather than noun, but nevertheless feels quite comfortable hugging him.

In none of her investigations has she come across a picture of Rose Tyler [possibly owing to the Bad Wolf virus; see X2.10, "Love & Monsters"].

• *Sylvia Noble.* Not noticeably more pleasant than the first time we saw her. She scathes her daughter for being unemployed and impractical; for her part, Donna takes it all in stoic silence. After the botched wedding ["The Runaway Bride"], Donna came back temporarily. It's been at least a year since then.

Sylvia sometimes treats her father as a naughty child. It turns out she has some friends of her own, the Wednesday Group.

• *Wilfred Mott.* By sheer coincidence [sort of – see the miasma concerning Dalek Caan's manipulations in X4.13, "Journey's End"], it turns out that the cheery Monarchist, alien-fearing insomniac in "Voyage of the Damned" is actually Donna's granddad. His hat bears the badge of his Parachute Regiment [see X4.17, "The End of Time Part One"]. There's a hill close to their house where he likes to stargaze every night; he stoutly affirms to Donna that aliens exist. When Donna's not around, he whiles away his watches listening to music [Gene Pitney in the script, Dusty Springfield on the soundtrack, "24 Hours from Tulsa" in either case].

He and Donna share an easy, comfortable camaraderie, but they skirt around some difficult subjects. She still hasn't told him about her Christmas, and he refers to 'whatsisname Lance'. Seeing his granddaughter waving down from an alien spaceship utterly delights him; he waves back and does an endearingly enthusiastic happy-dance and a piercing whistle.

• *Rose Tyler.* Donna asks a seemingly random woman in the street to pass a message on to Sylvia... whereupon Rose nods and continues staring moodily off in the distance. Then she softly and suddenly fades away.

• *The Shadow Proclamation.* They seem to enforce intergalactic law concerning less-developed worlds such as Earth.

How Does This Play in Pyongyang?

continued from Page 9...

Space Museum".) When Peter Capaldi was launched as the new Doctor on a global tour, he was addressed as this and asked if the name could somehow be used in the English-language original, hence X10.0, "The Return of Doctor Mysterio". At its peak, the series was shown in as many countries as have taken it in the Moffat years, something easily overlooked in the fanfare over the series's new incarnation as a "mega-brand" (the BBC's word, not ours).

Doctor Who differs from most of the popular dramas and Light Entertainment shows being distributed by the Corporation, in that the sales pitch seems to have affected the content, most noticeably once Innes Lloyd took over as producer in early 1966. (Just a reminder for newcomers: not all television made in Britain is BBC and for most of the last 60 years the commercial body, ITV, was a loose amalgamation of smaller stations.) Telerecordings of *The Avengers* in its Cathy Gale years were proving popular in America – to the extent that production moved to all-film thereafter – and Lew Grade's ITC were making things explicitly for export even before there *was* an ITV on which to show them to the ostensible original market. (The full story of this would have to start with Hannah Weinstein's company Sapphire Films and the concatenation of a US flour manufacturer and a disused film studio in Richmond.)

Lloyd consciously mimicked many of the features of these series, not least the contemporary London settings, internationally-accented casts and action set-pieces. The programme's erstwhile trademark villains, the Daleks, had been removed because their copyright-claiming creator was trying to pitch a series to American producers (3.4, "The Daleks' Master Plan" has more on the abortive *U.N.C.L.E.* connection), which made everyone think that the biggest untapped market was theirs for the asking. Watch the introduction to "The Tomb of the Cybermen" (5.1) where they go onto film to make the TARDIS set as big as possible and laboriously re-introduce the programme's core concepts – as if anyone watching in Britain, 1967, didn't know all of this already – before re-introducing the series's newly-promoted chief baddies.

To be fair, the ratings slide in Britain wasn't just because of these changes. Nonetheless, this was only the first time that anticipating what overseas viewers might want in a British-made space-time family adventure serial (that American or German series competing for international sales can't or wouldn't think to attempt) influenced the content. (Accounting for the otherwise pointless Bill Filer in 8.3, "The Claws of Axos" is hard without thinking of how long that story's gestation had been and what people were thinking when it was first commissioned.)

Whilst British screens had been filled with imported film series – many of them deeply strange – making drama all on film was unusual, if not unheard-of, for BBC productions. The Children's department of the BBC had made a few film serials (notably *Man Dog* and *The Changes*), and there were a couple made for schools, but only ITC had been doing it in significant quantities with an eye for foreign markets. (A very domestic and parochial 60s cop-show, *Gideon's Way*, had an episode entitled "Subway to Revenge"... even though it was about people being pushed under Tube trains, and was manifestly filmed on the London Underground or studio mock-ups with accurate insignia and layouts. A "subway" in Britain is a pedestrian underpass.) The BBC's last attempt had been the underwhelming Michel Rennie vehicle *The Third Man* in 1963.

After 1974, Euston Films, a division of Thames Television, made film series explicitly and aggressively for the domestic market. Their big hits, *The Sweeney* (the very name being cockney rhyming-slang), *Minder* (see Volumes 5 and 6), *Widows* and *Danger: UXB* were made to look cinematic, but made fewer concessions to non-British viewers (although they flogged *The Sweeney* to 50-odd countries). As we'll see in **What Difference Did Field-Removed Video Make?** under X4.15, "Planet of the Dead", before international standards for recorded images were in place, 16mm or 35mm telecine was as important as being in English for cracking America – and redubbing film into French, German or Arabic was significantly less fiddly than messing with the sound signal on videotape. BBC's black-and-white output had been relatively easy to transfer to film but, once 625-line PAL colour became standard, things had to change. There was a brief notion of using the accidental all-film production of "Spearhead from Space" (7.1) as a template for further productions, but the producer was transferred to other duties and they were giddy with the possibilities of CSO, a video-only technique, so it died on the vine. There were problems converting British VT to

continued on Page 13...

UNIT/Torchwood There's no sign of them. [That might seem strange on paper, but Adipose Industries isn't doing anything genuinely dangerous until the Doctor shows up and threatens them. Indeed, if a million people are on this treatment and only *one* goes into uncontrolled parthenogenesis beforehand, it has a much lower failure rate than any human medical treatments. Nonetheless, conspiracy-theory websites have commented upon Adipose Industries, so they might be in Torchwood's "Mostly Harmless" file.]

The Non-Humans

• *Adipose.* [Let's cut Davies and company some slack, and assume that using human surrogates to incubate Adipose entails some genetic transfer, which is why the baby Adipose end up as bipeds with faces and hands, much like us, when they emerge from a human. Otherwise, we'd have to ask why Foster didn't consider using other species (cattle? Vocci?) as hosts before deciding to trick humans, in violation of galactic law.]

Their breeding planet has mysteriously vanished. [See X4.12, "The Stolen Earth" for why.] Their technology involves items the Doctor dubs a bioflip digital-stitch; each gold capsule adapts itself to the customer, and while they sleep a kilogram worth of fat congeals into an Adipose and runs away, once per night for an unspecified period. [Miss Foster's sales-pitch includes the idea of a 'mobilising lipase', which sounds dead scientific but could only be *part* of the process even if true.] The main engine for this is the Inducer, a tremendous computer core installed in the Adipose building; it's protected by triple deadlocks and has a setting for 'Levitation Post', so all the baby Adipose can float up to the nursery ship. The Inducer activates the pendants given to all customers, and relays the signal for the ingested substance to start parthenogenesis.

As the name suggests, the Adipose are composed of fat tissue. Other tissues can be utilised under emergency conditions, though it makes the newborns ill. A complete human body can produce about a dozen infants. It's not indicated whether the squat little white babies resemble their adult forms. [X4.18, "The End of Time Part Two" suggests they do, unless there's an under-aged Adipose running around a bar. Conversely, the original conception of the Shadow Proclamation scene in "The Stolen Earth" would have included a 15-foot adult version. Presumably,

their reproduction cycles typically work along much the same lines as seen here.] The babies seem to have an instinctive comprehension of where to go, as they efficiently head out to the waiting vans. The company uses a decal like a red version of the Lazarus/Saxon green spiral-of-circles [X3.6, "The Lazarus Experiment" et seq.].

The Adipose First Family has hired Miss Foster, whose real name is Matron Cofelia of the Five-Straighten Classabindi Nursery Fleet, intergalactic class, to administrate creation of the baby Adipose on Earth. She seems to prepare in advance for impressive explanations to her foes. [We can't think of any other reason why she keeps a baby Adipose in a desk drawer, other than to whip it out for dramatic effect.] The First Family kills Foster as a liability [even though Earth has had experience with aliens – perhaps the Shadow Proclamation guidelines include rules about disclosure. Either way, it would make more sense if the players here aren't aware, somehow, of the very public alien invasions of Great Britain.]

Planet Notes

• *Earth* is still a 'Level Five' [17.2, "City of Death" et seq.] world, so seeding alien embryos here is a no-no. Miss Foster assumes that any aliens checking up on her would have contacted the Shadow Proclamation. Although Foster's plans are brought to fruition sooner than expected, a million prospective Adipose surrogates are implanted in London and presumably spawn the Adipose babies.

History

• *Dating.* It's a Tuesday when the episode starts – Sylvia goes out the next day with her 'Wednesday girls'. Adipose victim Stacy mentions having started the course of pills on Thursday and 'five days' later, she's dumping her feller. [She might have obtained them on Thursday and started Friday morning, which makes that problem walk away.] It seems to get dark before 6.30. Venus is visible in the evening sky. Donna's father Geoff Noble has died since her failed wedding. [Script editor Gary Russell's tie-in novel, *The Glamour Chase*, suggests he died on 15th May, 2008.

[Following the whole Year Ahead procedure started in "Aliens of London" (X1.4), it should now be 2009. Sylvia's comment about how nobody's unemployed any more is suggestive: in our world, the global economic meltdown trig-

How Does This Play in Pyongyang?

continued from Page 11...

America's NTSC system – but fewer than the reverse.

As you'll perhaps recall from the photos of Tom Baker, a Wirrn, a Dalek, a Voc et al queuing at the US Embassy for Visas, America as a whole was invited to jump on the *Doctor Who* bandwagon. By and large, they passed. Time-Life (see below) had earlier offered the Pertwee episodes to commercial stations that had little or no idea what to do with them. The simple fact that this was a series of serials seemed to elude people, so the timetabling was all out of whack. This cock-up led to one of the most distinctive features of the later PBS transmissions, but we'll come to that. Time-Life had started co-funding prestigious BBC documentaries after their South American ventures went off the boil. These were also all-film.

Year Zero for BBC exports was 1977. The majority of national networks had upgraded to colour transmission, even if production was slower in some countries than needed to keep viewers happy. BBC Television was a respected brand and had been making high-profile co-productions, mainly documentaries. Although international trade in programming had been going since the late 1950s, when American film companies switched to filming TV series and ITC had done everything possible to grab a slice of the US market, the BBC only started its own showcase expositions in the late 1970s. Trade fairs had been a good way to grab a cheap few hours of programming, as anything displayed at an international television event had already paid for itself in its native country, so was offered for as low as the rights-lawyers and agents would allow. Other nations had run them, hence all the "presented for television by Peggy Miller" European and Soviet stuff we got shoved on in school holidays, but the BBC seriously rethought its own export drive around the year of the Queen's much-hyped Silver Jubilee and held its own expo. The first such event was in Brighton and, by all accounts, a low-rent affair attended by fewer than 30 buyers. This was also the period when *Target*, an all-film action-drama firmly in the Euston mould, was the BBC's tentative toe in these waters. (As you'll know from Volume 4, the consequences of this for *Doctor Who* were immense.)

Nonetheless, the big prize was in sight. As we explained in **Why Didn't They Just Spend More Money?** (12.2, "The Ark in Space"), the BBC was strapped for cash in the latter half of the decade after a big splurge (people had bought colour sets and the requisite colour licenses) had led to a five-year spike in more extravagant productions, which was now the reservoir of material to sell. If you've wondered why *Are You Being Served?* is in perpetual rerun around the world (and, frankly, we'd rather it wasn't), it was down to those first buyers cherry-picking. Thus, when most overseas buyers took *Doctor Who* in 1977, they were getting Jon Pertwee and the first three years of Tom Baker as one package.

Of course, this being the BBC, any revenue from such sales went into collective departmental pots rather than to the specific series. The priority was always to make programmes that appealed to a section of the licence-fee-paying public (especially if that section didn't appeal to advertisers, and thus didn't get much attention from ITV). A series catching on in Australia wouldn't suddenly start winking at Australian viewers or introducing characters from Brisbane or Perth, heavens no. If, however, it was plausible that a new series might have appeal to viewers from a specific nation, that country's TV companies might have been asked, hypothetically, if they wanted to pitch in for co-production and defray some of the overheads, especially if they wanted to make an all-film drama series of the kind the BBC started making in large numbers. This went double for ITV companies, who felt like they were constantly playing catch-up with the BBC, hence the alarming number of 80s filmed series about how terrible the British aristocracy were, and what fabulous clothes they wore while being horrible to India and the poor. Which brings us to PBS.

For non-American readers who may have wondered why Cookie Monster sometimes wears a velvet jacket, a quick catch-up. America has a form of commercial-free network funded by the public, not exactly like the BBC. PBS was launched in its current configuration in 1970, with a hefty contribution from Time-Life Television (who were moving back into domestic US cable after some unsatisfactory collaborations overseas). It is sort of a network, sort of not; many statewide (or not) broadcasters were interlinked under the Public Service Broadcasting name and logo, some with additional funding from their state legislature.

Time-Life had a deal with the BBC, concerning

continued on Page 15...

gered by the sub-prime mortgage scandal was brewing in late summer 2008 and, by Christmas, Woolworths and Virgin Megastore had been high-profile casualties. Alternatively, if you want an "in-universe" reason for 2008 to be a big year for massive losses, the Doctor used Rory's phone to reset every stock exchange to zero (X5.1, "The Eleventh Hour"), probably causing the trouble President Obama was supposed to have a plan to fix (X4.17, "The End of Time Part One"). Venus is at its closest to Earth, 25 million miles away, so 2009 is a safe bet – but as the recession's effects aren't apparent yet, it must be fairly early in the year. And, sure enough – in the alternate timeline of "Turn Left" (X4.11), the Adipose incident happens in March.

[At this point, there's no sign of side effects from the recent shakeups (alien invasions becoming expected and understood, the American President and British PM dying under highly suspicious circumstances, stuff like that). Sylvia seems to think Donna should have no trouble finding a job. It'll all be visibly different in 18 months.]

The Analysis

The Big Picture There's a character in this story (the journalist) called "Penny Carter", but not the one originally planned. The next companion after Martha was to have been a sort of Bridget Jones figure – looking for Mr Right, but fairly certain it wasn't a skinny alien with retro sideys. She was to have just been dumped when the Doctor careered into her life. In fact, although Davies and others invariably use the name "Bridget Jones" in this connexion, the irresistible comparison, especially in view of the casting decisions of Series 1 and 2 and the name "Mott" coming back, is *Linda Green*.

However, the series cited in the Tone Meeting as a template was a different relationship-based comedy-drama: *Cold Feet*. This was about three couples (or three blokes and three women depending on what stage the story was at) who lived in aspirational purple-and-cerise houses and is in no way to be muddled up with *Coupling*, Steven Moffat's farce about three couples who lived in similar flats and met in a bar like that. *Cold Feet* was a rom-com resolutely grounded in supermarkets, mortgages etc. and featured men coming to terms with being 40. Already it's hard to recall this, but a home like Stacy's in this story was the almost-within-reach model for a lot of real

people's interior decor. However much the episode resembles fantasy, and the homes have a slightly garish *Edward Scissorhands* look, it was identifiably like what umpteen makeover programmes were encouraging people to do with their personal spaces.

Therein lies the key to this story. The Adipose are a violation of the ultimate personal space, the one being made over more assertively (in TV shows such as *Ten Years Younger* and *Would Like to Meet*) than ever before: the body. This shouldn't surprise us. Ever since the Yeti-in-the-loo formula became a staple of *Doctor Who*, the pretentions towards control and safety within the home were a legitimate target for the programme to exploit and make scary. As we've seen (notably in **Was 'Yeti-in-the-Loo' the Worst Idea Ever?** under 5.5, "The Web of Fear"), there are diminishing returns on this if it's done too often in rapid succession. Once the arrival of aliens in London on Christmas has become routine enough for jokes ("Voyage of the Damned"), the only way to make it work again is to raise the stakes.

The original of this was Davies's attempt to write a story about alien-derived Botox injections gone horribly wrong, having already satirised it with Lady Cassandra (X1.2, "The End of the World"; X2.1, "New Earth"). It mutated from there into the fad diet theme; the name "Adipose" was derived from the scientific word for fat cells, adipose tissue. However, there is a popular rapid diet pill called *Adios*, which is essentially a diuretic and reduces water retention. This aspect isn't mentioned in the TV ads with young women in sequinned shorts strutting their funky stuff without frequent bathroom breaks. Quick-fix metabolic diet pills have been a staple of weight-loss fads for generations; the first and most notorious were amphetamine-based and had side-effects that included hyperactivity, heart problems, mood-swings and withdrawal symptoms (the original 1988 *Hairspray* made Divine's growled threat "Ma diet pill's wearing awff" a much-sampled line).

In the early 90s, there was a fad for deliberate ingestion of tapeworm eggs. The most recent pills do indeed metabolise away body fat, but in some cases removed the brown fat necessary for maintaining the body's core temperature and homeostasis. It is, once again, a quick fix, a means to undo the effects of a lack of restraint and conform to some idea of what is acceptable, much as the

How Does This Play in Pyongyang?

continued from Page 13...

distribution and financial backing for projects such as James Burke's *Connections* and Alastair Cooke's *America*. Cooke had begun as the *Manchester Guardian* correspondent in Washington before working for the BBC and writing the weekly *Letter from America* for over half a century, but this series got him known in the US, so he became the host of reworked BBC dramas under the title *Masterpiece Theater*, hence the *Sesame Street* spoof *Monsterpiece Theater*. (This strand was originally the classic novel adaptations – often produced by either Barry Letts or Terrance Dicks – and a few original dramas set in the time of extravagant facial-hair, but later comprised almost all the tiresome village detective things nobody under 60 watches. These got a whole new network, called "Masterpiece". They even made an all-American version of *Antiques Roadshow* quite unrecognisable from the Fiona Bruce series.)

So, from 1978 onward, PBS became the natural American home of *Doctor Who*. To make sure the casual viewer was up-to-speed, they allowed a semi-retired actor called Howard da Silva to narrate; to make room for *this,* they hacked chunks out of each episode. These adapted episodes, converted to 525-line NTSC, included the last colour broadcast of 8.2, "The Mind of Evil" and most of 7.3, "The Ambassadors of Death" (on Buffalo's local station). Some clips of these, grabbed almost at the last minute before the BBC wanted their property back once the number of transmissions was up, were the only remaining colour footage prior to the chroma-dot breakthrough. Iowa's PBS station (Iowa Public Television) had already been showing it for a while, intact, and continued after Mr da Silva had been put out to pasture.

In some areas, PBS is funded directly by donations, and they occasionally rattle the tin with special treats, often the US premieres of key episodes of hit shows. *Doctor Who* has been a reliable temptation. IPTV has been showing the series almost continuously since the start, and still uses it in pledge-drives: their most recent big coup – the publisher of this guidebook often co-hosts the pledge drive, and talked them into it – was to be the first PBS station to net the rights to broadcast the recovered episodes of 5.5, "The Web of Fear". (That makes it the first transmissions of episodes two, four, five and six since 1976 in Nigeria – a fairly meaningless achievement in a world of DVDs and downloads, but one takes what one can get.)

What this means for *Doctor Who* is that there's a direct correlation between a programme's success with enthusiastic viewers and that station's survival and few British series have had such enthusiastic supporters in America's heartland. This is a large part of why the original series persisted after the disastrous feedback for "Time and the Rani" (24.1). It's also been a significant bellwether for the BBC Wales series.

That's been a mixed blessing. It means that the old episodes were in circulation all the years the BBC weren't making any new ones, and maintained a proven market for new ones – PBS pledge drives aid the BBC in determining what to try out overseas next. On the other hand, it established an idea that this series was exclusively for the kind of people who dress up in multi-coloured scarves. Anyone who knew the name *Doctor Who* in America pre-2006 had an idea of wobbly sets and English-accented rubber monsters. It was often shown in a context of detectives in small villages, worthy popular science shows, adaptations of books people pretend to have read and Lawrence Welk reruns on Saturday nights. In some regions, it was on at Breakfast-time; some stopped halfway through Baker's run of episodes and cycled from "Robot" (12.1) to "The Invasion of Time" (15.6) over and over. In some, they bought new series up to Sylvester McCoy. Unlike *The BBC Shakespeare* or *Nova* (the US name for the BBC/WGBH composite we call *Horizon*), there was merchandising to offer in return for donations. Nobody thought to make *Brideshead Revisited* action-figures or *Miss Marple* pizza-cutters.

When the new episodes were being pushed, this earlier impression was the main reason not to bother. However, the loyal PBS stations sometimes refused to get into a bidding-war over the Eccleston and Tennant episodes, partly because they're perpetually cash-starved (especially after the 2008 recession, which led to legislatures hacking their support off at the knees) and partly because they feared that other networks (notably Syfy) would claim them. Moreover, in the increasingly mercantile BBC, there were moves to launch global outlets. There were digital channels, in Europe and Australasia, which were more like iPlayer (the digital catch-up service) but needed

continued on Page 17...

brutal "decluttering" removed people's pasts and made everyone's homes look like everyone else's. As we have just mentioned, a lot of slightly prurient evening television, especially on BBC2 and Channel 4, ridiculed people for not conforming and sent in alleged "experts" to be callously stern and "sort out" their lives, whether they wanted sorting out or not. (See X1.12, "Bad Wolf" for the ghastly Trinny and Susannah.)

As the dialogue indicates, Miss Foster was meant to be redolent of *Supernanny* (then at the height of its popularity in the States, already on the skids in the UK). In this, a plump (and probably rather nice) lady called Jo Frost, with no formal qualifications but a bit of experience, was made to adopt a stern persona with glasses she didn't need – and a tight suit that did her few favours – and get tough with "problem" children whose parents weren't, on the slanted evidence given to us, up to it. She was a grotesque parody of *Mary Poppins* – the Disney one, not the real character from the books (X6.0, "A Christmas Carol"; X8.12, "Death in Heaven").

Each episode had the same script – an outsider is shown bad behaviour and counters it for a week by being strict and forbidding, then lectures the parents on using "the naughty step" and magically cures everyone. Then she comes back a few months later in her own clothes and everything's perfect. Once again, control-freakery combines with a "normal" person surrendering responsibility to some external force. Diet pills, camp burglars breaking in and remodelling your house without you knowing it, posh harpies slagging off your clothes, or a woman with no children tapping into a BDSM cosplay fantasy and telling you you're a bad parent are all part of the same syndrome. Admitting to needing help gives permission, after such an "intervention", to be selfish. Stacy is using her newfound confidence to dump her "he'll-do-for-now" boyfriend.

Yet, following the progression we've mentioned several times (most recently in **Who are You Calling a Monster?** under "The Lazarus Experiment"), taking control of one's status and relationships is hubris when something wants to treat you as meat. What makes this particularly uncomfortable is the sheer familiarity (in every sense) of the concept; a new, blameless little life comes into the world at the cost of a bit of dignity, as with all babies. The problem is when it ends the life of the host, and it's more noticeable when the host is male. This taps into a genuine concern not just about sex-roles, but the extent to which a parent, especially a mother, can be considered an individual either when expecting a baby or, more controversially, when raising one. Note, for instance, the very similar set-ups of 12.2, "The Ark in Space" and *Alien*. In both cases, the character who becomes infected with an insectoid lifeform is removed from having any agency once the "conception" happens. (The engineer Dune, in "The Ark in Space", is frozen and only gets dialogue when the Wirrn-infected Noah has his memories in episode three. Kane in *Alien* is recklessly curious – usually the solution in SF, but the cause of all ills in horror – but, being played by John Hurt, makes more of an impression before this than the number of lines would indicate. After being, in effect, raped, he's unconscious until just before dying when the critter hatches out of him.)

Another story-aspect that wasn't universal is the low opinion of the press, something firmly taken for granted in Britain. Even back in the 1930s, there were satires on this (*Scoop*, mentioned in the write-up for "Voyage of the Damned") and little of what Fleet Street hacks got up to thereafter did much to improve their image. The recent investigations and trials of Murdoch employees over their phone-hacking activities were no surprise to anyone who has seen these agencies being fined, condemned and penalised for far worse crimes against people who aren't wealthy film-stars, including 97 dead football fans and their friends libelled after the Hillsborough disaster. *The Observer*, mentioned in this episode, is generally regarded these days as one of the more ethical titles (although a glance back at the 1970s indicates that some of the former owners were less-than-clean), and even *this* paper is treated as suspect by many people. "Suspect", not "the enemy": we're not a Third World dictatorship.

In passing, let's note the similarity to the whole window-cleaner's cradle sequence and an episode of *Some Mothers do Have 'Em* that was as close as they got to a stunt going wrong. This sequence was originally conceived for X3.1, "Smith and Jones" as part of Davies's continuing effort to prove his "vertical" vs "horizontal" theory of action television. The mime sequence where the Doctor and Donna converse silently across a different conversation is a throw-back to the signal-chats Jack and Henriette have in *Casanova*. The

How Does This Play in Pyongyang?

continued from Page 15...

subscriptions (a model abandoned in 2015 with a mumbled comment that it was always just an experiment).

Now we have Britbox and the so-called "BBC America", which resembles genuine BBC broadcasts mainly in the number of trailers for Graham Norton. The channel has copious adverts for knee-braces or diabetes medication and trailers for *Broadchurch* and *Downton Abbey* (not actually BBC programmes) interspersed with programmes, including heavily-edited versions of BBC Wales *Who*. They censor most films they show.[1] It's strictly commercial. BBCA is on the majority of US cable packages. It's co-run by BBC Worldwide (the international/commercial subdivision that handles merchandising) and the AMC network and became sufficiently lucrative to fund programmes such as the Canadian *Orphan Black* (see **Working for the Yankee Dollar?** under X6.1, "The Impossible Astronaut"). UK readers might want to think of this network as a less-good version of Dave, and non-British readers will have to accept that, yes, there's a television station called "Dave"[2].

Elsewhere, the black and white episodes were running until the late 1970s. We have heard eye-witness reports of bored kids in New Zealand grumbling about watching episode four of 4.2, "The Tenth Planet" *again*. Australia's rerun policy was to show it after schools, alongside *Danger Mouse* and the like. When new episodes premiered, they were trailed in the breaks between reruns (any UK fan whose supply of 625-line PAL tapes of 70s stories began here has probably encountered the idiotic things continuity announcers said over the end credits, especially 15.3, "Image of the Fendahl"). As with all English-speaking territories other than Britain, the episodes were bought on the understanding that they could be shown a number of times each. Unlike the people who'd originally paid for it, Anglophone viewers in other countries got umpteen reruns, making it as familiar as any perennially-repeated imported show was in the UK. Although America's main channels ignored it, Australia and New Zealand put it on with mainstream programming, removing the taint of "cult" or "geek" at least until the late 1980s. You didn't need to go out of your way to find it.

So for a lot of nations (54 during the 20th Anniversary in 1983), there was at last a vague awareness of the series's habits and basics. Just as viewers in Britain in the pre-digital age were generally able to identify the sets, costumes and theme-tunes of *Belle and Sebastian* or *The Young Doctors*, but not the specific episodes or characters, so the writers of *The Simpsons* could assume that a bloke with big hair, a scarf and a hat was identifiable as low-rent cable filler alongside the Spanish-speaking bee-man (we're back to "The Web Planet"). The series's folk-memory lurks behind the use of phone booths for time travel in *Bill and Ted's Excellent Adventure* and *The Suite Life of Zach and Cody* among many others. This caused a degree of consumer-resistance.

However, with all the other allegedly-similar series being cancelled or going off the rails (as the die-hards saw it[3]), by 2009 *Doctor Who* was almost the only game in town. A couple of Hugo-winning stories didn't hurt.[4] Nonetheless, overseas showings of *Doctor Who* have too often been targeted at self-identified "Geek" audiences rather than, as with Britain, the general public. The BBC has always seen *Doctor Who* as a drama version of the Swiss Army knife, but, for export purposes and that lucrative merchandising revenue, it's been sold as a very specialised tool for a particular job. Or, to be purely accurate, two overlapping jobs, as the series conveyed a positive idea of Britain while (at least on BBC America) removing anything too specifically British to pass unchallenged. The repeats of "The Hand of Fear" (14.2) lose the amusing material with the Doctor and Sarah in the quarry, discussing whether Croydon has a "season" and demonstrating pace-bowling prowess, for example.

Many other countries ran the episodes without such impact. Finland never had much success running it.[5] A couple tried it briefly and gave up. As we mentioned in Volume 6, Radio Television Luxembourg ran the McCoy episodes in Germany (and in German) in the late 1980s, in a Sunday lunchtime slot. (Some of the pussyfooting about De Flores and his chums being Nazis – 25.3, "Silver Nemesis" – was in deference to this potential new market.) "The Ice Warriors" (5.3) was shown to German TV executives in 1968, but declined. The new series was offered in a German translation in 2008 and rapidly taken up by Fox (not quite the same as the US or UK stations of the same name) along with *Torchwood* and *The Sarah Jane Adventures*. The best source for this is a website

continued on Page 19...

ABOUT TIME 2008-2009

Doctor and Donna crossing each other's paths without seeing one another is very like the start of the grim *You've Got Mail*.

Finally, as we mentioned in **Things to Notice**, the sequence of the Adipose amassing to make the mothership connection alludes to, among other things, the ship from the climax of *Close Encounters of the Third Kind*, the characteristic right-angle arms-raise of Eva Peron (returned to the wider public consciousness by Elaine Paige in *Evita* 20 years before Madonna in the film version), and a Wile E Coyote-style realisation that she's about to fall. Their voices recall Morph, a claymation character from the 70s (recently revived) whose success as an insert in Tony Hart's post *Vision On* show *Take Hart* led to a whole series in the *Magic Roundabout* slot before the news in the 80s, and to the animators eventually launching Aardman Studios, home of Wallace and Gromit. Hindsight makes it seem as if the Adipose look and voice was tried out in the spoof advert for "Ekto-Shine" in X2.12, "Army of Ghosts".

Plus, there was a 1991 advert, a landmark in its day, for the things a milkman could do that buying plastic or card cartons in a cornershop denied the customer. This had a Jedi milko raising bicycles and righting garden gnomes as he led a procession of dancing bottles down a street to the accompaniment of Jack Hylton's "Grasshopper Dance". The CGI work was by a company called Silicon Graphics and won a few awards, but try getting your milk delivered in the UK these days. Following this, a number of other adverts used small toy-like beings. The specific reference Davies made to the effects team was the 2007 Vauxhall Corsa advert with the "C'mon" knitted puppets – a group of small CG monsters instead of one big one.

English Lessons

• *Watchdog* (n.): Originally a section of 70s news-lite *Nationwide* dealing with consumer rights and unfair trading practices (notably the Pyramid Selling scams of the era, see 16.2, "The Pirate Planet"), this was the replacement for "Consumer Unit", often the occasion for allegedly-comic ditties by Richard Stilgoe. Then it outlived the parent show and was generally presented by Hugh Scully (who went on to found *Antiques Roadshow*), then, Lynne Faulds-Wood, whose insistence that "a small child could have an accident with that" became the butt of parodies. (For maximum

effect, it has to be said in a Miss Jean Brodie accent.) Notoriously, Anne Robinson turned hosting the series into her personal crusade. She left to do *The Weakest Link* (X1.12, "Bad Wolf"), but returned in 2009 and stayed for another seven years. So anything where some member of the public suspected a rip-off would be natural territory for them.

• *Health and Safety* (n.): As you will recall from last story's discussion of conkers ("Voyage of the Damned"), there are many urban myths surrounding the Health and Safety Executive, often promulgated by opponents of the EU and tabloid newspapers (assuming they are not the same thing). In the UK, the main cause of death in the workplace is unsafe practices, a situation that has nonetheless improved since small boys were sent up chimneys. However, "Health and Safety" is a convenient excuse for employers and organisations to wriggle out of anything they don't feel like doing, and the advent of US-style claims lawyers has made many institutions curtail their former benefits, notably school trips and inter-company sport. Most workplaces have periodic Risk Assessments, based on the *a small child could have an accident with that* principle, so the term "Health and Safety" is often associated with fussiness or being a killjoy. See X7.10, "Hide".

• *The Observer* (n.): the world's oldest Sunday newspaper, started in 1791. In 1993, it was bought by the trust that runs *The Guardian*, but it was originally very pro-Government and anti-radical. Science coverage is not what it does best. Think of a less stuffy *New York Times* Sunday edition.

• *Strathclyde* (n.): The bit of West Scotland with Glasgow in it, around the River Clyde. It also includes Argyll. Rather a long walk for a small girl from Chiswick.

• *Crèche* (n.): This is a bit like a kindergarten but usually run by employers, or contractees thereof, to allow employees with small children to work normal hours whilst keeping an eye on the sprogs at breaks. The kindergarten model is not the only kind of nursery schooling available in Britain, nor the most well-established, since the idea of "nursery" as a place where a professional looked after small children is as old as castles and feudalism.

• *Notting Hill* (n.): Someone from nearby Chiswick would see Notting Hill as where the Yuppies start. Apart from the Carnival (op cit. in

How Does This Play in Pyongyang?

continued from Page 17...

called "Timelash" (obviously old-skool fans are still around). On the back of this export drive, older iterations of the series have been broadcast and released on DVD; India has just got started – it's potentially the biggest audience on the planet and, conveniently, one where English is widely spoken. Viewers of Japan's NKH were reportedly confused about the programme's status as family fun and showed it late at night, then got complaints that it wasn't scary enough for horror-slots. They cancelled it.

In America, *Doctor Who* is once again known-about, if not extensively watched by, uncommitted viewers. Jodie Whittaker was on the cover of *Entertainment Weekly*, as well as special editions of *TV Guide* and *Newsweek*. BBC America's commitment to marketing the Davies series, streets ahead of the then-Sci-Fi Channel's lamentable efforts, led to a massive upswing of goodwill and interest among the public. Once Matt Smith's tenure began, that paid off in the sheer number of high-school students engaged in the series, referencing it in graduation speeches and openly wearing *Doctor Who* or Dalek T-Shirts. All of that would have been unthinkable in the mainstream of the 1980s, the era of Anoraknophobia (see Volume 6) but these days, your average American teenager is at least vaguely aware of the programme's basics and doesn't demonstrate an urge to run screaming from the room when it's mentioned. BBCA's target audience is 16-25 year olds, so any talk of it being a kid's show in its native land is hushed-up. This caused problems with Series 10's resolute attempts to recapture its natural constituency. There was a noticeable downslide of public interest after the anniversary blitz, despite the ratings spike, but general awareness, if not full comprehension, of *Doctor Who* among America's youth is almost certainly the highest it's ever been.

Coupled with that, any comic store or DVD retailer will have some of the increasingly daft merchandising. The peculiar chain of Goth-lite boutiques, Hot Topic, carried a bewildering panoply of TARDIS socks, plush fezzes, smart-alecky T-shirts and felt K9s. Imported, slightly outdated copies of *Doctor Who Magazine* can be found in some normal newsagents, or in specialist shops alongside the IDW comics, BBC Books and objects too tacky for even the Stamp Centre (see **What are the Biggest Merchandising Disasters of the**

Twenty-First Century? under X5.3, "Victory of the Daleks").

The flipside of this is if you consider the series in absolute numbers – first broadcast in the US happens on BBC America, where *The Return of Doctor Mysterio* netting 1.7 viewers was enough to set a record for the channel. But then, eventually, came Series 10. Moreover, the new *Doctor Who* episodes are also offered *the very next day* on Amazon, a development sure to send older fans into competing shivers of delight and despair, if they lived through the dark days of watching new episodes months after the fact on grubby videotape funnelled through the fan underground. Then again, we're living in an era where a show's influence can outweigh the raw numbers of eyeballs watching brand-new episodes – AMC's *Mad Men*, an evergreen critical darling, only averaged two, maybe 2.5 million per episode on initial broadcast. You can still find reports of viewers watching *Doctor Who* on the inevitable PBS reruns, and the Tennant episodes were briefly picked up and heavily promoted by Disney XD, so the potential audience for these is still growing while the Moffat-produced stories and Chibnall material is being shown elsewhere. The streaming of almost all extant episodes on Twitch in Spring 2018 triggered a resurgence of interest in the older stories, so iTunes et al have been getting a fair bit of traffic for 25-minute episodes.

France's experience of the BBC Wales series is pretty typical of most non-English-speaking territories. The series is on, often in minority channels, and those people who know about it tend to be either very enthusiastic or not at all. Those who are converse online, and get background on the earlier series if they've just stumbled across it (as seems to be the most common method of encountering it). Most nations bought it along with other big hitters from the BBC (*Top Gear*, *Sherlock* and *Call the Midwife* – not everyone's taken to *Mrs Brown's Boys*, oddly enough), plus ITV and Channel 4 shows that somehow get bundled with them. A subset of the devoted handful gripe if the series isn't tailored exclusively for them (so, for example, River Song routinely says *ce-n'est pas l'heur*, i.e., "not yet", despite some French geeks assuming that everyone watching knows what "Spoiler" means). Nonetheless, the BBC attempts to pitch all forms of *Doctor Who* for the widest audience possible in each country, but has accept-

continued on Page 21...

Volume 8) and Portobello Market, the W10 area is known for trendy companies that employ young mums and big houses owned by the kinds of people who might have an au pair (see Series 7). It's got a bit gentrified since its 60s heyday as a cheap bohemian backwater (see the film *Performance* for more), home to Michael Moorcock and Hawkwind... and Tom Baker c.1975.

• *Long streak of...* (n. sl.): The usual phrase would not, as Donna does here, have ended with "nothing". (See *Take the Mickey* with X4.3, "Planet of the Ood".)

Oh, Isn't That...?

• *Sarah Lancashire* (Miss Foster). As with last year's season-opener, TV royalty from *Coronation Street*. She was Raquel the barmaid, dotingly loyal to her much-older husband Alec. After this, understandably, she tended to go for roles that weren't dim and right northern, like, such as in Paul Abbott's *Clocking Off* (in a sort-of relationship with a neighbour played by Christopher Eccleston), and as a cool younger barrister in a firm of stuffy incompetent-but-tricky old pros in *Chambers*. There have also been a number of one-off roles, and she's now famous as herself rather than for that breakthrough role. She's married to a Very Important TV Executive, so she can afford to only take roles she'd like. More recently, she starred in the headline-grabbing *Happy Valley*.

Things That Don't Make Sense Adipose Industries has – on its own merits, it seems, without benefit of hypnotism, coercion, drugs or alien influence – signed up a million customers, out of a city with a population of nine million, in under a year. No company has that successful a start-up, especially with just 50 operators making 40 calls a day each. You can tell that an alien set up the company, as its employees meekly hand over a list of customers to two investigators simultaneously. Then again, neither the Doctor nor Donna leave with a printout of all million customers in the London area, so it can't be very complete. The Doctor apparently took it into his head to investigate this company even though he's no idea what they're up to. The home-made detector he uses makes it clear he's alien-hunting (it must be calibrated to ignore him and every other alien in London), but on what grounds did he suspect extraterrestrial involvement with a diet plan? (And how alien *are* these Adipose? Human fatty tissue isn't just lipids,

it's in cells with nucleii and mitochondria.)

Each of these customers has been given a pendant that, if fiddled with idly as Donna does while waiting for Stacy, will prematurely trigger a parthenogenesis and kill a nearby Adipose client. How has not happened before now? The odds against two Adipose customers in London being in the same building simultaneously in the last month aren't astronomical. There should have been a wave of hapless customers exploding into tiny milk-white people. Tube passengers turning into dozens of Lilliputians on CCTV in a confined space would be conspicuous.

In light of "Turn Left", we should also ask why the Adipose have only gone for the UK, when there's a country across the Pond with such a bigger market for weight-reduction products. Britain simply isn't the most practical place to be doing this; it's not even the most likely spot in Western Europe. The one thing that makes the UK preferable is that it takes exactly one kilo to make one baby Adipose, while America has stuck to a weird calibration of Edward III's body-parts for its measuring system. All the same, Germany or Mexico would have been much better targets.

There's no obvious reason for Adipose Industries to occupy a 15-storey office block. The pendants aren't manufactured on-site, they've farmed out the babies to their own customers; the pills are alien tech (and if not, they'd be made in a sterile factory somewhere, not in a costly London high-rise office building). Moreover, they've dead-locked the entire building and fitted reinforced glass throughout, which rather suggests a purpose-built edifice. (Once again, we have to posit a very obliging body providing start-up funding for alien insurrections – see 4.8, "The Faceless Ones"; X2.7, "The Idiot's Lantern" and alternate *Sarah Jane Adventures*.)

Let's assume the rest of the tower block is slated for storage of fat-babies. About a million have been born each day for the last few weeks, after a trial run lasting a year. Even averaged across the whole year, we're talking 4,000 babies a night being collected, seemingly with just the one van and two guards driving it.

The company need so little office space, in fact, Miss Foster and her grunts know immediately which bathroom to check for infiltrators. (Although we'd like it if Foster and the grunts just went round the other floors making her "we know you're in here, I warn you, I'm not a patient

How Does This Play in Pyongyang?

continued from Page 19...

ed that it would be a minority-interest compared to Clarkson's comedy hate-crimes or endless Agatha Christies.

BBC Cymru made sure that a French-language version of their revised series was available as soon as possible, not least because they were securing co-production money from the Canadian Broadcasting Corporation. Thus France received the new episodes at around the same time as America or Australia. However, these were relegated to a relatively lowly network: France, like Britain at the time, had terrestrial networks (the old UK term for analogue broadcasts) with a degree of state funding (if not direct control) and a number of cable and digital-only ones, some commercial and some within the France Television family. France4, one of the digital-only options, was rebranding as a self-consciously "edgy" digital channel and became the home for the imported dramas less obviously of universal appeal. Most imports land up on France3, then a terrestrial network universally available; this is the home of *Inspecteur Barnaby* (AKA *Midsomer Murders*) and countless other British-made whodunits (and some frankly bonkers German ones). Oddly, though, France3 elected to run *Torchwood*, so the various television magazines ran explanations of what *Doctor Who* was for people without access to it. There was a degree of head-patting condescension, lots of *ils sont fous, ces Anglais* clichés. When Kylie Minogue made a guest appearance as part of her comeback from cancer, this made *Who* newsworthy, often with passing comments about the series's resemblance to France's favourite UK imports, *The Avengers* (or, as they pragmatically call it, *Chapeau Melon et Boittes de Cuire* – "bowler hat and leather boots" – still massively popular) and *Monty Python's Flying Circus*. Yet it remained a word-of-mouth hit.

Analogue station TF1 gave it a whirl in the mid-1980s, under the aegis of *Temps X* (see 23.2, "Mindwarp"). They'd had a go with some Tom Baker episodes in 1978, but nobody noticed (see 17.2, "City of Death"). The repackaged Target novelisations had pictures of Igor and Grichka Bogdanoff, silver-jumpsuited presenters and putative public faces of all things futuristic (and mumbo-jumbo).[6] Nothing came of this either, despite France's respect and enthusiasm for SF in general and interest in non-US forms of pop-culture. After

Temps X was dropped, there were random repeats in children's slots early in the morning. However, once the rights to the two Peter Cushing Dalek films were bought by French distributors Studio Canal, the 60s widescreen versions became more known than the 70s 4:3 ratio adventures the rest of the world adored (or tolerated).

Most Anglophone television there is redubbed by one of two Belgian-run agencies, Dubbing Brothers or Nice Fellow. The former handled *Doctor Who*, and the majority of humanoid characters come out sounding approximately like the originals. However, David Manet made Eccleston's Doctor sound as if he smoked 60 *Galois* in a day. He retained the role after the regeneration, altering his pitch and making a good job of keeping up with Tennant's machine-gun delivery. The majority of the puns fail to make it across the Channel, but it was this version of the Doctor who caught on with French fans, to the extent that Eccleston has become akin to the Brigadier or Leela: part of the background to be looked up online. France4 treats new episodes as big events, but these days its output is divided between sports, children's television and late-night docusoaps and gigs. *Doctor Who* gets put on as repeats in strange hours, or in semi-regular weekend slots capable of being pre-empted if France is doing well in rugby or tennis, and sometimes the reruns come in odd orders. One week in May 2014 saw "Le Collocateur" (X5.11, "The Lodger") three times. Things developed as fan-pressure made itself felt: the 2018 episodes were shown VO (i.e. undubbed, in Yorkshire-accented English) in the small hours of the Friday after each Sunday premiere, interspersed with the French versions of the end of Series 10 so they had a Christmas episode.

For many fans, the DVDs are a better bet; after an online petition from the fan website beansontoast.fr, the early ones were reissued with the original English soundtrack as an option. Marc Weiss, as the eleventh Doctor, makes that character more cheeky and authoritative than Matt Smith ever managed to sound (and can pronounce "Metebelis" properly; X7.10, "Le Fantôme de Caliburn"). Whilst earlier Scottish characters were allocated the equally-distinctive Marseilles accent (notably Dr Constantine in X1.9, "L'Enfant Vide"/"The Empty Child"), Amy Pond is mercifully generic-sounding.

One odd feature of the redubbing is that songs

continued on Page 23...

woman" speech for half an hour each until they finally hit the right stall. Besides, as Donna and Penny are in adjacent stalls, for over eight hours, they each ought to have intuited that they weren't alone. Donna's phone might have been a bit of a hint. As would the occasional flush.) It's as if Penny *wants* to be caught; she's sneaking around after introducing herself at the briefing.

When Miss Foster points her sonic device at the window-cleaner cable, she aims for the one on her left (right as seen from outside the building), but the one on her *right* (left as seen from mid-air outside the tower-block) snaps instead. This wouldn't be so bad, but *Doctor Who Confidential* spent eight minutes demonstrating that Davies is such a great writer because he clearly defines all the visually-based action-sequences in his scripts, and used this very sequence to tell all budding writers to try it for themselves. Then he posted the script online so we could mark his homework.

Given that Matron just tried to murder a million people on orders from her employers, she seems daft to presume they'll deal fairly with her. She's meticulous about every other aspect of this operation, yet has no back-up plan, escape route or Kompromat. The Doctor's plan is to hide patiently in a cupboard for hours on end. Yes, this incarnation. Why is there an Adipose Industries plaque on the inside of the cupboard door and not the outside?

It's against the rules of Davies-era *Who* for a sonic screwdriver to open a deadlock seal. But when Miss Foster "triple deadlocks" the building's core, the Doctor accesses it with her sonic pen. All right, maybe individual deadlocks are calibrated for individual opening devices (like keys and locks), but this isn't said. And if so, why can't the Doctor's screwdriver *make* deadlocks, which would have been very handy in any number of stories? Or, if Miss Foster's sonic pen is genuinely superior to the Doctor's, um, tool, why does he throw it away so casually? It's in a bin with the keys to a Toyota.

According to Sylvia, Donna took a job with the Health and Safety Executive but left after two days, going onto Jobseeker's Allowance. This is, in fact, impossible. The Department of Work and Pensions would have zealously refused to give any money to someone who has voluntarily left a job or been fired, and it would have been six months and a lot of intensive questioning and probing before she got a penny. Donna's 100 wpm would

get her £120 a day whenever she wanted it so why bother with JSA? Why is Sylvia's hair in curlers in the morning and straight (as per usual) when she goes out with her mates that night?

It's a bit odd that, after a year or more of looking for the Doctor, Donna can't hear a mysterious wheezing groaning sound ten feet behind her as she walks from her car. An allotment on a hill overlooking London is a pretty lousy place for stargazing, as the city's light-pollution often turns the sky orange (as we see when Donna's stomping towards Wilf, in his first scene). A bit of shade would be a good idea. (It's quite possible to star-gaze in the UK even in built-up areas – the present authors have managed it in Trafalgar Square.)

Finally (just for the record), we noticed that Stacy and Roger have made-up addresses in a real bit of London, Haringey (see "The Idiot's Lantern") and there's another underneath it on the screen, but while the two we *see* are in N4 5DB and 5DE and "Melanie Darnforth" is in N8, they all have the same phone area code, (020) 7946, which isn't right at all. Haringey's Outer London and gets an (020) 8 prefix. Fair enough if it's deliberately done to avoid real people getting rung up (see "The Stolen Earth"), but it left a subliminal *eh* impression, which we cite now to acknowledge the unsung BBC employees who get paid to do this sort of thing.

Critique At risk of damning with faint praise, this episode delivers exactly what was expected of it. By now we've become familiar with the competing impulses of series openers – just setting the stage versus being independent stories in their own right. Although it has a lot of jobs to do and does them efficiently it has an élan about it. It's occasionally a string of sight-gags about flying saucers and blobby aliens bursting from people's bodies – like a cute version of *Alien* paired with a *Looney Tunes* version of *Close Encounters* – but that's why this story's more than just the sum of the tasks it has to perform.

Davies is doing just as much as he usually handles in a season opener – establish the new companion, character beats, merchandising monster – but it's certainly the most relaxed example we've yet seen. It also provides outright comedy without being misjudged or lax. It looks assured and stylish without being in-your-face. It provides a different kind of alien intervention into mundane British life, conceptually and visually, and

How Does This Play in Pyongyang?

continued from Page 21...

have to be subtitled or, when sung by a character, the voice-artist has to approximate phonetic English (X7.9, "Cold War", or "Destruction Mutuelle Assurée" has Clara warbling "hong ree lark ze olf" with subtitles translating the lyrics into French). Smith's episodes are also noteworthy for everyone accepting that the series is called *Doctor Who,* but, when everyone's called upon to spend a good chunk of every episode shouting "Doctor Who?", repeating "*Docteur qui?*", which sounds enough like "Duck-Turkey" to be amusing to native English-speakers the first 60 times (especially in X7.16, "The Time of the Doctor").

As you probably knew, the 50th anniversary episode was broadcast simultaneously on every one of these networks. There was no facility for local translations so, for once, everyone had to watch the English-language original. Many viewers look on the untranslated episodes as a means to improve their English, as well as bone-up on the British way of life that get lost in all the off-the-shelf clichés of beefeaters and Tower Bridge. The rights to the translations are sometimes owned by bodies other than the BBC. Similarly, the DVD sub-titling (in English for hard-of-hearing viewers) is the responsibility of the distributors (usually Warner Bros and 2Entertain or Pup), another obstacle for some (including many PBS stations legally obliged to offer closed captioning for all transmissions). Redubbing is costly and time-con-suming compared to subtitles, but is considered more accessible for the casual viewer. Whereas the vogue for miserable Scandinavian cop-shows has added cachet to subtitled drama in Britain (with the folk-memory of *The Singing Ringing Tree, The Water Margin* and *The Flashing Blade*[7] making redubbed imports intrinsically ludicrous to the point that the last famous one, *Monkey,* was delib-erately done in funny voices), it's seen as the poor relation in France and Asia.

The Netherlands, Belgium and, apparently, most Scandinavian countries except Finland show *Doctor Who* with subtitles, causing fewer time-lags between episodes being shown in the UK and locally. Serious fans in nations where the redub-bing process is the norm have been known to do deals to obtain the subtitled version, but the streaming of video – legally or otherwise – allows even shorter short-cuts. A computer-savvy fan with a proxy server can get live online episodes (as was happening in Russia as early as 2006).

Let's pause here: there's an obvious problem with redubbed episodes of a series that relies on verbal humour and local, topical allusions to dif-ferentiate from the generic staples of umpteen other series. Anything that doesn't immediately fit with the lip-synch and plot-exposition is sacri-ficed. It's especially noticeable in the Tennant epi-sodes, when his rapid delivery doesn't allow screen-time for the more measured redubbers to convey anything more elaborate than the bare bones of the plot. Just as BBC America's versions of the hour-long episodes remove any reason to watch these rather than the *Star Trek* or *Buffy* epi-sodes they're riffing on, so barely any of the best jokes in English make it into the French, German or other redubbed versions we've seen, but occa-sionally new ones are added. Some of the humour comes across unscathed (especially the sight-gags), but the impression is that, far from being a parody of That Kind of Show (as viewers in Britain are encouraged to see it, see **Is Kylie From Planet Zog?** under X4.0, "Voyage of the Damned"), it's simply a nimbler, odder specimen of that genre.

Anyone who saw the unedited version of the 2012 Olympic opening ceremony (especially if it's compared with the trimmed NBC version with the uncomprehending commentators – see X6.13, "The Wedding of River Song") will have realised that there is a specific and carefully-garbled notion of Britishness, for export purposes, and a lived experience of anyone resident in the UK. These barely overlap. The Olympics, as with the previous year's regal events, were tailored to fit a pre-existing narrative and when anything didn't fit it was ignored until – as with the civil unrest in August 2011, it was too big to disregard and all the overseas commentary was asking why they didn't see it coming. The British-made series that do best in exports all fit the same fairy-tale – and yet not even David Cameron thought *Downton Abbey* was anything like real conditions in Britain either in the 1920s or now. Davies-era *Doctor Who* was often about the gap between that export-friendly story and what things are really like: *Torchwood* doubly so, as it revelled in squalor and kept on about how Wales differed from England.

For a small percentage of viewers – the kinds of people who refuse to stay mainly in the hotel and go to the obvious tourist attractions when visiting a new country – this isn't enough. The wonders of

continued on Page 25...

23

doesn't drop a ball. Perhaps that's why it feels slightly routine.

The phrase that keeps coming up in *Doctor Who Confidential* this year (apart from "marvellous") is "bigger and better" and that's how this episode gets away with delaying both the expected meeting of Doctor and Companion and any significant fantasy elements in the first quarter of the story. It's almost a routine comedy-drama, of the kind found on ITV on Sundays, until Stacy dies... and even after this, the bulk of the first three-quarters is Screwball Comedy (as per Tate's last appearance) until Matron opens up a panel in her office to reveal a Bond-Villain super-computer.

Nonetheless, we're not in conventional drama at any stage, but something more garish and cartoony. It's especially noticeable after seven years of the flinty, oily look in vogue these days, but even compared to a knowingly lurid episode from last year, X3.12, "The Sound of Drums", this week's trip to *Doctor Who* Britain is like being trapped in a nine-year-old girl's toy-cupboard. The sequence in Stacy's living room is almost hallucinatorily saturated, with the wallpaper, her blouse and make-up and even Tate's hair regraded in post-production. It's impossible to say any one element is "wrong", it's all pushed up to 11 and slammed together in our faces. The TARDIS scene in the back-alley, with a different Director of Photography, looks reassuringly normal because it's only as over-coloured as Series 3.

Within this context, anything is possible but the team's not making any assumptions about the casual viewer's acquiescence. Instead, every element of the story is slipped in slowly and methodically, so that the progress from the mundane world to the finale's slapstick is made incrementally. There are flashes of something more than basic storytelling (oddly enough, the bits BBC America thought were surplus to requirements), but very little of the self-indulgence so frequent in episodes that creep over 42 minutes of screen-time. The set-piece window-cleaner cradle sequence drags on a bit, and the build-up to the Adipose mass emergence is slower than it perhaps ought to be, but the overall pacing is judged to a turn. It's hard not to be won over by Donna's determination to find the Doctor but practically everyone went into the episode knowing her and knowing that she'd be leaving with him at the end so it's the effort put into delaying this and providing a non-formulaic way for them to meet cute

that gets all the attention. And we finally have a companion who loves the Doctor's life but thinks of him just as a good chum. After all the unrequited love, requited love, companions pairing off, and the Doctor's multiple marriages in the BBC Wales series, this season will be refreshingly unromantic (if you ignore Billie Piper standing around dreamily gazing off into the distance).

Where this story – and Series 4 overall – scored was in the use of Wilf. Although bringing back Bernard Cribbins was a last-minute emergency measure, having a semi-infantilised adult for Sylvia to bully makes her treatment of Donna slightly more plausible and gives the children watching an identification figure. As most of the first-night audience were watching as a family, this is crucial. Somehow, Sylvia treating Geoff like that wouldn't have worked dramatically, and the shared secret with Donna about the Doctor would have seemed odd as a father-daughter bond. A rebellious grandad siding with Donna against an authority figure who doesn't know what's going on, and cheering his granddaughter on, resembles how parents (and teachers, and politicians, and the news) seem to have an arbitrary idea of what's important. If Sylvia can brow-beat a WWII veteran, one who, like many kids, wears a bright red knitted hat and looks skyward, her treatment of the otherwise headstrong Donna makes sense. (Well, almost.) Later episodes mention Geoff as the big influence in Donna's childhood, but he's more potent as an absence, the "nice bloke" the Doctor mentions when Donna finally gets married. Plus, for a lot of the parents watching with their kids, Bernard Cribbins is a British childhood personified.

It's a mark of the programme's success in this phase that something with so much *right* with it can seem samey, but it's hard to find anyone going into the first episode of a new series who wasn't expecting most of what we got. *Doctor Who* has slid into a comfortable groove, only different from being in a rut because they keep upping the ante on the budget and cinematic look of the series. The pattern of the episodes is securely locked-in, with a present-day romp followed by a celebrity historical (with Pompeii as the celebrity), a simple story on a kerr-azee alien planet, a two-part return to Earth and some old monsters and so on. Just as we sort of know where we're going with this episode's plot, we know where the series as a whole will have a two-parter, an "experimental" tenth

How Does This Play in Pyongyang?

continued from Page 23...

online result in a subset of fans who are writing fanfic and need to know what Britain's really like, or who are asking questions about the differences between *Doctor Who* and other space-opera shows or other representations of Britain.

Traditionally, the whole premise of *Doctor Who* is that the misfits, the curious kids who don't buy the official line, are the ones with the right idea. International fandom is being formed by people who apply this to even *Doctor Who* as they are given it by BBC Worldwide and their local broadcasters.

episode, a Doctor-lite one and a few celebrity cameos in Part Twelve. It's hard to argue with success, but let's acknowledge the challenge of keeping things fresh while maintaining a hit property.

One last problem (if you can call it that): this is just about the last time Davies's London, as a place exactly like the real one except for the occasional presence of aliens, comes across as plausible. By the time Donna comes home again, let alone the series finale, we deserve to see some thought put into how the acceptance of alien life has altered people's ways of thinking. *The Sarah Jane Adventures* picks up the slack, but not everyone is watching that. In later years, the series ducks the question by removing this year's adventures from the timeline. That means that the next alien invasion has to be bigger and more consequential, so the season finale is rather less unexpected than it perhaps ought to have been. The team seem to know that this is the last time they can get away with a story like this without some kind of change in the series, so they're a little reckless. (ATMOS is never publicly stated to be alien; that story ends with a hint of a global change in habits that's never followed up).

On its own terms, though, without worrying about how it fits into the series as a whole, it hits every note. It works as an episode, and entertains in ways only *Doctor Who* can. It's only later that we see how it set up mysteries and developments rather than relying on this element to keep people watching a story with few merits of its own (as would become the norm for season-openers later).

The Lore

Written by Russell T Davies. Directed by James Strong. Viewing figures: (BBC1) 9.1 million (and an 88% AI), (BBC3 repeats) 1.4 (87% AI) and 0.7 million.

Repeats and Overseas Promotion As we mentioned, *Le Retour de Donna Noble*. In German, *Es Lebe das Fett* (Long Live the Fat).

Alternate Versions Ah! The edit of this episode shown to the press a few days before transmission lacked one key scene. It contained no hint that Rose would be back, so the surprise was kept until broadcast. The allotment sequence was originally shot with Howard Attfield as Geoff Noble. Graeme Harper directed both the Cribbins version and Rose's brief stay in this dimension during the shoot for "Turn Left". The original allotment scene is on the box-set DVD.

BBC America cuts the cat-flap scene, trims Sylvia's rant about Donna's career-plans, Wilf's Strathclyde anecdote and the Doctor talking to himself in the TARDIS.

Production

• After Puppy-Love Girl and Rebound Girl, the obvious next step for a long-term companion was a sort of Bridget Jones figure – a distraction from the Doctor's complicated love-life rather than the focus of it. A set-up for Penny Carter, as the new girl was to have been called, involved discovering her boyfriend *in flagrante* (as far as could be shown on Saturdays at 7.00pm) and walking past the TARDIS just before aliens arrive. One notion briefly tossed around was a portal from another world and thousands of small aliens pouring through: this was rejected as too much like *Primeval* (but see "Planet of the Dead"). Another idea, one Davies had first thought up in the abortive 2000 relaunch talks, was a group of elderly alien-hunters, a version of which became the story for Penny's grandad. (We'll see a version of that in "The End of Time Part One".) They had someone in mind for Penny (and there's still speculation over who that might have been), but already a wild card was coming into play...

• After "The Runaway Bride" was broadcast, Catherine Tate had talks with Jane Tranter at the BBC about future projects and the conversation kept coming back to how much fun *Doctor Who* had been. Davies had sketched out Penny to the authors working on Series 4 scripts, and a rough consensus emerged that she was a bit like Donna. Davies, as usual, had to establish Penny quickly by debuting her in a fast-moving but relatively "routine" *Doctor Who* adventure.

• Tate and David Tennant had, since their collaboration in 2006, become something of a double-act, recording a *Comic Relief* sketch with Lauren Cooper and a supply teacher she thinks is the Doctor, as well as a radio chat-show (*Chain Reaction*, in which the interviewee one week interviews someone else next week, so on until the last interviews the first), in which Tennant forecast the first line on his obituary. By then talks were over and, although neither could say anything, Tate and Tennant knew that Donna would be back. Despite trying to keep Donna's return secret, the news was out within hours of Martha's surprise walk-out at the end of "Last of the Time Lords" (X3.13) on 30th June, 2007.

Meanwhile, Davies was piecing together a season finale with a team-up of all the former companions in their new, improved lives, and hoped that Donna would also make an appearance. When Tate was sounded out about this in March, it quickly became apparent that she'd be glad to do a whole year. Penny became Donna-with-the-Big-Picture, her name given to the hapless reporter in this episode. Davies continued to put together ideas about aliens using anxieties over body-image to invade present-day Britain, even as he supervised scripts for the earlier stories in production: the Pompeii escapade they'd been putting off since Series 1, a return engagement with the Ood and a meeting with Agatha Christie. The season opener was to have been part of the same production-block as the Pompeii episode, after Block Two, the Ood story and the Christie romp. (Block One, the Christmas Special, was expected to be out of the way by the time Block Three began.)

• As Donna had a bit of previous with the Doctor, the meeting could be delayed for comic effect, altering the pacing. Rather than play against Tate's established comic reputation right from the start, Davies opted to try to make Donna the emotional core of an otherwise comedic episode – so,

to some extent, the alien menace had to be almost place-holders. After a notion of a Botox-like alien that made tentacles erupt from faces, the Adipose came about as a relatively benign horde, resembling the spider-robots in *Stargate SG-1* if they'd been made of marshmallow. Similar technology had been used in the Orc army sequences of the *Lord of the Rings* films, so was known to be doable. A package called "Massive" was the final choice and The Mill started work on tests. With this sucker-punch in place, the projected second episode, "Planet of the Ood", could be a more gruelling experience for the Doctor's new companion.

• As we know from Davies's big book of emails to and from Benjamin Cook, the boss was having a rough time writing his own scripts while micromanaging everyone else's and attempting to salvage *Torchwood*. This script was so late, and the Pompeii escapade took such a lot of preparation, that Phil Collinson approached James Strong during editing of "Voyage of the Damned" so that Colin Teague could concentrate on the logistics of shooting in Rome. He and Collinson went on recces around Cardiff in September, and the Y-junction (shot from the highest available crane) was selected after looking for two close parallel streets as the script specified.

Much of the discussion for this episode centred on the cradle-chase sequence. Strong took stunt coordinator Tom Lucy to, as it were, road-test the commercial cradles. They were all slower than required (and one broke down and kept Lucy in mid-air), so what we see often uses sped-up longshots of a real cradle in between a prop cradle containing the stars. Instead of the conversation we see where the Doctor brings the pen and the screwdriver together, Matron's big exposition was slated for the roof (the cradle only went down a bit at first and the Doctor's head peeped over the rim); this was more complicated and expensive than the cradle scene we got. The idea of placing battery-operated climbing Spider-Man toys under the actors' clothing to simulate the Adipose eruptions was floated, but instead the more traditional bladder mechanism was used.

• Location recording began on 4th October, making this the fifth story in this year's run to be started. The following evening was spent in Waterloo Gardens, Tremorfa, a bit of Cardiff that looks vaguely like North London, at a building called Glan Rhymni. Stacy's domestic setting was selected for its colour scheme, being a show-home, while the bathroom's interior was a display (real bathrooms are hard to film in, even if you can find the right one). Stacy's death-by-diet-pill was done as a second-unit shoot, directed by Collinson after a day testing and attaching the inflatable bladders under Jessica Gunning's cloth-ing. For CGI purposes, some scenes needed Gunning to have crosses drawn on her abdomen. In this and a few other scenes (such as Miss Foster pulling one out of her desk), a knitted Adipose was provided for eyelines. Most of the team took the weekend off, although Tennant was back at Upper Boat on Sunday to record "Time Crash".

• Tuesday 9th was the start of the elaborate procedure for the cradle sequence. The roof selected for this was the British Gas offices at Helmont House, in central Cardiff. Several of the shots of the Doctor and Donna opening/trying to open the window were executed on the roof with no window there (Tate got the giggles hitting a non-existent window with a spanner) to get the background of a city at night and the right acous-tics. The cradle was rock-steady, but the camera, on a crane, moved according to the needs of each shot.

As the cradle was lowered, the stars were replaced by regular Doctor-double Gordon Seed (coached in cradle-operation, in case of problems) and Jo McLaren as Donna. However, the Adipose building was a composite of several office-blocks in the city and, on the next night, the team was at the South Block of Dominion's Arcade in Queen Street (which, by now, you probably know is one of the main streets in Cardiff city centre) for scenes involving Our Heroes being seen from inside Miss Foster's office. The next night included the silent conversation when Donna meets the Doctor. Although the script outlines about a para-graph of conversation, nobody had thought to work out how Donna would actually convey this without words; everyone assumed that Tate would be up to the challenge. As it turned out, she was. All the dialogue was scripted (and there was slightly more), but not how to mime "internet". On Saturday evening, when the Newport offices of Picture Finance weren't in use, the team asked a few of the employees to stick around as extras on the cubicle sequences well into the small hours. The remaining cast completed the first confrontation between the Doctor and Matron Cofelia as dawn broke.

• After a Sunday off, the production moved to the increasingly-familiar location in the basement of the Millennium Stadium (last seen when Donna and the Doctor rode Segways in "The Runaway Bride") and Davies and Strong texted each other on how to write out the guards. On the 16th (and into the 17th), the crew went to Bar Icon, Cockermouth Street for Sylvia's friends experienc-ing the downside of the Adipose "miracle".

• By now, it was evident that Howard Attfield was too ill to continue as Donna's father. It seems that Collinson suggested casting Bernard Cribbins as Donna's grandad to take over. It was still a couple of months until the transmission of "Voyage of the Damned", meaning that – hypo-thetically – "Stan" the newspaper-vendor could be recast (Cribbins was tightly framed, and could be replaced without recalling Kylie Minogue from Australia). Cribbins had been a hit with the pro-duction team and they were already thinking of having him back anyway.

Cribbins was, apparently, more interested in travelling *with* the Doctor than being the support-crew back at home (he'd get his wish in "The End of Time Part One"). If we take the emails between Davies and Cook at face-value, the money to reshoot came from insurance. (Attfield's illness didn't allow for cover, but an injury did, and Attfield seems to have broken his leg at some stage – which, by the Byzantine workings of television production law, released monies for a remount.)

• Although Donna was still getting used to the Doctor's lifestyle, Tate had already acclimatised to the extent that running-shoes became part of the character's "look". Everyone forgot that the earlier scenes had shown Donna wearing her posh work-place shoes when the first take of the stairwell conversation had been shot with Donna wearing trainers. (As it turns out, Donna's heels are almost invisible in the finished version anyway.)

• By the time shooting resumed on 19th November, Howard Attfield had died. Strong took a break from working on an episode of *Bonekickers* to drive from Bristol to Cardiff for the remounted stargazing scene, but torrential rain prevented this so, eventually, Graeme Harper fit it in with work on "Turn Left". Harper also shot the highly secret scenes of Donna meeting Rose in this episode and as part of the alt-universe version of "The Runaway Bride" that night.

• As per the last two years, the Christmas Special included a trailer for the new series, in expectation of an Easter Saturday start. As it turned out, Easter Saturday's timetable was busy, and it was suggested that the series could start a week later, on 12th April instead. This would have collided with the end of *Torchwood* Series 2, so it was eventually shown on 5th, but starting at 6.20pm... more or less the usual start-time for Tom Baker episodes, but considerably earlier than usual for the relaunched series.

• The ratings were expected to take a hit. As it turned out, only the Grand National (the single biggest horse-race of the year) got a bigger audience that day, but it wasn't quite the start they had hoped for. The most talked-about element was the one the production team had kept from the review DVDs and press showing: Rose's return. Tennant and Tate had been on Graham Norton's show the night before and, on both BBC1 and BBC 4, selected highlights from the career of the recently-deceased Verity Lambert were shown that night, as was BBC3's *Doctor Who Confidential* – so it was hard to avoid knowing that the series was back even if you'd missed the various trailers running over the previous three weeks. The episode's credits include a dedication to Attfield.

X4.2: "The Fires of Pompeii"

(12th April, 2008)

Which One is This? It's implicit in the title. "Woe, woe and thrice woe."

Firsts and Lasts For the first time in the new series (and the first since 22.4, "The Two Doctors" back in the mid-80s), the main cast go abroad. David Tennant and Catherine Tate really were packed off to Italy, and the effects team and set-dressers managed to blag two days in the legendary Cinecittà studios.

We have, in rapid succession, the first appearances of Karen Gillan and Peter Capaldi – they here play, respectively, a Soothsayer and a Pompeii merchant. In Capaldi's case, it's the first time that someone did a *Who* having already won an Oscar (for *Franz Kafka's It's a Wonderful Life*).

This is the first story to go into detail about Fixed Points in History. (We'll try to make sense of it in the essay.)

Watch Out For...
• This word for this episode is "epic". It has more extras, more elaborate sets, a bigger scale and a more momentous decision for the Doctor

than anything we've seen since the relaunch. The Doctor's decision is Tennant's very own "Have I that right?" moment (12.4, "Genesis of the Daleks"), and Donna makes it with him. The size of the shoot was similarly ambitious, as were the effects. It's even a bigger episode in running-time, a shade under 49 minutes. This is the high-water mark of the Davies era as far as non-Special episodes go, and the subsequent efforts to make *Doctor Who* on a comparable scale have come at the cost of the number of episodes per fiscal year.

• Many of the sets were constructed for the HBO series *Rome* (2005-2007), hence the soundtrack including a quick homage to that show when the Doctor and Donna step from the TARDIS. Otherwise, this genuinely looks like a real location-shoot in ancient Pompeii (as far as we can tell, without the real thing for comparison). One set, of course, wasn't: a big *Ave* for our old friend the Temple of Peace as the Sybil's chamber. And keep an eye on Caecilius's fishtank – we'll see that again in a fortnight.

However, on the main set, there are five streets filled with extras, chickens and one donkey. It crops up a lot. Less obvious is the attention to detail, even using cages with rabbits that we can barely see. This is as ambitious a shoot as they have attempted to date – all the more impressive because the Italy locations were used for just one day and one night, with technical set-up between these, and after delays with getting the dressings and effects materiel driven from Cardiff to Rome.

• Yes... chickens! It was a standing joke that 70s BBC Costume Dramas going for that authentic period feel always chucked in a chicken, either a Buff Orpington running around in the background or a roasted one being pulled apart and masticated by a thesp with every confidence in the glue holding his false beard on. Nothing said "this is quality drama and we've done all the research" like strategically-positioned hens. *Doctor Who* was no exception[8], so this story's use of them, after so long a gap, is profoundly reassuring.

• The cast includes David Tennant, Peter Capaldi and Karen Gillan. This means that for almost half the episode, there are at least two Scots trying to sound like they come from southern England in any given scene. Gillan's few lines are especially funny with hindsight, as is her Kate Bush impression when doing the whole Sisterhood of Karn bit (13.5, "The Brain of Morbius").

What Constitutes a Fixed Point?

We've discussed how Time was said to work in two key phases of the programme's development, the very beginning (**Can You Rewrite History, Even One Line?** under 1.6, "The Aztecs") and the conceptual rethink of Barry Letts and Terrance Dicks (**How Does Time Work, How Did it Use to Work and What Changed?** under 9.1, "Day of the Daleks"). The new series has brought in some new regular features, some self-consistent and some wildly altering from story to story as the mood takes any individual writer. We'll deal with Steven Moffat's idiosyncratic approach in Volume 10 (**Is Time Like Bolognese Sauce Now?** under X5.5, "Flesh and Stone"), but the one part of Welsh *Who*'s repertoire one might have expected to remain constant would be Fixed Points.

Not so; this subject changes whenever you take your eyes off it.

The nearest we ever got to such a concept in the original series was the beginning of "Time-Flight" (19.7), in which there was zero possibility of going back and rescuing Adric before his death, and the Doctor treated the topic as not up for discussion. There had been theoretical conversations about what would happen if someone changed history ("The Aztecs", of course, but also 2.7. "The Space Museum" and 2.9, "The Time Meddler") and the Doctor's once-rigid policy about not causing known events was bending slightly (2.4, "The Romans"; 2.8, "The Chase").

"Day of the Daleks" is the first time that events in our own time (or near-future, if you prefer) were shown to be malleable. What's interesting is that this still cleaves to the orthodoxy of the era: that only certain points were alterable. The majority of SF writers who touched on this were clear on the existence of particular moments of destiny that could have gone either of two ways. (The best mass-audience version of this is the film *Quest for Love*, in which Joan Collins gets a lecture with a blackboard and chalk about six months before "Day of the Daleks".)

What theoretical physicists were saying was more radical – namely that *all* moments were switching-points between different possible outcomes. Once this filtered into popular culture, we got Alternate Histories being written by anyone who could put in the time to research other potential sequences of events. It became the first-thought notion of any bored writer trying to avoid typecasting and a relaunched *Doctor Who* needed to clamp down on these. Thus, in "Rise of the Cybermen" (X2.5), we're told that even the TARDIS can't travel between realities and this is somehow because there aren't any Time Lords left.

The very first time Rose goes into Earth's past (X1.3, "The Unquiet Dead"), she's told that it's possible for the world to end in 1869. It doesn't though, and by the end of the story Charles Dickens has the same biography as can be found in any textbook. Her next trip back results in time going wrong because she rescued her father from a car-accident. We discussed the discrepancies between this and any other *Doctor Who* story ever broadcast in the last volume (**The Reapers – Errr... What?** under X1.8, "Father's Day"). What that story suggests is that the presence of the Doctor and the TARDIS tends to unfix events, as evidenced by the way the Doctor responds to a pair of wrong futures (X1.7, "The Long Game"; X1.12, "Bad Wolf") and assumes his own guilt for causing the latter. As it turns out, the Daleks are as much to blame as anyone, since they have been amended to have Time Lord-ish abilities.

Thus when, in the middle of wiping out all opposition prior to detonating the Crucible and annihilating all matter in all possible universes (X4.16, "The Waters of Mars"), one Dalek stops and refrains from exterminating a small girl because it can somehow smell that she's connected to a fixed point in time from half a century in the future, we have to ask... *Uh?* Adelaide Brook's destiny, to be killed at Bowie Base One, somehow over-rides the Dalek imperative to destroy everything that could ever exist, ever (X4.12, "The Stolen Earth"). The Dalek apparently has a Time Lord-like sensitivity to such matters (see **What's Happened to the Daleks?** under X1.6, "Dalek").

There seems little logic to this Dalek's priorities until we ask about the precise nature of these Fixed Points. Assuming a linear, causal time-flow for a moment, the existence of such an instant in a time-line contingent on so many possible variations earlier on seems nonsensical. However, the problem becomes more interesting if we re-frame it. If it's not the *event* that is fixed so much as the *point at which it happens*, we might be getting somewhere.

The dialogue in "The Wedding of River Song" (X6.13) is confusing and contradicts much of what we see in the episode itself, but one notion is helpful here. Lake Silencio, Good Friday 2011, is a "Still Point" in time, and thus any event witnessed there becomes a Fixed Point. This requires two things: an

continued on Page 31...

• As all the publicity mentioned, the name "Caecilius" was a joke on the Cambridge O-Level Latin courses that Davies recalled from school. It was the name of the father in a "typical family" booklet set in Pompeii, with the rest of the family also having the names we get here. Meanwhile, anyone over 12 should have guessed that "Lucius Petrus Dextrus" would have a stone right arm (and be somehow connected to a wolf – see later this year) and "Sister Spurina" lives with smoke. It's a script littered with *Asterix*-style gags, including many about the TARDIS translation system.

• There's a reference to every adventure the TARDIS crew has ever had in Italy. The Doctor denies any involvement with the Fire (2.4, "The Romans"), while Donna's questioning of the TARDIS translation systems and near-sacrifice suspiciously resembles Sarah's experiences in 14.1, "The Masque of Mandragora", as does the hokey soothsaying. The "modern art" gag, of course, is from 17.2, "City of Death".

• The Mill have excelled themselves in a pyroclastic eruption simulation beyond anything computer animation had yet achieved. They also make the Pyroviles – stone Centurions with magma coursing through their joints – look like what Ray Harryhausen might have wanted to have done. One shot with these creatures has the Doctor take one on with a water-pistol, a juxtaposition you simply won't get anywhere else.

• For all the tearjerking pathos of the climax, and the quasi-messianic way the Doctor reaches out a hand from the over-lit TARDIS to rescue the family (and will be back to haunt us in X9.5, "The Girl Who Died"), the following scene veers uneasily from horror to contemplation to an awkward line where Caecilius invents the word "Volcano". That Capaldi just about pulls it off augured well...

The Continuity

The Doctor tries, unsuccessfully, to bring Donna to ancient Rome for a treat.

As a Time Lord, he has a natural awareness of Fixed Points – what can be changed in history and what mustn't. [That said, it's interesting that as soon as he realises that it's Pompeii on Volcano Day, he wants to leave right away. He doesn't intuitively sense that their departure would avert the eruption, so prevent the Fixed Point in question. See also, however, the twelfth Doctor's ability to innately sense the outcome of key historical decisions in X8.7, "Kill the Moon".] Upon confronting the High Priestess, he demands that the species he's up against identify itself, threatening to call in the Shadow Proclamation.

Yet again, he's enjoying ghastly puns, including reusing the 'armless' one [from X1.1, "Rose", and indeed 14.2, "The Hand of Fear"] and an even worse one on the Appian Way. (Donna: 'Where are we going now?', Doctor: 'Into the volcano'; 'No way'; 'Yes, way. Appian Way.') He tells Metella not to mention to anyone that he was there [maybe the Shadow Proclamation would take a dim view of his killing 20,000 people, even in the interest of preserving history; more likely it's a way of preserving the Fixed Point through restricting information].

He jokes with Quintus that he won't mention the Lucius escapade to Caecilius if Quintus doesn't tell his dad [side note to say that when Tennant whispers this, he goes into his Barty Crouch Jr. voice]. He cheekily says it's all right for 'just us girls' when Spurina says men aren't allowed in the Temple of Sibyl. [With any earlier Doctors, this would have been an opportunity for comedy drag.]

• *Background.* He's very bitter at being the only Time Lord left [so he's not quite over X3.13, "Last of the Time Lords"]. Lucius taps the Doctor's mind and see that Gallifrey 'burned' [X1.2, "The End of the World" etc.].

He's met the Sibyl and thinks she danced a wonderful tarantella. [As this is an enormous anachronism, she must have been massively powerful.] She apparently 'had a bit of a thing' for the Doctor, who told her it would never last... only to be told that she knew. He finds a quote from *Fawlty Towers* ['She's from Barcelona'] irresistible. Ditto *Spartacus*.

One of the soothsayers says that the Doctor's real name is hidden in the 'cascade of Medusa herself'. [What this might have to do with the Medusa Cascade in X4.12, "The Stolen Earth" is never made clear.]

• *Ethics.* He seems to refrain from killing all the Pyroviles until they formally announce that they plan to kill everybody else first. [For once, he doesn't try the usual "please let me take you somewhere suitable in my TARDIS", he just gets on with destroying everything.] Even after spouting off about Pompeii's destruction being fixed, it appals him to realise that he personally needs to choose between saving Pompeii or the world. [At

What Constitutes a Fixed Point?

continued from Page 29...

event and a witness. There may be any number of such Stillnesses in interstellar space, or when no intelligent conscious observers were around or nothing's happening. It would appear that the fixing of a Fixed Point is itself something that requires a Time Lord or similar, and a moment that is, however this works, a Still Point in spacetime. Once this has happens, news of it can be allowed to emerge – in fact *has* to – via conscious observers. (If you haven't already, see our comments on X3.10, "Blink" and **What *is* the Blinovitch Limitation Effect?** under 20.3, "Mawdryn Undead".)

The implication is that it's the nature and quality of the time at this node of the spacetime continuum that is significant, rather than the scale or possible consequences of the activity there and then. So the Daleks can wipe out all matter in the Cosmos, and the Still Point at what ought to have been Mars in December 2059 might still be there, just with no Bowie Base One disaster to occur there and become a Fixed Point. Hooray! That's all settled.

Except... if the nature of the time and space is all that fixes a point, it ought to be irrelevant who does what there, so why hesitate to shoot Adelaide? It cannot possibly be as straightforward as even this mystical supposition of properties of time at different places suggests. After all, if nothing happens at such a node, and nobody's alive to see it not-happen anyway, the consequences are negligible. We need more data.

Oddly enough, the first use of the words "a fixed point in time" occur before "The Fires of Pompeii" (X4.2), the official introduction of the concept. The very first Fixed Point, one so anomalous that even the TARDIS flees in terror, is Captain Jack Harkness. He keeps coming back from the dead because something's gone wrong with his personal timeline, and the Doctor identifies him as having become a Fixed Point (X3.11, "Utopia"). This is curious for a number of reasons: if he were indeed fixed in time, he probably wouldn't be able to remember anything that happened to him after coming back from being exterminated (X1.13, "The Parting of the Ways"); he wouldn't be getting any older (X3.13, "Last of the Time Lords"); and he certainly couldn't have grown the Victorian-style sideys we see in flashback sequences in *Torchwood*.

This becomes more complex the more baroque Jack's many deaths become. When he's just shot,

stabbed or zapped, there are wounds that undo themselves and he just sits up and gasps. However, in *Children of Earth*, his "deaths" include being encased in concrete and having all his flesh scoured off in an explosion caused when someone put a bomb inside him. What's stated in the dialogue is that he's aware of what's happening to his "corpse" each time. There's a continuity of consciousness. Where the limits of the body to which that consciousness is linked might be – bleeding, haircuts, trips to the toilet and so on – is irrelevant. The body "resets" to a state just before the fatal injury (no mention of illnesses, though: would cancer affect him?) What might therefore be happening is a localised Still Point with an inbuilt conscious observer. Jack might well be a complex spacetime phenomenon in a greatcoat, but one itself capable of being transported to other times and places via a Vortex manipulator or a more contrite TARDIS.

We might at this point reinforce the comparison, made in **What Happens in a Regeneration?** under 11.5, "Planet of the Spiders", between Jack's apparent immortality and those of Rassilon (20.7, "The Five Doctors") and Mawdryn ("Mawdryn Undead"). This isn't entirely satisfactory as a resolution, though, as in those cases the desire to end was the most clearly-defined feature. If consciousness were the key, a combination of head-traumas, drugs or the kind of mind-transference common in *Doctor Who* would let the body stop.

A comparison of the first two Fixed Points to unequivocally fit the pattern isn't much help either. It's the release of information that's the problem when the Bowie Base One survivors show up safe in London. Had the Doctor taken them to live out their days on a desert island or a pleasure planet in the far future, he would have got away with it. On Volcano Day, however, the Doctor rescues the Caecilius family and tells them not to mention his actions. They commission a marble frieze of the Doctor, Donna and the TARDIS and train Quintus as a medic. That's going to have a knock-on effect on its own: saving lives that should have ended. The frieze isn't Caecilius's own work – he trades in marble but isn't a mason. The influential visitors from Alexandria might well ask about the oddly-dressed Household Gods. Information about the Doctor and Donna stands a good chance of seeping out from the immediate family. Nothing untoward happens.

continued on Page 33...

ABOUT TIME 2008-2009

least, that's how he describes, but it's an inherent false dichotomy – it's not as if Pompeii would survive if the Pyroviles succeeded.]

After the shock of sealing Pompeii's fate, he stomps off without even thinking to try to save anyone; he seems paralysed by the notion that changing history even to save his own people would be unacceptably dangerous. None of Donna's arguments about saving *someone* work, but her tears do. Afterward, he tells Donna with a perfectly blank expression that she's right: he needs someone to stop him.

[We hear a lot about the Doctor's ability to change things being mainly governed by fear of consequences. His decision to save the Caecilius family is the first step towards the more drastic rupture of history on compassionate grounds, after he has breached a Fixed Point and lived: X4.16, "The Waters of Mars"; X7.15, "The Day of the Doctor". In a very odd moment at the end of "The Girl Who Died", it occurs to him that regenerating into a Caecilius look-a-like was a hint from his subconscious that this ought to happen more often. We conclude from this that the Doctor never met Mr Frobisher from *Torchwood* (also played by Capaldi), because that would be quite a different message: *I'm the Doctor and I peddle children to alien junkies except my own, because I shoot them first.* But see 20.1, "Arc of Infinity".]

• *Inventory: Sonic Screwdriver.* It unties knots on Donna's wrists and knocks over marble carvings. It also locks the door of the capsule.

• *Inventory: Psychic Paper.* It convinces Caecilius that the Doctor is a 'marble inspector'.

• *Inventory: Other.* The Doctor puts away his water-pistol in his inside jacket pocket [making the terrible Appian Way joke] and later gets it out of his back trouser pocket. [Since you've caught us on a good day, we can *maybe* treat this as an extension of his having inter-dimensional pockets; X3.0, "The Runaway Bride".]

We also have a brass telescope [per Season Eighteen, and rather than those souped-up opera glasses in X1.9, "The Empty Child"]. He also takes a valuable Roman coin from behind Quintus's ear.

The TARDIS It's confirmed that the TARDIS can and does translate written languages for companions, with Roman text rendered for Donna as English. When Donna attempts the first bit of genuine Latin she can think of ["Veni, vidi, vici" – Julius Caesar tossed it off after a successful war],

the local vendor concludes that she's Welsh and says he can't understand her. Caecilius seems to have the same problem with the Doctor's Latin tags. [Perhaps we're meant to conclude that back in X2.4, "The Girl in the Fireplace", Reinette realises she's addressing an "Englishman" by his accent, and attempts to address him in that language. Which would explain the "Monsieur" line. We first speculated on this in 1.8, "The Reign of Terror".]

When the Doctor dematerialises the first time, the console grates a bit. When leaving the villa and arriving again, the process takes longer than usual, with the dematerialisation sound well into its cycle before Donna even gets to the door and the sound (and a brilliant blue-white light) preceding the appearance of the police box shell by a good ten seconds.

The Supporting Cast

• *Donna.* Upon noting that Roman signs are in English, she asks in bewilderment whether they've landed in Epcot. Thereupon, she decides on an empirical test of the translation system, to resolve a question the Doctor admits had never occurred to him. [By comparison, Rose was annoyed with the translator-function and Martha didn't ask.]

She *almost* suggests that she doesn't know what 'Veni, vidi, vici' means [since she's aware the main danger of Vesuvius wasn't the lava so much as the volcanic ash that choked everyone – Pliny the Elder, in a harbour boat at the time, died of it and so did most of the immediate survivors – we'll give her the benefit of the doubt.]. She picked up the phrase from her dad, who used to say it coming back from football. [Presumably on those occasions when West Ham won, before she was old enough to go with him.] She also knows that Rome is built on seven hills.

Most of the episode involves her questioning all the unwritten rules concerning interference in established historical events. The Doctor's various tactics of "they'll think you're mad," "I'm a Time Lord, I know how this works," and "Let's just leave now before we die" fail to convince her. Once they really *have* established that everyone on Earth will die if they don't destroy Pompeii, she takes symbolic responsibility for erupting the volcano with the Doctor. After Vesuvius has erupted, she urges the Doctor to save one family if that's all he can do; her response to his refusal has Donna as furious as we'll ever see her. By the time he comes round,

What Constitutes a Fixed Point?

continued from Page 31...

To be honest, the supposedly catastrophic results of the later transgression aren't clear. A clairvoyant on a bus foretold the death of this particular Doctor *before* this rupturing of causality (X4.15, "Planet of the Dead"), so the Doctor's personal future wasn't affected one way or the other. Apparently, the Doctor messing with a Fixed Point was itself a Fixed Point. So whatever terrible things that followed were themselves pre-ordained, so can't be considered to be the consequences of his decision. Time becomes unpredictable in predictable, predicted ways. The Ood develop eldritch powers (X4.17, "The End of Time Part One", and compare it to the Sybilline Sisterhood's almost unerring accuracy leading up to another potentially-ruptured Fixed Point), but we knew all along this species had some psychic ability. The Doctor seems to think it's been precipitated by a century, but he really hasn't much idea about the Ood when he first encounters them (X2.8, "The Impossible Planet"), so their potential as Time Lord replacements and Rassilon giving the Master some jewellery seem to be consequences of Adelaide shooting herself in London. But that's it. The sky doesn't fall down, but the Ood Elder becomes Sir Basil Exposition and the Doctor's death happens exactly as predicted. Everything else is as it should be.

Apparently.

Everything that happens to the *next* Doctor seems to involve the nature of time altering from the set rules of even the earlier BBC Wales episodes. The space-time Vortex changes its appearance (X7.0, "The Doctor, the Widow and the Wardrobe" confirms what we saw in the titles and the end of X5.13, "The Big Bang"), and Cracks in space-time that allow Prisoner Zero to emerge and individuals to be removed from history without any knock-on effects open and eventually swallow the universe (Series 5's overall plot). Moreover, next time a Fixed Point is ruptured, everything goes wildly wrong and the dead all convene on the same point in Earth's time. The precise details of what happens to fix it are a bit obscure, because the episode is more concerned with River Song than ontology. The explanation given in the ancillary material, never on screen, is that marrying River sets up a new timeline that alters the progression from Lake Silencio *for her* and thus re-sets time. That would work better if the Doctor had never met her future selves, but

never mind. It's a matter of historical record that the Doctor died there that day and she, his apparent widow, did it. The key point is, again, information. A Silent witnesses the Doctor being shot according to plan and reports to base, so time flows normally thereafter. That the event witnessed isn't exactly what's really happening is a minor point, it seems.[12]

That so many people *know* that he isn't dead doesn't seem to worry anyone either. The Daleks know how to contact him; so do UNIT and Madame Vastra. In fact, Series 7 is one long sequence of contradictions to the end of Series 6 but, as far as we can tell, the universe is still a going concern. (Although the Vortex has altered and changes colour from episode to episode, until it completely changes once we're shot of the Ponds.) Arguably, this universe isn't quite the same as the one before "The Big Bang", because the Doctor extrapolated everything in it from the contents of the Pandorica (and possibly the traditional small piece of fairy cake). The entire cosmos is now a story Amy Pond tells. That small detail seems to have been forgotten (see **Who Narrates This Series?** under 23.1, "The Mysterious Planet" for more in this vein) and everything seems to be exactly as it was beforehand.

We have possible confirmation of the working hypothesis from *The Sarah Jane Adventures*. In "The Temptation of Sarah Jane Smith", the apparently complimentary concept of "weak points" in space-time gets aired in its fullest form. These appear to be small ruptures which, when tampered with by time-travellers, open up fissures and allow both the advent of malign beings from other dimensions (see **Should the Trickster have a Dead Bird on His Head?** under "The Wedding of Sarah Jane Smith") and ghastly alternate timelines.

An interesting sideline is that Sarah mentions other weak points and that they often locate around places of worship. This is interesting. We have often suggested that conscious observers and in particular concerted mental effort and awareness seems to be bound up with time travel (a notion explored in **How Does the TARDIS Work?** under 1.3, "The Edge of Destruction" and **What *is* the Blinovitch Limitation Effect?** among others), and we tried *ever* so hard to make sense of the seemingly-ludicrous piece of Whitaker-Science underlying 4.9, "The Evil of the Daleks" by similar means. If, as we tentatively concluded in

continued on Page 35...

she's run out of arguments and is simply standing there crying.

Like Martha, she likes hugging the Doctor at random intervals; unlike Martha, she doesn't seem to seek any more intimacy than that. There's a hint she too appreciates terrible puns, with a very laboured one about *Rocky IV*. She chimes in with the Doctor's "I am Spartacus" joke. When arguing with the designated driver about interfering with history, she pulls rank on the "kids" he's used to travelling with. Her immediate response to the volcano is to go into the nearest amphitheatre and warn the public about the danger. When the eruption has begun she tries this again.

She takes being tied up on a sacrificial altar in her stride, along with the Doctor's just-in-the-nick-of-time appearance. [Her assumption of the latter might be why she's so bellicose when shouting at a woman with a knife.]

• *The Shadow Proclamation.* [The Doctor expects his invoking the Shadow Proclamation's name to be meaningful, suggesting the group has existed for far longer than hitherto suggested. The Proclamation refers to Pyrovilla's disappearance as a 'cold case' in "The Stolen Earth".]

The Non-Humans

• *Pyroviles.* Natives of Pyrovillia [another of those too-appropriate planet names; see 2.8, "The Chase" for some classics]. Their pod crashed on Earth 'thousands of years' ago, turning the occupants to dust. Humans who inhaled this became hosts for the renascent aliens. The smaller Vesuvian eruption 17 years before woke them all up, and their spores activated latent human psychic ability even as their bodies slowly petrified. Eventually, they become anthropomorphic ten metre rock beings, with magma to bind the carapace. These have crests on the heads, resembling Roman helmets, and the eyes and mouth, plus a few fissures around the joints, glow orange. They have fire-breath and, when at full size, can crush rocks underfoot.

[Why the afflicted humans start petrifying from the right fore-arm first is unclear, but compare to the method by which Amy began transforming into a Weeping Angel in X5.4, "The Time of Angels". It's a curious coincidence if it isn't connected, but so's Karen Gillan being involved in both cases. The internal evidence suggests that this transmogrification is unconnected to Petrifold Regression (X2.1, "New Earth").]

Humans in the process of conversion can access prophesies of the near-future with precision, and can divine buried memories when within eye-contact of the subject. Longer-term, they foresee a future in which Pompeii supplants Rome as the centre of a post-human empire lasting for millennia. Their vision doesn't forecast the city's destruction, since it was this very eruption that caused the space-time crack that reverberates back and gave them their sight. The infection is especially strong amongst those who deliberately exposed themselves to the smoke, such as the Sybilline Sisterhood and the city's Augur. A bucket of water shatters a Pyrovile 'foot-soldier' [almost like the Witch in *The Wizard of Oz*], and even the Doctor's water pistol stings the partly-human priestess hybrid and one of the foot-soldiers.

They have technology that can use circuit boards carved from marble. These form the components of an energy converter.

Planet Notes *Pyrovillia.* Something vanished their home planet as well [see last story]. They crash landed here when looking for somewhere else to go. [We can presume that Earth has something they want or need, if they're sticking around here instead of going to Venus, which is much hotter with plenty of recent-ish volcanic activity. Perhaps it's just the presence of humanoid forms they can possess, or that Venusian aikido works on giant rock-beasts. Io, a moon of Jupiter with volcanic activity and no fictional pesky locals (to date) would also be a good bolt-hole.]

History

• *Dating.* [The date the Doctor gives, '23rd August', '79AD', is the day before the eruption as usually stated, based on Pliny. There's some evidence that it might have been 17th October. They're still around on the day itself, the first of three days of falling ash and pumice. The final scene, said to be six months later, is as the contracts for the grain-store in Alexandria are being awarded. The earlier earthquake in Pompeii was a real historical event, relatively smaller but significant enough that the town was still rebuilding when it was covered.]

Donna says that the Doctor 'saved me in 2008'. [If the 'saved me' phrasing refers back to events in "The Runaway Bride", that happened at Christmas 2007. Given the "year ahead" model that's been in place ever since X1.4, "Aliens of London", she

What Constitutes a Fixed Point?

continued from Page 33...

the essay with "Day of the Daleks", a Time Lord, post-Time War Dalek or similarly "time sensitive" being (the term is only used in 18.5, "Warriors' Gate", but applies to the Tharils and Romana alike, so seems to be applicable here) somehow fixes a version of events as the "correct" one by being in the vicinity, a large enough concentration of un-time-sensitive consciousnesses might have a simi-lar (or opposite) effect. Or, more likely, such a patch of wobbly spacetime might produce miraculous-seeming events and attract the faithful. Or, most likely, the two effects reinforce one another.

What constitutes stillness in an expanding universe? The model that seems to fit best is some kind of standing wave. If it is somehow a quality of spacetime, and the accident of a bit of matter with conscious observers and a passing Time Lord (or equivalent) on it passing through is circumstantial, we might wonder about superstrings or whatever. It makes a nice mental image: an 11-dimensional "string" being vibrated like a washing-line between two poles, so that nodes that don't move as much are created by wobbling it at exactly the right fre-quency. It's probably not that. Besides, mass isn't unrelated to spacetime; Einstein said so. Something as big as a planet is going to bend the continuum, making gravity happen (sort of). It also doesn't help us if were looking for any regu-larities between the known Fixed Points. August 72 AD. March 2011. December 2059. Perhaps 65 million BC. All in this solar system, as it whirls around the galactic hub in a universe red-shifting away from the rest of itself.

Two of these events, Pompeii and the extinction of the dinosaurs, are marked by very big explo-sions. We're told in "The Fires of Pompeii" that a blast equivalent to 20 atomic warheads is enough to make rifts in time. The destruction of Bowie Base One isn't quite on that scale, but is a fairly hefty bang. Perhaps it's the damage to spacetime that sets these three events apart, coming as they do at otherwise Still Points. This doesn't account for the relatively straightforward effects they seem to have had (or not) compared to the immense dent in reality caused by the not-very-big gunfire when River done shot her old man down. However, that event is a concatenation of several Time Lord-or-equivalent beings, including the *Teselecta*, a Silent, River (two of her, in fact) and the Doctor. The one remaining anomalous Fixed Point was caused by the biggest temporal anom-aly we've ever seen, the Bad Wolf, resurrecting Jack without due caution.

Until new episodes re-open this matter, we are having difficulty finding any regularities between the events stated on screen to come into this charmed circle. The chances are that any such episodes will complicate matters further, just as the more we find out about the Weeping Angels, the less sense any of it makes (see **What's With These Angels?** under X5.4, "The Time of Angels"). For the moment, our tentative theory is that it needs someone a bit like a Time Lord, a Still Point and something to bruise time (probably a massive explosion) to make an event a Fixed Point. The more drastic the consequences of events happen-ing thereabouts, the more likely we are to know about it, so information is bound up in it as well.

We'll pick up this thread in a few episodes' time, with **How is This Not a Parallel Universe?** under X4.11, "Turn Left".

should now originate from 2009. Maybe she means that she lived through 2008 as part of her questioning the definition of 'history', or this is when she thinks "Partners in Crime" (X4.1) was happening. Or she's one of those people who hasn't quite adjusted to the new year, like continu-ing to sign your cheques with the previous one.]

The Doctor says that clothes are no problem in ancient Rome, because it's like Soho. [It's a bit fun-nier if you know that the Big Finish audio *The Fires of Vulcan* had Mel's attempts to sort out her anachronistic clothing driving the plot. For three episodes. Then everything just blows up.] As schoolkids used to all know, dormice and ants in honey were genuine Roman delicacies.

The Analysis

The Big Picture The prologue: titter ye not...

In 2000, Big Finish audios released a four-part adventure by Steve Lyons called *The Fires of Vulcan*. In this, predestination is a bigger problem than usual for the seventh Doctor and Mel, because the TARDIS is unearthed in the ruins of Pompeii in 1980 (and placed in custody of UNIT officer Muriel Frost; see X1.4, "Aliens of London"). There's a rivalry between groups of religious/pro-phetic cults, as happened more mutedly in the TV story, and the Doctor is forced to take on a gladi-ator, a combat interrupted by the entirely natural eruption of Vesuvius. The audio time travellers

ABOUT TIME 2008-2009

engage more with the different mind-set of people from this culture, as might be expected.

At the core of the television story is an attempt to resolve one of the big problems in *Doctor Who*: that Earth's history is somehow sacrosanct, yet the Doctor and chums happily alter the events of the future, present-day and other planets. Barry Letts had attempted a fudge with the unspecified details of the Blinovitch Limitation Effect (9.1, "Day of the Daleks"), but this story required a coherent explanation for all previous stories and any new ones. The *New Adventures* and BBC Books novels had touched upon the concept of Fixed Points in history. Notably, the historical event in *The Final Sanction* (1999) by, er, Steve Lyons involved one of those, as well as a war between humans and an aquatic race who wore glorified spacesuits when attacking on land. Not at all like the Hath (X4.6, "The Doctor's Daughter"). No, indeed, in that one it was Zoe who was abducted by the fish-like Selacians, not Martha.

Doctor Who had already changed its mind on this issue before *Star Trek* began, so the *Trek* idea that all of Earth's history was equally vulnerable – even the bits that hadn't happened on the day of broadcast – wasn't tenable. The compromise that had come about by unspoken consensus: anything in our past that was made to happen as recorded by visitors (e.g. the *Mary Celeste* being evacuated after a Dalek assault, "The Chase") came under the same heading as the improbable-but-handy coincidence of the whole universe having English accents and the relaunched series needed to deal with it. The idea of a special kind of time-space event that was untouchable gave all other adventures in history the potential to end unexpectedly, while making it possible that any other world or time could be equally set in stone. As a tactical move this was significant.

Making a known event – taught in most schools and available in popular culture – the site for a discussion of Utilitarianism was precisely what had been needed since Series 2 if not earlier. It's a more than unusually blunt version of the trolley problem, a philosophical problem much favoured in university ethics classes. Is sacrificing a numerically-smaller number of people to save a larger group ethically necessary? (We'll get other, more obviously rigged versions in X6.10, "The Girl Who Waited"; X8.7, "Kill the Moon" and X9.8, "The Zygon Inversion". See also **Does This Universe have an Ethical Standard?** under 12.1,

"Robot".) We've seen the ways that calculating the relative morality of small, personal losses to big abstract ones has been treated when discussing X1.8, "Father's Day" and its closest source, Harlan Ellison's *Star Trek* episode "City on the Edge of Forever", and will revisit it with "Turn Left".

Although the destruction of Pompeii and Herculaneum was described in detail by eye-witness Pliny the Younger (the nephew of Pliny the Elder, who died organising an escape), the ruins were, for obvious reasons, not immediately apparent. It was only in 1599 that a plausible site was found; excavation began in 1748. Excavations continued (and are still proceeding) and our old chum Edward Bulwer-Lytton (7.2, "Doctor Who and the Silurians") wrote a bestseller, *The Last Days of Pompeii,* that set the tone for most twentieth-century fiction about the city, making an explicit connection between the supposed lax morals of the residents and the suddenness of their deaths and erasure of their city from the map. The city's documents and leftovers, a snapshot of daily life in the first century captured *in media res* (bach), continue to provide surprising insights into the normality and practical details of a working city. It's a setting that keeps coming back into fashion, with Robert Harris's book in 2003 and a risible film from 2014. A more measured approach came in a 2003 docu-drama, *Pompeii: the Last Day*, which was shown as Davies was getting his pitch for a revised *Doctor Who* together. One shot from that, of the moon seen through plumes of ash, was borrowed for this episode.

The city's fall had been done as Hollywood spectacle and used as a parable for San Francisco and Los Angeles but, in early 70s Britain, it was mainly known as a pretext for a bawdy sitcom. *Up Pompeii!* had been a hit around the time Davies would have been just about able to realise that the jokes were rude (it went out on Mondays at 9.25 pm, just before *Doomwatch* in the same weeks when 7.3, "The Ambassadors of Death" and 7.4, "Inferno" were on Saturdays). It used the Roman-era setting as a background for Frankie Howerd's usual schtick[9], and endless bedhopping and slapstick farce. His character, Lurcio the slave, broke the fourth wall and talked to us, raising his huge eyebrows at accidental double-entendres from other characters and trying to talk posh then dropping into conversational camp cockney. This wasn't unprecedented, as we saw with "The

Romans" (and – oh look – Max Adrian plays Lurcio's master, Ludicrus Sextus, with the same zeal he put into playing Priam in another Hartnell adventure in not-quite-real history, 3.3, "The Myth Makers").

Two almost-simultaneous films, both with Jon Pertwee in, had come out in 1964. *A Funny Thing Happened on the Way to the Forum* was a Broadway hit brought to the big screen by Dick Lester between Beatles flicks, but *Carry On Cleo* was repeated at least once a year on BBC1 in the late 70s. As you will recall from earlier volumes, fully comprehending *Doctor Who* without a grounding in the *Carry On* films is a forlorn task. As the *Asterix* series had yet to make it across the channel at the time, *Carry On Cleo* was the first use of those sarcastic anachronisms anyone in Britain had encountered – a slave-trading firm is called "Marcus & Spencius", for example. *Up Pompeii!* was itself turned into a feature film which used the volcano as a way to keep the farce going for as long as possible without the conventional resolution. The series as written by *Carry On* scriptwriter Talbot Rothwell and a one-off special, *Further Up Pompeii*, went out in 1975, shortly before before *I, Claudius* began production.

Asterix first showed up in the UK in a weird translation in a short-lived boys' paper called *Ranger*, in amid the gosh-wow technology and the fondly-remembered *Trigan Empire* Roman-style space-opera. This version made out it was about ancient Britons sticking it to the *Vir* (Latin for "Man"; tidy, that), and failed to get in any but the most obvious jokes. Eventually, it got a proper rendition, with good equivalents of the gag-names[10], and the first animated version was redubbed with surprising fidelity and shown on BBC1 in school holidays. For anyone who's managed to get to reading-age without encountering this, it's a series of adventures in comic-strip books about a small village of Gauls that Caesar has perpetually failed to conquer when he veni'd, vide'd and vice'd the rest of France. Their druid, Getafix (or "Panoramix" in the original), devised a super-strength potion that is for Asterix what spinach is for Popeye. The parable of defying US domination of European culture is never rammed down the reader's throat, but it's worth noting that the live-action films are sufficiently successful for them not to bother with an English-language version (Obelix, the giant friend of the pint-sized hero, is played by Gerard Depardieu), and that Parc Asterix is more popular with French families

than Disneyland Paris.

A similar jokey reworking of antiquity was used in *Hercules: The Legendary Journeys*, and its slightly less playful spin-off *Xena: Warrior Princess*. That also played on the market-with-wickerwork-and-narrow-windey-streets-full-of-extras-and-chickens vibe we see here, and the music often used a similar wordless melisma for supernatural shenanigans that the Sisterhood has provided for them in the score for this episode. That slightly mucky, lived-in look for the locations was also in the HBO series *Rome* (for which these sets had been built), and was something Davies was keen to have as "accessible" for the audience he had in mind, rather than the Hollywood gigantism or the BBC ack-torrs in clean TV studios he associated with *I, Claudius* and adaptations of Shakespeare in the 1970s. Davies had been throwing around concepts for a story set in Pompeii since the first season, originally scheduling one in as a work-out for the new three-person team in the slot eventually given to X1.11, "Boom Town" (hence the Volcano Day jokes in "The Empty Child"). He had already used the idea of inhaling the volcanic dust from Pompeii in *Casanova*, where it had been a cocaine analogue as part of depicting 1780s Naples (built near the site of Pompeii) as a prototype for contemporary California.

Of course, there was a real Sybilline cult, and genuine Vestal Virgins, but the look of this lot is more obviously influenced by the Sisterhood of Karn ("The Brain of Morbius"): another gang of fire-worshipping psychic goth-chicks in red gowns. The high priestess is addressed as "Reverend Mother"; this is usually a term for senior Catholic nuns, but if we're talking about women who can see the future, it's maybe more directly from *Dune*. (The shots of her seen through gauze seem very like the early episodes of 5.2, "The Abominable Snowmen", which keep Padmasambhava from plain sight until the plot has thickened.) If we're counting *Doctor Who* references, then Metulla calling the TARDIS a "temple" is a pretty obvious allusion to Katerina's annoying habit, in the episode of "The Daleks' Master Plan" (3.4) that had just been rediscovered and reissued in 2004.

As we mentioned earlier, the Cambridge O-Level Latin course used booklets using a "typical" family of Pompeiians. The father, Caecilius, was a trader; he and wife Metulla, son Quintus and two slaves (neither called "Rhombus") all lived in a villa. In reality, Lucius Caecilius Iucunda (who would have been called "Iucunda") and a family a bit like this lived in a well-preserved estate, now visitable, on which the set for the episode was based. It had a good specimen of a shrine to Household Gods and another to Jupiter. He wasn't a marble trader, but a sort of fixer for auction-loans, but his Household Gods annex was well-preserved. Sadly, the evidence seems to indicate that he was long dead by the time the volcano erupted (most likely in the previous event 17 years earlier).

And regarding the whole concept of people in Pompeii turning to stone... this is, of course, a joke on the archaeological techniques used to reconstruct its inhabitants. Over the hundreds of years since the town was buried, most of the bodies had decomposed, leaving gaps in the ash layers. The Victorians worked out that plaster-of-Paris could be poured into these gaps to create a cast model, thus making solid rock copies of the dead. Equally obviously, the idea of humans becoming slowly petrified was used as one of the futuristic ailments in X2.1, "New Earth", and "petrifold regression" was re-used in Jacqueline Rayner's BBC Books novel *The Stone Rose*. The "positions" gag about the falling statues every time the earth trembles is manifestly pinched from the Disney rendering of *Mary Poppins*.

English Lessons

• *Soho* (n.): The bohemian/sleazy bit of London from 1750-ish to a couple of years ago: still the hub of what little film-making we have left (especially digital effects houses such as The Mill and Framestore), and with a higher concentration of gay bars than most of Britain, but not what it was. The name is a hunting term because, before the various waves of refugees settled there, it was Henry VIII's private estate.

• *Lovely Jubbly* (interj.): The slogan for Jubbly, a frozen drink in a tetrahedronal cardboard container from the early 60s, revived as a catchphrase by Del-Boy in *Only Fools and Horses* (see Volume 7). It's usually used to mean "Result!" or "Score!"

• *TK Maxx* (n.) a cheap clothing outlet, equivalent to the US TJ Maxx.

• *Sunshine* (n): A mock-friendly term of address, often used when asserting authority (much like "Matey", although that's more Home Counties and "sunshine" tended to be northern, the peak use being in the late 1970s). Associated with Eric Morecambe and Paul Daniels, thence Gene Hunt

in *Life on Mars*. (A further Eric Morecambe allusion comes when the Doctor, saving the bust from toppling when he first appears at Casa Caecilius, pats the cheeks exactly the same way Eric would do to Ernie Wise.)

Welsh Lessons

• *There's Lovely!* (interj.) is the clichéd exultation of comedy Welshmen (see, for example, Evans in 5.5, "The Web of Fear"). They would also append *look you* or *isn't it?* to a sentence, as a rough equivalent of "you see", and call everyone "Boyo". (See 10.5, "The Green Death" for some ripe examples of off-the-shelf Taff-speak.)

Latin Lessons

• *Appian Way*: All roads lead to Rome, but this one goes there directly. It passed near Pompeii.

• *Etruscans*: People from a different bit of what's now Italy, who had invaded Pompeii a few centuries back but weren't quite as disreputable in the first century as the dialogue suggests. Certainly not as dodgy as the early Christians, who probably really did burn Rome in 64 (contrary to what "The Romans" suggests).

• *Morituri Te Salutant*: We who are about to die salute you.

• *Hypercaust*: (n): A form of underfloor heating, usually fuelled by burning wood to heat water but in this – apparently unique – case it is geothermal.

• *Sesterces*: Unit of currency, a quarter of a Denarius. Fifteen sesterces (or sestercii if you're posh), the amount the trader got for the TARDIS, is about ten days' pay for a Roman soldier, a week's-worth of wheat or the cost of a decent tunic. Shortly after this time, production transferred to Lugdunum (Lyon, France).

• *Thermopolium*: A place where hot food was kept hot for sale to the public, cheap, and with drinks and (possibly) girls. The most famous one in Pompeii was right next to the bath-house, where all strata of society could get cleaned and pampered. Both venues used the plentiful heat from the mountain, but while a bath-house was relatively salubrious, the graffiti unearthed at Pompeii's thermopolia suggest that Caecilius was rightly concerned about his son's reputation.

Oh, Isn't That...?

• *Karen Gillan* (Soothsayer). At the time of her appearance, she'd not been in much of anything yet, just a bit of modelling. You'll see more of her in the next volume playing Amy Pond, a part that also began with her arm turning to stone (see X5.5, "Flesh and Stone"). Or, if you prefer, she's the bald blue one in *Guardians of the Galaxy*. She gets about ten seconds in *The Big Short,* rather more in the recent *Jumanji* reboot, but she's parlayed all this into a directing career.

• *Phil Cornwell* (Stallholder). The one who did the Eccleston imitation on *Dead Ringers*. He appeared in several of the later *Comic Strip* films, notably *Detective on the Edge of a Nervous Breakdown*. He was the voice(s) of the alien puppet Gilbert in the late 80s (25.2, "The Happiness Patrol") and several *Spitting Image* characters. But more, much more, he was half of the regular cast of *Stella Street*, the all-star suburban sitcom.

• *Tracy Childs* (Metella, Caecilius's wife). She's from *Howard's Way* (see 21.4, "Resurrection of the Daleks"; 22.2, "Vengeance on Varos"). She'd done many one-off dramas before that, notably the BBC production of Brecht's *Baal* (the one with David Bowie). Big Finish listeners might be acquainted with her as Elizabeth Klein, a Nazi schemer and sometimes-seventh Doctor companion who debuted in *Colditz* (also featuring David Tennant as Kurtz, a German officer who threatens to rape Ace – no, seriously).

• *Peter Capaldi* (Caecilius, marble trader). Lots of things, including the 1996 *Neverwhere* (the original, as the book was an adaptation of the TV script) as the Angel Islington. Before that, we could suggest you watch *The Crow Road* or *Local Hero*, but if you're really brave try Ken Russell's *The Lair of the White Worm*[11]. He pops up later as John Frobisher in *Torchwood: Children of Earth*. He directed an Oscar-winning short film, *Franz Kafka's It's a Wonderful Life*, starring Richard E Grant (see X7.6, "The Snowmen" et seq. and A4, "The Curse of Fatal Death"). At the time of broadcast, he was Malcolm Tucker: the inventively foulmouthed puppet-master of the clueless minister in *The Thick of It* and its related feature film *In the Loop*. He did a devastating spoof of the kinds of documentary Mark Gatiss always does for BBC4, entitled *The Cricklewood Greats*, which shows a genuine love for the films being ridiculed. He got to be the Doctor between 2013 and 2017, a mere 40 years after bombarding the BBC with letters about *Doctor Who*.

• *Phil Davis* (Lucius Petrus Dextrus, petrifying Chief Augur). Most recently, he was the Devil in the last BBC series of *Being Human*, but his breakthrough role was Chalky in *Quadrophenia*. You'll

have seen him in things as diverse as *Notes on a Scandal, Alien*[3], *Bleak House* and the first episode of *Sherlock*. He was King John in *Robin of Sherwood*.

Things That Don't Make Sense The Doctor gets away with removing *this* family from the predestined doom of the city and then makes a huge song and dance about doing the same for the three survivors of Bowie Base One ("The Waters of Mars") as if it's unprecedented and a huge moral dilemma. Even if Adelaide Brooke *must* die to fulfil that Fixed Point, surely he could remove the others and order them to live out their days in silent obscurity? (Not that this family does: the shrine to the new Household Gods must have entailed them telling someone about their visitors and Quintus, as a healer, must affect history a bit.)

For an upwardly-mobile householder such as Caecilius, having a house-guest called "Spartacus" just as a civic dignitary shows up is like... well, the nearest we can come up with is if they'd done an episode of *Bewitched* in which Darren's playing host to an important client for his advertising company and a Mr and Mrs Leon Trotsky pay a call. And then they claim that Mrs Spartacus is from Barcelona, a city named after the family that produced Hannibal and which was founded by Rome's great rival, Carthage.

The Sisters send out a not-even-slightly-conspicuous attack-squad led by Not-Amy-Pond-At-All (is her name "Stagna"?) to get Donna because she made a false prophesy. Like she's such a threat. But Lucius *also* sent a raiding party to the same address at the same time. Quite apart from their being astonishingly thin-skinned, the Pyroviles' agents – especially for telepaths, and prophets – aren't exactly masters of joined-up thinking.

Why is there a Sybiline Temple in Pompeii in the first place? Everyone who wanted the future foretold used to leave the city and sail out a few miles to the nearby island of Cumea. (That provided the framing narrative of *I, Claudius*: it's not as if there wasn't anyone on the production team who'd read the novel or seen the 1975 BBC adaptation. See X3.11, "Utopia".)

It's undoubtedly to make the story more family-friendly, but there is a distinct lack of slaves for a family this wealthy. Rhombus might be one, as might the lad in the yellow toga, but we might expect a couple more in such a moderately well-to-do household. Either way, while the Doctor saves Caecilius's family, these people are left to die.

On the other hand, a purple dress in AD 79?

Being "Born to the Purple" meant wealth beyond anything provincial Pompeii could muster – murex shells were crushed in vast numbers to produce tiny amounts of dye, so this was conspicuous consumption *in extremis* (boyo). It was reserved for the Imperial family, not the likes of Donna, and definitely not something Metella might lend to unexpected house-guests.

Lucius's right arm has become completely stone as far as his shoulder, but otherwise he seems unchanged. All right, but even the full-blown Pyroviles who stomp about have more flexibility than his right arm. Why should he be so singular? Moreover, how does he *walk* with such a hefty appendage? Wouldn't he list to port?

We'll leave aside any quibbles about red-hot beings ten feet tall fitting tiny (to them) marble slabs inlaid with melty metal in a pod too small for any of them to get in through the door, and wonder why beings who survived the crash by becoming dust and getting ingested by local humans should be stopped by a volcano turning them to dust.

All right, it's done for comedic effect, but two buckets of water suffice to extinguish and shatter a ten foot walking volcano. Later, the Doctor's self-replenishing water-pistol causes a severe sting to a big Pyrovile and the Mother Superior, somehow.

Moreover, the Pyrovile that comes into the Villa is glowing, and rises from a hole in the ground that leads to the lava-stream, but casts a shadow when lit by the relatively small candles we see Caecilius blow out at dawn. Similarly, Quintus and the Doctor cast big impressive shadows on a wall when en route to Lucius's lair, despite Quintus's torch being brighter than anything else around (and the moonlight is blue, the light with a Doctor-shaped hole in is yellow).

Whence comes the white light before the TARDIS has properly started materialising for Caecilius and his family? And, when Vesuvius erupts, we hear a plate glass window smash in Casa Caecilius. Last reader to spot a problem with that has to take a school trip to see glass-blowing.

More a problem with the Cambridge Exam Board c.1967, but why is "Quintus" the elder of two children? There was a banker called Lucius Caecilius Iucundus, on whom the booklet and thus this Caecilius was based, but he had an elder son, named after himself but with his (better-connected) wife's name and a younger called "Quintus". No daughter, it appears, and he died in the earlier earthquake of 62 AD. (Since that booklet was written, there's been a popular chocolate-hazelnut sandwich spread called "Nutella", making every reference to his mother sound silly.) So if the comment at the end of the episode about how "you" will be remembered is a reference to the Cambridge course, the well-preserved house in Stabiae Street and all the documentation about Iucundus's business affairs – rather than the Doctor talking about Pompeii in general – then Evelina's been written out of history.

If a Time Lord sees all the possible futures subtending from any choice, all the time, how does the Doctor *ever* make a mistake? We had this as a rhetorical ploy (X1.13, "The Parting of the Ways") but apparently he's always been like that. This makes a lot of earlier stories, some quite significant (e.g. 12.4, "Genesis of the Daleks"), a bit weird in retrospect.

"Foss" (Street) is from a Latin word for earthworks, so the market trader would sound Welsh to himself giving directions there. Similarly, Caecilius claims that the possession of modern art will give the family "status". The Latin graffito (*nunc*) on the walls behind the Stallholder's pitch could be the work of Celts (with step-ladders?). There are others visible, but this is notable if not nonsensical. That Quintus has an unmistakeable Welsh accent in some scenes is also unfortunate. The jury's out on whether the Romans could have got oranges from China.

Pedantry compels us to point out that it wasn't so much fire as lava/volcanic ash that was the problem, so "The Ashes of Pompeii" or "The Smothering of Pompeii" would make for a more accurate title. (But it starts off a classical elemental theme for this year, with "The Poison Sky", "The Stolen Earth" and "The Waters of Mars". Let's pretend that this was deliberate, and not just more proof that they pilfered *The Fires of Vulcan*.)

Critique The wonder is that Moran, Teague and Davies pulled it off at all, let alone with any flair, considering the list of included elements. This episode: sorted out the translation system they've been casually playing with for three seasons; includes the tick-box of prophecy components that Davies wanted for his year endgame; reintroduces several of the "new companion" perspectives; sets up the principles of "fixed points" that Moffat used so extensively (and which is somewhere under all the other stuff leading to the regeneration); incorporates Davies's wish-list of Soothsayers, effects and *Asterix* gags... and still tells a more or less coherent costume drama about Pompeii.

It's only when you stop and examine it that you realise how few speaking-role characters were in the street scenes and how few there are *at all*, considering that we're being presented with a story about a whole city dying. Even the comedy stallholder (the under-used Phil Cornwall) has a bearing on the plot. The Caecilius family are (as with the O-Level Latin book) exemplars, a "typical" Pompeiian family representing all the different aspects of everyday life before it was interrupted. Although this story tries to follow the usual Celebrity Historical procedure of making jokes about how all cultures and times are interchangeable (while ignoring the grating noise of Sydney Newman turning in his grave), it lands up putting more effort into establishing life in 72 AD as unlike ours than has been evident in the "alien" cultures of late. Sybils, Household Gods and a belief that Vulcan has punished the Pompeiians establishes a world of thought-patterns and customs, a culture, quickly and effectively.

This is what should have been happening in "The Shakespeare Code" (X3.2), but there was no hint there that, within recent memory, people had been burned at the stake for their beliefs and were being arrested and tortured. (The slightly anachronistic Bedlam sequence was the main concession to this being a radically different time.) Although the majority of the period details in "The Fires of Pompeii" are gags, such as the snack of ants in honey and dormice, they knit together. It helps that, in this case, we get to see the belief-system working in an improbably practical way and that this is the threat to the Doctor. The lava-monsters are just window-dressing.

That the Pyroviles are largely gratuitous, and there because the team thinks all *Doctor Who* needs monsters (ideally ones that look good in plastic figure form), is rammed in our faces by the entirely redundant Lucius. Phil Davis is always good value, but he's there in the same capacity as the semi-famous guest leads in Tom Baker stories: as a mouthpiece for mute, mumbling, shambling hordes (or, back then, implied hordes represented by three tall blokes in latex). We later discover that the Pyroviles can talk for themselves *and* they have the Sybils to talk for them. In a story already visually unlike any previous *Doctor Who* – and anything else on television at that time – another

digitally-realised monster might have been surplus to requirements, but these things are such a breath of fresh air from the standard (usually Paul Kasey in a boiler-suit with a rubber animal-head), it's hard to condemn it. We get the Ood back next week and Sontarans after that, then the Hath (oh dear), so giant flaming stone men are as much a welcome change as the Adipose were last time.

They do muddy the narrative, though. At one point, two separate sets of human agents for the Pyroviles trip each other up and give the Doctor his big breakthrough. As we said in **Things That Don't Make Sense**, this isn't especially farsighted of either faction. There's a rather odd subplot of gender rivalries that shows potential, but was interrupted by routine *Doctor Who* business. It seems to have some connection to the plot, and is presented as a "cause" and most of what follows as "effects", but isn't explicitly connected to it. Instead, it's mainly there as a pretext for Lucius and Evelina to have a sooth-off using the Doctor's secrets (and clues to the Big Bad). As is often the case with Davies-era stories, this could have benefitted from either one more redraft or three fewer.

So we've got quick, effective world-building and memorable, well-motivated aliens and their human agents. All of this, however, services a story about the Doctor showing Donna that space-time travel comes with a price. The Pyroviles provide a dilemma akin to Barbara wanting to rewrite history in "The Aztecs" (1.6) and the Doctor *not* wanting to in "Genesis of the Daleks". Next week, by contrast, we'll get a story about the Doctor showing Donna that, um, space-time travel comes with a price. For all that they're ramming home the "arc" elements and an idea of Donna undergoing a steep learning-curve (like Rose, Mickey, Martha and Jackie), there's an underlying redundancy in that Donna, more than most, begins each new adventure the same way she began (in "Partners in Crime"). The one time she shows any sign of having developed as a result of her travels is the first one recorded, "The Unicorn and the Wasp" (X4.7), and the only time we see her assimilating a different outlook on screen is the one time they have a logical reason for a reset button (X4.9, "Forest of the Dead"). Donna's more interesting the more the writers thought she was going to be Penny.

To some extent, therefore, the other cast-members are almost part of the scenery, and hindsight makes two of the performances more interesting than they were at the time. Karen Gillan was cast to be conspicuous (an odd decision, given the character's main job of spying on people), but hearing her talk posh is a hoot. Peter Capaldi is obviously relishing being on *Doctor Who* (although he was probably thinking this was as good as it would get) and is a convincing patriarch. It's a thankless part, and legend has it the role of John Frobisher in "Children of Earth" was offered to Capaldi as a reward for "wasting" him on this. The grinding change of gears as he goes from observing his city die to coining the word "volcano" could have been even more tasteless with another performer. Nonetheless, he, like everyone else, is there as almost part of a pageant, and the "celebrity" in this historical is the CG volcano.

This, like everything else in this story, looks *astonishing*. We have a genuine epic on our hands and, even if the linkages between set-pieces get tenuous, this is head and shoulders better than anything else on telly that night. The figures preserved in the excavations are sometimes a bit abstract for most people: showing the interrupted lives in a family-friendly way is sort of what the series was created to do. This isn't just pushing *Doctor Who* to its limits, it's stretching what popular TV drama can do. The starting-point, the 2003 docu-drama *Pompeii: the Last Days,* was rather worthy and used voice-over commentary, but this episode does as close to a family-friendly tragedy as you can get before the watershed. To have done more would have required a longer episode... and nobody would have wanted a downer like this on Christmas Day.

The Lore

Written by James Moran. Directed by Colin Teague. Viewing figures: (BBC1) 9.0 million (and an 87% AI), (BBC3 repeats) 1.0 and 0.5 million (both AI's 89%).

Repeats and Overseas Promotion *La Chute de Pompéï* ("The Fall of Pompeii"), *Die Feuer von Pompeji.*

Alternate versions Not every overseas showing has the tag scene six months later, in Rome.

Production

• They'd been wanting to do a Pompeii story since Series 1. "The Empty Child" had referenced "Volcano Day", and the proposed episode 11 might have been exactly this, had they been able to achieve it (instead, "Boom Town" was purposefully the cheap episode that year). It didn't look as though they could do justice to the idea in the budget and, more crucially, time allotted. Nonetheless, when the new series had been a hit and the BBC were expecting more, the idea kept coming back, and Series 4 seemed like the last chance to do it before the key personnel all left. James Moran had written a successful low-budget feature film and a 24-style episode of *Torchwood* ("Sleeper"), so he was given this project, under Davies's supervision.

In the meantime, Mark Gatiss's slightly cheaper yarn about Nazis and Spitfires was being held in reserve. (We'll pick up that tale in X5.3, "Victory of the Daleks".) Confirmation from the BBC for extra funds for the requisite effects and overseas shooting came late in the day (towards the end of April 2007), and the story began to fall into place for Davies once the idea of soothsayers came to the forefront. There were obvious consequences of this; the location work would have to be quick and with as few actors and technicians as possible (cf. "City of Death"), and they'd need at least one story later in the year light on effects and sets, to free up time and budget for this and the two-part Dalek epic at the end of the year. As you probably knew, Davies took a hit for the team and wrote X4.10, "Midnight" and X4.11, "Turn Left" within these restrictions. However, his workload was starting to get out of hand, as he had three drama series and *Doctor Who Confidential* to oversee. The scripts for the season-opener were delayed so much, the production block for that and the Pompeii episode was split.

• Phil Collinson asked James Strong to take over as director for "Partners in Crime", leaving Colin Teague free to handle the complex logistics for a trip to Rome and some ambitious effects-shots even by recent standards. The team had scored a genuine coup: Cinecittà. The near-legendary film complex in Rome had housed Italian cinema's great films of the 50s and 60s, as well as industrial quantities of cheap-and-cheerful gladiator movies, schlock horror flicks, Spaghetti Westerns and copyright-infringement-adjacent reworkings of Hollywood hits.

More to the point, the HBO bonkbuster *Rome* had been made there, and the street sets were still up. The studio's administration were interested in attracting productions from the UK (there were plans for expanding British production facilities and offering fiscal goodies, but these would take time to deliver). The relatively low budget and small resources of even BBC Wales *Doctor Who* was a sprat to catch a mackerel, especially as the series had such a good global publicity machine. There was a brief window in mid-September when a light crew and minimal cast could duck in, refit the sets slightly, shoot for two days and leg it back to Cardiff.

• The plan was to keep it all as a surprise. However, five weeks before the planned shoot, an electrical fire broke out (killing some of the staff, but looking for a while as if it was going to be far worse). The Roman police and media nonchalantly mentioned to *Variety* that *Doctor Who* was one of the productions that might have been affected. It turned out this wasn't the case, but the complex was severely damaged.

This was mid-August; 13th and 14th September were to be the two days of actual shooting, after a period of set-dressing. As will become typical of overseas jaunts in this phase, there was trouble getting the equipment to the right place, with hold-ups at customs for the effects team (all those explosives, taking a day to negotiate) and a delay in Switzerland for the lorry with the other stuff (including the TARDIS). The street scenes included the eruption, for which a woofer (a sort of mortar) was filled with cork chips. Conveniently for anyone explaining to international readers the heat of Rome in September, it was 28°C or 82°F.

• Collinson and Tracie Simpson had been to Rome several times during the lead-in time for this shoot, and he recommended a restaurant for the cast on their visit; according to Tennant on the DVD commentary, this turned out to have rats on the night they went. On 15th, Tennant and a small team went to Pompeii itself for *Doctor Who Confidential*, accompanied by The Mill's Dave Houghton, there to take plate shots.

• The next location was less celebrated but familiar: the Temple of Peace in Cardiff's University block is probably the most frequently-used and familiar setting for BBC Wales's *Doctor Who*, and this time actually used as a temple, for the Pyrovile-infected Sybils. A few lines were added as this episode was reslotted ahead of the Ood story.

• Older fans will be gratified that the increasing acceptance of quarries as locations continued with this story, but not everything that looked like a quarry was one. To begin the Vesuvius scenes, the crew went to the Clearwell Caves (as seen in X2.0, "The Christmas Invasion" and X2.9, "The Satan Pit") on the 28th for the sequences in the rock-tunnel and beneath the Caecilius villa. However, October began with a genuine quarry (Morlais, near Merthyr Tidfyl) for various shots of the rocky pass, the hillside and the base of Vesuvius. UK residents may recall that the summer of 2007 was pretty miserable, so the lowering skies weren't added in post – in fact they had trouble matching Italian sunshine from footage shot before this to the gloom. The volcano's interior was faked in the Comex quarry at Taffs Well on the 2nd (the owners had bulldozed a patch especially for them) and that was about it.

• The Mill had prepared a couple of designs for the Pyroviles (previously called "Pyrovillaxians"), the one chosen being more centurion-like. There was a plan to use an effect to make the Doctor's water-pistol shoot like a super-soaker, but Davies thought the feeble stream it made in real life was funnier. The BBC's Pronunciation Unit, which has been advising newsreaders and actors since the 1920s on foreign names and languages, offered help with the Latin names and words – although nobody really knows how Romans spoke the words they've left written down and the thinking on the most likely pronunciations has changed even since Davies's dad taught it at school.

• On transmission, the end-credits were a one-off return to the scroll method, but with the cast in order of appearance. Later that day, BBC4 repeated the 2003 drama-documentary *Pompeii: The Last Day* which had prompted the original "Volcano Day" comment in Series 1. The *Radio Times* write-up included a shot of the Cambridge Latin O-Level booklet about Caecilius and a quote from long-time fan and cast-member Peter Capaldi saying that he'd agreed to take a part in *Doctor Who* without looking at a script.

X4.3: "Planet of the Ood"

(19th April, 2008)

Which One is This? Pink-Eye and the Brain.

Firsts and Lasts It's the end of a trilogy of stories set in the same time-period (as per X3.3, "Gridlock" last year), with the forty-second century getting another visit after X2.8, "The Impossible Planet" and X3.7, "42". The Ood aren't afflicted by any ultimate-source-of-all-evil this time, so we have our first recurring friendly aliens since the show's return.

It's also the first episode this year to be under 48 minutes long. We're a full five minutes shorter this week.

Watch Out For...

• Well, kids, this is the Big Moral Message story of the season. That moral is: *slavery is baaad, m'kay?* The Doctor helps overthrow it, a bit, after which everything will be peachy. Something was made online of the Doctor-Donna exchange about overseas manufacturing (Donna: "I haven't got slaves", Doctor: "Who do you think made your clothes?", Donna: "Is that why you travel round with a human at your side?... so you can take cheap shots?"), but it's difficult to take seriously an argument that takes three lines of script and has no impact on the plot whatsoever.

• Still, what this story lacks in subtlety, it makes up for in child-friendly punishment for baddies. The security chief is given a literal taste of his own medicine and gassed with his own equipment but the climax has the slave corporation-owner turning into an Ood in an appealingly yukky manner. However, the grand guignol also includes one of the key goodies (Dr Ryder), who is pushed into the Giant Pulsating Brain and presumably killed, despite being the Real Hero of the story, and deserving all the thanks that the Ood spend the last five minutes lavishing on the Doctor and Donna. The plot of the story, such as it is, entails Our Heroes discovering what Ryder knew and acted upon *all along*, then just being around when it all gets resolved.

• Old meets new as the rather wonderful planet-laden sky is digitally matted on to a quarry to give us Ood Sphere location shots. Then we go to the main base, shot in yet another disused factory, and observe battles conducted with practical machine-guns. (Here's where we mention that this was directed by Graeme Harper, who made a point of not using ray-guns back in the 80s.)

• After last week's episode, where Tennant and Tate were supposedly inside a volcano but their breath was visibly misting, we have everyone trying to look cold on a snow-planet where the sun is shining brightly. If it had rained, all the paper the team use to simulate snow would have gone mushy.

The Continuity

The Doctor He can hear the telepathic Ood song, even when Donna can't [see **Can He Read Smells?** in Volume 7]. It's strong enough to start giving him a headache. He does a mind-meld to let Donna hear the Oodsong when she asks him to, taking pains to make sure she isn't overwhelmed.

When Donna waxes philosophical about humanity's impact on the universe, he shies away from any absolute answers. [Compare to X1.10, "The Doctor Dances," when he concludes a similar conversation with a cheeky double-entendre or 15.2, "The Invisible Enemy", where he briefly admits to thinking of humans as a plague. See also X2.0, "The Christmas Invasion", where humans are the real monsters.] The sight of snow delights him [it seems that Tennant is never around any real snow unless an Ood is involved].

• *Background.* He tells Donna that he wasn't paying much attention when he met the Ood before, as he was "busy". [A reasonable assessment of X2.8-2.9, "The Impossible Planet"/"The Satan Pit". He at first refers to the Ood as the 'servants of humans', so it's possible he overlooked the entire slavery aspect last time. At any rate, he knew the name "Friends of the Ood", although this is a familiar formulation.]

For once, he passes up the chance to namedrop when Donna mentions Houdini [c.f. 11.5, "Planet of the Spiders"; 12.5, "Revenge of the Cybermen"; X11.8, "The Witchfinders"].

• *Ethics.* He thinks he owes the Ood for having let them all die last time ["The Satan Pit"], and calmly goes about turning the society upside-down. When Donna starts getting angry about a slave-owning society, he teases her about modern clothing manufacture. Then he apologises when she accuses him of taking cheap shots.

How Can Science Salvage Badly-Made Planets?

One of the drawbacks of the cut-and-paste approach to storytelling (the so-called "shopping lists" the executive producer gives a writer) is that we get anomalies. We had the Ood coming back, because they looked like everyone's idea of a *Doctor Who* monster and the heads had cost a bundle to make, so had to be re-used. But Keith Temple, the writer of "Planet of the Ood", was also told to set it on an ice-planet, because umpteen other films and shows had used ice-planets and *Doctor Who* hadn't yet (well, except for A5, "The Infinite Quest", but people kept forgetting that).

For those of us raised on 1970s *Doctor Who*, where the conditions of a world fed into the story-telling right from the start, obvious mismatches such as this can be distracting. Take a relatively simple tale such as "The Mutants" (9.4) or "The Caves of Androzani" (21.6), where the basic knowledge every child watching had picked up from the Moon landings or news items about pollution was deployed in a conceptually exciting and intriguing way (regardless of the execution), then compare it to The Mill's persistent inability to get phases of the Moon right, and you'll see why experienced viewers get a little peeved.

This is especially aggravating, as the Davies-era makers did seem to be trying. The throwaway science lessons about Faraday Cages (X4.14, "Planet of the Dead"), the action of acetic acid on calcium carbonate (X1.5, "World War Three"), Happy Primes (X3.7, "42") and the life-cycle of a star (X1.2, "The End of the World") indicate, if nothing else, that the Davies regime was trying to stick to the original plan from 1962's conferences. The Moffat Babies weren't as scrupulous, indeed one of his first acts was to refuse to have the series associated with a schools science initiative (as we'll explore in the next volume). Series 7, among some gratingly stupid planets (see below), had two stories where Chris Chibnall applied the sort of thinking that was standard in the Letts-Hinchcliffe-Williams years and the result was refreshingly solid. As executive producer, he hired actual scientists to advise on things (e.g X11.4, "Arachnids in the UK").

In fact, this is one side of a tug-of-war that's been going on since the start, when writers who worked well in cop-shows or soaps just pilfered anything cool they'd seen in a film or comic-strip, regardless of how any piece of the collage-world they were making related to any other piece. Terry Nation notoriously said that if he invented a planet and decided to make the rocks talk, nobody could gainsay him because it was *his* planet.

Terrance Dicks, Robert Holmes, Douglas Adams and Christopher H Bidmead took the opposite position: that a well-thought-out world allowed for multiple plot-lines and options, of which they preferred the most interesting one that could be done on time and on budget, but they had Plans B-K ready if anything went wrong. When there was a tension between a writer who put in things because he felt like it and a script editor who wanted lived-in worlds that made sense, the results were usually engaging, especially if the set-designer was on the ball.

A large part of the appeal of 70s *Who* was trying to follow the Doctor's reasoning on what the new place he'd landed up in was like. Rather than just apparently plucking information out of thin air as happens most times now, we'd see what he saw (and be told what he and his chums could feel or smell), and admire his speed in making deductions we might *just* have been able to make if given more time. Indeed, go back a few years, and it's Ian and Barbara who do this reasoning and the Doctor marks their homework. It involved knowing how our world works and keeping good faith with the audience.

It's not especially hard and, in many ways, the 1960s and 1970s were the ideal time to be doing it, because jet travel was opening up this planet to just such an approach. People were aware that the different time-zones existed, moreso after the cost of international phone calls came down, so how Earth works was laid bare for the public. (But see 5.4, "The Enemy of the World" for a story written just before jet-lag caught on as a concept.) Documentary crews could show people the less-well-known parts for the first time, and then for the first time in colour. From the 80s onward, the homogenisation of these formerly distinct places kicked in. In place of the Victorian adventure-yarn's emphasis on the exotic as glamorous and strange (but ultimately there for the benefit of Europeans, as far as the writers were concerned), there was now an interest in the otherness of other cultures – from the small-scale (England discovering Mediterranean cookery and seeing Alan Whicker visit Bali) to wholesale anthropology. The writers still got a lot wrong (exactly what "constellation" means is a perennial niggle), but they checked the details on which the stories hinged, and made sure the viewers knew that such details were checkable.

continued on Page 47...

• *Inventory: Sonic Screwdriver.* The Doctor has a go at using it to lock himself in a cage [whatever technique ought to have worked in X4.1, "Partners in Crime" doesn't here either].

• *Inventory: Psychic Paper.* The Doctor whips it out to claim that he and Donna are investors. Curiously, whatever it's showing is compatible with Donna's ad-libbed claim that they're from the Noble Corporation.

• *Inventory: Other.* A stethoscope. [Most likely the same one from "Partners in Crime". In fact, we wonder if it's the one Jackie borrowed from Tina the Cleaner's lodger in "The Christmas Invasion", and which Martha – who may well have been that lodger – used on Jack in X3.11, "Utopia".]

The TARDIS The Doctor tells Donna he set it for random coordinates. [There's a lot of speculation in the behind-the-scenes piece in *Doctor Who Magazine* #395 that the TARDIS landed there because She picked up a telepathic trace, and wanted to give the Doctor a chance to assuage his guilt about letting the Ood get sucked into a black hole. Well, that might be possible. Last time we saw this happen, the Doctor also wound up coming into conflict with a bunch of slavers and resolving the problem by not interfering. Does this always happen when he tosses a coin to set the controls? (Odd that Graeme Harper, *de facto* director of 18.5, "Warriors' Gate", didn't make this connection.)]

The Supporting Cast

• *Donna.* Sensibly, she has a heavy coat ready to go [part of her luggage in "Partners in Crime"?] when it turns out they've landed on an ice planet. [She retrieves it so fast, it's tempting to think that it was on the TARDIS hat-rack.] They patiently explain that no, they're not married – and yet, Donna is later quite huffy about being assumed to be single.

She does well at not being overwhelmed, and tries to comfort a dying Ood in the snow as best she can. She makes the logical assumption that one speaks to an Ood through what she calls its 'Persil Ball'.

Her realisation that different societies can be even more horrifying than her own upsets her no end, and she sobs that she wants to go home. Once it's clear the Ood will be all right, she tells the Doctor she definitely wants to stay with him after all.

She was born in Chiswick. [If we presume that Donna is as old as Catherine Tate, or perhaps a little younger, there was indeed a maternity hospital in Chiswick that her mum might easily have used. It closed in 1974, so that gives us some idea of the dating.] She has an earsplitting whistle picked up from West Ham games, where she went 'every Saturday'. [Last episode she said that only her dad cared about the footie, but perhaps not. A couple of weeks from now, she'll have been a Fulham fan for years. And if she went "every" Saturday, it would mean that on alternate weeks; when the team played away, she and her dad would be travelling all over the country.] Being given psychic access to a telepathic song agonises her so much she begs the Doctor to take it away.

The disappearing bees mystery ["Partners in Crime"] is still bothering her.

The Supporting Cast (Evil)

• *Ood Operations.* [Well, that *seems* to be what the company in question calls itself.]

They argue that it's all right to enslave Ood, because Ood had no civilisation in the first place. An artificial telepathic field dampener has kept the Ood from 'connecting' for decades. The Big Brain is kept in Warehouse 15. Part of the compound involves the shipping area where containers full of Ood are packed for delivery, while another includes the processing areas for lobotomising newly reared Ood. As you would expect of any slave-holding race, they have safeguards against possible uprising. There are sufficient gas canisters to kill an entire batch of Ood and explosives to destroy the Big Brain as a last-ditch option.

The economy hasn't been going brilliantly, so Halpern – the company CEO, apparently – has had to cut the price to 50 credits, a figure that at least one of his salesman regards as absurdly low. Both domestic and military buyers have uses for Ood. As part of the sales push, they're having an investors' seminar exactly like twenty-first-century ones, right down to a seemingly-useless map of the facility. They're not at all surprised to see pro-Ood infiltrators and Halpen presumes they're from Friends of the Ood.

The company has sufficient resources invested in rockets that Halpen thinks could go into cargo instead. [What happens to it once all the core staff and would-be investors are dead in a slave rebellion is anyone's guess, but some company out

How Can Science Salvage Badly-Made Planets?

continued from Page 45...

The one thing we were never told back then was "just accept it". The Doctor used to save planets by encouraging people to ask questions and get a bigger perspective. This was one of the traditions the first BBC Wales series maintained, but then the Doctor started just waving his screwdriver around like a tricorder and not telling us what he was looking for or why. (Why *does* he do this, anyway? It's not as if there's any kind of readout or screen. The notorious Series 9 gimmick of sonic sunglasses actually makes more sense, but would surely give anyone wearing them a sinus headache like nobody's business.)

Paradoxically, it's never been easier for viewers to check things. On Saturday nights in the 1960s and 1970s, anything one might want to verify or investigate further had to wait until the library opened on Monday. Yet this kind of viewer interaction, despite a last-ditch attempt to justify the existence of *Doctor Who Confidential* by lacing the backstage goss with pedagoguery, isn't encouraged. If anything, it's resented by the production team facing a barrage of grumbles, just as when they get basic history wrong.

So, in the Whittaker-era spirit of *rapprochement* between fandoms old and new, we'll apply the thought-processes of old-style *Doctor Who* to some more planets in an attempt to resolve the apparent contradictions. We'll ask the questions the Doctor used to ask before he became concerned with impressing girls.

1. How can beings with tiny feet, exposed (and moist) skin and only one hand free have evolved on an ice-planet?
(X4.3, "Planet of the Ood"; X4.17, "The End of Time Part One")

The Ood are, we're told, natives of an ice planet. So they're moist, glistening, hairless, skinny iceworld residents... not *impossible*, but it needs their skin-dampness and dangly bits to be wax-based rather than water. The most logical way this could work is that they have formaldehyde for blood, or diethyline glycol (as used in Liebfraumilch and car engines). Maybe it's a relatively straightforward alcohol. We'll talk a bit more about their body temperature and chemistry in a moment, but we don't see their breath (if they have any) misting. Then again, we don't see Donna's or Solana's either.

They have *remarkably* small feet for iceworld inhabitants as well. They must slip over a lot, and get stuck in snow more than a few inches deep. (Big feet or paws spread the weight and allow even people wearing heavy furs and big backpacks to walk on snow – those tennis-racquet things Arctic explorers have on their feet are for this.) This would be awkward enough if they had both hands free, but they don't. Even if we assume that having a major portion of your brain hanging out of your nose doesn't lead to neural frostbite, this is a bit haphazard. The Ood aren't exactly adapted for hunting, either, so that they must forage on all the foliage that's so abundant on ice planets.

Plus, they're very trusting – or so Donna guesses; we haven't anything to go on. So there may never have been any predators on this planet. That's remarkably unlikely as, with no vegetation to speak of and no sign of how the Ood would eat such plants, it would be logical to assume that anything with the ability to eat Ood would have become very good at it. The Ood can't outrun humans. (Who aren't especially well-adapted for snow either, but have invented shoes and guns. And can use both hands. And have hair. And wear clothes thicker than pyjamas in the snow.) The only way this works is for the Ood to have always been top of the food-chain, *or* to have been inedible to everything else on the planet.

Err... what else *is* there? Once again, we only see a tiny part within walking distance of where the TARDIS lands and are left to assume that the whole world's like this. So let's look for evidence beyond what the showrunner said in *Confidential* that the whole of Ood Sphere is ice. Well, the Doctor says it is, but he has no idea what planet he's on when he makes this rash statement. Halpen comments on the weather as if it being cold is unusual. He grew up there. The humans found the brain under the northern glacier (a perfectly natural place to keep an exposed cerebral cortex) 200 years ago. So part of the planet's been cold for a couple of centuries. A century later, the world's much the same, except that a city's been built. (There's no way to know how long "a century" is on Ood Sphere, as their year is never specified, but the Doctor reacts as if it's not as long as all that. Let's say for now it's about as long as ours.) That's about it.

The air's breathable to humans, which suggests

continued on Page 49...

there was reckless enough to sell slavers insurance. As Solana, a PA, correctly points out, the fact that Earth has refrained from asking questions about how the Ood are treated indicates they're aware but don't wish to know the answers. It does also suggest that the model of slavery involved is more Imperial British than American South, if people aren't generally aware of the treatment of Ood; perhaps Halpen's trying to push into the civilian markets because no one else has yet.

[How the Ood lobotomies are carried out isn't made clear; it might clear up a few details if some of the more unsavoury employees (medically trained staff who can cut off bits of Ood without simply killing them) have been sent out of town temporarily to make everything seem shiny in case the buyers poke around. But somebody must be around to do a post-mortem on an Ood, and Halpen doesn't expect Ryder to do it. Maybe these guards have basic anatomical knowledge sufficient to handle these sorts of jobs; if Ryder is the only one with any idea what's happening with red-eye, its inexplicability to everyone else would be justified.]

The Non Humans

• *Ood.* [As with 'Voord' (1.5, "The Keys of Marinus"), nobody seems quite sure of the grammar here. Is it one Ood, two Oods, or one Ood, two Ood, or is the species name being used when people talk about 'The Ood'?]

It emerges that Ood have a three-brained structure; A) whatever's in their humanoid headspace, B) the small front brain, normally hand-held – it's chopped off and replaced with a translator globe, a form of lobotomy that conditions the Ood to obey humans, and C) a 30s-style Giant Pulsating Brain linking them all together unless surgically altered. [Again, Danny was clearly wrong when info-dumping to Rose a couple of years ago.] The Brain can consume a person dropped into it; the company has limiting its influence with telepathic fences. Unafflicted, unmodified Ood share a telepathic 'song'. Once the Brain is liberated, even Donna can hear the Oodsong.

Here the Ood have some self-awareness as individuals [in stark contrast to what we were told in "The Impossible Planet"] rather than a collective herd-mind. One is identified as Ood Sigma [he'll be back in X4.16, "The Waters of Mars"]. He seems to accompany Halpern everywhere – but is secretly a ringleader [so to speak] of the plan to overthrow human rule. Clandestine efforts to increase the Brain's influence have resulted in some Ood exhibiting the 'Red-Eye' condition (their eyes literally turn red) and trying to kill everyone.

As this episode progresses, a new type of infection makes the Ood in question show signs of rabies. So far, it's only affected the Ood on the Ood Sphere [consistent with the info dump the Doctor provides at the end]. The symptoms are a manifestation of the Ood's subconscious tendencies, with expression of anger and rage. Ood Sigma's actions may result from another, more rational tendency.

Hundreds of thousands of Ood are shipped off the Ood-sphere; there's about 2000 to a batch. Breeding farms can make up this quantity again without too much trouble. A planned advert indicates that the Ood may have had their own space travel at one point [it may be unwise to take this too seriously]. The translators can be equipped with various voices for the purchaser's pleasure.

The Doctor doesn't know how many hearts they have, but identifies the injured Ood in the snow as male. [Perhaps it's pheromones, although in the snow this would be hard to detect. If, as is hinted, they are related to the Sensorites, their hearts may be in the centre.]

There's a crucial line in which Ood Sigma explains that natural Ood mustn't kill [which explains a lot about this story]. They deal with Halpen by turning him into an Ood; this requires years of dosing him with Ood-graft biological compound treatments. Halpen notices no symptoms besides his hair falling out, until he's peeling off his scalp and literally sneezing out his brains.

[The graphics department gave us a significant detail not elaborated on in the dialogue or visibly on screen: Ood Food comes in packets marked 'Toxic to Humans'. This may or may not confirm the speculation in this story's essay about their biochemistry.]

Planet Notes

• *Ood Sphere.* An ice world in close proximity to a gas giant with a ring-system and several other sizeable and/or nearby planetary bodies. [See **Things That Don't Make Sense** and this story's essay concerning the many, many things that are off about such a species coming from this planet.] The Doctor notes that it's the same neck of the woods as the Sense Sphere [1.7, "The Sensorites"].

How Can Science Salvage Badly-Made Planets?

continued from Page 47...

that photosynthesis or something similar is going on or has until very recently. That, in turn, suggests a lot of life with chemistry like ourselves. (Even if you start off with an atmosphere 80% nitrogen and 20% oxygen, or near enough, the odds of it staying like our air without a constant cycling through organisms using the carbon, oxygen and nitrogen aren't good. All sorts of reducing elements, notably carbon and iron, would ordinarily bond with the oxygen and remove it from use unless something is cycling it, like things breathing and plants photosynthesising. It's more likely that the nitrogen and oxygen would settle into laughing gas, nitrous oxide, than that these gases would spontaneously stay at arm's length, as they do on Earth because of the whole respiration process.)

A world that's all ice all the time isn't going to have humans just grumbling about a bit of snow – there are enough moons of gas-giants in our solar system to make this sort of thing a fertile area for speculation on what could live there and the low-temperature chemistry involved is now quite well-established. The residents of a world that's always been cold are as likely to breathe chlorine or hydrogen cyanide as anything else. (Do the Birastrops come from such a planet? 13.5, "The Brain of Morbius", if you didn't know.) That's assuming such a world has an atmosphere at all.

A more likely model for life on a ball of ice is the Jovian moon Europa. This appears to be heated from within by Jupiter's gravity and radiation (the daddy-planet's chucking out microwaves amongst everything else), and could conceivably have liquid water under the icy crust. Enceladus, a similar world orbiting Saturn, is similarly slushy within and spurts out water periodically (if you recall 10.4, "Planet of the Daleks", the fact that serious science journals have used the word "icecano" will cause a wry smile).

The current best-guess is an ocean under the ice that is almost a saturate solution of Epsom Salts (so, like a very cold flotation tank, but at least your skin wouldn't wrinkle as you died of hypothermia). Inside such a world, there might be methane clathrates and something analogous to the Antarctic red algae on the bottom of glaciers (and the annelid worms that can feed on this) or more. There wouldn't be a lot of light for photosynthesis, but there might be localised heat-sources and nutrient vents such as at the bottom of the oceans on Earth. The point about such an ecology is that it's protected from the worst of the radiation, but cut off from everything else. Intelligent residents wouldn't know about stars or other planets. It would be a good place for a story (ideally a Big Finish audio, as it would be dark all the time), but it's not this story's setting. Ood Sphere is nothing like the real ice worlds we know.

It *is*, however, very like a couple of well-known made-up worlds. Gethen in *The Left Hand of Darkness* is probably the most celebrated prose SF conception (and among the most likely sources of the prophetic circle in "The End of Time Part One"), but on screen we have the ice planet Hoth from *The Empire Strikes Back*. Various hobbyists have tried reverse-engineering the ecology of a world from what we see here and all seem to end up saying that it must only have changed from being more Earth-like in the last few thousand years (perhaps due to all those asteroids). In *Star Trek: Enterprise*, the Andorians (the blue guys with white hair and cute little antennae) were themselves retrofitted into being elfin tricksters trying to wrest power from the Vulcans and given an appropriately Tolkienesque world and Le Guinnish culture. This is the most likely source of what we see in "Planet of the Ood", right down to the rock-bridge and nearby gas-giant.

So if the gravity and radiation and air and magnetic field are like Earth's, and the Ood are natives, it probably only became an ice-world relatively recently. There are a lot of ways this could have happened: that gas-giant we see might have made the orbit shift outwards from its star; something might have changed the world's albedo (reflectivity of sunlight) – once this started, the nice white reflective ice and fog made it bounce back more light, which made it colder, which made more ice and fog and so on; the star might have cooled down for a bit; something could have blocked sunlight for a short spell (clouds of interstellar matter can do that – we're due for an encounter in about ten thousand years); it could be a world with a very eccentric orbit (see 9.4, "The Mutants"; 16.1, "The Ribos Operation"). What's interesting is that this allows us to speculate on what the world in which the Ood developed was like. One obvious clue: these are almost exactly the sort of space-squid creatures Margaret Atwood is always blethering about as proof that her dystopias aren't SF because she's famous.

continued on Page 51...

ABOUT TIME 2008-2009

History

• *Dating*. It's the year '4126'. The Second Great and Bountiful Human Empire [cf X1.2, "The End of the World"; X1.7, "The Long Game"] now stretches into three galaxies. Earth's a 'bit full' at this point. The Doctor says he's been to the system containing the Ood Sphere 'years ago, ages'. [It's not clear whether he means his time, chronological time, or both. "The Sensorites" was set in the twenty-eighth century, but happened in his first incarnation.]

Human corporate culture is similar enough to the twenty-first-century version that Donna's claim to be from 'the Noble Corporation, PLC, Limited, Intergalactic' meets with no comment. Ood Operations is a family-run business; Halpen's grandfather ran it at some point. Riffs on Andy Warhol's images are still used as standard industrial décor. Homer Simpson's 'D'oh!' is among the Ood's voice options. People, or at least slavers, know about the mass slaughters for foot-and-mouth disease. Hair tonic and baldness still exist.

Slavery is accepted as part of how an empire works. [It's tempting to see the debate in 23.3, "Terror of the Vervoids", set about 1,150 years before, as being impossible now that someone has found a suitable species and established some kind of imperium, even though the near-contemporaneous "The Mutants" (9.4) shows Earth's first empire in a rapid decline.] Ood Operations was established after the Brain was found under the Ood-Sphere's northern glacier, and a psychic baffle placed around it to make the Ood more tractable.

The Analysis

The Big Picture Well, the anti-slavery thread to this story is hardly subtle. The attempt to link a literal or figurative song to the oppressed is especially familiar with African American accounts. Spirituals, Blues, Jazz and what was called "Race Music" (until Alan Freed renamed it "Rock 'n' Roll") all get linked back to abduction from one culture and accommodations made with others. In current Western popular culture, this is the most often represented version of slavery and, perhaps inevitably, attempts to dramatise the historical link between types of music and four centuries of oppression simplify this connection (we think of the TV version of Alex Haley's *Roots* where Chicken George apparently invents the

Blues on his deathbed). It's not unique to African American experience, of course – transported Jacobite rebels (4.4, "The Highlanders") were set to work in Virginia, Kentucky and the Caribbean, and it was around that time that an Act of Parliament proclaimed bagpipes to be an illegal weapon. The resemblance of Bluegrass and Pibroch is well-established. Similarly, the Portuguese-speaking world has Fado, the Greek response to Turkish dominion was Rembetika. We could list lots more, but the point is that slavery, self-identity and a "secret" song are a found symbol, there to be used. (Oddly, though, Murray Gold opted for something more like John Dowland's *Lachrimae* – an Elizabethan emo classic – for the "sad" song and Ennio Morricone for the "Freedom" version.)

Similarly, telepathy pops up a lot as a side-effect of oppression in rather more cases than one might think. It was, after all, one of the off-the-shelf ideas derived from 40s *Astounding Science Fiction* that mutants were likely to be superior, and superiority means psychic gifts, and that there was a sort of trade-off of mental abilities and physical strength or attractiveness. Thus, the parables of racial oppression (meant to get the assumed readership to side with the underdogs) conveyed that fearful "normals" were hunting them, but they'd found others of their kind to form a resistance, or underground railroad, or one day would establish a homeland. Again, not exactly subtle, and with a large New York Jewish presence in the writing and readership of this and similar papers, you can see where this is heading. Just to complete the circle, telepathy is often described as analogous to song, weaving thoughts into shapes and collaborating, harmonising and so forth. Telepaths are, traditionally, pacifists and gentle, so would not resist enslavement and would, once indoctrinated, know what to do without laborious training or all that faffing about with literacy. (How useful they'd be as slaves is another matter.)

Ergo, apparently, telepathic slaves would have a song to sing and anyone sympathetic would hear it and be moved to act. This is as obvious a move as having squid-faced aliens with glowing red eyes (as we said last time, they're the twenty-first-century equivalent of Alpha Centauri – 9.2, "The Curse of Peladon" – as the first-thought cliché *Doctor Who*-style alien[13]). Plus, in a classic example of what we've taken to calling "Zog-think" (see **Is Kylie from Planet Zog?** under X4.0, "Voyage

How Can Science Salvage Badly-Made Planets?

continued from Page 49...

If Ood Sphere had been mainly aquatic, almost all the stupidity of their design goes away: the dangly brain-section doesn't need a hand to hold it, the exposed tentacles and skin are a more useful surface (and better for scooping up whatever equivalent to krill they sift) and song – as with cetaceans on Earth – is a better way to communicate over distances. (Except they're telepathic. Whatever that means.) Donna and Halpen comment on the smell of the Ood, but don't elaborate. Again, waxy sebaceous secretions, possibly aldehydes, and alcohol/glyceride blood to prevent freezing would be handy for deep-sea life. (If they aren't hunters, they might have been bottom-feeders, so risked explosive decompression if they came to the surface – also a risk for flying sharks.) Aquatic life tends towards unsaturated lipids. (You know from what you spread on your toast that saturated ones, like butter, go hard in cold temperatures, but unsaturated ones stay flexible.)

Then there's that snow. It isn't quite like our usual ice-crystals in formation, but it settles (eventually) and covers a dead Ood. If the atmosphere is pretty much Earthlike, rather than something like Titan (a world so cold that hydrocarbons are filling the roles water does on this planet, although 90 Kelvin temperature and 1.5 atmospheres at sea-level probably rule out the potentially picturesque lilac methane snow), it's a safe bet that this is water-ice. But might it be water-ice with added extras? People in arctic regions of Earth mix methanol or isopropane with water to keep engines and wires from icing up, but these freeze far lower than the probable temperature that day. The conditions for this don't fit what Halpen's wearing – not even a hat. The atmosphere isn't ignited by his ship, so high-level aerosol methane or benzene aren't around (methane's response to infra-red makes it a greenhouse gas, rather militating against the whole "ice-world" thing). If the Ood are using something like alcohol or propane to avoid freezing their tentacles off, they might be brewing it themselves (you'd think a more ruminant-like gut would be handy, but they are a bit slim for the conventional model we know) or the wherewithal is environmentally ready-to hand.

As we know that rogue Ood are chased by dogs, their body-chemistry can't be *too* exotic. Perhaps the tentacle-like things on their faces are exterior digestive apparatus. If the have something midway between a cow's caecum (the mini-stomach used to break down plant matter) and a gin-still, they could take in air and snow plus a bit of carbon from somewhere and let those friendly bacteria we hear about in yoghurt adverts brew up a nutrient-cum-antifreeze. Maybe Halpen's banned alcohol on the base not for fear of drunken staff, but in case it fortifies the livestock and permits more escape bids. The alcohol route seems not to be working too well for the amount we see the Ood eating (i.e. nothing, ever), so if they live on snow and air (plus a few other unseen supplements) and not constant grazing, we're back to oils. These are a bit high-maintenance, but doable with a daily one-off meal and just about in keeping with a former life aquatic. Of course, there may be airborne plankton outside the complex's perimeter. Either way, oil or alcohol or even some benzene-derivative, the fact that their priests congregate in confined spaces with naked flames is slightly worrying.

Those feet are still a problem. Whereas the paddle-like feet of their alleged cousins the Sensorites (1.7, "The Sensorites", would you believe?) look good for residents of either deserts or oceans, that is also a better adaptation for snow than what we see here. Of course, if they are concerned about conserving heat, then the amount of skin-surface becomes an issue (see **How Hard is It to be the Wrong Size?** under 16.6, "The Armageddon Factor"). A humanoid body works less well as aquatic life than a squid body with a human head, which gives us pause. All the things that make it plausible for beings to have cephalopod-like features and live on an ice-world make it far less practical to resemble humans in so many other ways. They've adapted to living out of the water, with all the abrupt weight and load on the joints hitherto spared them when they floated, but are bipedal and upright, a really bad posture for living on tundra and supporting unaccustomed body-weight. Think about walruses. Even if we're assuming that the Ood aren't mammals – and thus don't need rolls of fat to survive – they'd still be better off as quadrupeds. This, of course, leaves part of their brains dragging along the icy floor, so there might be a reason for their gait and convenient similarity to humans. This all suggests a very rapid, very recent environmental catastrophe making sea-life unsustainable in a few generations and just before the humans arrived. That's suspiciously good tim-

continued on Page 53...

of the Damned"), once their Giant Pulsating Brain (another *Astounding* favourite – see 24.1, "Time and the Rani") is freed, the Ood unlock the next level and get clairvoyance to add to telepathy, because these things are all equally possible in that sort of story. As with the remarkably similar "Warriors' Gate" (18.5), asking how precognitive aliens managed to get themselves enslaved is almost beside the point. As beings on another plane, with access to what might crudely be termed the Big Picture, they seemingly have some plan beyond mere human comprehension. In other words, shut up and watch the pretty pictures.

We're in parable-land, kids, so everyone has to have appropriate fates. In that week's *Doctor Who Confidential*, Davies talked about the way bad characters "earn" their deaths by crossing a line. He gleefully comments on Solana making a choice not to help and *therefore* being bumped off (and we note that the script's ostensible author, Keith Temple, is nowhere in this programme).

Moreover, Halpen getting turned into an Ood is justified by making the script give him one last chance, but cheerfully ignoring it. This is Roald Dahl plotting: we ought to be thankful that the Ood Song doesn't have lyrics beginning *Oompa Loompa Loompitty-Doo*. The point we have to make, once again, is that for the majority of the target audience this is entirely as it should be. For all the new series' affectations of teen-drama, space-opera and family viewing, the British public long ago accepted that *Doctor Who* is mainly for children. Halpen's icky transformation was designed with ten-year-old boys in mind.

That's why the story doesn't start with Halpen finding out what it's like being an Ood. It would be possible to make a different kind of morality-tale, with a vengeful Doctor making his stunts at the end of "The Family of Blood" (X3.9) something of a routine, but after that set-up, he and Donna would have been further from the story's centre than even the broadcast episode shows. As the story reveals, the Ood lack even the agency to take the rights we (and the Doctor) assume to be theirs and it needs a human plant within Halpen's company to make anything happen. The Red-Eye "infection" makes individuals violent, but is presented as being precisely the contagion the O-O personnel believe it to be. It's not shown as a responsible reaction to oppression.

Twentieth-century liberation movements fol-

lowed the line of thought that imperialism was a form of brutality, dehumanising and oppressing people to the point that armed uprisings were proportionate, the only response comprehensible to the colonial powers. Nineteenth-century thinking was that universal rights should be explained to everyone who has not yet realised that their rights were being stolen – ending slavery needed Abolitionists to make things happen. "Planet of the Ood", to avoid patronising a non-existent racial group (and thus implicitly real ones), has to have the story hinge on the Ood knowing their own strength and being frustrated in attempts to exercise it while the barrier is working. To be understandable to children and inattentive adults, the story requires a visual logic, with glowing eyes and froth meaning uncontrollable violence, and the standing around in circles with hands raised meaning controlled empathy. Plus there's the auditory coding of the Ood Song, operatic and "natural", against the sampled, chopped-up vocal of the processed Ood. Throwing an ex-human in would simply not have worked in that context, and would have made the story another condescending tale of how the oppressed need an outcast oppressor to make things work for them. That story almost functions independently of the Doctor and Donna, which makes things awkward for anyone used to the Doctor being the story's catalyst.

From that perspective, the fact that this lacks the relative nuance of 2.2, "The Dalek Invasion of Earth" (in which the Daleks occupied London despite a Resistance movement, and raised their right appendages at 45 degrees when proclaiming a "Final Solution") is irrelevant. For many people watching in that first-night audience (and their household had to pay a Licence Fee to get it made, don't forget), this was the first time these ideas had been put before them. Anything more than mild annoyance about the brevity of the "Who makes your clothes?" exchange ignores the fact that it happened at all, at prime time on a Saturday in front of an audience who may never have considered this. Admittedly, this is now Series 4 and the time for such an entry-level parable might really have been Series 2 – perhaps instead of the two-parter that introduced the Ood.

Indeed, conceptually, we're not too far from "New Earth" (X2.1), where beings bred for the utility of cynical "benefactors" (the Cat-Nuns) became conscious, contagious, angry and trouble-

How Can Science Salvage Badly-Made Planets?

continued from Page 51...

ing on humanity's part.

The Ood may have had human genetic material introduced as part of a project to create a slave race. Four-fingered, unwebbed hands with opposable thumbs are a remarkably useful feature... and so unlike what would suit either snow-dwelling or aquatic life-forms as to be improbable. That's creepy, but consistent with what we've been shown. Changing Halpen into one so quickly suggests a certain proximity. Then again, given that they have psychic abilities and are clairvoyant, it might have been a Time Lord entering the food chain some time in the past. (Some have gone the other way and speculated that the Ood are the universe seeking to replace the Time Lords. If they really are like octopuses on Earth, then they would have two hearts. Maybe this is the hidden secret of the ancient Gallifreyans: that they are descended from singing cuttlefish with bits of their brains hanging from their noses.)

2. How can anything we see in "The Rings of Akhaten" work?

(X7.8, "The Rings of Akhaten")

It's a challenge to salvage any sense from this story but if we combine some of the apparent Science Fails and look carefully at what's on screen, there's a slim hope. It involves legitimate Newtonian physics, off-the-shelf space-opera gubbins and a sprinkling of Whitaker-Science (see **What Planet was David Whitaker On?** under 5.7, "The Wheel in Space").

The first clue is that "Grandfather", despite looking like a brown dwarf (a recently-discovered type of very small dim star) until it turns into the Great Pumpkin, is lit from another of those mysterious off-screen sources. Look carefully and you'll see that the left side has a blue-white tinge, as if a bigger, brighter object is out of shot. If this orange thing is a planet (and the Doctor vaguely gestures towards it while mentioning that the locals believe all life began on "this planet") rather than a star, the scale of the ring-system and suchlike contracts considerably. The various trips the Doctor, Merry and Clara make in their furious flycycle cease to require decades. They still would have to take a lot longer than the story suggests, unless this amphitheatre's audience are incredibly patient and tolerate delays long enough to raise families in, between the start of the ceremony and the end of the story.

However, we can make it work by looking into another apparently stupid detail. We'll talk about Hohmann Transfer Orbits in a tic (no, it'll be fun), but how is everyone breathing?

Quite apart from the voyages between asteroids (or whatever they are – see later) being possible without spacesuits, there's a remarkable lack of any vegetation on any of these rocky worldlets. If each one had a force-field, that'd be genre-acceptable, if not kosher science, but we don't even have that. So the air must be abundant. It's looking as if Grandfather is pumping out oxygen. (Maybe nitrogen too, but not necessarily. It's interesting that this is the first pseudo-mediaeval/quasi-Egyptian religious cult not to use candles, censers or naked flames of any kind.) What's keeping the air from dissipating out into space? Well, note that we only see the system from two angles, neither looking out from the Great Pumpkin. Note also that we're told there are seven worlds, and the inhabitants regard this as the start of all civilisations. We're supposed to be thinking of Ptolemaic cosmology and *Harmonia Mundi*. In which case, there's something obvious keeping the air in: a giant crystal sphere.

It has to be crystal for the light from that off-stage star to be illuminating everyone even when Grandfather is extinguished by Clara's Magic Storytelling Leaf (another triumph of dead tree technology over electronic media). Suppose for a moment that some ancient race built shells around planets to give a bit more *lebensraum* and populate the moons of a nearby gas-giant. They might have demolished a few moons to make the shell. It's perhaps an old enough world that the moons broke up and formed rings. (When a moon's orbit gets too close to its planet, the tug-of-war between gravity and the velocity of orbit gets too great. At a certain proximity, called the Roche Limit, the moon breaks up. So whatever was going on in *The Sarah Jane Adventures* must have needed more than just a tractor-beam.)

Each fragment of former moon now has a city or something on it. The world they orbit is most likely surrounded by methane or ammonia and, with the sphere acting as a greenhouse and things in the upper atmosphere using the carbon and letting the oxygen out, there's a breathable supply of air. How much air? Well, assuming a world smaller but denser than Saturn, as appears

continued on Page 55...

some and went on the attack, killing anyone they touched. The difference is... difference. The Ood don't look entirely human, and children's fantasy series do like to deploy the homily that we shouldn't judge by appearances. Doing that in "New Earth" would have overloaded an already messy season-opener, one in which one subplot had to be kicked into the long grass until next time (see **Was Series 2 Supposed to have been Like This?** under X2.11, "Fear Her"). Nonetheless, it's possible now, and the Ood costumes and prosthetics were in storage to be used.

Because, however much we dignify this as a meditation on slavery and mutual respect, this is as much as anything an excuse to bring the Ood back and discuss all the things people wanted to know after their last outing. The introduction of this race was a pragmatic move: they were cheaper than refurbishing the Slitheen suits (see Volume 7 for the full story) and replaced the Raxacoricofallapatorian relics as the cultists who would be possessed by the Beast. The idea that a slave species (the fact that this exists as a second-hand concept is pretty horrible in itself) is telepathic is, as we've hinted above, very familiar, but it's not an immediately obvious connection. Yet it had to be so, for the earlier story to function even as clumsily as it did. That Donna dismisses the plot of the previous Ood story as stupid is all the commentary that needs here. The rest of this episode tries to recover at least some idea of how a species as potent as the Ood could have become livestock.

That's another strange thing about this story. Everyone who comments on it in the Making-Of stuff compares the conditions of Ood retail not to the Triangle Trade, but to battery farming. The ethics of food production had been in the news once again when this story was being put together, including a return of the protests over the transport of veal-calves to France in inhumane conditions (as if what happened to them at the end of the journey was any more pleasant). Chicken-farming was getting a high-profile protest led by TV Chef-turned-farmer Hugh Fernley-Whittingstall (who'd got Jamie Oliver – see X2.3, "School Reunion" – to use his clout with Sainsbury's, the supermarket chain he advertised, to change their suppliers).

Slavery, in this story, is subordinated to a wider issue of consumerism. After all, with three separate tie-in magazines, DVDs, assorted action-figures and strawberry yoghurts all available in your local Sainsbury's or Tesco at the time of transmission, it would have been difficult for BBC Wales's cash-cow *Doctor Who* to slag off capitalism. Never mind "who makes your clothes?", the environmental and human-rights track-record of the Chinese manufacturers of "Destroyed Cassandra" and the Dalek Sec Voice-Changer might not have borne scrutiny.

We might at this point mention an old American hymn, "Can the Circle be Unbroken?" (or variations on the title). The lyrics don't really work as a "source", and it's hard to make a direct connection, but it did give a title to Mildred Taylor's second book in the series that began with *Roll of Thunder, Hear My Cry*, about Africa-American sharecropper farmers in the 1930s. That book was on the GCSE syllabus shortly before this story was made.

The erroneous stuff about the Amygdala, and the afflicted specimens going berserk, seems to be a vestigial memory from the Reavers in *Serenity* and its source-series, *Firefly*. We've been here before ("Utopia"). It's probably worth mentioning, even if it's almost too obvious to claim as any kind of insight, that the calm-voiced servitors whose eyes go red as they overcome their conditioning to go on a killing-spree is the second call-back to "The Robots of Death" (14.5) in four episodes (X4.0, "Voyage of the Damned"). Their frenzy when chained up after going rogue was intended by Keith Temple to recall *28 Days Later*, but it's only apparent once you've been told this.

Additional Sources BBC website info: According to the Ood Operations Sales and Information Pack, you can buy a variety of the creatures – Household Ood, Pilot Ood, Personal Trainer Ood and Military Ood. There's a 15% discount if you buy ten.

English Lessons

• *Take the Mickey* (v.t.): It's the politer version of an expression you're not allowed to say on BBC One at 7.00pm. "Mickey" as in "micturation", if that helps.

• *Rough Guide* (n.): A British travel guide series. The idea is that rather than ticking off a country and adding to your carbon footprint, you stick around and look into it a bit longer. They also did handbooks for science, technology and suchlike, and some scholarly World Music CDs.

• *Persil ball* (n.): It's for laundry detergent

How Can Science Salvage Badly-Made Planets?

continued from Page 53...

to be the case, and that the Doctor's vantage-point is about a quarter of a million kilometres away (or else Clara would be a *lot* older by the time the commuting between planetoids ends) and that's the outer limit, more or less, and with school maths telling us that the volume of a sphere is $4/3\ \pi\ r^3$, we get, er... 6.45×10^{17} cubic kilometres of air. All at room-temperature, rather than the usual single-figures-above-Absolute-Zero. As Big Dumb Objects (the technical term for *Ringworld* or *Rendezvous with Rama* sort of artificial worlds) go, this is compact and bijou, but still ample for storytelling. We'll take it on trust that the pressure's even, and that there's some way to get the carbon back into the food-chain.

If there's air, there'll be drag on those bits of rock flying around. The big ones will create a backwash that would disrupt the orbits of the littler ones. This isn't a recipe for stable long-term ring-systems. Neither is the way the Doctor can stand on a tiny one as if it had the mass of Earth. They all seem to have agreed on a direction for "down" that's at right-angles to the direction for "in" towards their humungous jack-o-lantern *and* to the direction of spin the planetesimals have all adopted or retained. Localised gravity-generators? If such a thing were possible (and in *Doctor Who* there are precedents, making 4.6, "The Moonbase" the one time that the film convention of opening the airlocks and losing your Earth-like weight actually works – cf X4.16, "The Waters of Mars"; X8.7, "Kill The Moon"), these rocks would all pull on each other as well. They might use that to hold the rings together, rather than them aggregating at the Trojan points or – if that star's the nearest and biggest other mass – Lagrange points within the sphere. These days, we'll have to explain those terms.

There are zones where gravitational equilibrium between big objects makes small objects tend to stick around if they've got there. They don't stay absolutely stuck in space, but relative to the big bodies they keep the same approximate distance. If it's a planet and a big moon, then the Lagrange points (AKA "Libration points") move around the planet at the same rate as the moon, but in a different orbit. The Lagrange zones are handy balance-points when two unequal but large masses (a planet and a big moon) are in a stable orbit. (The L5 point is the preferred locale for those cylindrical colonies that were in 70s textbooks on

how we'd be living now, but L2 is a good bet for where the Cybermen were in 6.3, "The Invasion" or the Daleks in X5.3, "Victory of the Daleks".)

All other things being equal, a system this old with two massive objects in play would have landed up like that rather than the neat circular rings we see. If the star's a long way off, as with Saturn, this is less of a concern, but then we're back to the ice-world problems we discussed *re* Ood Sphere unless the sphere was specifically made to heat the system up like a greenhouse. Maybe that accounts for the lack of vegetation (assuming there's only one way to grow plants), if they actively want loads of CO_2. Saturn's rings are kept in line by the action of shepherd moons, larger bodies that braid the gravitational pull of the ice-lumps on one another with their own, probably causing the banding (the famous Cassini Division and others). If each rock in the Akhaten rings has its own 1g field, these fields have to be very localised – or else the rocks would reform back into a planet in a relatively short period.

Yet no such force can be uniting the rings, as the inner ones orbit Grandfather faster than the outer ones (paradoxically, by moving slower they take less time to complete an orbit), as would naturally happen in a frictionless one-central-mass set-up. That causes another problem with the jet-bikes. The Doctor and, more alarmingly, Clara, navigate between inner and outer lumps as if it's a simple matter of pointing at the destination and revving up. As we touched on in "Frontier in Space" (10.3), the way to get from a high orbit to a low one is to slow down. Moreover, as all these bodies are in their own individual orbits, any journey between them involves aiming to be at where your destination is *going* to be when you and it both arrive. Doing as we see our heroes do here – pointing at where the temple is at the start of their (long) journey and firing the engines – is stupid.

It might be better, as there's air between these islands, to rig up a sail and slow yourself down that way – making a graceful arc-section of an ellipse tangential to both your starting orbit and finishing orbit and timed to take as long to get there as your destination does. As Grandfather isn't a star, there isn't a solar wind (although if our earlier speculation about the atmosphere holds, there might be something similar and maybe stronger), but if the heat's coming from off to one side – from that star over yonder that's unevenly warm-

continued on Page 57...

("Persil Washes Whiter"), and they do look quite similar. The idea was to put the powder in the plastic sphere and pop that in the tub with the laundry, to avoid clagging up that drawer where the powder would normally go. They've not been used for about 15 years, so the BBC was able to use the term.

• *D'oh* (interj.): Yes, all of the publicity material says this was nicked from *The Simpsons* but, appropriately given the proximity to the Sense Sphere, it was used a lot and much earlier by Peter Glaze in *Crackerjack* (you know the drill), and before that James Findlayson in the Laurel and Hardy films.

• *West Ham* (n.) A district of East London, west of East Ham but, in this instance, they mean West Ham United FC, a football club whose glory days were in the1960s and early 70s. Their home back then was the Upton Park stadium (technically, the "Boleyn", and messily redeveloped – it's about 200 yards from The Who Shop), but they somehow wangled a deal to take over the Olympic Stadium in Stratford, about a mile north. The fans are no more happy about that than anyone else is. It's a bit of a step from Chiswick, so we presume that Geoff Noble was originally from out east, and refused to switch allegiance to the nearer Fulham or the Hammers's arch-rivals Chelsea. Remember this for Series 11.

• *PLC* (n.): A public limited company, formed after 1981. It's a bit like the US publicly traded companies. The alternative is a private limited company (with the suffix "Limited") or an American-style corporation. Donna seems to think a company can be all three at once, despite them all being mutually-exclusive entities, and Solana accepts this. So maybe tri-galactic corporate law is very different in the forty-second century, despite the story's strenuous efforts to suggest otherwise.

Oh, Isn't That...?

• *Tim McInnerny* (Halpen, CEO of Ood Operations) is, these days, often playing suave corporate villains like this one, but spent a lot of the 80s as Percy in various iterations of *Blackadder*, except the last one where he was Captain Darling. He was also, perhaps appropriately, Franz Kafka in *The Young Indiana Jones Adventures*, a series that has many casting decisions that readers of these books might want to investigate. Oh, and the usual *Game of Thrones* stint and *Notting Hill*.

• *Ayesha Dharker* (Solana Mercurio, Ood Operations PA). She played Tara Mandal on *Coronation Street*. Plus the Queen of Naboo in *Attack of the Clones*, but we won't tell.

Things That Don't Make Sense "Thank you, DoctorDonna, for standing there while our actual liberator, you know, wossisface, died inside our Giant Pulsating Brain. And while one of our own turned our enslaver into Oodkind. We will always honour you for, er, whatever it was you did."

The origins of the Ood make little sense (see the essay). This is a species, after all, that has language, telepathy, fire, toolmaking and so on, but they haven't figured out pockets to hold their dangly brain-bits in. Not even a papoose. They've figured out one-handed firemaking, tool-making, cave-excavation and so on, but not the cerebral jockstrap. (If, as we speculate in the essay, the moisture on their exposed brains and tentacles is oil or wax or alcohol or anti-freeze, getting that close to a naked flame would be risky, but that's more a problem for X4.17, "The End of Time Part One".) Neither did the humans who dress them in Mao suits. Because one-handed slaves are *so* useful around the house.

It's a problem we've already had with the Tharils (18.5, "Warriors' Gate") and will have again with the Janus (X9.10, "Face the Raven"); there may well be a good logical reason why entire races of clairvoyants can be enslaved in the first place. We can't think of one right now, though.

The Doctor tells Solana that 'a species born to serve could never evolve'. Species born to serve have evolved many times on Earth, usually as symbiotes or getting something out of the deal – think of those birds that pick the teeth of hippos. Consider the mitochondria within every cell of your body, or intestinal flora. Or, more embarrassingly the Doctor's used it as a metaphor before, there are Pilot Fish ("The Christmas Invasion"). And apart from the Ood having impractical feet for an ice-world, Solana's stilettos are a bit silly for someone who works on a planet like this.

As always, we have no idea how many pints of milk you can get for one Credit, so we're not really able to assess the tri-galactic economy. However, it's in crisis, we're told, and the slavers of Ood Operations have cut their prices to rock-bottom: 50 Cred per head. Why? The Ood only come from *one* planet. They have to be shipped across three galaxies. They appear unable to breed

---

How Can Science Salvage Badly-Made Planets?

continued from Page 55...

ing the goldfish bowl they've built around the planet – there might be a complex meteorology. In fact, if there's air between the worldlets but not a lot of gravitational pull unless you're right up close, then you might as well build wings out of cardboard and flap between planets. Take snacks, it'll take a while.

Maybe the angular momentum of each planetoid is enough to counteract localised hurricanes and keep them all in nice neat orbits. It's possible. Just. The Doctor and Clara can stand upright on the outside of the first one they visit, so there isn't as much of a breeze as one might expect. Moreover, with briefly-adjacent space-islands the journey will expand while you're on it if you're not careful, making a trip to a further-in or further-out world easier than to a neighbouring orbit unless you slingshot around a bigger object (such as the dirty great planet at the system's core). It might be quicker to rendezvous with your target on the other side of Grandfather in half a year from when you set out. Taxi-drivers would do complex equations to calculate a route – much as Thames boatmen in Elizabethan times would charge more for an apparently shorter journey against the tide – and offer seasonal discounts if a big lump of rock is conveniently due allowing a shorter trip via completely the opposite direction. See, Hohmann Transfer Orbits *are* fun.

This model accounts for most of the daftness in the words and pictures we get, although there is a small matter of there being two sets of rings with, apparently, two different ecliptic planes around the same planet. We can get around that by having the rings come from elsewhere rather than being by-products of the planet's formation – they aren't in the same relation to Grandfather as planets are to their sun. If the planetoids were a moon that split up when it orbited inside Roche's limit, they'd most likely all be around the planet's equator unless there was a collision at some point.

There are, however, two distinct belts of planetoids in two different orbits at a 30° slant to one another, and planets only have one Roche limit and one equator. So they were both the result of disintegrating moons, each in a different, unusual orbit. Two different moons underwent orbital decay and broke up, and the fragments were in orbits at an angle to each other and, apparently, don't intersect. (Had a collision between them shattered both of them, they would be in a com-

promise orbit in a single band.) As we've concluded that nothing in this planet's set-up is natural, there must be some kind of cultural reason for this to have been done deliberately. If the proportions of the orbital distance are arranged as some kind of octave, as Kepler tried to prove about our Solar System, then the inner ring's alignment to the outer's may be a conscious attempt at discord – again, more interesting than what we got and a complete contradiction of the story's theme of music to set the culture in cosmic harmony.

If the dialogue and pictures are right, and Planet Grandad is one of the seven worlds, where are the other six? Unlike the Ptolemaic model of concentric crystal spheres pushed by angels, possibly there are seven planets orbiting the star as they always did, each inside a sphere. Maybe the planet's atmosphere being infected by a story-eating parasite got it quarantined. Quite apart from the full implications of the peculiar economic set-up where objects acquire value through stories (like in *Bagpuss*) and the presence of the Hop Pyleen brothers (X1.2, "The End of the World", they obviously go from system to system hoping to catch a stellar extinction), there are many aspects of the episode that could, if approached the right way, be more interesting than the confused and embarrassing story we got. There's still a lot that doesn't even make sense on its own terms – the Doctor and Clara show up one afternoon and end the oldest known civilisation in the universe, who thank him by returning her ring.

Of course, with this and Trenzalore, there is a small detail we ought to acknowledge: if they have more than a pair of large masses around which the location of the story is orbiting, we have ourselves a Three Body Problem, and anyone attempting to predict the motion of the smaller worlds might as well sacrifice pigeons and look at their intestines for answers. We discussed this in **The Obvious Question... How Old is He?** under 16.5, "The Power of Kroll" even before the question of how many suns Gallifrey orbits was resolved.

3. How can it be Winter Solstice for eight centuries on the trot?

(X7.14, "The Name of the Doctor"; X7. 16, "The Time of the Doctor")

When seen from space, Trenzalore doesn't seem especially weird. It's got a moderate-sized star an

continued on Page 59...

anywhere else. The once-bountiful Human Empire is running on a commodity that Ood Operations controls utterly. So, one would imagine, they could ask any price, but instead feel pressured to offer massive discounts. With the fortunes and power he ought to be wielding, Halpen could buy and sell planets (we know a guy – see 16.1, "The Ribos Operation"). The other weird thing about this economy is that space travel appears to be free. Quite apart from abolitionists and Friends of the Ood, Mr Halpen ought to be worried that anyone with the spacefaring equivalent of a U-Haul could whisk off his prize merchandise.

Also, Halpen confirms that Ood are sold to the military. What possible use are they, even if their innate inability to cause harm is overcome? They can't work on production-lines either, unless they avoid leaning over. (Apart from anything else, footsoldiers unable to wear helmets...) Military Ood, apart from apparently contradicting the rest of the story, are themselves going to destabilise a lot of the Tri-galactic political system by abruptly not working (X7.13, "Nightmare in Silver" hints that this could be a problem real soon). And the security risks involved with having telepathic soldiers or munitions workers must have been absurdly high. If the intelligence community knew that all of the Ood in three galaxies were in touch with a central brain on their homeworld, the Ood Sphere would have been bombed to bits as a basic precaution.

Then one day, after two centuries of prosperity, an entire inter-galactic economy collapses after a system that's been stable for generations folds up. The Doctor's awfully confident the humans will supply all the Ood with rockets and let them come home. More importantly, if removing the hindbrains is as much like lobotomy as the Doctor thinks, he's leaving a race of brain-damaged individuals to put their lives back together themselves. Which leaves the question of what exactly the hindbrains actually *do*, if the oldest and most experienced Ood got along so well without them.

The Doctor also claims that the amygdala is the bit of the brain that contains the personality. Unfortunately, not so; it actually controls baser responses like anger, fear and aggression. That is, it does for humans and the more complex brains among terrestrial mammals. Fair enough, it could be anything in a different species with such a radically different neural configuration. A bigger

worry is how a portion of an alien brain he's seeing for the first time is instantly recognisable as something that lurks under the main cortex in humans. Someone, a human most likely, must have known enough about what the Ood brain was like to have constructed the prototype for the Persil Ball voice-box. They even knew that the species was telepathic. The voice-box doesn't inhibit this ability (Danny said so: "The Impossible Planet") and yet they developed a method of translating thoughts into English using neurosurgical techniques and didn't bother to block any potential gang-up-on-the-enslavers psychic message? Who builds electronics for slaves that kill anyone they touch?

If Halpern wants a post-mortem on the rabid Ood, isn't machine-gunning the poor devil for five seconds likely to reduce the useful information they might get? Speaking of which... isn't it peculiar that the Red-Eye symptom that meant "ancient alien force taking over" in "The Satan Pit" is the same as the Brain reasserting itself? Red-Eye is treated like an infectious condition, but no effort is made to disinfect the visitors to the complex who might spread it to other Ood colonies. They even talk about "the classic foot and mouth solution", but nobody washes their shoes or even puts on a paper mask.

We'll go easy on the way in which the soldiers just miraculously stop fighting, and assume, as with Donna, they can hear the Oodsong once the circle is broken, and are moved to quit. (Look, we have to graft on such an explanation, because the scene shows the hitherto-murderous Ood simply standing around waving their hands in the air like they just don't care. The human slave-traders and mercenaries, who've been getting slaughtered until about five seconds before, accept this and carefully place their sub machine guns on the snow, mill about and look slightly embarrassed.)

And... you give the Ood comedy voice-balls that sound like Homer Simpson, and nobody mentions Zoidberg?

Critique This story, as we've examined in **The Big Picture**, has a lot of elements and an overall shape that seasoned cult-TV viewers of the 90s would be joining in with almost from the opening shot. It's so familiar that, for that audience, it can hardly be said to have been a "first viewing" even in April 2008. The criteria for that sub-section of the BBC1 viewership are how well it's executed, and wheth-

How Can Science Salvage Badly-Made Planets?

continued from Page 57...

appropriate distance away, a few neighbouring planets, and is either blue (like Earth) or brown (like post-apocalyptic, over-populated Earth in Series 1) depending on whether there's been an endless war in its past. (How a war can be endless and over will not tax us, as the "endless" part was prevented from even starting, and was only Madame Kovarian's rather hyperbolic justification for creating River Song.) It has Earth-like gravity and atmosphere. The weather, like the clothing of the locals, is sort of an all-purpose Northern European Winter, part Finland, part Switzerland.

And yet, it always seems to be night. This could just have been a sampling anomaly, with everything that happens being within a three-hour window, and then the next visit a similar three-hour event three centuries later and so on. Then the Doctor takes Clara up to the top of the bell-tower to watch the sunrise and sunset while he's talking continuity. It seems it's not just the hats and snow that are Scandinavian – this is the land of the Midnight Sun. Again, a picturesque version of an Earth phenomenon, but... it's been like that for a while. It's an arresting image, one good enough for Stephen King to allude to in a recent novel (Mile 81), but it can't work the way we're sold it. You can't have Midnight Sun for more than a small part of a planet's year. Certainly not a planet so like Earth in every other respect.

On our world, this is the result of the axial tilt of 26 degrees. All actual planets in our system are orbiting the sun in the same plane, called the ecliptic, around the sun's equator. (Pluto doesn't, but that isn't exactly a planet.) Earth's orbit, whilst not precisely circular, doesn't swing back and forth enough to cause seasons (we get closest to the sun around 3rd January). Those are the result or the obliquity of the daily spin (around the axis of "true" north and "true" south) to the plane of the yearly orbit. So we get solstices and equinoxes at different phases of the progress around the sun, depending on which pole is pointing where relative to the star we orbit, and thence seasons and weather. You probably knew that.

What we've seen of Trenzalore doesn't make it seem as if it's that different – if a world is so far away that its year lasts hundreds of times longer than ours, its star would look like a tiny point, and Trenzalore's doesn't. Even if it did, that would take it too far from a star like ours to be inhabitable. Moreover, it would mean that the only bit of this whole Earth-sized world we saw was a village right at the pole. It would be a bit colder than what we saw. No sunlight for... well, let's call it 800 years. (The dialogue's a bit vague but, taken with X6.1, "The Impossible Astronaut", wherein the Doctor spent 200-odd years in the same trousers and didn't look any older, we have to assume an immense time for him to have visibly aged more than the slight impact five centuries had in 18.1, "The Leisure Hive". Also, there's repeated clues that twelfth Doctor is over two thousand years old – X8.1, "Deep Breath"; X8.8, "Mummy on the Orient Express"; X9.5, "The Girl Who Died".)

On the opposite pole, no night for just as long. One long hot summer day lasting eight centuries. You'd think there'd be a bit of an anticyclone. This village should be flattened by winds and considerably colder than the Antarctic in midwinter. We have snow on the ground for as long as the Doctor's there, but none ever falls. The rest of the planet wouldn't be much more hospitable, as nothing could grow and the air wouldn't be breathable even if it started out as like ours. (As it is, the matter of what everyone eats and how it gets there is never resolved, because the story shows us a planet consisting of one village very far from fields, fishing, trade-routes or even a Tesco. There's talk of farmers and barns, but it's the set-up for a silly gag.)

One possible solution is that the planet is itself orbiting another. If Trenzalore is revolving around a bigger world which is, like Uranus, spinning at right-angles to the ecliptic (north pointing "inwards"), and if the axis of Trenzalore's rotation is about 90 degrees out-of-true from the plane of its orbit around the primary, then they would in effect have two types of "year"; the period of orbit around the primary and the period of the primary's orbit around its sun. One pole (let's call it "south" for now) could be pointed at the primary at all times and the other away from it – which would be why we never see a thumping great planet in the sky over Christmas. (However long the primary takes to make a circuit, the main problem is the relationship between the Trenzalore's rotation and its progress around the primary, the day and year. Understandably, nobody seems to bother with calendars here.) The majority of big-enough moons so far examined have captured rotation, like our moon's, so always show the same face to the primary (because the unevenly distrib-

continued on Page 61...

er the components are put together in a new and interesting combination.

On that score, it's somewhat above average. There's nothing here under-par, and all the effects shots and set-pieces are pretty and tight. That's enough for the nation's eight-year-olds and their grannies; a plot would be almost surplus to requirements. What's missing, even compared to an under-performing old-series story such as "The Krotons" (6.4) or a good one like "Horror of Fang Rock" (15.1) is a sense of the rules changing – of this environment being substantially different from any other TV drama with similar ingredients. The grabber-chase is efficiently done but, as with the cradle sequence in "Partners in Crime", it could almost have been in any action-adventure series. The Doctor could be running around any warehouse in Liverpool or Deptford; Ood Operations could be any people-trafficking cartel.

Until we get yet another off-the-shelf staple – a Giant Pulsating Brain – it would take very few alterations to make this a historical drama or cop show about Eastern Europe. Sure, not many of those would have been family viewing for Saturday teatime between *The Kids are All Right* and *I'll Do Anything* (this being the peak of John Barrowman's ownership of Saturday evenings), but the Ood are there to be scary and/or poignant-looking, with humans as the agents of their liberation. Members of this species are born telepathic, but have this facility, this innate sense of community, surgically removed. We never get any sense of *what* they lost, how it feels to have this violation, what a culture like that might have been like – that's not this story's job. Instead, it's a collage of images from other sources used to disguise a fairly routine story, one that might have been new to small children, but which wimps out of making any sustained or original comment about why humans blind themselves to inhumanity for the sake of convenience.

Instead, the focus is on Donna's reaction to visiting an alien planet as seen on TV. The spaceship, the ice-planet, the space-squids and the Giant Pulsating Brain are all there for her to look at and us to watch her looking at. That this is as much a tableau or pageant as a story with a sequential plot is shoved in our faces by the climax, where the Doctor and Donna stand by as someone else saves the Ood, and look on as Halpern gets a Roald Dahl-style comeuppance. As Davies comments in *Confidential*, every human

victim "earns" a nasty death by doing something villain-like, and Halpern's fate is designed ruthlessly to be talked about in school playgrounds the following Monday.

This is what makes "Horror of Fang Rock" a useful comparison: everyone there (except the Doctor and Leela) gets killed in increasingly moralistic ways, but as a consequence of the story energetically juxtaposing two sets of narrative conventions. The plot is driven by the intersections (or collisions) between "Who Goes There"/ *The Thing from Another World* and a John Galsworthy/Anthony Trollope narrative about coercion. The "normal" costume drama material is inserted *within* the logic of a Science Fictional narrative, and the various visual cues (wing-collars and jars of Bovril, electronic burbles and *Top of the Pops* effects) are made to perform specific tasks unlike their conventional uses. The conventional human characters all suffer the consequences of misreading the situation according to the codes and conventions of their era, but the situation is a reasonably well worked-out set of circumstances following basic schoolkid science (and the reasoning process of an experienced SF reader who'd been working on the BBC Classic Serials).

The Rutan's biology and technology are intrinsic to how it operates, what it does and how the Doctor uses a lighthouse to kill it. The Ood, as we'll see in this story's essay, have features that flatly contradict their imputed background. Nothing in the story *needs* them to come from an ice planet or works better that way; Davies simply told Keith Temple and The Mill that Ood Sphere is an ice-planet on a whim. We have (to date) never seen Ruta 3, but the fact that it's an ice-world was crucial to the plot of "Horror". Everything that happens from the moment the fog sets in is a consequence of this fact. The Rutan is, we might say, a load-bearing alien; the Ood are almost purely decorative. They could have been Slitheen, Hath or Adipose, for all the difference it would have made. The story's all about the slavers, who are all one-note caricatures. The Doctor and Donna serve to explain to the viewers that the Ood smell and how their Song makes Donna feel and to give the slavers an excuse to prove their nastiness.

With the brief they were given, neither Keith Temple nor Graeme Harper can be criticised. A "shopping-list" approach can be the start of the problems, but a duff writer or inept director can

How Can Science Salvage Badly-Made Planets?

continued from Page 59...

uted mass makes the heavier bits point towards the "bottom", where the gravity-source it orbits is), but whatever knocked the primary for six may only have happened recently (in cosmic terms, anything under three billion years is "recent") and so Trenzalore's rotation has yet to adjust.[14] Does this get us out of all the other problems we've identified?

Maybe. If the primary is, like Jupiter, chucking out radiation on all frequencies then it, rather than the star, would be the main source of energy. That might well account for only the part of the world pointing away from the bigger planet being populated. If the star's big, bright but distant, it could illuminate dimly but be just a countervailing force for weather systems. A bigger star might be on its last legs and expanding after billions of years of not being all that much cop, or it could have been always a bit less warm than a more compact and massive one (although then you'd expect it to be a bit redder).

We may be back to a very long year, but without the distance from the star being enough to make the planet uninhabitable. The climate, on the bits of Trenzalore that aren't lethally irradiated, would be milder than expected for a world so distant from the star and less polarised than a perpetually frozen north and lit-up south as speculated upon above. Of course, this would have its own consequences a bit unlike what we got shown: if Trenzalore's magnetic field is strong enough to block most of the radiation from both the star and the planet it orbits, such a "hot" world nearby would make for spectacular aurorae. If they're big enough and powerful enough, these could be what the farmers use to grow crops in perpetual night-time.

Don't like that? There are good reasons not to, especially the effect this unseen primary world would have on the orbits of those profuse spaceships making a ring-system at the start of the Christmas episode. They'd have to be constantly adjusting their positions, which rather defeats the object of orbiting. And the radiation would make things change over time. Well, what if the star's tidal forces and big planet make the core of the moon-as-big-as-a-planet especially active, and allow exciting geothermal phenomena (keeping with the northern European theme if nothing else)? The first time we saw Trenzalore, it was looking a bit more volcanic. Perhaps the habitable pole

is only possible during certain parts of the primary's year. Then again, they had just endured a "never-ending" war.

If this is all true, then life for anyone living on Trenzalore's equator would be interesting. If the orbit around the primary planet is significantly longer or shorter than the basic day, then the stars will be in different places every night. Their mythology would be interesting. Navigation would be a challenge, especially on the choppy seas such a climate would cause. If the main source of warmth is the world's core rather than the sun, then the whole ecosystem would be affected: photosynthesis still needs light, but the oceans would be more like the freakish micro-climates of the thermal vents (which makes the likelihood of an oxygen-rich atmosphere developing unaided a lot lower).

That works as a model, but does it match everything we see on screen? Well, no. For a start, there's a ring-system at the beginning of the episode that vanishes later on. That could be the vast number of spaceships orbiting as seen from a distance... except that there's another ring of spaceships nearer the "camera". Maybe one's close scrutiny satellites and the outer one's geostationary motherships. Then there's a peculiar shot when the Doctor opens the doors of the TARDIS to show Handles that this planet isn't Gallifrey, and we see the planet and its star and, between them, another planet seemingly lit from a *different star* out of shot to the top right of the CGI fake-camera. It's about eight minutes twenty into the episode, just before the Papal Mainframe shows up. We could dismiss this as the latest in a string of daft goofs by The Mill/Milk on this score (especially at Christmas), but let's take it at face value and assume a binary star system.[15] This makes the odds of a perpetually dark world fall through the floor. Unless, of course, something *very* peculiar is happening...

Trenzalore has a lot of wood, but not much metal. It might be a very light planet or it could be a very dense small one, the core of a former gas-giant. Such a world could withstand a lot of tidal forces so, if we're really gagging to keep all the details we see and hear within the bounds of possibility (if not probability), this planet might be at the barycentre of two equal-sized stars. The pair of stars orbit the same focal point in space, a gravitationally stable one; either nice neat circular orbits (rare in the universe, but we did say they had

continued on Page 63...

compound the felony (e.g. 21.1, "Warriors of the Deep" or 22.4, "The Two Doctors"), and if you get both at once on a producer's pet project, it can be unspeakable (19.7, "Time Flight"; 2.5, "The Web Planet"). Here, by contrast, we have an episode that's as good as it could ever have been and which manages some interesting crinkles and grace-notes.

And here we have to talk about Murray Gold. His recent scores have been intrusive or generic – or both – and for much of this episode, we're on familiar ground. Almost all of Halpern's scenes have a slidey 70s bass, a trio of French horns (or synth equivalent) and a triangle, more or less holding up a big banner saying "John Barry Bond-Villain Music", and a lot of the stuff about ice uses sounds like milk-bottles with water in being tapped. But at key moments, he and the dubbing mixer co-operate in making a soundscape that tells a story slightly athwart what we're seeing or being told in the dialogue. The soundtrack of a story with a plot-element that gets called a "song" was always going to need extra effort, but the interesting bit *isn't* the rather formulaic vocal Donna is vouchsafed a listen to, via the Doctor, but what's done with the same voice electronically in earlier scenes, plus what they do with Catherine Tate's voice saying "broken" when the unprocessed Ood rise. Unlike the dialogue or action, it makes the Doctor-Donna's part in freeing the Ood more than just bearing witness and distracting the guards.

Many stories have blurred the edges between "special sound" (as they used to credit it in the 60s and 70s) and music, often to great effect. (Brian Hodgson did both when they wanted to shave the budgets for "The Krotons"; 5.7, "The Wheel in Space" and 6.1, The Dominators"); Dudley Simpson and Dick Mills liaised on many 70s stories, but the one with the most co-ordinated sound-worlds are 13.3, "Pyramids of Mars" and 14.5, "The Robots of Death". Mills and Malcolm Clarke made 19.6, "Earthshock" as much a sonic environment as an action-adventure narrative.) With the bombast of Gold's scores, the work of Paul McFadden et al on the other sound elements is less obvious than in the old days, and many of the sounds used are recycled Radiophonica from those days anyway – but here it's more than usually worthy of close attention. Of course, if you do then you spot how, as with Rose's appearance in "Partners in Crime", Gold occasionally slaps a dif-ferent music cue over one that was running under a scene, like switching the channel on a radio, but by now this is almost a familiar feature rather than an aesthetically-clumsy glitch. The "your song is nearly ended" scene is an especially obvious example.

None of the performances is out-of-key (well, except maybe the yuppie slavers), but pay particular attention to Adrian Rawlins as Dr Ryder. He's there to be inconspicuous (mostly), but offers little hints of the character's motivation throughout; his accent becomes noticeably more northern once he's outed as a Friend of the Ood, for example. Everyone here knows exactly what they are doing, what's expected of them, how this story goes. It's a matter of how good a job everyone makes of a story that's barely worth that much effort. It's not a complete waste of everyone's time – not entirely perfunctory – but as close as *Doctor Who* should ever get to being "routine". That clichés only get to be clichés because they work is itself a cliché – whether it *always* works is another matter. We gave this story's near-twin, "The Sensorites", a lot of leeway for being the source of what would soon become the most hackneyed ideas in *Doctor Who,* so it's only right that we shouldn't be satisfied just because a slicker, more cinematic adventure allows us to settle in to a warm sense of familiarity and contentment. The subject-matter isn't something that should be cosy or reassuring.

The Lore

Written by Keith Temple. Directed by Graeme Harper. Viewing figures: (BBC1) 7.8 million, (BBC3 repeats) 1.3 and 0.6 million. First night AIs were 87%, but 89% for BBC3's first repeat.

Repeats and Overseas Promotion *Le Chant des Oods* ("The Song of the Oods"), *Immer zu Diensten* ("Always at Your Service" – some of you will now be imagining an Ood remake of *You Rang, M'Lord?*).

Production

• Keith Temple had met Russell T Davies at a BBC Drama reception and they had got reminiscing about the Philip Hinchcliffe era of *Doctor Who,* so Temple was on Davies's radar. After writing for pretty much all the major soaps and a number of

How Can Science Salvage Badly-Made Planets?

continued from Page 61...

identical mass) or, more excitingly, two identical eccentric elliptical orbits – both stars approach, rotate around and leave the same point of equilibrium over thousands of years.

A planet that drifted to this still point would get stuck there, unless the orbits of the stars altered. That might give us the timescale for the Doctor to have seen the sun rise in the same place for centuries but, as you're probably already thinking, it allows all sorts of other possible stories with more potential for tension and wonder than whether Clara's turkey will be cooked in time. For starters, anyone trying to prove Copernicus right would be in for a hard time if they just materialised on a planet like this, rather than seeing it from outside first. Then there's the environmental cost of *two* big stars approaching and causing big tides, stripping away the atmosphere and raising the mean temperature implacably. And they might well have streams of particles, their solar winds, crossing at this point. In fact, the pull of two suns might

well lead to a bit of bulging around the equator. It would also lead to more than one dawn per rotation (see 3.1, "Galaxy 4").

Of course, this would make the other planet we see very vulnerable, and causes problems when the Doctor first visits and lands by switching off the anti-gravs and making the TARDIS fall – we have no guarantee that the nearest heaviest object is the planet and not either of the stars. And eventually either the stars' masses will become imbalanced or they'll collide. We're forced to conclude that the only viable mechanism for this is that the TARDIS only ever shows up on days when the sunrise and sunset are minutes apart, but that this is only as common there as it is on Earth. Perhaps She's reacting to having been human for a few hours (X6.4, "The Doctor's Wife") by going into a sulky teenage phase.

4. How can sharks fly in breathable air?
(X6.0, "A Christmas Carol")

That's just bollocks.

long-running dramas, Temple was an experienced pro. Davies had a few ideas of things he wanted to see, and gave Temple the list of ingredients (a return of the Ood, an ice-planet, evil human slavers and something under the ice making the Ood rebellious; this later became a Giant Pulsating Brain as per 24.1, "Time and the Rani").

After their hastily-improvised debut as replacements for the Slitheen in "The Impossible Planet", the Ood prosthetics and suits were still useable. Davies and the nation's schoolkids had liked them, so a return engagement was more a matter of *when* than if. At one point, the team were interested in making this a two-parter, possibly bringing back Ida Scott (X2.9, "The Satan Pit" had ended with her being rescued, at the expense of the 50 or so Ood being left to perish), and perhaps with a quest across the tundra for the (just one more time) Giant Pulsating Brain.

• This story was recorded in the same block as "The Unicorn and the Wasp" (X4.7), so was directed by Graeme Harper and produced by Susie Liggatt. The Agatha Christie story got priority because they wanted good weather (despite 2007's pretty abysmal summer) but, as it turned out, the second half of the production block had more sunshine. The snowscape scenes were especially bright, even before the white surface reflect-

ed back sunlight and caused a few sunburns.

• Recording began on Tuesday, 21st August, with a scene in Reception, shot at Upper Boat while Donna was investigating a locked room in Lady Eddy's house ("The Unicorn and the Wasp") and Her Majesty was fleeing a falling ocean-liner (X4.0, "Voyage of the Damned") down marble stairs in Llandaff. The Reception scenes continued the next day – Tate had not seen the Ood before and compared them to her cat.

• After all the planets with beaches of recent years, the crew went retro – the ice-plains of an alien world were realised in a quarry, specifically one in Trefil, near Tredegar, rather further out from Cardiff than usual. A company called "Snow Business" does this for films all the time, so they and the BBC Wales effects team sprayed water on a patch of hilltop being used, then covered this with paper-snow. The Brecon Beacons, the hill-range that defines south Wales (as mentioned in X1.3, "The Unquiet Dead"), formed the backdrop in some shots. Despite the heat and sunshine, Tate was swaddled in a fur-lined parka as the leads and Ood trudged through paper-snow on August 23rd.

• The following day was the start of work at the warehouse, really the Twin Peaks aircraft-hanger at RAF St Athol (a familiar location we'll see again as Demons Run in X6.7, "A Good Man Goes to War", Area 51 in X6.2, "Day of the Moon" and others). There was a degree of improvisation with the claw-chase, but the action had also been roughed out in a crude CG "pre-vis" so that everyone had an idea of what the post-production claw would look like. Tennant had to find different ways of dodging and fleeing around corners, but with limits to where the claw could "physically" go. If you've read the Production material for "Colony in Space" (8.4) or "Utopia", it will be absolutely no surprise at all that Harper used a Quad bike instead of a camera dolly.

• Tuesday the 28th was the start of a complicated four-day shoot at the Aberthaw Cement Works. The locations here were in four parts of the complex, labelled A-D. Detailed descriptions of what was shot where and for which scene would take a while and not really help anyone. It's worth noting that the rotating drums were kept rotating because this was a working day there, and the cast and crew had to follow stringent safety procedures – wearing hard hats and goggles if not in shot. The other cast often aided the Ood surreptitiously, as their prosthetics made seeing difficult enough without slippery surfaces. The Hero Ood, Paul Kasey, also had motors in his head, making it hard for him to hear cues or directions. Temple visited the location on one of these days, commenting that the industrial landscape resembled his upbringing in the North East.

• As you may have seen in the DVD extras, Tennant and Gardner spent a lot of Friday stuck in traffic trying to get to Blackpool to switch on the illuminations – eventually getting a police escort. (Tennant was in the headlines, as this was when the news of his stint at the Royal Shakespeare Company broke, launching fevered speculation about a possible regeneration – see **What Were the Strangest Online Theories?** under X4.12, "The Stolen Earth" – then a hasty announcement of the 2009 Specials.)

• Saturday, 1st September had everyone back at Upper Boat for scenes in the Executive Office; they completed those on Monday. Tuesday and Wednesday were the days for Warehouse 15 and the Factory front. The latter were shot at the Hynix building in Newport (slightly further away from Cardiff than the usual 45-mile radius and, again, smothered in paper-snow), then they went to Pontypool for the Warehouse at the Johnsey Industrial Estate, which had doubled as the

innards of Starship *Titanic* in "Voyage of the Damned" some six weeks before. James O'Dee doubled for Ryder in the fall. By 7th September, all the principle photography was done (ending with the Doctor and Donna in "quality" handcuffs, at Hensol Castle), and the preparations for going to Rome were being finalised.

• On examining the footage, the last stage of Halpern's transformation looked like a bad sneeze, having been shot facing McInnerny. It was replaced with a new side-on shot of a stand-in: the Best Boy, Peter Chester, was the right build and face-shape (and had a shaved head), so was recruited to be the stunt-Ood for the revised spit-take. With the move from second to third place in the running-order, the dialogue in the TARDIS needed to be re-done, so that was fixed on 16th November in amongst pick-up work on the Agatha Christie story.

• The BBC1 schedule for Saturdays had been slightly adjusted because of a new National Lottery show, so the broadcast of this episode began at 6.20pm again, after the previous week's move to 6.45. It was still the second-most-watched thing on that day.

X4.4: "The Sontaran Stratagem"

(26th April, 2008)

Which One is This? Martha Clones.

Firsts and Lasts Yes, this is the first time we've seen the Sontarans in the twenty-first century (our last sight of them was 22.4, "The Two Doctors" back in 1985). They get a new war-chant, *Sontar-HA!*, done like a Haka (even down to the hand-gestures – readers from non-Rugby-playing backwaters can investigate **The Big Picture**). It's therefore the first of many occasions on which Dan Starkey will be smothered in latex (here he's Commander Skorr; later he'll be Strax). At long last, their world is called "Sontar" – something never said on screen until now, but used in *Doctor Who Magazine* comic strips since 1980.

For all the talk we've had of how the Sontarans are a cloned army of thousands of millions, this is the first time we've seen more than a handful, and actually caught them in the act of cloning. Thus, this is the first "evil twin" episode we've had since

Must All Three Series Correlate Properly?

Just as we'd finally sorted it out, the advent of two spin-off drama series at the end of 2006 moved the whole continuity/canon debate up a notch. It seemed as if *Doctor Who* admirers were obliged to watch (if not enjoy) both *Torchwood* and *The Sarah Jane Adventures* to fully comprehend their preferred series. Some were dismayed at this as, officially, *Torchwood* was not for children and *SJA* was exclusively for them, while *Doctor Who* attempted to appeal to all ages.

The coexistence of these other storylines meant that *Doctor Who* could go to other times/planets, while the Yeti-in-the-loo portfolio was offloaded on one spin-off set in Cardiff, another ostensibly in London but shot in Cardiff. In practice, it meant a lot more overlap, as locations that were shoved at us as *come to exciting Cardiff* in *Torchwood* were re-used as "look, just pretend it's London" in *SJA* and *Who*, whilst the TARDIS found reasons to keep landing in the present day and avoid anything that looked a bit otherworldly. Paradoxically, more thought went into planet-building in *The Sarah Jane Adventures* than Davies-era *Who*.

The antipathy – or apathy – toward the spin-offs exists partly because of the shows' own failings, but also just because they're aimed at different audiences than the *Doctor Who* whole. During the airing of *Torchwood* Series 1, certain quarters of fandom radiated disgust and bitterness – some because of its (many) low points, but also just because it wasn't a type of show that they would have normally chosen to watch, and yet felt dragooned to doing just that out of loyalty. *The Sarah Jane Adventures* was far more respected and beloved, but a certain portion of adult viewers simply weren't interested in watching a kid's show, no matter how well it's done. And the general public was less likely to just stumble across something shown at 4.35pm on a weekday.

They were all made to be shown on different BBC channels, some inaccessible to many viewers, albeit with non-digital viewers getting a chance to catch up at odd hours a week or so later. Both *Torchwood* and *SJA* were conceived in part as ways to tempt viewers onto the BBC channels you could only get with a special decoder, prior to that being the only way you could watch any television in Britain in 2012. (See **Why is Trinity Wells on Jackie's Telly?** under X1.4, "Aliens of London".)

A 2006 promo for the exciting world of digital telly explicitly said "you like *Doctor Who*, don't you? Well *Torchwood*'s on BBC3" to a teenage boy whose ethnicity is still being debated. (If you don't see why that's relevant, you must have slept through the gibberish being yelled about the first year of Jodie Whittaker.) It was explicitly – in many ways – a show aimed at BBC3's 16-25 demographic. The spin-offs, like the online content, were enticements toward a new "platform" the BBC was keen to promote, with some of the *mana* of *Doctor Who* attached. (This goes double for *Class*, as by then BBC3 had gone so far down the "yoof" road, it wasn't even broadcast on digital television and had to be accessed with a computer or smartphone. More people saw it on BBC America, and that was only half a million people for the episode with the Doctor in.) The BBC2 early-evening repeats of *Torchwood* Series 2 had the swearing and gore cut down, for kids who were watching because Martha was joining. (Sadly, the best joke in either series was a well-timed F-bomb in *TW*: "Something Borrowed", so these viewers missed that.) Eventually, *Torchwood* Series 3 (AKA *Children of Earth*) was made for BBC1, as a five-day event shown at 9.00pm Monday-Friday in July.

As such, *Children of Earth* is the only manifestation of the spin-offs to even come close to *Doctor Who* in the ratings. This is significant, as a big reason people had for sidelining the CBBC and BBC3 series as irrelevant was simple access. Only a tiny, minuscule minority of people who watch any of these series are the paid-up convention-going fans. When, in 2009, *Comic Relief* did a skit with Ronnie Corbett as a baby Slitheen materialising in Sarah Jane's attic, John Barrowman had to come on and explain to the British Public what *The Sarah Jane Adventures* was (he should have stuck around to apologise afterwards).

Overseas, access to any of these series on analogue was a turkey-shoot (France showed *Torchwood* but hid *Doctor Who*; America doesn't appear to have taken to Sarah Jane). The situation's muddied further by *Torchwood* Series 4 (AKA *Miracle Day*), made by US network Starz (sic) and so not always legally tethered to the other programmes, but shown on BBC1 to rapidly-dwindling ratings and public apathy and buried in America on a relatively obscure subscription service. It's been almost completely forgotten.

It's certainly not come up in any subsequent *Doctor Who*. A lot of this is simply that incoming new-broom showrunners have applied their own criteria, their own head-canons, and discarded anything they didn't grow up with or create them-

continued on Page 67...

65

"The Caves of Androzani" (21.6).

It's the first time on screen, following a complaint from the real-life United Nations (X1.4, "Aliens of London"), that UNIT is named as "Unified Intelligence Taskforce" (despite the script reiterating that the UN funds them). This is the first story directed by Douglas McKinnon, later the utility director for the Moffat Era.

Donna identifies herself as "Supertemp" for the first time. And this is the first of three episodes with the credit "... and Freema Agyeman".

Watch Out For...

• Sarah Jane or no Sarah Jane, two idiot journalists in a month (the first being in X4.1, "Partners in Crime") just makes it look like the production staff have something against the profession (can't think why...). The doomed one in the teaser here dies because she gets in a car that she *knows* is programmed to cause serious and inexplicable deaths, because she went to confront the perpetrators, a crowd of red-pyjama'd cultists.

Although the scene is quite daft, it at least infodumps to new viewers what UNIT is, and how ATMOS can be used to kill, and looks like a real big-budget thriller's pre-credit sequence. But, as it's a journalist and this is British television, most viewers knew she was toast. In fact, she's just as expendable as the lorry-driver who delivers the exposition about International Electromatics in episode one of "The Invasion" (6.3), and gets shot as soon as his function's over. See how many other resemblances between that story and this you can spot before we point them all out.

• The Doctor and Donna have an exchange about someone having "put a dent in" the 1980s, perhaps an on-screen Michael Grade sneer just as he left the BBC under a cloud (again). Later, the Doctor confesses that he worked for UNIT "back in the 70s, or was it the 80s?" – a cute in-joke about the alleged uncertainty of UNIT Dating, but against the grain of the new series (*The Sarah Jane Adventures* especially) piling on copious piles of evidence that any thoughts of it actually happening in the 80s are hogwash.

• Oh goody, Martha's back! Going through a tricky transitional phase in which she's trying to variously define herself as a soldier, a doctor or a scientist. Catherine Tate is all that keeps Martha's initial reconciliation scene with the Doctor from being hugely awkward.

• If this had been a traditional four-parter, the timing's almost right to have made the taking-off-the-helmet part the first cliffhanger.

• The Rattigan laboratories are, as the Doctor notes, exciting places full of fancy tech and genius. Therefore, we spend about 20 seconds in them before they shift the scene to a big dull room with nothing much in it besides a potted plant, a spacehopper and an industrial-design teleport.

• The cliffhanger: Martha's asleep, Donna and the Doctor are relatively safe, the Sontarans are in orbit waiting... but *Wilf's* in danger. They've figured out where the viewers' priorities lie.

The Continuity

The Doctor As in "School Reunion" (X2.3), he doesn't like to see his companions fighting, but is almost more uncomfortable when they're getting along well and teasing him instead. Being saluted puts him out. He's oddly compelled by the idea of a hothouse for geniuses.

When he thinks Donna's going home, he rattles off a list of Exciting Tourist Destinations [one strongly suspects him of memorising in advance]: "The Fifteenth Broken Moon of the Medusa Cascade, the lightning skies of Cotter Palluni's World, the diamond coral reefs of Kaata Flo Ko". Her apparent leaving distresses but doesn't surprise him, and he thanks her for being brilliant and saving his life in so many ways. [The comment is odder than usual this time, given that – putting aside X3.0, "The Runaway Bride" – Donna hasn't so much saved his life as that of people around him. Compare his straight-faced statement to Wilf that Donna kept him safe rather than the other way round – was he that miserable travelling alone? The idea seems to be, rightly or wrongly, that his post-Rose sulk made him a bit of a monster until Donna told him to stop.]

• *Background.* The Doctor never resigned from UNIT, so is still technically on staff. He also can't remember whether he had all the adventures with the Brigadier in the 70s or 80s. [The long version of our explanation is a goodish chunk of Volume 3B. The short version: they were set just after the broadcast date in the 70s.] Nevertheless, he knows that UNIT keeps files on the Sontarans, and that there's a 'Code Red Sontarans' designation. [Aside from a spectral cameo when Linx abducted scientists (11.1, "The Time Warrior"), there's no on-screen engagement between UNIT and the Sontarans, so we presume the Doctor's

Must All Three Series Correlate Properly?

continued from Page 65...

selves. It's entirely understandable that Steven Moffat, de-facto creator of Captain Jack, might want to allude to the character as something other than the donor of a Vortex Manipulator, but he didn't. Neither was *Class* in any way alluded to in Series 10. Chris Chibnall, ostensibly in charge of the first two years of *Torchwood*, has made a version of *Doctor Who* that resembles *The Sarah Jane Adventures* and so far has steadfastly avoided any reference to anything else supposedly in the loop. Not even *TW*: "Countrycide".

[We'll pause here and mention that links between *Doctor Who*, *Torchwood* and *The Sarah Jane Adventures* are plentiful and deliberate. An earlier iteration of this essay proceeded to list them. For three solid paragraphs. The writers of all three shows weren't just encouraged to connect the series, they were carefully overseen to remove any potential snags about the dating (with the One Year Ahead thing from "Aliens of London" uppermost in their minds). Directors and set-dressers may have goofed on the details, especially in *Torchwood*'s first year, and a few lines slipped through, but they were accidents. They may have had the same effect on first-time UK viewers as the things that stop 7.2, "Doctor Who and the Silurians" being any later than a year after transmission, but the intention was to keep in step with the main series. Focussing on the discrepancies while grossly ignoring the deliberate connections between the shows doesn't get us anywhere – the second *Torchwood* series seems to be set in 2007, 2009 and 2010 if you follow this line of reasoning neurotically.]

Those inter-series ties that did occur in *Doctor Who* are almost all covered in this book or the previous two; the others are, by definition, pretty redundant as anyone who cared would most likely have seen the relevant stories. As matters turned out, *SJA* – its viewing-figures bolstered by ageing fans, not all of them parents – made more explicit links to the 70s stories than *Torchwood*, which riffed on BBC Wales episodes. They exist, though, in such profusion that it seems implausible, and would baffle some people, to suggest that they're not all part of the same package. So, of course, we'll look at the case for exactly that.

The most obvious thing to state about the spin-offs is that they *are* spin-offs. For the original intended audience(s), the assumption is that everyone watching *Torchwood*, *SJA* or *Class* watched *Doctor Who*. You can, in fact, find people who migrated over to *Doctor Who* after watching *Torchwood* first, and weren't confused (at least, no more so than any other *Torchwood* viewer). Not many, and practically none in Britain, but such people exist and stood a good chance of eventually being bought-in to the essential premise of *Doctor Who*. But, if you turned in to any of the spin-offs out of a sense of obligation or genuine enthusiasm, you could be assumed to know the continuity references – or at least prepared to look them up. Obviously, references to the spin-offs in *Doctor Who* are vastly outweighed by the ways these subsidiaries frantically allude to the original series. Apart from the coda to "The End of Time Part Two", they only matter in "The Stolen Earth"/"Journey's End". Not even a quick mention of Martha's recent past in Cardiff is considered necessary in "The Stolen Earth".

While big developments in *Doctor Who* warrant a brief mention at least in the other two, nobody in *Torchwood* or *Doctor Who* mentions the Sun going out, approaching meteors, mass abductions of kids from video-game arcades or the Moon leaving its orbit – and that's just in the first year of *The Sarah Jane Adventures*. True, Martha and Donna mention in passing that Cardiff is experiencing weirdness – by which they mean literally apocalyptic events, explosions in the city centre on a scale unseen since the IRA campaigns of the 70s (each as big as the 7/7 bombings; look at how much changed after that morning), plagues, Romans and a nuclear power station having a meltdown. Or just the stuff in X1.11, "Boom Town". All are pretty big events that in our world would be discussed for years and change global governmental policies. Even so, if you squint hard and assume that just because something's not said aloud, it doesn't automatically follow that it doesn't exist, it's a workable model. Well, it's workable for all of *The Sarah Jane Adventures* and *Torchwood* Series 1 and 2. If anything, you might wonder why the shows don't cite each other's developments more often than they do. In some ways, this is to be expected, as all three franchises entail humans forgetting what's not in front of them (see **How Can Anyone Not Know About Aliens?** under X3.1, "Smith and Jones").

Bits of contradictions remain, such as the malign faerie forces in *TW*: "Small Worlds" being called "the Mara", with no attempt to accommo-

continued on Page 69...

exile included a few spoilers about who was in the area and likely to attack.] He guesses, or recalls, that Sontarans are probably using copper excitation to disable guns.

The Sontarans know of legends saying the Doctor led the battle in the Last Great Time War.

• *Ethics*. He's not happy about UNIT's current manifestation, including its profusion of guns. Nevertheless, he has no problem ordering them to lay on a Jeep [see, it *is* like the old days] for his convenience [or perhaps this incarnation just isn't fond of driving].

• *Inventory: Sonic Screwdriver*. It toasts the Sontaran teleport, but only temporarily. The ATMOS deadlock thwarts the sonic for a while, but once the Doctor knows it's Sontaran, he makes some progress – if by progress we mean "accidentally activating the system".

• *Inventory: Other*. The glasses are pulled out for close-up examination of the ATMOS rig and the Rattigan Academy's terraforming equipment.

The TARDIS The Doctor's giving Donna rudimentary lessons in TARDIS-flying. In case of accident, he has the usual big rubber mallet on hand. The Doctor really did keep Martha's mobile [X3.13, "Last of the Time Lords"]. There's even a handy little holder for it on the console.

He prefers keeping his sophisticated time machine out of the way when there's unknown dangers on the loose.

The Supporting Cast

• *Donna* has decided not to do that neck-snap thing when Martha's around. She's supportive of Martha and tosses in some bon mots about the Doctor where appropriate. She seems discomfited about the Doctor having turned Martha into a soldier. Finding the alien-control proof in the paperwork is an accomplishment she's understandably smug about.

Her first experience of UNIT is watching soldiers arrest everybody working in a factory, which she compares to Guantanamo Bay, and wraps up a tirade saying that if they're gonna salute the Doctor, they can salute her too. When the Doctor misunderstands a statement and thinks she's going home, she watches with massive amusement as he stumbles through bribes and Thank You's.

Upon returning home, she's very glad to see her granddad again and runs to him for a wordless hug. She admits to her beloved Gramps that the Doctor is amazing and dazzling, but would rather not tell the Doctor that. She trusts him with her life.

She's a little embarrassed by her childhood nickname of 'The Little General'. Later on, she used to bring home a weekly-changing selection of boys, including one 'Matthew Richards' who wore nail polish [not unusual in the 80s] and now lives in Kilburn with a man. There's a hefty hint she's sold a couple of the ATMOS systems to friends of hers.

• *Wilf*. A bout of Spanish flu laid him up during Donna's wedding [hence his non-appearance in "The Runaway Bride"]. He's pleased that all his suspicions about aliens were quite right, but wants to know whether the Doctor will keep his granddaughter safe. It does rather thrill him to have met a proper alien.

He advises Donna not to tell Sylvia about the whole travelling-in-time-and-space business. Meantime, Sylvia's been trying to keep him on a macrobiotic diet, which he's been cheerfully defying by nipping off to the petrol station for pork pies. [He may have a valid license then. Without Donna around, maybe they've been sharing the blue car – but it's Chiswick, so there's probably one a short walk away. It would be in character for him to tell himself that walking to a Wild Bean is exercise and the pie is his reward, then eating it in the car to avoid detection.]

• *Martha*. She's engaged to Tom Milligan [the doctor from "Last of the Time Lords"]. He's bought her a ring, but has gone into paediatrics in Africa. [It doesn't seem to bother Martha unduly, or indeed at all.] Oddly, it's only after she's stopped being a companion that she gets to do the traditional ear-splitting scream, when the Sontarans do something unspecified to her.

Donna's appearance as the new companion embarrasses and slightly hurts Martha, but she warms up to her camaraderie quickly enough. She returns the favour, characteristically, by warning Donna that terrible things can happen to companions' families nowadays.

[In case you skipped it, Martha was off in Cardiff for three episodes of *Torchwood* Series 2 ("Reset", "Dead Man Walking" and "A Day in the Death"), which is where Jack's odd habit of referring to her London-ish croak as 'the voice of a nightingale' starts. In this, it emerges that her medical degree was fast-tracked, and UNIT head-

Must All Three Series Correlate Properly?

continued from Page 67...

date the identically-named psychic entity from 19.3, "Kinda" and 20.2, "Snakedance". Even that, however, is as it should be – both are named after beings in belief-systems that existed thousands of years before even Hartnell episodes.

There's also the matter of the Black Archive(s). In *The Sarah Jane Adventures,* the first mention of a specifically UNIT facility (rather than the one that contains plans of gizmos they can't get to work) comes in "Enemy of the Bane", where it's an anonymous-looking warehouse miles from anywhere and with ID passes, red-beret-wearing armed guards and miles of files. By the time of *SJA*: "Death of the Doctor", they have moved their British operations to UNIT Base 5, Snowdonia, but can still drive a tank to Ealing. However, by X7.15, "The Day of the Doctor", UNIT's Black Archive has been in the Tower of London since... well, the guard's been there 15 years and Kate Lethbridge Stewart thinks the Doctor doesn't know about it, even though her dad was entirely unsurprised that Sarah did. Perhaps the *SJA* one was Doctor-bait for the less important stuff, while the real goodies (and a nuclear warhead safeguard readied to destroy London if needed, which the Doctor would probably frown upon) were under the Tower. (Before anyone brings up the call-centre in X11.11, "Resolution", look carefully at the stuff flickering by on the laptop Lin uses under Dalek control.)

Torchwood: Children of Earth complicates matters in a more sizeable way. In this, a group of aliens – the 456 – regularly freeze Earth's children in place, and make them uniformly speak pronouncements such as "We are coming... back!" With the entire world at stake, Earth's governments try to harvest 10% of the world's children for the 456 – soldiers take to the streets and grab screaming kids to meet their quotas, even as community members form mobs to stop them. The baddies don't succeed, but it's unbelievable that Luke Smith and his chums wouldn't notice anything untoward at his school around the time *Children of Earth* takes place. Or that the Doctor wouldn't weigh in on the topic (unless it's a Fixed Point that he's reluctant to go near).

There's a token acknowledgment on *Doctor Who,* at least, when Captain Jack tries to find happiness in the bottom of his shot glass in "The End of Time Part Two", seemingly following Ianto's death in *Children of Earth,* but that's it. It's remarkably un-remarked-upon in the other series. Then

again, other than its epilogue, *Children of Earth* restricts itself to a five-day span. Its horrific repercussions are the sort of thing that would topple governments – but you can slip the core of it in-between the corresponding *Doctor Who* (at least, under Davies) and *The Sarah Jane Adventures* seasons without too much hassle, if that's your idea of a good time.

The same can't be said of the ten-part *Torchwood: Miracle Day,* which happens in 2011 and entails – wait for it – death being suspended across the whole of Earth, civil liberties being quashed and governments forming incineration centres, to forcibly cremate the undead. That state of affairs continues for *two months* or more. At a pinch, it could take place after *The Sarah Jane Adventures* has concluded. But it's absurd that the Doctor never hears about this, or takes notice, or that Amy and Rory (or Martha) never phone him in a frothy panic to *do something already, because there's no death, and Earth is going to hell in a hand-basket.* If there's no death in 2011, his own death at Lake Silencio's even less of a Fixed Point. (See Series 6, in which everyone acts as if mortality still works. Well, except when time is stuck in one second of one day – X6.13, "The Wedding of River Song" – and then resets with everything normal.)

In all of this, *Miracle Day* most overtly parts ways from *Doctor Who.* It's simply incompatible with everything around it. Davies was very strict on not ever having the Doctor appear in *Torchwood,* even allowing for the discontinuity between the end of Series 1 of that and the way Jack finds the TARDIS in "Utopia" (X3.11). Now he had finally made a US-backed series and kept the two main characters (and a few supporting ones) and his copyrighted brand-name, but barely anything else. What's remarkable is that *Miracle Day* is at arm's length even from *Torchwood* series 1-3. *Children of Earth* effectively ended the story that began in 2006, and Jack got a happy ending on a date with Alonzo Frame.

But... let's assume for the moment that *Miracle Day* is on a separate time track. Where and when did this deviation/rupture occur? The most likely place is when the whole of spacetime went wobbly, after the Doctor messed with a Fixed Point in "The Waters of Mars" (X4.16). Granted, the Naismiths still remember Torchwood in "The End of Time" (in the past tense, so *Children of Earth* was in play), so events on Bowie Base One didn't

continued on Page 71...

hunted her to become chief medical officer – they both look upwards when Jack suggests friends in high places. In this capacity, she contacts Torchwood about a big pharma corporation's new breakthrough, which cures everything by reactivating genes ("Reset" is arguably the series' best single episode but still has clunking logical flaws), using alien insects who would normally lay eggs in animals but enslaving them. The project-head finds that TARDIS travel has already caused chromosomal changes and lymphocyte augmentation within Martha, and tries to patent her blood.

[The Torchwood medic, Owen Harper, dies in the ensuing mêlée and Martha is seconded as a replacement. The Resurrection Glove partly restores Owen to life, but he's on restricted duties, so Martha gets to act as the wailing-wall for all the long-term relationship hassles – hence Gwen and Ianto's subsequent shock at her apparent death (X4.12, "The Stolen Earth"). Her family are now almost over their ordeal ("Last of the Time Lords"), and she's well over the Doctor.]

Martha seems to be fairly high up in the UNIT hierarchy, having Security Clearance Level One. [As you may recall from Volume 3B, the usual rank for an intelligence officer is Lieutenant; Jo Grant would have outranked Benton, but Mike Yates could give her orders. Harry Sullivan, Martha's nearest precursor, was already one in the Royal Navy. Martha's access in the next episode and "The Stolen Earth" indicates she's at least a Captain. Back in *Torchwood*, Ianto, on seeing her pass, called her 'Ma'am' and seemed flustered at someone so high-up visiting (but not even slightly perturbed that his old Canary Wharf colleague Abiola – Martha's identical cousin – apparently rose from the dead). Anyone who wishes to imagine Harry appearing in *Torchwood* can do so on their own time.]

• *Sylvia* got her car back despite the girl Donna asked to take a message fading out ["Partners in Crime"]. She's acerbic towards Donna for disappearing for days, condescending to Wilf for eating pork pies despite her strictures and apoplectic when she sees the Doctor again ["The Runaway Bride"].

UNIT It's officially 'Unified Intelligence Taskforce' now, led by Colonel Mace in the UK with a base at Tower Bridge [X2.0, "The Christmas Invasion" et seq.]. A journalist can contact with UNIT over an ordinary mobile connection. [The implication

is that they use reporters as eyes and ears, something we are led to believe was UNIT policy by Season Thirteen, although "The Android Invasion" (13.4) suggests that it was in place before Sarah blundered into the Doctor's life.] Ahead of the regular army's policies [at least in the UK], they send women in to front-line combat.

Mace has read the many files on the Doctor, so insists on saluting him as well as handing over a UNIT jeep for his disposal. They're still using the Greyhound/Trap designations but in reverse [see **English Lessons**]. There's a Code Red system and extensive files on alien threats. [The Doctor knows that it includes the Sontarans, so he may have compiled it for them during that strange phase when he had a functioning TARDIS, but still hung around HQ conducting experiments on ESP and building flying cars (11.5, "Planet of the Spiders"). It would make sense if the Doctor gave UNIT a parting gift of this kind along with the Brigadier's Space-Time Telegraph (12.5, "Revenge of the Cybermen"; 13.1, "Terror of the Zygons"; X7.15, "The Day of the Doctor") as part of a phased withdrawal.

[Otherwise, the underlying implication is that UNIT is currently reinventing itself. As we mentioned under "Last of the Time Lords", there's good reason to suspect that the Master seriously compromised the organisation. Senior staff have died in every UNIT story since the revival. Here, we see a colonel who respects the Doctor as a legend, plus a lot of red-beret foot soldiers and Martha Jones. If this is the team left to analyse the ATMOS equipment, it's no wonder that they decided to call the Doctor in. It does get us around the problem of why UNIT policy for soldiers who meddle with alien tech is promotion instead of court-martial; anyone who survives the experience probably has the curiosity and ability that the organisation needs to encourage right now. That said, this is such a marked contrast from what we see in *Torchwood*'s flashbackapalooza TW: "Fragments" and the strange comments Kate Stewart makes in X7.4, "The Power of Three", we've got an essay on it with the next episode.]

They've finally worked out that soldiers on recce ought to go in pairs.

Torchwood Does not come up at all. [From hints about the timeline in X4.11, "Turn Left," we can reconstruct a version of events. Martha and Jack

Must All Three Series Correlate Properly?

continued from Page 69...

entirely unfix events. And, if this Fixed Point rupture had somehow peeled off the three series into separate – oh, all right – universes (see **Is This the Star Trek Universe?** under X4.6, "The Doctor's Daughter"), the Doctor's farewell tour of companions wouldn't quite work. Again, Jack is off-world and getting over Ianto's death – so the end of *Children of Earth* happened for him, if not the rest of the planet.

One episode later, though, and the past's been altered to include invasions of Earth by some improbable monsters that were historical details in 2008. That episode (X5.1, "The Eleventh Hour") has history-eating Cracks and the first mention of the Silence but, perhaps more significantly, the spacetime vortex has changed. We'll be speculating later about whether the violent regeneration in "The End of Time" is in part an assassination attempt by the Kovarian Schism, but *something* seems to have done a lot of damage. It's confirmed that the Vortex is what that white swirly thing in "The Doctor, The Widow and the Wardrobe" (X7.0), but it changes shortly thereafter, when Clara shows up.

Something's clearly amiss when the Doctor's timeline is messed up twice in rapid succession, especially as the means by which this is done, the TARDIS-tomb of Trenzalore, is prevented from ever happening by an unscheduled new set of regenerations (X7.16, "The Time of the Doctor"). The Doctor's past is rewritten wholesale twice in that episode (X7.14, "The Name of the Doctor") and now includes a whole new incarnation that allows us to shear everything since then off from the other series and indeed earlier versions of this one. Add to this the anomalies following the Doctor's failure to be killed properly at Lake Silencio ("The Wedding of River Song") and we have the cosmos rebooted twice, and the Doctor's past altered three times (so that the Time War went to penalties; "The Day of the Doctor" again) and...

You see the problem: There are almost *too many* likely causes for such a discontinuity between the three narratives. Moffat-era stories barely manage continuity between each other. You can more easily draw a line under most of the Eccleston and Tennant eras – and *Torchwood* and *The Sarah Jane Adventures* – all in one go, and claim that the Cracks in Time/the Bowie Base One fiasco/Impossible Girl scrubbed their key events from history, than you can put *Torchwood* and *The Sarah Jane Adventures* onto separate time tracks when they're so heavily intertwined. If you embrace one spin-off, you have to have the other.

Let's not forget that the first time the Doctor told us that old episodes available on DVD never happened was in X5.6, "Vampires in Venice", where the absence of a giant steam-driven Cyberman trashing London in 1851 (X4.14, "The Next Doctor") and the Daleks conquering Earth after dragging it to the Medusa Cascade (X4.12-4.13, "The Stolen Earth"/"Journey's End") is because of this Crack. As an entire year of *SJA* is set in a post-Dalek world, where everyone knows about aliens, while the revival of a Dalek in "Resolution" (set on New Year's Day, 2019) needed the Doctor to explain to people who were alive in 2009 what the thing *was*, we have to assume that these stories are still erased.

That would work fairly smoothly had not the Doctor who fixed the Crack shown up in *SJA* ("Death of the Doctor") talking about Amy and Rory's honeymoon. Davies wrote that episode so he, at least, thinks it's all still in play. "Death of the Doctor" follows logically from *SJA:* "The Wedding of Sarah Jane Smith" and has plentiful references back to 70s stories (although the shape of the TARDIS key causes trouble). In this story, the Doctor is manifestly the one from Series 5, but he's talking to Clyde, Rani, Sarah and Jo about events in the *SJA* world, and Sarah remembers her last glimpse of the Tennant version in "The End of Time". The Doctor's farewell tour incorporated trips to every single former companion (except maybe Adric).

While it's customary to try not to giggle at fans who refuse to accept *Children of Earth* because Ianto dying is too sad, we've almost reached the point where the writers are doing something very similar. (We'll pick this up in **Was There a Martian Time-Slip?** under "The Waters of Mars".) The Doctor can recall some of the things we saw happen to him even if they've been removed from history, but not all; the current state of affairs is that Captain Jack is immortal and around somewhere for Ashildr to meet one day (X9.6, "The Woman Who Lived"). Or, at least, *a* Captain Jack...

So the three Davies-era series *don't* entirely correlate properly, but fair enough – it's more than the Moffat *Doctor Who* does with the Davies version and *certainly* the Chibnall version, and definitely more than Big Finish and the *DWM* comic-strip do.

continued on Page 73...

have kept in touch (evident from the phone call in "The Stolen Earth"). UNIT's already investigating, since Jo Nakashima's been in touch with them about ATMOS already. Martha decides to call the Doctor and consequently tells Cardiff they needn't worry about it, so Jack stays out of the way.]

The Non-Humans

• *Sontarans.* They're seriously annoyed that they weren't allowed to join in the Last Great Time War, as it was 'the finest war in history'. [We don't know why they were excluded from the war – perhaps their earlier attempt to invade Gallifrey (15.6, "The Invasion of Time") made them untrustworthy. The brouhaha over the Kartz-Reimer experiments ("The Two Doctors") can't have helped.] They're aware that the Doctor was involved in the war, and that he's now the last Time Lord.

On the outside, little has changed since their first three appearances [what was going on with the tall, skinny ones in "The Two Doctors" is anyone's guess], but there have been developments within the culture of this apparently interchange-able clone-species. From being an androgynous race who hatch in thousands and had only read about species with two different sexes, they have become sexist dorks. From a race from a high-gravity world adapted perfectly to load-bearing, they have become short and sensitive about their height.

They chant *Sontar-Ha!* before battle now, although they have amassed a vast army they don't bother to use, and instead infiltrate Earth with clones and/or brainwashed workers [it is unclear what 'processing' entails, and whether the UNIT squaddies can recover], indispensable gad-gets that turn on customers, and similar tactics associated with small incursionary forces of the kind the Brigadier dealt with once a month. Nonetheless, they are still under 150 cm tall, have three digits on each hand, look like toads with facial hair and wear rubber spacesuits with hel-mets that fit their hemispherical heads exactly.

Being whacked on the probic vent [see every story since "The Time Warrior"] with a squash-ball knocks them out.

Their culture is honour-based as ever; the Doctor's taunts provoke Staal to come talk to him head-on. Sontarans would rather be court-mar-tialled than show pain. It's not hard for Staal to fix a teleport the Doctor fried. They're puzzled how

humans can tell each other apart.

Their spaceship is maintaining orbit at 556.3, sector 270. As with some parts of the Rattigan Academy, it is suffused in a pink light.

The Sontarans' human ally, Luke Rattigan, is a very annoying ex-child genius who's publicly credited with inventing ATMOS. [It must be *mostly* his, since the Doctor can't tell at first it's of alien origin and even states that it's just a bit ahead of its time.] Rattigan is known for having been a child millionaire, inventing the Fountain 6 search engine when he was 12. [Actor Ryan Sampson was born in 1985; that dating suggests he staked out the market before Google showed up. Perhaps this explains why everyone the Doctor trusts uses unfamiliar-looking alternatives whenever the BBC needs to show a search page.] Now he runs the Rattigan Academy, for similar budding geniuses.

General Staal of the Tenth Sontaran Battle Fleet, known as Staal the Undefeated, is running the operation. His second is Commander Skorr of the Tenth Sontaran Battle Fleet, known as Skorr the Blood-Bringer. [We've not witnessed this habit of epithets ("Someone the Something") before, but with the finite potential Sontaran-sounding names (see **Are All Alien Names a Bit Silly?** under 9.2. "The Curse of Peladon") and the sheer number of Sontarans, it's probably a good move.]

It takes time, it seems, but they can brainwash UNIT soldiers into being dupes. [Perhaps UNIT soldiers don't get psychic training. It appears to be the same process they used to hypnotise all the Polish labourers, which may have been quicker on unprepared subjects. Linx could do it in "The Time Warrior" with a hand-held gadget in sec-onds, but on someone who could barely read; we never saw how long it took him to condition sci-entists.] There's a minor translation holdup, since they don't know the expression "it's cool".

For more complicated operations, they have equipment to create a body that can be imprinted with a captive's memories. [This technique has apparently been reserved for the first time anyone with alien-hunting experience showed up.]

The ATMOS system is deadlocked [the stan-dard villain operating procedure by now, to hold up the plot for the necessary 45 minutes]. There are 17 ATMOS factories across the globe, but they're all sent to Great Britain for depot. [We'll presume the basic systems do what they're said to, and the English factory just installs the killer deadlock programs.] The sophisticated world-

Must All Three Series Correlate Properly?

continued from Page 71...

Our question, remains: "It absolutely necessary to watch all four shows to get the most out of *Doctor Who*?" The answer to that, at least, has to be a resounding "no". The people making *Doctor Who* assume that they are catering to an audience at least six times bigger than that for the other shows, and meticulously (if occasionally implausibly) insert exposition. The most obvious example is, of course, "The Stolen Earth" and the ways people discuss continuity in combat situations. Everything you need to follow that story is there in that story (unless it's not anywhere). There was a token effort at autonomy in the early phase of *Torchwood*, so that you could watch if you'd somehow missed *Doctor Who*, but having a whole episode of Canary Wharf fall-out with the runner-up monsters ("Cyberwoman", the longest drama ever to be based on fan-art) somewhat undid this.

While aliens from *Doctor Who* have shown up in *SJA*, none but a soft-porn version of the Cybermen have been in *Torchwood*. (Well, okay... the script to *TW*: "End of Days" also hints at Abbadon being the son of the Beast from X2.9, "The Satan Pit". Both stories aired in the same year.) The production team placed a deliberate embargo on the Daleks and Cybermen showing up on Sarah Jane's porch – the reasoning being that, if it were played straight, those villains would massacre everyone. Or, they'd be defeated by a 60 year old and her teenage friends, at which point everyone would wonder why they give the Doctor so much trouble. They also took steps to keep *Torchwood* at arm's-length from the other two shows.

So, with the exception of the Sontarans, all the *Doctor Who* monsters the Bannerman Road Scooby Gang met were created by Russell T Davies, while Gareth Roberts fashioned some new-ish foes from very familiar materials; not just the Trickster (he or his agents appear on all three shows; multiple *SJA* stories, X4.11, "Turn Left" and *TW: Miracle Day*), but Mr Smith himself, who was based on a smart rock not a million miles from being a Kroton, plus a cosmic force from before time (take that, Matt Jones – "The Satan Pit") which was like the Mandragora Helix (14.1, "The Masque of Mandragora"), but chose to possess Russ Abbott in Ealing instead of Hieronymus in Quattrocento Italy. And in a rare case of *SJA/Torchwood* crossover, the pink sparkly alien Maria sees in Sarah's driveway in the pilot episode also shows up in Cardiff giving Tosh temporary telepathy (and girl-on-girl action, because it's *Torchwood* Series 1).

We have the tangential question, then, of "should I bother at all?" Now that the first two spin-offs are long gone and the third is in a let-us-never-speak-of-this-again limbo, this is more a matter of individual choice than it was in 2009. There's as much to be gained as there is to be annoyed at. The tonal differences between the series are greater than between individual episodes of each. (Although, if we're discussing tone and spin-offs, 18.7a, "K9 & Company" is two totally different series tied up in a sack and made to fight to the death for 45 minutes.)

The series have three distinct identities – *The Sarah Jane Adventures* went out afternoons on CBBC, so naturally is fairly chaste and gore-averse (although less so than most things on that channel); *Torchwood* is a post-watershed series slathered in blood, human treachery and sex; *Doctor Who*, as made these days, exists in a curious middle. There's no hardcore throbbing and pulsing, but it's not above Amy trying to seduce the Doctor the night before her wedding (X5.5, "Flesh and Stone"), or intimating at sex with a paving stone (X2.10, "Love & Monsters"). It's more overt than it was in black and white or when Sarah was a companion, but only by degrees.

It's a situation that's probably unique in television history. We can't think of any other example of an all-ages show spawning one spin-off for eight to 12 year-olds and two more, aggressively targeted at 16-25s with gore, sex and not much else. It's awkward and unwieldly when taken as a whole, especially if you're a parent weighing whether your little *Doctor Who* fan's request to watch *Torchwood* (i.e. bloodspurting murders, bedhopping and an alien that feeds off orgasms – *TW*: "Day One"). The 2008 attempts at Kiddy-*Torchwood* lost a lot of viewers because, even with explosions and popular characters from the TARDIS along, it was a bit slow and rather silly.

The ways in which the characters react when they return to the parent series are interesting indications of the growth they've experienced on their own series. The Jack of *Torchwood*'s first series is moody, tortured and withdrawn – certainly not the character *Doctor Who* audiences had come to know, lacking his *joi de vivre*. But this falls after Jack's spent a century on Earth waiting for the Doctor to return, and all the horror he's experienced with Torchwood (among other

continued on Page 75...

73

destroying tech is all hidden away in temporal pockets [a neat trick beyond the rather limited time-corridor technology Linx used].

They use Cordolaine signals to excite the copper casings of bullets and make guns jam [at last, a retcon for 3.10, "The War Machines" and their magic spotlight].

History

• *Dating*. It's a few days after "Partners in Crime" – long enough for Sylvia to have become irritated, but not so long that she's surprised by Donna's reappearance.

While teaching Donna to steer the TARDIS, the Doctor informs her that someone put a dent in the 80s. [How seriously anyone should take this is left to the viewer's discretion.]

The Analysis

The Big Picture ("The Sontaran Stratagem" and "The Poison Sky")

As we mentioned at the start, this story follows a very obvious template. The Doctor comes to London in pretty much our time and finds that a consumer electrical product has become indispensable while he's been away. UNIT have been looking into the factory where it's made, but nobody can quite see how the gizmo works. The public face is an arrogant inventor, but he's merely the contact for some old enemies of the Doctor's who've finally decided to grab present-day Earth. The factory workers turn out to be superhumanly strong and tireless, but unable to answer simple questions. Once the Doctor finds out who's *really* behind it, the planned stealthy assault is ramped up and the world is paralysed. UNIT attempt a missile strike with worldwide collaboration, but the Doctor enlists the aid of the betrayed genius who now wants revenge for being duped.

Even if the name "International Electromatics" didn't ring a bell in "Rise of the Cybermen" (X2.5), you'll see that the combination of personal communications tech and mass hypnosis (from 6.3, "The Invasion") was deployed there and in "The Sound of Drums" (X3.12). They blurred the lines between the alien menace and the famous inventor to make first the Cybermen, then the Master, combine Tobias Vaughn's plot functions in the 1968 story with the vast army he thought he controlled. Vaughn was the forerunner of the Delgado Master as well as any number of Tom Baker's

adversaries: a veteran character-actor as front man for a rampaging mob of mute or near-mute monsters (something Kevin Stoney had also done in his other great proto-Master role as Mavic Chen in 3.4, "The Daleks' Master Plan"). If you like this kind of story, then 7.1, "Spearhead From Space" is almost exactly the same, with only slight changes to make it work as 8.1, "Terror of the Autons" and "Partners in Crime". (It took a few more to create 6.5, "The Seeds of Death", but even this is surprisingly close.) Those slight variations made each story memorable for different things, but satnav was to 2008 what transistor radios were to 1968. We've come full circle.

In fact, this story follows that template so exactly, the Sontarans have to behave ostentatiously out-of-character to make it work. This being episodes four and five, it's time for more companion-family-friction and/or the return of a famous old monster. A case could be made that plotting a season was now almost slot-monster-A-into-tab-B and it's true that the sneaky peak at the Judoon at the end of "The Runaway Bride" had proved that the Sontarans were well-enough remembered to warrant such a return.

This one is a bit strange, though. There's Sontaran cloning technology and a doppelgänger of a companion. There's a story here about aliens using satnavs to render Earth defenceless, which could have worked with other vintage aliens or some new ones. Either of these would work with just one stranded Sontaran but, these days we expect big armies, especially with a race whose vast numbers were part of their usual sales-pitch but never *quite* arrived on screen. There's also a story about the Sontarans deciding to attack Earth *en masse* and humiliate the Doctor. The Doctor keeps commenting on how little this plot resembles the usual Sontaran M.O. Making all three work is an uphill struggle and there's a load more stuff they've chosen to address. Since we're in full Yeti-in-the-loo mode for these two episodes, it has to latch on to something recognisable and here it has picked two very obvious targets: satnavs and Polish migrant workers.

The initial arrival of posh-voiced, supernaturally calm backseat drivers on the dashboard was accompanied by endless newspaper stories of people relying on them and landing up in rivers, on footpaths or hopelessly lost. Whilst America's roads make enough sense to warrant such a device, the cities of Britain – most of which pre-

Must All Three Series Correlate Properly?

continued from Page 73...

things, there's the matter of his boss slaughtering their teammates, then blowing his own brains out; *TW*: "Fragments"). He's more broody in *Torchwood*, true, but he's not the same person who sashayed around space and time with the Doctor and Rose. (See also *Angel*, *Torchwood*'s spiritual forefather.) If anything, the more we learn of Jack's past, the more his *Torchwood* persona comes across as the genuine article, suggesting he was partly faking it for the Doctor's benefit (although there's the scene at the end of X1.10, "The Doctor Dances" where he's alone with a computer facing certain death, with a degree of panache that rather puts the lie to this).

Conversely, Sarah Jane Smith becomes so Doctor-like in *The Sarah Jane Adventures* that seeing her whimpering when confronted with Daleks in "Journey's End" is unsettling. It might seem against the grain of someone who only whimpered once a story, usually when she thought the Doctor was dead (which itself happened once a story), but parenthood does that. Just about every family has an elderly relative who will attest that while they don't mind dying themselves, they worry about what will happen to their offspring. Martha Jones has no such excuse and seems to forget everything that happened in Cardiff when she calls in the Doctor for help with ATMOS. She even looks surprised when Donna thinks of what would have been her "other" self's first move. It's almost as if the joke about the Brigadier having his memory wiped after each alien invasion were true and standard UNIT procedure. The Martha from those three *Torchwood* episodes would have made "The Doctor's Daughter" much more interesting.

If you wish to view *Torchwood* and *The Sarah Jane Adventures* as apocrypha, there's nothing stopping you: you can set aside the veins running between them and *Doctor Who* Series 1-4. The easiest way of doing that, however, is to not actually watch the spin-offs, which folded quite a long time ago now. The decreasing influence of those shows over the years – and that nagging impulse to treat them as separate entities – is because they're lapsed properties, not to a deliberate strategy to cleave them apart. The BBC has no motivation to keep pushing them alongside new *Doctor Who* seasons (it barely mustered the energy to promote *Class* when it was new).

Everyone has the right to pick and choose – except those of us paid to write books about it. We strive to minimise the number of divergent continuities and make all the time-lines fit. We also have to account for all of these meta-canonical series. We watch *Class* so you don't have to.

---

date steam – have crinkles and one-way systems beyond the processing power of the chips in the TomToms and Garmins bought by (or for) early adopters. Satnavs were toys, real drivers didn't need them. Eventually, as with pocket calculators, the ability to manage without one became seen as freakish. The AA (Automobile Association, the ones with the black and yellow TARDIS-like boxes on roadsides between 1912 and 1968) and RAC got on board, lessening the disparity between how the world looks on Google Maps and what it's like driving around the UK.

Now, most people use apps on their phones anyway, so this story's as dated as the woefully wrong idea of what the 2012 Olympics would be like (X2.11, "Fear Her"). Nonetheless, unlike mobile phones *re.* Lumic or Saxon, people are disquieted about surrendering so much control to a machine they acknowledge that they don't entirely comprehend. (People *think* they've got the measure of mobile phones and haven't quite acclimatised to how far the information they disclose is itself a product to be sold.) Killer satnavs were an idea that cropped up in thrillers – especially long-running hi-tech TV shows with initials for names – because of the amount of trust people invest in a machine that sounds almost human.

Moreover, the extent to which car-ownership is treated as a right and not a privilege is one that might confuse any future generations watching this. Whether or not humans are the root cause of Global Warming, this isn't helping – but everyone wants everyone else to change their ways first. Everyone, outside a few backward areas, sort-of knows that CO_2 emissions are destabilising a dynamic system by retaining more energy than hitherto. Getting anyone to accept individual responsibility requires some sort of crisis to get the whole industrialised world to say "1-2-3-GO!" and change, just as smoking or slavery stopped looking normal. Or, as many people hope, some kind of magic technological fix will come along and remove guilt so drivers can carry on as before. An earlier draft of this story had everyone fitting

ABOUT TIME 2008-2009

magic carbon-capture chimneypots, a suggestion being made seriously even now.

The real anomaly in the first episode is the sequence with Treppa, the Polish(-ish) migrant worker who repeats "I come to do my job" and has some kind of tachycardia that allows him to pull 24-hour shifts. It's uncomfortable for British viewers in that there's a perceived hostility outside the main cities to migrant workers from former Soviet nations – many of whom were, as their countries joined the EU, allowed to work in the UK and often took lower-paid work than they are trained to do and worked longer hours than is usual. In most urban areas, the words *Polski Sklep* have become as familiar as *kebabish*[16] as specialist shops selling imported East European foodstuffs take over disused pubs and add another new flavour. There are a few right-wing parties and the usual lurid tabloid headlines fuelling such discomfort, but Catholic churches reversed the downward trend in their attendances and primary schools facing closure a few years ago with the dropping birthrate had to expand. Neo-Nazi groups opposing immigration were wrongfooted by tall blond taxpayers, but the old saw about coming over and taking "our" jobs persists.

After the whole Referendum unpleasantness, actual violence against these guest-workers increased, but nobody expected that in 2008. That the BBC, and especially *Doctor Who*, appeared to be playing up to this stereotype seemed odd. Instead, the Yeti-in-the-Loo format means that something new but becoming familiar has to be made suspect, even if it's people rather than gadgets. Note how Martha goes out of her way to reassure Treppa that she's not questioning his visa. This scene doesn't go anywhere (which may be as well) and looks as if it's setting up an army of cloned factory workers. One line later on suggests that they are all under hypnosis (which somehow cures them of all known ailments), but this looks like the start of a different storyline from what we get.

Instead, we have a doppelgänger of Martha. This sort of thing is usually a way for an actor in a long-running franchise to do something slightly different once in a while, like possession or alternate universes, but it's noteworthy that Martha and Evil-Martha are almost completely indistinguishable. The traditional doppelgänger story is about the reactions of people around it, the uncertainty of whether someone is the same one day as

the next, and reflects the tension between the supposedly-stable "personality" (which is a set of social functions, a performance, rather than hardwired) and how mutable people really are. The clone has a set of pre-set loyalties and a task to perform, but the grafted-on personality and memories make her question this.

Back when stories about brainwashing were a staple of spy shows and paranoid fantasies (either entertainment or supposedly-serious concerns of politicians and the media), you'd get a variation on this type of thing every so often where the victim would, somehow, be weaned off mind-control by showing him or her pictures of puppies or something – and then next week, everything would be back to normal. *Doctor Who* handles this better than most by taking it as read that anyone hypnotised or possessed that well is probably going to die before the story's out; the exception being regular characters, although it's noteworthy that the two most effective possessions ended with Dodo and Sarah being written out of the series. (Those would be 3.10, "The War Machines" and 14.2, "The Hand of Fear" – the latter not explicitly connected to Eldrad making Sarah a potential killer and causing a reactor to melt down.) This time, once Bad-Martha is exposed, they could have just had her drop dead – but, instead, we get the sort of scene you'd normally have when a possessed/brainwashed regular is deprogrammed, and it's Good-Martha doing it to her. The generic set-pieces are being included because you "have to" use them, but the logic that underlay them originally, the causal linkages that make a plot flow from the premise, are lost in the mists of TV-convention-history.

You will notice that Luke Rattigan's accent wanders across the Atlantic in mid-word a few times. The script said nothing about him being American (indeed, an on-screen readout has him going to a primary school), but did suggest his personal style was Silicon Valley casual in contrast to his uniformed cult-like academicians. Suspicion of the whizz-kid billionaires who developed software rather than social skills is almost universal – but as the story comes from 2008, the onset of widespread social media and the reports of these creators' sinister beliefs (they all seem to be Ayn Rand fans) making such an obnoxious little squirt either a wannabe Californian or a real one who came to Britain for tax-breaks was intuitively obvious. By that same reasoning, mad scientists with big drills were always given German accents (4.5, "The Underwater Menace"; 7.4, "Inferno"; 13.2, "Planet of Evil"). Rattigan's Academy, with the jumpsuited Future Homemakers of Gemini doing their exercises on the lawn, is a straight steal from the unloved Bond flick *Moonraker*.

Colonel Mace's speech is closely analogous to (if not explicitly modelled upon) the pep-talk Colonel Tim Collins gave to the 1st Battalion of the Royal Irish Regiment in Kuwait just before the British forces went to Iraq in 2003. The official version is that they wanted something like Bill Pulman's much-ridiculed speech in *Independence Day*. On the other side, the Sontaran chanting-and-punching is explicitly referred to (not least by Christopher Ryan) as the "Haka". That was a Maori war-dance, now used as an intimidating ritual by New Zealand's rugby side, the All-Blacks. Many of the players have been Maori, but seeing stocky white guys sticking their tongues out and doing sumo-stomps while reciting a threat is always amusing and, in the 70s, gave them a psychological advantage that translated into a run of victories. Rugby players these days tend to be shaven-headed with cauliflower ears and no discernible necks. Or women.

English Lessons

• *Left hand down*: Steering something more complicated than a car, but being instructed like a learner driver, is a running gag in various media. The most famous is Lt Phillips in *The Navy Lark* (see Volume 3 for the thing Jon Pertwee was most famous for pre-*Who* and X3.1, "Smith and Jones" for more on Leslie Phillips) constantly crashing HMS *Troutbridge*.

• *Who's she? The cat's mother?*: A phrase used by women who object to being spoken of in the third person within earshot. First used in print in about 1913, and considered obsolete by Eric Partridge in the 1960s, but it has all the hallmarks of being something a Victorian nanny would say (like "Mind your Ps and Qs"), an attempt to extirpate unthinking rudeness.

• *Prawn* (n.): What Americans call shrimp. (English shrimps are a bit different.) Prawn cocktail was a swanky dish c.1962, then a popular flavour for crisps. (See also 15.2, "The Invisible Enemy".) Thus it was a handy U-certificate insult, alongside near-analogues "pranny" and "prat" (the latter being formerly a term for backside, as in "pratfall") for use in 80s children's television.

• *Pork Pie* (n.): Consultation with Americans indicates that the British concept of a "proper" pork pie is unfamiliar, as they have something that's like a chicken pot-pie but with pork and peas, heated up before eating. That's not a pork pie as we understand it. They must be served cold and only use chopped pork and pork jelly, no vegetables. You can have big ones to slice, but the norm is an individual drum-shaped one; it's often eaten as a picnic item or a snack for long car journeys, and the translucent jelly surrounding the meat is many people's favourite part. The pastry is resilient but flaky and, when cut in half, the whole thing holds together as a semi-cylindrical lump. The pork is peppery, but whether or not it's been cured is up to individual manufacturers. It's generally agreed that the best come from around the Leicestershire town of Melton Mowbray (although the recipe is not Protected Geographical Indication-worthy, like Champagne) and are hand-made – but the ones in petrol-stations are mass-produced. Appropriately, considering Wilf's attempted deception, rhyming-slang for fibbing is "telling porkie pies" or just "porkies".

• *Man Flu* (n): Because real men don't take time off work for just a cold.

• *Dunce* (n.): The schoolboy (or later, schoolgirl) who makes such a stupid mistake as to be forced to sit in the corner with a conical white cap bearing the letter D. Oddly, though, the name is thought to derive from the brilliant Mediaeval Scots philosopher Thomas Duns Scotius; when the Reformation came, his style of logic-chopping was, at best, outdated. His status as a fashion-victim was confirmed when his Aristotelian notion of refining thought through geometry by wearing a conical "thinking cap" became a schoolmaster's method of humiliation-as-paedagogy. But we still think of wizards as wearing conical hats...

• *Squash* (n.): The game Luke plays with the small rubber ball and the slimmed-down racquet; long associated with the high-finance world and 80s market types in adverts aimed at Gordon Gekko wannabes. It's tactically more like high-speed snooker than tennis, and involves bouncing the ball off a wall. Fans of *Sherlock* (which we assume includes quite a few of you) will recall the use of a squash-ball in the armpit to simulate death.

• *Michael Palin* (n.): In a classic example of comedian enantiodromia, Palin, formerly of *Monty Python's Flying Circus* and thus one of the participants in the "Whicker's Island" sketch, has replaced Alan Whicker as the BBC's globetrotting documentarian. (Just as Stephen Fry is now Robert Robinson to six decimal places, Griff Rhys Jones makes programmes about ecclesiastical architecture like the Donald Sinden one he parodied in 1980, Hugh Laurie makes a living pretending to be American...) Palin began his new career in 1988 with *Around the World in 80 Days*, then did *Pole to Pole* and several others. He is now Sir Michael, a literal knight who went 'Ni'.

• *Kickabout* (n.): Playing football for fun rather than to score goals; no need to form teams or change clothes, jumpers for goalposts...

• *Trap* (n): As we didn't have this feature in Volume 3, it's worth pointing out that the UNIT radio callsigns are thematically linked. In greyhound racing, the dogs are penned in traps, metal cages with a mesh door that opens upwards in an instant, so they all start simultaneously – as with racehorses, the number and pattern of each allows the punters to identify their chosen animal. (See the cover and sleevenotes of Blur's album *Parklife* for what we mean – there are usually eight traps.) What's odd about this story's use of these is that rather than the leader (i.e. the Brigadier) being identified as 'Greyhound' and all subordinates and locations numbered as 'Trap One', 'Trap Two' and so on, the pantechnicon mobile base is 'Trap One' and Ross is 'Greyhound 40', Martha 'Greyhound 16' and so on.

Oh, Isn't That...?

• *Christopher Ryan* (General Staal). Apart from Marshall in *Absolutely Fabulous* and Mike, the Cool Person from *The Young Ones*, he was Lord Kiv in "Mindwarp" (23.2). He rejoined *Young Ones* co-stars Rik Mayall and Nigel Planer in an episode of *Spongebob Squarepants* (it was the one about chimps auditing Sandy's experiments) but, unlike them, didn't get a credit.

• *Christian Cooke* (Private Ross Jenkins) followed this with the juve lead in the hapless ITV *Buffy*-clone *Demons* and then was in *Trinity*. He has worked since. Before that, he'd been in misbegotten postmodern soap *Echo Beach* (half of a duplex with a comedy-drama called *Moving Wallpaper* about people making a soap they hate, called "Echo Beach").

• *Ryan Sampson* (Luke Rattigan, boy genius) was then appearing in a sitcom called *After You've Gone*, a series with more writers than viewers, alongside three much more famous regulars. He'd had a pilot on BBC3 and a reasonable-sized part

in *Plebs*. He's not really American, you know.

• *Rupert Holliday Evans* (Colonel Mace). Amidst the usual cop-shows and odd historical drama, he was Harry Enfield's Double-Take Brother.

X4.5: "The Poison Sky"

(3rd May, 2008)

Which One is This? Sex Lives of the Potato Men. The most annoying boy genius since Adric blows himself up to save the Doctor. Just like Adric.

Firsts and Lasts After the crisis ends, two UNIT officers snog whilst on duty. Against all expectations, one's male and the other's female.

Watch Out For...

• Donna wanders around a spaceship and makes a Vulcan salute to open the doors.

• Colonel Mace lets the Doctor use him as comic relief until it's time for a rousing speech, when suddenly Earth's technology is easily a match for the Sontarans. This pleases both sides.

• We have reached the point at which Davies's fake BBC news updates can be assumed to be part of the story, so we have a Trinity Wells newscast that none of the characters appear to be watching. In a pinch, perhaps we're seeing the feed from Wilf's telly. *Newsnight*'s Kirsty Wark pops into the BBC newsroom, for some reason, as this story's celebrity Jeremiah.

• The mobile phone obsession is given full rein, as the Doctor spends much of this episode talking his companion through what to do. By the end of this year, it will have got out of hand, so to speak, as the Doctor's mobile number will be released to the public.

The Continuity

The Doctor He's taking pains to keep the military out of the battle as much as possible [as per 25.1, "Remembrance of the Daleks"]. He gets angry with Mace for not breaking protocol on an open channel in front of the troops and addressing the compromised Trap 40 as 'Ross'.

He does the official "give the companion a TARDIS key" bit [he wasn't expecting to do it now, so presumably this key is one of his own]. It's an important little ritual to him, and he's slightly put out when Donna tells him to get on with saving the world. Being stuck on Earth like 'an ordinary

What Happened to UNIT?

Anyone coming to the much-hyped 1970s "Golden Age" of UNIT adventures after only having seen the BBC Wales episodes is in for a bit of a shock. Not so much what we'll politely call the pioneering special effects, nor the unashamedly heterodox music... no, the big surprise is that UNIT is the most homespun "international" outfit in television history. Even the possibly-related US rival to that claim, the United Network Council for Law Enforcement (*The Man from UNCLE*, but you probably guessed that), had an English boss and a Russian (played by a Scotsman) among all those Yanks.[17]

UNIT under Lethbridge Stewart seems barely able to muster an on-screen tea-lady, but can lay on (as they tend to say) air-strikes, interruptions to the National Grid, worldwide emergency broadcasts and troops galore. As a Brigadier, he ought – in theory – to be in charge of a brigade (approximately 5,000 soldiers). At their lowest ebb (9.5, "The Time Monster"), they're so under-staffed that Sgt Benton can't be allowed his day off because someone has to go and inspect a prototype teleport, although even when doing routine security for a summit meeting, they just happen to have anti-tank weapons handy (9.1, "Day of the Daleks"). They seem to be swatting away invasions and threats to humanity once every four to six weeks, but hardly seem equipped to defend Walmington on Sea[18]. Compared to the state of play under Colonel Mace – who, with all those action-movie resources, was out of his depth dealing with a small band of Sontarans who weren't even invading, just nesting – the success-rate of Glam-era UNIT is astonishing. What's happened?

The evidence on screen and in the dialogue is abundant, if a touch contradictory, but we have a timeline and sequence of events. Practically every "contemporary" UNIT story is set about 18 months after broadcast. (We'll point you in the direction of **When are the UNIT Stories Set?** in Volume 3 for details and **Was There a Martian Time-Slip?** under X4.16, The Waters of Mars", for the freaky outliers.) Before the new series and the *Sarah Jane* spin-off (which among other things allows us to date Sarah Jane's birth within a month), you could try arguing that the UNIT stories were all set in The Future; these days, there's too much evidence against it for anyone to maintain this position for long.

The second point is that since the Nestenes made what appears to have been their third attempt to capture London (X1.1, "Rose"), the timeline has been changed, several times. We have a drastic shift when Harriet Jones's "Golden Age" is aborted, although this might wind up restoring a previous baseline (X2.0, "The Christmas Invasion" and **He Remembers This *How*?** under X1.5, "World War Three"). The version of 2012 we saw in X1.6, "Dalek" belongs in this aberrant future. Then we have the whole mess with Earth being plonked inside a giant machine and Daleks flying around in plain sight (X4.12, "The Stolen Earth") which, despite being attached to a Fixed Point ("The Waters of Mars") is made to go away (X5.3, "Victory of the Daleks"). It's never mentioned again in *Doctor Who*, but forms the basis for several plots in *SJA*. That near-future has the public fully aware of aliens and Sir Alastair Lethbridge Stewart claiming to be writing his memoirs at long last. However, the Dalek invasion was effaced from history and stayed that way even as far as "Resolution" (X11.11). We have an essay in the Appendix for this volume where the apparently-canonical animated episodes and BBC Wales spin-off series seem to make a plausible case for a big change in Galactic policy towards Earth, the consequences of which seem to have affected UNIT and Torchwood (**What Happened in 1972?** under "Dreamland"). Apart from the whole Dalek thing, nothing in the Moffat era contradicted any of those – indeed, one major piece of supporting evidence comes from the pen of the head-man himself, so we'll start there.

In "Day of the Moon" (X6.2), we have a lot of evidence that President Richard Nixon was so affected by an encounter with the Doctor, he began recording all his phone-calls and Oval Office transactions and visiting Area 51. Although the president was under the impression that the experts helping him were from Scotland Yard, he assigned a rogue FBI agent, Canton Delaware III, to supervise and liaise. Given Nixon's antagonism towards J Edgar Hoover, this is peculiar. It's especially odd, as "The Sound of Drums" (X3.12) suggests that a First Contact Treaty in 1968 handed a mandate to UNIT, meaning the group was already in existence a year earlier. The Doctor never invokes UNIT as some form of affidavit (he'd be messing with his own timeline if he did), but claiming an official post with the Met was risky with Torchwood looking out for him.

However, both Canton and Nixon are able to use Area 51 despite it being associated with the US Army's infiltration by aliens (the Alliance of

continued on Page 81...

person' initially disgusts him, then he apologises to Martha.

He has an easier time coping with the fouled air than Donna [no, they don't actually say "respiratory bypass system"]. Teleporting leaves a metallic tang in the air he can taste. [If you wish to believe this is zanium powder, we really can't stop you – 21.7, "The Twin Dilemma". Alternatively, on the strength of Missy's ramblings in X9.1, "The Magician's Apprentice", perhaps Time Lords have a sort of synaesthesia, and that gravity and such-like manifest themselves as what seems like a metallic taste. Or it's the Quantum Entanglement Rice Krispies from *The Sarah Jane Adventures*.]

• *Background.* He says he earned the authority to speak on behalf of the Earth a long time ago.

Without being on the Sontaran ship himself, he can talk Donna through it to the teleport juncture and deadlocking the systems open. [Perhaps the ships are as standardised as their inhabitants.] He's sure that none of the nukes NATO can throw at the Sontaran ships will even scratch the surface.

• *Ethics.* He seems to rather enjoy the process of baiting Sontarans with insults about their honour. How far he anticipated the Sontarans taking the TARDIS with Donna aboard, and based his plan on her being smuggled into their base, is unclear.

Having neglected to offer the Sontarans a choice until after the Earth is safe, he goes up to the Sontaran ship with the atmospheric converter to offer them one. He doesn't expect to survive the experience but won't [or can't] take Martha's advice to send it up on delay. [Since Luke takes over before the countdown's done, we've no idea whether he'd have any last-minute crisis of nerve as his last incarnation did.]

• *Inventory: Sonic Screwdriver.* He uses it as a telly remote control, setting up a vid-call between the UNIT headquarters and the Sontarans, and flipping to CBeebies for a bit when he gets bored. It detects alien technology [as he knows what he's looking for this time, or the bodged-together detector in X4.1, "Partners in Crime" would have been unnecessarily frivolous].

• *Inventory: Other.* He borrows a phone from a passing UNIT trooper.

The TARDIS Its shielding is sufficient against normal Sontaran scanning. The external shell can be teleported like any other object. It relays the Doctor's call to the Sontarans to the scanner for Donna's benefit. Just before Donna pulls up the

Doctor on the TARDIS scanner, we see another soundless shot of Rose shouting [following on from "Partners in Crime"].

The Doctor's severed hand, the one that caused him so much trouble when the Master nicked it in X3.11, "Utopia," is being kept in the console room. It starts bubbling when the TARDIS abruptly takes off, both of which occurrences catch the Doctor off-guard [see the next episode].

The Supporting Cast

• *The Brigadier.* Colonel Mace explains that, unfortunately, Sir Alastair cannot help because he's stuck in Peru. [The Brigadier returns, later this same year, in *SJA:* "Enemy of the Bane".]

• *Donna.* She agrees with her grandad, and doesn't tip off Sylvia about her adventuring in time and space. Sylvia begs Donna not to go with the Doctor, but Wilf insists that she go, so Donna does exactly that.

She learnt to use the TARDIS scanner to pick up the UNIT-Sontaran communication. The correct pronunciation of 'Sontaran' eludes her throughout. She doesn't know how to mend a fuse. She admires the way Martha looks in the Doctor's coat [if you want to write slash, this is a gimme]. It's certainly her who invites Martha along in the TARDIS, not the Doctor.

• *Martha.* Technically, she's an evil clone for most of this episode. Her mum always says "never put off to tomorrow what you can do today, because you don't know how long you've got".

Donna interprets Martha's comment that wearing the Doctor's coat – that it's like dressing up in dad's clothes – as a sign that we're definitely in post-crush era. Martha really, truly, wasn't planning to travel in the TARDIS again, even if she has missed it, insisting to the Doctor that there's someone back home who needs her.

• *Wilf.* He tells Sylvia to trust Donna's promise that they'll be all right, even while they're choking to death. He's thoroughly keen on Donna's travelling. [One wonders whether his injunction that Donna not tell her mother is as much for Sylvia's sake; his daughter is enough of a worrier to keep an axe on hand, so she'd be downright panicky hearing what Donna's really been up to as of late.]

It looks as though he's putting sticky tape on all the windows in one scene [see 8.3, "The Claws of Axos" and any story set in the Blitz].

• *Sylvia.* Keeps an axe about the place – she claims – to deal with 'burglars'.

What Happened to UNIT?

continued from Page 79...

Shades; "Dreamland" again) and the Doctor seems to know all about its facilities c.1969. The most sensible interpretation of all this is that Area 51 is being run as a sort of US version of Torchwood but, somehow, unaware of the Doctor. Despite the treaty agreement of 1968 giving UNIT overall control of all First Contact situations rather than national governments, the very personal nature of the apparent threat – phone calls directly to the Oval Office – means this has to be handled in-house, meaning a pre-existing set-up with no official existence. UNIT's involvement would make it impossible to keep a lid on such a matter, even within a few months of its Charter. As a former vice president, Nixon *might* have known more about Area 51 than his boss, Eisenhower (even though the latter was a former general).

Henry Van Statten ("Dalek") spirits away some of their goodies for his private collection, but the Doctor recognised them. Ergo, he knew about this organisation before he met Rose, so could factor it into his plans without giving the Brig and his younger self any more anachronistic trouble than necessary. This is all starting to look as if, after 1972, all of this came under UNIT jurisdiction. We could conjecture that Canton became the American version of the Brigadier, and that he sent Bill Filer to agree a policy towards the Master (8.3, "The Claws of Axos"). We could even speculate that the Doctor thereafter read about Roswell in UNIT's new files.

The point is that the eleventh Doctor's older self set up a rendezvous at a Still Point and left a clue that the puzzle would be solved in 1969, so scrupulously avoiding UNIT in this year means that they must already be fairly well-established. If they were any less organised, Nixon – scared as he was – might have chanced involving an agency dedicated to exactly the sort of problem he was facing. The Doctor, realising that anything so bad as to require a trip two centuries into his personal past and located around such a delicate patch of spacetime (**What Constitutes a Fixed Point?** under X4.2, "The Fires of Pompeii"), has even more to fear from paradoxes than normal.

Staying with the "Dalek" timeline for a second, Adam is forthright in his views that aliens keep visiting, but thinks anyone hearing him say so will dismiss him as a nutter. He insists that the United Nations is hushing it all up. As we all know, the big change between UNIT in their Dudley Simpson-scored heyday and now is that they've been rebranded as the *Unified* Intelligence Taskforce rather than United Nations. They aren't allowed to wear blue UN-style berets (26.1, "Battlefield"), but Martha tells us they got megabucks funding from the UN.

So what, exactly, was unified with what? Clearly, it's not just a lot of national anti-alien squads banded together, as Torchwood seems to be ploughing its own furrow merrily ("seems" being the operative word: see below). UNIT Mk II has regular army back-up, but a distinct uniform. They have, in one version, a New York office ("The Stolen Earth") and a base under the Tower of London. They have the suicidal Osterhagen Key (X4.13, "Journey's End"). They've got bloody *Cloudbase*. The *Valiant* is quite the most disproportionate response to anything hitherto faced by UNIT. Admittedly, it became the Master's vanity project and he had an ulterior motive for a base over the Fjords where the Toclafane were due to arrive, but it got nodded through despite him trying to avoid disrupting the delicate Archangel hypnotic signal. As ways to avoid drawing attention to yourself go, this is a major fail. All the signs are that this was a pre-existing scheme he co-opted and subtly altered when, as a Defence Procurement minister, he found out about it. So if the MoD had that kind of money available to give to UNIT as a matter of course, there must have been some justification.

Which is odd, as, if we look through the annals of UNIT's encounters with extraterrestrial threats, Axos seems to be pretty much the last big one before the Slitheen. The new mantra of "Homeworld security" is a bit hollow when you consider that practically everything UNIT, Torchwood or Sarah Jane Smith had encountered *after* 1972 is either a home-grown threat or something that's been around for centuries waking up. There's a heavily-shielded Cyber-fleet in 1988 (25.3, "Silver Nemesis"), but they're literally not on the radar and are back-up for a scavenger-hunt. The only actual invasion they directly faced was the Kraals (13.4, "The Android Invasion") – which, as we'll argue in that other essay, seems not to have happened anyway. There seems to have been a moratorium on visits to Earth until 2006. UNIT, as Earth's first line of defence against alien invaders, was almost entirely redundant after the World Peace talks finally panned out ("Day of the Daleks"; 8.2, 'The Mind of Evil') and the planet's reconfigured status as a Level Five world under

continued on Page 83...

UNIT 'Trap One' is for the UNIT leader nowadays. The *Valiant* is still around; its contact is 'Hawk Major'. It has a tremendous laser [similar in design to the one Torchwood had in X2.0, "The Christmas Invasion"; the script said it was the same one, which raises dozens of questions about Harry Saxon and Captain Jack].

Their reaction to being told that it's the Sontarans is to pull in NATO for a Defcon One, so that they can shoot up the aliens with nukes. [We're left to infer that people with Priority One clearance like Martha have access to entertaining backdoor features in the combined missile defence launch, such as the untraceable 'No' command that freezes the entire system. The programmers must have been erring on the side of caution.]

Colonel Mace sends troops into combat, but he's sufficiently in the thick of things to confront Skorr and – apparently well-briefed – gives his opponent the order to face him when being shot. [The conference-call scene has Mace dismissing the Doctor's idea of 'diplomacy', but this incident implies that he's prepared to see the aliens' world-views as valid. He's shocked at actually seeing one, but refers to them as 'Warriors of Sontar', so those files must be fairly detailed.] We have no idea if Captain Price is disciplined for snogging Mace, her superior officer, in a combat zone.

They have sufficient armaments to muster bullets clad in rad-steel rather than copper [26.1, "Battlefield" established that UNIT keeps a wide selection of bullets on hand]. They now wear black fatigues and send women in to combat.

The Non-Humans

• *Sontarans.* Their ship orbits 5000 miles above the planet. [The Sontarans must have a goodish idea of Earth's alien defence strategy; the factory is as much bait for the *Valiant* as centre for the battle. Indeed, their basic knowledge of Earth goes into the details of what can be downloaded onto a phone used by a UNIT officer with Level One clearance, and what fear does to human sweat. They must also have had a sample of Martha's DNA and a good idea of her hairstyle and scars to make the clone. All of this indicates a long-laid plan with a good deal of reconnaissance.]

This lot must have three fingers [that's the configuration on the door Donna uses; cf. 11.1, "The Time Warrior"]. A mallet to the probic vent will down a Sontaran. Staal claims he is the first Sontaran to capture a TARDIS. [Storr actually got there first, by capturing the whole of Gallifrey (15.6, "The Invasion of Time"), but to what degree do the Sontarans know that?]

The fumes they're using to terraform the planet into a Sontaran hatchery is lethal to humans at 80% density. It includes all the usual greenhouse gases, and a 10% solution of something the Doctor calls clonefeed: a caesofine concentration with one part of Bosteen, two parts Probic 5. He compares it to amniotic fluid and the food for Sontaran clones of humans. The Sontaran tech that created the duplicate Martha isn't perfect; she has reduced iris contraction and slightly thinner hair follicles on her left temple. Waking up the original slowly kills the spare.

Rattigan has been colluding with the Sontarans so they will relocate him and his followers to a colony world, Castor 36. In truth, Staal's group intends on using the hapless humans for target practice. [Castor, Alpha Geminorum, is actually six stars, including an eclipsing binary pair that rotate around a common point once a day, near enough, so any planets in that neighbourhood would be flung about like pinballs. Whether the Sontarans were lying to Luke about there being a viable planet there is an open question.]

The Doctor knows the Sontarans will respond to his call under Jurisdiction Two of the Intergalactic Rules of Engagement [possibly this relates back to the Shadow Proclamation, again]. 'Basic Sontaran Stratagem One' is to kill everyone in sight. They've no objection to dying in battle, especially if they take the Doctor with them. The Doctor's offer to let them leave and not tell High Command what happened isn't heeded.

• *Speelfoxes.* Apparently make Slimebait run. [Whether they're related to Speelsnapes (22.6, "Revelation of the Daleks") is unclear.]

• *Slimebait* reputedly run from speelfoxes.

Planet Notes

• *Earth.* The list of areas in the 'worldwide nuclear grid', which can be coordinated against extraterrestrial invaders, includes North America [presumably a dual Canadian-US system], the UK, France, India *and* Pakistan (!), China, and [of all places] North Korea. In the Doctor's view, the nuclear launch would have started an interstellar war [presumably owing to Sontaran reprisals]. Jodrell Bank traces the ATMOS signal that set off all the cars. People stop using cars afterwards, at least in London. For a bit.

What Happened to UNIT?

continued from Page 81...

mixed local and galactic supervision settled down. Perhaps this was the reason for those talks that required the Brigadier to keep popping over to Geneva in 1976, until he abruptly gave it all up and became a schoolmaster (20.3, "Mawdryn Undead").

However, we may not have the whole picture. We don't know, for example, what UNIT did when Mondas showed up (4.2, "The Tenth Planet"). That was December 1986, and it's confirmed in 22.1, "Attack of the Cybermen". The fact that Ace didn't know about it suggests a fairly good cover-up. If we're to believe the Atraxi's records (X5.1, "The Eleventh Hour"), Earth was, at some point(s) before 2008, invaded by the Hath, the Ood and some archaeologists' remains in spacesuits. The Daleks claimed to have left Replicants of major politicians in 1980s Earth (21.4, "Resurrection of the Daleks").

Something pretty big must have happened in the interim, for the sort of sanctions UNIT has at its disposal for theft of alien tech we see in *Torchwood* (*TW:* "Fragments"). In this, a flashback dated "Five years ago" (and the next episode is stated explicitly to immediately follow and take place in 2009) has Toshiko Sato captured by UNIT, locked in a cell, incommunicado and told she has no rights. It's obviously based on Camp X-Ray, but it's somewhere in Britain. This violates so many Human Rights conventions, even Captain Jack (whose treatment of a suspected sleeper in an earlier episode would have had *24*'s Jack Bauer saying "steady on") is forced to act. Whatever he does is so effective that both Torchwood 1 (Canary Wharf) and UNIT are happy to let Tosh dissect the alien pig (X1.4, "Aliens of London"). That was a fortnight after Owen Harper joined (Tosh covered for him because he was drunk, as *TW:* "Exit Wounds" tells us) which was "Four Years Ago". So the situation with UNIT operating well outside UN supervision predates the UN having to vote on Britain getting to shoot missiles at a faked alien threat. It's not the Slitheen situation that creates this sense of crisis.

One oblique sidelight we can recruit, if not as evidence then as a significant space where evidence ought to be, is the similarity of the seemingly UNIT-less history in Pete's World ("Rise of the Cybermen" et seq.) which lacked, it seems, an invasion from Mondas or a failed one from Telos ("The Tenth Planet"; 6.3, "The Invasion"). Everything else is more or less the same, although we were given reason to believe that the earlier event, and its defeat, was a significant part of UNIT's prestige

and influence. It would be possible to conclude from this that the Doctor's presence caused the majority of invasions and threats UNIT faced back when spherical television sets seemed smart (see **How and Why is the Doctor Exiled to Earth?** under 9.5, "The Time Monster"), but it's also possible to speculate on whether the Time War bulldozed away the majority of these incidents. The trouble with that is that people keep talking about them, and their consequences are obvious throughout the twenty-first century stories. In fact, almost all of them are, which makes the three that *really* made things awkward more suspiciously absent.

There was a lot of *X Files* inspired fan-fic wherein UNIT collected alien tech and reverse-engineered it to provide excitingly futuristic gadgets like the ones in the *Doctor Who* version of the near-future as seen on TV. Everything we see in the new series makes it clear that, while Torchwood might play such shabby tricks, UNIT endeavours to keep it all out of the hands of anyone untrustworthy – as did whatever equivalent body ought to have investigated John Lumic ("Rise of the Cybermen"). The only time the original UNIT allowed a situation like that in many episodes of *Torchwood,* where private individuals got alien goodies (or even the anomalous timeline of "Dalek"), was 13.6, "The Seeds of Doom" – a grubby, shambolic and, frankly, ludicrous scenario with an obsessive millionaire and day-trips to Antarctica. Although the decision to depose Harriet Jones could have caused all the changes in the global anti-alien network that we see in bodies set up after Christmas 2006, this doesn't have any influence on pre-existing UNIT or Torchwood procedures.

If we take the "Intelligence" part of the name at face value, this is a worldwide security and surveillance operation (no wonder Nixon was wary) coordinating any number of apparently unrelated monitoring systems to show up such anomalies. Look at the car-death data Martha collates when she starts noticing ATMOS (X4.4, "The Sontaran Stratagem"). What this suggests is way beyond anything Edward Snowden would have dared speculate. If the UN could organise something on this scale, it's amazing that any wars or conflicts happened *at all* after 1976. What we're looking at is something far beyond the capabilities of any peacekeeping force or mandated security operations. It may be part-funded by the UN, but the

continued on Page 85...

History

• *Dating.* [The end scene is clearly a few days after the crisis resolves. Everyone's changed clothes and the reaction to ATMOS seems to be becoming permanent.]

The Doctor confirms in passing that the Sontaran-Rutan war has now been going on for '50,000 years'. He believes, rightly or wrongly, that the Sontaran gambit here indicates they're losing the war.

The Analysis

English Lessons

• *Back of the Net* (interj.): Football commentator cliché for a goal being scored, used as a triumphant "mission accomplished" or "top that". It usually has the same intonation that Donna gives to 'back of the neck'. The official start of this as a meme, rather than just a fairly familiar turn of phrase, was the use of it in a different context – referring to his love life – in Series 2 episode one of *I'm Alan Partridge*.

• *Clone* (n. sl.): It was an American thing originally but, we gather, more commented-on here – in the late 1970s, many young gay men started looking similar: short hair, moustaches, white T-shirts and earrings. Freddie Mercury and the cowboy from Village People were the first prominent examples then, for a few years, hundreds of them showed up on *Top of the Pops*, usually as backing dancers for disco divas. (There was also that thing with different coloured hankies in different pockets, denoting different preferences, but nobody in Britain ever fully understood that.)

Oh, Isn't That...?

• *Kirsty Wark.* As per usual, someone who wasn't quite right was picked for the fake BBC newsreading. As one of the main hosts of *Newsnight*, the terribly-solemn late evening BBC2 current affairs series, she interviews senior figures and – back then – would spend alternate Fridays discussing new novels and films with a panel of increasingly randomly-selected critics. She may have read headlines in the middle of this, but didn't pop into the main newsroom to do live updates on News 24 (as it was then, the digital-only rolling news service – until all BBC became digital-only in 2012 – and which became BBC News Channel in 2009).

Things That Don't Make Sense ("The Sontaran Stratagem" and "The Poison Sky")
We've touched upon this, but there's really something spellbinding about the way People in the Know keep using vehicles fitted with ATMOS. A journalist dies doing so in the teaser, then the Doctor and Ross jaunt about in another one – even though only half of the world's cars have been converted, so there should be some hundreds of millions of non-ATMOS ones available. Ross finds a safe car quickly enough when "The Poison Sky" opens.

But if we're asking about ATMOS... the *real* problem is how something fitted after the fact to already-roadworthy cars can not only over-ride the engines and central locking of new cars, but can lock and rev up older models with no actual connection to the mechanical door controls, steering-column, brakes, gearbox and – to judge by Jo Nakashima's death – seatbelts. If you're going to suggest it's some kind of nanotechnology, the obvious question is why they bother with cars at all and don't just make it rain clonefeed.

Speaking of which, the precise details of the titular stratagem are hard to fathom. The Sontarans need a planet on which to breed. All right, that makes a sort of sense, but why does it have to be Earth? If they want the added thrill of a glorious fight while eliminating humanity, why hide from them and use missiles and gas, plus sneaky subterfuges and double-agents? Moreover, we were always told how rapidly the Sontarans could muster an army, ten million in ten minutes. Yet, for the first time, we see Sontarans using teleports. If they are that bothered about producing fully-trained troops, surely they could convert these into photocopiers and mass-produce Staals, Skorrs and Skrees.

Why are conditions aboard the Sontaran vessel so like that of Earth? Since they evolved in a high-gravity environment (which would also make it hard for Donna to stand up), the air would have a completely different composition. Maybe they've decided to acclimatise to Earth by setting the gravity in their ship abnormally low, as you might expect if they were expecting an infantry operation in vast numbers – but they aren't.

UNIT's employing idiots as grunts. Two of them see two boiler-suited goons, and don't take them into custody. The goons escort them into a locked room and lock it behind them. Their radios are dead, but they proceed. They then confront a force-grown humanoid, and neglect to report it.

What Happened to UNIT?

continued from Page 83...

Unified Intelligence Taskforce is out of their league. It's also probably illegal. If the United Nations knew about the detention facility, their own lawyers would have been among the first to complain about breaches of their Human Rights conventions.

If the British government's somewhat pragmatic response to the 456 arrival in 1965 (*TW*: "Children of Earth") is any indication, the main effect of UNIT has been to keep politicians out of such matters. We looked into this in **How Can Anyone *Not* Know About Aliens?** in Volume 8, so we'll take the list of all the potential interested parties as read. This entire matter has been put under international military jurisdiction. But look at the other bit of the name: it's an Intelligence Taskforce. Not just soldiers, but information (especially science); not a dedicated army, but a smaller nucleus that has the right and duty to augment its numbers with regular army *ad hoc*. It's odd that Kate Stewart announces that letting the science lead is a shift of emphasis (X7.4, "The Power of Three"), even though it was Martha Jones spotting a pattern in apparently unrelated deaths worldwide that caused the raids on the ATMOS distribution plant. Indeed, letting the science lead is the hallmark of both iterations of Captain Magambo's smaller, funkier UK UNIT.

The first time we see this, in the aberrant chronology of "Turn Left" (X4.11), the bulk of the military are running a police-state and whisking off affable foreigners. This leaves a small core of well-protected researchers trying to figure out the TARDIS. The first and most interesting discovery we make in this story is that when the Racnoss was attacking, a UNIT squad were already en route to H. C. Clements and, in the revised version, got there too late to save the Doctor. This indicates that they were pretty much on the ball. Magambo's first reaction when a bus goes missing amid a lot of dimensional flux is to drag along her own scientific advisor to the site, even though it's barely half a mile from the Tower of London (X4.15, "Planet of the Dead"). Indeed, the only times when UNIT *doesn't* let science lead and clamps down on curiosity are in the first two series of *Torchwood*. It's possible, as we explored in the previous essay, that the two series had diverged by this stage and the jump-start at the end of Series 5 rewrote history, but it sounds as if the UNIT Kate was reforming was the one that locked up Tosh rather than the

one that let her dissect space-piggy. Neither of these is either of the ones Magambo led.

Having a Captain in charge of the entire national operation in either reality makes little sense, so we might assume that this is a smaller part of an overall operational body. The fact that anyone as high-up as her is liaising with the anonymous expert who's recruited Donna (yes, we know it's Rose Tyler, but she doesn't) is possibly more surprising than if Magambo was as high-up as it got. This UNIT seems to allow its officers a degree of autonomy, as we can tell from when the Daleks attack New York. The BBC's website (the one we see Mickey using in "World War Three") indicates that New York has supplanted Geneva as the overall high command.

This makes a bit more sense of the speed with which the Security Council votes to allow the missiles, but the size of their alien booty-haul compared to the ones in *Torchwood*, *SJA* or even X7.15, "The Day of the Doctor" makes it look as if this was a recent development (or one of the staff had an eBay account and no morals). Even their UK Base 5, under Mount Snowdon, is better-appointed (this is in *SJA*: "Death of the Doctor", where we also discover that they have a Moonbase). Britain has been invaded so often, withstood so many attacks and accumulated so much exciting leftover ordinance, it would make sense to allow this branch a lot more leeway, even though the Slitheen killed the majority of their experts and the Sycorax compromised their operational staffing. It's Geneva again in "The Sound of Drums" though.

If we're to take the 1968 Charter as a clue, then the formation of UNIT happened just as the novelisation of 5.5, "The Web of Fear" suggests – with Colonel Lethbridge Stewart proposing an international network of experts and soldiers to deal with anything like this happening again. It's hard to see this chain of events leading to what happened to Tosh, though. If there's no external threat making UNIT get so bad-ass, and if, according to that website, they have only a hazy idea about Torchwood, what was going on during that 30-year hiatus between invasions? The website offers no direct clues, but it's tangentially interesting for another reason. All of this material was written by Joseph Lidster, who was writing up the flavour-text around the same time as his work on a Big Finish *UNIT* audio series. Nicholas Courtney's part as Sir Alastair was to advise newcomer Colonel Emily Chaudhry on the proper care and

continued on Page 87...

And along comes an honest-to-badness alien, and they slag him off to his face.

Martha's clone can breathe in the toxic gas because she's a Sontaran clone. Harris and Grey can breathe in the toxic gas because they're, er, hypnotised. For that matter, how does hypnosis stop anyone from needing sick days?

And, Martha's certain that the 52 worldwide deaths were poison, because... err... she checked biopsies and found no toxins. QED. The test was overseen by Rattigan, but took place at 5.00am in the UK. Whoever was driving then would have been more noticeable than any unexplained death at, say, 7.00am. Actually, why test (or have) a "kill the drivers quickly" option at all? The point of the scheme, we're told in the second episode, is to emit enough gas to turn Earth into a Sontaran hatchery. After that, everyone dies anyway.

So, the Doctor shows up at UNIT saying he's got a clever plan and don't shoot anything, then he can't make it work, then he calls the Sontarans for a chat in defiance of Mace's request that Earth experts should handle it, then he accomplishes nothing... and then he's shocked to find out that with air pollution at 60%, and nearly a deadly 80% for the whole human race, Mace plans to shoot at the baddies with nukes. What did he *think* was going to happen?

Why does so much of the Sontaran plan hinge on cloning a highly-placed UNIT operative and keeping "her" safe, when all this agent has to do is press a NO button on a phone? Then, as Evil Martha makes a quick download of highly-sensitive material onto her phone, so she can somehow control all atomic weapons on the planet from her mobile, the smog gets worse and worse, but UNIT keep the door of their van wide open. And as she has Security Clearance One, she's on a very short list of suspects, if not the *only* suspect, but nobody at UNIT works this out. Last time Earth prepared to defend itself with a coordinated missile strike, it took a UN vote (X1.5, "World War Three"). Now it needs just Martha saying 'Code Red'.

Cordolaine signals can't work the way everyone says, or else A) the guns would explode or B) the bullets would fall out with a trickle of cordite. (We'll assume, to spare the blushes of whoever wrote this bit, that 'copper surface' means the casings and not a spray-on paint or bullets galvanised like O Level Chemistry experiments.) More peculiarly, once UNIT switch to steel casings, the Sontarans' armour isn't enough to protect them.

Fifty thousand years of space warfare, and they haven't got around to inventing Kevlar? Either way, Ross explains to UNIT that bullets don't work around Sontarans. Nevertheless, in a misguided salute to tradition, they try shooting aliens with standard weapons anyway.

In Luke's bio, the address for the Rattigan Academy is given as Richmond, but the view of London we see from the front drive is more Sydenham/Blackheath. (The London skyline seems to be the exact reverse of Martha's view of the city after teleporting down from the *Valiant* in X3.12, "The Sound of Drums".) Then two minutes later, it's ten miles outside London and Donna's house is on the way. Richmond isn't ten miles outside London but, wherever the warehouse is, it's not in the heart of the city.

The same bio cites Luke as comprehending quantum mechanics before starting Primary School in 1990. If he's supposed to be American, why was he at a primary (not an "elementary school") and how does he know where Chiswick is and how to pronounce it? To weigh in on Rattigan and the Doctor's grammar-spat (Rattigan: 'If only that was possible', the Doctor: 'If only that *were* possible. Conditional clause.'), 'If only that *were* possible' is in the subjunctive mood with a conditional clause; the Doctor simply saying 'Conditional Clause' isn't a sentence. (How's *that* for grammar-pedantry?) Moreover, there isn't any way that 'ATMOS' is an acronym for 'Atmospheric Emission System". (The on-screen subtitles for the DVD claim it's 'omission', but that's nonsensical even by the standards of a CO_2 filter that's got a TARDIS-like reservoir of other gases hidden a second out of phase.) Ross calling the Land Rover a 'jeep' is just wrong (the Doctor does it too, but he doubtless remembers that UNIT had actual jeeps way back when).

Staal, with his tin hat on, can smell human fear from ten feet away. Later, a very frightened Donna, presumably wearing perfume or deodorant, hides three feet from a whole bunch of them.

We might also ask in what ways society's been turned on its head if no one needs to worry about carbon emissions; the Doctor ponders the implications of the oil running out that much faster, but its impact goes way beyond that. If the ATMOS systems work at all, it would be retroengineered and installed in every emissions-creating factory in the world, not just cars. There would be all sorts of manufacturing upheavals that would

What Happened to UNIT?

continued from Page 85...

running of UNIT. The metaplot involved the British government attempting to replace our favourite paramilitary organisation with a nasty home-grown pack of xenophobes (ICIS, if you really must know – pronounced "Isis", so inadvertently funnier now), and if there's anyone disappointed that UNIT and Torchwood never had an explosive show-down, the storyline here will probably be satisfactory (even if it's difficult to reconcile with anything broadcast since). Someone on the *Doctor Who* production staff must have been talking to them, as the story where Albion Hospital appears and No. 10 blows up appeared a good month before the telly story. (Oh, and the villain of the piece is David Tennant.) With the amount of Big Finish influence on the thinking at BBC Wales (see X2.5, "Rise of the Cybermen" for a really big example), it's tempting to think that a similar scenario was being floated for future use, but never quite made it to our screens. Is there any hint of it in what was broadcast?

Hardly. Even Jack refers to UNIT as "the acceptable face of intelligence-gathering on aliens", although this is partly for Martha's benefit (*TW:* "Reset"), but he's busily reconfiguring the Cardiff Scooby-gang to disown and make up for the Canary Wharf mob. That episode opens one intriguing possibility though: Torchwood aren't the only government-sanctioned, off-the-books agency using alien tech, and the nefarious activities of The Pharm (who were using endoparasitic ETs to cure all ills, then bumping off the failures) would have been even more lucrative than Global Chemicals (10.5, "The Green Death"). In both cases, there is pressure brought at Cabinet level for Our Heroes to back off. A pharmaceutical combine of any size these days is bigger and wealthier than almost any national government. Professor Copley, head of this outfit, is savvy enough to spot Martha's turbo-charged immune system as being the result of time-travel. How exactly *anyone* has that sort of expertise is a question that opens a whole can of worms about the security of captured alien technology, but it links up to something we've sarcastically suggested in various **Things That Don't Make Sense** entries.

If you look at all the companies and Public-Private Partnerships (a common solution to infra-structural needs under New Labour) in *Doctor Who* and the spin-offs (especially *The Sarah Jane Adventures*), it looks as if there really *is* a venture

capital network for aliens requiring start-up funds to form businesses to invade by stealth. (See, for example, 4.8, "The Faceless Ones" for a medium-sized airline that seemed to turn a profit despite all their passengers vanishing, or X2.7, "The Idiot's Lantern" for a significant cash injection and sudden spurt in manufacturing capacity for a street-corner electrical supplier.) This almost makes sense of the problem with UNIT UK's "funding partners" mentioned by Call-Centre Polly in "Resolution". People read this as a clumsy political gag, but the legal aspects of allowing alien billion-aires access to Earth's defences and Britain's infra-structure might have come to light during nego-tiations over some aspect of foreign policy and an injunction served. It's not that UNIT isn't operating, despite the sadly plausible detail of alien tech col-lection now being privatised, but that the public's access to them is more restricted than when Jo Nakajima could get them on the blower and they had a number close to that of a pizza delivery service ("The Sontaran Stratagem", "Planet of the Dead").

If someone like Mr Copper (X4.0, "Voyage of the Damned") can set up a network in under nine months ("The Stolen Earth"), he must have had help. For things such as Bubbleshock (*SJA:* "Invasion of the Bane") or Deffry Vale School (X2.3, "School Reunion") to have occurred, there has to have been local help. It may not always have been willing (the Master managed to co-opt a plastics factory without any boardroom shenanigans; 8.1, "Terror of the Autons") but it makes more sense than not that a network of expats might exist. After all, Cardiff has a lot of unwilling immigrants and not all of them are man-eating Weevils or clouds of pink sparkles that make Welsh teenagers shag themselves to death (if you skipped *Torchwood*, accept our assurances that these were indeed among the items that came through the Hellmouth). Unwilling immigrants might well have set up a self-help group.

Of course, there's a world of difference between something making sense and reflecting the real-world experiences of people we know, and what we get on screen. It's evident that there is a change in the nature of UNIT beyond the name-change, and that it took place during a phase when we have no indication of any significant incursions by extraterrestrials. The activities of other agencies connected with alien impact on

continued on Page 89...

affect just about every product on the market. Great Britain would be experiencing a technological boom (and yet the nation's economy goes from booming in "Partners in Crime" to crashed in X4.17, "The End of Time, Part One").

What makes it worse is that the Doctor seems to think ATMOS works by molecular conversion of carbon monoxide into less problematic particles. (Like Cyanogen? Ethane? Carbon Dioxide?) The uses of a device that makes molecular conversion cost-effective are literally astronomical (such an advance would have cold fusion as a handy side-effect and would, if programmable, be the *Star Trek* replicator). In effect, therefore, even if the temporal pocket technology remains obscure for a few years, the world after this story is going to be post-scarcity economics and limitless energy – goodbye OPEC, Gazprom and manufacturing as we know it. If this had happened in 2009, then by now we'd be in the Troughton era's twenty-first century rather than that of "Resolution" (X11.11).

One story-aspect that *doesn't* need explaining is that Luke happens to have an atmospheric converter lying around (given the creation of ATMOS, it's an obvious spinoff). We'll even write off the atmospheric flame-boil as a special effect. But, according to the Doctor, the Rattigan Academy workshops are full of terraforming equipment, and yet the students seem so shocked to hear that Luke plans to move to another world. What did they *think* they were working on? Then again, in a situation in which the entire planet is choking to death, and the cleverest bloke they know explains a plan to allow them all to survive, they leave because they've abruptly started believing him evil and sick. Just Rattigan's bad luck to be training a batch of geniuses with high moral fibre.

How are spaceships leaving vapour-trails in a vacuum? How volatile is caesofine gas if ground-to-air engagements really might set it off? Given that the Sontarans are 50,000 miles away (so, outside the atmosphere), it must be either the flash or the EMP that would ignite the atmosphere. Luckily, there isn't a single lightning strike anywhere on the whole planet for at least a day.

But the biggest problem is one the script makes noises about, then dodges addressing. Why is Donna so keen to carry on travelling with the Doctor? We have a flashback montage of her adventures and it's all *horrible*. When hanging from a thin wire 150 feet in the air is the one example that doesn't involve her being appalled

by either the Doctor's ethics or those of slavers and aliens, you have to wonder what stops her from pulling a Tegan and walking out on him (21.4, "Resurrection of the Daleks"). Earlier that day, she'd been disgusted that Martha had joined the army as a result of hanging out with the Time Lord. Then she visits her family after learning from the ex-companion about what TARDIS travel does to your loved ones.

Critique ("The Sontaran Stratagem" and "The Poison Sky") All the things that the Davies-era series did well are done well here. It's expensive-looking, crystallises a vague sense of unease about a recent development (and tries to create one about a different trend in an unpleasant, uncomfortable way – see our comments on Treppa in **The Big Picture**), has jokes and action-scenes (and a joke about the lack of an action-scene) and delivers things we were often told about, but couldn't be realised on screen in the 1970s.

Where it falls down is by making these the surface features of an incoherent narrative that's a parade of events rather than a story, and by making the supposed focus of the entire enterprise – Martha and Donna interacting and adding a warm fuzzy glow to the Doctor's adventures – so quick, glib and intrusive.

Like a lot of Davies-era *Who*, it's a Big Monster story that might have been much improved by not having the monsters in it. This is a story about UNIT, and has to have all the Yeti-in-the-loo rituals of stealthy insurrection leading to a pitched battle at the end, which simply isn't what the Sontarans are for. A completely new alien race might have shown them off to better effect. It's not just that the Sontarans behave out-of-character compared to their earlier outings, it's that they are presented to us in *this very story* as war-obsessed, but spend two episodes tiptoeing around not starting anything.

As a re-introduction to these aliens, it might have been better to show them in an all-out assault on a different planet, rather than as a relatively easy target for UNIT. It would have fit the arc better if the Sontarans had explained that their closest breeding-planet had gone unexpectedly missing. The opportunity was right there, but that would have made it an obvious retread of "Partners in Crime". However, this set-up means that the Sontarans are fighting to defend their families and future generations – something normally used as

What Happened to UNIT?

continued from Page 87...

Earth's institutions are hazily sketched-in, and, whilst it would be obvious that such activities would impact on how UNIT goes about its business, we have no proof. As we said, one aspect of this transformation is the result of changes happening off-world for which we have ample evidence but as we have one unaccountable absence we might throw another one at the problem. Even if you don't follow the unauthorised spin-offs, there is a character in the broadcast episodes who is called "Kate" and is the Brigadier's hitherto-unmentioned daughter. If, as "The Bells of Saint John" (X7.7) might suggest, we can discard *Downtime*, then we have even more reason than otherwise to ask where she's been all this time.

It may also be the case that the Doctor wasn't the only stranded alien recruited (willingly or otherwise) to such a body. Don't forget, in "Spearhead from Space" (7.1), we see Liz and the Doctor in a makeshift lab, apparently in someone's garage, but the equipment they're using seems to include bits of alien gadgetry – obsessive prop-spotters will know the Xeron Freezing Machine (2.7, "The Space Museum") from many other guest appearances, and there's a blue object we'll also see in "Colony in Space" (8.4). So who got this stuff and from where? Was Liz a replacement for an earlier alien advisor? What happened to this person?

Virgin Books's *New Adventures* had a proto-UNIT at work in World War II. Presumably, things would have gone very differently had the Nazis obtained alien technology, but we are confronted with the problem of what Torchwood did (and didn't) do to aid Churchill. The events of "Victory of the Daleks" (X5.3) indicate a lack of any other offworld ordinance available to him, so quite what was going on is anyone's guess. Nonetheless, if Broadsword, the UK extraterrestrial applications team, is one of a number of similar national initiatives, then these might be what were unified. In that case, we have a lot of trouble with the antagonistic forces pooling their resources and intelligence (in both senses) – never mind Operation Overcast/Paperclip and the start of NASA, this is an enormous task and might involve several people otherwise scheduled for execution for war-crimes getting hired by their former enemies. Using the then-fashionable United Nations as a justification and pretext for this might have made sense in the 1950s, but we're told it didn't get started until 1968. Fan-lore and spinoffery suggests that Group

Captain "Chunky" Gilmore was a driving-force here, after the events of "Remembrance of the Daleks" (25.1).

For obvious reasons, near-misses are more exciting television than easily-averted potential crises, so the gap between Axos and the Slitheen may well have entailed a number of thwarted invasions that we didn't get to see just because they were too boring and the Doctor wasn't needed. This would justify an increase in spending and resources up to what we finally get, but the question is then why this abruptly stopped and the Doctor had to assist a version of UNIT that was tooled-up and funded, trained better than ever and yet needing his help nowadays.

[That doesn't make the need for defences any less: just as the precautions against the 2009 H1N1 virus ("Swine Flu") meant that the tabloid hysteria seemed overblown and caused those same tabloids and their Parliamentary mouthpieces to decry the waste of public money on a "false alarm", so the lack of successful alien attacks might have led to the "Resolution" situation being politically popular – had anyone known about it. Our only evidence about whether anything else has changed is Karl's claim (X11.1, "The Woman Who Fell to Earth") that "We don't get aliens in Sheffield". Not that they don't land, or don't exist, just not in Yorkshire. Then again, *someone* gave Tzin-Sha a hunting permit, so the Shadow Proclamation might be in trouble.]

Obviously, after 2007, this is easier to explain if we stick to Britain, as Torchwood rather exceeds its brief by causing two simultaneous invasions and closing down its London branch. The situation we see makes a lot more sense if, apart from Torchwood and perhaps Van Statten and a few lesser collectors, all other such bodies were brought into UNIT's jurisdiction in 1968 and given more responsibility after 1972. This being the case, the big question is how the Nestenes and Slitheens got as far as they did with the best-protected nation, and why successive US Presidents failed to take the hint from Nixon's actions and let Britain get on with this sort of thing unimpeded.

The biggest threat to Earth after this is Harold Saxon. Only UNIT personnel and Martha's family know what actually happened next (as they were on *Valiant*, so remember the Year That Never Was), and if America is as traumatised by a President being assassinated on live TV as in 1963, this

continued on Page 91...

an excuse for the humans being inhumane (see, for instance, X5.9, "Cold Blood").

Still, they're back, after the false alarm of the Judoon, and in the numbers we were always promised but never quite got before. They look a lot better than the last couple of outings, with some thought going into them beyond just running a Robert Holmes script through a photocopier. The redesign is respectful of all the reasons they caught on in the first place and there is obvious love in the costumes, digitally-realised spaceships and prostheses. Visually, it's everything one could have hoped for. But they have little or no connection to the story's starting-point: scary sat-navs.

In fact, there's a lot of brute force making the assorted ingredients in this story seem to work together when they don't quite fit. As we mentioned in **The Big Picture**, this has a lot of elements from a story about mind-control, and places them in the sequence you'd expect such a story to follow, but then makes it a story about cloning instead, because they've chucked the Sontarans into a generic-alien-menace vacancy and want to use their backstory. The hypnosis-breaking plot works best if it's someone the audience knows, so Martha gets that gig and we're supposed to be concerned even when, a draft or two later, it's an evil clone of her being "cured" by the original. The whole sales-pitch of this story was that Martha and Donna finally meet, but they do so many of each other's plot functions, it would have worked better with one or the other written out. Yet Davies maintained that the companion relationships are why people watch, so they expend a lot of screen-time on these, if very little thought.

The Doctor needs a companion sarcastic, smart and tough enough to stand up to him. Unfortunately, in this adventure he has two and neither of them does it. Freema Agyeman's main job is to stand around as a bland unassuming clone and have a touch of emotional blather about how much she cares for her family – both of which she accomplishes with aplomb, given the material. For anyone who'd just seen her in *Torchwood*, the way the character snaps back into a less sharp, less confident Martha is a let-down, but *Doctor Who*-only viewers needed a familiar yardstick against which to measure Agyeman's other role in this story. She's also playing an Evil Martha who's not especially evil. Instead of

Agyeman doing the Laugh That Begins with an N, we have her trying to extract pathos from Evil Martha knowing what a wonderful person Normal Martha is.

Indeed, Skorr tells her (and thus us) that Martha is to be protected at all costs, so we know that – although her return was the big selling-point of this episode – she's in no jeopardy at all. In this two-parter and the episode that follows, we're supposed to be intrigued about how Martha's return will affect the Doctor-Donna dynamic, but it doesn't. Neither is she especially different from last year. Nor does the cloned Martha materially affect the plot. Most of what the original does here is redundant; Jo Nakashima uncovers the conspiracy and alerts UNIT, Donna finds the anomalous lack of sick-days. Denied even Manic Martha shouting *nossing in ze vorld ken schtopp me now!*, it's hard to see why they included her. Some have speculated on a contractual obligation side to this, but Agyeman did a full 13 episodes and three of *Torchwood* and will be back again at the end of this year.

Donna's main role is to turn on a teleporter, but at least she accomplishes it with some style. She's the ostensible audience focus, so we get a long, *long* scene of her returning home with all her adventures preying on her mind, but most people seem to have been more interested in Wilf. The logic of these scenes is that it's analogous to Rose telling Jackie that the Doctor's shown her a better way to live (X1.13, "The Parting of the Ways") but, as all her flashbacks are to how grim life with the Doctor is (because the production team are going dark and playing against Catherine Tate's perceived comic persona), it's Wilf who tells her to stay on the TARDIS. Sylvia is a more malignant, abusive version of Chrissie Jackson (Maria's annoying mum in *The Sarah Jane Adventures*) and the logic of teen-drama is that eventually Donna will stand up to her and declare independence. Don't hold your breath – it's never gonna happen. By using Wilf as the other child in the household, we at least get a version of such a scene in "The Stolen Earth" (X4.12).

We're also presented with a revised version of UNIT resembling their first outing (appropriately, as so much of the rest of this story resembles 6.3, "The Invasion") and promised a serious consideration of how the Doctor's values differ from those of the military. Don't hold your breath for that either. If we're supposed to be siding with the

What Happened to UNIT?

continued from Page 89...

would cause a significant upsurge of political will to support anti-alien action. This doesn't explain why it was so firmly in place and well-funded *before* the Slitheen incursion, though. Perhaps there was a massive (but very secret) invasion threat in the 1990s, but the version of the Doctor who helped them with that hasn't happened yet.

Doctor against career soldiers, despite him turning his companions into exactly that, it might have been better to use a fictionalised version of the regular British army – but a lot of the real ones watch the series and pay licence fees. If the idea was to suggest that the Doctor was hypocritical in having been with UNIT in the 70s (which they murmur about, then forget), it needs audiences to be on the same page with regard to the Brigadier and Benton.

Instead, we have a fresh group so that all viewers, of any level of fannishness, are on the same page. Nu-*Who* gets nu-UNIT – NUNIT. The cosiness of the *Dad's Army* version of UNIT was faintly ludicrous, but suited *Doctor Who* at the time; we can make a direct comparison between Colonel Mace's refusal to break the chain of command and refer to Greyhound 40 as "Ross" with the botched pathos of the third cliffhanger to "The Time Monster" (9.5). In that incident, after a lot of semi-comic mucking about with knights in armour, Roundheads and a bottle of Moroccan Burgundy (don't ask), they have to make a cliffhanger out of a V1 rocket landing and Captain Yates gets hit. The end credits roll on the Brigadier yelling "Mike" into his RT. All that did was highlight that 70s UNIT had about eight soldiers at its disposal and they all went to the pub together after every invasion (plus that standards have dropped since 7.3, "The Ambassadors of Death" in many other ways). If they'd wanted to make a point about Mace's reaction to Ross's death, they could have mentioned that Mace has to break it to the relatives while the Doctor just swans off into time and space. As things stand, we just cut from the magic instant terraforming stink-bomb to everyone deciding to walk (whenever this was, a week later or something) and Martha getting trapped as the TARDIS leaves. This obvious loading of the dice, skipping any scene that would complicate the script's big gestures about how terrible commanding officers are, is a cheap trick.

It doesn't help that the virtue we're supposed to see in the Doctor's approach – seeing the other species as just that, another species rather than "*Doctor Who* monsters" to be shot at – is what Mace does at the end, respecting their code by insisting on shooting one facing him rather than in the back. Apart from one brief comment to Ross about how the Sontarans must see humans as stretched-out and oddly-coloured, this story assumes "human" to be such a universal standard that Sontarans must, *by definition*, feel inferior because of their height and must, *of course*, believe females to be inferior because they're all rather blokeish. The Doctor's supposedly superior knowledge and experience, plus his cosmopolitan viewpoint that's constantly being talked about rather than demonstrated, amounts to "I'm the Doctor, they're the monsters, so I have to do whatever's necessary to end this in under two episodes". They hold off explicitly stating it this way (at least until X8.9, "Flatline"), but it's there. Wilf's idea that aliens are all green and want our women isn't so far from this that they can make jokes about it with a clear conscience.

Similarly, this is a Doctor whose defining trait – the reason he supposedly "needs" human girls mooning after him – is a lack of restraint or emotional intelligence. That makes him the worst possible person to guide Luke Rattigan away from the Dark Side. A brainy but gauche teenage lad who needs experienced, empathic normal folks to guide him might have made a good story, but *The Sarah Jane Adventures* already did that – and he's called "Luke" too – so they make him Mark Zuckerberg, Elon Musk and Jeff Bezos all in one, which means an embarrassing cod-American accent. It's not just that he's a stereotype, or that it's playing to tabloid clichés of clever boys being sinister and cold, or that he is, fundamentally, a very boring character – it's that he's redundant. They've opted for a Tobias Vaughn-style human face for an alien attack (as was so often the case in Tom Baker stories), but with aliens who can talk perfectly well (and more interestingly) and aren't just shambling hordes.

Once again, the model they're following is one that required the set-pieces when the story they're telling doesn't, so we have the set-pieces with no reason for them to be there except nostalgia. Anyone who is nostalgic for these elements is probably making unwelcome comparisons, while everyone else was wondering why entire scenes and characters were there.

One model they could have followed is having the Sontarans, devised as a critique of militarism as an end in itself, set against either a more flexible, funky human counterforce or a Doctor who embodies whatever definition of "human" the guest-villains lack. It worked in 1973, after all. But in this phase of the series, the Doctor is himself supposed to be a warrior and humanity's defining characteristic is a wounded-animal aggression against the other. What we've got is really three sets of Sontarans (as conceived in the 70s) fighting it out. Martha claims she's trying to humanise UNIT from within but she's doing a terrible job if nobody notices she's been replaced by an evil clone reporting to a race that's bombast incarnate.

If you judge these two episodes by the production-team's goals as stated in *Doctor Who Confidential*, then it's a failure. It's a good-looking, watchable failure, though. But if they'd succeeded, it's hard to see whether the story would have been any better or more memorable.

Sontar Meh.

The Lore

Written by Helen Raynor. Directed by Douglas McKinnon. Viewing figures: (*The Sontaran Stratagem*) (BBC1) 7.1 million, (BBC3 repeats) 1.0 and 0.5 million, with an AI of 87%. (*The Poison Sky*) (BBC1) 6.5 million, (BBC3 repeats) 1.1 and 0.5 million, with an AI of 88%.

Repeats and overseas promotion In the French version ("A.T.M.O.S." 1 & 2), the aliens are called "Sontarians" and Donna's mispronunciation is "Centimes" (pron. *son-teem*), 1/100th of a Euro or Franc. The German title for "The Sontaran Stratagem", *Dicke Luft*, literally means "fat/thick skies" but is, we're told, an expression meaning "trouble brewing". *Mörderischer Himmel* is murderous skies, but "Himmel" also means "Heaven".

Production

• Time and again, lists in *Doctor Who Magazine* or the *Radio Times* cited a list of the "big five" old monsters (Daleks, Cybermen, Ice Warriors, Yeti and Sontarans) until it took on the status of fact, so when the first trailers for Series 3 showed the Judoon stomping up a staircase, many people assumed that it was the Sontarans returning at last. Even though it turned out not to be, the general impression in the media and among fans was that it was "when" rather than "if" they would come back. (The Ice Warriors had to wait until X7.9, "Cold War", although X4.16, "The Waters of Mars" hinted that they were still around. The Yeti have never officially returned, but Series 7 offered us a surrogate.)

On top of this, Russell T Davies was planning to bring Martha Jones back into *Doctor Who* after her secondment to Torchwood and wanted to probe the Doctor's involvement with UNIT. As a spine for all this, there was a notion of a sinister new form of carbon-capture device – apparently a chimney-flue – and an oddly motivated workforce. Despite the hostile reception she had received in some quarters for her previous two-parter with a shopping list (X3.4-3.5, "Daleks in Manhattan"/"Evolution of the Daleks"), former script editor Helen Raynor was given this crowded brief. In discussions, the "sinister chimney" idea was replaced with a more easily-understood menace, SatNav devices, but it was only late on that the cloned workforce became hypnotised instead.

The cloning aspect of the script was reallocated to a new development: an Evil Martha subplot. Raynor had intended to call the gullible child-prodigy "Luke Marlow", as a tip of the hat to a young fan she knew (hardly the most flattering gesture, one might think), but Davies had the surname "Rattigan" left over after renaming Matron Cathelia as "Miss Foster". ("Partners in Crime": he would later call a similar character "Miss Hartigan" – X4.14, "The Next Doctor" – so his usual sense of nominative determinism was clearly in play. What the estate of Sir Terence Rattigan, a playwright of some distinction, made of this is unknown, but it's not a very common name.) Much of the script had scenes-we-would-like-to-see elements, such as more than one helmet-less Sontaran in a shot, UNIT finally getting guns to work against aliens and a large number of identical-height troopers.

• This production block was allocated to Susie Liggat, who had supervised production of X4.3, "Planet of the Ood" while Phil Collinson was handling the logistics of the Pompeii story. Collinson was finally getting a rest (a similar situation to X3.8-3.9, "Human Nature"/"The Family of Blood"). The director chosen was a veteran of many popular ITV dramas, Douglas McKinnon, whose last main credit had been Steven Moffat's *Jekyll*. He'd worked with Liggat before. Among many preparatory tasks for the producer and director was finding enough short actors to play an army of Sontarans. (Davies teased Freema Agyeman that, at last, she could tower over a monster. Catherine Tate wasn't sure if there were real people inside the costumes.)

• Neill Gorton, prosthetics designer, was as keen as anyone to retain all the features of the original John Friedlander make-up and James Acheson design for the Sontarans. Although the armour was less quilted-looking and more like the Stillsuits from *Dune*, it was agreed that the 1973 look was impossible to beat. One detail from later iterations was retained, however: Staal's facial hair was a reference to Field Major Styke in "The Two Doctors". The body-armour was based on a cast of Christopher Ryan, as Staal, but with enough give to fit all the actors recruited. Dan Starkey, as Skorr, was a huge fan of the series and an experienced stage actor, but this was his television debut.

• The first scenes to be shot were at the Rattigan Academy (it's Margam County Park, near Port Talbot, really) on Tuesday, 23rd October. The location hadn't been used in *Doctor Who* to date, but viewers of *The Sarah Jane Adventures* and *Torchwood* would have seen it as a gorgon-infested nunnery and a wedding venue. In real life, it is only one of these. (Some of the staff claim to recall Eccleston and Piper shooting there in 2004, but we can't find anything to substantiate this. Port Talbot's not so far from Cardiff that they would have needed to use the hotel as a hotel when pretending that Swansea was Victorian Cardiff in X1.3, "The Unquiet Dead".) Friday was interior work in Luke's lab (this section of the mansion was rebuilt in the 1970s after a fire).

• On Saturday, the team relocated to Pontypool, to the Usk Valley Business Park. As this complex boasts the longest corridor in the UK, it has inevitably been in *Doctor Who* before (X3.1, "Smith and Jones"). Most of the ATMOS plant was in this location but, as parts were still in use as a chemical plant, the timetabling of this and the other site

used for the invasion plan was tricky.

The Clone Tank was Caecilius's fishtank from "The Fires of Pompeii" (X4.2) and had been filled with a gruel of carrageenan, kids' powder-paint and glitter for both Ruari Mears (as the half-formed creature) and Mariam Nundy (and Clone Martha) to rise from. Mears, near blind from the mask and unable to hear even when out of the goop, compared the immersion to a sensory deprivation tank (but said it was preferable to the full-body wax he'd had to undergo in preparation). Agyeman also had to rise from it and accidentally swallowed a mouthful on the way down, but continued with the take.

Martha's disco bedstead was apparently the berth used *TW*: "Cyberwoman", and the teleport was the same one from Margam. Meanwhile, Ailsa Berk had drilled the Sontarans in how to move, starting a few weeks earlier when the extras were cast. (One was, in fact, from the accounts department of BBC Wales.) The prostheses for the speaking-role Sontarans took two to three hours to put on. The armour was lighter than it looks, but was still restricting, especially for anyone plumper than Ryan.

• On Hallowe'en, work began on Donna's house, back at the location around Nant Fawr Road. When Sylvia smashes the car window with a rubber axe, it is in fact Danny Hargreaves in a pink angora sweater, his hand shaved for the occasion. (Jacqueline King would have loved to do it, but, even with sugar-glass, it was an insurance hassle.)

• Following a request from his son, McKinnon arranged an unscripted shot from inside the TARDIS prop onto the street, with Tate in the doorway.

• The remaining ATMOS factory material was made in a less picturesque bit of Port Talbot, at Orion Electric (the production line and office overlooking it) on 9th November. The following day, the car-park of this factory was used as a supermarket car-park for the cliffhanger. As the wind was very variable, the scenes with smoke were complicated and took a lot of time to match up for continuity purposes.

• Another Sunday off (at least, not recording: the stars and production team were busy in the run-up to the Christmas episode's launch), then to Studio 5 of Upper Boat for the interior of UNIT's bigger-on-the-inside removal van. (The Mill had to augment the location footage of the articulated lorry, to make the interior dimensions less ludicrous; at the same time, the factory was digitally augmented.)

• A weekend away and then the underwhelming explosion of the UNIT Land Rover and Jo Nakashima's death were shot on the familiar Dock location in Cardiff, used so often in *Torchwood* and with the bridge that featured in "Army of Ghosts" (X2.12). The car's 60mph dive into the bay required a large pneumatic cannon to propel it into the water, in a populated area, at night. They had one shot at this, after three weeks' preparation, but several cameras were in strategic positions. They also had a crane and a diver to recover the stripped-out car before the Dock was due to be used again in the small hours. On 22nd November, news broke that Verity Lambert, the original producer of *Doctor Who*, had died.

• A few additional pick-ups came in December, notably a new insert of Rose yelling silently on the TARDIS screen (recorded on 5th as part of recording X4.11, "Turn Left" for use in X4.10, "Midnight", but only added to this episode in April 2008 after broadcast of "Partners in Crime"), and some more TARDIS interiors on 18th during work on X4.6, "The Doctor's Daughter". This was mainly Donna alone in the Ship. The scene had been written as Donna using a high-heeled shoe on the probic vent, but Tate had opted to wear trainers for most episodes, so the TARDIS mallet was used (the shoe gag was saved for the Sontarans' return in *The Sarah Jane Adventures*). Donna's mispronunciation was a throw-back to an on-set discussion in the making of "The Time Warrior" (Kevin Lindsay had over-ruled the director, on the grounds that he was a Sontaran, so ought to know).

• Post-production work included stretching the UNIT mobile command, adding veins to Mears as the embryo-creature and setting the sky aflame, but The Mill added freebies, such as the Sontaran single-pilot scout ships. They were allocated money to augment the smoke effects but the practical effects on the ground during the shoot had worked better than expected. The scripted insert of a bit of kids telly in the Sontaran Haka was planned to be *Shaun the Sheep,* but instead they used *Tommy Zoom*. One final addition was an exterior shot of the Rattigan Academy on 29th February, again using Upper Boat. This was also the day *Newsnight's* Kirsty Wark recorded her doom-laden bulletin. McKinnon knew her socially and that she'd be thrilled to be in the series.

• By now, it was traditional for the two-part returning-monster story to get a *Radio Times* cover, so Staal glowered at readers from the 22nd April edition.

X4.6: "The Doctor's Daughter"

(10th May, 2008)

Which One is This? Jenny from the Bloc: There's a plot, of sorts, but this is mainly notable for the future Mrs Tennant being pert at great length. And a drowning fish.

Firsts and Lasts Worryingly, this is the first time Donna insists she couldn't possibly imagine ever going back to live a normal life again, and she's going to travel with the Doctor forever. Everyone at home thinks: *she's doomed.*

To date, this is the last time Stephen Greenhorn wrote an episode. As with his previous go (X3.6, "The Lazarus Experiment"), it's more than slightly reminiscent of a specific *Star Trek* story (see **The Big Picture**).

Watch Out For...

• The one thing here that justifies bringing Martha back, only to be sidelined, is a scene where she becomes a mascot to an army of roly-poly fish-heads called the Hath. The main point is that she can understand their bubbly speech, which normal humans can't. And they can understand hers. Hooray! Except... this makes a lot of other stories where mutual incomprehension was the cause of conflict look a bit silly. (We might mention the Foamasi, 18.1, "The Leisure Hive", but that looks silly in so many ways already.) The scene plays to those of us without even GCSE Hath as Peck saying to his/her commanding officer something like: *she followed me home, can I keep her, Dad, huh? Can I? Huh?* and everyone else stoking Martha and saying *You're a cute little fellah, aren't you? Let's call him Spot.*

It also means that we are denied the poignancy of Peck's death scene as Martha was experiencing it. His (her?) dying words are, for us, "Ubble-ubble-ubbleooop", not as big a tearjerker for us as for her. All we see is an aquatic life-form, equipped with breathing apparatus, drowning – which raises awkward questions about how so many people read the script without anyone saying "hang on..."

[NB: for the subsequent DVD release, they

Is This the *Star Trek* Universe?

Once, nobody who knew either series well could take this question seriously. *Star Trek* and its unending stream of tie-in works and reboots was a self-contained fictional universe running by rules that seemed almost designed to annoy anyone raised on original-series *Doctor Who*. It was a world of over-achievers, with top marks in the Academy, all gollywhacking around the Galaxy to see it on their terms – not those of the worlds they briefly visited and sorted out. Everyone belonged to an orderly Federation (not entirely unlike the United States), and alien-ness was just skin-deep. Even the Borg, of whom more later, could eventually be incorporated into the set-up.

The one attempt at showing any dissent, the Maquis, were reined in and made part of the overarching brotherhood of man-like-beings. The 90s series were perfect product, smooth, efficient and largely unsurprising. Fans of these even found the occasional rough edges and oddness of the original *Trek* embarrassing, whereas this is generally the one iteration that hardcore *Doctor Who* fans really warmed to (more for nostalgia, and the ritual and familiarity of the 75 episodes shown over and again[19], than the content *per se*).

The planets visited in *Doctor Who* were supposed to be exotic, but the world of *Star Trek* was genuinely alien to us. There were all the various ethnic stereotypes in the original and the assorted semi-alien crewmembers later on, but no British accents (unless you're prepared to countenance whatever the hell James Doohan was doing[20] – when we *did* finally get someone who spoke properly, he was supposed to be French). Later, we had ships filled with brilliant engineers, but not a single one of them was from India. Comic-relief crooks aside, nobody is "just getting by". Nobody "just works here" – they are all dedicated beyond anything you ever see outside religious cults. Everything is free and abundant; no waiting-lists, queues, price-rises or cut-price supermarket own-brand versions. Nothing's homemade or second-hand. The big thing you spot if you grew up in the UK is that everything works perfectly first time. The world of *Trek*, like the self-image of the nation that made it, was a Utopia – and Utopias are, by definition, bland and tedious if not outright terrifying.

Seen from the other side of the equation, people who accepted *Star Trek* as normality-plus sometimes struggled with the worldview that old *Doctor Who* espoused by implication. The Universe was filled with malignant horrors, rarely amenable to reason or an appeal to their better natures. They often didn't *have* better natures. Humans were capable of atrocities. Earth was constantly under threat from invaders or the results of human or alien miscalculations. Worse, the people making the decisions weren't the clean-cut over-achievers of Starfleet, but a bunch of losers and chancers – ordinary people muddling through as best they could. Politicians were venal and self-interested and corporations were invariably evil and ruthless. The programme's original formulation had no higher authority than the Doctor himself; later versions had UNIT and the Time Lords as resented, misguided obstacles for him rather than a reassuring framework and back-up as the Federation was for Kirk et al.

Looked at in this light, "The Space Pirates" (6.6) is especially revealing. On the one hand, it is made up of off-the-shelf elements from B-Westerns, the consensus-future of international co-operation and FTL travel, and the sort of model-work the BBC used when the satellite feed from Cape Kennedy wasn't available[21]. Everyone has a funny accent except the Doctor and Zoe, because it's The Future and there won't be a Top Nation any more (although, unlike any other Troughton story except 5.1, "The Tomb of the Cybermen", something almost like an American accent is used for people whose job involved flying spaceships).

It sort of fits in with early 60s puppet shows such as *Space Patrol* or *Fireball XL5* in the ways it sets professionals in sharp uniforms against comic-relief amateurs dressed like saddle-tramps. But, if you look at it from the perspective of the average BBC1 viewer in 1969, it's obvious that the gleaming white space-patrol ship is staffed by idiots, and the clapped-out old banger with the ludicrous "so-larr toaster" is normality. People scrabbling around to make enough money is reality, bureaucrats with better equipment and no imagination are the bad guys, QED. The reports of viewer reaction state that the space-walks and models – the things we think of now as the padding – were the most popular element because nobody'd seen anything like them. Now that we have run into *Star Trek*, it's impossible to see "The Space Pirates" clearly, even if we had more than the one episode nobody cares for much. What people now expect is that Hermack and Warne are going to be the heroes.

The Federation was also inescapably blokey.

continued on Page 97...

made sure to redub a resounding tinkle of breaking glass to reinforce Peck's unfortunate situation. On first transmission, there was bubbling and slurping, and we needed to listen very carefully to off-air recordings for anything that might have been the stupidly-fragile life-support equipment failing in slurry.]

• The frontier world Messaline has been at war for generations, and looks remarkably like a primary school built in the 1890s. The genetic magi-mix includes a Random Accent Distribution-inator, meaning the humans all seem to come from different bits of Britain despite being born grown-up seconds before they start talking. (As the name "Messaline" is the surname of one of the actors who managed to get Dalek voices wrong – 9.1, "Day of the Daleks" – this is almost appropriate.) Cobb seems to be about 60, whilst everyone else on the planet seems to be about 20. This flagrant, clue-like anomaly looks like it's going somewhere, but don't get your hopes up.

• The scene where the Doctor distracts someone with a clockwork mouse is the kind of thing anyone old enough to remember Tom Baker thinks all *Doctor Who* used to be like. Appropriately, the rest of the episode is running up and down corridors, getting locked up in cells and Martha wandering around a quarry.

• There's one of those *girl in leather trousers does backflips to get past security lasers* scenes. The thinking, one suspects, is that nobody watching would have seen *Jay and Silent Bob Strike Back*. The girl in question is the eponymous daughter, who is introduced, made a big thing of, killed, resurrected and completely forgotten next episode and evermore. That resurrection is, like much of the rest of the episode, a straight steal from the Genesis Device from *Star Trek II: Wrath of Khan*.

• ... yes, you read that right, it's our *second* magic instant terraforming bomb in as many episodes. None of that scientifically-accurate 20,000 years of mulching and algae to get a breathable atmosphere stuff, we're using that BBC Wales standby of Sparkly Pixie-Dust technology, which is why many viewers thought that the "slain" Jenny was regenerating. Look carefully, though, and it's clearly Lime Green Sparkly Pixie-Dust and not the Orange Sparkly Pixie-Dust associated with Gallifreyan life-force.

• British viewers will also be aware that Jenny's "birth" strongly resembles the perplexingly-popular talent-oid series *Stars in Their Eyes*, wherein a member of the public walks into luminous dry-ice in a glittery shower-stall and, with the magic of editing, emerges made-up and dressed as the pop star they are going to emulate (usually Marti Pellow from Wet Wet Wet). However, anyone thinking that would have had a worse time with Richard Lazarus's rejuvenation in Greenhorn's previous script.

The Continuity

The Doctor Somehow, he can tell by feel when a machine takes a tissue sample and extrapolates it. The process gives subjects a Y-shaped scar, but he doesn't appear to have this later on [so presumably his Wolverine quick-healing factor kicked in]

He spends most of the story trying not to become close to Jenny, and softens up just in time for her tragically predictable/predictably tragic demise. Nevertheless, he can't resist saying "no, don't do that" whenever Jenny's done something particularly violent. He properly warms to her when she sorts out some lasers by, erm, being ostentatiously physically adroit. [His reaction is written as if she had done something mentally agile, rather than gymnastics.]

[The Doctor doesn't stick around for Jenny's funeral, never checks up on the planet afterwards and leaves thinking she's dead. However, by "Death in Heaven" (X8.12), Clara references Jenny as separate from the Doctor's children and grandchildren who are "assumed to be dead". Did the Doctor air suspicions about Jenny's survival, or is Clara remembering one of her multiple selves' experiences?]

He finally calls Martha 'Doctor Jones' when saying goodbye to her.

• *Background.* Some time in the past, he was a father. He's very vague when explaining it to Donna, but he 'lost all that a long time ago, along with everything else'. When he looks at Jenny, he says, 'I can see them. The hole they left, all the pain that filled it.'

To him, being a Time Lord is as much a cultural experience as a biological one with 'a sum of knowledge, a code, a shared history, a shared suffering'. [This last one is probably a reference to the War (unless everyone else on the planet thought that 20.1, "Arc of Infinity" was as excruciating as we did).] He also says that the Time Lords aren't 'for' anything in particular.

• *Ethics.* Unsurprisingly, blatant announce-

Is This the *Star Trek* Universe?

continued from Page 95...

The assumed audience for *Trek* was young men with a military/engineering bent. This assumption is the whole reason Slash fiction began. *Doctor Who* was conceived in 1962/3 as a series for the whole family and, in its original line-up, reflected this in the TARDIS crew. Although once Barbara had left, the tendency was towards younger women as the usual assistant/companion, this was achieved by reconfiguring the Doctor himself to incorporate many of the matronly, common-sense attributes of the sensibly-shod schoolmarm. At the same time, the crossover from "family" to "children" began to make the programme's profile less like that of any usual drama series. Nonetheless, when *Doctor Who* did a story about the Gunfight at the OK Corral (3.8, "The Gunfighters"), it was parodic in parts, but also very much "straight" drama in the real Tombstone, as opposed to the goofy unreality of *Trek*'s essay on the topic ("Shadow of the Gun").

Oil and water, then. Nobody would think that, even being occasionally set in the same time-period and planets near Earth, there was any prospect or reason to mix the two. But people did. The all-engulfing tendency of fan-ficcers to do crossovers means that we've been having stories about these worlds colliding since the mid-70s. Both series are, it must be said, pretty shameless in making use of other fictional settings and milieux, albeit with peculiar results in original *Trek* (all those planets that "just happen" to be Prohibition Era Chicago, Nazi Germany, Imperial Rome, Greek Mythology...). Once again, the tendency has been for *Doctor Who* to do it more on the original's terms, and *Trek* to enclose the society and setting inside the *Trek* rule-book. If this traditional demarcation of approaches were to hold good, then you might expect the TARDIS to materialise aboard the USS *Enterprise* in a *Doctor Who* story, but the crew of said ship to make a holodeck game of playing at being characters from BBC television back in the era of 2D broadcasts (like in the Diane Duane novel *My Enemy, My Ally*).

As we've often said, you can date any TV space franchise by what it thinks come fitted as standard for the capital-F "Future", and anything made in the 1960s (and not a slightly risible dystopia) will look like footnotes to *Destination Moon*. English-language franchises starting in the same period assume a rough couple of centuries, and then a magical breakthrough to some Faster Than Light space-engine with no intervening stages such as Generation Starships. Where the differences lie is in how desirable this model of the future seems. We see in Volume 3 how first *Doomwatch*, and then *Star Trek*, become what lazy writers first think of when they try to pay bills by knocking off a quick *Who*. *Star Trek* had an initial impact simply by taking a lot of the printed SF staples and putting them on screen for the first time... or rather for the first time with an adequate budget and no concessions to toy manufacturers.

Most of what *Doctor Who* writers after 1970 borrowed from *Trek* was itself borrowed from the *Lensman* series, the *Foundation* trilogy, *Voyage of the Space Beagle* and a whole tradition of over 30 years'-worth of prose which had itself generated parodies and no-hang-on-a-sec rethinks. The two most influential script-editors after David Whitaker's founding year, Terrance Dicks and Robert Holmes, were steeped in this stuff back when everyone else thought of childcare when they heard the name "Spock". Some of the writers working with them used the public's new familiarity with starships and teleports as a short-cut, others had few ideas beyond these hand-me-downs, but Holmes and Dicks were a few jumps ahead and had read, or thought up, the rethinks before the BBC1 viewership had been introduced to the concepts.

Whatever the causes of this compulsion to put one TV series "inside" another, there's no reason why it should be either of these. 1960s visions of the future are much of a muchness, either optimistic and broadly Fabianist or pessimistic and quasi-Soviet. It's not as if there are only two television series set in space, or with the capacity to incorporate other fictions within itself as these two have done. It could be argued, for example, that the near-future space operatics of both shows can be squeezed into the mid-60s German series *Raumpatrouille*, since this sets up a World Space Authority compatible with any *Doctor Who* story set between 2100 and 2800.[22] We've seen how the sheer promiscuity of *Doctor Who* and the powerful impact of prior British SF material came to make different aspects of the series so intuitively compatible with *Quatermass* and *Dan Dare* (see **What Kind of Future Did We Expect?** under 2.2, "The Dalek Invasion of Earth" and **Is This the Quatermass Continuum?** under 15.3, "Image of the Fendahl") as to warrant essays. This is often the

continued on Page 99...

ments of intentional genocide get on his nerves. In a moment of unexpected honesty, he tells Jenny that after a while, killing infects and one can never be rid of it again.

The genetic duplication process offends him. So does killing people out of mere intellectual sloppiness. Having observed the extreme willingness of the Messalines to resort to mythological thinking, he picks up a gun, lets everyone think that he's about to shoot Cobb with it, and then tosses it aside and tells them to make the foundation of their society 'a man who never would'. [So, not the least delusions of godhood then.]

• *Inventory: Sonic Screwdriver.* It finds the secret map Easter Egg and unlocks level two. Donna's mobile is given the Superphone upgrade, so it can call Martha's.

• *Inventory: Other.* There's the usual glasses and the stethoscope. Also a grey clockwork mouse that the Doctor uses first to distract a guard, then to test scary destructive lasers that tragically disintegrate it. He also carries a pad of paper and pen.

The TARDIS The Doctor informs us that She's instituted a paradox: they arrived on Messaline because of Jenny's existence there, but arrived some time too early and ending up creating her instead. There wasn't and isn't a forthcoming explanation as to how this worked, except that his hand is there bubbling away like billy-oh. [Every other instance of the TARDIS creating a loop such as this is either because the fate of the Universe is at stake (X3.13a, "Time Crash"), or the Doctor's well-being is in jeopardy (X4.8, "Silence in the Library" et seq.) There has not, to date, been any consequence of this story's events, but we can't rule it out.]

The Supporting Cast
• *Donna.* She wasn't perturbed by the Doctor having a disembodied hand in the TARDIS, but is slightly freaked to learn it's his.

While she encourages the Doctor to accept Jenny, up to half-ordering the Time Lord to take her along as a companion, she's appalled by the idea of anyone using her biology to have children.

In keeping with the "Supertemp" theme we've been hearing this season, this week she deduces the improbable structure of the Messaline society from the numerical plaques about the place. She tells the Doctor with a perfectly straight face that she worked out the Dewey Decimal system in two

days, during a six-month period as a temp in Hounslow Library. [There's several reasons it's tempting to place this between X3.0, "The Runaway Bride" and X4.1, "Partners in Crime", including the aptness of a companion trying to find the Doctor by working at a library.] By the end of the story, she's convinced that she'll never go back to normal life ever again.

Rather than assuming, she asks the Doctor for the feminine form of 'Time Lord' is [c.f. X8.12, "Death in Heaven"]. Once more, she objects to being considered the Doctor's "woman".

Her friend Nerys apparently fathered twins with a turkey baster. [That's the same Nerys who was Donna's arch-rival in "The Runaway Bride".]

• *Martha.* Self-confident enough about her medical skills to be sure that she can fix an alien's dislocated shoulder first go. She's rather more shouty and sobby than when she was a full-time companion; when first confronted by the Hath, she asks, 'I'm Dr Martha Jones – who the hell are you?'

Here Martha disobeys the Doctor's instructions to stay put, and – against her new chum Peck's misgivings – leaves the safety of the Hath camp to investigate the Source. This directly results in Peck's death by drowning, when he gives his life to save her. His death distresses her, but she refrains from mentioning it to either the Doctor or Donna. However much she still enjoys stepping out into new worlds, life in the TARDIS is currently a bit much for her, and she gets the Doctor to drop her at home.

Planet Notes
• *Messaline.* The planet has three moons and lots of mud. The atmosphere is largely a nitrogen/oxygen blend, with high ozone levels. There are also some radiation spikes, high enough to hurt a human in the short term.

The colonists arrived in a fusion-drive transport spaceship. Their reproduction is via machines, which recombine the genetic 46 chromosomes of a human into two sets of 23, then shuffles and deals. It works by taking a tissue sample from the person in question, creating a Y-shaped scar. People who lack these have 'clean' hands and there's a strong cultural imperative to put them in the genetics machine right away. Jenny refers to herself as a Generation 5000 soldier. [This is more likely the number of her cohort than a date. Force-cloning humans was beyond even the Bi-Al

Is This the *Star Trek* Universe?

continued from Page 97...

case when we have one overarching media version of The Future that is in the ascendant.

To be blunt, the degree of consensus between individual *Doctor Who* writers is more noticeable on this score than in the compatibility of one future-set adventure of the TARDIS crew and another broadcast a year earlier or later – the details of *Trek* chronology and *Who* timelines differ less across series than examples within each series contradict each other. Even though the depiction of the twenty-third century in *Doctor Who* is sketchy, the details we get don't allow for the utopian set-up of the Federation (unless the minority view of the dating for 9.2, "The Curse of Peladon" is right) or Starfleet.

The number of times in the Pertwee years when we can read "Vulcan" for "Venusian" when discussing neck-pinches or Shanghorns makes the possibility of interaction at least plausible. Could the future history of *Star Trek* have taken place in the same chronology that had the Silurians, the Ice Warriors and the Daemons? To begin with, the dates for *Trek* are fairly clearly set out, and the events in Earth's neck of the woods at the same dates in *Doctor Who* rule out an United Federation of Planets, Vulcans, Klingons or seemingly-interchangeable-humanoids-with-onesies-and-funny-foreheads, even a San Francisco for Starfleet to use as a base (see **Whatever Happened to the USA?** under 4.6, "The Moonbase"). Although the Eugenics Wars of the 1990s seem to have slid down the same temporal back-of-a-settee as Mars Probe 7 landing in the early 70s (see **Was There a Martian Time-Slip?** under X4.16, "The Waters of Mars"), the rest of the timeline of pre-Kirk space-travel requires a lot of *Doctor Who* events supposedly at the same time not to have happened. Two are conspicuously absent.

You'd think enslavement by the Daleks in 2157 would have made the fledgling Federation less of an attractive prospect for the surviving population of Earth. You'd think that the Cybermen would have provided a neat dress-rehearsal for encounters with the Borg. What's worth noting about *Doctor Who*'s future is that, despite the repeated bad experiences Earth's population kept having with aliens, the basic assumption was that they weren't *all* bad. It was still worth trying to find the positives. Nonetheless, the humans keep their guard up. The touchy-feely UFP is the result of an Earth whose only encounters with extraterrestrial life have been positive, mutually-enriching exchanges of point-of-view and leisurewear. The problem of there being an Earth colony some time in the twenty-first century called "Vulcan" is relatively trivial (4.3, "The Power of the Daleks"). The planet was obviously named after the one in the old TV series, itself named after a figure from Roman mythology.

The sequence of events outlined in the film *Star Trek: First Contact* is less tractable. For this to be the very start of space-warp technology on Earth, so close to the posited dates for "The Power of the Daleks", "Nightmare of Eden" (17.4) or the definite, repeatedly-stated date of "The Moonbase" is awkward at the very least. If 2062 is the dawn of space-flight as we see it, and the eponymous First Contact from the planet Vulcan... the *other* planet Vulcan, why is everyone taking it so much for granted as something generations old by 2090? And why, in 2070, are the Cybermen more of a historical given, from a century earlier, than a near-terminal World War III in the 2050s that nobody in *Doctor Who* ever talks about? (Mind you, nobody in these stories talks about that day in 2047 when the Moon hatched and a space-chicken laid another egg as big as itself; X8.7, "Kill the Moon". Most viewers have also agreed never to speak of this again.)

For many decades neither series mentioned the existence of the other. There was one specific incident where the *Enterprise* database seemed more than usually knowledgeable about the cast of *Doctor Who* (*TNG*: "The Neutral Zone", in which Claire Raymond's descendants include William Hartnell, Patrick Troughton, Jon Pertwee, Tom Baker, Peter Davidson – sic – and Colin Baker), but not once, in the original 26-year run of *Doctor Who*, did anyone say anything about boldly going, beaming up or not wearing red shirts if you want to survive to the end of the episode.

The BBC Wales series has mentioned *Star Trek* fairly often, but in contexts where it's presented as purely fictional; the entire point of the Spock references in "The Empty Child" (X1.9) is so that Rose can establish that Jack doesn't have much knowledge of pop culture of the twentieth century, suggesting that *Star Trek* is just as ubiquitous in the *Doctor Who* universe and just as fictional. Ditto the Doctor's Vulcan salute in X2.11, "Fear Her". Ditto the Klingon language being a stigma of losers in X6.11, "The God Complex". Ditto Craig's comments

continued on Page 101...

Foundation's abilities c.5000 AD; see 15.2, "The Invisible Enemy"].

The machines force-grow and educate; Jenny comes out with a working knowledge of the local weaponry and the inculcated outlook of a soldier, plus one of several possible English accents. Names are assigned later. General Cobb indicates that the machines have many different settings; there could be colonists rather than soldiers. [See **History** for a possible way to account for this.]

The Hath and Humans were meant to colonise the planet together. Phase One went well; robot drones built an underground city that the planetary terraforming would expose. After the mission commander's death, it all went very wrong, with no agreement on who ought to take over. The one part of their shared background is a creation myth about the Source, which both sides believe controls the planet's destiny. [We can guess that the rapid generational turnover was intended to aid rapid colonisation, so would have been a virtue rather than a flaw.] On the human side, it's resulted in something quite like a religion, in which the garbled memories of the terraforming gas has been romanticised into a story about the importance of the Breath of God. [A 'she' in this version; perhaps the mission commander was female, or the chief scientist.] Both camps seem to have anti-war factions, but the pacifists haven't stopped hostilities.

The Non-Humans

• *Time Lords.* The Doctor denies that looking like Earth's ape-descended species implies any more than a superficial somatic resemblance. Nonetheless, Jenny is born with two hearts [see Volumes 1 and 2, and **When Did the Doctor Get a Second Heart?** under 6.1, "The Dominators"]. A bullet between these kills her, but doesn't mess up her T-shirt. [For reasons we'll elaborate in **Things That Don't Make Sense**, the fact that the machinery works on the Doctor is A) indicative of Gallifreyan biology being more like mammalian terrestrial life than we are sometimes led to expect, and B) deeply bonkers.]

• *Hath.* Fish-headed humanoids, generally at least six feet tall. They wear boots and combat gear and have four-fingered hands and opposable thumbs. They appear to have shoulders like ours, which can get dislocated. All we see of their skin is the neck and head of a fish, with pulsating gills [in whichever Hath is nearest the camera], blueish

scales on top and pinkish below. They're each equipped with a fitted black leather facemask, in which is mounted a glass cylinder that is slightly luminous and contains green bubbling liquid. [The bubbles are loud and correspond to the half of the conversation Martha has with them, so we're led to assume this is their speech.] They also have bulbous noses, like baboons or elephant seals. They reproduce in the same way as the humans.

We're told that they arrived on this world with the humans. [This pushes the question of their origin further into the background. The next time we see them, it's in a montage of invasions of Earth prior to 2008 – X5.1, "The Eleventh Hour" – which raises all sorts of questions, but makes more sense than the Ood invasion we also missed according to the Atraxi records. A Hath appears in the background at the bar where Jack meets Alonso in X4.18, "The End of Time Part Two". Another appears in the Maldorvarium in X9.1, "The Magician's Apprentice".]

History

• *Dating.* It's 6012-07-24 [just go straight to **Things That Don't Make Sense**]. If Donna's right, this means it's Space Date 24th July, 6012. The colonists and Hath used the New Byzantium Calendar, which is Space Date/Year/Month/Day in format. [The old one ceased trading when Constantinople fell to the Ottomans in the 1450s, by our calendar. Even if they started a new one today, that would put this at 8027 at the earliest.

[If this is the one used by the Persian Empire, who never actually conquered Byzantium but were never averse to rewriting history in their favour, this may just be our one with 561 years added, starting from Cyrus the Great. That would put us at 5583 AD, so at least it's not the sodding fifty-first century again. This might well mean that what looks like genetic anagrams is a refinement of the Kilbracken Technique ("The Invisible Enemy"), so the people produced won't live long anyway.

[Alternatively, if this calendar's name indicates that it's a refinement of an Old Byzantium Calendar, that suggests Earth origin. If they are using one from a planet called "New Byzantium", it may have been named by humans, but there's no guarantee that the people here aren't from Planet Zog. (Early scripts named them as 'Takrans' rather than humans, for what that's worth.) With

Is This the *Star Trek* Universe?

continued from Page 99...

on the teleporter in X6.12, "Closing Time". Both Davies and Moffat were very clear on this one; Chibnall's been silent.

Of course, if we keep on this road, we have to wonder whether Craig and Chloe are familiar with any "local" equivalent to *Doctor Who*, and that way madness lies. From the point of view of the tie-in material, *Doctor Who* has generally treated *Star Trek* as fictional: Big Finish's "Bang-Bang-a-Boom!" did a vicious parody of *Deep Space Nine* and the Eurovision Song Contest; Kate Orman's *The Left-Handed Hummingbird* had Benny mistaking *Next Generation* for a documentary. (One exception to all of this was IDW's *Star Trek: The Next Generation/Doctor Who* comic-book crossover.) Oddly enough, *Star Trek* references tend to treat *Doctor Who* as real; several of the novels have surreptitious cameos of *Doctor Who* characters, and the Temporal Cold War borrows ideas from *Doctor Who* up to and including the dimensionally-transcendental time machine.

US television's cultural imperialism made it seem that the makers of *Star Trek*, especially in the 90s, could act as if they could engulf any other television series or set of stories "inside" their all-conquering juggernaut, while the BBC, even today, presents *Doctor Who* as happening in more-or-less "our" world – a world where there was a show that those-people-over-there watched seriously, but that everyone had heard of and – if nothing else – at least enjoyed the quirky, shambolic 60s *Trek*. (See **Is Kylie from Planet Zog?** under X4.0, "Voyage of the Damned" for what the BBC and Davies in particular assumed about the viewers' tastes.) We all know the difference between *Star Trek* and reality, even if we're actually just characters in *Doctor Who*. Of course, some characters in *Doctor Who* are also characters in other things (26.2, "Ghost Light", for example, has Mrs Grose from *The Turn of the Screw* in an earlier incident in her career) and some are kept ambiguous (see 25.1, "Remembrance of the Daleks" and "Image of the Fendahl").

As is now well-documented, the Borg are as much as anything a thought-experiment in how much difference the Federation format and *Star Trek* itself can accommodate. They first appeared in an episode of *Star Trek: The Next Generation* with the otherwise inappropriate title "Q Who". These beefed-up cyborgs are not nice and, after the long string of episodes about getting the Klingons and the Romulans to sing from the Federation hymn-sheet, they seemed to be beings with, as Terrance Dicks said of the Daleks, no redeeming features. In short, *Doctor Who* monsters. Specifically, the Cybermen as originally conceived in 1966. Although they are all about assimilation and smoothing over differences between species, the Borg aren't themselves capable of co-existing with the all-assimilating Federation. They even go around saying "Resistance is futile", a cliché so hoary that Douglas Adams parodied it in the pilot episode of *Hitchhiker's* (and the Mondas Cybermen said it more interestingly). The Lumic-model Cybermen (X2.5, "Rise of the Cybermen" et seq) returned the compliment by giving them oddly Borg-like catch-phrases and faculties, and their latest upgrade (X7.13, "Nightmare in Silver") is *TNG*: "The Best of Both Worlds" in Alton Towers. With the Mule. "World Enough and Time" and "The Doctor Falls" (X10.11, X10.12) took this further.

It's noteworthy that they played "Q Who" and all subsequent Borg stories relatively straight, whereas *Doctor Who* never borrowed from *Trek* without a wry smile or a barely-concealed sneer (see, just for starters, 17.3, "The Creature From the Pit" for a contemptuous point-for-point revision of *Trek*: "Devil in the Dark" or 9.4, "The Mutants" for how a typical *Trek* scenario would have played out if Starfleet were run by jobsworths and the Doctor wandered in one day). It's taken as read by everyone except Kit Pedler that what we can loosely call the Federation model is laughably optimistic.

For all that Davies made sure his writers and designers avoided anything overtly *Trek*-like, to the extent that they delayed visiting an alien world for a whole year and explicitly stated that the Hospital in X2.1, "New Earth" had to avoid looking anything like American series (not that this stopped the quarantine area resembling the Borg collective, green light and all), the associations and cumulative details in the BBC Wales version of *Who* are inflected with *Trek*. Some have very similar plots and situations (Stephen Greenhorn's two efforts are noticeable, but try watching X7.15, "The Day of the Doctor" and the *Next Generation* finale "All Good Things" back to back. Billie Piper is more or less playing Q.) It's also inflected with a lot of late 70s films, BBC sitcoms and Australian soaps and, as we said, promiscuous. However, if the Chula spaceship's technology in "The Doctor Dances" (X1.10), seems, shall we say, enterprising, it's not a

continued on Page 103...

ABOUT TIME 2008-2009

this production team, the former is more likely, so this date could be as close as the fifty-sixth century, but it could just as well be The Space Year 17000 (12.4, "Genesis of the Daleks").]

Rightly or wrongly, the humans have equipment with UNIT decals on them.

The Analysis

The Big Picture As we've mentioned above and will again in **The Lore**, the root of this story was in a comment Stephen Greenhorn made in *Doctor Who Magazine* about the unchanging nature of the Doctor. Davies called his bluff and commissioned a story where the Doctor undergoes an irrevocable change. Acquiring a daughter by conventional means was unpalatable (see **Does He... You Know... Dance?** under X3.4, "Daleks in Manhattan"), so it had to entail a maguffin. In many series, the protagonist gains a daughter only to lose her at the end of the episode (usually by discovering that she wasn't really his and it was a con, or in gunfire). It's as much a staple as the *They Might be Giants* episode (see X4.14, "The Next Doctor"), the amnesia episode (usually when the hero is tempted to give it all up and have a normal life – see X3.8, "Human Nature") and the imposter episode (X4.4, "The Sontaran Stratagem").

Inevitably, we have to mention *Star Trek*. This sort of thing didn't happen much in the original series (someone vetoed McCoy's daughter being one of the space-hippies in "The Way to Eden", although the rest of the episode and indeed Season Three proceeded with few such second-thoughts). In *Star Trek II: The Wrath of Khan*, Kirk turned out to have had a son he didn't know about, and who hated everything he stood for, but then just as abruptly died in the next film along. We'll return to this film in a moment, but consider also *The Next Generation* episode "The Offspring". In this, Data the android builds an avatar of himself, to see whether there's more to him than his construction and programming. It is given female characteristics and called "Lal". Obviously, being female, Lal gets messed up by emotions and has to shut down, but is absorbed into Data's memory-core, supposedly to change him forever. And yet, in the very next episode, he's the same as always, unable to use contractions.

For Jenny to *really* make a change to the Doctor's life, she would have to survive and travel

with the Doctor and Donna – and this was impossible, given the big plan afoot to do something with Donna at the end of the series. To shelve this was out of the question: Catherine Tate was so in-demand, her committing to one year was enough of a surprise. Ironically, a big change was to come by accident in two episodes' time, when yet another time-travel gimmick refreshed yet another TV-show staple and gave the Doctor a wife he hadn't met yet (X4.8, "Silence in the Library" et seq.).

So Davies both caused this story to be and prevented it from coming to fruition. He also imposed the Hath as a cute idea for an alien race that communicate in burbles. As we mentioned under "The Fires of Pompeii" (X4.2), a suspiciously-similar race, the Selacians, had already appeared in two BBC Books novels by Steve Lyons. The second of these, *The Final Sanction*, was about the Doctor not being able to change history and thus made the humans' military set-up impossible to oppose. "The Doctor's Daughter", by contrast, is supposedly a commentary on the Doctor's own revulsion at war – having been in a fairly big one lately – and yet is within a series that constantly make a big point of all his friends becoming soldiers one way or another. Greenhorn and Davies are at cross-purposes here and inevitably the one in charge will get the last word. Pacifism is therefore hypocritical folly; the showrunner has spoken, and there's an end to it.

One feature of this story that is seldom commented upon is that the entire story follows logically (as much as anything *can* in this format) from the central conceit of a machine that makes large numbers of grown-ups. It's an image used a lot in advertising, but not as often as it seems in films. Even *Star Wars Episode II: Attack of the Clones* had the eponymous clones growing up faster than usual (whatever "usual" means when Skywalker *pere et fils* both seem to reach adulthood in three years), but from embryo to hundreds of kid Boba Fetts to hundreds of Jango-a-likes. The most common manifestation is hundreds of the same face, a notion best used in *Being John Malkovich* (see X4.17, "The End of Time Part One").

Artificially-created adults, since Frankenstein's Monster (from a novel intended as, amongst other things, a critique of Lockean education theories), are more normally made one at a time. Inside the machine, the soldiers receive an implanted education limited to what they need to know to fight.

Is This the *Star Trek* Universe?

continued from Page 101...

sign that fifty-first century aliens belong in the same narrative, the same "ontic sphere", as twenty-fourth century humans. The Daleks and the Imperial forces in *Star Wars* both seem like futuristic versions of 30s Germany, but they aren't in any way causally related within the fiction.

You're getting the picture. Despite a significant lack of any awareness of the other version of history even as a fiction to play with, neither twenty-third century allows the possibility of the other. Nobody in *Star Trek* seems to have heard of *Doctor Who* or even the BBC, whilst nobody in original-series *Doctor Who* knew that *Trek* had been on telly. The revived series acknowledges it as the general public's default idea of "The Future" but nobody in *Star Trek* has ever heard of *Star Trek*, therefore that future cannot follow from a present that has "Closing Time" in it. QED. Slam dunk. Sorted.

But there's a wild card we can play. After decades of stories where the protagonists have striven, successfully, to prevent alterations to "the" timeline we've had two drastic revisions to the *Trek* chronology that weren't reset at the end of the episode. *Star Trek: Enterprise* started the final season with a run of episodes that acknowledged how borderline-fascistic the Federation can look to anyone not enamoured of it. (The only-slightly-revised version of the triumphalist and historically-dodgy Soviet-free history of spaceflight was chilling. But not as good as *Blakes 7*, the definitive "evil" Federation.) The next version of the franchise to come our way (after a decent interval for people to forget the last episode) was a feature film that peeled off a second track of *Trek* continuity that is contingent on the first, but in which everything after Kirk left Starfleet Academy is up for grabs, and so they can remake any story they like. Leonard Nimoy pops up as "Spock Prime", the only person in this palimpsest who recalls how things "ought" to unfold, then gets to watch his homeworld get destroyed as a consequence of (ahem) a Time War. And now there's *Star Trek: Discovery*. Or not, depending on who you ask.

As we will see in a later essay, the world of "The Ambassadors of Death" (7.3) significantly differs from that of every other UNIT-era story (except, perhaps, 13.4, "The Android Invasion" and possibly 26.1, "Battlefield"). This has been a source of slight embarrassment, and occasional efforts to discuss it end in a decision to grin sheepishly and change

the subject. The key point is that we end this story with a British-led space programme landing people on Mars in the early 1970s and making a worldwide telecast of a First Contact with immeasurably wise and powerful aliens in a garden centre. Apart from the television aspect (and it's hinted that John Wakefield's been asked to prevent the transmission going any further than that room), there's a lot of interesting ways that situation can develop – none of them compatible with any other *Doctor Who* story set after 1970.

This sets up an entirely different question: how exactly the TARDIS managed to end up in a different universe when this shouldn't be possible any more, but that's an order of magnitude down as a problem. (IDW's solution, for what it's worth, is that the Lumic-universe Cybermen picked the Next Generation model of *Trek* to visit because they hope to team up with – and then betray – the Borg. The Doctor fell through that gateway and his vague memory of a Kirk-Tom Baker encounter was a "ghost" memory of a deleted timeline.) It's not beyond the range of possibility that the Doctor was going to an alternate universe that he's already visited pre-Time War. The only other one he'd definitively gone to hails from 7.4, "Inferno" and that's hardly a tourist spot, but we have strong hints that he was going to pay a lot of visits to Avillion ("Battlefield") in later lives.

In a few essays from now, we'll get into the whole knotty issue of alternate universes and altered timelines (**How is This Not an Alternate Universe?** under "Turn Left"), but there's one pocket-universe we have to take into account: the Land of Fiction (6.2, "The Mind Robber"). If that story were to have been made now, with a free hand and unlimited money for rights issues to be resolved, it's probable that the Karkus would have been replaced by Spock. If any story made up by humans is amenable to being realised in this realm, then long-running franchises must be there. (After all, the story's author, Peter Ling, started off with the fact that he'd written for *Crossroads* and had to answer mail sent to the characters.) Indeed, if Zoe and her friends were following any TV series at the hot-house for child genii in The City, it would most likely be *Trek*. There, now you've got a mental image of her life before going to the Wheel as a hybrid of *Muppet Babies* and *The Big Bang Theory*. You may need a shower.

(You may start wondering if there's some sort of

continued on Page 105...

This is a more common idea. Its most detailed use in legitimate printed SF was John Scalzi's *Old Man's War* and sequels, where the disparity between having access to facts/skills and having any personal experience or even a name is specifically used in a military context. However, it has been common as a critique of educational practices since William Blake. From the utilitarian advantages of schools to create a workforce for the industrial age (as ridiculed by Dickens in *Hard Times* – see "The Next Doctor" again) to the Teaching Machines in 6.4, "The Krotons" (and possibly 2.5, "The Web Planet") and the "Speedlearn" system in "The General", an episode of *The Prisoner*, this has been a persistent criticism. Army satires from *The Good Soldier Svejk* to *Catch 22* have touched on it. However, the more complex form of parthenogenesis introduced here is one that allows individual differences and that lets Jenny stand out. It also lets the rest of the story's premise flow on so that this is less a string of set-pieces than usual.

There *are*, however, set-pieces. One in particular stands out. The image of a girl in tight clothes doing gymnastics to evade security lasers is one that can be dated to the otherwise pointless film *Entrapment,* but soon was a cliché in advertising and pop videos. Britney Spears's other hit "Toxic" (see X1.2, "The End of the World") used it and it was ridiculed by Kevin Smith and dozens of cartoons. The use of lasers as easily-broken beams for security is well-established in real museums (see 17.2, "City of Death" for a very famous example), but lethal lasers capable of evaporating clockwork mice are still only found in films.

Back to *Wrath of Khan*. In this, the Doomsday Machine is a gadget called the Genesis Device which created life from dead rock in seconds through the magic of "proto-matter" and, thus, kills anyone in the wake of its detonation. Luckily, Spock's nobly sacrificed himself to get the *Enterprise* to safety, so they do a space burial-at-sea and his body lands on the planet they've made come to life – so there's a sequel where he's resurrected. Apart from engendering any number of noble sacrifices where the hero is denied a last cuddle with the soon-to-be-dead chum because of thick anti-radiation glass (X4.18, "The End of Time Part Two" riffs on this), this story's scenario must strike even the most *Trek*-blind reader as a bit familiar.

The main source of the iconography of this story, though, is 70s *Doctor Who* (or at least a folk-memory of it). More overtly fannish writers have replicated specific incidents or storylines (see X3.7, "42"; X2.8, "The Impossible Planet"; as well as reintroductions of old characters or aliens), Greenhorn is channelling a whole half-remembered tradition and marrying it to a sort-of-impression of *Next Generation* plotting. We will pick up on this in the **Critique**, but as with the last two years of the old series, there is a sense of this being written within a set of intuitive associations of ideas and images.

English Lessons [Just to reiterate, General Cobb's accent is a real one, from Bristol (home of Dave Prowse and Cary Grant), in the South West of England just next to Wales. It's the accent people were using in X8.9, "Flatline", which was set in that city because *Being Human* was, or something. Robert Newton's attempt at this accent in *Treasure Island* led to the idea that pirates talk a specific way. In fact, as so much of New England was populated by people who sailed from there, and named so many places after West Country towns, it's possible that this slurring of consonants and slightly strangled vowels is the origin of the standard American accent. (Bristolians are notorious for their inability to pronounce the letter T – referring to their home town as "Brissle", for example). Anyway, just to be clear, this is what actors trying to sound rural or nautical are usually attempting to emulate – see Volume 3B for an exhaustive look at "Mummerset" and "Pigbins" and **What are the Dodgiest Accents in the Series?** under 4.1, "The Smugglers". That story is set in Cornwall, further to the south and west, so you now have a yardstick for comparison.]

• *Kew Gardens* (n.): Technically that's the Royal Botanical Gardens, Kew. It's in Richmond (a couple of tube stops from Chiswick), which is now in South West London but was, in 1759, south west of London, and has vast Victorian greenhouses, Regency arboreta and space-age conservation spaces, plus 30,000 plant species being conserved and bred. If you've ever seen the Trooping of the Colour and wonder what happens to all the horse manure, there's your answer.

• *Chinese Whispers* (n.): The British expression for the game Americans call "telephone".

• *Nut-Job* (n.): Lunatic, in a term generally agreed to have originated in 70s school soap *Grange Hill* (the apparent origin of a lot of Donna's

Is This the *Star Trek* Universe?

continued from Page 103...

metaleptic "bleed through" of real elements of one reality into another's fiction, much as the Flash of Earth-1, as DC Comics told us in the 60s, grew up reading the adventures of his predecessor, the Flash of Earth-2, in comic-book form. Cervantez did that joke better.)

So the old DC standby of the "Boom Tube" might be in play, but otherwise there's no crossover between *Star Trek* and *Doctor Who*. Except one comic series, by a company that, briefly, had the rights to both: IDW. However, this story makes it clear that even if there has been the occasion incursion between the two spaces (there's been at least one other; the Doctor is shown meeting Kirk, back when he was still wearing a scarf and carting round jelly babies – the Doctor, not Kirk, that is), they're explicitly parallel, or at least alternate, realities. It's noticeable that the Doctor's trio never say "Blimey! It's just like *Star Trek* on telly". That's not the only comic to have the rights simultaneously. In the next essay, we'll be having a look at a messed-up incident where the Doctor and Kirk did exactly the same things in one of the freakiest manifestations of non-television *Who*.

---

slang – see also "Flippin' 'Eck" in X11.11, "Resolution"). It's appropriate as "cob" is an old word for a hazelnut. (In which case, it's lucky they didn't make a pun on "kernel".)

• *Miss Saigon* (n): Most of you will know that this is a musical based on *Madame Butterfly* (see 27.0, "The TV Movie", if you must), and more of you than is statistically likely will know that John Barrowman and Naoko Mori were in the West End production in the late 90s.

Oh, Isn't That...?

• *Nigel Terry* (General Cobb). Best known as King Arthur in John Boorman's *Excalibur*. He'd been doing telly since the late 60s – check out his turn as a hippy in *Randall and Hopkirk (Deceased)* and a stand-out part in *The Lion in Winter*. He had the title role in Derek Jarman's *Caravaggio* and did a few other arthouse projects (another Jarman and a couple of Greenaways) in between the usual cop-show rounds. The last starring role on television we can think of is a mini-series, *The Mushroom Picker*, in which he played an earthy Russian with an even more singular accent.

• *Georgia Moffett* (Jenny). She'd done some Big Finish work (in "Red Dawn" and "City of Spires", and as Avril Fenman, a Bernice Summerfield villain) and had a high-profile part in *The Bill*. In real life, she's Peter Davison's daughter (the *Radio Times* made hay out of this at the time). Everyone involved strenuously denied that her casting was at all a publicity stunt. She and David Tennant keep details of their relationship quiet, but they're now married and have children. She was an instrumental producer (and also appeared as herself, very pregnant) of her father's spoof *The Five(ish) Doctors Reboot*.

• *Joseph Dempsie* (Cline). Chris Miles off *Skins*.

He also landed up in *Game of Thrones* as Gendry, an apprentice blacksmith and bastard of the king.

Things That Don't Make Sense *[Brace yourselves, gang: apart from the frequent and obvious science-fails and logical flaws, this story manages to screw up basic character-continuity for the regulars, something we're told was the Davies era's key strength. We'll be here a while.]*

Taste aside, there's a basic problem with that catchpenny title. Jenny is a rearrangement of the Doctor's chromosomal information into a different configuration, with no genetic input from anyone else. This makes her his sister, not daughter.

The Hath and the Humans arrived together on the same ship, and appear to have come from the same place, yet they have no means of communication. Wouldn't a translator-machine be more useful than a genetic kaleidoscope and assault troops? If the Monoids could manage it (3.6, "The Ark"), there shouldn't be any difficulty. At the very least, a slate and some chalk might have been an idea. How can Martha's new best friend be called "Peck"? They can't pronounce the word and don't do the verb.

Jenny announces herself as "Generation 5000". By the time we get to Cobb's HQ, Generation 6680 have been wiped out. Assuming about an hour, *tops*, that would mean that the Progenerators have stepped up and produced 1680 generations of soldiers since Jenny was born, but only 4999 before her. That suggests the war's been going hours, not days.

Either way, the only way the "Chinese Whispers" story works is if the *entire first generation* were killed in the first attack and couldn't pass along the background of the human-Hath conflict. In which case, who set this all up? How did they all

ABOUT TIME 2008-2009

lose touch with the centre of the spaceship? They know of the Source as the basis for all their creation myths but, somewhere along the line, a series of tunnels and an imposing laser-beam trap separate everyone from it. There are at least four different routes, so it's not tremendously hard to find. Why hide the mapping information so well that only a Time Lord with a sonic screwdriver can pull it up? It's certainly curious that there's only one written record in the entire facility and that everyone's been depending on word-of-mouth for the whole week.

Still not sure what we're getting at? Ask two more obvious questions: How old is Cobb? And if all soldiers get identical brain-tattoos at birth, how did *he* get to be a general? (Or, if not, why aren't there many more officers?) The only way this story stands up to even cursory analysis is if it wasn't an accident or series of unfortunate misunderstandings, but a concerted effort at genocide and a project to selectively breed super-soldiers. The story-logic would work much better if Cobb had cold-bloodedly engineered a war to both wipe out another race and kill anyone of his own considered genetically inferior to his chosen breed, making him Davros Mk II ("Genesis of the Daleks"). Just one problem: that's not what we get here. This culture requires a Fiendish Mastermind at the heart of it, and there isn't one.

Actually, for the story to work *at all* and nobody to think there was anything odd about the Doctor or Cobb being the only humanoids not looking like extras from *Hollyoaks*, we'll assume a rapid ageing for anyone who survives their first day on the planet. So inviting Jenny along might extend her lifespan into months, but she's hardly guaranteed a long and happy life even if the Doctor does some kind of stabilising like with the Yoghurt-People in X6.5, "The Rebel Flesh".

In a planet that has so much reflective glass and metal, why is a corridor full of lasers so daunting? Who put the lasers there? Nobody building this place thought there'd be a war the following afternoon.

Quite apart from Time Lords having a mere 46 chromosomes and being diploid (which isn't standard even on Earth; bees, frogs and geckos have different arrangements and wheat, rice and potatoes have three sets, which is why we harvest them for food) and yet still having a repertoire of faces and hair-colours to choose from during a dozen regenerations, we know from *TW*: "Reset"

that time travel has reconfigured Martha's genes and immune-system. The Doctor's accumulated a significantly larger quota of cosmic air-miles. The Untempered Schism also does a lot of remodelling (X3.12, "The Sound of Drums"; X6.7, "A Good Man Goes to War"). Yet no alarms go off and the locals think the Doctor's one of them.

Generations of genocidal fury leads heavily-armed Hath to come along and, er... grab Martha to take home with them. She hasn't *said* anything yet, so the fact that she later turns out to understand Hath burbles is irrelevant. Is she spared and taken to their HQ because she has a vaguely military-looking leather jacket?

Hath frontline troops are born equipped with breathing apparatus, which is fine, but that apparatus has a prominent and luminous piece of glass, with not even a metal grille to protect it. (Perhaps this is a form of intimidation, like those Highland regiments whose ferocity and bravery supposedly extended to going into battle in kilts with no undergarments – their reputation being their biggest weapon. When *Carry On Up the Khyber* is our best hope of making sense of an episode, we're in real trouble.) Nevertheless, the humans don't have any such equipment, so a gas attack would have ended this silly war untold generations before, like last Tuesday.

How did we get here? To make people in seconds is one thing (the nutrients required to turn a few scraped cells into a person, at least, might explain where all the bodies go). To make them able to stand up, as anyone with experience of babies, long-term confinement to bed or astronauts returning after spells in null-g will tell you, is less likely. Then there's the random accent allocation of all these neonate squaddies. If they're getting rubber-stamped education, they ought to all sound roughly the same. (Of course, if this *was* a hasty retrofit of a pre-existing machine to colonise a new world, perhaps it had a record of extinct cultures to draw on. But it's not new or strange, because they've got a magic stink-bomb to makeover the planet. Anyway, it's a bit daft to make an entire planet's population from the same templates, without the shuffling and diversification from having two different parents.) But the machinery was there and they rejigged it to create soldiers. In minutes. And the rejiggerers made all their readimade infantry aware of how to fire guns, walk, speak, kick-box and whatever – but not tell the time.

Nor do they get briefed with any clear idea of the mission-objective. They know the Hath arrived with the human colonists but nothing more obvious like what they want and why they look so much like humans. (That's a point... why *do* they look so much like humans? They've got feet and hands – add your own fish-finger jokes – and load-bearing legs and spines. The Doctor finds in the records that they were on the ship when it landed, so it can't be the result of a situation like *The Fly* where someone got into a teleport with a haddock. If they can run and jump, they must be used to gravity, so they can't actually be aquatic – something confirmed by Martha's examination of their bone-structure. That just makes their breathing arrangements, a face-mask but nothing on their gills, even stupider.)

It grates that the Doctor explains accelerated progenation not to Donna, who we've no reason to think would know this stuff, but to Dr Jones. Who is kidnapped before being able to remind casual viewers (and, apparently, the Doctor) that she's a medic and, to judge by *Torchwood* and X3.6, "The Lazarus Experiment", a specialist geneticist. Donna, however, comprehends this because her "best mate" Nerys did something similar. *That* Nerys (X3.0, "The Runaway Bride")?

What's going on with the clothes-dispenser in the Generator? Everyone else is wearing a uniform that's, well, uniform. Jenny, on the other hand, has a tight T-shirt and leather trousers. And eyeliner. Perhaps there's a Combat Barbie gene in the Doctor's DNA that over-rides the system. (But we know from X3.5, "Evolution of the Daleks" that Time Lord DNA makes people wear grey flannel.)

The planet was made ready with robots programmed to construct stained-glass and Edwardian brickwork. (And equipment with UNIT markings. No, really.) Why couldn't the robots have been reconfigured to do all the fighting? (Don't give us that Three Laws stuff: if they can build genetic shaker-makers that can imprint everything a soldier needs in seconds, they can bodge up something like Sir Killalot from *Robot Wars*. Even Kroagnon did it in 24.2, "Paradise Towers", and he was dead at the time.)

Hooray! Another magic terraforming sparkly-thing has made the land fertile, but Martha says it's radioactive out there. Not to worry, as the atmosphere's 80/20 Nitrogen/Oxygen, and there's a few stray bougainvillea. Martha can smell these, despite her clothes still being manky from her having been chin-deep in gunk after a day being petted by guppies. (She hasn't got a cold from crossing a stormy planet at night in wet clothes – at least we have a retcon on that from *Torchwood*.)

Martha comments about there being a lot of ozone. With that and the composition of the atmosphere being 80% nitrogen, it's unlikely that this is naturally-occurring, or else it would have bonded differently – ozone is three oxygen molecules sticking together despite all the other things they could have paired off with (like girls dancing around their handbags at the school disco) – so maybe it was a deliberately-created means to preserve surface conditions from hard UV, as it does on Earth now there's been life to generate free oxygen for 600 million years. This planet's atmosphere is manifestly unnatural. Ergo, the Source must be the *second* phase of the terraforming.

Moreover, Donna makes a reference to clearing away topsoil. If any thought had gone into this, at all, the opposite would have been the case. Topsoil is probably the most precious substance on Earth. (And unique as far as we know, so all those aliens coming here for methane or silicon – X1.1, "Rose"; 19.2, "Four to Doomsday" to cite especially silly instances – ought to have been after this. It takes 800 to 1200 years to turn smectite clay and leftover biomass into useable topsoil, through the agency of worms and bacteria – 1/4 the weight of any amount of this is bacteria, which is why things grow in it so much better.)

Building a city underneath what's apparently oozy, unpleasant mud with sinkholes, and *then* terraforming the planet, seems a bit backwards. What changed in the interim that the Doctor can terraform the planet *now*, yet nobody bothered to do it on arrival. If there was some sort of time-delay, the creational myths would likely have included that ("the Source will reshape this entire planet, but it will take so long to do"), which would have changed the dynamic of the war no end.

Three moons and a lot of sloshy mud. Anyone who can't see trouble there ought to watch 21.6, "The Caves of Androzani" (if only to restore your enthusiasm for *Doctor Who* after this). A lot of sloshy mud... and yet the aquatic species is fighting the monkey-related ones on land, ceding the home advantage.

Donna, who claims to have memorised all of Dewey Decimal (proof of her secret wonderfulness, apparently), is completely wrong about how Americans mess up writing dates. If she'd said "France", it would have made more sense. If you don't know how it's done in Britain, Series 5 will need a lot of explaining.

General Cobb tries to shoot the Doctor because... why? For costing him the opportunity to commit genocide, maybe? Whatever his motives, he uses a gun that leaves no mark on Jenny, and doesn't penetrate through to the Doctor. Jenny, despite having two hearts, is killed by a chest-wound. Let's be generous and assume that Martha has read the UNIT files on regeneration – even so, with her never having seen the Doctor regenerate, she's absolutely certain that Jenny is finished *and tells the Doctor*, who has regenerated many times.

The Doctor's release of the terraforming gas in such a confined space should have killed everyone present. People need air to breathe (methane and ammonia, presumably kept separate by chilling it but potentially making hydrogen cyanide; see 13.5, "The Brain of Morbius") and ATP to make muscles work. This stuff converts any carbon-based mass into new forms and will be the mother of all carcinogens. (If you're going to pilfer the Genesis Device from *Star Trek*, you should also have the vaguely sciencey explanation and address Bones's worries about what it'll do to any living matter within its field.)

Jenny's on her bier for a very long time – generations, if the story's to be believed. If this war's had a casualty-rate sufficient to warrant this whole story then there must be a lot of dead bodies around. This is perhaps a better way of creating a viable ecology on a new world than a bottle full of farts and nanobots, so long as they remembered to pack some worms, but we don't actually see any corpses. But however long it took to set up her memorial, supposedly the great healing ceremony of Human and Hath after, er, call it seven thousand generations of warfare, the Doctor couldn't be arsed to stick around and do a eulogy or see his daughter interred. What a git!

Jenny breathed in what looks like two percent of the total amount that we're led to believe made a whole planet viable in as long as it took for the Doctor to think about shooting Cobb. She seems none the worse for all that nanotech running around in her, giving her the biome of a small country. If Time Lords are immune to being turned into trees, then the plot of 22.3, "The Mark of the Rani" would have been different, if not as memorable.

And as at least one person involved in this book

used Hounslow public library – when did they *ever* had anyone capable of getting the Dewey Decimal system right?

Critique As we've tried to argue across the entire *About Time* project, the context in which a story is first shown is always significant. We now have a slightly different perspective on the cast dynamic, but that wasn't there at the time. What is clear, however, is that this was planned and built up as being a traumatic incident that would alter the Doctor's life, but landed up as Just Another Episode. What happened?

The obvious point is that it followed a big two-parter with old monsters, Martha and UNIT coming back. A single-episode story would struggle to be more special than *that*, but they don't help their cause by Martha's entire sub-plot looking like an afterthought, and punctuating it with her talking about it as just like old times, i.e., same-old-same-old. Chucking Martha in leaves Donna in turn simply *there*, clogging up scenes that should just have been the Doctor and Jenny, until the whole number-sequence clue slots into place. Quite apart from the way the Hath all pet Martha, treating her as a spectacle (something online fans have cited as yet another race-fail, but is more conceptually baffling than anything – they've seen humans before), this is the sort of subplot Donna was created to do. So if we posit a version of this with no Martha, and the plot clarified to Donna bonding with the Hath and observing the numerical sequence that somehow eluded the Doctor (because she's in a different bit of the city), and the Doctor getting to actually know his instant family – does it become the epic trauma everyone intended?

Not really. They still don't have enough time to make this count. Here is where the old format of four 25 minute episodes, once a week, could have helped. What many people fail to notice about this format is that for every half-hour of screen-time, there is 167½ hours of between-time, for reflection and discussion (in school playgrounds, around the proverbial water-cooler and now online), so the idea of the Doctor acquiring a daughter would have properly sunk in before he lost her. Think of how a gap between episodes made the concept of River Song seem interesting when it was first mooted (X4.8, "Silence in the Library"; X4.9, "Forest of the Dead"), in ways that a one-off episode could never have done.

The way the story is punctuated would suit four weekly episodes. Part One, the Doctor meets Jenny in a war-zone, usual companion is lost behind enemy lines, Doctor and Jenny face firing squad; Part Two, Doctor accepts responsibility for Jenny, usual companion's intervention makes the Hath launch an attack, Jenny caught between Doctor and Cobb has to make a choice; Part Three, laser backflip malarkey, usual companion loses only friend in dangerous night-time crossing of quarry location, all parties reunited and Doctor realises war's been going on for days rather than centuries; Part Four, Jenny dies unexpectedly and Doctor looks likely to get revenge on whole planet. Or, maybe, Jenny becomes new companion.

After all, comparison with Season Twenty (where a story like this would have stood head and shoulder above everything except 20.2, "Snakedance" and maybe 20.5, "Enlightenment") shows that soap-like dealings with a suspicious newcomer aboard the TARDIS make a good narrative hook. If this had been how Turlough was introduced, the whole Black Guardian plotline would have been a lot stronger. Structurally, the plot is sound, but there is simply no way – in under an hour of screen time, all in one burst – to make it seem to count to the Doctor as much as the production team intended. It doesn't help that the next thing we see is the Doctor taking Martha home and chatting about old times like nothing's happened – and then, in the throw-forward, the Doctor and Donna have a carefree romp in 1920s England with Agatha Christie and a wasp.

The conceit around which the plot hangs is neat: accelerated reproduction on a new planet means that a folklore can develop across generations in under a week. It's a good way to use the gimmick to give the Doctor a daughter without any relationship hassles, and follow-through of other consequences. Donna figuring it out gives her a plot purpose besides mere commentary, and amplifies the "supertemp" theme that there's something odd about her. The conceptual breakthrough, even in this cluttered episode, is a rug-pulled-from-under-the-viewer moment that only *Doctor Who* can do. Imagine that as a cliffhanger. Again, a four-part hypothetical version might have introduced the New Byzantium Calendar in passing weeks earlier so that Donna was just slightly faster than the viewers, like the Doctor ought to be, rather than having information we were denied that the Doctor can seemingly pluck out of

the air. But that's like complaining that they didn't really go to another planet to film it. Given the limits of what they can do these days, the only two measures that work are *could this have been done any better?* and *should this even have been attempted on screen?* We are veering towards a "No" on both counts.

Everyone involved does at least as much as could have been expected. As a story more than usually about running up and down corridors and across a quarry (you see why we latched onto a Davison comparison, quite apart from stunt-casting), the locations were slightly more interesting that they might have been. We note that Newbridge Memorial Hall was used again in "Nightmare in Silver" (X7.13), which confirms the impression of a slightly beaux-arts flatpack colony-kit (or, if you prefer, that Messaline was blown up by Porridge). Georgia Moffett is stellar and manages to upstage Catherine Tate, something neither Daniel Craig nor Tony Blair managed. Hindsight, however, makes it feel at times as if we're watching Mr and Mrs Tennant's first date, which is *slightly* uncomfortable.

There are two big glitches in what we see, as opposed to comparison with doing it as a Big Finish audio, a book or a 1983 four-parter. One is the Hath. Conceptually, an interesting opponent, even if we can't hear what they have to say but... why are they fighting onland? There's clearly a reason for this, but it seems to have been lost in rewrites. The unique feature about them is squandered in both the plot and the literally ridiculous scene of Peck's death – six-year-olds were pointing at the screen and laughing. So instead, they become exactly the kind of generic *Doctor Who* monsters we were told time and again we'd never get any more. They are there to give the humans a hard time *and nothing else*. We get no backstory for them, Martha doesn't tell us what she's learned about them, and they might as well be humans with blue faces for all the difference their species makes to what they want and how they fight.

The other is General Cobb. He is the only old person native to this planet. What is his story? His motivation as far as we can see is that he's... err... a soldier. Well, so's everyone else on this planet, so why's he different and what makes him look 70 when he's maybe four days old? If he'd ever got a line that wasn't unreflective xenophobia, this might have been redeemable, but there isn't time for that with so much else going on, and so many soap-ish plots for the TARDIS crew to unpick with a planet at war reduced to a backdrop. Nigel Terry (as Cobb) gives as good a performance as the part-as-written deserves, but nobody could have given it what it needs: a drastic rethink and an extra episode. Cobb's there to be a nasty general who can't see beyond his mission-brief. That sort of thing was good enough for the Hartnell era 2.7, "The Space Museum", 4.2, "The Tenth Planet"), but even by the 70s it was so hokey a cliché that it had to be subverted almost immediately (16.6, "The Armageddon Factor"). Even Colonel Mace was more textured than this (see last story).

Meanwhile, we get a lot of what ought to be the usual Doctor-Donna angsting with the Time War and loneliness, but the quality of it this time is a notch higher. Donna's old life is more vivid in dialogue in a tunnel than in faux-Chiswick location material with Wilf and Sylvia. The sequence about "dad-shock" shows her having learned from her odd life to date, and allows a different perspective on what we thought we knew about the Doctor's past. If, as we gather, Greenhorn had less intervention than other writers in the Davies stable, we have an idea of why this scene works when so many similar ones seem perfunctory. Maybe he could have been allowed a hand in the Sontaran two-parter: it would have saved the redundancy of the Doctor here explaining terra-forming to Donna and Martha all over again. Almost every piece of this story functions – some of it really well – but, as a whole, it doesn't work.

As we've been dealing with hypotheticals drawn from comparisons with wobbly-set-era Who, let's imagine how we'd think of Robert Holmes if the two scripts he wrote for Derrick Sherwin were all we had. "The Krotons" (6.4) is an odd mix of schoolboy chemistry, space-opera concepts taken seriously and murky politics; "The Space Pirates" (6.6) is an over-ambitious satire on bureaucracy, with some genuine pathos in the later episodes and a couple of cliffhangers straight out of Saturday Morning serials, marred by a director who didn't get Doctor Who and let everyone do silly voices and overlong model-shots. Only under Barry Letts did Holmes come to full flower as the programme's single-best writer ever (whatever Mark Lawson thinks). There are incidents in both "The Doctor's Daughter" and "The Lazarus Experiment" that are out-of-keeping, seeming to come from better stories where the companion's story-arc wasn't tripping everything up. Greenhorn seems to be the victim of the BBC

Wales way of doing things. Nonetheless, this time around few of the mistakes were his – certainly fewer than in his hastily-commissioned Series 3 effort. Working under the Moffat regime wouldn't have done him many favours, but perhaps one day Greenhorn might return to surprise everyone.

The Lore

Written by Stephen Greenhorn. Directed by Alice Troughton. Viewing figures (BBC1) 7.3 million (AI 88%), (BBC3 repeats) 1.4 million.

Repeats and overseas promotion La Fille du Docteur, Der Doktorvater.

Alternate versions As we mentioned, most versions after the initial transmission make more effort to suggest that Hath Peck's breathing apparatus has been damaged in the slurry. BBC America doesn't.

Production

• This whole thing began as a dare: Stephen Greenhorn had incautiously said in a Doctor Who Magazine interview about his previous script (X3.6, "The Lazarus Experiment") that the stakes for the Doctor were never high because he could always get out unscathed, without undergoing any real change or loss. Russell T Davies called his bluff and proposed a scenario where in the Doctor – by non-icky means – acquired a daughter who disagreed with him about everything. He also saddled Greenhorn with the idea of a race who talked in bubbles and an underground war (so much cheaper to shoot).

Over several drafts other ideas – such as the seven-day "eternal" war and the arboretum – evolved, but the scripts stuck with the idea that the daughter ought to die, because writing her into subsequent episodes was too tricky. According to legend, Steven Moffat spoke up and said that killing her was a cliché, so they went with the option of having her seem dead and then escaping to unbroadcast sequels. On top of all this, Greenhorn had to incorporate Martha and Donna, so the numerical pattern became more significant and the Hath got more to do. The dialogue for these aliens was written out so the actors had a vague idea of what was going on, and Greenhorn sardonically named the two main characters after

Clarke Gable and Gregory Peck. Their human antagonists were apparently called "Takrans" in some iterations, but this was dropped as the only people using the word would be gurgling. Later scripts mentioned "New Byzantium", so the humans probably started from Earth anyway.

• Block 6 was this story and X4.10, "Midnight" (originally planned as the eighth story of the year), the latter double-banked with X4.11, "Turn Left". After two episodes each for *The Sarah Jane Adventures* and *Torchwood*, Alice Troughton – who'd directed *EastEnders* and *Holby City* and some theatre – was given this block. Other than casting Jenny, the big problem was the laser-barrier stunt. This was rigorously storyboarded and a professional gymnast, Belinda McGinley, was recruited. Meanwhile, as Moffat was now chummy with Peter Davison, the idea of Georgia Moffett as the eponymous daughter was becoming more plausible and attractive. She'd not really watched the old series (her dad had left before she was born), but her young son Tyler was addicted to the new version.

• More behind-the-scenes changes were afoot. Julie Gardner was planning a move to the US in a little over a year, and on the day that the cameras started rolling for this, it was announced that Piers Wenger would replace her at BBC Wales's Drama Department. Meanwhile, Tracie Simpson – whose lacquered fingernails launched a million fevered speculations (X3.13, "Last of the Time Lords") – moved on from the post of production manager, but would be back in another capacity later.

• The recce for the locations (slightly more far-flung than normal this time) was on 1st December. Shooting began on 11th December at the studios of Upper Boat, the same day that Tennant and Tate had been in Newport for the opening and closing scenes of "Midnight". The location work began with a night-shoot at Bridgend, at the Aberbaiden open-cast colliery near Kenfig Hill. (The traditional coal mines associated with South Wales, as seen in 10.5, "The Green Death" and 16.2, "The Pirate Planet", have mainly closed or been turned into museums.) These scenes only required Freema Agyeman and Paul Kasey as Martha and Peck, plus their stunt-doubles. (Tennant was off doing *Top Gear* and promoting the impending Christmas Special.) A pit was dug and filled with wood-chip, and Agyeman was given a wet-suit – but in December in South Wales it was, inevitably, a bit miserable. (One report claims it was -5°C, so Agyeman was warm-

er in the pool than outside.)

• Shooting at the next selected location, the Marble Room at Cardiff's City Hall on the 13th, was complicated by a picket line protesting at planned school closures. Several of the proposed scenes were reallocated to later in the shoot along with material in the humans' camp. Most of this was in the Celewyn Colliers' Institute & Memorial Hall on Newbridge High Street. (You'll see more of the "Memo" in "Nightmare in Silver". Perhaps appropriately, it was built after World War I to commemorate local boys fallen in battle.) The crew went there on the Friday and resumed on Monday, with Tuesday spent partly on the Hath Encampment scenes planned for City Hall. They proceeded on Wednesday and the beginning of Thursday before moving on to Pontypool.

[NB If all these Welsh place-names are bewildering, and the relationship between one weirdly-spelled town and another is confusing in the abstract, the best heuristic we have come up for South Wales is as follows: Imagine a clock-face and that everything from 9.00 to 4.00 is coastline. (There's a reason that so many alien worlds look like rainy beaches these days.) Draw a line between 10.00 and 2.00 and that's mountains. Cardiff is at 5.00 and Barry is coming up for 6.00. Each hour is about fifteen miles. Swansea is at 9.00, and Port Talbot is roughly 8.00. Usk, home of so many handy quarries, is at 2.00. Now draw a circle midway between the numbers and the centre (which is the Rhondda Valley). On that inner circle put Pontypool at 2.00, Bridgend at 7.00, Merthyr Tydfil at Noon. Newbridge is due north of Cardiff and west-south-west of Pontypool.]

So, Mamhilad Industrial Park, Pontypool, formerly where ICI and DuPont had a base, became a spaceship with corridors and a vague smell of bougainvillea. Then on Saturday 21st, the crew moved to Swansea to shoot the floral abundance and Jenny's "death" in the giant spearhead-shaped greenhouse-cum-garden-centre Plantasia (it's about 200 yards from the old town library that became The Library two episodes later). "Voyage of the Damned" came and went and the team reconvened in the Rhondda Heritage Park, near Pontypridd. (Oh, er, continue the line from Pontypool to Newbridge and draw another line from Cardiff directly North West. South Wales has a lot of rivers and streams so a lot of bridges, meaning a lot of names are "pont-y-something".)

• January 8th and 9th were back at Mamhilad,

and involved Jenny flipping over lasers. This entailed the professional gymnast (in a wig and heavy boots) and several takes from different angles, after two days' rehearsals for Moffett to get her start and end shots looking like the same person as was doing the flips. The fake machine-guns had gas-burners and could be used repeatedly without reloading, so there were fewer delays between takes. Then on the 10th and 11th, the team increased their carbon footprint by using the underground Barry Shooting Range as the locale for the pre-credit scenes. This was, Tennant reported, warmer but a bit smelly.

For the big explosion, Danny Hargreaves rigged up a two-stage pyrotechnic for a sheet of flame and the barricade being blown away, making it look like one more devastating blast. As it was, the camera crew withdrew to a safe distance and locked-off the camera, leaving the cast to leg it on cue. A week later, the last pieces were added; Martha returning home (Mark St., Cardiff) and a pick-up shot of more greenery at Roath Conservatory, because the reactions of Martha and Donna to Jenny's death hadn't been captured.

• A few scenes were trimmed, partly for timing but also because it was decided – perhaps unfairly – that dialogue that worked on the page didn't suit the mood. Jenny, in the middle of the escape, questions the local creation-myth about the Creator sighing (as if disappointed by her creation – see what they did there?), while the Doctor finds the cellophane map we later see him consulting. This conversation was referred back to in her death scene (see, it could have been even longer). Another trim loses Cobb being told about the Doctor's call to Martha, confirming, in the general's eyes, that these people are Hath collaborators.

• Although he was credited with having reprieved Jenny, Moffat claimed later not to have realized this and, indeed, seemed to have forgotten this episode had happened when he came to write "A Good Man Goes to War" (X6.7) and introduced a character with the same name (Jenny Flint). He later had Clara mention the original Jenny when posing as the Doctor ("Death in Heaven"). Davies later quipped that a first-time space-pilot leaving a planet with three moons probably crashed and died seconds after we last see her. The joke rubbed Georgia Moffett the wrong way, so Big Finish's Jenny – The Doctor's Daughter boxset, in which she reprises the role, opens with Jenny avoiding that very fate.

X4.7: "The Unicorn and the Wasp"

(17th May 2008)

Which One is This? Agatha Christie meets The Man in The Brown Suit.

Firsts and Lasts One of the footmen in the first scene after the titles is Tennant's dad. Due to the cut made to X3.0, "The Runaway Bride", this is Sandy McDonald's screen debut (just as Graeme Harper's director credit comes on screen).

This is the first time since 2005 that we've met a famous British person from the past who hasn't been on the currency. (If that had been the sole criterion, then Newton, Darwin, Austen, Wellington, Faraday, Elgar, Elizabeth Fry, James Watt, Florence Nightingale, Adam Smith and, um, Sir John Houblon are still available. George Stephenson was grabbed in 22.3, "The Mark of the Rani", a story which also featured a painting by forthcoming banknote star JMW Turner, but not the same one shortly to be used in the £20, The Fighting Temeraire, as seen in episode six of 15.6, "The Invasion of Time").[23]

This was the first episode this year to begin transmission at the former usual time of 7.00pm; it's been wandering around from 6.20 to 6.45 and will be 7.10 later on.

Plus, Donna gives a first on-screen shout-out to Planet Zog.

Watch Out For...
• Oh look, it's Christopher Benjamin playing the slightly stuffy older gentleman he always plays on Doctor Who (see, naturally, 7.4, "Inferno" and 14.6, "The Talons of Weng-Chiang"). Like all of the suspects in the first murder, he gets to do a flashback scene where what he says and what we see are different. His, however, has another flashback inside it and it's apparently a moving version of a hand-tinted postcard. This might pretend to be a straightforward Agatha Christie pastiche, but stay on your toes.

• And of course the *real* murderer was the one who wasn't seen doing anything dodgy in the flashbacks. The only two who don't get a flashback are the crime author herself and Donna – something all the more noticeable, given how much of Donna's time from here on out is going

Are All the Comic-Strip Adventures Fair Game?

If you only joined the party with Eccleston, or thereafter, the strangeness of the earlier off-screen *Doctor Who* formats will take a bit of getting used to. When Santa Claus showed up in X9.0, "Last Christmas", most people were correct in assuming it was some kind of hoax, hallucination or humbug. When the William Hartnell Doctor and his grandchildren John and Gillian met him in 1965, It was for real and for true. That was in the early, relatively sensible stages of *TV Comic*'s version of the series. We might safely have relegated this to the same limbo that contains the World Distributors annuals, embarrassing cash-in singles and the serialised strips that came with ice-lollies or chocolate bars – but for one thing. Bits of those later strips have been cannibalised for broadcast episodes written by long-term fans.

For overseas readers, we have to make one thing clear: what people in Britain meant by a "comic" isn't what Stan Lee et al meant, nor was it much like *Love & Rockets*, *Maus*, *Persepolis* or a French *bande desinée*. Instead, we're talking about something for ten-year-olds and under, in a booklet (more like a small newspaper, on the same grade of paper) bigger than anything Marvel or DC put out, and with up to 15 monochrome one or two-page drawn stories, each with a regular character with some kind of oddity or gimmick.

They were often kids who took a particular aspect of childhood too far, and would end up either being spanked or treated to what was invariably called a "slap-up meal" (featuring sausage and mash, ice-cream and cake – rationing was a recent memory). If not actually children, the characters had child-like aspects: Desperate Dan in *The Dandy* was (and is) a 30s B-picture-style cowboy, but he lives in Dundee with his auntie. (His slap-up treat is a cow pie: literally, a pastry the size of a bathtub with bovine horns and tail emerging from the crust.) Biffo the Bear was, er, a bear. In bright red lederhosen, of course. This genre began in the 1930s with *The Dandy* and *The Beano* (see X7.8, "The Rings of Akhaten") and peaked in the 1970s, the era of *Whizzer & Chips*, *Cor!!* and *Sparky* (just don't mention the cover-strip for the latter).

There's been comic-strip *Doctor Who* since there's been television episodes (more or less), but it was slotted into a format about as far from the near-contemporary Steve Ditko-era *The Amazing Spider-Man* as that was from *Archie* (the American *Archie*, not the robot from *The Lion*). Neither was it exactly like the three-panel strips you still get in newspaper "funnies" (although the *Daily Express* wanted to run one of these and, when denied the likenesses of the cast, included a white-haired Doctor with a police box in the long-running "4D Jones"; the BBC very firmly asked them to stop). There were action-comics, but these too had up to a dozen two- or three-page episodes of different heroes. Britain had been doing this in text since the Victorian era (see 6.2, "The Mind Robber"), but pictorially, after World War II gave a new form of derring-do legitimacy, the one to beat had been *The Eagle* (see **What Kind of Future Did We Expect?** under 2.2, "The Dalek Invasion of Earth"). *Dan Dare – Pilot of the Future* set new standards in quality (artwork and world-building alike) and Anglocentric Space-Opera became part of the UK schoolkid vocabulary alongside disgusting school dinners and Nazi stormtroopers shouting *Aieeeeee!!!* as they died (usually within three panels of exclaiming *For you, Tommy, ze war is over*). By 1965, the action-comics were getting a bit weird (notably one called *The Lion* – the clearest way to delineate the difference between British and American comics would be a detailed comparison of morally-ambivalent crimebuster "The Spider" and Spider-Man, but we'll just offer this as someone's postgrad thesis and steer the rest of you online). Time-travel, gadgetry, aliens and spies were all more normal than Americans or pop music in this world.

The first legitimate strip[27], and probably the most influential on the broadcast episodes, was a Dalek-only strip in *TV Century 21* from 1964: it visually resembled *Dan Dare* (no surprise there, given how much the 50s British space-hero's adventures with the Therons and the Treens had influenced Terry Nation's seven-part TV script), but with the Daleks as almost the heroes. These had a scale and epic ambition far beyond anything possible on screen. They were in full colour and had adventures that spanned centuries and galaxies. (The nearest comparison is the near-contemporary *Trigan Empire* strip beginning in *Ranger* and ending in *Look and Learn*.)

David Whitaker, the series's original story-editor, had more than a small input into the scripts for the comics, although the precise amount is disputed. Some sources, including Wikipedia, claim that Alan Fennell – regular *Thunderbirds* scriptwriter and later one of the mainstays of the *TV Comic* strip) – was main author on the early serials.

continued on Page 115...

113

to entail flashbacks of one type or another. Even the Doctor has one, to ninth-century Belgium.

• It's possible, if you squint, to see Oscar potential in Carey Mulligan's turn as Sally Sparrow in "Blink" (X3.10), but you'd be hard-pressed to forecast the eponymous Unicorn getting one for *The Theory of Everything* a mere seven years later. Felicity Jones is all right, but the part requires her to fade into the background somewhat. That's getting harder.

• The villain, we're told, has absorbed the ground-rules and set-pieces of "typical" Country-House murders (what are, slightly loosely these days, called the "tropes" of the form). In fact, none of the plot functions that way, and the story really makes sense if – and only if – a telepathic werewasp has somehow learned how a BBC Wales *Doctor Who* "celebrity historical" is supposed to work. Anyone who wishes to "re-imagine" an improved version of "Timelash" (22.5) with a giant wasp generated on a BBC Micro can do so on their own time.

• The story's climax is a car-chase but, this being 1926, not a particularly fast one. This allows for dialogue fixing another continuity point about how time works nowadays, which is going to be important in future stories. Or you can just look at the pretty bruum-cars. (Agatha drives a 1925 Bullnose Morris. Professor Peach's vehicle, borrowed by the Doctor, is a Sunbeam 14/40 tourer of similar vintage.)

The Continuity

The Doctor He smells the air ('grass and lemonade, and a little bit of mint'), and from this tells Donna that it 'must be the 1920s'. [It's *just* possible that he can tell the year by scent, as some sort of synaesthesia, in which case the twenties do indeed smell like mint. We refer you to **Can He Read Smells?** under X2.8, "The Impossible Planet", and Missy's curious description of artificial gravity in X9.1, "The Magician's Apprentice". Or it could just be the Pimms. Donna's probably correct to tease him for cheating by spotting a vintage car, but check *Ethics*.]

He drinks lime and soda, then lemonade, but doesn't slap down his companion ordering cocktails [unlike the last time he was partying in the era; 19.5, "Black Orchid"]. At least one of Christie's stories fooled him properly, to his delight. Donna's comment that 'all the decent men are on the other

bus', i.e. gay, makes him mutter 'or Time Lords'.

Cyanide can kill the Doctor [and perhaps all Time Lords], but he survives via an odd mix of domestic ingredients: ginger pop [we refer you to 13.4, "The Android Invasion" for the lack of apparent effect of ginger beer on Time Lords], protein (walnuts), salt (anchovies – straight salt is too salty) and a good resounding shock to reverse the inhibited enzymes. Donna kissing him is sufficiently surprising to do the trick, and he belches out a blackish-grey smoke [as if the orange pixy dust had gone off]. He comments he should do the detox more often.

He says that not knowing how one will be remembered, but hoping for the best, is what keeps him travelling.

• *Background.* Even before showing up, he's au fait with the biographical details of Christie's life. [Meeting Christie was an adventure he suggested to Martha before she left in X3.13, "Last of the Time Lords," so he might have been planning this trip for a while.]

• *Ethics.* [It's distinctly possible that he's up to his old tricks of knowing *exactly* what he's getting into without mentioning it: there's the info dump; his certitude – without real evidence – that the real culprit was alien; the regulation magnifying glass and willingness to impersonate a policeman and his deduction, when Agatha drives off, that time is in flux. He might even, before or after what we see, have genuinely shown up at the reception he mentions to Lady Eddison via the psychic paper. The script could have it either way: see **English Lessons** for why we doubt it.] He spikes the soup with pepper, but only as a bluff to drive out the Vespiform.

This time it's Christie who rebukes him for enjoying destruction too much, and he doesn't even look properly guilty about it. Donna more-or-less murdering the Vespiform upsets him; he claims the wasp wasn't responsible for its actions. It cheers him to think that Christie remembered at least part of the Vespiform adventure. [So he's not that concerned about anachronism. Perhaps he didn't object to Donna's chatter because she's due for a bout of amnesia; anyway, he doesn't seem much sorry to have called her "Dame" by mistake or let slip that she'll live a long time.]

• *Inventory: Psychic Paper.* It seems to "charm" Lady Eddison more strongly than usual, as she's apparently convinced that she's met the Doctor at an ambassador's reception. Later on, he uses it as

Are All the Comic-Strip Adventures Fair Game?

continued from Page 113...

Elements of these colourful tales of cosmic calamities filtered into the broadcast Dalek tales and feature-film adaptations, including small details such as "Rels" (although *what* the Daleks measured in these changed) and bigger matters such as a civil war breaking out between hard-liners and more human Daleks, plus the advent of the Dalek Emperor. The look of this major character changed between the strip and 4.9, "The Evil of the Daleks" (by Whitaker), but later on Davros adopted this title and disguised himself as the *TV 21* version (25.1, "Remembrance of the Daleks"). We told more of that part of the story in **Why Did We Countdown to TV Action?** under 8.3, "The Claws of Axos".

BBC viewers had to wait until Eccleston's Last Stand to see anything approximating the 60s comics (X1.12, "Bad Wolf"). The rights for the Daleks were negotiated on behalf of Nation independently of what the BBC could do, so this strip formed part of his stable of spin-offs, including the deeply strange *Dalek Pocketbook & Authentic Space Travellers' Guide* and a few annuals. The continuity between these peculiar books and the *Dalek Chronicles* (as the strip is now usually called) is watertight. Resemblance to what we saw on screen, less so. There was little outright contradiction, but the Dalek franchise was rumbling on in its own direction and the Doctor only occasionally stumbled into it.

This meant that when the publishers of *TV Comic* acquired the rights to *Doctor Who,* they came without the Daleks, just as the Doctor and all the other series-paraphernalia were left out of the *TV Century 21* strip. (Well, almost all... the Mechanoids' off-screen activities were more impressive than their clumsy bumblings in 2.8, "The Chase"). *TV Comic* was firmly within the other tradition of British comics, the one-page slapstick stuff with its roots in the 1930s. Among the earliest and weirdest of the pre-war titles was *Radio Fun*. This, as the name implies, drew what the characters on BBC radio comedies and dramas ought to have looked like (almost like the actors but not always), and put these individuals into the sort of antics that DC Thompson's papers (the aforementioned *Beano* and *Dandy,* plus *The Topper, The Beezer* and more parochial strips for their main paper, Scotland's *Sunday Post*) routinely did. *TV Comic,* which began in 1951, carried on this slightly unsettling habit and made up stories about not only fictional characters from television, but the real-life stars.

So when *TV Comic* did something approaching a *Doctor Who* strip, alongside *Ken Dodd's Diddymen* (see 24.3, "Delta and the Bannermen"), it was inevitably a little more outlandish than the broadcast episodes, but entirely in line with the rest of the comic. This Doctor travelled with two entirely new grandchildren, John and Gillian, and frequently encountered characters and situations from folklore: notably the Pied Piper and the aforementioned Santa Claus. (Not "Father Christmas" as everyone in Britain still called him reflexively then; he is explicitly "Santa Claus".) He also met the Trods, who were like supermarket own-brand Daleks.

The writers and artists seemed not to be paying very close attention to the BBC's own stories (possibly wise, after they were caught trying to lift the plot of 1.2, "The Daleks"), nor even to each other. When the Zarbi returned weeks after being vanquished from Vortis in 2.5, "The Web Planet", the Doctor somehow squeezed into a robot Zarbi costume and flew. Neville Main, the original artist (and occasional author too) made heavy weather or telling simple stories, with little or no attempt to make the kids likeable or even distinct. Oddly, though, the second story, *The Therovian Quest,* was considered interesting enough to be recycled five years later when *Joe 90 TV Adventure* (yet another revamp of *TV Century 21*) launched a *Star Trek* strip. As this is literally a tale about gathering moss, this indicates how little anyone in Britain knew about the USS *Enterprise* (which is pink in this version, redrawn by Ron Turner – he also did the last 50 or so episodes of the Dalek strip).

Bill Mevin took the strip into gaudy space adventure, and John Canning tried to make action and characters work in this cramped format, but throughout this phase it was hard to reconcile with the television series (especially once John Wiles and Donald Tosh were running the TV show, around the same time as Mevin's stint). The most anyone now will admit was that these stories had charm. As the show and strip changed hands, the strip started looking a little more like the series. The Doctor turned into Patrick Troughton (sort of), although he kept that bloody hat for three more years on paper than he was allowed to on screen. John and Gillian stuck by him as he took on increasingly familiar opponents – notably the Mondas-model Cybermen, with his Utility Belt

continued on Page 117...

proof of police credentials.

• *Inventory: Other.* He has the obligatory magnifying glass and a test tube capable of holding venom of giant wasp. When investigating morphic residue, he wears his glasses.

The TARDIS The Doctor jemmies open a grill in the console room, under which is a big chest of objects all starting with the letter "C". [Odd that a Gallifreyan ship's cupboards are alphabetised in English, but we'll let it slide.] This includes a Cyberman chest plate, the Carrionite globe [X3.2, "The Shakespeare Code"], a bust of Caesar, and a facsimile edition of *Death in the Clouds* from the year Five Billion. [If Christie really is the best-selling novelist of all time as the story claims, this might have been a special reissue at a gift shop for the Satellite Five guests, meaning he picked it up during X1.2, "The End of the World". Or maybe the hospital at New New York *did* have a gift shop after all (X2.1, "New Earth").]

The Supporting Cast
• *Donna.* When needs must, her confidence in her not-at-all-a-couple relationship with the Doctor is so solid, a kiss is the perfect shock.

In a complete reversal of "Planet of the Ood" (X4.3), she mocks the idea of Planet Zog and rushes back into the TARDIS to fetch appropriate flapper apparel. [The deleted closing scene from the previous story had Donna suggests they go find a bright new world.] Her drink of choice is a Sidecar cocktail, then an orange juice before dinner.

She's offended when the Doctor refers to her as a 'plucky young girl'. She correctly guesses that two of the men present, Roger and Davenport, are gay – which slightly disappoints her, as she seems to approve of Roger's looks. She also seems disconcerted at the idea of there being a real Noddy.

Meeting Agatha Christie delights Donna and she's familiar with several of the author's works [most likely from telly]. It amuses her to spout off names and concepts that she knows Christie will use later, and she several times claims a joshing copyright. [She has all the references the Doctor had with Shakespeare in X3.2, "The Shakespeare Code".] *Murder on the Orient Express* was one of her favourites. She thinks that meeting Dickens and ghosts at Christmas would be preposterous [X1.3, "The Unquiet Dead"].

She doesn't seem to feel guilty about killing a murdering alien wasp with the traditional schoolboy method of a magnifying glass, telling the Doctor that she "couldn't help herself". Her Belgian accent's even worse than Albert Finney's.

It's long enough since "The Runaway Bride" that she can talk to Agatha about Lance and say that she's moved on from her cheating fiancé.

The Supporting Cast (Evil Under The Sun)
• *Golightly.* In the 1880s, a Vespiform came to Delhi and masqueraded as a human to learn about humanity. Under the name 'Christopher', he and Lady Eddison fell in love and he told her his true history. She didn't mind, but he drowned in a flood in 1885 leaving her with only the Firestone necklace [actually a Vespiform telepathic recorder]. As Vespiforms can interbreed with humans, Eddison's pregnancy resulted in a healthy and apparently human boy who was accordingly put in an orphanage run by the Christian Fathers. For the next 40 years, he lived a very quiet and peaceful life as a country vicar.

Unfortunately, the sight of a couple of boys stealing from his church angered him so much, he finally accessed his alien heritage and connected with the telepathic recorder – from which, among other things, he absorbed a thorough understanding of the motifs of Agatha Christie's writing style via his mother, who was wearing the recorder at the time. [Reading between the lines, it's suggested that the telepathic recorder was intended as an heirloom to give Golightly a mental template for coping with his heritage; Christopher's untimely death meant that an appropriate understanding was never installed.] When in the process of transmogrifying, he speaks with a high-pitched buzzing noise like a wasp.

Once Roger is dead, he's the heir presumptive to the Eddison fortune. [If nobody knew Golightly was in line to inherit, then it leaves the murders apparently unconnected unless Lady Eddy figures it out and acknowledges him spontaneously. If she does, he gets the title and anyone who accuses him of the murders will wonder why someone went to such lengths to cover up something he wanted known. There is, within the framework of the story-format he's imbibed, a logic to *some* of his crimes that fits this pattern (less so Miss Chandrakala's death or poisoning the Doctor).]

It appears that even in his human form he's conscious of what he can do and has done in wasp form. The recorder's hold to the template is so

Are All the Comic-Strip Adventures Fair Game?

continued from Page 115...

(yes, exactly like Adam West's Batman) and Jet-Pack.

Then, once Nation had gone to America with a plan to make the Daleks big Hollywood stars (look, it *could* have worked), the BBC stopped making stories with them in, so the rights were renegotiated and the Trods decided not to bother trying to conquer the Universe any more. At last, and after near-misses with the Sky Ray cards and Cadet Sweet Cigarette cards, the Doctor we saw on telly was fighting the Daleks in a comic. (He won, by the way.) John and Gillian, despite bravely seeing off literal space-pirates (they and the Doctor walked the plank wearing space-helmets, but no pressure suits – Gillian's mini-skirt apparently being enough to spare her the same fate as Katerina in 3.4, "The Dalek's' Master Plan"), were packed off to Zebedee University and Jamie McCrimmon showed up with no explanation.

Amazingly, the BBC not only had a veto on this sort of thing, but the then-junior script editor, Terrance Dicks, had to be consulted on all of this crossover merchandising. This passage of concepts and characters from screen to page was strictly one-way: unlike the *TV 21* Dalek strip, there wasn't any hint of trying out ideas too broad and deep for the small screen. What happened was that the writers were strongly advised to watch the programme and keep roughly within its tone; to colour-in within the lines, so to speak. There was a line and Dicks told them when it was being crossed, but no story-ideas were floated in the comics to test their suitability for television (unlike what has happened with other series more recently). Nothing too expensive, but the production-team's wish-list got a trial run with Jamie marvelling at it as he would if it had "really" happened on BBC1. Many ideas were too bonkers for television, and we'll come to those, but prior to 2007 nothing remotely resembling *TV Comic* ever cropped up in *Doctor Who* as the BBC and most of the viewers understood it.

But this was to change. Suddenly and terribly, the Time Lord was faced with one of the most ludicrous threats his drawn incarnation had faced – unconvincing, green-faced, snaggletoothed witches. Forty years on from their first encounter with the Doctor, John and Gillian, we saw something very like these supernatural menaces in X3.2, "The Shakespeare Code". Witches had used magic from a book of spells in a strip running while the on-screen Doctor dealt with the aftermath of Salamander having his mistress assassinated for stealing the proof that he had blackmailed senior public officials (5.4, "The Enemy of the World"). In 2007, Mother Bloodtide used a form of sorcery that the Doctor (and writer Gareth Roberts) struggled to keep within the bounds of what was possible in *Doctor Who*, rather than ignore such niceties as Roger Noel Cook did in 1967. But so what? Figures like these are part of folklore, in the public domain. They were a cliché when Shakespeare used them. At least David Tennant didn't use a ray-gun on them, as the drawn Patrick Troughton was wont to do.[28]

Five weeks later, we got another threat markedly similar to one faced by the *TV Comic* Doctor. The Family of Blood built an army from straw and sacking and molecular fringe technology. Walking scarecrows weren't new in 1969 either (*Worzel Gummidge* had been in print since the 1940s), and there had been many stories with housemaids called "Martha". In the following year, we were treated to a giant killer wasp very like the ones the Quarks used in the strip, but menacing Agatha Christie.

Any individual instance of a barmy idea returning might just have been coincidence, or a half-buried memory from when *DWM* reprinted these as kitsch fillers in the 90s – even if we didn't know that the authors concerned, Roberts and Paul Cornell, were fond of the silliness of these story-ideas. These came after two season-finales that seemed oddly-familiar to anyone following *DWM*'s own strip in the run-up to the return of the series in 2005, as we'll see. With the Macra coming back unexpectedly (X3.3, "Gridlock"), it seemed for a while that older fans could legitimately ask: *will we ever see the Trods?*

Some might counter this by suggesting that the Macra differ from the Trods, or Ice-Apes or any other drawn manifestation of 60s *Doctor Who* by being on-screen and thus canonical. But then, 4.7, "The Macra Terror" is currently represented by about ten seconds of fuzzy, embarrassing footage and an audio-recording that contradicts much of "Gridlock". If that were the criterion, then arguably the 30-second 1967 cinema commercial for the Walls "Sky Ray" lolly with the cards that make up a story about an odd-looking Doctor fighting the Daleks with giant mechanical ants has about as good a claim. (The latter half of Series 7 even had

continued on Page 119...

117

strong that when Agatha takes the necklace, she can control Golightly's wasp form to some extent. When Donna tosses the necklace into the lake he dives in after it in his wasp form and drowns. Before dying, he releases Agatha rather than killing her.

The Non-Humans

• *Vespiform.* They leave morphic residue – a leftover from genetic re-encoding for certain species – that looks like Krillitane oil [X2.3, "School Reunion"] or Tate and Lyle Golden Syrup. Their hives are in the Silfax Galaxy. Golightly [whether he's typical of the species or not] has remained human for 40 years. Telepathic recorders seem a crucial part of the life-cycle of the Vespiforms; Golightly's going so wrong enables the Doctor to absolve him of his actions.

Their transport methods involve something that looks like a purple shooting star. [It's the same shade as the lights on the Adipose collection van, the Sontaran ship and Rattigan Academy's nocturnal lighting, some of the tunnels on Messaline and a few things we'll see later. If this were a Moffat season, this would be a Big Clue.]

History

• *Dating.* In our universe, Agatha's amnesia would set this in December 1926. [Only it's not, because it's genuinely meant to be summertime, instead of as usual when the production team films in summer and tries to pass it off as winter. We might call it early August, the calendar date when filming took place.] The mansion is a short drive from somewhere called 'Silent Pool' [the obvious inference is that we're near Guildford, in Surrey; see 19.4, "The Visitation"].

Agatha Christie, we're told, is the best-selling novelist of all time, and they're still publishing her in the year Five Billion. [There is, as you might expect, a special subsection we can do here, with the titles of Christie books crowbarred into the dialogue for people to feel clever for spotting. How many did you get? In the cut pre-credit scene, we got *The Man in the Brown Suit*. Then we have Professor Peach's 'why didn't they ask...? Heavens!' thighslapper (the original was 'Evans'), *Murder is Easy* (well, the BBC put out a special script extract with the line, so it was intended to be in there), *The Body in the Library*, *N or M?*, *Nemesis*, *Cat Among the Pigeons*, *Dead Man's Folly*, *They Do It with Mirrors*, *Appointment with Death*,

Cards on the Table, *Sparkling Cyanide*, *Endless Night*, *Crooked House*, *Taken at the Flood*, *The Moving Finger*, *Death Comes as the End* and (oh dear) *Murder at the Vicar's Rage*. Tee and to some extent hee.

[There's also a rundown of plot-points used by this episode and catch-phrases (leetle grey cells) and so on. Donna explicitly compares the situation to *Murder on the Orient Express*, Christie makes a cheeky reference to her already-published *The Secret Adversary*, there's a vase of yellow irises (a radio drama), Clemency is seen reading *The Murder of Roger Ackroyd*, and of course there's the Doctor's copy of *Death in the Clouds* at the end. Russell T Davies pondered inserting a reference to the original title of *And Then There Were None,* but decided against it. Donna inadvertently inspires Miss Marple as well.

[As we've noted, history has been tweaked somewhat so that teddy bears were common in the 1880s and golliwogs weren't. This has now happened enough times to stop counting towards **Things That Don't Make Sense**, since it's arguably deliberate and is foregrounded in both this and X7.6, "The Snowmen". (See the essay with X3.2, "The Shakespeare Code" for our reasoning.) The precise fate of the Robertson's Marmalade factory is unclear; perhaps it blew up and was replaced by a banana plantation. Nonetheless, *Noddy* still exists in Donna's childhood but not in her reality, so evil golliwogs may well be something she read about as a child.]

There are apparently lots of amorphous insectoid lifeforms, but none in the Earth's galactic vector. [The Isop Galaxy has a few; 2.5, "The Web Planet".]

The Analysis

The Big Picture It's a Celebrity Historical. By now everyone knows the score; we meet a famous person in their context, the Doctor bibbles about how brilliant that person is, and then we get a bog-standard *Doctor Who* alien showing up. The last adventure without such extraterrestrial malarkey was "Black Orchid", a story we'll be mentioning a few times. In that, the Doctor, the TARDIS and the irritating alien teenagers he travelled with were the interruptions to a "normality" culled straight from period dramas.

In most cases since "The Highlanders" (4.4), however, the Doctor has brought a generic *Doctor*

Are All the Comic-Strip Adventures Fair Game?

continued from Page 117...

a Doctor resembling this Troughton-Hartnell compromise.) Anyone who remembered the Macra in any detail was likely to know about the Trods or Martha the Maid (a Jetsons-style robot housekeeper the Doctor patented, handy with a broom to beat up Quarks).

A more practical consideration might be the ownership of rights. Most of the TV series writers went along with the usual practice of a small consideration if something they invented got re-used, but some (and one in particular springs to mind) wrangled better deals. What has been singular about the BBC Wales series in this regard is that everyone gets a credit for their babies: Malcolm Hulke is credited when the Silurians come back, even though Madame Vastra is so unlike what he invented as to be effectively a new race (see **Reptiles with Tits?** under X5.9, "Cold Blood"). The Robert Holmes estate got a tidy windfall from the Flashmob of Doom (X5.12, "The Pandorica Opens") bringing Sontarans and Nestenes together at last.

The situation with the works of Mervyn Haisman and Henry Lincoln is cloudy. The Ice-Apes were *TV Comic*'s way of skirting their dodgy claim to have invented that particular version of the Abominable Snowman, and Steven Moffat seems to have found another (X7.6, "The Snowmen" and that episode's essay, *The* **Great Intelligence or Just** *a* **Great Intelligence?**). Notice that when the end-credits rolled on X7.14, "The Name of the Doctor", Hulke and Holmes got credits, Haisman and Lincoln didn't. As you will have read in Volume 2, the reason that the authors of 6.1, "The Dominators" tried to take out an injunction to prevent it being broadcast was that *TV Comic* rights came under the same licensing arrangements as any other *Doctor Who* monster, whereas Haisman and Lincoln had Terry Nation-scale ambitions for merchandising the Quarks. *TV Comic* had the Quarks in almost alternate stories, without their masters the Dominators, and doing all sorts of weird schemes. Although other, even more questionable, claims were made concerning the re-use of Brigadier Lethbridge Stewart (developed from a character in 5.5, "The Web of Fear"), the *Doctor Who* production office has happily re-used the Yeti (20.7, "The Five Doctors"), so the situation can't be as big a legal minefield as all that.

There's just one comic-strip adventure that has a rock-solid case to have included concepts and images later to show up on screen. In 1971-2,

Nestlé issued a fairly ordinary slab of chocolate wrapped in one of 15 covers, each an episode of *Doctor Who Fights Masterplan Q*. This has a good claim to be the most Pertwee-ish adventure, like, *evah*. Magic crystals, dinosaurs, teleports, Bessie, the Master, it's all there (except the Brigadier).[29] It's just about as close to a statistical average Barry Letts/Terrance Dicks storyline as you can imagine (they should have gone the whole hog and given it the statistical average title, "Planet in Space"), but no author is credited. Had it come out 20 years later we'd suspect Gary Russell (see below), that's how many on-screen concepts are yoked together in so short a time. But it pre-dates most of them, so we have to conclude that – as with the *TV Comic* Season 6B – Dicks was at very least consulted and possibly road-tested ideas here.

The situation with *Doctor Who Magazine* is more complex because it is, in effect, two different publications. One was the upgraded version of Marvel UK's *Doctor Who Weekly* and occasionally did crossover stories with very minor Marvel Universe personnel. After mid-1995, it became a different publication owned by Panini, the sticker-album people (although still technically a Marvel publication). The BBC's relationship with this magazine has been complicated, especially since the global resurgence of interest in the series. We might assume that nothing from the pioneering early days of the *DWM* strip is likely to show up on screen (apart from a sight-gag inclusion of Abslom Daak in X8.5, "Time Heist", and the ninth Doctor quoting him in X1.12, "Bad Wolf").

Now that Marvel is owned by Disney, they have far more crossover material than they know what to do with already. The 1979-vintage Marvel UK writers were largely clueless about the series, and reallocated stock Marvel-style stories to the Doctor and famous aliens. (This included the Quarks, now reunited with the Dominators and setting off earthquakes like before. Strangely, no lawsuits followed.) Panini had no such rights and were unlikely to do team-up stories with David Ginola, but were able to use material invented for the earlier strips as well as on-screen events and characters and things they made up. It seemed as if the two storylines could rumble on independently of one another. That's not exactly what's happened.

Small elements of the Marvel UK strips have seeped onto the screen, so that the Sontarans do indeed have a home planet called "Sontar" (X4.4,

continued on Page 121...

Who-ness with him, which means that – despite the endless talk about "the flexibility of the format" – only one kind of story can be told in such period settings. Space monsters show up in something from a type of BBC historical drama. The pioneer of this is David Whitaker's attempt to hybridise the Daleks and *The Forsyte Saga* (4.9, "The Evil of the Daleks"). The next was 6.7, "The War Games", where all the different time-zones were subordinated to the "outside" story of nasty aliens, including one of the Doctor's own kind, trying to avoid them mixing; the same plot shows up in 10.2, "Carnival of Monsters" and is used to allegorise *Doctor Who* itself.

As "The Unicorn and the Wasp" is a Gareth Roberts story, listening out for a reference to the 1973 one is almost obligatory. It's not hard, as the "period" flavouring in "Carnival" was 1920s Posh (to the extent of going port out and, presumably, starboard home[24]). And, lo, Pertwee's Doctor gets period slang wrong almost exactly as Donna does here. The point is that, "Carnival" – along with Robert Holmes's next historical/space-opera mash-up, 11.1, "The Time Warrior" – was the template of getting the kind of BBC costume-drama aesthetic (and decades of practice) into *Doctor Who*. It was a cheap way to make exotic-looking locales from the abundant stock sets and costumes, plus all the actors were on firm ground and wouldn't mispronounce spacey-sounding words. Apart from "Black Orchid", there hadn't been a story set in Earth's past that didn't have the run-of-the-mill *Doctor Who* plot yet again but with the dresses and lamps changed. At the end of the day, "Human Nature"/"The Family of Blood" (X3.8-3.9) would have been the same story set in 1981, 1800 or 1641. "The Mark of the Rani" (22.3) is in most essentials "The Masque of Mandragora" (14.1), but with Kate O'Mara as Hieronymous.

Where "The Unicorn and the Wasp" differs from the routine, it's more to do with the author than the setting, or the author's use of the setting. Count how many ways the Doctor uses "British" pejoratively, to denote how everyone refuses to acknowledge pain or loss. Gareth Roberts had played with the literal inability to feel physical pain in his first script for *Randall and Hopkirk (Deceased)*, mainly for comic effect in a Tex Avery style fight, but the plot was motivated by a scientist avoiding bereavement (Sir Derek Jacobi – X3.11, "Utopia" – got to use lines from 17.4, "Nightmare of Eden"). The pragmatic, stoic reac-

tions of previous generations is in stark contrast to the self-flagellation of current Westerners, who seem if anything less able to cope after the post-war boom in tranquillisers and psychobabble.

Is repression a sensible long-term policy? Evidently not, although advocates of various therapeutic procedures make it seem as if it is a binary either-or. The normal British reaction to extreme situations is gallows humour and a semi-ironic attempt to make the best of things. The now notorious *Keep Calm and Carry On* poster was never used as planned: it was intended to be posted in the event of a Nazi invasion. More typical is the end of *Monty Python's Life of Brian*, where Mr Cheeky's reaction to crucifixion (and, for later service personnel, in sinking ships in the Falklands or shelled in the Gulf) was to whistle and sing "Always Look on the Bright Side of Life". However, Roberts tends to make his stories hinge on more extreme reactions. From his second novel *Tragedy Day* to X6.12, "Closing Time", he has made the combination of anguish and psycho-sensitive technology too powerful to control.

Thus, a famous author known to have undergone a fugue state and come to her senses hundreds of miles away is a suitable narrative hook. The author is herself associated with tales of terribly well-bred people masking pent-up emotions and keeping secrets... until someone gets killed. Although Christie was observing changes in British life until her last few new books in the 1960s (before dusting off her reserve-stock to leave her beneficiaries something), her work is associated with inter-war country-houses and resorts. Roberts has a bit of previous here with *The English Way of Death*, a 1995 Missing Adventures novel pastiching these and Season Seventeen.

Christie's frustration and uncertainty at being merely a peddler of fantasies and pastimes is a matter of record, but it's the flipside of the self-deprecating comments Roberts made (and made Shakespeare share) about his composite *Love's Labour's Won* last time around (X3.2, "The Shakespeare Code"). This script has the formal properties of a TV adaptation of Christie, but any attempt to emulate the prose style is played for laughs. The fact that we have a comedy episode set in the 1920s-as-seen-on-TV means that hints of Wodehouse are in the air (although he was writing books about the antics of aristocrats), while the "criminal gains entry to country houses as an aristocratic guest" is more like the Raffles

Are All the Comic-Strip Adventures Fair Game?

continued from Page 119...

"The Sontaran Stratagem"), but any attempt to suggest that Peter Capaldi's character in *Torchwood: Children of Earth* was a Whifferdill should be kept to yourselves. (Frobisher, the shape-shifting private eye stuck in the form of a penguin, later got his moment in Big Finish continuity under the auspices of Robert Shearman.)

The more obvious legacy of the comic in this phase is way in which the re-use of old monsters from the series in team-up stories has occasionally come into vogue on screen as well as on the page. Even in *DWM*'s earliest phase, when *Doctor Who* was still popular with the general public, the continuity-led stories indicated a captive audience who were all up-to-speed on the series lore (or wanted to be). The writers were often less clued-up than the readers, but the main object of this this phase of *Doctor Who Weekly/Monthly* was to educate younger readers in the whole previous 17 years of the series (since there was no chance that any of the episodes would ever be seen again). It was thus a roughly level playing-field for young *Doctor Who* fans and aspiring Marvel writers and artists. Some of the writers would meet with *DWM* editor Jeremy Bentham and get a bit of background on old episodes (mainly names of characters or monsters), then write their usual sort of stuff. The results were messy and magnificent in equal measure. Predictably, Alan Moore is responsible for the worst shambles (see **Did Rassilon Know Omega?** under 14.3, "The Deadly Assassin"); equally predictably Grant Morrison later attempted to combine lots of past elements in as daft a way as possible (see **What's All This About Planet 14?** under 6.3, "The Invasion" and a reference in X10.12, "The Doctor Falls").

Meanwhile, on BBC1, the new generation of writers who'd come in after John Nathan-Turner's purge of the 1970s giants were equally unfamiliar with the programme's past, but had helpful hints from fans – one in particular – about what would be sure-fire popular returning baddies. *DWM* had more scope for epic adventures, but in many regards there was little to differentiate the thought-processes of the script-writers in both media. Once freed from the cumbersome television series after 1989, the *DWM* strip might have become more elaborate, but these stories were a bit intricate even when the Doctor they were trying to draw was Peter Davison. It almost went both ways, as Pat Mills, experienced comic writer who

had worked on the *DWM* strip as well as many better-known titles, spent ages being strung along by script-editor Eric Saward over "The Song of the Space Whale" (see 20.3, "Mawdryn Undead" for the fall-out over this).

As with the broadcast version, there was a strange assumption that the Time Lords were intrinsically interesting; unlike the telly stories, everyone soon started looking like six-year-olds dressing up as the Doctor and his chums as Mick Austin took over the artwork. The period around the programme's twentieth anniversary was the lowest point. Some of the strips for Colin Baker's Doctor, by contrast, were among the best of any (and arguably the best stories for that character), but after the series was put in hiatus in 1985, the quality dropped. This was when someone decided that a female Draconian would need a Red Sonja bikini, because the concept of "mammal" was lost on the people making the decisions. We had to wait until 2010 for a similar error on screen (but keep reading). Things slowly improved and strips by experienced fan writers – many of them working for Virgin Books's *New Adventures* line – were run in amongst increasingly erudite articles.

Unsurprisingly, the 1996 Paul McGann TV Movie rudely disrupted this idyllic state. The BBC took the book rights from Virgin (heirs to WH Allen, owners of the Target Books brand that had kept the novelisations coming since 1974) and rebooted with *The Eight Doctors*, apparently thinking that they needed to get everyone up to speed on decades of backstory in one fell swoop. The magazine wasn't messed with by them, partly because the Marvel UK staff had been on good terms with the production office and kept the flame lit since 1989, but mainly because Marvel UK was itself being reconfigured with Panini. On the plus side, they knew that this magazine had survived against the odds and made money without a programme to sustain it. The internal thinking shifted, however, when Gary Gillett – not a big fan of the strips or the NAs, which he viewed as "product" rather than a legitimate source of stories in the absence of a TV show – was installed as *DWM* supremo.

Where Marvel had originally seen the strips as the magazine's *raison d'etre*, with articles as a side-salad, the comic adventures were now having to earn their keep. One interesting effect was that a secondary serial, written by Alan Barnes (A5, "The

continued on Page 123...

books (written by Conan Doyle's brother in law) than anything Christie did – few of her books involve professional criminals. The formula here is the one Christie made a name for herself by subverting.

The popular impression that Christie stories are all essentially 20s and 30s cosy mysteries isn't that far wrong – she updated her references (rationing becomes a running theme in the appropriate decades) and made some more adventurous, but she did indeed tell much the same type of story throughout her career. However, 1926 is a little early for the concept of Christie stories as a definable type, explicitly differentiated from the plethora of mystery stories on the market that decade. So much of this story's impact depends on the audience's sense of those 66 mysteries, even though the six novels she'd *then* published could hardly support that storytelling weight. But to set the story much later, you'd need a rather more hefty examination into what elements really *do* go into a Christie novel, which wouldn't neatly fit into a single story anyway. There isn't much room to include her usual touchstones of, say, children's rhymes, match-making, small-town gossip and the economics of country houses. The format requires that we boil it all down to a country house and a twist ending.

Well, that isn't quite right. Purists condemned *The Murder of Roger Ackroyd* for pulling rabbits out of hats and being insoluble using just the information available to the reader-as-sleuth. Two of the novels that Christie had published as the story opens, *The Secret Adversary* and *The Man in the Brown Suit*, are straight-up international espionage adventures; in fact, averaging out the novels she'd written up to 1926 suggests something more like a spy thriller than a cosy manor. The Vespiform's got as much chance of turning out a scenario for Bulldog Drummond as for Poirot. On screen, the impression of Christie and her work is aimed cold-bloodedly at an audience presumed to have only read a couple of her novels, if that, or perhaps seen an adaptation or two, and have an image of what this sort of thing *ought* to be like rather than anything about the actual personage the story supposedly commemorates. In which regard, it is exactly like every other celebrity historical.

Christie's disappearance for ten days in December 1926 did happen essentially as described, shortly after she discovered her original husband was having an affair. It was a considerable scandal, sparking an intensive search and national uproar. It was catnip for the press, much as the Lindberg kidnapping was for the US. There was a film about it in the 70s. Quite a lot of books have been written on the matter; the official diagnosis was simple emotional breakdown, but more unfriendly theories suggested she set it all up herself to gain public sympathy or just publicity. Her autobiography is reticent on the matter, though it describes graphically the trauma of her husband's adultery.

Aside from presenting an obvious story-telling hook, it's indicative of the production team's priorities that they first looked at her biography rather than her fiction. As someone known internationally (more than for her books than for the television or film versions, for a change), she lived a peculiar enough life to be an ideal pick for a pseudo-historical. In many ways, Christie was a more interesting character herself than any of her creations: after a childhood straight out of a Victorian novel, she worked in nursing and pharmacy during the Great War, picking up a knowledge of poisons along the way; travelled abroad as often as she could (she took up surfing in South Africa), and aided on the digs of her archaeologist second husband. (For a dim echo of this, look to the character of Bea Nelson-Stanley in *SJA*: "Eye of the Gorgon".) Everyone in this story knows of Mrs Christie's reputation, but the only person from this world who's read any of her books is Clemency, which is what causes the trouble. "Agatha Christie" is, in this story, a semi-mythical figure much as Robin Hood was in the suspiciously-similar "Robot of Sherwood" (X8.3).

So instead, the role-model for the country-house murder is that most enduring of reductive plot-led puzzles: the 1940s board-game *Cluedo*. As the name implies, this is a variant on Ludo with stock, almost archetypal characters and a limited repertoire of murder weapons. Note the colour-coding of the Miss Scarlet-ish Robina and the vaguely Mrs Peacock-like Lady Eddison, the presence of a housekeeper, a colonel, a vicar and a professor. Donna alludes to it, but the game is often cited as a criticism of the more perfunctorily-written specimens of the format.

There were many other ways to write a story with Agatha Christie Westmacott as a character once Phil Collinson had proposed having her as the focus of a story. 1940s Egypt might have been

Are All the Comic-Strip Adventures Fair Game?

continued from Page 121...

Infinite Quest") and illustrated by the distinctive Adrian Salmon, detailed a history of the Silurians (and their interactions with the Mondas Cybermen, whose strip this officially was) that surprisingly made a degree of sense. Meanwhile, former *DWM* editor Gary Russell both novelised the TV Movie and scripted a *Doctor Who* comic strip in the *Radio Times* that was seen by far more people than would ever see or read any other fannish output.

For much of the 1990s, the strip was written or edited by Scott Grey. He genuinely seems to have preferred writing stories that only work as comics, whist retaining a fan's knowledge of what can be woven into a *Doctor Who* story. Once Barnes replaced Gillett (and the botched relaunch of the TV series faded from public memory), the strip became more of a selling-point. Other writers came in and out, many of them names you'll know, and reprints of the *TV Comic* and *TV21* strips had been worked into *DWM* or – in the early years of the decade – given their own collections by Marvel in *Doctor Who Classic Comics*. Although there was a sense of kitsch giggling at the old strips, this aspect of the series's heritage was being reclaimed alongside merchandising and the old episodes now available on video. The official strip itself hinted at aspects of this. As a serial drawn by people who had some idea of what the television episodes were like, it punched well above its weight visually. From 1990 onwards, *DWM* writers and artists spent 16 years trying to show what *Doctor Who* would be like if they ever got a chance to do it. Then they did.

Cornell, Roberts and Russell T Davies have all been involved in one capacity or another with the strip(s) in *DWM*(s). We discussed the porousness of "Human Nature" and "The Family of Blood" in **How Many Times has This Story Happened?** and we mentioned in the notes that "The Shakespeare Code" ran vaguely parallel to *DWM*'s Roberts-written "A Groat'sworth of Wit". There was also "The Lodger", in which the Tennant Doctor stayed with Mickey Smith for a fortnight, a scenario Roberts reworked (with some of the same incidents and a lot of the same simmering resentment by an ordinary bloke being outshone by a paragon) for Matt Smith's first series (X5.11, "The Lodger", oddly enough). A more curious case is the last strip the magazine ran with the McGann Doctor, "The Flood". Davies was consulted on this and drafted an ending where the Doctor regenerates into Eccleston,

but he is not the official author. Indeed, Martin Geraghty made efforts to tie the strip to earlier *DWM* stories that later broadcast Davies scripts contradict.

Nonetheless, the sequences of the Cybermen infiltrating Camden Market across a dimensional breach are notably similar to X2.12, "Army of Ghosts", while the Doctor's solution, to absorb the space-time vortex and blow his antagonists to perdition, is *very* like what Rose did to become the Bad Wolf in X1.13, "The Parting of the Ways". The original ending, sketched and scripted but not used, has the regeneration we assumed at the time immediately preceded X1.1, "Rose". That version of the Doctor's off-screen past before visiting the Powell Estate is now off the menu, and the non-BBC1 material to support the Anniversary episode has, at least, a better claim to be canonical than the published strip.

Yet more by luck than judgement, the Time War version of the Doctor is distinct from the one who escorted Izzy back home and contemplated wearing a leather jacket to replace his lost velvet one. Adding a whole new Doctor to the back-catalogue allows all the off-screen adventures of the eighth Doctor to remain viable as possible pasts – even the officially-sanctioned novels with the "other" Time War when he destroyed Gallifrey and the Daleks rebuilt Skaro. We note, however, that in "Night of the Doctor", released online and as a DVD extra, the dying McGann Doctor only names his Big Finish companions, not the ones from the novels or the comics.

One of the arguments offered in favour of the cumbersome "Season 6B" theory (see **Was There a Season 6B?** under 22.4, "The Two Doctors") is that it allows the amusingly ludicrous antics of the *TV Comic* Doctor full rein. After a career zapping robot spiders with lasers, managing pop groups and impaling Father Time on a cuckoo from a giant clock, the Doctor evades the Time Lords by taking up residence in a swish London hotel and appearing on TV panel-shows explaining mysteries. Hiding in plain sight obviously works, as he deals with time-paradoxes, alien visits to Earth and naughty schoolboys before the High Council lure him into a trap with walking scarecrows and force a regeneration six weeks before the broadcast of 7.1, "Spearhead from Space". Dicks had been consulted on the impending changes and subsequent drawn adventures of the new Doctor,

continued on Page 125...

costlier, but less of a procrustean formula to put a living person inside a stereotypical fiction. Moreso than Shakespeare or Dickens in their respective pastiches, Christie here is a landmark to be visited and re-purposed like the London Eye (X1.1, "Rose"), the Shard (X7.7, "The Bells of Saint John") or the Post Office Tower (3.10, "The War Machines").

Every generation of viewers gets the Christie they deserve. In the early 60s, we had Margaret Rutherford's bizarre swashbuckling Miss Marple, in a number of films which eschewed the plots and were great fun if you didn't know the books (or did and hated them, or just accepted the films as that cohort of character-actors having fun). The 1970s saw big-budget all-star feature-film adaptations of varying quality and fidelity. The 1974 *Murder on the Orient Express* was roundly ridiculed (although it got an Oscar for the Ravel-pastiche score by Richard Rodney Bennett – 1.6, "The Aztecs"), but there isn't a lot to choose between Albert Finney's Poirot and the supposedly-definitive David Suchet version on telly from the 80s onwards. The Hollywood Miss Marple, Angela Lansbury, adapted the character to the extent that *Murder, She Wrote* seemed like a good idea. The Peter Ustinov Poirot films are another way of knowing if it's coming up to Christmas; the flashback style in this episode seems to spoof the one in *Death on the Nile*.

In the 80s, as we said, the trend for feature-length TV adaptations of crime (on film and as "authentically" as possible) made Joan Hickson's Marple part of the work-creation scheme for actors famous enough to be the obvious suspect on BBC1, just as Jeremy Brett's unsurpassed Sherlock Holmes was for Granada and Suchet's Poirot for LWT. For American and European audiences, any face they recognised was in the frame – if in doubt, Peter Davison dunnit. But by the twenty-first century, there was nothing left in this format and any new adaptations had to be more radical. Whereas the approach to Sherlock Holmes was to place the emblematic features in another context and rethink the character within a modern format (hence DCI Bulman, Dr House and Mr Monk, then a string of knock-offs), the ITV series *Marple* took that character and put her in stories made of other Christie books remixed apparently at random.

The calculation was that viewers weren't concerned with the plot so much as the atmosphere – the familiar elements done well and the little old lady solving crimes originally solved by Tommy and Tuppence or Poirot. It was of a piece with the then-contemporary cosy crime series (set in some freakish neverland like the US idea of England) also being made by the conglomerated ITV1, *Midsomer Murders* and the notorious *Rosemary and Thyme* (see **Oh, Isn't That...?**), where what happens is less important than famous faces, nice gardens and a maguffin. Then this too was superseded and the current modish Christie at time of writing is "dark" renditions, occasionally returning to the books but going out of their way to shock the little old ladies who were supposedly the main target audience of previous iterations. Whether overseas companies buy these remains to be seen.

As it happens, Agatha Christie currently *is* the best-selling novelist of all time, owing to decades of reliable marketability combined with her work ethic – she turned out more than a book a year averaged over a career lasting a half-century, resulting in book sales that numbered into the billions. Admittedly, people read Christie for other things than just the plot. As the Doctor repeatedly points out, it's motivation that makes the books function, the journey rather than the destination. Christie wrote the books in draft, then decided who the most interesting killer was, rewriting accordingly. However, her books are slowly disappearing from libraries in London, so we can't guarantee that this much-cited statistic will last.

Davies says that he suggested a giant wasp after remembering the paperback cover for *Death in the Clouds* (a wasp is in the novel, but purely as a red herring). There's nothing to suggest that Christie paid close attention to that book's cover art and the plot of that book is quite different from this adventure anyway. Her short story "Wasps' Nest" isn't any closer, although a trick with cyanide crystals is a mite reminiscent of the Doctor's bluff with the pepper. It's the only story that Christie herself adapted for television, in 1937. (For obvious reasons, this live performance no longer exists. The knowingly Art Deco 1991 version with David Suchet included a garden fête and Peter Capaldi.)

Christie's own favourite of her books was *The Mysterious Mr. Quin* (inspired by Italian harlequinade, so guess what his first name is). He's a Byronic traveller with ambiguous but positive motives, comes and goes at peculiar intervals,

Are All the Comic-Strip Adventures Fair Game?

continued from Page 123...

absurd as many of them were to be, at least kept within touching-distance of what kids watching would have seen (unlike earlier romps, where the Doctor kept a Cyberman disguise-kit handy on the off-chance).

The new Doctor was exiled to present-day England and worked with someone purportedly the same Brigadier as Nicholas Courtney was playing (however much weight he seemed to have put on for the strip). And we have to ask whether the levitation ability the Doctor learns in December 1970's strip is any more ridiculous than the "transmigration of object" in 7.3, "The Ambassadors of Death". Most of the stories in that year's strips were *Doomwatch*-ish, but not far from Season Seven's formula of government research stations where things were going wrong.

One or two went further than quarries and refineries, but not as far as submissions being considered by Dicks at the time (see **What *Else* Wasn't Made?** under 17.6, "Shada"). One strip was by Alan Fennell, and is closer in tone to the three seven-part broadcast stories that year than what we had after the Master showed up in 1971. Most of the scripts, as for the year before, were by Roger Noel Cook, whose previous use of the format to do whatever he felt like had been constrained by the need to link to the on-screen change. They weren't all as memorably barking mad as before, but still strained at the limits of what John Canning could draw and any comic could contain in a weekly strip.

When the rights were transferred to *Countdown to TV Action* (the last gasp of the *TV21*-style format), the artwork and ambition improved, but the exile-to-Earth was too constricting for the writers – just as it was beginning to be on screen. This phase moved the Pertwee Doctor (and the Master, and the Daleks) off into the sort of thing the BBC could never have afforded, but it never did as much violence to the core concepts of the series as *TV Comic*. In some ways, *The Sarah Jane Adventures* mixed space-operatics and domesticity more like *Countdown* than any *Doctor Who* other than, perhaps, X1.5, "World War Three". (However, the closest any individual story ever comes would be those stories that also resemble another 70s precursor, *The Tomorrow People*. At its best, this series looked and felt like the *Countdown* version of *Doctor Who*; at worst, *SJA* resembles the 1990s reboot of *The Tomorrow People*. Nothing

from Cardiff is as dire as the 2014 reboot of the reboot.) The BBC Wales version of *Doctor Who* can approximate a comic more smoothly than anything hitherto and has authors (and a couple of directors) steeped in these traditions. They could, after a bit of haggling over rights, take anything from any drawn iteration of the series. If they so chose. Anything.

As we discussed under X3.1, "Smith and Jones", the Judoon were deemed appropriate for *Doctor Who* on telly, but the almost-identical space-cows in Gareth Roberts's *DWM* debut ("The Lunar Strangers") were dismissed as "silly". What's going on? There's two different ways to grade any idea: the expected age-range of each audience and the expected background knowledge of the series. Plotting these on a graph in 1993-4 would have revealed two very tight concentrations of *DWM* readers, the relatively large but casual residue of the few children (as a percentage of UK children) still watching in 1989, and the hardcore of active fans, mainly in their 20s and 30s. The latter were more vocal. Both sets of readers were uncomfortable with the idea of the other being anything to do with them. By 2007, we're back to the series being a national obsession and only one viewer in 500 knew what the Macra were beforehand.

If anyone is seeking to plunder the past for more than a famous monster coming back, the source of an idea is less important than how well they can "sell" it to the casual viewer. What would have appealed to a *DWM* reader in 1995 and what would have appealed to a *TV Comic* reader in 1965 are radically different. As we mentioned, Roberts had a *DWM* strip about Shakespeare and psychic forces in 2006, a year before the broadcast of his television go with *TV Comic*-style witches (although the commissions for these weren't in that order); his comic version of "The Lodger" changed less than might have been expected, because by this phase *DWM* was assuming a similar readership to the viewership of the BBC Wales series. Capaldi *DWM* strips were more amenable to newcomers than the involuted TV series under Moffat.

By contrast, the most recent additions to the Doctor's comic adventures have assumed a need to explain everything from scratch. Sometimes this was done adroitly with the minimum needed for the story in hand, as Titan Books have been doing. They were granted the US comic rights after a peculiar spell with indie publisher IDW. This is

continued on Page 127...

seems to have a flexible relationship with time and is prone to showing up at dangerous times. We see him paired with a companion, Mr Satterthwaite, who drops in and out of his life much like, say, Sarah Jane's relationship to the third Doctor or Clara with the twelfth. The stories teeter between Christie's usual no-nonsense plots and magical realism, atmospheric tales that leave one guessing – the effect is cumulative and makes the final story downright lyrical, with a conclusion that would have fit neatly enough into the tenth Doctor's character trajectory. This is all a much more obvious plot hook if you're interested in Christie's literary life and, since the older Christie talks about the Doctor being a "harlequin" in the deleted scenes, someone on the production team had the character in mind. *The Passing of Mr Quin* was the first Christie story adapted for the screen, in 1928.

If anything, Donna's discovery of the giant wasp resembles a scene from the notorious 1979 film *The Swarm,* in which Katherine Ross hallucinates a huge bee behind a door after nearly two hours of combating millions of small ones (and some atrocious dialogue). However, if we're looking for innocuous-looking humans transforming into giant insects and killing everyone in a period drama, we should bear in mind the mesmerically-awful 1967 Tigon production *Blood Beast Terror* in which Wanda Ventham (4.8, "The Faceless Ones"; 15.3, "Image of the Fendahl"; 24.1, "Time and the Rani") isn't just a were-moth, she's a Franken-were-moth made from a number of different species stitched together. (SPOILER: Peter Cushing lights a bonfire and she can't resist flying into it.) There is another precedent we'll cover in this story's essay on *TV Comic* et al, so we'll just rejoice that the Doctor wasn't armed with lasers and move on. Wasps and slightly dim girls new to India finding forbidden romance is a connection made in *A Passage to India* (see X2.6, "The Age of Steel" for more on Mrs Moore).

The Doctor's poisoning was borrowed from one of Gareth Roberts's own comics: the ninth Doctor's first *DWM* strip, "The Love Invasion". In this, the Doctor survives poison gas by eating a chicken-chocolate sandwich. Golightly's line "Don't make me angry" is, of course, a reference to Bill Bixby's portrayal of David Banner in *The Incredible Hulk*, a series that surprised parents of ten-year-old boys by having plots and acting and that. Arnold Golightly's transmogrification resembles the way Bixby was periodically replaced by Lou Ferrigno

as the Hulk. A bit. We note that a few of the character-names are producers or directors with whom Roberts has worked, so the Unicorn may have been named after the boss of *Brookside*, Phil Redmond, for example. The Doctor's eccentric touch of yelling "Maiden!" as if it means a lot and then saying it doesn't mean anything is – as you will have noticed – stolen from umpteen times Tom Baker did that sort of thing

Additional Sources The Doctor mentions going deep into the Ardennes after an insane computer kidnapped Charlemagne – the BBC website related this Beligan adventure under this episode's listing, as part of the expanded content. It features a thoroughly unconvincing shopping-obsessed version of Donna, but a story where the Doctor goes out of his way to say he doesn't like celery isn't a complete waste of space.

The DVD contains the un-used top-and-tail sequences with Daphne Oxenford [24.4, "Dragonfire"] as the dying Agatha *almost* remembering the events of this story, and the Doctor and Donna coming to visit her and show the book we see Donna being shown in the revised end-scene. Their removal is just as well – somehow, despite a long and absorbing life, Christie's entire existence has become haunted by the Doctor in a way that's impossible to reconcile with the real-life version, not least because you'd expect her to have written more science fiction. (Actually, there were a couple of borderline short stories.) They do, however, intriguingly have Christie explicitly referring to the Doctor as the Harlequin several times; see **The Big Picture** for more...

English Lessons

• *The Professor with the lead pipe in the library* is a formulation from the board game *Cluedo* (or *Clue* in the US). In both versions of the game, it's Professor Plum rather than Peach. That's the role Tom Baker played when they adapted the game into a TV series. Professor Peach was, of course, Benny Hill in *The Italian Job*.

• *Slapper* (n. sl.): a cheap slut; the term is often associated with the mythical "Essex Girl" (see Volume 7).

• *On the other bus* (sl.): Ever so gay.

• *The Ambassador's Reception*: noted in society for their host's exquisite taste. The 90s advert for Ferrero Rocher was a kitsch classic and provided a final iconic role for John Abineri (7.3, "The

Are All the Comic-Strip Adventures Fair Game?

continued from Page 125...

almost closing the circle, as Titan was set up by many of the people responsible for the early Marvel *Doctor Who* strips, and is run by the people who own the Forbidden Planet chain of comic/merchandising boutiques. Early attempts at a Capaldi strip were a bit weird even compared to his broadcast episodes, but they are more widely available than the IDW comics. (It would help if anyone could draw him: we had Doctors apparently played by Nicholas Parsons, Joyce Grenfell and Hughie Green.) The Titan ones stepped away from that model, offering up adventures with new companions right from the start, but it's too early yet to know what will come of it. The purposeful effort to stay away from on-screen continuity as much as possible did it credit – the eleventh Doctor rendition was far more appealing and believable than much of the material Matt Smith had to say on screen.

IDW's stint is an object-lesson in how to kill the goose that laid the golden egg. It's also a salutary example of the flow of ideas between comics and TV going very wrong. IDW got the US rights to a *Doctor Who* comic on condition that they didn't go toe-to-toe with Panini, so only die-hards in Britain sought these out as imports. It took the new series catching on in America (in a small way, at least) to make this happen and, as with *TV Comic*, one did wonder if the people who commissioned this had ever seen the series. These combined reprints of specially-curated Marvel-era *DWM* strips (largely Tom Baker on through some of the Sylvester McCoys) along with bespoke material (we can hardly call it "new" or "original", but it was written for this comic and no other) by a variety of authors – some UK and some US, but so often excruciatingly fannish. That's not "fannish" as in knowing what worked and what didn't from experience, it's "fannish" as in a collect-the-set mentality of old monsters and situations (see **Wot? No Chelonians?** under X5.12, "The Pandorica Opens"). The first of these stories, by Gary Russell and published later as "Agent Provocateur", wasn't helped by variable artwork that made Martha look like eight different women in six episodes (not all of them even human).

Being licensed, the IDW comics required someone at the BBC to sign off on them – making it a bit strange that nobody in the loop averted unconscious replication of story-ideas or incidents. This means that such apparent goofs as a Jack the Ripper storyline coming just before Madame Vastra nonchalantly mentions offing him ("Ripper's Curse", cf. X6.7, "A Good Man Goes to War"), and a one-episode story ("Little Blue Box") being a reworking of Philip K Dick's "Imposter" at around the same time that X5.3, "Victory of the Daleks" did it to Professor Bracewell.

There must have been some hint, one would think, when Tony Lee was writing "Body Snatched" that X6.5, "The Rebel Flesh" was in the works. Likewise, "Sky Jacks" by Andy Diggle and Eddie Robson vis-à-vis X7.11, "Journey to the Centre of the TARDIS". "When Worlds Collide" manages to get in Sontarans in period clothes, alien time-phased theme parks and Nazis just as Series 6 takes a mid-season break. Then again, it has a Western town and a dinosaur called Kevin who briefly joins the TARDIS crew and then goes to live on a spaceship (X7.3, "A Town Called Mercy"; X7.2, "Dinosaurs on a Spaceship"). Even the vague thread in "Agent Provocateur" of an un-named Something removing the populations of whole planets and Series 4's "missing worlds" arc is a bit dodgy.

The 2013 year-long "arc", "Prisoners of Time" is all about the Master trying to rewrite the Doctor's entire timeline (rather as the Great Intelligence did in "The Name of the Doctor") and then the current model summoning his past selves to defeat this menace (as he did in X7.15, "The Day of the Doctor"[30]). That the Master's tool in this is Adam (X1.6, 'Dalek') and he is defeated by Frobisher disguising himself as a time-vortex manipulator, indicates that keeping the number of continuity references up to some kind of quota has more priority than second-guessing what BBC Wales might have up their sleeves in the immediate future. Precedent is not the same as influence, and any one of these might be an interesting coincidence, but these are just the most blatant examples of a regular phenomenon.

Lee became established as the main writer, as well as contributing to the Big Finish audios. Although elements of old adventures (generally old monsters in team-up combos that hadn't been tried on screen) were almost mandatory, very few actual ideas for stories were unfamiliar to long-term fans. "Run, Doctor, Run" was essentially the end of 19.1, "Castrovalva" without the plot. (That might seem like an insult, until you recall the stupidity of the plot.) The most characteristic adventure was Lee's *The Forgotten*, in which the Tennant

continued on Page 129...

Ambassadors of Death" and others) as the waiter carrying the tray of these chocolate nutballs.

• *Cut of your Jib* (n.): the way particular sails are trimmed, i.e. how one goes about things. 'Colour' is wrong, as is...

• *Chin chin* (interj.): Cheers, bottoms up, goodbye. Not what you say on meeting someone.

• *Ginger Beer* (n. & sl.): A perfectly innocent and often child-friendly drink composed of semi-fermented ginger and sugar. Enid Blyton's *Famous Five* books are supposed to have endless jugs of the stuff (although this is largely an invention of the *Comic Strip* parody "Five Go Mad in Dorset"). More to the point, it's become rhyming slang for "queer", and therefore a slightly peculiar expression to be shouting at the footman (especially as his reaction is anachronistic).

• *Noddy* (n.): And as we were just mentioning Enid Blyton, it's a book series about a small wooden boy who drives a cute little car around Toytown. Nobody's quite sure what he's supposed to be, but he has a red Phrygian cap (like the Smurfs) with a little bell on the end – so when he nods (which he does a lot, hence the name), it rings. (In France, he's called "Oui-Oui", which amuses British schoolkids more than anything in these twee books.) As befits something rather stiltedly innocent from a less enlightened time, people find unconscious innuendoes and probably-conscious racism in them now. Various animated versions have struggled to avoid using the naughty golliwogs at all and sidestep the tendency for the whole thing to look extraordinarily gay.

• *PC Plod* (n.): Yet another Enid Blyton reference. The plump copper in *Noddy* became the politest derogatory name for the fuzz (and Military Police, the red-caps from the Ministry of Defence, are "MOD Plods").

• *Belgian Bun* (n.): A small joke. The pastries called Belgian buns have about as much to do with Belgium as Danish pastries have with Denmark, French fries do with France, English Muffins with England or Swedish Fish with Sweden or fish; they're iced sultana-filled buns treats topped off with a cherry.

• *Do a Bunk* (v. sl): abscond, escape, leg it.

• *Buzzed Off* (v.sl.): Left. "Buzz off" is a kid's way of saying "go away".

• *Pip Pip* (interj.): Goodbye (not used since about 1950 in the UK). So not what you say when you want someone to do something post-haste, as Donna seems to think. She's *really* off-beam with

her period slang this week, which is odd considering how dated most of her usual expressions are.

• *Nobs* (n. sl.): Nobility. Also a homophone for "knobs", as in "dicks", "willies" et cetera.

• *It's a fair cop* (n.): What apprehended criminals say in cheap fiction from inter-war Britain, or post-war American films set in fog-bound London.

• *Dame* (n.): the formal title for a Dame of the British Empire, the female equivalent of a knighthood. (The usual form is to attach "Sir" or "Dame" to the first name – *not*, the surname. Derek Jacobi, for example, is Sir Derek, not "Sir Jacobi". The first name is usually the same as the one on the birth certificate, although some leeway is allowed with contractions such as Dame Judi Dench, Sir Mick Jagger, or stage names such as Sir Cliff Richard. Or, indeed, Dame Agatha Christie, rather than "Dame Agatha Mallowan" as it would more properly have been by the time she got the gong. This is entirely permissible, as a knighthood or damehood is a name-change sanctioned by the reigning monarch and the Prime Minister, so as legal as it gets. Thus, the *New York Times* referring to Sir Paul McCartney as "Mr" is hopelessly wrong.)

• *Railway station bookstall romances* is more of an insult than it might seem. The advent of the railways seventy years before had altered the nature of the novel, making serialisation in magazines a viable business model but placing the emphasis on cliffhangers and plot-twists (as Dickens demonstrates). The shops at railway stations, notably WH Smith's, often sold out-of-copyright older titles in cheap paper-bound editions and Routledge started commissioning original works specifically for travellers, priced at 6d (i.e. the cost of a chocolate bar). They weren't the most demanding reads. As Modernism developed in post-World War I culture, these books were dismissed as tawdry and dated. We are still a few years ahead of Penguin Books launching with an Andre Maurois novel and redeeming the idea of affordable paperbacks being worth anyone's time. As we saw in the flashbacks, Christie's works were hardbacks to begin with, so this is a sneering dismissal of her career.

Oh, Isn't That...?

• *Felicity Kendal* (Lady Eddison) is still getting royalties for endless repeats of *The Good Life,* in which she and Richard Briers (24.2, "Paradise Towers") attempted self-sufficiency in the suburbs

Are All the Comic-Strip Adventures Fair Game?

continued from Page 127...

Doctor has lost his memory and is wandering around a museum of his old foes, each exhibit reminding him of an encounter in one of his earlier lives that wasn't worth showing on telly, with a BBC Wales monster being defeated by an old series Doctor and appropriate companions (Davison, Tegan and Turlough against the Judoon, that sort of thing). So as plot went, it was a retread of Terrance Dicks's BBC novel *The Eight Doctors*.

Lee would do it again in "Dead Man's Hand". The ingredients of the stories were all from the television series, with the majority of the ones shown to us rather than just mentioned being from BBC Wales stories (and photos). There's an unspoken assumption that recombining everything from the old episodes is intrinsically a good idea, that people will like a story in proportion to how much continuity there is per page. This was also a flaw in the worst of the *DWM* strips (those later Davisons with the stumpy legs and endless Gallifreyan machinations – oh, look, the editor from that period, Richard Starkings, wrote for IDW's strip too). The only people who could be impressed by this are people who already knew the original stories and, unsurprisingly, many of them weren't impressed at all. (However, they were hardly the comic's primary audience.)

Conversely, all the malarkey with Enochian speech and Dr John Dee is the kind of shtick Alan Moore's been riding and, when combined with moving trees ("Don't Sit on the Grass"), might have come from a late 80s *Swamp Thing* or early 90s *Hellblazer*. Bolting it on to BBC Wales *Who* was slightly awkward (although not as clumsy as X8.10, "In the Forest of the Night"). Brandon Seifert's "The Doctor and the Nurse" made better use of the way people read comics than most of these, and told a story that was theoretically possible on screen, but would have been an incident in a more bloated story. (In fact, the same emphasis on character interaction during odd incidents rather than plot-plot-plot makes it almost compatible with X7.4, "The Power of Three" and its side-dish "Pond Life". All three could have been remixed so that the Beer Deluge of 1814 – featured in the comic – replaces the Zygons in the Café Royale and the Ood in the bathroom could have been slotted into the year-long wait for the story to start properly.) Nonetheless, these stories showed that the comic medium could do things with the *Doctor Who* toolkit that no other comics

and few other forms of *Doctor Who* could attempt. They just chose not to, most of the time.

The "Final Sacrifice" conclusion to the big tenth Doctor storyline, with two original companions, reads like a warmed-over remix of Big Finish's Charley Pollard and the Shade/Fey storyline from *DWM*, with Torchwood thrown into the mix for good measure. As a publication where the most exciting and trumpeted thing that could happen was a crossover with *Star Trek: The Next Generation*, there's something a little too safe about all this. In a fan-run series, there was always a slight sense that the stories were purposely avoiding anything that BBC Wales could re-use, not least because many of the writers seemed to be holding back more televisual story ideas for when (rather than "if"), they got the phone-call from Russell T Davies or Steven Moffat. Holding back ideas that might have worked on television ought to have meant more creative use of ideas that would only have been possible in a comic, just as Big Finish, Virgin and BBC Books might have attempted in their media.

Whereas once the limits of what was possible in a studio in London gave the writers and artists of *TV 21* et al free rein, just as the Target novelisations had bigger effects budgets and casts of thousands, today BBC Wales has the facilities and legal right to cherry-pick anything. IDW often acted as if only the ability to use the likenesses of dead actors separated them from the television adventures – and the artists weren't always too sure about what the things and people in the reference-photos were like on screen.

For a time, Titan kept comics with storylines of each of the tenth, eleventh and twelfth Doctors running concurrently. Each had companions exclusive to the comics, and happily staked out their own patch of ground whatever was happening with the TV series. It remains to be seen how popular these will continue to be with either the new US fan base or comic-readers hitherto uninterested in the series. They must think there is a market for all of these adjacent titles – indeed, they seemed to be selling better than the other merchandise has since the 50th anniversary boom fizzled out. That said, a significant pruning occurred with the advent of the thirteenth Doctor, with the aforementioned comics going on hiatus to put more focus on just the Whittaker series.

For the most part, the Ice-Apes, Robot 2K,

continued on Page 131...

(see 8.4, "Colony in Space"; 10.5, "The Green Death"). It's called *Good Neighbors* (sic) in America, because there an awful and forgotten Larry Hagman sitcom had used the proper name. Nonetheless, as you might recall from X3.10, "Blink", she'd been in an ITV detective series, *Rosemary and Thyme,* recently and was by now as known for work on stage, as muse of Sir Tom Stoppard in his 90s purple patch. She'd been in the first Merchant-Ivory film, *Shakespeare Wallah,* based loosely on her family's work, then did the rounds of those late 60s ITC series, often pretending to be French.

• *Fenella Woolgar* (Agatha Christie). She'd been the Honourable Agatha Runcible in Stephen Fry's *Bright Young Things,* which had included Tennant. She also appeared with him in *He Knew He Was Right.* Later on she'd be cast in the ITV series *Agatha Christie's Poirot.* When this episode went out, she had just had a small but significant part in Woody Allen's *Scoop,* but a year earlier she'd been in Steven Moffat's *Jekyll.* She was more recently reunited with Felicity Jones in *Cheerful Weather for the Wedding,* but nobody saw that.

• *Christopher Benjamin* (Colonel Hugh Curbishley). It's a long list, notable for playing bosses (the best being *It Takes a Worried Man*), though for our purposes his turn as Jago in 14.6, "The Talons of Weng-Chiang" has to be noted. (See also 7.4, "Inferno".) He has two separate roles in *The Prisoner,* one or both of which might be his character from *Danger Man.* Oh, and he's in *Hawk the Slayer.*

• *David Quilter* (the butler Greeves) was PC Tanner in *Softly Softly* back in the 60s.

• *Felicity Jones* (Robina Redmond/the Unicorn) was Catherine in an ITV *Northanger Abbey* and Cordelia in the already-forgotten film of *Brideshead Revisited.* She made more of an impression in *The Amazing Spider-Man 2* as Felicia Hardy. After that, an Oscar nod for *The Theory of Everything* made people forget the curious Julie Taymor film of *The Tempest.* Then came her lead role in *Rogue One* and playing Ruth Bader Ginsberg. The original target audience for this episode would most likely have remembered her from *The Worst Witch,* if at all, but at the time of first broadcast she wasn't even the most famous Felicity in the cast.

• *Tom Goodman-Hill* (Rev Arnold Golightly) was in *Ideal* (see Volume 7 and X8.1, "Deep Breath") and played Lilburne in *The Devil's Whore.* He was also in *The League of Extraordinary*

Gentlemen, but we'll forgive him. At the time this was made, he was Sir Lancelot in the production of *Spamalot* with Peter Davison as King Arthur.

Things That Don't Make Sense Even if we accept that an alien has adopted the "rules" of a Christie novel (before most of them were written, and contradicting the ones that had) as its model for human behaviour, the sequence of events is a bit strange. He/it murders people according to how the plot would progress and acts as though the murderer being caught is part of the package. Okay, but this requires a plot to be predictable by anyone with access to all the facts – *including that the killer is a were-wasp from beyond the stars.* Even Agatha Christie never pulled out a surprise like that.

In short, patterning this after a Christie story means the crime has to be soluble but, to do *that,* someone needs to figure out that they are in a *Doctor Who* adventure. The Doctor's offhand reaction to Donna's questions about Dickens and Noddy indicate that *he* does... but as the Doctor's arrival was a surprise to everyone (except maybe him), the only logical explanation within the story's own terms is that Golightly knew that the Doctor was planning to crash the party and solve the case – with the added information that he could survive cyanide poisoning. But only the Doctor himself could have done that. Therefore, it was *YOU,* Doctor, who orchestrated the whole affair and thus caused four deaths, a nervous breakdown and the end of a long-established title.

Actually, why poison the Doctor at all? He wasn't on the guest-list, so Golightly cannot have included him into the plot.

How did Peach (unless he's a professor of xenobiology, and the word didn't exist then) figure *any* of this out? If all he's deduced is that Lady Eddington had a son before Roger, what made him investigate that? What convinced her to let him check on any of her past, given that this secret was likely to emerge? Only Golightly stands to gain from Peach's enquiries – so why hide the documents and look so embarrassed when the vicar walks in?

Even if we conjecture that – as a Vespiform with a download of all of Agatha Christie's novels as a guide to life (again, ahead of most them being written) – Golightly actively *wants* to be caught, he has to have set this up long before last Thursday, the first day he received said download.

Are All the Comic-Strip Adventures Fair Game?

continued from Page 129...

Frobisher, the Trods and the Pied Piper belong in a reservoir of indulgent childhood memories along with Fluid Neutralisers, the Denys Fisher Leela, the Jotastar Top Trumps cards and so forth. With hindsight, we can see vague similarities between stupid things in the strips and stupid things done this century on screen – anyone who remembers the "Flower Power" strip from late 1967 will think that Cybermen and pollen should never be combined (X8.12, "Death in Heaven") – but few are as obvious slam-dunk influences as the Series 3 ones. The *DWM* strips are perhaps more likely to be alluded to. It isn't unknown for characters from these to crop up in Big Finish projects or be alluded to on screen. There was a degree of crossover between the early Marvel-era strips and the McGann phase ones, notably with the small town of Stockbridge, and one resident, Maxwell Edison (not the serial-killer from the Beatles song) was given his moment of audio glory, played by Mark Williams months before giving an almost-identical performance as Rory's dad (X7.2, "Dinosaurs on a Spaceship").

One small thing leaves us uncertain as to whether we've seen the last of these strange neglected corners of the fan-memory: Clara, pretending to be the Doctor ("Death in Heaven"), told the Cybermen that s/he had grandchildren whose fates were unknown. Grandchildren? Plural? Are two of them left languishing on the planet Zebedee waiting to be picked up from school?

The coincidence of Golightly coming to Lady Edison's gaff is improbable, unless he A) started seeking his mother before realising he was a wasp in a wig, B) made his intentions known to the local bishop years before, and C) saw the ad in the *Church Times* when the previous incumbent died or retired. Peach therefore had a different reason for investigating Golightly's relationship to the Curbishleys and we're back at square one.

For that matter, how did Golightly figure out that Peach had figured it out? How does he later on figure out that Miss Chandrakala has figured out that Peach has figured it out? And how does a wasp hold a lead pipe?

Moreover, the Reverend must have switched denominations as an adult: "Christian Fathers" suggest a Catholic orphanage. but he's wearing a CofE collar and the church looks more Protestant than Catholic (a Catholic church would have locked up all the metal, not left it on the altar). If so, why does he cross himself on encountering the Professor's body as if for the first time? He's also gone 40 years without encountering pepper, despite all the cucumber sandwiches a stereotypical Vicar's Wife makes for cricket matches. (And just because a Vespiform *resembles* a terrestrial wasp, it doesn't mean that pipparene would work as an insecticide on a being from the Silfex galaxy. After all, the Doctor looks human, but we wouldn't recommend using walnuts and anchovies should one of our readers suffer arsenic poisoning.)

As mentioned: if you're watching the broadcast version, then the record playing immediately after the titles, "Twentieth Century Blues" (the one that starts curiously like the *Doctor Who* theme) was written by Noel Coward in 1931 for *Cavalcade*. Al Bowlly's recording of Ray Noble's "Love is the Sweetest Thing" (heard in the flashback to Roger's tryst with Davenport) came a year after that.

Why is everyone astounded that Sir Hugh is able-bodied, when he visibly legged it from the wasp at dinner? Why is the Unicorn so called? Is there a calling-card or something? We're just told that there's a clever notorious international jewel thief (© *Top Cat*, 1962) called "The Unicorn", so how do they even know it's always the same person?

How does a household with gardeners and footmen allow a giant wasp to noisily hover outside a bedroom window without comment? How does it fly past six bedroom doors in a narrow corridor without anyone hearing?

Now, we've got the usual questions that crop up when the police are kept out of an investigation. The decaying corpses of Professor Peach, Miss Chandrakala and Roger are somewhere around the house in high summer. Eventually, a coroner is required before they can be carted away (the scion and the servant could be buried on the grounds, but a professor must be attached to a university and his disappearance would be noticed). Once the deaths are explained (with aliens, were-wasp vicars, a female jewel-thief and the disappearance and amnesia of a famous author adding to the paperwork), this all has to be kept out of the papers, along with why the police weren't called and how a fake inspector and an ageing flapper managed to fool everyone. Even the aristocracy can't keep something like this quiet in 1926.

Miss Chandrakala is killed by a cornice that's light enough to move when the deceased breathes. Mrs Christie is very relaxed about being called "Agatha". Whilst most of her dialogue was in period, no sooner has "toilet" betrayed the fake Robina as common than Agatha uses the term "fallen pregnant", characteristic of the East End of London until the 1960s.[25] It's slightly silly that no one asks Chief Inspector Smith why he prefers going by the name "the Doctor".

We've got the usual question for stories with giant insects: the inverse-square law; how does it fly; how much does it need to eat, etc. (see **How Hard is It to be the Wrong Size?** under 16.6, "The Armageddon Factor"). Leaving that stuff aside, there's one shot that doesn't even make sense on its own terms: when the wasp somehow hovers from behind an archway to in front of it without battering its wings (it's just after the "they do it with mirrors" bit). Granted, the shapeshifting itself isn't much more implausible than normal, and the wasp form could contain all of its human form mass, but would need much bigger wings (see 2.5, "The Web Planet", if you dare). To have impregnated Clemency, Christopher has to have had compatible DNA (which suggests that it possessed, or killed and ate, a real human to make a template). So Golightly isn't just a hologram, but a somatically human option. Thus losing its sting in a door when attacking Donna would have meant losing a body-part in human form. Which has grown back just under a minute later.

And why is transforming into something with disproportionately small wings that make a buzzing sound accompanied by slurring sibilants and doing a Bruce Forsythe impression?[26] The Vespiform dives into the lake to retrieve the necklace because... someone told him the episode needed a climax or something. One might think it a good idea to turn back into a human instead of diving into water as a wasp; we know from the "show yerself!" scene that the transformation can be accomplished very quickly.

And... a writer, a show-runner, a script-editor and a whole cast and crew seem to think that "insectivorous" means "like an insect" rather than "insect-eating", unless the Doctor's trying to tell us that the Silfex galaxy is populated by space-aardvarks and space-starlings, which is why the one insectoid life-form has fled here to avoid being eaten. If that's the case, why Mutter's Spiral and not the Isop galaxy?

Critique It seems that the whole world adores 1920s English country-house murders. The whole world except British teenagers, film-buffs, crime novelists and, well, anyone in the UK who isn't a little old lady at heart. American television companies (and others in Europe) have a troubling tendency to think that all Britain is good for, apart from devising formats for shows they clone, is period murder mysteries. Whole channels are devoted to it, often the same ones who, with differing degrees of enthusiasm, put out Doctor Who occasionally. "The Unicorn and the Wasp" is, therefore, one of the leading contenders for "most obvious story". So let's congratulate the BBC Wales team for waiting until they had a good enough reason to bow to the inevitable.

If it had to be done, this is the way to do it. Except, maybe, the giant CGI wasp. Everything around it is a showcase for things the BBC can do almost effortlessly and US companies mess up grotesquely when they try. Watching it with hindsight messes it up slightly, because you're unavoidably aware of Felicity Jones and the extraordinary ten years she has ahead of her; at the time the main thing people noticed (other than her rotten cockney accent) was how much the camera loved her. Until the climax, nobody put a foot wrong and everything is at least as good as it needs to be. Usually far better, even.

What's also very obvious now is that the script and directing are pulling in opposite directions. Gareth Roberts is writing a Graham Williams-era story where elements from another kind BBC drama are inserted within a Doctor Who framework and made to look ridiculous (a template might be 16.3, "The Stones of Blood" riffing on the staples of Hammer films, but from a space-operatic viewpoint). Graeme Harper is directing it as a mystery, with multiple cameras at the dinner-table for seemingly-unguarded reaction-shots, and using the ludicrous Doctor Who-ish monster as a distortion of that normality. Ordinarily, this would make every scene hover on a knife-edge of which set of generic codes, acting tricks and editing decisions would prevail – but this story alternates, except when doing something else entirely (such as the parodic flashbacks). It's customary to use words such as "energy" and "pace" when discussing Harper's work, but this story gets a new kind of (ahem) buzz from this uncertainty. It's as if the episode itself is afraid that it'll be found out. Where it all falls down is at the atrocious on-screen transformation of a vicar into a wasp (to be fair, it's hard to imagine how this could *ever* have worked without going all *Alien* on us) and the subsequent inept car-chase. The latter could have worked if played straight but edited and scored over-earnestly (as per 24.3, "Delta and the Bannermen"), but the inclusion of an earnest discussion of Fixed Points and temporal flux kills the scene stone dead. This abrupt departure from the self-consciously frivolous tone of the preceding half hour probably seemed appropriate when supervising the script, but it's the start of this Doctor's habit of choosing the *worst* possible times for a fanwank conversation (see X4.13, "Journey's End" for a doozy). We were letting a Christie-pastiche with space-monsters wash over us, then it abruptly resembled the worst excesses of 1980s *Doctor Who* – but in an old car rather than running up and down corridors.

Letting it wash over us is the best option for a story such as this. If you apply even the amount of attention one needs to watch a straight Agatha Christie adaptation, it's like pouring tea into tissue paper. The "spot the title" game allows viewers to *think* they're staying engaged, but it distracts from a script that doesn't hold together even on its own peculiar terms. Instead, the look and tone of the piece is what matters – and this is appealing, mixing all the positives of such a work (the sumptuous look and costumes, the performances, the dialogue's many good gags) in a way that later attempts at "can't-fail" generic pastiches get catastrophically wrong. Looking good and ticking off genre clichés might seem like a minimum requirement, but X6.3, "The Curse of the Black Spot" and X7.3, "A Town Called Mercy" (to name but two) couldn't even get that right. For the most part, this story finds the right tone – but there is one often-cited caveat we have to discuss...

Agatha Christie was a real person, with relatives alive today who remember her. She died during transmission of 13.5, "The Brain of Morbius" (two days after Part Two). For all that the production team sought (and deployed) the approval of her grandson when making and publicising this episode, it seems to many fundamentally tasteless to caricature her the way earlier stories did HG Wells or George Stephenson. It's easy to imagine the makers of "Rosa" (X11.3) being shown this and told "not like that, please". It's especially crass to use a famous incident involving apparent mental illness (although, with hindsight, she got off lightly compared to Marilyn Monroe in X6.0, "A

Christmas Carol"). The suppressed ending with 1976 Agatha being finally cured of her nightmares would have been redemptive and perhaps more elegant, but the original opening scene was clumsy and misjudged. Fenella Woolgar and Daphne Oxenford (in the cut scenes as the old Agatha, erroneously called "Mrs Christie") give the part dignity and insight, but many would think that it should never have been tried.

What were the alternatives, though? If *any* fictional Country House murder happened in a 1920s story, you'd have inevitable comments about the Christie cycle and *Cluedo*. A coy, smarmy reference to it (such as Professor Lasky visibly reading *Murder on the Orient Express*; 23.3, "Terror of the Vervoids") would have been a bit annoying. The options became limited the moment they decided to do a story with the Doctor meeting Agatha Christie, and a full-blown pastiche – rather than meeting her in Egypt on a dig in the 1940s – was the only practical way. The known memory-loss incident in 1926 keeps things fairly straightforward, and then it's just a matter of finding the right *Doctor Who*-style element to introduce. All right, the Vespiform may have been a mistake but this production team have decided to steer clear of inventing anything that isn't a recognisable Earth creature – besides, the storyline of a famous author being stuck inside one of his own stories worked well enough for Charles Dickens. The difference is that Dickens conveniently died the following summer, but Christie threw herself into writing murder mysteries for half a century. Given the situation described here, she would have avoided such settings and stories and become an alcoholic. Even without all the doubletalk about temporal flux, there isn't a way from *that* ending to the real-world situation that inspired the entire story.

An episode with so many fun moments ought not to have been tainted by such concerns. For all its conceptual misjudgements, it's better that this episode exists than not. After later goofs, that age of Celebrity Historicals as a mainstay of *Doctor Who* passed (as it did in 1986, 1965 and the tie-in novels), so this is now a benchmark for how they used to work and what sort of storytelling they allow... or forbid.

ABOUT TIME 2008-2009

The Lore

Written by Gareth Roberts. Directed by Graeme Harper. Viewing figures: (BBC1) 8.7 million, (BBC3 repeats) 0.8 and 0.6 million, with an AI of 86%.

Repeats and Overseas Promotion *Agatha Christie Mène L'enquête, Das Einhorn und Die Wespe*

Alternate Versions The DVD replaces the (slightly anachronistic) Noel Coward record just after the titles with something less expensive.

Production

• Phil Collinson suggested that the Doctor could meet Agatha Christie; Martha's departure in "Last of the Time Lords" (X3.13) had a line added of the Doctor thinking it might be fun. Given the options available for such an idea, Russell T Davies settled on having a country-house murder with Christie as a real-life participant in a pastiche of the TV adaptations of her work, and that Gareth Roberts should write it.

One option was the older Christie as a Marple-esque figure in the 1960s, but the 1926 disappearance and the general *Jeeves and Wooster* ambience seemed like a better idea. As cream teas on the lawn came with the deal, wasps seemed like an appropriate style of alien menace (because an alien menace was unavoidable in a Celebrity Historical). They recalled the cover of the late 60s Fontana edition of *Death in the Clouds*, with a cover painting of a Cessna and a wasp for no good reason, and Roberts – no fan of wasps – went through all the possible ways to kill them before settling on drowning. The discovery of Christie's car at Silent Pool, Surrey, provided a means to tie this to the amnesia, but an attempt to have Christie as a murder suspect was abandoned. Over the course of several drafts, the script developed into one of the few attempts at a purely comedic episode (Davies was still struggling to keep what would become X4.1, "Partners in Crime" relatively straightforward) and they made a game of inserting Christie book titles into the dialogue.

By the time of the Tone Meeting in June, this was being reined in slightly as plans to re-introduce Donna had consolidated and the season-opener was made the official "funny" one. David

Tennant had asked that the original ending, with Christie holding the Vespiform at bay at the water's edge and the Doctor driving into it to save her, be amended to make the Doctor less cold-blooded. (It would also have been a logistical nightmare. The vintage cars hired for the episode had less-than-ideal brakes, especially on a muddy lakeside, and were too fragile and expensive to dent convincingly.)

• Although Christie's much-publicised disappearance was in December 1926, the team thought that a sunny Country House setting, as seen on TV (many, many times) would work better for the casual viewer, so this story was moved to the start of the production year – just after the Christmas episode – to be recorded in August in the same block as X4.3, "Planet of the Ood" (conceived of as the second story to be shown). During the late stages of recording X4.0, "Voyage of the Damned", Tennant had been commuting between Cardiff, his flat in London and his mother at a hospice in Scotland. There were plans to record without the Doctor if necessary, and although Tennant's mother died shortly before work on this episode began, he elected to continue working around the funeral planning.

• The read-through for Block Two (this episode and "Planet of the Ood") was on 7th and the shoot began the next day at Llansanor Court, seen a few times in *Who*-related episodes – not least as the eponymous Torchwood House in X2.0, "Tooth and Claw", and later as Lady Me's palatial gaff in X9.6, "The Woman Who Lived". As they shot this, another unit completed the Doctorless Bridge scenes for "Voyage of the Damned". The first day was the rooftop and some scenes at the side of the house but began with the flashback to Charlemagne's Belgium. The lawn sequences were shot the following day. As luck would have it, the otherwise dismal summer of 2007 was relieved by a perfect sunny day.

• As we've mentioned, Tennant has brought his father along: Sandy McDonald was given a non-speaking role as one of the footmen. In order to give maximum screen-time to all the potential suspects and victims, every exchange was shot multiple times to allow optimum coverage (routine procedure for real murder-mysteries, but unusual for modern *Doctor Who*). The week ended with the first scenes in the Drawing Room. As the Doctor interviewed each character one-on-one, the actors playing the suspects queued outside feeling, as Woolgar and Kendal said on the DVD commentary, like they were waiting outside the Headmaster's office.

• Monday 13th was the day the team returned to Tredegar House (last seen as 10 Downing Street in X3.12, "The Sound of Drums"). The cast were instructed to stay in character throughout each take, even if they thought they were out of shot, two cameras were running to maximise coverage. A day off followed, then back to Llansanor Court for two days of the Sitting Room location and then the 18th was the day of the Exterior (for the bathroom window and the patch of ground under it), the fields, the lawn again and the inserts of everyone in their bedrooms. By now the drizzle had returned, and a gazebo from elsewhere on the grounds was placed under the window for Agatha's chat with Donna. The 21st had three episodes being shot, with a first visit to the locked room along with the Reception at Ood Operations and the Buckingham Palace steps and fake news reports for "Voyage of the Damned". Then came two weeks where the director and stars were on Ood-Sphere.

• On 6th September, the crew made a trip to Pen Y Lon road for the low-speed car chase. For this, the crew rented a 1925 Bullnose Morris for Agatha and a Sunbeam 14/40 Tourer of the same vintage for Professor Peach's car. The gearing on these was markedly different from modern vehicles, and the clutch and brake were swapped over compared to now. Woolgar and Tennant were coached in how to avoid damaging these cars, and it got a bit competitive as the night shoot proceeded. A second unit, led by that episode's producer, Susie Liggatt, swung a roughly wasp-shaped bolster into the lake to make the appropriate-sized splash for the CG Vespiform. On the next day, they went to Hensol Castle – another familiar location – for the hotel exterior in Harrogate and the bedroom interior where Dame Agatha spent her last hours. This was also where the younger version of Lady Eddy was wistfully gazing out of a window in India. There then followed a few days off before the stars flew to Rome.

• When examining the rushes, it seemed a bit of a downer to start the story with Agatha in 1976 (it also removed any tension – even though the Doctor, Donna and Agatha logically must have survived). Thus a new end-scene was fashioned from dialogue in the old one and shot over two months later, with a facsimile book in the TARDIS cupboards. On the same day (16th November),

they reworked the locked-room scene while at work on the TARDIS scene in "Planet of the Ood" and a couple of others from the same episode.

• The episode was shown at 7.00pm, in the now-normal Barrowman sandwich, and over the end credits it was announced that, as with last year, there would be a week off for the Eurovision Song Contest. Unlike X3.7, "42", they didn't fashion a new trailer but instead stuck with the throw-forward of X4.8, "Silence in the Library" and a mention of the Trailer-maker on the website. (The *Radio Times* reminded everyone that the 2004 BBC-financed film about Christie's later life would be on BBC4 at 8.30. It's got Mark Gatiss in, like every British film then.) A few hours later, the press reported a leak of that episode's plot in some detail – conveniently introducing the public to the term "spoilers" just in time for River Song's debut.

Then the big news stories started breaking: Davies was stepping down, Steven Moffat was his successor and Tennant's commitments to the RSC meant a year with just four Specials (or five, if the already-announced Christmas 2008 episode was included). The usual un-named "sources" reported various permutations of the programme's future. The truth was more complicated and less certain than any of these pundits suggested. Moffat was courting Tennant to stay on for another year after the Specials. Some within the BBC were unsure if the series was worth retaining without Davies.

X4.8: "Silence in the Library"
(31st May, 2008)

Which One is This? Skeletons in spacesuits. After last week's familiar locale, we get a bigger library with an alarming lack of bodies – and a River runs through it.

Firsts and Lasts ... in which we introduce Professor River Song. Mind you, as far as she's concerned, this is pretty much her last adventure. Nonetheless, like K9 – another gimmicky one-off character who became the defining feature of a particular phase of the series – she'll be back, with several catch-phrases (River's first line, in fact, is "Hello, Sweetie"). Unlike K9, River persists in rather matronly flirting and always shoots to kill.

This was the first episode broadcast after its author, Steven Moffat, was announced as the anointed heir of Russell T. Some of the Moffat repertoire comes onto the board here (tune in next week for the remaining pieces)... it's the first story featuring something with a swivelling top that has a human face on (see the Smilers in X5.2, "The Beast Below", and the Spoonfaces in X7.7, "The Bells of Saint John"), plus scary spacesuited strangers with reflective visors (X6.1, "The Impossible Astronaut" and so forth), and the first appearance of River's diary with the TARDIS cover (it'll crop up as late as Series 10).

It's the start of the whole "sonic screwdriver doesn't work on wood" set-up we'll see getting hammered into the ground over the next seven years, as well as futuristic tech made, apparently, from polished oak or walnut.

And, according to the DVD commentary, this is the first time Tennant did up all four buttons in the blue suit. Gosh!

Watch Out For...

• In the finest traditions of the 70s episodes, the teaser pre-credit sequence is reworked with context about halfway through. (Those wishing to argue that modern *Who* uses a refined television grammar that earlier audiences couldn't have followed might like to compare this opening and its subsequent reconfiguration with 12.2, "The Ark in Space" or 14.3, "The Deadly Assassin". That's far from the only straight steal from Robert Holmes in this episode.) This teaser is that a little girl with a make-believe library sees it getting visitors. If you haven't worked out who the girl's new imaginary friend is, the whole of Moffat's *Who* career must have passed you by.

• After *Torchwood* made the fannish term "retcon" a plot-point, here we have the great unwashed brought up-to-speed on the concept of "Spoilers". The Doctor explains it to Donna, and then we hear it twice more in this episode and a lot thereafter. A *lot*.

In fact, with one thing and another, the dialogue in this episode is very repetitive. Because the story is – at risk of a spoiler of our own – about electronically-recorded memories playing out, the last two minutes of the episode are two recently-deceased characters repeating their lines over and over as people run around. Confusingly, with hindsight, the girl's dad gets to call her "Sweetie".

• The "throw-forward" (trailer, in English) omits any mention or sign of Donna. With River Song's foreknowledge including something horri-

ble happening to Donna, and the recording of her face and voice claiming that she has joined all the other vanished Librarians, it genuinely looks as if they might have killed her off. To add to the confusion, one line, out of context, has an angry Doctor saying "You've just killed someone I liked".

The Continuity

The Doctor Upon bringing Donna to the biggest library in the universe, the first authors he mentions are Jeffrey Archer, Bridget Jones and Monty Python [if it's some sort of joke on Donna's reading tastes, it falls completely flat]. He likes the scent of books. They've landed in the biographies section, a favourite of his.

When Donna teases him about being sent a message sealed with a kiss, he looks confused and asks if everyone doesn't do that.

While naturally curious about River Song, it takes absurdly long for him to understand that she's meeting him out of chronological order. Her knowledge of the TARDIS's Emergency Programme One, combined with her possession of a sonic screwdriver that's unmistakably of TARDIS manufacture, worries him no end.

In this century, he has no problem admitting he's a time traveller. As a matter of principle, he and Donna simultaneously accept Mr Lux contracts of their life rights – then rip them into pieces.

• *Background.* Sometimes he seems very familiar with the Library, sometimes basic things about it come as complete surprises. [The logical inference from this and other anomalies is that the Doctor, of all people, has read *about* the Library but hasn't been there. That's why he spouts all sorts of info-dumpery in the first episode, but doesn't know that there's a Moon that talks about rhubarb puddings in the second. The fact that such a famous place was shut for a century is itself lost on him; that's weird, like knowing about the Library of Alexandria, but not the fire that destroyed it.] Likewise, he has some general knowledge about the Vashta Nerada.

• *Foreground.* As will be the case in River Song's later/earlier meetings, there's a sequence where they compare notes on what they remember having done. He will, at some point, meet her at the Wreck of the *Byzantium* [X5.4, "The Time of Angels"] and a picnic at Asgard [this is probably what the business of the gold dress was about in

What Were the Best Online Extras?

In **Was 2006 the Annus Mirabilis?** In Volume 7, we suggested that one of the underpinnings of all the televised goodies was the role of the *Doctor Who* BBC website(s). At the time, these included a dozen different in-universe websites, loads of games, and everything else down to – and including – lots of shiny desktop wallpapers.

In addition to this was all the lovingly built-up content from the prior years of the BBC Cult website, in which *Doctor Who* already had pride of place by a large margin, with several ebook releases of old Virgin novels and two fan-written guides to the series. Fast-forward to the anniversary year and what's odd is how much of this older material was still on hand to bulk up the site; the version of Pong that was whipped up to make the release of a script page from "The Next Doctor" just a little more challenging than looking at a news article was still to be found in the eleventh Doctor's Games tab, right underneath all the quizzes and "How to Make a Cube". And the link that led back to something that's recognisably the pre-2005 website was still right there on the main page.

By Jodie Whittaker's first season, we had a site so slackly-run that they forgot to tell anyone that the Daleks were returning even after it had been a news item on various BBC news sites and stated in a trailer they'd neglected to paste in (the worst goof was for X11.9, "It Takes You Away", where preview clips were marked *this item will be ready shortly* hours after the episode had aired in the US). How did things slide so badly?

Well, it's a fairly involved and somewhat sordid story, but let's start where it begins: the BBC Cult site. In 1998, someone had the bright idea of using a chunk of the BBC's website assets to cover some of the geekier programmes. In practice, this meant American shows: *Voyager*, *3rd Rock from the Sun*, and *The X Files*, but also *Seinfeld*, *Larry Sanders* and *The Simpsons*. If you were in Britain at the time, this constellation of series makes absolute sense (except *Seinfeld*, although a lot of people pretended to like it to seem cosmopolitan). A lot of it is the supposed cachet of getting all the American references, and that quintessentially 90s association of "minority interest" and "foreign" with "cool" (see **What's All This Stuff About Anoraks?** under 24.1, "Time and the Rani"). Nevertheless, they knew their target audience; the first British programme to have pride of place on the Cult front page was *Doctor Who* (updated with a snazzy blue background rather than the quick-and-plain black that used earlier; pay attention to backgrounds in

this account, they'll be important). This was summer of 1998, as people were pondering what the BBC might be doing for the 35th anniversary (answer: ditching all continuity in the books range and releasing 5.3, "The Ice Warriors" on VHS), with an invite for readers to write in for the first time by participating in the new *Doctor Who* forums.

But it didn't really get exciting until 2000, when James Goss started heading an off-shoot website that focused solely on *Doctor Who*. New material started coming thick and fast, with several online webcasts (a reworked version of 17.6, "Shada", and a new Colin Baker story called "Real Time"). There was even an overly ambitious attempt to reboot the series ("Death Comes to Time", an item that even the most diligent of *Doctor Who* timeline obsessives never, ever managed to coherently explain or fit with any other content and with which few really bothered.)

We've discussed the hassle that so many teams jostling to get *Doctor Who* caused for any of them getting it at all. (See the essay with A5, "The Infinite Quest" and compare to Doug Naylor's attempt to get a *Red Dwarf* movie before eventually chucking it in and returning to television, or the hassle that Douglas Adams had with his *Hitchhiker* script in Hollywood.) Russell T Davies had been trying to sell a new version of the show since 2000. This kept falling through for a lot of reasons. To cut a long story mercifully short, BBC Worldwide's failure to get anything off the ground offered an opportunity. This is where the "Scream of the Shalka" webcast comes in.

It was meant to be the biggest project the Cult site had yet seen, inaugurating the fandom's coming to terms with no televised *Who* ever again, and restarting it in a new format for a new century. Unfortunately, one of the side effects of the BBC's organisational structure (creating lots of little sub-units who had no idea what other people are doing) was that this arrived September 2003, just as the BBC announced that the proper *Doctor Who* series was coming back, and got lost in the hype over a new television series.

It was an understandable mistake and all parties behaved themselves in public. Well, almost. When queried on the issue, Davies would dodge by slagging off Richard E. Grant as having phoned in his performance (for anyone wondering why an obvious candidate for a guest appearance was away from the show so long, this may well have

continued on Page 139...

B1, "Night and the Doctor". It's rendered as a short story in *The Legends of River Song* anthology]

[(NB: for the sake of keeping things simple, we're disregarding River's involvement in the Big Finish audios. In those, she manages to hang out with the McGann Doctor a lot as well as many of the previous versions, always finding some means of obscuring her identity with them – up to and including a psychic wimple. Those stories are contradicted, a bit, by River's claim that the Doctor here is "younger than I've ever seen you".]

• *Ethics.* After telling Donna they were going to the beach [it could almost qualify as a Moffat running-gag if the beach was going to be Rio (X5.8, "The Hungry Earth" and X7.3, "A Town Called Mercy") or Space Florida (X5.13, "The Big Bang") – in fact, almost *any* story where they aren't shooting on the Welsh coast for real], he switched tracks when River's psychic paper message came through, but lies about the real reason until Donna forces the info out of him. He generally tries to keep his companions away from major plot developments of their future, though he notes he's not very good at that.

Despite working out what the real threat is by halfway through the episode, he keeps this information under wraps until after people have started dying. It doesn't bother him when River Song wants to shut off the stuttering Data Ghosts. The practice of donating one's face after death worries him even less. Later on, he tells Donna that she's safe from the Vashta Nerada to "shut her up" [like that was going to work] and teleports her to the TARDIS against her inclinations.

• *Inventory: Sonic Screwdriver.* It can increase the mesh-density of the suits, theoretically then less penetrable by Vashta Nerada. [It's not much good with cellulose fibres. The procedure the Doctor seems to describe when confronted with a wood door is the resonance-frequency trick Moffat detailed back in X1.9, "The Empty Child".]

Upon receiving a teleport, the TARDIS sends an automatic confirmation signal to the screwdriver.

Here it's established that the Doctor will give River Song one of his sonic screwdrivers. The one she carries is considerably more faded and battered than his, but is clearly not his later models. [X5.1, "The Eleventh Hour"; X7.15, "The Day of the Doctor"; X9.12, "Hell Bent". We see River's screwdriver brand-new in X9.13, "The Husbands of River Song" at the start of a long night, so it must have had a lot of use.]

• *Inventory: Psychic Paper.* As in X2.1, "New Earth," the Doctor receives a long-distance call via psychic paper. ["Library" isn't much use for temporal coordination, so there must be something else on it besides the message he shows to Donna.]

• *Inventory: Other.* He uses his glasses to examine the sphere up close, then neglects to remove them. It would appear he's ceased carrying a torch [unless we're meant to read some alpha male message into his confiscating Mr Lux's].

The TARDIS The TARDIS "recognises" [perhaps because the Doctor configured it that way] if Donna teleports inside, but nobody else. The TARDIS is so programmed that five hours after said teleport, Emergency Programme One will activate [consistent with the "four-and-a-half" hour timeframe in X2.4, "The Girl in the Fireplace"]. However it doesn't really work, since Donna materialises halfway and then vanishes with a scream. [We can't say this contradicts X1.12, "Bad Wolf" since she hadn't properly arrived, but see **Things That Don't Make Sense** and **The Big Picture**.]

[Now for the timey-wimey faff... River's message arrived at a point designated by the Ship (a detail explained in X5.12, "The Pandorica Opens"), so the TARDIS seems to have stage-managed her arrival into the Doctor's life right at the end of hers and thus all subsequent encounters. Therefore, everything in Series 5 and after results from this misdirected message.

[If we take this and other such uses of the TARDIS coms at face value, the Doctor must have a stockpile of messages that the TARDIS has always-already received, and buffers for the right moment. The sequence of events in X4.6, "The Doctor's Daughter" and X8.5, "Time Heist" require *that* particular incarnation to do things on *that* particular day to allow the message to be sent/ have been sent in the first place. However, the messages received in X6.4, "The Doctor's Wife"; X6.9, "Night Terrors"; "The Big Bang" and the various SOS messages the Doctor has responded to when looking like Tom Baker – 13.2, "Planet of Evil"; 15.2, "The Invisible Enemy"; 17.3, "The Creature From the Pit" – must be at the Ship's discretion. This, once again, suggests that the TARDIS is manipulating the Doctor. See **Why Do Time Lords Always Meet in Sequence?** under 22.3, "The Mark of the Rani". It's possible that the

What Were the Best Online Extras?

continued from Page 137...

something to do with it) and writer Paul Cornell played the stalwart fanboy (he was already a shoo-in to write for the televised version, more than enough reason not to rock the boat). It wasn't *entirely* ignored. For one, the Interpretation of the Master – played by Sir Derek Jacobi – was, unfortunately for purist Delgado fans, rather more in line with the slap-slap kiss-kiss slash of the new series. "Shalka" was released at the end of 2003 as a slightly embarrassing oddity and everyone started speculating about who the *next* ninth Doctor would be.

Meanwhile, the BBC shook up their websites and shut down a lot, including the Cult websites (cue a massive amount of internal politicking; accounts make it seem like the Cult/technology-friendly crowd are duking it out with the higher-ups for the soul and future of the BBC), as the notorious "BBC Trust" started messing with everything to look as if they were doing something. Everything except, and this is an important *except*, for the *Doctor Who* website. Goss and what was left of the BBC Cult team had nothing else to work on, so we got two years of top-notch website content. This started off with a real-life version of Clive's website from X1.1, "Rose" (which included the two sections we see in the episode, plus a funny, frightening and downright touching guest-book, with entries sent in by the general public).

For the first two seasons of the show's return, the BBC made a lot of little websites that expanded on the show's existence. These were timed so as to be updated and posted in sync with the episodes being aired. For the generation of Internet-savvy kids coming to *Doctor Who* for the first time, it became a ritual to look for these as soon as the episode had aired – checking out the full spoiler version of the Fear Factor, see what curious bits of lore there might be in the Fact Files. (Little bits of info, largely just simple continuity explanations for the new fans, but with a couple of behind-the-scenes facts to freshen it up. James Moran saying that the TARDIS-as-an-artwork in X4.2, "The Fires of Pompeii" was a deliberate allusion to 17.2, "City of Death", for instance.) There might be a new game, too. (Indeed, there was a fresh one for nearly every story in 2006; Flash games, but well programmed and sometimes fairly involved – the one for X2.11, "Fear Her", in which a crayon Doctor has to play connect-the-dots and avoid being erased from existence by

the scribble monsters, is considerably more suspenseful than the actual episode if you play with the sound down. The backstory behind these: the BBC awarded an external contractor £150,000 to get these done properly, and got their money's worth.)

Goss went in 2007, the website visibly trod water the next year and then went into a bit of a decline. The red-and-gold Tennant design stuck around until Matt Smith, when they gave it a face-lift that brought back a colour-scheme like the blue-green Eccleston-era one and tidied up the site in a few other ways. Yet, generally, at that point all the energy started to go into making fancy games. Aside from a few good short stories by reliable *Who* stalwarts, nothing interesting happened there any more – and the URL changed from bbc.co.uk/doctorwho to bbc.co.uk/programmes/b006q2x0 to fall in line with the rest of the BBC programme websites.

The next notable development was the 50th anniversary website, which was really just a news feed with a giftshop. Anyone looking for information on the recovered nine-episode haul of Season Five clicked on the BBC's official outlet in October 2013 and saw a pre-determined list of ten monsters from which you were to pick the scariest (regardless of whether *any* of those ten genuinely did it for you as a child). In the meantime, a great deal of material on the BBC site is now tricky to find if you don't know *precisely* what you're looking for, accessible only through the Wayback Machine or just gone entirely.

Nevertheless, those two years were a brilliant time to be a *Doctor Who* fan of any sort and that went double for the ones who liked the website. So here's a quartet of the best features from the early days.

1. Ebooks

The section dealing with *Doctor Who* books was a large and wonderful place once. There were previews of the ongoing BBC book line, with witty tagline descriptions and extracts from the most recent books (quite well picked extracts, by and large; it's remarkable how promising the first chapter of *Deadly Reunion* seems in comparison with the rest of the novel). There were interviews with the authors, dozens of them. By the time the PDA range was cancelled (that's the Past Doctor Adventures: stories about Hartnell to McCoy, the

continued on Page 141...

Time Lords' absence might be connected to the Doctor's newly-acquired problem of dealing with the consequences of things he's yet to do.]

The Supporting Cast

• *Donna.* She claims to have learned how to kick down doors to "surprise" boyfriends. [We know from Lance (X3.0, "The Runaway Bride") that she doesn't necessarily have the best judgement in men, but it doesn't quite fit the version of her love-life Wilf gave us. She also neglected to use this handy skill when Stacy was screaming for help; X4.1, "Partners in Crime".]

By her own admission, she agrees with the Doctor's nickname of 'Pretty Boy' rather too quickly and covers this by saying that his looks are only 'meh'. She's surprised by the idea of time travellers meeting out of chronological order, and concerned that River knows of her ultimate fate but isn't talking [see, of course, X4.13, "Journey's End"].

The Nodes freak her out more than flesh-eating shadows.

• *River Song.* We're informed right off the bat that she's a keen liar and can't be trusted. Nevertheless, most of her interactions regarding the Doctor seem honest, but flirtatious. His older self habitually comes running when River summons him.

[It's unclear whether she's met this incarnation of the Doctor before – she mentions him having young eyes, not a completely different face, and recognises him on sight. Then again, the ninth Doctor says he's '900' in X1.4, "Aliens of London", but the tenth is only '906' in "The End of Time", which suggests the Tennant Doctor only lived six years. If so, he can't be *that* much younger in spirit if River has met this version before; it seems just as likely that she's astonished to meet an incarnation *so* young compared to the last one she met: the Capaldi Doctor, by the time she meets him, is at least a thousand years older. We also know from X9.13, "The Husbands of River Song" that River has photos of the previous Doctors' faces. Either way, she goes a while presuming that that Pretty Boy is pretending not to know her on purpose, rather than confront the idea that he genuinely hasn't met her yet. The reasons for this will be revealed down the road.]

When the Doctor finally explains that he doesn't know her, River looks stricken. Nonetheless, she still trusts him implicitly and

absolutely. She knows enough about Donna that she's obviously pained by her future. There's chicken in River's lunch [so she's not vegetarian and archaeological packed-lunches have gone lo-tech – cf 5.1, "The Tomb of the Cybermen"; 16.3, "The Stones of Blood"]. She's obviously pained by her knowledge of Donna's future, but needs to be told who this stroppy ginge is.

In purely personal asides that may not be reliable... she says she's professor at an as-yet unnamed university. She's dated androids and thinks "they're rubbish". She's been paid quite a large sum for arranging this exclusive archaeological expedition, but refused to sign Mr Lux's contract. How seriously we should take her claim that she fancies everyone in the room except Lux isn't clear, but she saves the sweet talk for the Doctor. Donna doesn't even get a look-in.

River's diary is a dark blue, with a cover modelled to resemble a stylized police box. When searching for earlier points in her life, she flips towards the left. The two of them apparently compare diaries a lot in his future. Nevertheless, he's not allowed a peek because of rules he will set up for himself.

[Moffat's stated that River's "squareness gun" is indeed the one from "The Empty Child"; Jack left it in the TARDIS and River found it in the Doctor's personal future. Presumably it still has the same battery problems, as she doesn't think to use it for safety-sweeping. Nor does she replace the portion of wall she removed with the "rewind" function, a mistake that makes this story a two-parter.]

Planet Notes

• *The Library.* A library the size of the planet, the biggest in history; the index computer occupies the planet's core. The whole place is the project of another family-run corporation, Felman Lux. Three generations ago, the computer running the system sent out a message saying "The lights are going out" with a data extract saying "4022 saved. No survivors." There were 4022 customers that day. It locked down the planet so securely it's taken a century to break back in.

The Library was sturdily built; after a hundred years, everything still looks fresh and dust-free, and the computer Nodes are in working order. These Nodes are made of stone, or something that looks like it, with a space where an appropriate human face – donated by dead volunteers – can be modelled on top.

What Were the Best Online Extras?

continued from Page 139...

equivalent of the Virgin *Missing Adventures*), they'd had a rudimentary message board set up for people to discuss the latest release.

This wasn't the best of it, though. There were was full copies of various choice VIrgin *New Adventures* and *Missing Adventures*, rereleased one by one with fresh new illustrations: *Human Nature*, *Nightshade*, *The Scales of Injustice*, *The Empire of Glass*, *The Well-Mannered War*, *Lungbarrow*, *The Sands of Time*, and *The Dying Days*. All of these featured commentary by the writers. (Paul Cornell actually did two, after the television rendering of *Human Nature*; by now the Tennant main page section of the website, done up in teal and orange, was already being differentiated from the Eccles-and-older areas of the website, which were all in the bluish-green that characterised his TARDIS lighting, with separate main pages for both. So the new site had information on the new episode, and the old site had information on the old book, with easy linkage back and forth...) It was a delightful, evident connection between the old and the new.

These all vanished from the BBC website at the end of 2010. Six months later, the BBC started testing out e-books on demand and these days an increasing number of authors are having their old books getting back into print. Which is good. But these eight were freely available to the public.

2. The Actually-Quite-Good Dalek Game

In the interests of strict accuracy, we must note that the pre-Eccleston iteration of the website had some games; an electronic version of Top Trumps (we spoke about this in Volumes 3b and 6) and a frankly absurd time-travelling tennis game where one could play as John Lennon and Shakespeare at Wimbledon. Those were relatively simple Flash games without much depth to them, sort of like the Google Doodle one for the 50th anniversary.

"The Last Dalek" was different. It went up on the BBC website just after "Dalek" (X1.6), to best capitalise on fan excitement (as we've mentioned, updates were very closely tied to the broadcast of the actual episodes under Davies; flavour text about all the stories was appearing on Mickey's website up through X1.11, "Boom Town"). It was far more involved than anything that had shown up before: easily worth an hour of play, especially if you took the new game-plus option that let you destroy everything with the big endgame gun. For a generation of kids just coming of age with the

Internet, it was exciting and a reassuring sign that the programme-makers were just as interested in what was happening off-screen as on. It looked just right. And you got to play as the Dalek.

For quite a while, it wasn't clear whether there was even going to *be* a Dalek episode, which makes pulling together a solid and entertaining game even more impressive. The continuity was tight, too; it's explicitly presented as a version of "Dalek" with no Rose standoff to get in the way of the Dalek shooting things, so there's references to Van Statten, the alien hairdryer and the Doctor's desperate last stand. The ending, in which a ghostly Christopher Eccleston swears he'll not leave his TARDIS unprotected and tries hopelessly to stop you from making the Daleks the Lords of Time, is at least as affecting as anything broadcast this century.

It was so solid a platformer, in fact, that they went back and did it again with K9 wandering through Eccleston and Tennant episodes. That version's considerably more surreal.

But the tie-in websites themselves were the best, as you'd never know what you were going to get...

3. Weird Associated Websites

Mickey Smith was a godsend for this purpose, as he provided a narrative hook for all this extra content. The idea was, he took over Clive's website after "Rose". (Old-skool fans will have recognised the "fanzine-as-alien-conspiracy" joke inherent in the setup.) In practice, this meant a series of exciting, sometimes acerbic, sometimes naive commentaries on the episodes as they happened, with odd tie-ins (an essay by a young Adam, Mickey's attempts to make sense of the events of X1.8, "Father's Day" 30 years on without even knowing as much as the Doctor and Rose do). His characterisation on the website is miles ahead of what we got on screen. The version of the site for Series 2 was lighter and definitely more child-focused; Noel Clarke recorded several video messages to introduce the games, and explain to the viewer how important it was to chase the Clockwork Robots or break into the Deffry Vale website by acing their aptitude test. For the parallel universe game, you even got instructions from Ricky.

Yet Clive's wasn't the only website: the other function of Mickey's website was to serve as a

continued on Page 143...

Biographies are at the equator. Fission cells designed to outlast suns fuel the lighting. Index points are associated with teleports. There are wooden-looking flying security globes with embedded lenses. These have an unspecified connection to the girl talking to Dr Moon.

It's quieter on Sundays. The Library system can look for life forms, but isn't designed to scan for more than 1,000,000,000,000 life forms on the planet at once. One of the Courtesy Nodes requests that mobile comm units be switched off.

It's four days by spaceship from the expedition's starting-off point to the Library. It's apparently possible to confuse the ship's toilet with its escape pods.

The Non-Humans

• *Vashta Nerada.* Swarms of microscopic beings that live in shadows, and look like shadows themselves. They inhabit 'Earth and a billion other worlds', passing unnoticed because they mainly subsist on 'road kill'. In sufficient numbers, they can devour a person in seconds. Light doesn't kill them but can slow them down, as does a tightly woven spacesuit. The best option, according to the Doctor: run away.

History

• *Dating.* [Bloody Nora! If the baseline chronology of River Song is reliable and linear, this is some considerable time after 5145, the year named in "The Pandorica Opens" (X5.12), as River is a Professor now. She currently has no Vortex Manipulator that we can see, so let's run with the idea that the Doctor played fair at the end of "The Husbands of River Song" (X9.13) and took her back to base in the same time she left. So that's 5343, plus however long it takes to build a restaurant on a crash-site plus four years for the booking of a balcony-seat then 24 years (we'll assume they all use Earth-standard years, as they seem to have embraced Christmas across the 12 galaxies). Therefore, if River *isn't* time travelling at present it could be as late as 5371. Not a Sunday, apparently.

[But... the Doctor here says it's the 'fifty-first century', and does the same during the *Byzantium* crisis in X5.4, "The Time of Angels". He doesn't know about the Library being self-quarantined for a century, so perhaps he's naming the century in which the Library was built/operative and it's now only the fifty-*second* century (in line with the hard

dates given in X6.7, "A Good Man Goes to War" and "The Pandorica Opens"). We're fairly safe in assuming that the Library doesn't have a long tenure prior to becoming isolated, since – we learn next episode – Cal is Lux's aunt, not his great-great-great aunt or older. How we square that against the Library's fame is a different matter.]

River claims the Library's teleport machinery is now 'ancient'. [And yet the systems work better than anything anyone else has encountered. River's standard of "ancient" is questionable, as she has experience of digs in the future – among other things, we now know she excavated the ruined spaceship under the restaurant on Darillium some 400 years after being on the crashing ship.]

Alternatives to books include fiction-mist, holovids and direct-to-brain downloads, apparently. Nonetheless, the haptic and olfactory features of books have prevailed over Kindles and the like. Modes of data storage have expanded tremendously. It's considered ordinary to donate one's face after death, no more disturbing than endowing a park bench. Generations in the 5000s seem as long as they are today, and Sundays remain meaningfully distinct from other days of the week. They still have recognisable chicken legs as a snack.

The Felman Lux Corp. is family-owned [possibly after the same model as Ood Operations a millennium earlier]. It seems there's no such thing as sexual harassment legislation in this century.

Spacesuit hardware includes neural relays that can briefly retain an individual's consciousness after death. The data patterns begin to degenerate fairly quickly into a looped piece of dialogue – mere minutes in most cases.

The Analysis

The Big Picture ("Silence in the Library" and "Forest of the Dead") As is often the case, if this had been an old-style "Where Did This Come From?" entry, we could simply have pointed you at Volume 4, especially the stories written by Robert Holmes. Whole sequences, and the general tendency of the first episode, are recognisably transplanted into this script. We mentioned the pre-credit sequence being shown again with context, a hook you ought to know from "The Ark in Space" and "The Deadly Assassin" but compare

What Were the Best Online Extras?

continued from Page 141...

clearing house for the new URLs. The second one, and one of the better ones, was a UNIT website put up shortly before the broadcast of "Aliens of London" (X1.4). At this point, it played coy with the whole "aliens are our business" angle and only offered little teasers about UNIT being set up in 1968 – although there was quite a good joke post-dated to 10th March about asking people to please not pirate a file that looked like "something they would most want to download".

After the climatic "buffalo" in X1.5, "World War Three", fans rushed off to try out that password (if they didn't get the hint from the episode itself, Mickey had posted it on his website) and were greeting with a series of deeply sarcastic UNIT message boards, some of which bewailed the existence of Mickey's website. It kept updating until "The Christmas Invasion" (X2.0), presumably so that Davies could make his own decisions about how to tell stories about modern-day Britain coming to terms with aliens... which he never quite got around to doing.

There were lots of other websites by the time "Doomsday" aired (X2.13). A couple were educational (the tie-in for "The Christmas Invasion" had some actual facts about space as well as in-jokes about British Rocket Group). By the end of it, they could even do a parody one – Millingdale Ice Cream was a website about a fictional ice cream company that existed merely to play an ice cream truck jingle version of the swoopy Flavia theme, and whet viewer's appetites with silly ice cream flavours – satsuma Christmas Surprise and the like. Then the Graphics department thought it'd be funny to use it in the background of X2.10, "Love & Monsters", so "Madame du Popadom" ice cream is probably now canonical.

Goss had hoped for "dozens" of websites for Series 2 – in practice it worked out to about one per episode, with an accompanying game, but that's still more than then we'd had before or since. From "The Christmas Invasion" on, most of the story content on these was written by Joseph Lidster. Goss had hired him after a chat in a pub and compliments about a Big Finish audio (probably "The Rapture"), and was kept on long enough to write Martha's Myspace – which showed a much more laidback, free-and-easy character than the one we actually got to enjoy on the show.

As we said, Goss left soon after that as well, and that's about when this sort of thing ended – they revamped the look of the website and kept making games, but a lot of energy was now going into the *Torchwood* tie-in websites instead. For whatever reason, Moffat was never as interested in this form of storytelling (even though Lidster ended up doing website content for *Sherlock*), so the website under him largely became a clearing-house.

After the end of *Doctor Who Confidential*, it has also been the one-stop location for behind-the-scenes stuff and interviews, but these are less involving. There is, however, a lot of effort put into getting younger users to develop their own games from available components released through the site and unlocked as they appear on telly. This is a remnant of the educational remit of the more complicated professionally-made games we'll get to in a moment.

4. Fear Forecasters

Long before liveblogging became an acceptable way to behave during all new television broadcasts (if it ever did), the BBC website crew came up with a nice and simple concept. Shiny new *Doctor Who* was bound to be scary, so some sort of forewarning for impressionable families might be helpful. Enter the Fear Forecasters: Amy, Harry, Samuel and Adam, aged 5 to 13, and their mums and dads. They got to watch the new episode *before anyone else* (and to their credit, the kids always seemed to find this as exciting as it should be), commenting on its scariness throughout, and at the end of it the four children would average out their Fear Factor to offer an estimate of how scary a story was, on a one to five scale. (Theoretically, that is, although in practice nothing scored lower than a two. Since you're curious, "The Impossible Planet" scored as the single scariest episode ever.)

And for the first few Forecasts, that was pretty much all there was to it, with a transcriber dutifully taking down minute-by-minute notes about "these aliens are really freaky" and "that's scary!" But it quickly evolved into something rather more special – as close to an unmediated look at a family watching *Doctor Who* as you're likely to get. Amy commenting that the golden cloud in "The Doctor Dances" were obviously faeries, one of the dads stoutly pretending not to have had a crush on Elisabeth Sladen and being teased about it through "School Reunion", the kids recognising

continued on Page 145...

Miss Evangelista's investigating a silent and hither-to-unsuspected door and coming unstuck to Sarah in "Ark" Part One, then compare the cliff-hanger to that episode's (not so much the Wirrn coming out of the closet, but the discovery that Sarah has become part of the world-machine).

What's interesting is that the conceptual basis for the teleport in each story is different. Back when broadcasting people was first used in stories, it was analogous to television; people or objects were scanned and broken down, the components sent and reassembled. This is the origin of *The Fly*, a story lurking behind "The Ark in Space", and the source of all Dr McCoy's objections to the transporter beams in *Star Trek*. In the 90s, the various reiterations of *Trek* took the digital model and posited teleports working by processing people and things as information, to be manipulated and downloaded (except when the episode needed something else, sometimes involving Reg Barclay – see X3.6, "The Lazarus Experiment"). There were transporter malfunction stories in the Shatner series (let off the hook because the best one, in "The Enemy Within", was written by Richard Matheson and thus sacrosanct) but the spin-offs contradicted each other with merry abandon. The cast felt like playing different characters one week and they'd done "possession" and "Alternate Universe" already that year? Just give them a glitchy beam-up. Similarly, in place of the Kirk-Spock-McCoy staple of we've-found-a-planet-that-resembles-an-RKO-backlot-populated-by-people-in-stock-costumes, the Frenchman who drank Earl Grey kept getting stuck in the Holodeck.

Eventually, they crossbred these set-pieces, and in *Star Trek: Deep Space Nine* we got an episode where people were saved in the holodeck as characters after a transporter malfunction (it was called "Our Man Bashir", a Bond spoof less amusing than even Roger Moore). Only the physical appearances of the regulars was stored, their minds were somehow kept in separate files.

So we've got electronically-created fantasy-worlds and teleports somehow working the same way and mental processes running independently of bodies in a different computer... we mentioned "The Deadly Assassin", didn't we? For those just joining us, this gave us the low-down on how Gallifrey normally functioned and included the APC net: a collective mind containing the stored consciousnesses of dead Time Lords, within which the Doctor's living mind interfaced within a mental landscape formed by his rival, the aptly-named Chancellor Goth. This was part of the Time Lords' mainframe, the Matrix. That name's been re-used since. The Wachowskis took the epistemological/ontological musings of the average bored eight-year-old and milked it for a trilogy (Morpheus, meet Dr Moon).

There were more mature, meticulous examinations of the basic ideas in authors such as Lewis Carroll, Philip K Dick and Bishop Berkeley, but a more apposite comparison – if not a direct influence – is Buster Keaton. His film *Sherlock Jr.* (1924) had an extended riff on the idea of someone from our world entering a film and being caught out by the edits. Three minutes of slapstick ensues before they get on with the plot, but the slapstick's all anyone remembers. Woody Allen inverted the idea with *The Purple Rose of Cairo* (1985), and had a 30s film interrupted by one of the characters walking out into the cinema and wondering why the usual movie grammar wasn't working (it didn't fade to black when he kissed someone, for example). The clearest precedent for what happens in this episode is the "Sprimpo" sketch from *Rutland Weekend Television* Series 2, where a woman is diagnosed with bad continuity: she sees a doctor about it and is told to cut out the next two weeks (after which she says she's very hungry).

However, a digitally-mediated afterlife is a notion that really starts with Dick's novel *Ubik* (1968) and then the 1976 *Doctor Who*-variety Matrix, but completely kicks in with cyberpunk, especially the compendium of what would soon become clichés, *Neuromancer* (1984). That version is essentially a jumped-up CD ROM of someone's recorded thoughts and habits that can be accessed, whereas the half-lifers in *Ubik* are still conscious, if increasingly vague (the best on-screen approximation being the Captain in *Dark Star*). This sort of thing will receive a thorough hammering by the end of Series 8 and the difference between memory and awareness is smudged even more than it is here, most perplexingly in "Dark Water" (X8.11). The confusion of mental interfacing with a digitally-created world and physically being teleported to an actual place that follows Donna's being saved is also at the start of the many things about "Heaven Sent" (X9.11) that resist any attempt to make sense of it.

People finding that "reality" was a film set was

What Were the Best Online Extras?

continued from Page 143...

Paul Cornell's name for "Human Nature" and cheering... it turned into an uninhibited, rambunctious, enthusiastic record. Endless joy at the opportunities the show offers for scatological jokes, snarky and adoring asides from the dads, lots of crisps and singing along to the theme tune. It's exactly the sort of viewing experience that the BBC was hoping to encourage.

This went on for five years, with the kids growing up, becoming more fannish, and switching from VHS to DVDs (they stopped reviewing at X4.15, "Planet of the Dead", probably for publicity reasons), but the feature hasn't been seen since. Quite why no one thought of doing this for Steven Moffat episodes is a question, especially as scaring small children seems to be his *raison d'etre*. (It should be noted in his favour that a Moffat episode always went down as being quite scary. Except for the one set in France, anyway.)

With everyone in the BBC using the series to prove that their guesses about how to transition synergistically into being a 360-degree multi-platform content-provider (or somesuch managementese) had turned out right for once, the website started to become almost the justification for the series. When the reworked BBC website became the home of iPlayer, the catch-up service for licence-fee-payers (and a few privileged tablet-owners overseas, mentioned in X7.16, "The Time of the Doctor"), inevitably *Doctor Who* was used to launch it. We saw when discussing the promotion of X4.0, "Voyage of the Damned" how the public's ability to see it any time in the following week was both mentioned whenever possible and – crucially – included when calculating the final ratings figures. Tennant's last two years were the place where the website bore the brunt of pre-publicity, in effect replacing *Totally Doctor Who*.

Following this, things went into, well, whatever the phase after overdrive is[32]. Piers Wenger, stepping into Julie Gardner's shoes, pitched the online material as being *as important as what was on telly*. To this end, the computer games of the eleventh Doctor were provided to the British public for free and, we were told, to be treated as canonical. The behind-the-scenes stuff of Matt Smith and Karen Gillan being scanned and modelled was included in *Doctor Who Confidential* (itself largely superseded by the online content and axed after X6.13, "The Wedding of River Song"). Worse, without having played the first of these games, *City of the*

Daleks, very little of X7.1, "Asylum of the Daleks" makes any sense (not that it entirely holds together even with this vital information). It didn't help that the BBC had another round of website cuts in 2011. Wenger was gone soon after this, and his eventual replacement, Brian Minchin, was a veteran of *The Sarah Jane Adventures* (the website for which was itself rather fun).

We'll just take this story up to the big Anniversary bash.

5. Comic Maker

Scarcely a month after "Last of the Time Lords" (X3.13), the team rolled out the virtual equivalent of Colorforms – you were given pictures of the Doctor and his companions, backgrounds and speech bubbles and were invited to make a comic out of them. It was a clever way to use the art assets now familiar to children from "The Infinite Quest", of course, but there was more to it than that – Davies gave the press an enthusiastic quote about children using it to make their own *Doctor Who*, and did a video tutorial telling kids how to do so. As artificial a format as it was, it worked; thousands of comics were made and posted to the BBC website, and eventually you could download and print them for yourself. Gardner observed that something about the show simply made people want to tell stories.

A year on, someone had the clever idea of asking professional *Doctor Who* writers to write their own comics with this software. These ranged from the silly to the sentimental to the surreal. (Keith Temple cheekily did a sequel to the subplot from "The Impossible Planet" that they could never have afforded to make for X4.3, "Planet of the Ood"; Helen Raynor wrote the Moxx of Balhoon prequel everyone had expected back in 2005, and Peter Anghelides turned in a surprisingly touching take on post-Time War angsting.) They also added a new treat – the Trailer Maker, which allowed you to cut and paste sound effects, Murray Gold's music, and clips from Tennant (and eventually some Eccleston) episodes to make short trailers. Tennant's fakeout regeneration was a favourite set piece.

[Incidentally, this wasn't the only time that Goss thriftily reused animation artwork from the children's production he'd produced – that same summer, the website did a competition in tandem with BBC Blast to allow a kid to actually create a

continued on Page 147...

a set-piece of many 60s adventure series. *The Avengers* did it with "Epic", *UFO* with "Mindbender", *The Monkees* did it three or four times and with the film *Head*. Of course *The Prisoner* did it – "Living in Harmony" most flagrantly – and any spy series where the baddies had made an exact replica of a familiar locale from the series is treading on this territory. Even *Star Trek* did it with "The Mark of Gideon".

However, for a *Doctor Who* precedent for this sort of self-conscious fictionality (as a sustained motif rather than as fleeting instances in Barry Letts or Graham Williams-produced stories), we refer you to 6.2, "The Mind Robber". Guess what, that's another computer with all the fiction ever written by humans in it and the companions interacting with characters. And guess what, we're told that the only way real people can escape being turned into caricature "fictionalised" versions of themselves (repeating things they said in life, earlier in the episode) is if the Doctor volunteers to replace the living mind in charge.

There's a double-bluff when the as-yet-anonymous girl asks the Doctor "are you in my television?", when it later turns out that she's the one inside an electronic image of a world. As we have noted before, the idea of people living inside the television is a very common one from the 1960s (back when sets were more box-like: see 10.2, "Carnival of Monsters"[31]). However, on-screen people talking at viewers directly is a popular paranoid delusion (associated with over-use of drugs as well as clinically-defined schizophrenia) and used by Moffat last time with the Doctor's "conversation" with Sally Sparrow. In the late 1960s, it was a running gag that the Troughton Doctor could see out of whatever monitor he was shown on, usually justified with recourse to futuristic two-way video communicators that happened to look like 60s tellies, but it's also latent in the revised title sequence.

A quick word about haunted libraries. Walter Benjamin commented on the idea of the "Library Angel", a form of providence that enabled the researcher to stumble upon exactly the right book by serendipity faster than any systematic search. This idea, and the Benjamin connection, was undoubtedly behind the memorable sequence in Wim Wenders's *Wings of Desire* of Berliners in the 1980s finding solace in books with help from the monochrome angels (which the film insists have long coats and ponytails and hang out at Nick

Cave gigs). This is characteristic of the ways that family films normally associate libraries and the dead. A rare example of malign spirits in the stacks is in *Ghostbusters* (and, yes, they hurl books around just like the sequence in the first episode).

However, for the association of small girl having a strop and books flying around, we might consider *The Exorcist* (1973) to be a more direct source, one parodied and riffed on often enough not to require anyone to have seen it (although millions did, and it was the benchmark for "scary" for anyone in school in 70s Britain). With many of the pop-cultural items we're listing, there's a residual linkage of images carried over from the original without any clear reasoning of why they belong together in this particular story. In the terms the premise affords, there is no reason why flying books should assail people in the real world when a girl who only exists as bits in the mainframe throws a wobbly, but that's the sort of thing that happens when these images usually coincide, so they put it in 'cos it looks dead cool.

The model of library seen here is not one any child in the UK would recognise from their local branch or the school library. You will struggle to find a publicly accessible library like this (even the real one in Swansea where this was filmed is less amply-stocked and a lot better lit.) The Library-with-a-capital-L is modelled on libraries that exist in the media, mainly American films. Those films are mainly about ghosts. (A whole TV series of Ray Bradbury adaptations entailed an opening sequence of a big spooky library. We might also include Jack Clayton's rendering of *Something Wicked This Way Comes*, again from the early 80s.) The episode title, "Silence in the Library", falls back on the folk-memory of librarians constantly saying *shhh* that now only exists in cartoons, and is as relevant to modern children as teachers in mortar-boards wielding canes or using chalk on blackboards.

Or, indeed, veiled Victorian governesses, another *idée fixe* of the author's we've now seen an awful lot more. The origin of the name "Evangelista" betrays the author's low opinion of the intellect of supermodels. Similarly, "intelligence" as a unitary property that can, like the colour or contrast on a television set, be raised or lowered independently of all other functions of personality, is a daft idea to which the Moffat will resort again, but one we know from other, more surprising contexts. One is the routine setting of

What Were the Best Online Extras?

continued from Page 145...

game. "Doctor in a Dash", a pretty bog-standard racing game, came out at the end of the year and had an intro that clearly has the same animated Doctor from "The Infinite Quest".]

They never got around to updating these for Matt Smith, and the software was gone by the Anniversary year, so you can't even read the professionally-done comics. The sole remnant of the trailers is a handful of blurry YouTube clips (the replacement Facebook app launched in October 2013, sticking a picture of your face into the title sequence – not the same at all, really). Those of us too young to recall seeing episodes that were later wiped can experience a little portion of the existential angst this causes by knowing that you once read a comic that not even the pro-level writer can see now. Still, it was a nice thought while it lasted, and the Comic Maker did get the website nominated for a BAFTA.

Even this wasn't entirely unprecedented. "Scream of the Shalka" had a website feature with paper doll versions of Alison, the Master and the Doctor that you were meant to print out and colour in yourself, complete with a scan of how to make the "*Blue Peter* Theatre" that was obviously taken from a 1977 *Radio Times* (see Volume 4).

6. Commentaries and Behind-the-Scenes Videos

The DVDs used to come in two forms; the "vanilla" ones just have the episodes and are released very soon after broadcast to catch the wave of public interest, then the box-sets had a few of the features we've been describing and the now-traditional commentaries and Video Diaries. This ended once Moffat's regime began making so many mini-episodes for the website and Comic Relief that there was no room, even had there been time.

However, even by Series 3 the amount of material generated exceeded orthodox commercial exploitation and the BBC's public service remit meant we got everything they couldn't squeeze onto discs by other means. Who gets to be on the commentary teams for each episode seems oddly haphazard. With the episodes covered in this book, there was a solution: record two sets of commentary and pick one for the DVD and one for online. As an odd side-effect of this, we've had a lot of work to do resolving discrepancies between two accounts of the making of a given episode.

Another has been that for various logistical reasons, the online commentary hasn't always been playable when we've had the DVD handy to put on or vice versa. Listened to on its own, there are odd gaps when everyone is watching and listening to an episode not included in the feed. Moreso than usual, these chats make the listener feel like an eavesdropper. You also have to remember what's on screen at any given time for the comments to make complete sense.

Because of the timetables of everyone involved, many of the online commentaries were made closer to transmission than the ones on the discs. This allows a few interesting sidelights, as well as reuniting people who've not seen each other for a while. The most cheerful aspect of this is that Freema Agyeman had caught up with her sleep and landed up acting as moderator in some of these, coaxing a shy Thomas Sangster (Tim Latimer) to talk on X3.8, "Human Nature" and refereeing a sort-of family reunion on X3.12, "The Sound of Drums".

One reason for deciding which commentary went where was simply concerns about how safely they could broadcast information about forthcoming episodes. The online commentaries were available immediately after broadcast of each week's adventure, whereas DVD box-sets have generally been fairly comprehensively spoiled. The same logic applied to which interview clips were in *Doctor Who Confidential* and which popped up on the website ahead of the broadcast. There is also the matter of value for money (something the BBC Trust make noises about in order to prove that they're worth funding themselves). Anyone who'd paid for the disc of X4.0, "Voyage of the Damned" would want to hear something more illuminating than Julie Gardner, Phil Collinson and Russell T Davies laughing for a solid minute over the word "jet-ski" and each pretending not to know who the other two were.

With the end of *Doctor Who Confidential*, some ten-minute pieces were posted on iPlayer and the website accompanying Series 8. These closely resembled the mini-pieces on the Series 7 box-set, but were promoted more heavily.

7. Guy Fawkes

The 2010 series had a big publicity blitz for the *Doctor Who Adventure Games*. These were one of the most complicated attempts to hitch the popu-

continued on Page 149...

ABOUT TIME 2008-2009

levels of various mental properties in android duplicates made by mad scientists (in our purlieu, we can include 13.4, "The Android Invasion" – again – and, not unrelated, *The Six Million Dollar Man* and its Fembots). The other is Role-Playing games, a subject on which Moffat has been unusually silent. Most forms of nerdish nostalgia have been soundly ridiculed in his blokey sitcoms.

To sum up so far, then: as has been the case before, Moffat has taken off-the-shelf *Star Trek* props and associations (which could be assumed, for anyone over 25, to be a "given" of television set in "the future"), half-remembered Tom Baker stories and a jumble of old films, and slotted them into a world-view that assumes computers, rather than television, to be the one thing every viewer recognises as how machines work. In this case, the mainframe, not BBC1 or physical books, is where fiction "exists". However, his model for a dreamscape into which Donna's disembodied "soul" is decanted is daytime television, with the caesurae (cuts, dissolves, channel-zapping) commented on rather than accepted. In the time-honoured tradition of *Doctor Who* writers, he subordinates any attempt to resolve these anomalies to a lot of fast-talking and running up and down corridors.

Yet this assumption that computers are normal, but books are scary, is one that the story can't square with the idea that the Doctor and Charlotte enjoy reading for its own sake and feel at home in libraries. Even the simple info-dump function of the Nodes had to be made creepy, just because. We'll see the rotating head thing again (and again) when Moffat takes over the series. This extends to the Vashta Nerada. For creepiness to have a seemingly-rational grounding, the darkness has to be a physical presence rather than being a mere absence of light. This is pretty much the *ne plus ultra* of BBC Wales's approach, a conceptual level of "ooh-scary" bordering on self-parody.

Meanwhile, the latest addition to the blank-faced threats (because the textbooks say that the "Uncanny Valley" feature of not-quite human faces is an infallible scare for kids) is space-suits. With lights inside the helmets (see X2.9, "The Satan Pit" for a sustained critique of this impractical and stupid notion). "The Ambassadors of Death" (7.3) is mainly remembered for having creepy spacesuited aliens who moved very slowly and reached out for people. This was recycled in "The Android Invasion".

Moffat will use this image yet again in X6.1, "The Impossible Astronaut". Some commentators noted that an early *Scooby Doo* episode used the skeletons-in-spacesuits thing, but it was older than that. Quite when the first use of this image might have been is debated (it seems to have been in 50s pulp covers often), but the most likely place for Moffat to have seen it is the 1969 Hammer Films attempt at a space western, *Moon Zero Two*. The first *Doctor Who* use was more recent, indeed on air at around the time the story was being written – Captain Kaliko's skeleton crew in A5, "The Infinite Quest". (However, look at the telesnaps of the dead Cybermen in 4.2, "The Tenth Planet" or the pilot on 20.4, "Terminus".)

Over the last few years, the Doctor had been dealing with the consequences of things he had yet to do (X3.2, "The Shakespeare Code" for example), so now the logical extension was to make this future more than one incident, and posit a whole future that begins where it ends. (We could cite all sorts of legitimate SF precursors, but Moffat is likely to have encountered this idea via *Red Dwarf*.) Creating a character who might be a significant player in the Doctor's future was itself a familiar move from the tie-in novels. Two obvious precedents are Iris Wildthyme and Bernice Summerfield. Both of these characters took on lives of their own outside the Doctor's literary adventures. Iris claimed to be the Doctor's ex and travelled through time and space in a 22 bus (a double-decker), often "remembering" versions of the past that don't tally with the broadcast episodes. She was plump and middle-aged (and all in all suspiciously like the character Elizabeth Spriggs – 24.2, "Paradise Towers" – played in the 90s revival of *The Tomorrow People*, bus and all). Benny Summerfield was a futuristic archaeology professor who liked a drink and tended to rough it with her students. She had a complex love-life and kept a diary, updated with Post-Its when the past changed. (She was the companion who had to babysit "John Smith" in the 1994 iteration of X3.8, "Human Nature".) Benny outlived the end of Virgin Books's hold on the *Doctor Who* rights and got her own spin-off novels, then a series of audio adventures in Big Finish's empire-building phase (where she was played by Lisa Bowerman of 26.4, "Survival" and A8, "Dreamland").

We have to admit, though, that the concept of a "rogue archaeologist" is barely novel. Even

What Were the Best Online Extras?

continued from Page 147...

larity of the series on television to the BBC's bids to diversify. A great deal of stress was put on the stories' canonical nature, the fidelity of the new Doctor and Amy's characterisation and the educational bonus of the game-play. Half an episode of *Doctor Who Confidential* was given over to the scanning process and modelling of the leads' game-avatars. (It was unkindly suggested that the digital Amy had a greater range of facial expressions that Karen Gillan's bog-eyed gawp and the binary-encoded Doctor walked more naturally than Matt Smith.) Moreover, the first game was a chance to show off their very expensive New Dalek Paradigm design (X5.3, "Victory of the Daleks" and accompanying essay) in a context where they looked most at home: software.

The BBC's most high-profile previous attempt at a *Doctor Who* computer game – the 1990s CD ROM *Destiny of the Doctors* – was, it has to be said, a shambles. The game-play was clumsy, the linking material (performed by Anthony Ainley as the Master) was at best perfunctory and it tried to synoptically include every Doctor and famous alien (supposedly what the fans wanted) and laboriously introduce it all for absolute newbies. It only reminded people of *Doctor Who* when it reminded the critics of why the series had been canned. But the new series of games were written by long-time associates of the BBC Wales series, Phil Ford and James Moran (X4.2, "The Fires of Pompeii"; X4.16, "The Waters of Mars"; X8.2, "Into the Dalek") and had supporting cast from the series, notably Big Finish veterans Barnaby Edwards and Nicholas Briggs. The music cues were retreads of broadcast scores. Much of the game-ware came from experienced manufacturers Sumo Digital, but in collusion with the new BBC Interactive franchise.

More importantly, it had support from other BBC departments. Sumo's head designer, Sean Millard, began his career with a Dalek game in the early 1990s but the chief creative brains on the series (called *The Adventure Games*) were Charles Cecil, Phil Ford and Steven Moffat. The look of each game was tried out on the showrunner, just as any other design decision for the broadcast series would be. Cecil's formidable CV as a games designer includes *Broken Sword*, so the project had credibility among gamers. The first *Adventure Games* release, *City of the Daleks*, re-introduced Skaro ahead of the TV series (X7.1, "Asylum of the Daleks" and the apparently contradictory X9.1, "The Magician's Apprentice") and in rapid succession led to three others: *Blood of the Cybermen*, *TARDIS* and *Shadows of the Vashta Narada*.

With the last of the games, *The Gunpowder Plot*, the educational remit was pushed in the publicity via more overt links with BBC Learning, makers of such Schools TV as now persists and the "Bitesize" section of the BBC website given to exam revision help. The head of BBC Learning at the time was Saul Nassé, who had previously been editor of the technology showcase series *Tomorrow's World* and before that, leader of the Bedfordshire Local Group of the *Doctor Who* Appreciation Society. The promotional material for the game had teachers' notes and links to the schools section of the BBC website. It won a special award from BAFTA Cymru. Unlike the other games, it had Rory in it (a popular move among reviewers) and a definite "slot" in between two broadcast episodes in Series 6. It got thumbs-up all around, so why was it the last?

Part of the problem was that it had three barely-overlapping audiences to please. The game was free to download for anyone in the UK, so needed to be for mouse and keyboard rather than adapted for custom-built machinery, and have glitch-free download without too much memory being eaten on Mum's laptop or the school computers. (Hard as it is to recall, smart phones and tablets were only starting to catch on when this began.) By design, the gameplay was simple enough for people who don't play many games (and the early stages have the player being taught to manipulate a Rory avatar before the main narrative begins).

Yet when looking up reviews for this piece, we found that most of the comments are from American gamers (who had to pay for it) unfamiliar with the series or the key incident of British history at risk from Sontaran-Rutan interference. Luckily, if you manage to get through the game without learning anything about 1605 London, you'll have picked up a lot of *Doctor Who* lore. Both the programme's history and that of Jacobean geopolitics are presented as plot-coupons for the individual player, although it's the stuff in the TARDIS that's useful for defeating aliens. That's right: the game's designed for single players, but it comes with class-notes.

Assuming, however, that you are ten years old, a

continued on Page 151...

before Indiana Jones, there were a few in SF and the often-associated idea of "space archaeologist" ties in with the idea of Mars as a surrogate Egypt that, rather than disappearing when Mariner IV showed craters, went underground in space-opera. It then, as with all 1940s skiffy clichés, became a staple of *Star Trek* and found a whole new audience. However, since 1981, the television idea of what real archaeologists do (wear chunky jumpers and drink real ale between doing very complicated things with computers) and what movie archaeologists do (destroy World Heritage Sites in order to recover ancient mystic artefacts and save the world while losing clothing – *Lara Croft: Tomb Raider* is probably the most ludicrous manifestation of this, but if *MacGyver* was doing it in 1989, it's pretty much a given) have diverged alarmingly.

Doctor Who was ahead of the curve and has always depicted archaeologists as a bit out-of-touch (e.g. 5.1, "The Tomb of the Cybermen"; 16.3, "The Stones of Blood"), in keeping with how the BBC had represented real-life ones (see our comments with 8.5, "The Daemons" re: Sir Mortimer Wheeler). River Song is a belated on-screen iteration of the off-the-peg notion of swashbuckling tomb-wreckers and, in keeping with how Moffat will handle other versions of science when he takes over, never seems to do any research or digging and absolutely never catalogues anything she unearths. She's also remarkably proximate to Vala (played by Claudia Black from *FarScape*), a character brought in for the last seasons of *Stargate SG-1* when it was hoovering up cast-members from cancelled rivals. That the start of her stint is an episode ending with alien treasure under Glastonbury Tor turning out to be a trap (see X5.12, "The Pandorica Opens") makes Claudia Black's amoral, flirtatious character seem like a clear role-model (see also X7.3, "A Town Called Mercy").

As we mentioned with "The Girl in the Fireplace", there's more than a passing similarity between this recurring Moffat storyline and the then-popular novel *The Time-Traveller's Wife*, but (as we also said) the idea of an out-of-synch relationship was hardly new even then. The most famous outside "cult" circles was of course Merlyn as conceived by TH White (a character who was lurking behind a lot of what would later become "Doctorish" traits, see 11.5, "Planet of the Spiders"; "The Stones of Blood"; and 26.1, "Battlefield" for

when it got most overt). By means of the debased Disney cartoon of *The Sword in the Stone* and Lerner and Lowe's typically crass reworking of the later books as the musical *Camelot*, this can be considered another popular-culture "given".

River Song's later appearances consolidated the notion everyone sort-of took from this adventure – that she was his future wife – but that's not the only possibility held open here. The second episode landed up being called "Forest of the Dead", but was hitherto "A River Song Ending" and "River's Run". The last of these alludes to the cyclic end/start or *Finnegans Wake*, where the book begins with the end of the sentence that starts at the end of the last paragraph. The first title was allegedly simply to provide a rude acronym; there are many records called "The River Song", but Moffat denies all knowledge of Dennis Wilson, Donovan, Joni Mitchell et al. Characters and people with "River" as a first name begin with, of course, River Phoenix but we have to mention River Tam in *Firefly*. Some have speculated that the name "River Song" is a play on Michael Flatley's once-inescapable Eurovision filler-show *Riverdance*. We can at least agree that having a character with that name in a 2008 episode is as unsurprising as someone called "Zoe" showing up in 1968.

English Lessons

• *Speak-your-weight machine* (n.). A device not seen since the 1960s, but still the axiomatic comparison for artificial voices. A set of bathroom-style scales formed the pedestal for a slot-machine with a complex arrangement of miniature gramophone recordings of numbers and phrases inset, so that the machine would tell the user something like "You weigh." "Eight." "Stone." "Eleven." "Pounds". The film version of *One-Way Pendulum* includes a choir of them.

Oh, Isn't That...?

• *Colin Salmon* (Dr. Moon). In the endless debates on whether the Daniel Craig Bond films are a reboot or a continuation with an old agent-name and number, Salmon's character Charles Robinson is Exhibit B after Judi Dench. You'll see him a lot if you watch British telly, even in things like *Rev* or one of Moffat's *Murder Most Horrid* episodes – or *Strictly Come Dancing*. He had been doing SF-adjacent projects since the early 90s (*Tomorrow Calling*, an adaptation of William

What Were the Best Online Extras?

continued from Page 149...

UK resident and have never played a computer-game before, but want to know all about pro-gramme-lore and Robert Catesby, the main fea-ture that would strike you is the set number of tasks to complete with little (optional) info-dumps along the way. However much you might want to just explore this odd-but-almost-known city or talk to people about something other than doctri-nal differences, this is all as rigidly-plotted as a 45-minute celebrity historical.

There is a preferred route through the game, with no option for history to go any differently if you make different choices given the information at hand. This has been a perennial bugbear of his-tory teachers with regard to software – the notion that whatever in fact happened was the optimum outcome. There is a walk-through online that enables the story to unfold in the smallest possi-ble time, just over two hours, without ever encoun-tering a Silent. (Although their gimmick is amne-sia, these eldritch horrors are somewhat perverse-ly employed to help players learn. They offer additional information without affecting the run of the game, so are totally absent from the walk-through.) Nonetheless, our hypothetical child player would have a feel for wooden London and the dawn of the modern age, and would have been thoroughly briefed on the functions of Black Rod. What an adult would notice on getting to the end is that the voice-cast includes some pretty big names: Phil Daniels, Ralf Little and Emilia Fox. (Little has, subsequently, been in broadcast *Doctor Who*; X10.2, "Smile".)

However, it's thought the internal ructions in BBC Wales brought about the cessation of the project. By the time this game emerged, almost 18 months after the first, the series was down two executive producers. The *Adventure Games* project had been closely associated with one of these, Piers Wenger, who soon took over a bigger plum job as head of Channel 4's drama department. Beth Willis, the other departing Exec, returned to her lucrative berth at Shine. By the time the flurry of replacements and other complications settled, all three of the lead actors had left. BBC Worldwide, now in overall charge of the games associated with BBC series, moved all of its gaming opera-tions to the US and games manufacturers moved from consoles to smartphones. The shambles of *The Eternity Clock* might warrant more commen-tary in a later volume, but the current state-of-the-

art is *Doctor Who Legacy* (a free download along the lines of *Candy Crush*, incorporating all Doctors for once) and tie-ups with Lego and Minecraft.

8. Adventure Calendar

Can you see what they've done there? It's like an Advent Calendar, but counting down to the *other* big event on 25th December, a new hour-long episode. Every day, from 1st December onward, they pop a new morsel on the site. Sometimes, these are games (the run-up to "Voyage of the Damned" had such delights as a jigsaw of starship *Titanic* that you completed to win a glimpse at a page of inconsequential script, plus the *Su-Doc-Who* pun everyone had already made came to fruition, with nine faces replacing the nine digits and a mugshot of Tennant as the prize). Sometimes it's behind-the-scenes photos. Occasionally, a new short story would be seri-alised, tying in with a recent episode (so Rupert Laight gave us the full story of the anecdote about Charlemagne, Madonna and a mad computer – X4.7, "The Unicorn and the Wasp").

2012 was notable mainly for the sneak preview of the new "Magic Roundabout" TARDIS console and Moffat interviews where he all-but admitted that the New Paradigm Daleks were a blunder. With *Doctor Who Confidential*'s demise, this is our main opportunity to see the cast giving each other tacky presents or chatting backstage. 2013 was the year when the fall-out from the Anniversary allowed them to almost completely ignore the forthcoming episode for the first two weeks, instead telling us about the Zygons (and claiming that the Savoy Hotel is in Paris, which is news to anyone who's taken a short-cut to Charing Cross station past the tradesman's entrance).

Admittedly, about 2/3 of this stuff would fail to make the grade as DVD extras or Easter Eggs, but the whole point of Advent Calendars is that you don't know what you're going to get each morn-ing; the ritual's cumulative effect is part of getting into the mood for the big event on Christmas Day. And, as with most things about Christmas, by 28th December it already seems an impossibly long time ago...

9. Bonus Material Superior to the Broadcast Episode Whence It Came

We discussed the *TARDISodes* in Volume 7; they were one-minute long clips made especially to be

continued on Page 153...

ABOUT TIME 2008-2009

Gibson's "The Gernsback Continuum" set in Blackpool, latterly the hapless *Hex,* and Avon in the Ben Aaronovitch/Marc Platt audio reworking of *Blakes* 7). You might, if you were unlucky, have seen *London Has Fallen,* where he was cast as the head of the Met to forestall any accusation that this atrociously racist film was racist. More recently, however, he's been General Zod on *Krypton.*

• *Talulah Riley* (Miss Evangelista). One of the young breakout leads in the 2007 revival of *St Trinian's* (along with Jodie Whittaker and Gemma Arterton), she was briefly married to Elon Musk. Twice. She's also been in *Westworld* and *Inception.*

• *Steve Pemberton* (Strackman Lux). Another of *The League of Gentlemen.* He'd played against Tennant before in a *Randall and Hopkirk (Deceased)* episode, and was a stalwart of the mystifyingly-popular ITV sitcom *Benidorm.* Most recently he did *Inside Number 9,* an anthology series with *League* colleague Reece Shearsmith (X9.9, "Sleep No More"), including an episode that managed to make cryptic crosswords even more unsettling...

• *Alex Kingston* (River Song) had been doing television since her stint as an extra in *Grange Hill,* but made the big time in the lead of *Moll Flanders* before giving America a shot and popping up on *ER* for a few years. More recently, she's been only the most overt borrowing from *Who* in the Greg Berlanti-produced DC comic adaptations.

X4.9: "Forest of the Dead"

(7th June, 2008)

Which One is This? Donna's on telly, so the Doctor runs up and down corridors with his new friend River instead.

Firsts and Lasts Chronologically, this is River Song's last appearance, except the posthumous one (X7.14, "The Name of the Doctor"). Here we have the Mysterious Victorian Governess with a Veil showing up; with variations and differing degrees of control over the situation, this figure will return as often as the Weeping Angels once Moffat gets his feet under the table. It's also the first time the Doctor opens the TARDIS door with a click of his fingers.

Watch Out For...

• That small girl's still playing with her telly remote, and now she channel-zaps between bits

of the story. In one sequence, the music cues from later in the episode (and later episodes) get chopped up to denote different groups of characters. Last week, she could see into the Library just by closing her eyes, but now she can cross between that and a separate place inside the same machine in which she lives where Donna's being conditioned by Dr Moon. If you're having trouble working out what's going on and what level of "reality" any one scene is going to be on this week, so was the author by the looks of things.

• Her front room has lots of vertically-striped things, like bar-codes, and a few paintings she appears to have done, including a blonde girl and a wolf. Some viewers got excited about this on first broadcast.

• The shot of the girl watching Donna watching Miss Evangelista remove her veil is peculiar: the girl is spending more and more of this episode as a model of how they want viewers to react, but she doesn't hide behind the sofa as cliché demands – perhaps because the Picasso-like distortions are more like a gag on BBC3's software-driven sketch-show *The Wrong Door* (see X8.1, "Deep Breath") than actually scary. She doesn't switch over, though, the story just goes on without her like in any other *Doctor Who* episode. (Josh and Ella, Donna's not-real kids, seem to have figured it out by making a Plasticene model without a face for their mum.)

Similarly, the reveal of the multiple copies of the same boy and girl is a bit of a cheat, as we've not been allowed to register anything out-of-the-ordinary before this; it's like the whole "Perception Filter" thing that's going to get out of hand for a few years after this, but it's more brazen. It is, however, a lot more effective. Meanwhile, Donna's reaction to this revelation is: "But I've been *dieting*".

• Plus, we get a textbook example of how to use one exposition to cover another. The Doctor works out that the spores were in the books while we almost-but-not-quite notice that Other Dave has said the same thing four times running.

• Donna abruptly turns out to be very maternal in the Doctor's absence. You're watching for it now, because it's not a trait we'll see in any of her other stories. Note that she's wearing the same wedding-dress as in X3.0, "The Runaway Bride".

• That whole would-be mythical scene at the end where the Doctor snaps open the TARDIS doors: no subsequent version got quite so excru-

What Were the Best Online Extras?

continued from Page 151...

played on phones that could play video, usually prologues to the broadcast episode. In general, they widened out the story beyond the confines of wherever the Doctor and Rose had materialised, so that the people who found the ancient writings about Krop Tor were shown on a different planet discussing whether to investigate ("The Impossible Planet") or the events depicted in a wood-cut were shown to us with brief but effective special effects (X2.2, "Tooth and Claw"). Gareth Roberts did the scripts and they were neat and punchy. This sort of thing came back in the Moffat years with bits of prolepsis (backstory, in other words) from Series 6, showing Nixon receiving his first nuisance call (X6.1, "The Impossible Astronaut") and so on. One to note is the clip for X6.3, "The Curse of the Black Spot". It's moody, it's tense and acted to a T, and gives a real sense of being on a ship far from any hope of aid – everything the broadcast episode failed to manage.

Series 7 went one better, with a mini-serial of one-minute episodes stripped across a week. "Pond Life" is, as the name suggests, what Amy and Rory did between adventures, with the Doctor popping in and out and disrupting their semi-normal lives (she's an international model, he's a nurse...) in, well, wherever they were living this year. Chris Chibnall wrote this, and X7.4, "The Power of Three", and to be honest the stuff about Rory walking into the bathroom and finding an Ood sat on his toilet deserved screen-time more than the episode's rather trite ending. (An Ood in the loo... maybe they live in Tooting Bec now.)

Most of this material in fact looks to have been made as part of that episode, suggesting that they selected some scenes for the montage of a year passing and some for the website; the incident with the unseen Zygons at the Cafe Royale is of a piece with the Doctor fleeing Sontarans in "Pond Life" and less spectacular-looking. If we take it that the six months or so of "Pond Life" is in the year where he's popping in on the Cube in "The Power of Three", then it makes a bit more sense that Brian is also on hand to monitor the Cube when the Doctor's away.

By late 2013, this was itself part of the overall plan of the broadcast episodes. In between Strax reporting on various ingredients in the big show, we had two mini-episodes that help make sense of what we saw and one of these, "Night of the Doctor", was an event in itself. If you didn't know,

this is the hitherto unseen story of how John Hurt's Doctor comes into the story and stars Paul McGann. He is recognisably the same Doctor from the TV Movie (although when naming his former companions, Grace and Chang Lee are conspicuously absent) and has been trying to avoid being in the Time War until one person too many dies and he resolves to change.

Fortunately, he's dying (or dead) on Karn (13.5, "The Brain of Morbius", although that adds another can of worms to the problem of numbering the Doctors), and so the Sisterhood help him pick a suitable new persona to end the War. It sounds like a Big Finish audio, looks like one of the cheap episodes of *Babylon 5* set on the Drahzi Homeworld, but McGann's presence and their ability to have kept a surprise fed into the buzz surrounding "The Day of the Doctor". For some viewers, the expectations it raised were unmatchable by any single episode.

10. *The Five(ish) Doctors Reboot*

For all that the BBC's carpet-bombing of the British media in the week leading up to 23rd November, 2013 stressed the whole 50-years-ness of it all, they were mainly preoccupied with the eight most recent years and all the things from it they could sell. There was Mark Gatiss's *slightly* mendacious play "An Adventure in Space and Time", which teased us with sets and costumes from missing episodes that the rumour-mill said weren't as missing as they had been, but was notable mainly for suggesting that Paddy Russell was a man (3.5, "The Massacre"), that Sydney Newman and Mervyn Pinfield stuck around until 4.2, "The Tenth Planet" and that Heather Hartnell was also married to Leggy Mountbatten from *The Rutles*. There was an edition of the resolutely middle-brow BBC2 puff-programme *The Culture Show* in which Matthew Sweet went on at length about 17.5, "The Horns of Nimon" and the allegations in Richard Marson's book *JN-T* about 80s producer John Nathan-Turner (see volumes 5 and 6) while supposedly investigating how this series had managed such a grip on the national imagination.

By and large, though, this was a series whose real history began in 2005, if the coverage was any guide – you had to go to local radio to get anything more. Then, on the BBC's digital Red Button and the website, a small note of protest was heard...

continued on Page 155...

ciatingly smug as Tennant manages to be here. (Jenna Coleman comes closest in X7.15, "The Day of the Doctor" by doing it while wearing leather gloves. Maybe she was really the Master all along...)

The Continuity

The Doctor Somehow, he wiggles out of hand-cuffs at the end. [Maybe Lux went down and retrieved him.] He describes having four thousand minds in one head as being "like me". River insists that were the Doctor to have used his own brain as memory space for a data transfer this large, it would kill him, burn out his hearts *and* prevent him from regenerating.

• *Background.* When River whispers his name into his ear – to win his confidence in a crisis – his expression remains unchanged but he thereafter trusts her utterly. [The Doctor confirms that River whispered his name when they're alone, so that'd be a very odd time for them to be mutually lying about it. In X7.14, "The Name of the Doctor", whatever name he gave her works on the TARDIS, so it's definitely *a* name of his but – as the thing claiming to be Great Intelligence points out – he's had a few. It makes the scene a lot more entertaining if you imagine she's whispering "Basil Disco" as per X9.8, "The Zygon Inversion".]

Accounts of the Doctor within the Library are so terrifying, the Vashta Nerada refrain from attacking upon reading them. He's unaware that the Library has a Moon or that this Moon protects the operating system – this would seem to indicate that he's never actually been to this planet before.

•*Foreground.* He'll take River Song to the End of the Universe. [The events in X5.13, "Big Bang" *could* be construed that way, if you squint. She's not along for the ride in X8.4, "Listen" or X9.12, "Hell Bent", so was he cleaning up after X3.11, "Utopia" or is this a different End of the Universe? Did they serve Pears Gallumbits?]

• *Ethics.* He'd much sooner die than let River fry her brain as the conduit for a massive download, even if he doesn't know her yet.

His opinion about the morality of data ghosts swings dramatically upwards once he realises he can upload River into the core. At the end, he and Donna consider opening River's diary to see how their lives turn out. They agree not to try.

The TARDIS River Song tells him he can open the Ship by snapping his fingers. When he tries, it works.

• *Inventory: Sonic Screwdriver(s).* Generally speaking, most signals shouldn't interfere with the screwdriver. It takes a supercomputer the size of a moon to do so, although the Doctor hints that hairdryers do something to the settings. A quick screw can darken glass [see also X4.15, "Planet of the Dead"].

River's bulky one includes a Neural Relay just like the ones that don't work tremendously well all story. It also has red settings and dampers, unlike the Doctor's. Hers is the Doctor's creation [it's interesting that this one looks more like Tennant's screwdriver than any later models; he remembered it looking like this].

The Supporting Cast

• *Donna.* Here becomes part of a simulated world within the Library's computer core, one that – from Donna's perspective – includes at least seven years of memories. It takes her a while to stop noticing the anomalies. In her fantasy, she marries one Lee McAvoy. They have a son named Josh and a daughter named Ella. She's been dieting, apparently. She's at first distraught when her children suddenly vanish and the counterfeit world disappears. Nevertheless, once teleported out of the system, she's only slightly regretful and doesn't ascribe too much practical significance to her fantasy life.

She contemplates having imagined Lee, a handsome adoring man who could barely speak [not actually the case, it seems, the further the illusionary marriage goes] and wonders what to make of that; the Doctor has a Freudian slip and says that explains 'everything'. Due to a stroke of bad luck, she doesn't realise as they depart that Lee was a real person.

• *River Song.* She dies using her own mind as the memory space needed to transfer the 'saved' thousands of people back into physical form.

River relates that on their last night together, the Doctor got a haircut and a new suit, showed up on her doorstep, took her for a picnic at the Singing Towers of Darillium, and gave her "his" augmented screwdriver [with a neural relay she doesn't know about]. He also cried a lot, evidently knowing she'd soon have to go to her death at the Library. [The actual event behind the Darillium story – or some of it, at least – is less poignant, as

What Were the Best Online Extras?

continued from Page 153...

Peter Davison had already mentioned a few times that the term "Classic" for anything made before 1990 was a bit offputting, but the real surprise about his half-hour film *The Five(ish) Doctors* is how game everyone was to parody themselves. The plot is that he, Colin Baker and Sylvester McCoy are desperate to be in "The Day of the Doctor" (as is Paul McGann, but he won't admit this) and, after pestering Steven Moffat with phone calls, decide to take matters into their own hands. Around this simple storyline are sardonic comments on everything from Olivia Coleman being in every television drama that year (X5.1, "The Eleventh Hour") to the steep-admission fee for the guided tour of the studio complex. To list all the surprise cameos would be beside the point, but there's one who couldn't be in it (hence the name), so they allude to a previous no-show by the same performer (see 20.7, "The Five Doctors" for a hint). A cast such as this is only possible if it's not intended for release any other way.

The film was written and directed by Davison, and produced by his daughter, Georgia Tennant. The script alludes to her pregnancy, as well as Colin's stint on *I'm A Celebrity... Get Me Out of Here!*[33] and the peculiarly long shoot on *The Hobbit*. It's in-jokey, as might be expected, with on-screen gags about Adric, the regeneration in "The Caves of Androzani" (21.6) and lines from old scripts. The most interesting feature is that it did indeed use the sets for the 2013 Anniversary Special, and ends with a strong hint that one scene in the finished version actually did have the old Doctors hiding in plain sight. (Sadly, the dates don't work for this to be true.) The episode landed up vying with the official Anniversary Special for the Hugo award.

This was independently made, with some official help from BBC Wales, as part of the anniversary – yet is critical of it. It has the Anniversary Episode at the centre of the action (and thus was kept until after broadcast of that), and – as with John Hurt's Doctor slagging off the other two for catch-phrases and gimmicks – seems at times as if Moffat is aware of how corporate the whole series has become and what he would think of it all if he were just a viewer. It also crystallised a feeling a lot of people had that, with Moffat giving interview after interview, and the renewed focus on Hartnell (through the Gatiss play and his status as the original) and Troughton (with rediscovered episodes going on sale a month earlier amid a whole lot more hoo-hah), someone else was being unfairly sidelined.

we see in X9.13, "The Husbands of River Song". This, after a botched attempt to go there on the DVD extra "Last Night". The screwdriver's a custom-job.]

At the moment, she's nostalgic for the Doctor who makes armies run away screaming, and isn't all that comfortable with the younger version. She insists that "not one line!" of her history with the Doctor can be changed [1.6, "The Aztecs" and others]. River says that she trusts the Doctor to the End of the Universe – and they've been there.

The Doctor and Donna opt to leave River's diary at the Library. [The journal next appears, chronologically speaking, in X10.6, "Extremis". We think.]

River's idea of the perfect afterlife, it seems, is to tell stories about the Doctor and hang out with her archaeological buddies [yes, even Miss Evangelista], tuck someone else's children into bed and flounce around in white lace. [Maybe they even get in some reading.]

It appears she normally carries handcuffs. She looks rather saucy when the Doctor asks why.

[We'll next see River in X5.4, "The Time of Angels", but her post-death digital self later appears in X7.14, "The Name of the Doctor".]

• *River Song (posthumous digital self)*. [A word on the veracity of the digital River that exists at story's end... let's assume that consciousness can exist without a body and must be stored separately, but any memories created afterwards are somatically part of the individual's brain. Within the terms of this story, that works – except that Miss Evangelista isn't conscious and, unlike the Library patrons and staff, was never teleported. Her Data-Ghost is exactly that, a recording of her memories. She, Anita and the Daves were dead. Proper dead. Whatever the software in white might be, it's not their consciousnesses. So even if we stretch a point that the Doctor's old screwdriver and River Song's former status as an embryo exposed to Artron energy means that her recorded self is capable of new thoughts and awareness, the recording was very nearly degraded when the Doctor shoved it into the plughole. It's no more her than the TARDIS-like diary is – which, pre-

ABOUT TIME 2008-2009

sumably, is why the Doctor calls River's avatar an "echo" in "The Name of the Doctor".

[Along such lines, we note that digital-River, like Virtual-Donna, has had the control marked "Maternal Instinct" moved up a notch as – despite no previous or subsequent evidence of this – it seems all she ever wanted was a two-bedroom semi and two kids selected from a catalogue. This mucking about with the specs means that whoever these recordings used to be, they aren't even faithful copies of the dead. This wouldn't matter, except that we got a posthumous visit from this electronic plaster-cast of River ("The Name of the Doctor") and it was almost indistinguishable from her normal performance. This also means that whatever mechanism is editing the people now knows all the Doctor's secrets, or as many as were vouchsafed to this woman after her shotgun wedding to the Doctor (X6.13, "The Wedding of River Song"). Intriguingly, Dead-River has a virtual version of her diary even as the real one lies outside in Biographies. CAL might have the capacity to transfer physical texts into virtual ones in real time. Imagine how long it would have taken with a flatbed scanner.]

Planet Notes

• *The Library* is in the same "system" as the homeworld(s) of the Vashta Nerada [solar system? Galaxy? Galactic group? Dewey Decimal?], but had no native trees. [Presumably the air is also imported.] It's one big hub, with a massive mainframe as its core and a virus-scanner (the doctor moon) orbiting. It was built for benefit of Charlotte Abigail Lux – the youngest daughter of Strackman Lux's grandfather – when she was dying. Her mind was transferred into the Library's computer core, where it currently resides (a Node sometimes appears with her face), so she could be entertained by every book ever written.

The copy of Miss Evangelista in the mainframe has a warped face, but increased intelligence, because – she suspects – 'a decimal point shifted' in her IQ. By the time River is uploaded, Miss Evangelista has regained her proper face. [One wonders whether she kept the heightened IQ.] All the team-members who died in this adventure are preserved there, as Donna was.

The Non-Humans

• *Vashta Nerada*. The Doctor, somehow, realises that the Vashta Nerada live on 'all the worlds in this system'. They prefer to attack only in very large groups. Generally they live and die in forests, but the sheer amount of books in the Library meant that microspores were brought in and populated the shelves. They learn to communicate through the suits' comms.

The Analysis

English Lessons

• *Bless (interj.)*: It was common in that decade, less so now, to exclaim "bless", often with a slight tilt of the head and drawing the vowel out, when something cute appeared, such as cat pictures on the internet or school Nativity plays. We suggested in "The Sensorites" (1.8) that this was the appropriate reaction to that story's naïve invention of all the clichés for which less-indulgent reviewers condemn it. It is, therefore, almost the most aggravating thing to say to someone's face, especially to an adult with a stammer.

• *Gob (n.)*: Mouth. Hence "gobby" meaning chatty [as in X7.12, "The Crimson Horror" describing Tegan] and the verb form, meaning to spit phlegmatically as per 70s Punk concerts.

• *Nutter (n)*: Lunatic, but in the sense of obsessive exaggerations of common behaviour, such as people who go to conventions in costume or stand on street-corners yelling religious opinions.

Things That Don't Make Sense ("Silence in the Library"/"Forest of the Dead") [*As you're undoubtedly aware, River Song becomes a regular feature of the show, and cavernous discrepancies exist between this story and what we see and hear about her later. Most of these are immaterial to the matters as they play out here, so will be addressed at the appropriate time.*]

We have a huge problem of scale... we're in the fifty-somethingth century, long past the time of the Earth Empire from *The Mutants* (9.4) et al, and yet the sum total of human writing amounts to just enough to fill one planet's worth of shelves. You'd expect that much added per century (on just Earth at the moment, it's about two and a quarter million new titles per annum, and that's not counting self-published e-books, online fanfic and rejected works). Worse, on the day things went pear-shaped in the Library, there were – across the entire planet – a mere 4022 people, users *and* staff. The British Library has the capacity for a thousand visitors a day.

Why Can't Anyone Just Die?

Once again, we have an essay suggested by readers (see **Who Died and Made You Dalek Supreme?** under 11.3, "Death to the Daleks"). Several readers, in fact, who spotted what seemed to be an irksome trend in 2008 and requested some sort of commentary on it. Since then, it became both the norm for the series and the plot-arc of Series 8, to the extent that the Doctor's rant to the Fisher King at the climax of X9.4, "Before the Flood" seems like an on-screen rebuke to the then-showrunner about "Disney-Deaths".

Simply put, there never seemed to be a definitive end for any character. Not just the now-apparently-infinitely-regenerable Doctor or Captain Jack or Ashildr/Me... all characters were potentially immortal. They couldn't let anyone rest in peace.

In this reticence about such a basic fact, BBC Wales looked – to British eyes – very American. The reluctance of Americans to even say that someone has died, but to talk of the person "passing" – even in news bulletins – is part of a peculiar switch-around since Victorian times concerning the public visibility of sex and death. More noticeably, the disquiet about what is appropriate for Doctor Who has flipped, so that sometimes all we know about characters is their sexual preferences – when once all we'd know is how many people they'd killed or whether or not they feared getting slaughtered. When, as in "A Good Man Goes to War" (X6.7), those characters are soldiers (identified only as "The Fat One" and "The Thin One" – we could add Vastra to this list, as we really don't know much about what makes her tick beyond fancying Jenny), something very strange indeed has taken place.

It used to be fairly straightforward. A character required some reason to be in a story, because Equity made every speaking character more costly than non-speaking ones – so, if someone had dialogue but no further part in the story, they either decided to leave and get on with their lives or (more commonly in stories set far from anywhere) they got picked off. If the story had a fairly big budget, speaking-part characters could be mown down like the ripened wheat in spectacular ways. If the author was fairly adept, the loss of a well-drawn character was a major setback and a notably upsetting development for viewers. If not, at least death stopped people from disclosing potentially useful information.

In more pragmatic ways, death was a handy form of punctuation for storytelling. It enabled viewers to see someone else fail to do something

that Our Heroes had to attempt, giving us an idea of the stakes. On-screen carnage establishes the threat in each story as being credible and unremitting. In a series such as this, where the hero prevails mainly by wits and not heavy artillery or brute force, the inutility of brute force and ordinance has to be set up so that we wonder how the Doctor or his chums will talk an unreasoning force out of just adding them to the body-count. In a whodunit, the death of each potential suspect further limits the number of people it could be behind it all. Plus, it was an excuse for pretty special effects and a show-offy stunt. This last point is most pertinent when the producers think of Doctor Who as having a primary audience of ten year old boys.

However, even at its most pulpy, Doctor Who did things that conventional action-shows couldn't. They learned the lesson early. At the end of "The Daleks" (1.2), the Thals have stormed the city and Our Heroes have prevented a genocide – but, in so doing, cut power to the Baddies' life-support machines. The Doctor pities the Daleks, but can only watch them all die. Unfortunately (in this one regard), the ratings have perked up considerably over Christmas and the BBC wanted a rematch post-haste so that they could rake in the cash from the potential merchandising. Terry Nation, then at work on his next story for the series (1.5, "The Keys of Marinus"), sees the writing on the wall and moves heaven and Earth to suggest that, whatever happened to the Conscience of Marinus, a Ming-the-Merciless-style miraculous exit ensures that the world has not heard the last of Yartek, Leader of the Alien Voord. (Actually, at time of going to press, the Voord haven't been back on our screens. They weren't even considered worthy to show up at Stonehenge alongside the Drahvins, the Adherents of the Repeated Meme or the Chelonians; X5.12, "The Pandorica Opens". The Daleks, however, have been back from oblivion more often than John Travolta and flared trousers combined.)

Surprisingly enough, this sort of thing reached its nadir in Eric Saward's stint as script editor. Saward gleefully wrote in vast numbers of characters who were cannon-fodder and knew it, talking tough and making out they didn't mind imminent meaningless deaths. He nonchalantly brought back the Master year after year without bothering too much about the logic (to the extent of cutting

continued on Page 159...

Regardless, 4022 people vanished in an unexplained incident involving moving shadows that took minutes. What precautions would *you* take when sticking your nose in a century later? Maybe send in drones first. Possibly sample the air for micro-organisms. Perhaps take pictures. What you *don't* do is take in anything that might disturb any biological swabs, scans or analysis; chicken drumsticks and salad, that sort of thing. Eating a picnic on a planet with a potential bio-hazard is suicidally stupid. Even the team from *Bonekickers* were better archaeologists than this.

Can't the Doctor Moon be accessed independently? Going there first to ask for an assessment, thus avoiding the potentially deadly shadows or any other risks, seems like a good idea. A space-archaeologist with a clue, Professor Parry or Bernice Summerfield, would have done just that.

Because, yes... the Library has a moon-sized virus checker, built to support and aid the main computer core (and protect the child-bride within). Yet the Lux family and corporation evidently don't know what happened at the Library a century ago. How is that possible? If the Doctor Moon collaborated in, or in any way noticed, the storage of 4022 extra minds inside the mainframe, why didn't it send an account? And if not, wouldn't it log some details? They have a tech expert orbiting the site, yet not so much as a SYNTAX ERROR message reached Lux HQ.

And, with an entire century to consider the problem and three generations spent hacking the seals, no-one has made the obvious connection between a bloody great computer and a message *4022 Saved*. Obviously, one would think, software was going to be a significant factor in this investigation, and yet somehow *not* telling anyone that the main operating system was a relative was regarded as a smart move. What's so shameful about something that happened centuries ago to save a child's life?

The obvious question, then: who picked this team? The Lux family has just worked out a way back into the Library and wants to know what happened there, but accompanying one of their own, Strackman Lux, is a slovenly archaeologist (and convicted criminal, we later discover) who won't sign her life-rights contract, a secretary too stupid to be trusted with a space-toilet and a trio of astro-campers armed with packed lunches. Are they, even Strackman, intended as an expendable tax write-off? Gilbert Horner (8.5, "The Daemons")

was under hypnosis when he got himself killed by such recklessness.

Maybe, when encountering people not in spacesuits, doing a quick medical scan on them before announcing that it's safe to breathe the air might help. And, why not say "this is a friend of mine"? With River pretending not to know the Doctor or Donna, why does nobody else want to check them for contamination, or accuse them of being nasty horrible aliens with designs on the Library's apparently devastating secret? Nasty horrible aliens, and environmental contamination, must rank among the possible causes of 4,000 deaths. The actual cause combines these two, but nobody makes the *slightest* gesture towards basic preliminary checks. Lara Croft would have taken more precautions than this bunch.

And, why not send a better-equipped squad? The technology available is, apparently, way behind what the Library's builders had centuries before. Certainly, there's spectrographic analysis – using lights, to register the anomalous shadows, just in case you ignored the "count the shadows" warning that someone used their dying moments to leave. As established in "The Time of Angels", the fifty-second century still has the gravity-globe illumination from the forty-second century (see also X2.8, "The Impossible Planet"). Or you could just have hand-held torches and get killed. After hearing "stay out of the shadows", Tennant and Tate walk out of the light so often that when they pull out the big *X Files* torches, it's hard to take seriously.

The Doctor says that those neural relays – the ones that trap dying minds in a loop intoning such memorable Last Words such as "ice cream"- allow the team to send "thought mail". Great! Why does nobody do this? At least three key plot-points, most notably when Miss Evangelista wanders off, rely on people being out-of-touch. Perhaps she's too stupid to think of sending a "look at this" message (despite being mentally linked to astronauts and a Professor) but River's team never seems to ping a message asking, "Where are you?" And River's in this hive-mind, so all the Doctor's secrets are available. (The Vashta Narada eat Miss E's flesh, suit and earrings, but leave just the bit with the data-core of her helmet. Are the space-suits made of bacon or something?)

The lifesign scan at the start stops counting at 1,000,000,000,000. If it has 13 digits available on the read-out, why not end on 9,999,999,999,999?

Why Can't Anyone Just Die?

continued from Page 157...

a vaguely plausible explanation of why 21.5, "Planet of Fire" wasn't terminal; when so much else of 22.3, "The Mark of the Rani" could have used such diligent pruning, it's puzzling why only this was edited). With Davros, there was the additional problem that Nation's revised deals with the BBC meant that he (Davros, not Nation) had to be in any Dalek story they did and seen to survive, since 12.4, "Genesis of the Daleks" had ended with this useful character unequivocally exterminated. As with Gerry Davis's stint as script editor and Season Eight's run of Master stories, we were in a phase when stories tended to end with companions asking "Have we seen the last of _____?" and the Doctor hesitating to give a definite reply.

The real surprise, given Saward's interest in the Cybermen, is that the conversion of minor characters into enemy troops is all off-screen or hinted. This is one aspect of the Cybermen that had been downplayed as the 60s wore on, but which was in keeping with the things he did well. It's nearly discussed in "Attack of the Cybermen" (22.1), but that gets lost in all the continuity-chatter.

However, the matter of what happens to dead bodies was increasingly the focus of stories, with even the prim Christopher H Bidmead incorporating it into the original drafts of 21.3, "Frontios". Anthropophagy was front and centre during Colin Baker's tenure. However much the series exploited old ideas of a "Soul" or a detachable consciousness and memory that could be preserved as software or exist independently of a physical location, this phase was more materialistic than ever. Even the dreamscape of the Time Lord afterlife, the Matrix, was physically entered through a door rather than interfaced with as before (23.4, "The Ultimate Foe"; 14.3, "The Deadly Assassin").

Depending on how you count it, two to five of the old series companions had been killed in the line of duty. Three, or two or one, were victims in the same story (3.4, "The Daleks' Master Plan": debate still rages in some circles as to whether Bret Vyon counts, and if not why Sara Kingdom is counted and not, say, Hugo Lang or Jackie Tyler). The three that are agreed to have been "proper" companions, Katerina, Adric and Peri, all perished on screen. Except... Peri was later said to have been spared and the evidence of her death faked (it's all in Season Twenty-Three's "Trial" storyline). We had all the plot implications of her death without the potential trauma to small kids. At least, that was

the theory – it's unclear how many people who watched the end of "Mindwarp" (23.2) stayed until the end of "The Ultimate Foe" (23.4). This is hardly unprecedented, though, as a glance at "The Android Invasion" (13.4) shows. For most plot purposes, it's pretty clear that Benton and Harry are toast – but, being series regulars and in a story directed by the producer from UNIT's glory days, Barry Letts, it's unthinkable that they could be anything other than bound hand and foot or locked in a cupboard.

People were killed for reasons other than just stopping them from advancing the plot, but they were killed nonetheless. This was enough of a series-feature to warrant a semi-serious essay on the death-tolls in old-form series (**Which Stories have the Best Body-Counts?** under, of course, 21.4, "Resurrection of the Daleks"). Stories in Season Twenty-Two expended a lot of effort in introducing several competing factions at the start and accounting for their fatal defeats at the end, leaving very little time for an actual plot or for them to be mourned. Some of the writers in Saward's stable objected to this approach (notably Christopher Bailey, interviewed in Tulloch and Alvorado's *Doctor Who: The Unfolding Text*), but the gallows humour that began to replace the bang-bang-you're-dead melodrama seemed to chime with the times. His successor, Andrew Cartmel, took that element and ran with it, but paused every so often to reflect that the victims of slapstick deaths had families. Indeed, the rites accompanying death became the focus of many stories.

This was the heritage that the Class of 2005 all knew and tried to recreate. The doomed Clive Finch described the Doctor as having "one constant companion... death" and died realising that he was finally part of the Doctor's story (X1.1, "Rose"). Series 1 is notable for having several characters ostentatiously not dying, but presents each as a surprising anomaly. Gwyneth the Housemaid miraculously withstands a fatal downloading of the Gelth into less-than-fresh corpses (X1.3, "The Unquiet Dead"), a fact that baffles the Doctor but not Dickens (whose own mortality is a given, because it's there in the textbooks). Suki's corpse grabs the Editor in X1.7, "The Long Game". The Doctor himself is a surprise to Jabe, as the Time Lords are all dead. The Daleks are – yet again – on the comeback trail after total extinction.

Two other non-deaths are more indicative of

continued on Page 161...

ABOUT TIME 2008-2009

If the scan is merely stopping when it hits the limit of all the single-cell organisms it can detect, oughtn't Donna's intestinal flora and toenail fungus swamp the scanner? There's that much life on her hair, which is why surgeons and forensic scientists not on US television shows wear bunny-suits and hairnets. Something that's been bugging us since "Rose" becomes absurdly obvious here: the Doctor uses a screwdriver as a tricorder but there isn't a read-out of any kind and even less room for one on River's clogged-up future version.

Most of what CAL does makes sense in terms of "she's a little kid and doesn't know any better", but who approved giving a little kid that sort of power in the first place? After all, it's possible to put someone *in* a computer hard drive without making them custodians of it. And, her library seems to have the books sorted by colour, not content or author. She's also, it appears, given free access to *every* book – not just the ones that get challenged by busybodies frightened that *To Kill a Mockingbird* will pollute the Vital Bodily Fluids of America's youth, but things a child *really* shouldn't read, such as *Last Exit to Brooklyn, Mein Kampf* and *The English Roses*.

Indeed, for a little girl who loved nothing better than books, Charlotte seems to spend an awful lot of time watching television. There isn't a book anywhere in her living room. All right, that television acts as a nexus for real events, but the timeframe goes wonky when hallucinated Charlotte watches events inside the Library on the same real-time monitor where she follows Donna's new life – even though Donna's experienced three or four years in the space of an hour. If CAL and dream-Charlotte are the same, she'd be aware of all of these simultaneously and know that she's not really in a house with a 1960s phone.

"Forest of the Dead" establishes that CAL isn't simply saving these people, it/she is messing with their recorded selves. Given the unknown nature of the catastrophe and the lack of time, this is an amazingly risky strategy. If we assume that it's little Charlotte wanting playmates, why isn't she playing with anyone? Why didn't the moon-sized Norton disc that talks like Colin Salmon stop any variations from whatever the usual teleport safeguards are? (Even by *Doctor Who* standards, a teleport fault-repair with the emergency default of caching people inside daytime television while it's buffering is a silly debugger.)

Why isn't Lee in the database under his name? If that isn't his name, why was he assigned one he can't pronounce?

For that matter, why is he so comfortable in Donna's recognisable suburban milieu from three thousand years before? If domestic bliss is a temporary holding-bay for preserved engrams, Evangelista-Plus saying "the world is wrong" just ensures that V-Donna has a miserable time rather than a holiday. It's never especially clear what she wants Donna to think or do. (The absence of a "do you wish to stay in cyberspace forever? Y/N." option seriously disempowers our companion, but what else is there for Donna to do? It's not like Agent Smith is around for her to kickbox in bullet-time.) If the augmented brain of the distorted bootleg of the bimbo's memories can hack the system that well, why not get a message out to the Doctor? And, how *does* Miss Evangelista's ghost know Donna's name? That revelation happens after Miss E dies.

There's a problem with the amount of time it takes the Doctor to get from the surface to the computer core; pure free fall would take a couple of days if we're discussing an Earth-sized body (see X3.0, "The Runaway Bride"). At the speed he's going, he might as well just have programmed a teleport to take him down. (We'll assume that the gravity is being maintained electronically – if not, compare this planet's core to 15.5, "Underworld" for why this might be a problem.)

The Vashta Nerada eat meat, usually roadkill. But with the Library isolated, and their forests pulped to make books, what has a whole planet of them been living on for the last century? After they negotiate an accord with the Doctor to keep possession of the Library what are they going to eat now? The Doctor tells the Vashta Narada to look him up, which makes depositing River Song's diary in the Biographies section something of an own-goal.

What precisely is going on at the climax? Four thousand-odd living minds use one living brain as a bus-bar, because the usual conduit – the mainframe for a world-sized institution – hasn't got the memory-space. It also requires the data to reconstitute the bodies in which these minds existed – all through a single biochemical relay. Even factoring in River's status as "human-plus" (X6.7, "A Good Man Goes to War"), this would take a while.

"Forest of the Dead" makes less and less sense as a title; the Vashta Nerada are still alive after all and books still aren't trees. And we're told, in the

Why Can't Anyone Just Die?

continued from Page 159...

what is to come, though. In the case of "The Doctor Dances" (X1.10), we have the first of many Steven Moffat stories where absolutely nobody has actually died, it was all a misunderstanding caused by faulty medical software. That seemed to work, so apparently it became his goal – and that of his posse of writers – to avoid any character's on-screen death being permanent unless the history books agree that s/he did (X2.4, "The Girl in the Fireplace"; X5.10, "Vincent and the Doctor") and sometimes not even then (X6.3, "The Curse of the Black Spot"; X7.2, "Dinosaurs on a Spaceship").

The other deathless freak was, of course, the resurrected Captain Jack (X1.13, "The Parting of the Ways" et seq.). His return from the death was primarily good housekeeping, making sure that this potentially useful (and, they hoped, popular) character was available for a return one day. Once the decision had been made to allow a spin-off, then Jack-as-Captain-Scarlet was as good a way as any to exploit this resurrection and make *Torchwood* just that little bit more like *Angel*. Meanwhile, although the plot-motor of X1.8, "Father's Day" is that Pete Tyler not dying makes the universe unravel, he's back next year anyway.

Series 2 exploits the handy have-your-cake-and-eat-it option of an Evil Parallel Universe, with Zeppelins (of course) and alternate versions of series regulars who can be killed on screen for maximum pathos. Just in case the full horror of what Cybermen do hadn't hit home with the death-camp iconography and Sally being converted on the eve of her wedding, we get Jackie being sliced 'n' diced and Ricky fried. Then Rose goes home to see her mum still alive and explain that Mickey's not around any more. Mickey staying in the other London is presented as being as good as death, since they can never return (but they do, and he does). However, looking at the interviews from the time, the decision had not only been taken not to ever kill off any of the series regulars, but to announce that this was to be the case.

At the start of "Army of Ghosts" (X2.12), Rose tells us that she "died" that day. As we stated in that story's write-up, posthumous narrators were very "in" that decade, so this narrative trick, the episode's title and the way everyone accepted the apparitions as the spirits of their deceased relatives fed into a huge sucker-punch the story had for anyone not paying attention. We've com-

mented before of fashions in horror-films, but this is something we ought to note here. The period we're talking about was the peak of "Paranormal Romance" and teenage books/series about unreachable dead hunks and stroppy girls who loved them. It was also the height of Zombie Apocalypse chic. The decision to aim BBC Wales's *Doctor Who* (itself back from the dead) at teenage girls made these sub-genres an obvious found-object.

Mortality became optional in popular culture once the struck-down-before-our-very-eyes Bobby Ewing came back in *Dallas*, but, as fantasy became more soap-like in the 1990s, we were provided with endless ways to make characters endless. "Soap-like" is a two-edged sword: in Britain it tends to mean grimly realistic and downbeat; American and Australian series are more prone to get all Magic Realist and include ghosts, curses and freaky prolepses. Whenever one of the miserable British soaps is having a ratings slump, there is a tendency to bring back a supposedly-dead character. The world-view of the sunnier imported soaps has influenced the more teen-orientated local ones, such as *Hollyoaks,* the ones with the same target audience as the revived *Doctor Who* and the spin-offs. The sort of magazines and websites for this slice of the populace had "true-life" accounts of supernatural encounters, ads for apps purporting to predict dating success based on "name-compatibility" and horoscopes.

It was more pronounced in the even more Goth-friendly spin-off. *Torchwood* began with someone killing people to test a resurrection device. That character (Suzi) later came back from the grave and the methodology allows another character (Owen) – not especially good at reaching out to people in life – a whole eight episodes after being shot at point-blank range to ask Tosh for a date. Another episode has a comic-relief wannabe saving Gwen from a car-crash after he'd died. Meanwhile, Jack's killed at least twice a week. The world-view of *Torchwood* is noticeably different from that of *Doctor Who* as it was or had ever been. This was amplified beyond recognition in *TW: Miracle Day* (see **Must All Three Series Correlate Properly?** under X4.4, "The Sontaran Stratagem"). Not everyone counts this but, nonetheless, presenting the absence of death as the worst thing imaginable – rather than punch-the-air time – was

continued on Page 163...

face of reason, fact or ontology, that "everybody lives". Either way, Lux's reactions at the end of the story are curious. He is overjoyed that the staff of the Library are back from their break, but unconcerned that the whole planet will be returned to the Vashta Nerada.

Finally... what exactly is happening when CAL flips on the TV remote and the books start flying around? The only way this works is if the Library has an auto-eject facility for any book on any shelf. Why would anyone have fitted that? As anti-intruder systems go it's not much cop. Maybe it's a very slow self-destruct.

Critique In the essay with "The Next Doctor" (X4.14), we're going to look at how this phase of *Doctor Who* assumes that the first broadcast has to be "sold" and include gimmicks that can be put in a one-line pitch – but also, apparently in contradiction to this, that any episode will be rerun a lot in the near future. This changes the storytelling. So far, up to this story, the BBC Wales team has made stories that work hard to justify the sales-pitch in each case, but which – apparently more by luck than judgement – function as well, if slightly differently, if you re-watch with the benefit of hindsight.

Not any more: this two-parter is the point at which a second viewing became such a radically different experience from the first that recapturing that initial experience requires mental effort for any (re)viewer with a functional memory. We've heard the jokes, we've done the jigsaw, found all the Easter Eggs, what matters now is how the elements fit together (or don't).

At first sight, in 2008, the main thread was a confused poppet imagining a library and finding intruders (the Doctor and Donna). The look of this library was intriguing, with Art Deco fittings and a similarly 1930s futuristic cityscape to suggest a whole world of books, and the child was floating around it with ease, so it seemed as if she was dreaming, except for the adult voice prompting her. It's clear what we're supposed to think, and a lot of effort goes into maintaining this pretence for as long as possible. The set-design is almost aggressively contemporary, right down to the telly showing CBBC and the retro 60s phone. Most overt is that there's a melancholy waltz played on a celeste – it's getting so that travelling back to 1990 and preventing Danny Elfman from doing the score for *Edward Scissorhands* is the

most sensible use of time travel.

The strain starts to show when the books start flying off the shelves for no good reason, other than to reinforce the impression that the girl's story is "outside" the Doctor's. It's more than slightly reminiscent of when the Doctor became convinced that the TARDIS had landed in the collective unconscious (2.8, "The Chase") and the Daleks were defeated by Count Dracula. In both cases, a momentary *frisson* is dragged on for three times its natural lifespan.

By the time that morphs into Donna being zapped into daytime television (with what seemed at first to be deliberately hokey music-cues for when we see the telly switch to different bits of the story – later in the series, we hear them used with no discernible irony), we've got a new mystery: who's this mad woman with all the hair, and how does she know the Doctor? The Lux Corporation has sent a team to investigate the abrupt disappearance of four thousand of its staff (a few years late) and we're assured that the predatory shadows link all of these riddles. As it turns out, they don't: even at the end of the second episode, we've been teased about River Song's past in ways that subsequent stories make an effort to resolve, but never quite manage.

On a *second* viewing, the pieces synch better but not perfectly: that living-room is needlessly decorated to look like that of the average BBC1 viewer in 2008 and the lack of any books is jarringly obvious once we've heard the ostensible reason the Girl's there. Little in the verbal account of what was going on matches the visual evidence. We're also supposed to think that the second episode's end has all the plot-resolution we need – except for the whole business about Professor Song being kicked into the long grass. Subsequent viewings make the way River talks about "her" Doctor frankly baffling, but there's the real problem for anyone looking at it now – if you like her as a character, and Alex Kingston's barnstorming performance, then this is the keystone to that whole arc and a rousing first/last hurrah for them. If, as many did, you found her annoying first go and unbearable on later appearances, that will taint how you look back on this adventure.

Hindsight also makes this an early example of Moffat-by-numbers, plugging something that all children are alleged to find scary into a set-up culled from 90s *Star Trek* and *Doctor Who* spin-offs – adding glitchy medical software, a perceptual

Why Can't Anyone Just Die?

continued from Page 161...

closer to 70s *Who* than to how *Doctor Who* was treating the topic in 2011.

Dodging the issue of death became Moffat's most distinctive trade-mark, here and in *Sherlock*. Even the most significant death in the series, the Doctor's regenerations, were reconfigured. We know from "The End of Time Part One" (X4.17) that Russell T Davies saw the distinct Doctors as individuals whose memories persisted, but whose selfhood went with each transformation. "The Doctor", as a concept, endures but that particular Doctor, the point-of-view and subjectivity, dies. Moffat sees it differently, and has other Time Lords (certainly the General in X8.12, "Hell Bent") waking up in new bodies with almost no side-effects. He has stated a few times that, in his view, regeneration is an accelerated accumulation of the sorts of changes we all go through, so that instead of stumbling across an old photo of yourself decades on and cringing, this perspective-shift happens in moments. Mortality is subordinate to embarrassment.

There have even been deceased characters talked into coming back after the Daleks had killed them. Professor Bracewell (X5.3, "Victory of the Daleks") was persuaded to not become a bomb by means of embarrassing recollections of his former sweetheart. Tasha Lem, whoever she was, managed to hold back the need to exterminate the Doctor by, um, observing Clara's willingness to die and holding on to her inner psychopath (as befits a space-pope). Tasha and the others were killed and converted into Dalek drones by the same process we saw in X7.1, "Asylum of the Daleks", which is also how the Cybermen possessed corpses at the end of the next year. So we'd seen the retention of personality after Dalek processing already, in the Clara-avatar Oswin. Before that, we'd seen Rory do it when he was converted into an Auton (X5.13, "The Big Bang"). Cyber-Brig ("Death in Heaven", X8.12) was hardly unprecedented, but it was seen as a new low.

That episode was hailed for finally introducing toughness on this issue after years of such indulgence. Osgood was executed for being a fangirl, it seemed. No second chances. No more safety-in-audience-approval. It was hailed by some as this century's Adric moment. But in a story that took the adage about old soldiers never dying to grotesque extremes, could anyone be sure? It quickly became a question of "how" rather than "whether"

she would be returned. Even blatant on-screen murder could be undone, as Strax's was (X6.7, "A Good Man Goes to War"; X7.6, "The Snowmen" et seq.) The revelation that Ingrid Oliver was to return as Osgood in Series 9 was less remarkable than Jenna Colman being back.

What *was* remarkable about this is that they made the plot hinge on grief and bereavement, although (as with the pernicious new classification in the real-life *Diagnostic and Statistical Manual for Mental Disorders*) bereavement lasting more than a few weeks is considered to be insanity rather than a normal reaction. This hardly matters, as Osgood was already safely packaged as a loony for liking science and dressing as Sylvester McCoy. What *did* matter was that a popular character was back despite being zapped, yet again.

Organised fandom and the public at large got the hang of this – Rory's 13 deaths didn't help – and interest in individual stories is at risk if the suspicion pervades that nobody is in any real danger. The significant irreversible deaths on screen in this phase were aberrant copies of regulars, the Flesh-copy "John Smith" (X6.5, "The Rebel Flesh"), the time-shifted Amy (X6.10, "The Girl Who Waited"), umpteen Claras and Rorys and the hallucinated River Song ("The Name of the Doctor" again). Danny Pink died, *twice*, but still appeared in the Christmas episode (X8.13, "Last Christmas"). Nobody was surprised when it was announced that Missy would be coming back in Series 9. After her seemingly endless death scene in X9.10, "Face the Raven", Clara was massively dead – but nobody believed it for a second. The question going into the two-part series finale was *how will they bring her back?*

The trailer for Series 10 offered the prospect of Bill not lasting long enough for Chris Chibnall to have to write her out, but nobody was fooled. Even announcing that she was a lesbian (back in the 90s, a sure sign that a character was not long for this world) didn't raise any expectations, fears or hopes. She was shot clean through the chest, kept on life-support for ten years, turned into a Cyberman, resurrected by her alien girlfriend, *then* brought back as a set of memories by the Glass Robots who record everyone who's ever died just to have a back-up (X10.11, "World Enough and Time"; X10.12, "The Doctor Falls"; X10.13, "Twice Upon a Time"). Any hope that things would drastically alter once Moffat left was forlorn, but things

continued on Page 165...

anomaly, a temporal paradox, Bob Holmes's Greatest Hits and a few *risqué* jokes – and hoping that a good enough director can cook the recipe properly. Not everyone finds libraries creepy; not every child was scared by shadows or the prospect of things under the bed. Very few people find space-suits intrinsically unsettling. No two children have the same fears. And yet, it *is* possible to exploit a known pre-existing icon of fear in a *Doctor Who* story that works for people who don't feel that way. The clowns in "The Greatest Show in the Galaxy" (25.4) were un-nerving because most of them were killer robots and one had sold his soul; if you were scared of clowns before, that was a (slightly dubious) bonus and the circus setting was arresting because it didn't look like an orthodox *Doctor Who* planet.

A space-suit is just a space-suit; a space-suit with a skull in it is arresting, but even a more convincing skull than the ones we get here (sorry, but they look rubbish) is a storytelling point rather than scary *per se*. This story relies too heavily on the idea that everyone will be scared just because it's a skeleton in a space-suit and that making them scared is the sole dimension of *Doctor Who*. The Vashta Narada are a conceptual monster with as real risk of looking as silly when realised on screen as the Scribble from "Fear Her" (X2.11) or the Snot-Monsters from "Sleep No More" (X9.9). Wisely, Moffat resisted the temptation to bring them back, but allowed their one re-use in a computer game: a medium and context more suitable than this. Libraries are, for many people, warm, exciting places and a sort of sanctuary – especially for the kind of kids who watch *Doctor Who*. Making an abandoned one ooh-scary is like attempting to make cardigans terrifying.

For the most part, the casting and directing saves a lot of potentially embarrassing scenes – but, for the plot to work, these have to be the most inattentive, incurious archaeologists in television history. They're less alert than contestants in *The Crystal Maze*, yet they've supposedly trained for this for a decade apiece and know their lives depend on keeping a sharp eye for details. They all seem to be more like roadies for a band playing in a pub – except their leader, who alternates between knowing things in advance and relying on the Doctor to do all their jobs.[34] They *do*, however, give a good impression of having known each other beforehand, except for the two interlopers from LuxCorp.

Nobody's bad, but especial praise has to be given to Talulah Riley for the thankless dual role of Miss Evangelista (she doesn't even get a first name); only once, very briefly, do we get a sense that Moffat wrote the role for Gina Bellman. It's significant that the circumstances of the character's death flatly contradict the supposed reason for the Data-Ghosts and her subsequent reincarnation as Lady Rosemary Exposition – the full implications of the technology and the story's premise haven't been thought through. (See **Things That Don't Make Sense** for a sketch of the reasons; there's more, but you'll have to ask us.) Most of the team become more than the sum of their parts, by performers fleshing out the scant clues in the script so that we're upset when each gets consumed and turned into catchphrases. Compare this to "The Rebel Flesh"/"The Almost People" (X6.5-X6.6), where we're almost bombarded with backstory about characters who never quite gel or seem to have met.

The Library seems like a real world partly because of the locations chosen and the fittings (the Pullman Car-style lettering makes it consistent, the Data Nodes make it exotic). It's not like any library children in the UK would have seen – it cleaves rather too hard to the US model, with a side-order of ancient libraries in films about two-fisted archaeologists – but it's like a consensus idea of a Very Big Library. The stage directions explicitly invoke Terry Gilliam and Moffat's profitably plundered his films before (X2.4, "The Girl in the Fireplace" being the most overt).

We can buy, for the time being, the notion that anyone setting up a definite-article Library would make it look like a 1930s film. The attempts at 2008 Britain are less convincing. Obviously, on a second viewing they're clearly not *intended* to be thoroughly realistic, but it's meant to fool Donna and show us that she's been fooled. The Donna of these two episodes is pretty much a generic companion with occasional hints of TV's Catherine Tate. All year, there have been moments where the details mentioned in one story clash with those of another (which football team does she support?), but it's down to Tate alone to make the character inside the CAL institute and married to Lee seem like the same one in episodes either side of it.

All the hallucinated "real world" material is unconvincing, because it's an attempt to straddle two mutually-exclusive forms of older *Doctor Who*: Yeti-in-the-Loo and Space-Satire. The for-

Why Can't Anyone Just Die?

continued from Page 163...

did change. Grace Sinclair dies in the first episode of Series 11 ("The Woman Who Fell to Earth") and it's her husband who is motivated first to get on with his life by travelling with the Doctor and, after a bit of a wobble, not to kill her killer. He still talks to her, though. And Grace's memory is used as an enticement to make him connect a discarded dimension back to our universe – a micro-cosmos that manifests as a frog with her voice (X11.9, "It Takes You Away"). Meanwhile, the Doctor's very strict with herself about killing people, and usually punishes wrongdoers with hygienic exile in space or time.

Does this mean that a return to Saward-style gratuitous massacres of supernumerary speaking-roles is the way to make the stories exciting again? Not really. They tried that in Series 9 as well, with obvious cannon-fodder (one even identified as a "grunt" with a number for a name; X9.9, "Sleep No More"), and even giving the uniformed sacrifices regional accents and making one profoundly deaf or another trans didn't make the survival or other-wise of these cookie-cutter characters very inter-esting. (Except that the one who was killed after suggesting they split up was, yet again, identified as a fangirl just before being slaughtered. That was in X9.4, "Before the Flood", but getting Joe Public to tell this and "Sleep No More" apart is tricky.) The only other characters who stayed dead were played by actors too busy and famous to come back (Jaye Griffiths, Colin McFarlane, Rebecca Front) or were secretly aliens.

The technologically-mediated persistence of personality after physical death had become sim-ply a given, whereas in older stories it was either a curse, a temporary expedient or a more oblique existential threat. The most characteristic 60s ver-sion was 6.2, "The Mind Robber", where a crude approximation of internal processes, a set of stock-phrases, gimmicks and logged "attribution" replaced anything like individuality. A "fiction-alised" Jamie or Zoe was as good as dead, just a story about them rather than actually them. The most 1970s response to the same problem was 12.2, "The Ark in Space" where people were filed in a sort of library and their genetic information, along with memory, were capable of being ingest-ed and transmitted to the next generation of Wirrn. Rather than the somewhat comforting notion, common to many religions, of an immate-rial essence remaining in the world, these stories

and others like them confronted child-viewers with the prospect of non-existence or, worse, not-being-me-but-existing.

The core audience for *Doctor Who* was, and remains, young. They are getting to grips with what "me" actually is. Threats to selfdom are more conceptual than simple hazards to life and limb. Early *Doctor Who* considered these in more detail than the recent version. Brainwashing, possession, surgical alteration and duplication were more common story-elements. The most unsettling one for many was not in the broadcast episodes, but the Terrance Dicks novelisations of the 1970s, wherein the Time Lords had an ultimate sanction: reversal of an individual's life-stream. Not only would the Doctor, or the Master, be dead, *he would never have existed*. This dread was at the heart of many Moffat-era stories. Amnesia was a fate worse than death.

This touches on the most significant point about storytelling in general, *Doctor Who* specifi-cally and Moffat's *Doctor Who* in particular. As might be expected, it is articulated most clearly as a joke: Donna points out that the Doctor's love of biographies is because they all end in deaths (X4.8, "Silence in the Library"). For the individual, unless converted into a Cyberman or downloaded into a giant mainframe (or, in Series 8, both at once), death is the end of a story. It provides a shape to a personal narrative, places perspective and meaning on what would otherwise be mere incidents.

Characters, and indeed those of us actually alive, tend to act more positively if they (we) assume this to be the one shot to get it right. (See also **Does Plot Matter?** under 6.4, "The Krotons".) People securely convinced that they will be rein-carnated or go to a better place after death can be very complacent, or terrifyingly reckless drivers. Most people assume that they are the main char-acters in their individual stories, and only reluc-tantly accept that their stories aren't very interest-ing. Given an unexpected reprieve, most people would choose to act differently as if this is The Plot, at last. The Moffat writers chose to prioritise narra-tive over simple mortality or consciousness. Series 5 has the supposed "triumph" of the Doctor surviv-ing his own erasure by becoming a character in a story, once the worst possible fate for anyone. And we know how reluctant Moffat has become finally, definitively to end his stories. (See **What's a 'Story'**

continued on Page 167...

165

mer works, when it works, by conveying an impression that the domestic world of the viewers, especially children, is weirder than we suppose and infinitely more dangerous. It's a close cousin of the 70s Public Information Films that warned us of the menaces lurking in the everyday, right up to Patrick Troughton telling us that polishing a wooden floor and putting a rug on it was lethal. As "Terror of the Autons" (8.1) showed, that always risks being daft or trippy (or both) unless handled with pseudo-documentary fidelity to the known world.

Space-Satire – amplifying contemporary and parochial concerns to the scale of Space Opera for comedic effect – also needs a delicate touch to avoid looking stupid. As "The Sun Makers" (15.4) showed, if the set-designers and actors get it into their heads to play it strictly for laughs, it gets a lot less amusing for the viewers. It also needs a writer steeped in both terms of the equation, or else it lands up like the later *Hitchhiker's Guide* books or the lowest ebbs of *Blakes 7*. World-building, even if done with the intent of poking fun at some small piece of British contemporary life, needs more thought than just making a collage of other TV shows. Eight-year-olds aren't the only people watching.

All the momentary effects in this story, the surprises, shocks and thrills (and, yes, scares) have to be symptoms of an underlying cause that, on reflection, seem to all ring true. The occasional pieces of familiar life have to be present in a future world for a reason and that reason has to chime with the reason for all the dream-imagery and running up and down corridors. Otherwise, you land up with a hot mess of discontinuous signifiers and botched retreads of "The Ark in Space" (i.e. X5.2, "The Beast Below" or, more cogently, X10.2, "Smile") without even a fig-leaf of 80s postmodernism. SF needs metanarrative, at least in the planning stages, a level of joined-up thinking that made "The Girl in the Fireplace" work when its absence in X8.1, "Deep Breath" – forgetting the *raison d'etre* of the Clockwork Robots – just made a silly story worse. Now that we know from later failures how close this story came to falling flat on its face, we can appreciate it more. This one took a risk and got away with it, narrowly or triumphantly according to taste, but "The Beast Below" slammed exactly the same ingredients together and failed.

The main thing missing for anyone watching it

now, compared to how viewers originally encountered it is, of course, a week between episodes. Predictably, the speculation over the various mysteries and how they related to each other and the overall "arc" of Series 4 led in peculiar directions, but we know most of the answers now and instead the abrupt shift of tone and content at the start of "Forest of the Dead" is now just stylistically interesting. That's a pretty big *just*, and the deft way in which television grammar is questioned and exploited is the main point of interest a decade on. Overseas viewers may have to take it on faith that daytime television looked like this in 2008 Britain, but it's such a good impersonation that perhaps British viewers didn't twig as fast as the rest what was really going on. The rug-pulling at the start of the second episode is, in fact, the missing pieces of the set-up being explained – but now that we know this, we can look at the pieces more in the abstract and appreciate the skill with which they were made. What's still arresting is the tonal shift between episodes, and the economy with which Donna's dream-world seems plausible even to her before the disruption can begin.

Holding it together, by an effort of sheer will, is director Euros Lyn. He and Director of Photography Rory Taylor have lit this to a T and he knows how to make the slow bits moody and the fast bits rousing. That sounds obvious, but a lot of directors, especially in subsequent Moffat two-parters, confuse movement for action and stasis for atmosphere, thinking that switching the lights off makes a scene scary. Even the perpetual BBC Wales problem of tag-scene after tag-scene is paced better (at least when watched without advert breaks).

But where the production really got lucky was in casting Alex Kingston. In later appearances, it's hard not to get the impression that she's having more fun than we are – whereas this first time around, River Song has just enough gravitas to make the flirting and Doctor-baiting seem like a natural side-effect of her ability. Later (or earlier), it seems as if the character is in the story just for that and we never again sense that she's earned these titles or jobs. Her "happy ending" of taking over as mother to computer-generated kids in not-2008 was a let-down even the first time, but at least it was a sidelight to the relentless libido-jokes. Even chummying up to Richard Nixon is more in-character than this (insofar as she can be said to have a "character" rather than a set of

Why Can't Anyone Just Die?

continued from Page 165...

Now? under X1.13a, "Pudsey Cutaway".)

Thus messing with people's time-lines became a more common threat than even extermination. If that doesn't scare anyone, altering perception and memory has potential and can be done without any costly explosions or ray-effects. It allows the same actor to play, in effect, multiple roles (which is another saving). After a while, though, it becomes a bit tangled. A messed-up time-line can be un-messed-up: that's what Clara did to become the ubiquitous cosmic soufflé nuisance (X7.14, "The Name of the Doctor"). History, and people, can be rewritten endlessly, with no fear of a literal deadline. There aren't many ways to lower the stakes more comprehensively than this.

In fact there's only one: have someone die on screen, then get an infinitely-extendable final-moment furlough. For Owen Harper in *Torchwood*, this was a curse; for Clara, it's a space-time *Thelma and Louise*. We're a very long way from 20.3, "Mawdryn Undead" or 15.5, "Underworld", when it was the doomed immortals on endless voyages saying "please make it stop", not the viewers.

Death renders people incommunicado; bereavement is the inability to ask any more questions or make any new experiences with that person. Just as gimmicking mobile phones so that a companion can call mum from Five Billion AD (not to mention fixing the TARDIS-navigation so they can always pop home for tea and a hug) lowers the stakes for anyone choosing to travel with the Doctor (as we argued in **RT Phone Home?** under X1.2, "The End of the World"), so having dead people on hand to chat about old times and, worse, ask about things that have only started happening posthumously dilutes the tension. *Doctor Who* spent most of the 2010s in denial about the finality of death, with even Gallifrey's destruction being revealed as a huge hoax and the Twelve Strikes and Out rule of regenerations dismissed as a slight inconvenience.

Even before the ritual cry of *Oh My God! They've Killed Rory! You Bastards!* and the wriggling out of the final-no-kidding-he's-dead end of the Doctor once a year for three years, Moffat was trying to resolve a reluctance to bump off his creations with the need to tell stories that have clear ends (usually bent back to form the beginnings). He teased us with the prospect of a final death for a main character at the start of each season, but even when he said "I'm not kidding" (as with the promotion for Series 6), he was kidding. Time travel means that characters can always be revisited at a point before their known deaths (which, in the case of Clara, means a potentially infinite time: "Hell Bent"). It also means that, *in extemis*, deaths can be undone as history changes. "The Wedding of River Song" (X6.13) begins with time stuck so that any number of dead characters are milling around simultaneously, but had a brief pause to mark that Brigadier Lethbridge-Stewart wouldn't be around any more. Two years later, they even undid this.

At least the deceased Brigadier was changed by the experience. Apart from the odd line here and there, we never hear Rory explain that he has been dead, resurrected as a Roman made of plastic and then killed another seven times, nor does he really process this (as the TARDIS arrives at his wedding breakfast, he mutters "I was plastic" and that's nearly it – one line in X6.1, "The Impossible Astronaut" – and then just a rather resigned "I'm dead... again" comment each time he thinks it's happened). He just goes back to being the sardonic husband of a supermodel. In his line of work (a nurse, as they sometimes remember), mortality and its consequences might come up in conversations and may well be something he would have reason to think about more deeply. But, apparently, not on camera.

The consequence of all of this is that the only Moffat-era character for whom a bereavement was absolute and a motive for action is Osgood, who is mourning, err... herself.

catch-phrases and plot-functions).

Here, she seems more rounded than later. Maybe that's because Moffat's writing specifically for Kingston. Or perhaps it's because River's first among equals in a team of close colleagues. It's those colleagues who come to the fore on a repeat viewing: once we're no longer concerned about who, if anyone, will survive, the small notes of difference in how they deal with a terminal illness

make them all more memorable than the relatively one-note River.

Similarly, Colin Salmon (as Dr Moon) has to walk a fine line between sinister and reassuring and was obviously scripted as a sort of anti-Doctor. It would have been possible to make his secret messages to CAL and attempts to "gaslight" Donna seem more serial-killer-ish. In another story that might have been the way to go, but with a time-paradox and predatory shadows in the mix, that might have over-egged it. This, ultimately, is the story's most significant feature; with enough in it to warrant (if not demand) repeated viewings, it wasn't swamped or confusing on first broadcast.

The Lore

Written by Steven Moffat. Directed by Euro Lyn. Viewing Figures ("Silence in the Library"): (BBC1) 6.3 million, (BBC3 repeats) 1.4 and 0.6 million. Viewing Figures ("Forest of the Dead"): (BBC1) 7.8 million, (BBC3 repeats) 0.8 and 0.5 million. AIs 89 throughout.

Repeats and Overseas Promotion *Bibliothèque des Ombres* (both episodes – as you will recall from X2.12, "Army of Ghosts", the word "Ombres" can mean "ghosts" or "shadows"), *Tödliche Stille* (deadly quiet), *Wald der Toten*.

Alternate Versions BBC America keeps it almost intact, but the "But I've been *dieting!*" line went missing and it ends with the Doctor finger-snapping the TARDIS open.

Production

• The usual procedure was for Steven Moffat to give Russell T Davies a vague, spoiler-free outline, then present a completed script subject to light tweaking rather than wholesale rewriting (unlike the other writers in the stable). When proposing a two-part story for Series 3, Moffat had mentioned a spooky library and some statues of angels, but work on *Jekyll* meant that he wasn't able to provide this; he had decided that the angels didn't fit and gave them their own one-episode Doctor-lite tale (X3.10, "Blink"). This had delayed the similar "Century House" idea for a year (see X4.10, "Midnight" for more on this) and alarmed Davies (who'd decided on robot angels as the menace for his Christmas episode, X4.0, "Voyage of the Damned"). One notion floated was that the library had windows to other times (like the mirrors in "The Girl in the Fireplace", but also very like the penultimate *Star Trek* episode, "All Our Yesterdays").

Moffat was keen to avoid spoilers about the forthcoming episodes where possible, but privately received some details of Donna's fate as and when he needed to know. The planet-sized library idea returned, but Davies was – once again – wrong-footed when Moffat's *fait accompli* script had Donna trapped in an alternate "what if" life with no memory of the Doctor (cf. X4.11, "Turn Left"). A flurry of emails towards the end of October resolved this: Davies factored this in as yet another clue about Donna's odd future (even though it doesn't exactly make sense as scripted). The name "River Song" was devised partly because one draft of the second episode needed a new name and – as they were usually referred to by acronym – it amused Moffat to call it "A River Song Ending". It was almost universally assumed that she was a future wife of the Doctor's, but it was left ambiguous.

• Meanwhile, Davies was sounding out Moffat on the possibility of a handover once Davies left the series. It was becoming apparent that the workload was affecting Davies's health, and potentially affecting the quality of the scripts and production of the three series over which he had final control. Tennant was taking time off to do the RSC productions after Series 4, so it was looking as if his departure would be sooner rather than later. (The plan for five Specials in 2009 in lieu of a full series was slowly coming together, and Tennant was contemplating making this his future after the RSC stint.)

With Julie Gardner already planning her departure and Phil Collinson considering a move, there was a sense of transition. Even production manager Tracie Simpson was going (see X3.13, "Last of the Time Lords" for her on-screen moment). Moffat was in the throes of adapting Herge's *Tintin* for the big screen, and had been offered more work by Steven Spielberg: taking time to write a two-part *Doctor Who* adventure was a bit of a problem. Spielberg is reported to have been entirely sympathetic with Moffat for turning down a chance to write the sequel in order to take over the series. (The eventual film was a hit, with later script contributions from Joe Cornish and Edgar Wright, but there's been no hint of a sequel.)

• With Moffat so busy, the first script was given to Euros Lyn (director of this block) on time, but the latter half was delayed. Small changes were made (Helen Raynor editing) mainly for practical purposes. The Nodes were, at one point, supposed to crawl on the floor and be adjuncts to a cybernetic librarian (perhaps resembling the Stephen Fry character from the then-current film

Mirrormask); Donna's fake children were called "Alan" and "Tracy" (with *Tintin* uppermost on his mind, maybe there was a *Thunderbirds* theme) and, crucially, CAL was a boy. Dr Moon was written as an old country doctor and initial casting ideas were Sir Ian McKellen (X7.6, "The Snowmen") and Sir Michael Gambon (X6.0, "A Christmas Carol").

As you may already have heard, the first thought for who should play River Song was Kate Winslet. However, Collinson had been sat next to Alex Kingston's agent at a dinner, and found out that she would be available to visit the UK and was keen on the series. A suggested subplot reported to have been trimmed was that Lee would, in real life, be a plump woman with a stammer – this was too complex to set up in a few lines and resolve along with everything else going on. As all of this crystallised, Moffat delivered the second episode on 1st December, 2007, three days before the tone meeting and a week before the first recce.

• The crew had a stroke of luck with the locations. The main library in Swansea had been a domed cylindrical building just opposite the Glyn Vivian Gallery in the east of the city; this was being converted into a specialist library for a new arts complex as a purpose-built new library was being completed across the city. For three weeks in early January, the old library was to be left empty. The team had been in the neighbourhood recently (Plantasia, used for the climax of X4.6, "The Doctor's Daughter", is literally around the corner) and both Lyn and Raynor had used it when revising for exams. By now, the first episode had been timed at 38 minutes, so Moffat was asked for new scenes (rather than, as with any other writer, Davies adding material); these appeared during recording and were worked into the locations already selected. The working title for the second episode, "Forest of the Night", was considered to be too close to "Midnight" (which was, by now, the next episode in the broadcast schedule); other options were considered.

• Recording work began at a familiar locale, Hensol Castle, on 15th January. Tennant was in London participating in an elaborate illusion with hypnotist Derren Brown (mentioned as UNIT's default explanation for oddities in public in X7.15, "The Day of the Doctor"). The shoot began with Donna and Dr Moon in the grounds of the CAL institute. It was Wales in January so, obviously, the weather was abysmal: Colin Salmon

needed a dark blue coat to be added to Dr Moon's signature "night sky" look (observe the moons and stars on his tie).

• With small children, there is a limit on how many hours they can do in a day and the delays for rain ate into these. They had four other children of similar build for the "reveal". As the day was almost a washout, a second unit took photos of Donna and her babies and a brief insert of her wedding was grabbed at St Catherine's Church nearby. Donna's dream-life continued in a house on Palace Road, Llandaff, across the road from the Girl's house (one used in *Torchwood* as Toshiko's pad).

On 18th (in with the end of recording "The Doctor's Daughter"), Lyn got the children playing Donna and Lee's kids (now renamed Josh and Ella as a wink at Moffat's son and his *Who*-mad schoolfriend) to run around the settee to seem as tired as if they'd been out playing in the park. Across the road, Tennant showed up in person to cue Eve Newton (as Charlotte) for her half of the conversation with the Doctor. The cartoon clip on the Girl's telly was a sneak preview of a new CBBC series *Pedro and Frankensheep*, not due for transmission until after the episode it was in aired. (A full list of the sources for everything CAL saw when channel-zapping is available on request, but life's too short: it's all BBC stuff except the horse-race.)

• Week Two began with a quick return to Palace Road. This was the day that Alex Kingston arrived for make-up tests and a first fitting. On Tuesday, they relocated to Dyffryn Gardens, which had doubled for Versailles in "The Girl in the Fireplace" and had been used in two *Torchwood* episodes (it's where Gwen and Rhys got married). This is where Donna arrived by ambulance and the late Professor Song was reunited with her team and met Charlotte and Dr Moon.

As Donna's brief materialisation in the TARDIS was recorded, the rest of the Song Expedition were getting costume fittings. The spacesuits were flame-retardant undersuits for Formula 1 drivers, while the helmets were constructed with fans to prevent overheating or asphyxia (almost all of the dialogue in scenes incorporating one or more archaeologist/Skeleton are redubbed in ADR). Choreographer Ailsa Berk was on hand to develop a walk for the Vashta Nerada in spacesuits. Instead of shorter actors with fake skull heads on top of their own, the actors in the suits were to wear masks. Most of the time the victims were played by doubles; Ruari Mears was in the suit formerly occupied by Proper Dave. While Tate was away doing remounts for "Turn Left" and pick-ups for the Sontaran two-parter, Tennant and the archaeologists ran up and down corridors at Upper Boat; the walkways were to be matted into the CG exterior shots of the Library. This was also the first time they shot the trip to the core, again using green-screen. The following day, Moffat brought the real Joshua to the set (he helped with a tracking shot across the stacks in the Blue Archive) and shadows were made to move using thick cardboard.

• Back to Swansea for more at Brangwyn Hall for the vast Foyer (lit to resemble the library in *Citizen Kane*) and the return of the four thousands library staff and patrons. These were, of course, doubled up and included some of Lyn's relatives. The Alcoa plant provided the innards of the planet-sized data-core for the next two days (as the scripts for the season finale were released on a need-to-know basis) and on the last day of January, as the news reports for the Sontaran two-parter and "Turn Left" were recorded at BBC Wales, the team took up residence in Swansea's library.

• February began with the Doctor meeting River Song. There was more shadow legerdemain with cardboard. Over the next week, various Blue Hall sequences were recorded, including the flying books sequence on 4th and 5th. The team had sourced a number of box-files the right size to pass for books (almost) and Danny Hargreaves's team at Any Effects had rigged some of the stacks with catapults and pneumatic pistons. The floor crew threw some books by hand when they needed to be seen to hit cast members.

• Meanwhile, backstage changes were being announced: Collinson had accepted a post at BBC Manchester, Moffat's accession to the top job was made public on 2nd and Tennant revealed his stint playing Hamlet and Richard II and the whole 2009 Specials scheme.

• The last full day of Blue Hall included Proper Dave acquiring extra shadows: this was done by the simple but lengthy process of multiple takes with light-sources in different places, superimposed in post-production. On 7th, they returned to the same location to end the Blue Hall and start the Red Hall (the same room lit differently, as you probably noticed). The under-run had been partly fixed with a couple of new extended scenes, the first of which was a TARDIS sequence with the

conversation about the Psychic Paper having a message with a little kiss. This was recorded on the 8th, but not used.

• One last morning at the Swansea Library took care of the Yellow Hall and the activation of the Self-Destruct, then back to Brangwyn Hall, this time for the old council chambers. These were redecorated with piles of books as the room Miss Evangelista finds and where her remains are discovered. Moffat had extended the scene of her recovery to add the Data Ghost scene, adding two minutes to the running-time. Another addition was when, in the atrium where the Doctor explains the Library to Donna, there is a handy scanner to detect life-forms.

• On 29th February, the usually unreliable tabloid *The Sun* managed a genuine scoop – someone had left the scripts lying around and they managed a spoiler of unprecedented accuracy. That it was a script by the incoming show-runner made it all the juicier. The concatenation of these stories kept the public interest high, but coloured all of Moffat's relations with the press as executive producer (especially in the run-up to Series 7). The other problems were closer to home: the proposed titles for the second episode included "River's Run", a Joycean allusion that Davies thought only made sense after you'd seen the episode; "Forest of the Night' (cf. X8.10, "In the Forest of the Night" and *In the Night Garden...*); "The Forest Wakes"; and "Saved". The eventual title was a compromise

• The episodes were both broadcast at 7.00pm, despite the start of the second-biggest football championship (after the World Cup), Euro 08, live coverage of which was split between BBC and ITV and usually on Saturdays. On 31st May, the main event on BBC1 was the two-part final of *I'd Do Anything*, with the last heat before the viewer vote for the eventual winner of the role of Nancy in a revival of *Oliver!* This required the station to move *Casualty* to an earlier transmission time to allow the results show, but they left *Doctor Who* in what used to be its usual slot. (The *Casualty* episode was about a comics convention, oddly enough).

The spoiler in *The Sun* seems to have piqued people's curiosity and the following week, aided by Spain vs Switzerland on BBC1 (delaying for a week the final of *The Kids are All Right*, the absence of which may also have helped), the ratings in the same slot were up by one and a half million. By now, there was a lot of odd speculation about the eventual resolution of the various story-arcs (see the essay with X4.12, "The Stolen Earth"), and it was even being suggested that the BBC1 station ident, showing animated neon figures supposedly leaving their moorings and walking down Blackpool's Golden Mile, was some kind of subtle hint. After all, they'd used that one exclusively before every episode so far that year...

X4.10: "Midnight"

(14th June, 2008)

Which One is This? The one without a monster. Or a companion for most of it.

Firsts and Lasts Davies tried something new for this year's Doctor-lite episode; whereas in previous seasons, the focus was on a guest character and the Doctor and company stayed largely off screen, this time Tennant and his co-star were split up. Catherine Tate was off doing "Turn Left" (X4.11) when this was being produced.

There's no sign of the TARDIS, either the console room or in box form; that's not happened since "Genesis of the Daleks" (12.4). Something else happens that hasn't occurred for even longer than that; director Alice Troughton, seeing that the script she'd been given ran more or less as a stage play (see **The Big Picture** and **Alternative Versions**), elected to shoot it more or less in chronological order. No one had done that since "The Ark in Space" (12.2) and that was an anomaly even then.

Instead of captions to denote elapsed time, we get "Kliks" (the local unit of distance). Also, when there's a thumping on the hull, this marks the only knock-knock joke around *Doctor Who* that has ever done that isn't unbearably twee. Not least because, this once, it doesn't refer to the Doctor.

Watch Out For...

• The majority of the menace here comes from simple things happening at the wrong time. Anyone occupied by the unseen alien force goes from mimicking what's just been said to pre-empting what is *about* to be said. The scariest moment in this story, and arguably in the whole of the new series, is simply David Tennant and Lesley Sharp talking cobblers very fast, in perfect synchrony. The words "Shamble bobble dibble dobble" have never been so terrifying.

• It's meant to be the effects-less one, so three-quarters of the episode takes place in one fairly small and drab grey room – but when The Mill's called upon to do CGI pick-up shots, they're lovelier than normal. On the other hand, the inevitable exploding machinery shots look strangely as if someone has overlaid pictures of sparks on the screen.

• The futuristic setting is a transparent fraud, as anyone who's travelled any distance by coach or budget airline will recognise. This allows gag-references to bad 70s Euro-pop, pointless health-warnings, neck-pillows and boring slide-shows. This anachronism is a neat way to have an in-character info-dump by a dry pedant in a cardigan, with a slide-projector.

• And it's Billie-Piper-blip-cameo time again, on a ship entertainment system a very long time in the future, as well as many systems away from the planet where Rose is looking for the Doctor. She looks perturbed.

The Continuity

The Doctor Likes travelling alone, or so he tells a lonely woman in need of such advice. He's convinced he can restrain the entity when they reach civilisation. [One wonders how he hoped to control a disembodied intelligence. He had a similar ambition in 5.5, "The Web of Fear", but the most recent precedent, X3.7, "42", didn't go so well.]

He sabotages the annoying entertainments and enjoys several hours making a bunch of tourists actually converse. Even in the middle of a crisis, he can't resist making Sky compliment his looks.

• *Background.* It seems that he's finally come to terms with Rose's parallel universe exile [Davies has said he was going for deliberate irony on that one]. When called upon to provide a name, he pulls out the usual John Smith pseudonym.

• *Ethics.* He's curt when offering to cut a deal with the entity who has already killed two people and possessed a third on purpose. It shames him to realise that a woman saved his life and he never bothered learning her name [see also the eleventh Doctor's outrage in X5.6, "The Vampires of Venice"].

It doesn't occur to him that asserting mental superiority over a group of panicky people might not win their trust. [Unlike the majority of times when the new-series Doctor is playing alpha male, here it backfires spectacularly.]

• *Inventory: Sonic Screwdriver.* Shuts off irritatingly hyperactive entertainment. The Doctor attempts using it to find the source of the knocking [unsuccessfully it seems].

• *Inventory: Psychic Paper.* The Doctor's now so carried away, the psychic paper allows him to give the Hostess and the Driver mutually contradictory stories about his identity in the space of 30 seconds. [Oddly, though, once an entity has possessed Sky Silvestry, he doesn't use the paper to bypass speech and get a clear line of communication with her or it. Nor does he flash it to claim some authority over his increasingly desperate fellow travellers.]

• *Inventory: Other.* You know the drill by now; he puts on glasses to look at computer screens and whips them off when he's not. [The sheer consistency of the way he uses them, for close-up detail work, suggests that he needs them more than he lets on in X3.13a, "Time Crash".] He's still carting the stethoscope around, but seems to have mislaid his torch again. [Either he has appropriate currency or the internal phones at the Leisure Palace don't need money.]

The Supporting Cast

• *Donna.* She's cheerfully unimpressed by the Doctor's description of the Sapphire Waterfall tourist brochure, but enjoys sunbathing and white bathrobes as much as anyone. Faced with a traumatised Time Lord, she goes for wry teasing and is taken off-guard when he takes it straight.

The Non-Humans

• *The Other Thing.* Well. Whatever is happening in this episode, the Doctor has no idea what it is, and doesn't even give it a name. [It's possibly shown up because of the new route that the craft took – we're informed that no one's ever passed over the specific part of ground that the Crusader 50 takes. This doesn't necessarily imply it was responsible for the truck breakdown, but we're given no other explanation. It does seem to be learning as it goes along. Some of the characters speculate on why it possesses Sky first, but we haven't any concrete evidence for the hypothesis it's attracted to the most frightened and lonely.]

Professor Hobbes, appropriately, is a materialist and declares that nothing can live on the planet's surface. This is certainly an exotic world, with X-tonic sunlight that evaporates human flesh and some kinds of metal in an instant. [So whatever the consciousness usually inhabits, if anything, it

probably isn't carbon-based. They do speak about diamonds, so inert carbon compounds seem to withstand this X-tonic ray. It may indeed be a form of modulated waveband within the radiation itself (after the events of "42", this is at least available as an explanation).

[One possibility: we have a planet full of crystalline structures and lots of high-energy radiation, just the sort of circumstances that could make the planet itself conscious. (Real-life chemistry suggests that silicon would be the next most plausible base for life after carbon, thanks to its propensity for chemical bonds.) If so, it'd make the Doctor's comment about the dangers of the Leisure Palace itself that much more explicable; one encounter with a big scary threatening entity is an incident, but if every part of the planet has the potential of tapping into this intelligence... The overwhelming bulk of Earth's mass is silicates, which are mixes of silicon, oxygen and whatever else, but this doesn't actually need an atmosphere to form. Oxygen can be metallic under the right conditions, and assuming that – since it's in Earth's air – it is only found in atmospheres is as crass as assuming that all atmospheres have to have it. We might note that it's Professor Hobbes who tells us that Crusader vehicles never stop and silicates need an atmosphere. Considering how reliable the rest of his dialogue is, you might wish to question that. Especially since an inexplicable earthquake happens right before Sky's possessed.]

• *Shamboni.* A species with big foreheads. Some of them work at tourist resorts.

Planet Notes

• *Midnight.* Its star is called Xion. A planet bathed in X-tonic rays and Galvanic radiation [however that works – in 13.5, "The Brain of Morbius", 'a belt of magnetic radiation' was the palpably false excuse Solon used for all the crashed spaceships], which is so lethal that sunbathing requires 15 solid feet of glass as protection – or a simple windshield made of Finitoglass, apparently. Despite the hazards, someone built a Leisure Palace and lowered it down from orbit for people to enjoy, complete with an anti-grav restaurant [more economically feasible if the gravity is low to start with]. Among the attractions is a Sapphire Waterfall [or a compound of silica with iron pigmentation, anyway], which falls over the Cliffs of Oblivion four hours away by bus-truck

What Were the Daftest Knock-Off Series?

[NB: as Mad Norwegian Press are already on our case about the word-count of this volume, we won't bother listing the shortcomings of *Torchwood* – that's a topic for a whole book – and like, everyone else, we'll just change the subject when anyone mentions *Class*.]

There were many US productions that seemed to have taken a hint or two from the PBS showings of *Doctor Who* in the 70s and 80s. We could also discuss at length the various ITV attempts at "me too" series, of which the most famous were the Gerry Anderson puppet shows, the most successful domestically was *The Tomorrow People* and the most interesting was *Ace of Wands*. The latter two are obvious comparisons, because they ran with the almost extinct series-of-serials approach that only *Doctor Who* was still doing in the 70s.

In the early years of the twenty-first century, before the money ran out, there were a lot of old shows revived in "serious" new formats – and a lot of new series that had obvious similarities to past hits – on both sides of the Atlantic. In America, for every critical success like the rethought *Battlestar Galactica,* there was a more obvious dud such as *Flash Gordon* or *The Bionic Woman*. (Actually, *Galactica* was pretty stupid too, but it was thought to be "about" something real, because there's a certain flavour of critic who can only handle SF if it's a grindingly obvious parable.)

Back in Blighty, though, the green light for any vaguely fantasy or effects/action show only really went on when *Doctor Who* managed to come back and not be crap. We'd had a few below-par fantasy shows of our own, in the bid for a UK version of *Buffy*. (For example *Hex*, which had undead girl-on-girl action in the school canteen, and yet somehow failed to win a big audience – see X1.7, "The Long Game"). You can tell that none of these caught on from the way that *Class* was being promoted as being like a British version of *Buffy* in 2016. Meanwhile, reboots of old shows were the Big New Thing (e.g. *Strictly Come Dancing* or *It's a Knockout*, to say nothing of Charlie Higson's *Randall and Hopkirk (Deceased)* – see **Why Now? Why Wales?** under X1.1, "Rose" for why many think we should say nothing of it).

Somehow, *Doctor Who* had got it right. Then the network chiefs saw two separate spin-off dramas making waves as well, and started casting around for anything a bit like that but not copyrighted. Saturday teatime went from being a graveyard slot to rapidly gaining notoriety as the ratings battlefield. Independent companies saw the mix of soap-like families, cheap(er) digital effects and already-known formats and thought "we'll have a bit of that."

The results weren't pretty.

Robin Hood (Tiger Aspect/BBC1 2006 – 2009 Saturday teatimes)

This series began with the worst possible endorsement. The series was shot on location in Hungary. It made the headlines when the local bandits stole the rushes and held them to ransom. Then they spontaneously decided to give them back. The joke went around that this was because they'd watched the tapes.

Once the episodes aired, in October 2006 in the *Doctor Who* slot on Saturdays (with a teaser before and after X2.13, "Doomsday"), this seemed less funny. For the first week, 8.6 million viewers tuned in. Later episodes averaged at 5.5 million in the first year (even with *Strictly Come Dancing* book-ending it), 4.6 million the second year. The very last episode, ignominiously moved to BBC2 because of Andy Murray getting through to the third round of Wimbledon, had 1.7 million viewers – few of whom were sobbing as Robin was betrayed and killed with a poisoned sword soon after finally killing the Sheriff. They'd managed to alienate the remaining fans while boring the general public.

They gave it a magazine with stickers and freebies – just like *Doctor Who Adventures,* but with a DVD ROM of games and pics in issue #1, but this just made it more obvious what was amiss. *Doctor Who* has different worlds and monsters each week and the central figures of the Doctor and Rose were popular and funny. *Robin Hood* was the same every time with a big cast of regulars, almost all of them more interesting than the ostensible hero. They had the perfect modern-style Robin Hood in the cast, but he was playing Gisborne. Richard Armitage's Guy indeed landed up as focal character in later series, after most people had stopped bothering, and he was the breakout star. Jonas Armstrong, as Robin, was sort of... there. If he had to share a screen with Sam Troughton (as Much) or Harry Lloyd (as Will Scarlett – see X3.8, "Human Nature" for proof of his versatility), Armstrong melted. Say what you like about Richard Greene in the 50s, he had a screen presence. Armstrong had a scowl.

Marian was even more anonymous, but wasn't

continued on Page 175...

173

from the Palace. Normally the route is through the Winter Witch Canyon, but a diamond-fall there blocked the way.

For all the bright sunlight everywhere, the entity suggests that Midnight is a very cold planet. [An odd statement for a native to make without a yardstick for comparison, so perhaps it is very old and the world has altered. It's apparently seismically stable – diamond rockfalls aside – and has no air. This may not always have been the case.]

The Crusader travels at least 251 kliks of a four-hour 500 klik trip, but a rescue craft of unidentified speed can reach them in only an hour. [We're invited to read 'kliks' as "clicks" and "clicks" as kilometres and "hour" as being one of ours, but that's not a given.

[If the planet itself is, as suggested, capable of sentience, we can speculate as to what it's composed of. A planet-sized jewel with hard UV sounds like a Hot Jupiter (a gas giant close to its star, currently the most numerous of the discovered exoplanet types), with the gases blown away and the metallic hydrogen or diamond core (as Uranus was supposed to have until they looked harder) exposed. Galvanic radiation implies a medium through which to work: perhaps it's composed of quartz (piezo-electric properties), silicon with impurities, or metallic oxygen for conductivity and magnetic flux. Or, if an atmosphere exists but is thin and toxic to humanoids, there could be some colloidal ferric dust suspended in the air, as used as the excuse for flying sharks (X6.0, "A Christmas Carol"). The view we get is too clear and the storm insufficiently abrasive for this to be exactly what's going on, but it might have "no air" the way our Moon does, with a tenuous halo of particles too thin to be called an atmosphere in all but the most technical sense.]

• *The Lost Moon of Poosh.* [See two episodes from now.] It's been missing so long, an undergraduate has written a paper on it.

History

• *Dating.* No one on screen ever mentions it. [There's a good argument for the fortieth century, although we'd hope that the retro fashions are cyclic rather than everyone dressing like that from now until AD Ten Trillion. (Dear Lord, this means sulky teenagers will be listening to The Cure until the Heat Death of the Universe – indeed, that might be what causes it. If 1.8, "The Sensorites" is to be believed, the wretched US boutique chain

Hot Topic will outlast London.)

[Within the BBC Wales chronology, there's nothing to stop this story from being in the twenty-sixth century (X8.3, "Robot of Sherwood") or the much-hyped fifty-first. However, taking the whole of the programme's future-history as at least uncontradicted on screen, the nearest analogy is 17.4, "Nightmare of Eden", which is stated as being late twenty-first or early twenty-second century. This might need a lot of backpeddling vis-à-vis the dates given in X4.16, "The Waters of Mars", but... it's complicated. (See **Was There a Martian Time-Slip?** under that story.) There's no clever, clean cold fusion or anti-matter drive for the charabanc; it runs on a micropetrol engine, which is silly on a planet-diamond that never had any organic life. But, we know from A5, "The Infinite Quest" that oil is used for all sorts of bizarre purposes in the fortieth century, including fuel for space ships.]

Rafaella Carra's 1978 hit "Do It, Do It Again" has persisted down the centuries. [So it's almost definitely an Earth colony in the future, and not another example of a humanoid society evolving along such similar lines, with similar names to ours and cardigans. (If, however, the people of Zog were sufficiently well-versed in 70s pop to have heard Wizzard – X4.0, "Voyage of the Damned" – all bets are off.)]

Humanity has budget intergalactic travel, allowing ordinary families easy access to the resorts of the cosmos. Aliens come up in casual conversation, but no one expresses surprise that the whole group on the Crusader are humans. Same-sex marriages are accepted as a matter of course. Peanuts are still *de rigueur* on flights. [They must have solved the current upswing in lethal peanut allergies, and yet the hostess still offers a warning that the peanuts contain nuts.] The packaged meals are still so flavourless as to make telling chicken from beef hard. [Or, it may really be some genetically hybridised force-grown meat: mixed flavours seem to be fashionable; peach and clementine might make a decent juice mix or a compound fruit grown that way.] The expression 'Wagons roll' has been revived for self-consciously ironic purposes. 'John Smith' isn't a plausible pseudonym. Someone named Ludovic Klein does abstract artistic installations for tourist buses.

In an exquisitely wrong bit of technobabble, the Crusader systems have a modem link for 3D

What Were the Daftest Knock-Off Series?

continued from Page 173...

the only woman in the cast this time: Djaq, a crop-haired Saracen lass in purple combat trousers (played by an Anglo-Indian actor, Anjali Jay) was handy with a Mongol bow and, like all Saracens, knew acupuncture. And how to make Greek Fire. And every language in existence. Meanwhile, Gisborne's sister Isabella landed up plotting against just about everyone as the original writing team were discarded. A plotline they'd spent most of the second series setting-up just went nowhere, while characters were abruptly ditched or left on-screen with no lines.

However, this was swamped by the 45-minute adventure format making a fight towards the end the main feature of each episode and by veteran scene-stealer Keith Allen as the Sheriff of Nottingham getting all the good lines and playing it with his customary, shall we say, ebullience. There was a hint of something more substantial in the way Robin's experiences in the Crusades had damaged him, and that the story moved to the Holy Land in the third series, yet everything else was so inconsistent that it seemed like an acci-dent. This series dropped (or mislaid) a few key characters and brought in Friar Tuck (who was a Ninja or something and played by David Harewood, Naismith from X4.16, "The End of Time Part One") and someone called Kate who took over the plot-functions of the written-out Djaq, Will *and* Marian. It didn't look like anyone making it was paying attention.

The press had fun with the obvious "Robin Hoodie" gags, noting that the whole "giving to the poor" part of the equation was being downplayed. This gang sounded more Tottenham than Nottingham, and looked more Boy Band than Merrie Men. That could have been interesting, but the whole thing looked tired from the second episode on. Older viewers who recalled the last Saturday night rendition of the story in the 80s found themselves taking back anything bad they'd ever said about Jason Connery's replace-ment Robin in the third year of *Robin of Sherwood*. Younger ones found other things to do. An early episode was written by Paul Cornell and directed by Graeme Harper – but every *Doctor Who* fan we know, especially the school-age ones, ended up watching David Attenborough on BBC2.

The Bottom Line: There's a reason Mark Gatiss seemed to be having such a good time writing

X8.3, "Robot of Sherwood". Revenge is a dish best served with a spoon.

Primeval (Impossible Pictures/M6 (France)/ ITV1 2007 – 2011, Saturday teatimes)

Sparkly holes in spacetime allow dinosaurs to run amok in present-day London. A small band of quirky experts tackle these and occasionally pop through the holes to visit the past. There are also holes to a nightmarish future, and these are the clue to the big conspiracy underlying all of this.

Admit it... once you read about the conspiracy thing, you sort of went cold on the idea. Another promising fantasy franchise sacrificed to the Curse of the Story Arc. This is especially true here, as the ostensible hero's ex-wife is the leader and she's hatched a plot that involves clones, brain implants, a program to predict where the sparkly holes will open and... we'll leave that for a while, because there's a lot else that went so wrong they had to reboot three times. Three.

Reboot 1 was the end of Series 1: they had a good cast but terrible characters, so they had Our Hero metaphorically tread on a butterfly during a trip to the Cretaceous era. When he got back, the same actors were playing different characters with the same names (except one) and the show's premise changed. The way that all non-white char-acters were dino-chow before getting any dia-logue had become notorious and was fixed. The sarcastic boss who had to cover it all up every week and justify expenses to the Home Office (Ben Miller, "Robot of Sherwood") got a big space-age complex for them. At the heart of it was Nick Cutter, the gloomy Scotsman with the Bond-villain ex. However much they made his revised team fun and heroic, Douglas Henshall played him as if he couldn't quite believe he'd been talked into star-ring in such an embarrassing series.

That's not the only similarity to Eccleston-era *Who*, as one of his sidekicks was a former teen pop star and stage-school brat: Hannah Spearitt from S-Club 7. Her character, Abby, had a pet flying liz-ard from the Jurassic which was one of the many digitally-realised creatures in the show. She would also remove clothing when the mood grabbed her. There was a will-they-won't-they thing with the Comedy Geek (Andrew-Lee Potts – not, as many people half-remember, Barney Harwood from *Totally Doctor Who*). So, Reboot 2a, Cutter realises that the wormholes were opening

continued on Page 177...

ABOUT TIME 2008-2009

vidgames. [Maybe this is a winking reference to Season Twenty-Three.]

The Analysis

The Big Picture A quick word on diamond planets. These were a staple of 70s SF novels, but more abundant in visual media, especially early computer games. *Jet Pac* in particular got a lot of mileage out of such worlds. However, the recent boom in exo-planet discoveries means that potential real examples have been in the news since this episode was made. 55 Cancri e (now called "Janssen") got a lot of people excited when it seemed to be just such a world, albeit eight times the mass of Earth, right up close to its star and with a "year" of 18 hours. Subsequent examination of the data reveals something less expected, and even less Earth-like, but it may well still be over 25% carbon under extraordinary pressure, as well as a great amount of oxygen and silicon. And it's tidally locked, so one side is always in daylight. One thing that any such planet would be is lifeless (as far as anything like us goes). The carbon and oxygen might look like suitable starting conditions, but they are in forms where they can't bond with anything else that might be around – diamonds are tight lattices of carbon, so are chemically inert under most circumstances.

Of course, we also have that old pulp standby of silicon-based life-forms (16.3, "The Stones of Blood"; 14.2, "The Hand of Fear"; and maybe 11.3, "Death to the Daleks"), but this time the story is strategically vague on the nature of the intelligence involved. What we can say is that the popular science journals of 2005-8 were given to reporting possible mechanisms by which such worlds could occur, ahead of data from the Kepler project. In short, it needs a star with either less oxygen or way more carbon than ours, so that the carbon in the planetesimals that coalesce to make worlds (X3.0, "The Runaway Bride") can't mix as much as it tends to otherwise. Our sun had more silicon than one of these, so this planet and the neighbours went down a different route and have a lot less carbon in the core inside than is needed. (Professor Hobbes is, of course, wrong about planets needing atmospheres to make silicates, but the star's halo of gases when forming needs to be like ours and was not like 55 Cancri e seems to have been.)

The dry theoretician, Hobbes (a name suggest-

ing a mechanistic world-view, see 11.1, "The Time Warrior" for his most famous quote inspiring a whole species) is suggestively like an earlier seen-it-all windbag, Captain Cook from 25.4, "The Greatest Show in the Galaxy". Like that story and others from the same period, this puts the previous generation's collective childhood through a distorting lens. It's all there: slide-shows by tedious middle-aged people in cardigans; seeing wonders through a window but not being allowed to stop and look or touch; the "typical" nuclear family (with a mum called "Val" who turns out to be a vengeful harpy under pressure); bored kids being told off for having imagination; bossy stewardesses and resorts with naff names. This is both a coach-trip (especially the school-arranged ones to dull, muddy patches of nowhere that once had a battle or settlement on it) and a package holiday (see 4.8, "The Faceless Ones").

If you recall Eric Idle's rant towards the end of the episode of *Python* that had "Summarise Proust", you've got a pretty good idea of how grim the latter could be. The stuff about the in-flight entertainment and peanuts is more akin to airline travel, but the experience of coach-journeys around excitingly foreign places is still familiar, especially to older viewers who signed up to such day-trips once road-travel to mainland Europe became easier. Indeed, a so-called Reality show, *Coach Trip*, refined this with the modish voting-off from umpteen other game-shows and docusoaps. The novelty was that it was couples rather than individuals who were discarded after each (relatively) glamorous or exotic city. They voted each other off with a soccer-style yellow-card/red-card system, over-ridden by the host if the rules were transgressed.

And, of course, coach-trips are an essential part of the alleged fun of a Holiday Camp. As you will recall from "The Macra Terror" (4.7) and "Delta and the Bannermen" (24.3), these were the not-quite-utopian pleasure resorts at coastal towns across Britain (and, as the 70s progressed, in Spain and Portugal), where low-cost enforced jollity and strictly-regimented relaxation were available in purpose-built futuristic townships. These were close to, but not *too* close to, famous seaside towns and historic monuments, so a coach trip to these places or local beauty-spots would form part of a week's entertainment. Although one version of this – the Mystery Tour – has been memorialised by the Beatles in *Magical Mystery Tour*, that

What Were the Daftest Knock-Off Series?

continued from Page 175...

throughout history, so all sorts of mythology was anachronistic crossovers. In comes a slinky archaeologist (Leila Rouass; see *SJA*: "Death of the Doctor" in Volume 10) and stories about knights in armour fighting "dragons" in Richmond High Street.

... and out goes Cutter (awkwardly, in mid-season, especially for viewers of the French version *Nick Cutter et les Portes du Temps*). Instead, we get a maverick cop (popular television admits of no other kind) with a motorbike and a cockernee accent; Jason Flemyng, fresh from screwing up the live remake of *The Quatermass Experiment*. Things perk up once the grumpy Scotsman is dumped, and for a run of six straight episodes, the series is as much fun as it always ought to have been – with playful jokes about its own premise (and those of other series) and genuinely good chases. The one saving grace of earlier episodes was Ben Miller, but now they all took turns at ridiculing earlier episodes.

Then it ends (sort of) on a literal cliffhanger: Cutter's mad ex has seen the polluted, evil future and has decided that the way to save the Earth is to prevent humanity, so she pops to Olduvai Gorge with a bottle of poison and is finally killed. But Abby and Comedy Geek Connor (yes, "Connor" and "Cutter" in the same show, confusing for casual viewers) are stranded hanging off an escarpment in the past...

At which point, the European co-producers bailed and a new team, briefly including BBC Worldwide, came in. This was supposed to have been the end and the two new stars had left, so they reboot *again* with a *new* sinister long-running conspiracy plot and – as is so often the case when a franchise sends out an SOS – a new regular fresh from a cancelled *Star Trek* spin-off. Alexander Siddig (formerly Julian Bashir) became a regular guest. Series 4 has seven episodes, Series 5 six, so it looks as if this was intended to be another 13-week run like before. However, this storyline ends abruptly with Burton, Siddig's character, realising that his conspiracy was part of mad Helen Cutter's mad plan of madness (even though she died at the end of Series 3), in a remarkably low-cost episode with killer ladybirds (written by Helen Raynor). And that was it. The plot involved creating the spacetime twinkly holes called "anomalies", (which made cataloguing them all seem a bit silly) by tricking the Comedy Geek into betraying his friends, then realising he was duped.

The team behind this had made documentaries about dinosaurs using computer effects and a lot of conjecture; the effects were mainly by The Mill, and as a result the team wrote in real dinosaurs and megatheria, offering an educational aspect to these romps. (What was never dwelt on was the sheer number of beings dragged from their rightful time and shot or electrocuted, and what effect their absence might have had on history.)

However, it was obvious early on that the effects were limited. One episode found a conveniently smooth and hairless mammoth in the textbooks, and used *that* because doing hair was too laborious. A series obviously intended as ITV's "answer" to *Doctor Who* just landed up as *Torchwood* for kids. A Victorian-set episode wherein Spring-Heeled Jack turned out to be a velociraptor simply shouldn't have been as dull as they made it. The problem with the final season is not so much that it just stopped, more that most viewers thought it was reruns of a series that had ended two years ago.

(NB: There was a Canadian spin-off, *Primeval: New World*. This fared even worse.)

The Bottom Line: It was done better in 1974 with the Brigadier and Sgt Benton taking on massively unconvincing rubber models.

Merlin (Shine/BBC Cymru Wales 2008 – 2012 Saturday teatimes)

A series about a nerdy English boy who trains to be a wizard. What *were* they thinking?

Well, partly, they were thinking that if Russell T Davies wasn't prepared to sanction a prequel to *Doctor Who* about a teenage Time Lord, they'd find someone prepared to do something similar from the public domain. The BBC had been thinking about it for a couple of years, auditioning a few treatments (including Chris Chibnall's one that mutated into his *Game of Thrones*-lite ITV flop *Camelot*).

The one they selected had four accredited "creators" (not counting Thomas Mallory, Geoffrey of Monmouth, Chretien de Troyes, Gododdin...), two of whom will be back with other can't-fail projects later in this piece. *Merlin* was set in a version of the Middle Ages where magic had been outlawed, but only the good guys were following this ban, leaving Camelot open to attack by any passing ne'er-

continued on Page 179...

was an event laid on for residents of a city, not part of a holiday already far from where the customers lived and worked. A trip from somewhere custom-made for relaxation or a specific (often grim) form of fun to a nearby "natural" or "authentic" was part of the package holiday. In the continental resorts, these would be things like Roman ruins or bullfights. Donna grumbled about this sort of thing in X4.1, "Partners in Crime".

This alerts us to an incidental story-detail: the Leisure Resort is the only inhabitable part of the planet (for humans and other orthodox life) and was literally dropped onto the surface. This is somewhat like the experience reported by people who went on the early package holidays to Spain and managed never to encounter anyone who wasn't English, or eat any foreign food, but it's also more like the new de luxe resorts in wildernesses such as the Sultanate of Dubai (see X4.15, "Planet of the Dead" and the "regeneration" of Beijing for the 2008 Olympics and other such prestige international events[35]).

However, the British reaction to short-haul flights has traditionally been bemusement; they exist in a strange hinterland between long-distance coach services ("long-distance" for a coach being five hours for a trip from, say, Swansea to London, a shade under 200 miles) and international jet flights. Most people wonder why anyone would bother with a plane to do a train's job (the main reason is a simpler fare-structure and fewer changes in mid-journey). As you may recall from "Nightmare of Eden", silly footling delays can escalate without passengers getting any information, even now but especially in the late 1970s. (Fit the Twelfth of *The Hitchhiker's Guide to the Galaxy* was based on a real example Douglas Adams encountered getting from London to Edinburgh, which also seems to have fed into "Nightmare of Eden".)

Coaches, on the other hand, have a curious mix of students, pensioners, *flaneurs*, people with low incomes, fugitives from small towns and people who just prefer coaches to trains or planes. You have more chance of getting an interesting conversation on one, although there is also the risk of outright nutters. Thus the irritations of long-haul air-travel (compulsory entertainment and peanuts, stewardesses who seem to be on autopilot themselves) and the oddities of National Express or Stagecoach (the main coach services in the UK) are combined here without either having much

logical connection to driving over a dangerous planet's surface.

For Davies, withdrawal into isolation seems to be among the cardinal sins: the Daleks are driven mad by their inability to touch rather than just being made that way (X2.13, "Doomsday"); residents of Satellite 5 are cocooned from the world and daren't ask questions (X1.7, "The Long Game"); learning about Earth from a few books and a reproduction liner in orbit is at best misleading (X4.0, "Voyage of the Damned") and so on. Conversely, small bands of formerly distant outsiders are powerful communities (e.g. LINDA in X2.10, "Love & Monsters", the entire world united by Martha's story in X3.13, "Last of the Time Lords", and assorted groups in his other projects, notably *Bob and Rose* and *The Second Coming*).

Here, and earlier in X3.3, "Gridlock", we get the downside of community bonding. Whilst the Doctor gets everyone talking to each other and this is initially a positive development, they form into a mob and hound a stranger to death. Groupthink can be a prison. (It's interesting to consider "Planet of the Dead" as a botched effort at rewriting "Midnight" with a happy ending.) The normal way such a story develops is with the Doctor talking people round, but here – just to twist the knife – his voice is taken from him and used as proof of his "wrongness". The Doctor's usual role is to persuade people to become who they might have been had things gone better for them. Both here and in X4.16, "The Waters of Mars", this is misguided and the Doctor's casual assumption that it will always work out for him (because it usually does) makes everything worse.

In interviews, Davies has claimed that "Darmok", an episode of *Star Trek: The Next Generation*, was his starting-point. Had he not said it, this would have been impossible to guess from the broadcast story. In the *Trek* yarn, first shown on BBC2 in late 1994, Picard and an alien converse using a vocabulary of stock phrases from the alien's mythology – but these are, grammatically, English-sounding and using verbs and nouns conventionally (so the result is like the Doctor's conversation with Lemuel Gulliver from 6.2, "The Mind Robber", where Gulliver was only able to say things he said in the book).

A more cogent comparison, if not an overt influence, is William Burroughs's often-cited comment: "language is a virus from outer space". He

What Were the Daftest Knock-Off Series?

continued from Page 177...

do-well with a book of incantations – about once a week, oddly enough. Good King Uther Pendragon (Anthony Head) was training his hunky blond son Arthur to take over, and frowned on his associations with the help, notably the serving-wench Guinevere (or Gwen, played by Angel Coulby) and nerdy Merlin (played by Colin Morgan from X4.10, "Midnight").

Merlin was being trained covertly by the in-house not-a-wizard-at-all-really Gaius (Richard Wilson, who anyone in Britain still thought of as Victor Meldrew, but you'll know from X1.9, "The Empty Child"). He was also getting coached by a dragon in a cave, played by a load of pixels and the voice of John Hurt. So apart from how Arthur's dalliance with a Person of Colour who works in the scullery started (and we'll ignore the derivation of the name "Guinevere" from the Welsh for "White Queen"), it all fits together and we have a formula. Wicked Queen of the Week comes along and puts a spell on Uther; Merlin asks both his mentors what to do, then does it, but tries not to take credit in case he's burned at the stake or forced into a crossover episode with *Robin Hood*.

Meanwhile, Uther's young ward Morgaine is everyone's BFF and, like, totally popular. The makers of the series claim to have had *Smallville* as their model, subverting the known, familiar version of the story to wrongfoot expectations (because that had worked out so well for the *Star Wars* prequels). Both Merlin and Morgaine are motivated by somehow knowing what they'll be like in the "proper" story later on rather than, you know, motivation. Later, like Lex in *Smallville*, she finds out she's the villain (and Uther's daughter). It is prophesied that her nemesis is a being called "Emrys", but we know that this is Merlin's (oh dear) Secret Identity.

Being put on BBC1 under the aegis of Julie Gardner's all-conquering BBC Wales Drama Department, it got the full promotional works, even a behind-the-scenes series; we got to see how the authentic Welsh castles were augmented by more picturesque ones in Kent and France, and how The Mill did all the dragon stuff. Fremantle, the Australian distribution company, sold it to well over a hundred countries, so from that point of view it was a success. How watched it was is another matter. Somehow, it never really caught light in America – nor really in Britain. It did adequately for the slot and the final episode, on Christmas Eve 2012, got favourable reception, but it's already almost forgotten. That might be just as well; this prequel to the Arthurian myth ends with Arthur dying.

The Bottom Line: Let us not go there – it is a silly place.

Demons (Shine/ITV1 2009 Saturday teatimes)

All right, so there's this London schoolkid who finds he's the Chosen One – no, please, keep reading – and destined to follow his late father into the secret brotherhood of Smiting. He finds this out from a bloke who drives an old American car, listens to Johnny Cash and talks roughly like a Southern preacher. When teaching the Chosen One how to smite demons, this bloke gets all Old Testament in his speech; *I smite thee, hell-fiend*, that sort of thing. Our Chosen One's girlfriend doesn't believe any of this, and is annoyed that he's spending so much time in a secret library of smitingness with Not-Giles-Really (who's even called "Rupert") and a blind concert pianist who is *the* Mina Harker from that Bram Stoker novel, somehow. Girlfriend is called Ruby, so when she gets into trouble they have an excuse to play that Kaiser Chiefs song. This as close to wit as the series gets.

The things that need smiting are Half-Lives, the eponymous demons, or at very least extras with rubber masks and hoodies. This is in fact one of the odd good things about the show: that what you saw was what you got. They simply hadn't got the budget for plentiful digital effects after the pilot (The Mill seem to have jumped ship early), so if you were seeing a creature attacking someone and a red bus driving past in the background, it's because they were shooting in a sidestreet in London early one morning and couldn't stop traffic or passers-by.

Like the earlier *Neverwhere*, this was a sort of purist approach to fantasy that could be dignified with comparison to Dogme 95, point the camera at what was there (especially odd corners of London) rather than resort to digital jiggery-pokery. Unlike *Neverwhere*, there wasn't a clever script, any internal logic, a mood of meta-reality or a sense that this was going somewhere. Instead, the occasional filler scenes of just a few chav goblins milling about a car-park were as significant (and interesting) as the rest. The assorted rubber-

continued on Page 181...

first used this in *The Ticket that Exploded* in 1962, but it caught on – partly via Laurie Anderson's song of that title – during the 1980s and was cited as prefiguring Richard Dawkins's idea of a "meme", or self-replicating habit. What little we see of the alleged alien in "Midnight" is directly comparable to how a meme transmits itself "virally". (That the meme concept and the phrase "language is a virus" have lives outside what their creators were thinking is proof of their validity.) The emphasis is kept off that, and remains on the effect it has on the other passengers. The self-righteous dad is called "Biff". Two episodes from now, Davros will be ranting in something called "The Crucible". The Doctor slips in to see Joe and Claude and gets a View From the Bridge. Do we really need to spell it out?

Maybe we do: Arthur Miller's spell as the King of Broadway results in a handful of plays still being taught in schools nearly seven decades on. *The Crucible* takes the mass-hysteria of the Salem Witch Trials of 1692 to depict how petty score-settling and a culture that believes it is right can result in people persecuting any non-conformist and believing things they would, as individuals, have dismissed. Peer-pressure makes ordinary people become a mob and demand the death of the misfit. Or, looked at the other way, one person is so arrogant that he (it's usually a "he") acts as if the rules don't apply to him.

Either way, being "right" is more a social phenomenon than a matter of fact or reason in such a situation. Once everything is seen through this filter, the smallest thing can be (mis)construed as further proof of guilt. Miller intended it as a comment not just on the McCarthy era's injustices and hysteria, but how groups of people under pressure in any society behave. A great many psychologists had tried to find some "factor" that had made reasonable people in Germany become monsters and had failed. (See earlier volumes for comments on Milgram and Zimbardo – especially "The Macra Terror" and 8.2, "The Mind of Evil" – or just look the psychologists up if you're just joining us.)

The "goblin men" lines that Dee Dee quotes are Christina Rossetti's poem "The Goblin Market". Published in 1862, the author intended it as a children's faerie tale, and was reportedly puzzled when critics objected to what they perceived as the adult treatment of sexual themes, including a troubled lesbian relationship. (So, not at all like

this story, then.) At a deeper level, the hint of possession and dabbling in other worlds, of being unable to return once beguiled, became a commonplace late-Victorian thread. (See Volumes 3 and 4 for more than you ever thought you'd need to know about Theosophy, the Hollow Earth theory, John Nevill Maskelyne and Bovril.) A sort-of version of the poem's story can be found in *Hellboy II: The Golden Army*. However, this poem is also a good analogy for the fears that we routinely get from the companion's mum about the Doctor. Once again, this story coming so close to "Journey's End" (X4.13) seems like a conversation the author's having with himself about the format of the series as it has become.

English Lessons

• *Kliks* (n.) A futuristic mis-spelling of "clicks", military-ese for kilometres. In a skiffy context, Heinlein used some remembered slang in *Starship Troopers*, so it crops up in a lot of 80s films with guns and spaceships. Anyone in the UK growing up with these films assumes that it's standard US terminology.

• *Second-Year Student* (n.) There seems to be some confusion on this: it simply means that Dee Dee is about halfway through her degree. Some commentary suggests that she's a postgrad (which would, in context, make sense of her accompanying the Professor as a factotum, rather than being part of a party travelling on a university-sponsored field-trip). The cast play it that way, but the script suggests something a touch more sordid.

• *Jethro* (n.) The names of the passengers denote things to a British viewer that aren't immediately obvious overseas. "Val" for example, suggests someone over 50 with slightly aspirational Working Class parents (although the definitive example, Valerie Singleton from *Blue Peter*, talked all posh and was far less frumpy than any Val you'd meet in real life).

Similarly, whilst the Biblical name "Jethro" might seem vaguely cool to the writers of *NCIS*, it is the quintessential yokel name, used by a rustic old relic in *The Archers* (father of Clarrie Grundy) and a colossally tedious stand-up comic. (Americans above a certain age will, most likely, remember Jethro Bodine, the well-intentioned idiot on *The Beverly Hillbillies*.) There is also the Prog Rock band "Jethro Tull", named after one of the inventors of the seed-drill, who can be roughly considered to be the nearest Britain got to a

What Were the Daftest Knock-Off Series?

continued from Page 179...

faced guest monsters included MacKenzie Crooke as a Teddy-Boy vampire hitman and Kevin (R) McNally (21.7, "The Twin Dilemma") as a vole-like critter who killed Rupert's wife. The make-up was risible, looking at best home-made, at worst like *The Mighty Boosh*.

Oh yes, the plot. Luke, the Chosen One (played by Christian Cooke, Ross from X4.4, "The Sontaran Stratagem", occasionally wearing a shirt) is being trained to make up for his father's betrayal. They stop short of giving him a lightsabre. Philip Glenister (see below) played the Obi-Wan in this, Rupert Galvin, with a dodgy American accent and breaks it not very gently that Luke is the great grandson of Abraham Van Helsing. Seriously. The Half-Lifes were about to broker a truce with Luke's dad when he died, and baby Luke was to have been given to them as a peace-offering. Mina's a vampire and can see when she drinks blood. Oh yes, only vampires can kill vampires, which makes the whole Smitery thing a bit silly, if they have to rely on the blind girl to smite the single most significant form of Half-Life.

Here's the strange part. This show can't have cost a lot, despite the guest-cast (all familiar faces in the UK but not worldwide – America doesn't get *Father Ted* or *One Foot in the Grave*[37]. Had Richard Wilson invested in Ostrich Farms or something?[38]). It looked cheap-and-cheerful, if not actually showing signs of enthusiasm among the cast. Most of its memorable moments were theatrical (at least, the ones that worked). Yet this, like the more obviously costly *Primeval*, got dumped by ITV1 as part of a mass cull of drama when advertising revenue plummeted after the 2008 crash and online marketing caught on.

There was a bid by Shine, the production company (which had friends in high places – founder Liz Murdoch is one of *those* Murdochs, although she tried to distance herself from NewsCorp) to get US distribution and backing via Sony, but it came just as the Sci-Fi Channel rebranded as Syfy and took to showing wrestling. BBC America buried it in their schedules. By this time the comments about Glenister's accent had hit home; he'd announced that even if it got a second series, he'd not be in it. As he was the main thing the few viewers it got said they'd liked, that was it. The show got smit.

The Bottom Line: It might have been easier to identify the people who liked it and perform it in their living-rooms.

Atlantis (Urban Myths Films/BBC Cymru Wales/BBC America 2013-14 – Saturday tea-times)

It's got Johnny Capps and Julian Murphy listed as creators, along with Howard Overman (who devised *Misfits*, the teen-superheroes-with-ASBOs series from Channel 4). Capps and Murphy gave us *Demons* and *Merlin*. The title was first announced as *Atlantis: the Legend Begins*, which gives you the idea of this being the sort of prequel-to-a-legend thing they did with Camelot.

In fact, it's *suspiciously* like *Merlin*. There's a plucky servant-girl whose name telegraphs her importance; this time it's Medusa, who becomes who we think she ought to be after opening Pandora's Box (because having Pandora in the story along with Jason and Pythagoras would have been silly). There's a grumpy old king with a stroppy kid (King Minos, played by a big hat with Alexander Siddig under it somewhere, and Ariadne). There's a mysterious mentor (no CGI dragon this time, just Juliet Stephenson trying to keep a straight face) who keeps telling Our Hero he has a Destiny, but it's a Surprise.

But it's not just a revamp of their former hit; they added a lot of their big flop too. Jason is from our time and got in a midget sub to find what happened to his father, only to wash up inside a well-known story and find he can speak classical Greek and doesn't need shirts. His guide to this new world is a slightly unreliable fat older bloke, Hercules, who takes credit for every battle Jason wins. Hercules is Mark Addy from *The Full Monty*, who stood in for John Goodman in the pointless *The Flintstones in Viva Rock Vegas* (he's in X11.10, "The Battle of Ranskoor Av Kolos"). That last film is a guide on how you should approach the version of antiquity herein. Hercules's job is to tell you when a scene is supposed to be funny. Jason wins fights by cheating: he has a super-power from somewhere that enables him to leap 30 yards, and can learn any weapon within seconds of first seeing it. That's because his dad is really...

Well, it got a second series, so we'll not mess it up for anyone who wants to watch it. It was about as surprising as when Mina in *Demons* turned out to be a vampire. However, a second series was all it

continued on Page 183...

home-grown Grateful Dead, but are more silage than psilocybin.

• *Previous* (n.) In British cop-shows, someone being described as having "a bit of previous" means that person has already been indicted. Whether any actual cop ever used the term before *The Sweeney* is unclear: "previous form" was more usual, we gather. It's come to denote someone having a track-record for whatever is being discussed.

Oh, Isn't That...?

• *Lesley Sharp* (Sky Silvestry). The other Rose in the Davies canon: co-starring with Alan Davies (no relation) in *Bob & Rose*. RTD had worked with her before that; she was co-star to Eccleston on *The Second Coming*. Latterly she co-starred with Suranne Jones (X6.4, "The Doctor's Wife") in *Scott and Bailey* – not, alas, a primer on fusion-reactor design (13.5, "The Brain of Morbius") but another cop show. In 1979, she did backing vocals on *7-Teen* by The Regents, and so was on *Top of the Pops* in a polka-dot mini around the time 17.6, "Shada" ought to have been on. You might also have seen her in *The Full Monty*, of course.

• *David Troughton* (Professor Hobbes). He's been in *Doctor Who* three times before, most famously as Jo's love-interest in 9.2, "The Curse of Peladon", plus a number of Big Finish audios. More significantly, he was Bob Buzzard in *A Very Peculiar Practice* (see also 17.5, "The Horns of Nimon" and most of Volume 5). He has recently stepped in as the new voice of Tony Archer, the ethical, organic farmer in Radio 4's *The Archers*. (That's sort of like getting a knighthood.) We're required to note that he's not related to this story's director; on the other hand, his dad was the Doctor.

• *Colin Morgan* (Jethro Cane). He'd had the odd acting role before, notably a part in Tate's 2007 Christmas special. Three months after this, he starred in the BBC's *Merlin*. (See this story's essay.)

• *Tony Bluto* (Driver Joe). An archetypal "Oh, Isn't That..." actor, usually playing fat blokes in cop shows or barmen in sitcoms. He's the dodgy accountant in the first episode of *Black Books*, if that helps, and he was in *Truly, Madly, Deeply*. (He co-wrote and co-starred in a low-budget film called *Redemption Road* that barely anyone saw, which exists to prove that he and Mark Benton are different people.)

• *Rakie Ayola* (Hostess). An ex-*Holby City* regular (Kyla Tyson). She was making *Holby* while recording of this story, so needed a scripted reason not to be around for an episode or so.

Things That Don't Make Sense Perhaps as a result of being written in a weekend without time for eleventy-dozen drafts, there's not a lot wrong with this script. We know so little about the entity that afflicts Sky, we can't say if anything's inconsistent. The main problem, from a plot-logic point of view, is that we've got no idea if killing Sky has any effect on it at all. It's apparently managed to live on a barren world drenched in toxic rays for an indeterminate number of years, so flinging it out of an airlock into, er, a barren world drenched with toxic rays might not be a solution.

In fact, had we never seen the Doctor before, there's no reason to suppose that there even is an entity rather than just a peculiar mass-hysteria or a distraught woman abruptly developing a telepathic ability she can't control. The evaporation of the cabin and Sky's pre-emptive mimicry are presented as causally linked through the agency of some alien on the planet's surface, as opposed to the crash-trauma finally tipping her over and unleashing her ability to guess what people are about to say. It's just that *the Doctor* says there's a psychic alien occupying Sky just before she/it starts making his life difficult, so we assume – this being *Doctor Who* – that this is indeed the case.

All right, let's say that there is. Why is the entity griping about the cold? If it's native, why complain about conditions there? It's like humans bitching about all the oxygen around Earth. On the other hand, if it's stranded there but comes from some other world, why antagonise the guy with the time-machine and detailed knowledge of aliens? If it exists as pure psychic force (whatever that means) or electromagnetic impulses, heat and cold ought not to matter or even be perceptible. If, on the other hand, it's really *Sky* saying that it was so cold and this isn't just a ruse, maybe there's something that finds living inside a human colder than living on the surface with all that radiation. So what's it doing on board this bus? (This being a genuinely alien being, its motives are barely worth trying to divine. Perhaps it was just bored and decided to set the humans against each other for a giggle.)

So we're left with a couple of basic practical issues. Donna's phone seems not to be plugged in, despite being a very good facsimile of a 90s handset that she's holding upside down. It's not espe-

What Were the Daftest Knock-Off Series?

continued from Page 181...

got, so whatever clever five-year story-arc they were working on will never come to pass... meaning that most of the first episode will remain incomprehensible, as this was all set-up for the big plotty *something* Juliet-the-not-Dragon refused to divulge.

A lot of the location work was shot in Morocco. It looks stunning the first time. After 13 weeks, it was obvious that they had spent a few days grabbing a lot of establishing shots and a few of the three flatsharing lads (Jason, Hercules and Pythagoras... er, they *do* know Pythagoras was a real person, don't they?) walking across a big concourse outside the palace, and shot the rest in Wales. Not just anywhere in Wales, they adapted a meat-packing factory in Chepstow specifically for this series.

Fifteen years earlier, Sam Raimi had realised that with the new computer effects, the sort of wire-work used in Hong Kong martial-arts films and a load of actors from *Neighbours* and *Shortland Street*, he could go to New Zealand and make a fun series mixing up Greek myths, pop-culture and sitcom. It was now possible to make the sort of series he would have enjoyed as a kid. The key difference between *Hercules: The Legendary Journey* and *Atlantis* is that *Hercules* has already happened. Capps and Murphy have cannily identified the sort of thing commissioning editors want to put on television and provided it, knowing that it will sell because it already has several times. Raimi worked mainly on instinct, opting to give minor character Xena her own series and improvising around production nightmares. Capps and Murphy left nothing to chance and allowed nothing fresh in.

The Bottom Line: Where's Professor Zaroff when you need him?

# # # # #

So that was Saturday teatime carved up as far as family-friendly fantasy-drama went. However, the success of *Doctor Who* got a lot of other projects off the ground, some after gathering dust for decades. There was an announcement almost immediately that ITV wanted to reboot *The Prisoner*. The usual un-named "sources" claimed that Christopher Eccleston was going to be Number Six. Eventually, a brief remake appeared

late on ITV's Saturday night schedule with Jim Caviezal in the lead, Sir Ian McKellen as Number Two week after week and various British actors putting on American accents to be likeable (because Fox paid for some of it). Sir Ian was, of course, English to the core as the villain. It had a *Lost* vibe to it and was filmed in Namibia.

Eventually, the series ended with the shock revelation that it was all a timey wimey trap and Number Two was Number Six after forty years in charge (and some elocution lessons). Nobody saw this coming – or saw it at all, if the ratings are to be believed. ITV1 moved it later and later in the Saturday night schedules as if trying to bury it. Meanwhile, the attempts to get *Blakes 7* back onto our screens have come and gone as often as new Doctors.

However, for really out-there series that wouldn't have made it to the screen had not *Doctor Who* been a hit, we have to look at BBC Wales's other shows. There are a few gambles that paid off – such as *Being Human* and *Sherlock* – but one team, using a lot of the same backstage talent as the episodes in this volume, made one series (well, one and a half) that was a huge hit, despite a ludicrous premise, and another on the back of *that* which went down with all hands. If you're following the behind-the-scenes details about the last three years of the Russell T Davies era, you really need to look at what else Julie Gardner was up to at the same time...

***Life on Mars/Ashes to Ashes* (Kudos/BBC Cymru Wales 2006-7, 2008-2010 Tuesday nights) and *Life on Mars* USA (NBC 2008)**
Before the return of *Doctor Who*, the characteristic shows on Saturday nights in the early years of the century were nostalgia-porn lists and kitsch; BBC2 did a set of reminiscence-oid shows *I* (heart logo) *1970* and so on to 1999. These were shown in 2000, so the last episode had people being inaccurately nostalgic about what had happened six months ago. Channel 4 did *Top Ten* lists of chart hits from specific years, then moved on to categories of TV (children's characters, animation, sitcoms...) which always ended up with *The Simpsons* winning. So while seeing someone born in 1972 on *I* (heart logo) *1970* waxing lyrical about Raleigh Choppers and Stuart Maconie beginning every rant with "What were that about?" got a bit samey and irritating to anyone who remembered what

continued on Page 185...

ABOUT TIME 2008-2009

cially smart to build a self-sealing passenger area without a self-sealing cabin as well (perhaps the Leisure Palace was cutting corners). We're left with the odd notion that a micro-petrol engine would work in hard vacuum (unless the micro-carburetta has its own supply of micro-air). Cast-iron in an airless waste with hard radiation seems a bit daft – it would be rather brittle and prone to cracks after a bit of buffeting, even with super-futuristic shock-absorbers. Wouldn't all that radiation make a rather better power-source?

One especially odd feature: we're told unequivocally that there is no air outside, and in the very next breath that there's a fire-exit at the rear, should anyone need to use it.

If they've got emergency space-suits (and the production design has a cupboard for these, rather stupidly located at the opposite side of the cabin), isn't this the obvious solution for isolating whatever's inside Sky or the Doctor? Conversely, we'll take it on faith that there's good reason why the bus to the Waterfall takes four hours, but the rescue party can make it to a hitherto uncharted region in under an hour (maybe they've got Thunderbird 1).

With so little information given, we shan't bother to ask why a planet saturated in dangerously bright sunlight is called "Midnight", although some people did. (For all we know, the same system may have a body called "Teatime".) This sunlight turns Joe and Claude to dust, but the passengers get exposed to it for two seconds when the Hostess opens the cabin door to check on the drivers, then a count of six when she hurls herself and Sky out of the airlock.

We'll accept with gritted teeth that Rose's cameo appearances so far this season have been plausible in terms of tracking down the Doctor, as they've been on Earth and a timeframe one might expect to find him. This story is set well in the future. How'd she track down these coordinates? It *almost* makes more sense if this was her first go at catching the Doctor, then another message in the Sontaran story, then popping over for "Partners in Crime" – at which point she realises something is deeply off with Donna and proceeds to "Turn Left". Almost, but not quite as the methodology described by Rose on Pete's World to physically send her to other dimensions in the same relative time (give or take those three added years mentioned in "Doomsday"). A message on some kind of interdimensional Skype might be picked up by the TARDIS comms, because the Ship's good at that sort of thing (although she occasionally delivers them at the wrong time to ensure annoying paradoxes), but not on the in-flight entertainment of a bus.

And regarding an upcoming plot point in X4.12, "The Stolen Earth"... we know that the Doctor puts back the Lost Moon of Poosh sometime after this episode is set. Perhaps Dee Dee finds it after all. But if these worlds all were pilfered to converge in a cube in the Earth year 2009 and the happy campers are from a world that has "Do It, Do It Again" in its past then, logically, she just has to look in the archives to find a mention of the other planets. If they were all put back in their correct times, then the Pyroviles and Adipose had no reason to come to Earth – so, for those stories to have happened, every stolen planet presumably dropped back in late 2009. Ergo, two Moons of Poosh must have been in the same orbit after that story until the fortieth century (or whenever), and the disappearance of one can't have been as mysterious as the arrival of its twin.

The episode is slightly rigged, with the Doctor uncharacteristically forgetting his usual methodology so that he gets into trouble with the bigots – all he needed to say when Sky started pre-empting his words is "See? It's identified me as the threat. I'm your best bet if you want to live."

The other remaining problem is that, in using the term "X-tonic" for the eldritch radiation on this world, Davies has unwittingly nicked the name of a well-established Chinese lighting manufacturer.

Critique This is very close to being the perfect *Doctor Who* story.

In fact, it's remarkably similar to the very first one: a disparate group of travellers are in a freakish situation and turn on each other, before deciding that the anonymous Doctor who seems to know so much is a bigger threat than the more obvious menace (1.1, "An Unearthly Child", if you were unclear). It's also similar to the third one, where a force inside their vehicle appears to be making people act out of character (this is in fact how the *Radio Times* pitched 1.3, "The Edge of Destruction", although even newcomers these days probably know what's really happening). We're right back to first principles here and the Doctor, who as usual embodies all we would like to think humanity is capable of being, is set

What Were the Daftest Knock-Off Series?

continued from Page 183...

these years were actually like, it established a set of handy shorthand icons for anyone wanting to caricature the period.

Meanwhile, writers on cop dramas were wishing they could take short-cuts like the writers of *The Sweeney* and *The Professionals* had been able to, and just have extremely violent boorish officers getting results without triggering an internal investigation once a week. The logical solution was to do a pastiche cop show set in the *I* (heart logo) 19-- version of the early 70s. As a result, *Life on Mars* (working title *Ford Cortina*) had a policeman from today hit by a car and waking up in a hallucinatory version of Manchester in 1973. Everything was brown, Wagon Wheels (a chocolate marshmallow biscuit launched in 1972) were bigger, everyone smoked and women were treated as objects.

DCI Sam Tyler (John Simm, between becoming famous and becoming the Master – X3.11, "Utopia" for those of you with short memories) was trying to figure out what was really going on whilst solving crimes and keeping his opposite number, Gene Hunt, from breaking all the rules Jack Regan got away with ignoring in *The Sweeney*. Sam got to make sardonic comments on our behalf: undercover in a wife-swapping ring, he and his maybe-love-interest Annie use the names "Tony and Cherie Blair", for example.

The interruptions to the superficial reality of this setting were increasingly trippy. The girl from Test Card F[39] would talk to Sam, although the memorably bonkers pre-credit sequence involving a spoof of *Camberwick Green*, a Hawkwind album-track, radio newsreaders talking about Sam's medication and a lollipop lady (school crossing warden) with something surprising written on her pole is probably the high spot of all five years. The strain of Sam being in every single scene got too much for Simm to commit to a third series.

The psychologist handling Sam's case was therefore flung into a 1981 London with the characters from Sam's supposed dream, and spent her first year convinced it wasn't real. The first series of *Ashes to Ashes* annoyed people who'd thought the depiction of 1973 was realistic by being just as much a travesty but of a period they actually remembered. More than this, it was set in the period when the police force was undergoing the investigations and reforms that made the 1973-style policing illegal. The debate on whether this hampered the effectiveness of the force was underscored by the representative of by-the-book twenty-first-century methods breaking every rule, because she thought it was just a bad dream and that she could save her parents from being killed.

The next two series messed with everyone's heads by breaking every generic rule: another twenty-first-century character killed his younger self and left our protagonist, Alex (Keeley Hawes; X8.5, "Time Heist"), to hide the body. A sniper kills a character clearly intended to be Ben Elton. Meanwhile, was Alex falling for Gene Hunt? No, but he was mesmerically wrong-headed, or so all the other characters kept telling us. The first episode played up to the fact that *Life on Mars* had made Hunt a folk-hero and went so far over-the-top as to need to be reined in later. In using records from the time, not all hits, they made a point of playing up that both Sam and Alex were stuck in someone else's nostalgia. But whose?

Unlike *Life on Mars*, we had whole scenes with Alex not around. It got the internet abuzz, as planned, but mostly about how it wasn't as good. The majority of critics remembered the Falklands/New Romantics period better and complained about the mistakes more, until they started wondering how many were deliberate. It didn't fit their preconceptions as closely as the drab, murky travesty of Glam-era Britain. (When London's then-Mayor, Boris Johnson, reminisced about life in 70s Britain, the things he claimed to recall were Sam Tyler's memories.)

The third series of *Ashes* – planned as the third series of *Life on Mars* and adapted slightly – gave an answer and investigated the minor characters; it began with an apparently recovered Alex in HMV in Oxford Street seeing Hunt on TV screens begging for her help in clearing his name. The investigator (Jim Keats, played by Daniel Hills from X6.9, "Night Terrors") is probably working for Satan (identified only as "Dave") and, by the end, Hunt is shown to have died in 1953, aged 20, and been pressed into service as a makeshift St Peter in a special Purgatory for police officers killed in the line of duty. Of course. This went out the same week that *Lost* ended the same way (*Last of the Summer Wine* also ended that month, but not quite in the same manner). This solution accounts for 95% of the weirdnesses that had people poring over every detail trying to figure it out.

continued on Page 187...

against mob hysteria and all we know humans can do if pushed onto the defensive.

Although David Tennant and Leslie Sharp cope admirably with some ridiculously difficult dialogue, in synch, this is an ensemble piece so it's invidious to pick any performance out from the rest. Everyone is listening to each other rather than waiting for a cue. The responses are in real time, not weeks or months later as can happen with current TV drama. This is as close as we'll get to how television drama was made in the 1950s and up to the 1990s. It's not quite like theatre, not quite like film and gives an intensity of performance equal to live drama but with cuts and retakes. It's especially impressive that the younger cast-members, who may not have done anything like this before, respond so well to this process. The retro production also entailed rehearsals and a script written in almost one draft. It would be silly to claim that this means that all modern *Doctor Who* ought to be made the way they did it at Lime Grove, but the pitch of concentration this allows and requires is exhilarating.

Compare this to the oddly similar "Voyage of the Damned" (X4.0), and the way the script works out all the consequences of the premise and how people would react – rather than worrying about what would look cool – is refreshingly direct. It's a clean, uncluttered script. It's entirely about dramatic potential between the characters. There are effects shots and they are, as usual, immaculate – but these have gone back to being narrative devices or scene-setting. They aren't what a story needs to be something only *Doctor Who* can do. *Primeval* could do CGI effects. *Buffy* could mix monsters, pop-culture gags and teen-angst. Stripping it back to the fundamentals – an alien environment that's spawned life unlike anything we know, ordinary people stuck in the middle of this and the Doctor fighting back with words and observation – was a reminder that all the gimmickry and post-production jiggery-pokery is a crutch.

Even Murray Gold, who'd been almost literally phoning it in since he moved to America earlier that year, throws in a few surprises. The scene where the passengers are "forced" to talk has a slightly counter-intuitive folksy acoustic guitar figure under the whole Shamboni anecdote, encouraging us to think the various people are bonding (but look at Sky hiding inside her novel and sulky Jethro joining in with the punchline).

The loungecore soundtrack of the opening scene hints at the same penned-in feeling as the grim entertainments on the bus, a sense of stifling enclosure. Swaddled against the harsh and unknowable nature of the planet, all that comfort is still a barricade and this is, underneath everything else, a basic base-under-siege story. More than that, the individuals are each under attack of some sort – and when the mechanical and environmental barricades fail, they are all on the defensive. The professor's name, "Hobbes", was aptly chosen. Every detail of the story and production pushes the idea that humans try to isolate themselves at times when they ought to be reaching out to each other.

There's a price to pay for this intensity, but it's a good problem to have. As with "An Unearthly Child" or 7.4, "Inferno" (and a few others but not many) this is a story to admire but not watch too often. Whereas one can settle back with a snack and put on – for example – "The Robots of Death" (14.5) or "The Idiot's Lantern" (X2.7) and maybe spot a detail that passed un-noticed or just have it on for company or nostalgia, "Midnight" requires complete attention and isn't something you can interrupt or let run while you check emails. It's too wordy, too strong, too – that word again – intense. This may be why it's less often cited as a highlight of this phase of the series. It's rarely on anyone's list of desert-island episodes, even if nobody seems to have a bad word for it. Certainly the less demanding, more ingratiating "Blink" (X3.10) has more champions, despite its many shortcomings.

Perfection, or anything that approaches it, is intimidating. But perhaps "perfect" isn't quite the right word when we're dealing with such a diverse and polymorphous series; perhaps the metaphor we need is "purity". Most of *Doctor Who* is an alloy, made resilient by its mixture. Or, even better, it's like a Cadbury's or Hershey's chocolate compared to the astringent 80% cocoa solid bars. It may not be what the aficionados consider the finest, but it's a lot easier to just eat and offer to children.

It's not as though "Midnight" were short on wit, charm, sense-of-wonder or familiar problems solved in a Doctorish way we all wish we could do, but the easy way this episode starts out has consequences from which the Doctor can't extricate himself. Part of what makes this episode special is that, for once, he can't sweet-talk his

What Were the Daftest Knock-Off Series?

continued from Page 185...

Another solution had been found when they adapted *Life on Mars* for the US. The writers thought that the set-up was insufficiently "mythic" and "sweeping". The pilot was considered a disaster, so we never really saw how Colm Meaney would have measured up to Philip Glenister as Gene Hunt; Harvey Keitel's reading of Hunt was odd. They gave him a daughter as Sam's love-interest. The main problem for most episodes was that, compared to Britain's move towards more scrupulous methodology, American police officers have become more unruly and bloodthirsty since the 70s. The writers couldn't deal with the ambiguity of the original, and gave the series the stupidest ending since Superman flew really fast around the world to make time go backwards...

See, they weren't in 1973 or 2008, but in the 2030s on a spaceship going to Mars and Sam was really Major Tom Tyler. Everyone was plugged into a game while in hibernation. Tom/Sam was on a hunt for his genes, see? Original series co-creator Matthew Graham (X2.11, "Fear Her"; X6.5-6.6, "The Rebel Flesh"/"The Almost People" – with Marshall Andrews from both *Life on Mars* and *Ashes to Ashes* as Buzzer) tried to be diplomatic on this.

More recently, *Dark Side of the Moon* was greenlit. This is the same premise, but a Moscow cop flung into 1979, under Brezhnev and with the KGB reducing what actual police work there was. However, as with America, the police now are more violent and slipshod than in the 70s, so the effect is more like sending Gene Hunt to 1951 Britain.

The Bottom Line: What were that about?

***Bonekickers* (Kudos/BBC Cymru Wales 2008 Wednesday evenings)**

Someone had to try it. Archaeology on British television comes in two flavours; earthy blokes and stolid bluestockings getting muddy in fields or big CGI reconstructions of lost cities. The most popular of the former was Channel 4's enduring *Time Team*, in which a crew get three whole days to dig up a farm or someone's garden and confirm or disprove a local story – viewers have learned as much about geophysics as about the Roman taste for fermented fish sauce. However, even this breakneck pace isn't enough for people whose idea of the science is more derived from *Tomb Raider* than from Sir Mortimer Wheeler. So the

good people who brought us *Life on Mars* devised a series about a team of experts from the fictional University of Wessex (see 10.1, "The Three Doctors" for another alumnus) who were as relentlessly "colourful" as the *Time Team* regulars. They seemed to spend all day every day being shot at or swinging from ropes over burning subterranean crucifixes. It looked like a parody of a non-existent better series based on the same premise, the kind of parody that's meaningless if you haven't seen the original. The BBC have sought to disown it (the DVD was released by ITV, their arch-rivals, possibly as a jeering reminder that not all of their dramas were much cop).

The team is led by Dr Gillian Magwilde, who is Julie Graham doing what Julie Graham does (pouting, being Scottish, frowning occasionally). Her mother had a breakdown looking for Excalibur, so she decided to fix this by, er, looking for Excalibur. That's the Big Story Arc. Her ex, Dr Ben Ergha, is still on the team and is Adrian Lester from *Hustle*. He's on autopilot for most of each episode. Comic relief and info-dumping come from Hugh Bonneville (just before *Downton Abbey* and long before X6.3, "The Curse of the Black Spot") as Dr Gregory Parton, who is K9 and Gene Hunt put into a blender and poured into a Barbour jacket and silly hat. As these characters have all known each other for ages we need a newbie, Vivian Davis. And as we've said "Excalibur" and "Vivian" in the same paragraph, you're wondering if she's going to be Magwilde's long-lost half-sister. Of *course* she is.

Viv is played by Gugu Mbatha-Raw (X3.1, "Smith and Jones" et seq.). She did get work again afterwards, though.

There's also a pompous Head of Department played by Michael Maloney, who is sort of Ben Miller in *Primeval* without the one-funny-line-per-week allocation. Every week, our dysfunctional team are in a race against time to stop other interested parties (usually religious cultists or political groups) from destroying crucial evidence that will prove them wrong. It starts with what looks like an authentic news item and ends with a gunfight or somesuch and there's usually a clue to Magwilde's quest along the way. "Dolly" Parton gets to be arrestably sexist and tell everyone the plot, and Ben has a moment to be all sympathetic about his ex's obsession and fear. Viv wears a woolly hat.

The set-up is a composite of all the things they *thought* were popular about *Life on Mars* and

continued on Page 189...

way out of a problem and his attempts to do so make matters worse. Even his sly but high-handed decision to shut off the 70s Euro-pop illustrates the way he's become used to being given command of a situation rather than earning it. In this story, even the throwaway gags have sharp edges. Because this was a story conceived to place the Doctor in an intractable situation and tell a story without recourse to set-piece explosions or crowd-scenes, monsters or effects, it keeps people watching – even relatively small children can find fun and surprises. There's less of an imperative to be "ooh scary" at every single turn, but to be unexpected. That makes the scares much more effective than when we are constantly being told "be scared" (e.g. X6.2, "Day of the Moon").

That's the paradox at work in BBC Wales *Doctor Who*. A lot of the writers have been middle-aged fans who think that if they reference earlier writers (let's be honest, nine times out of ten this means ripping off Robert Holmes), they are working in that tradition. They cling to their borrowed vocabulary and recreated favourite scenes like Linus blankets. There's a fannish mentality, especially prominent in the tie-in comics, novels and audios – a mistaken belief that the more allusions to old jokes or set-pieces you shove into a script, the more like *Doctor Who* it is. In fact, the fewer resources and less time writers have to get cute, the more they find themselves thinking like those earlier writers. They are forced to solve the same problems rather than merely doing cut-and-paste on favourite scripts.

Doctor Who is a grammar, not a vocabulary. "Midnight" has probably the fewest allusions to earlier stories of any Davies script, with only companion-names (and Rose's absence) being referred to, and the least fannish dialogue with regard to continuity comments. Yet this is the script most like something one of those old writers would have come up with. When forced to make a story with the companion absent and next to no money for effects, costumes, sets or non-speaking characters, in a weekend, Davies finally emerged from their shadows.

The Lore

Written by Russell T Davies. Directed by Alice Troughton. Viewing Figures: (BBC1) 8.1 million, (BBC3 repeats) 1.1 and 0.4 million. AIs 86 first go, 90 for the following Friday.

Repeats and Overseas Promotion *Die Stimmen, Un Passager de Trop*

Alternate Versions Salford University's Performing Arts students asked permission to stage a version of the script, and worked out a version largely intelligible even to non-viewers (they removed Donna and the tearful shots of Rose and used "Love Shack" rather than Italian pop, but the majority of the dialogue and story beats remained the same). This version of the story has since been played on pub circuits.

Production

• Although "executive producer" is more a pay-scale than a job-description, the US term "show-runner" (which was increasingly used to describe Davies's job) implies certain responsibilities, including taking a hit for the team. As with "Boom Town" (X1.11), "Love & Monsters" (X2.10) and "Turn Left" (X4.11), the initial objectives of this episode were administrative. It had to be a double-banked episode (in this case without Donna), quick to make and with minimal effects, location shooting or non-speaking parts. Davies says that he was interested in an alien thought-process revealed purely lexically and in undermining the Doctor's arrogance (something falteringly attempted in the Big Finish audio "Ish...").

• For a long time, the delayed "Century House" project looked likely to be the one filling this slot; as we understand it, the idea was a notoriously haunted house would be the subject of a live television investigation. (See our comments on *Most Haunted* in X2.12, "Army of Ghosts", on *GhostWatch* in X2.11, "Fear Her" and Reality TV with X1.12, "Bad Wolf", plus earlier discussion of the "Century House" proposal under X3.10, "Blink", the story that replaced it last time around.)

The arrival of Steven Moffat's haunted library scripts finally put the kybosh on this script, and Davies had been having trouble making Tom McCrae's story (from ideas suggested by Davies) function. As a glance at *The Writer's Tale* confirms, this gap came at a tricky time all round, with the press hounding Peter Fincham from his job as the head of BBC1 over a confected royal "scandal", Howard Attfield's condition deteriorating (see X4.1, "Partners in Crime"), the Rome shoot (X4.2, "The Fires of Pompeii") being leaked and causing a split of Block Three and Helen Raynor's Sontaran

What Were the Daftest Knock-Off Series?

continued from Page 187...

Torchwood, plus some snippets of actual archaeology in amongst the goofiness and scattershot plotting. It looked good enough on paper to get a classy cast, who had more fun filming it than anyone had watching the result. The first episode starts where *The Da Vinci Code* left off and goes weird from there on – Templars, Saracens in Somerset (see *Robin Hood*), beheadings, random Islamophobia and so on. 6.9 million people watched the first episode; by the penultimate part, it had lost three million of these. Most episodes were written by Matthew Graham, with Ashley Pharoah (co-creator of this and *Life on Mars/Ashes to Ashes*) writing one and the remaining episode by Tom McRae (X2.5-2.6, "Rise of the Cybermen"/"The Age of Steel"; X6.10, "The Girl Who Waited" and so on). Many episodes were directed by James Strong (see this volume and the last two) and one by Nick Hurran (see Series 6).

That's the real problem: it wasn't quite rotten enough to be a guilty pleasure, but it was too cheap, stupid, unpleasant and haphazardly-plotted to watch any other way.

The Bottom Line: When Julie Graham and Gugu Mbatha-Raw being sisters is the most sensible part, you've got problems.

---

script requiring CPR. And the delicate task of asking Moffat if he was able to take over *Doctor Who*.

• The idea of "space bus" was one Davies pieced together during this fraught period – but only when he chanced upon a film with a similar set-up while channel-zapping (*Jeepers Creepers II*) did the story gel as a contrast to how Hollywood did it. With a weekend to go before the first preparatory meetings for what was then episode eight, Davies hurtled through a first draft that was – barring a few pink pages after the read-through – practically the only one.

• As revealed in the Bumper Book of Emails, Benjamin Cook reminded Davies that this episode would be the fiftieth of the BBC Wales productions, so the space-bus was identified in the script as "Crusader 50". (As it turned out, the broadcast order was altered; this episode was number eight on the list but moved to tenth place; this didn't affect the production schedule, but meant that the in-joke stayed more in than planned.) The part of Sky was written partially with Lesley Sharp in mind; since *Doctor Who* had returned, Sharp had been in touch with Davies about possibly appearing and he had told her that he was waiting for a good enough character for her.

• The main set was the interior of the Crusader 50, made partially from a discarded light aircraft. Into this, the crew mounted practical props such as the flatscreen televisions and adjustable chairs. The look was supposed to evoke 1950s Pan Am or TWA jetliners, such as the Douglas DC4 as seen in *Zero Hour!* et al.[36] In the script, the exterior is explicitly compared to a SHADO patrol vehicle from Gerry Anderson's *UFO*.

• The timetable for recording was a bit complicated. Although this story and "Turn Left" were double-banked, this was part of the same block as "The Doctor's Daughter" (X4.6), but the shooting also dovetailed with the end of work on the Sontaran two-parter (while Freema Agyeman was available) and the remounts of "Partners in Crime" (X4.1). All three episodes had a rare read-through in London on the Friday before the start of Blocks Six and Seven (the propitious 23rd November).

• Sam Kelly, of *'Allo 'Allo* fame, had been cast as Professor Hobbes but broke his leg – so, over the weekend, David Troughton was asked to travel to Cardiff and fill in (he had just been doing a *Big Finish* audio that week). As location work began on "Turn Left" on Monday, the cast of "Midnight" spent a day rehearsing the old-fashioned way, with tape on the floor of a rehearsal room (see **60s Doctor Who – How was It Made?** under 1.8, "The Reign of Terror"). The real kernel of the story was the epic Scene 9, which was sub-divided into 9A to 9K and took about three-quarters of the script (44 out of 60 pages of the PDF copy released by the BBC). The rehearsal process and the way the nights were drawing in – most days the shooting would begin before dawn and end after dark, so the cast never saw daylight – added to the esprit de corps of this production.

• The production was to be conducted in an almost sequential manner, each scene recorded in roughly story-order. With the exception of the top-and-tail scenes in the Spa with Donna, the only out-of-sequence recording was the material using the cabin set, which was made on the second day of shooting. The first day, 27th November, was spent on the sequence where the passengers meet and are subjected to the grim entertainments on offer. Davies had suggested a 1940s cartoon, as he often found them unsettling, but had little hope of getting one: as it turned out, an archival 1935 Dave Fleisher *Betty Boop* was available without too many rights restrictions or costs. (It's on YouTube if you're at all interested, *Betty Boop and Grampy*, but the main noteworthy point is an earlier scene where she's rotoscoped onto a tracking shot of a model street.)

The *Top of the Pops* clip of Raffaella Carra was from an episode the BBC won't show now, 27th April, 1978 (Jimmy Savile presented it in a string vest), but the clip of "Do It, Do It Again" was repeated as the record spent the next month slowly climbing the charts to No. 9. The artistic installation was just one of those 60s oil-wheels you see in clips of Syd Barrett-era Pink Floyd.

• Wednesday the 28th was the only day on which the two pilots and the cabin set were needed. Unlike the passenger lounge, the cabin had windows open to the planet's sky, so there was a green-screen behind the glass and shielding. Once these scenes were in the can, there was a break while the Any Effects team rigged a panel to crumple next to where Sky would be cowering on the Thursday. That was also the day when sounds from outside disturbed the passengers (mainly achieved by having stage-hands thump the exterior of the set and the cast reacting as though they were coming from all over). The following day had the black-out and passengers flung around wildly (albeit not as wildly as it appeared, as it was shot with a tiltable camera-lens and supervised by stunt-arranger Crispin Layfield).

• For the following week, an autocue operator was on hand for Sky and the Doctor. The synchronous speech scenes used a few tricks, such as only saying bits of a long spiel on camera, post-synching to mimed performances and lots and lots of practice. Simultaneously reciting the square root of pi "simply" required a few test-runs before the cameras rolled. On the afternoon of the 5th, they performed the scenes of Sky saying things slightly ahead of the Doctor (and that afternoon Billie Piper took time off from "Turn Left" to record the desperate on-screen cry of *Doctor* for this episode, although it got a pre-emptive outing in "The Poison Sky"). On 7th, the the passengers tried to shove the Doctor out of the airlock. (Layfield was again on hand to prevent injuries and any shot not showing Tennant had the others wrestling with a big pillow.)

• Over the weekend the door of the airlock was rebuilt so that it would come apart, releasing carbon-dioxide to simulate explosive decompression, with room for Kirby Wires for Sharp and Ayola. The last part of the story to be made, on Tuesday the 11th (in fact, the small hours of the 12th) was Donna and the Doctor having a phone-chat at a spa in Newport (with underwater lighting added by the BBC).

• When the script for the two-part Library story came in, the similarity of the "dream" life of Donna and Lee and the unreal life of Donna-without-the-Doctor made it seem prudent to separate "Forest of the Dead" and "Turn Left", so "Midnight" became the tenth episode.

• On the day of transmission, the news broke that Davies had been awarded an OBE. Broadcast was moved slightly from the previous three weeks, starting at 7.10 to accommodate a *Weakest Link* special themed around *Blue Peter* (the 50th anniversary of which was the following October, if this makes any more sense), and before that the last episode ever of John Barrowman's *The Kids are All Right* – which was emphatically *not* ripped off from Dick and Dom's *Are You Smarter Than a Ten Year Old?* on Sky One. (It was ripped off from Jeff Foxworthy's *Are You Smarter Than a Fifth Grader?* on Fox.) Despite the frequent shuffling of the BBC1 timetable over this season, the episode got higher ratings than anything else on that night, even live football on ITV (Sweden vs Spain in Euro 2008, kick-off at 6pm our time).

X4.11: "Turn Left"

(21st June, 2008)

Which One is This? It's a Flippin' Wonderful Life

Firsts and Lasts Yes, Billie Piper has been popping up all season, but this is her first dialogue since "Doomsday" (X2.13). She takes advantage of it to enjoy being cagy. If you want to read it that she's flirting with Donna, there's enough evidence.

It's the last time we get to hear about Donna having something on her back. And that AMNN newscaster gets a name at last – Lachele Charles is henceforth credited as "Trinity Wells".

Watch Out For...

• The part of the Doctor is played by Billie Piper this week and they give her the spooky

"Flavia" theme, seemingly sung backwards then played in reverse.

• The Chinatown-in-space sequence at the start takes about two minutes of screen time. It seems several times longer. The singalong scene, however, is rather better – both Davies and Graeme Harper judge the moment and its abrupt cutoff perfectly. For anyone who grew up in 70s Britain, Bernard Cribbins performing *Bohemian Rhapsody* is about the most bizarre thing in the Davies years. (But listen closely: like most people in Britain, he feigns to believe that the lyric is "spare him his life and his pork-sausage tea" rather than "... from this monstrosity" as the printed lyrics and subtitles on the DVD claim.

(This sing-song gives Queen a good claim to be the band most favoured by BBC Wales: they've used three separate songs over the years rather than the one song over and over like with Slade.)

• There's a minor character called "Alice Coltrane". For any viewers who read *Mojo* or *Rolling Stone*, it seems briefly possible that the story's villain might be Carlos Santana. It isn't. Neither is it the often-mentioned Nerys. If anyone, it's Sylvia. (After Val last week, Lady Eddy in 1926, the Adipose and Sontarans using Earth as a nursery and Metella in Pompeii, mums are getting a really bad press this year. Don't expect any improvements soon.)

• The Doctor asks Donna, "What did [the mysterious woman] look like?", and Donna responds: "She was blonde." Observe Tennant's horrified expression: for all that Davies seems to have been writing for the Doctor/Rose shippers, it's an endearingly funny moment if you're in the other camp. Then comes the weirdest ending in the programme's history, as all writing everywhere turns into two words.

• ... oh, and the ending – in which the Doctor sees a wide swath of items render the words "Bad Wolf", and on this evidence declares "It's the end of the universe" – rather depends on the viewer having seen a series finale from three years ago. We pity anybody who might have come to this cold. It is, however, one of the odder cliffhangers of the revived series.

The Continuity

The Doctor Well, there's not too much to say about him in this one, for obvious reasons... but it horrifies him that Rose has returned with the Bad Wolf paraphernalia, and his response is to make immediate tracks for Earth in Donna's normal time. He enjoys exotic drinks almost as much as watching Donna's reactions to them.

• *Background.* [Much of the setup for why a big black beetle can latch onto someone's back and create an unreality is informed by *The Sarah Jane Adventures*; the Doctor has heard of the Trickster's Brigade and can identify the Time Beetle as one of its weapons. We'll pick up on this in A7, "The Wedding of Sarah Jane Smith".]

It seems that the heartbroken Doctor would, in a version of "The Runaway Bride" (X3.0) without Donna, have failed to leave the building quickly enough. UNIT retrieves his corpse several hours later, still clutching the sonic screwdriver, confirming all the vague hints we've ever had that a regeneration left too long won't happen at all. [Astonishingly, this suggests you can permanently murder any Time Lord you please with a conveniently full bathtub and good upper body strength.]

He's puzzled by the coincidences that have affected Donna, starting with her meeting him twice. The way her altered timeline seems to have created a viable alternate reality, apparently within days of the downloaded version of her making a real world inside a computer [X4.9, "Forest of the Dead"] alarms him most.

The TARDIS Once the Doctor dies, she seems to be letting go as well [presumably following Emergency Programme One from X1.13, "The Parting of the Ways"]. The lights have switched themselves off, the console sounds unhappy. Nevertheless, there's enough tech remaining for UNIT and Rose to work out what's on Donna's back, and power for her last-ditch trip.

After Shan Shen has been covered in Bad Wolf graffiti, the Cloister Bell goes off. [The fact that nobody else reacts to everything being written in English with just a two-word vocabulary reinforces the supposition that the Ship's ability to make lettering appear to change – as in X6.7, "A Good Man Goes To War" – is behind this alarming development. The difference between being a textual Babel Fish and outright induced hallucinations is a sliding scale. See **How Much of This is Happening?** under X5.6, "The Vampires in Venice" for more.] Even the words 'Police Box' change. The Doctor seems to think the end of the universe is at hand.

The Supporting Cast

• *Donna*. [This is her story in a way no companion's quite had before or since, if we set aside spin-off series. The nearest precedent is 3.5, "The Massacre", broadcast some 40 years before.]

When her mother nags about getting a safe local job instead of going out for temp position with a posh London firm [H.C. Clements, of course], Donna's initial reaction was to ignore her. She does rather suggest that she wouldn't mind if an executive noticed her. For some reason, she went to the Boat Show at Olympia with some of her mates.

The prospect of living in Leeds offends her, for some reason [there's really no need for her to spout off every Northern stereotype she can think of when they move in with the Colasantos]. Her response to her grandfather's gentle rebuke about her shouting is to say she's going to have a good try at making the world better that way. In practice, this ends up not going for much. She's deeply miserable and guilty that she doesn't have the opportunity to look after her grandfather the way she'd hoped.

She's easily convinced that she can prevent all this ghastly history and save the world by going back in time, and when she realises she has to die to accomplish this, she does so with scarcely a second thought. As Donna dies, Rose gives her two words to tell the Doctor; it's not clear how much memory Donna retains of the alternative, but she's able to tell the Doctor about "Bad Wolf".

• *Sylvia*. As unpleasant as usual. She mocks Donna's plans to work at a big professional office as an implausible attempt to get off with some posh blokes. [This is from the pre-change part of the timeline, which speaks volumes about Donna's hasty marriage to Lance in "The Runaway Bride"; apparently there's quite a lot of pressure on her already. She's certainly the oldest female companion we've seen on the new show.]

On the other hand, this version of Sylvia seems to soften under pressure; she gives up on Donna after the sacking and admits to grieving for her husband. When Donna despairs and asks her mother whether she's always been a disappointment, Sylvia bluntly tells her yes – which is the last we see of this version of her.

She doesn't seem to know *Bohemian Rhapsody*.

• *Wilf*. His slightly xenophobic stance on aliens is not at all improved by the increasing death toll caused by them. Nevertheless, he puts on a brave face during the evacuation, saying that they ought to show "a bit of wartime spirit". He likes both beer and singalongs. He appears to already know all the words to *Bohemian Rhapsody*. Even in the chaos of the evacuations, he's kept track of his beloved telescope – it's a sign of how depressed he's become when he ponders selling it.

He first shows temper when an obviously disturbed soldier pulls a gun on his beloved granddaughter for no apparent reason. [Under the circumstances, he's more than justified.] He's the first to realise what euphemism "labour camp" is covering, and grimly salutes their Italian host. His health deteriorates under the stress, but it seems he promised Donna's father that he'd take care of her, and he's determined to keep that promise. [We don't know if the promise happened in the standard timeline, but it seems plausible.]

• *Rose*. The Doctor's hair is one of his better features, in her opinion. She looks a lot older and her accent's become more RP; she's developed a more pronounced lisp and has acquired a lot of impressive-sounding time-technology patter. [At times it's almost as if Romana II had dressed in Martha's clothes.]

For reasons not elucidated to the viewer, she says that she's been pulled across dimensions because of reality going wrong. Rose consistently conceals her name for fear of changing the casual nexus; she's apparently crossed a good many realities to reach this one.

As soon as she finds out that the Doctor's dead, she knows something is very wrong and simultaneously starts studying Donna's back. The second time Donna sees her, she instructs Donna to use her winning raffle ticket and take a free luxury weekend. [This isn't ever explained but, as every other time anyone has a lottery ticket in this era of the series they win, it's no trick to think Rose made sure which one she got.]

Donna thinks that Rose is attempting to pick her up; Rose doesn't bother correcting this. [Why exactly Rose knows to send Donna out of London is another matter. Ignoring the possibility that this Rose knows she's in *Doctor Who,* the nearest we can find to a logical explanation for this shift in emphasis is that, for Rose, the time elapsed since her earlier yelling-silently-on-TV-screens plan to acting as the Doctor's stand-in is a lot longer than it was for Donna-in-the-normalverse. During this, she and her back-room team have apparently deduced that Donna is more important than it

How is This Not a Parallel Universe?

The Doctor is very clear that parallel worlds are sealed off from the universe he inhabits and that what's happened to Donna in "Turn Left" is unprecedented and weird. Earlier, Rose authoritatively stated that every universe is in danger from an as-yet unspecified threat, and that this is how she can visit Donna in her own private *idios kosmos*: a what-if world created by the Trickster and Donna's peculiar nature. Rose has considerably more freedom of movement in this World of Wrong than in the one she left at the end of "Doomsday" (X2.13), and can even pop back to see Donna-Prime on her deathbed to deliver a message.

Something very odd is happening and there are apparent inconsistencies even between stories by the same author, let alone between these scripts and what physics says ought to be happening. So we'll try to make it all work, but one thing is certain – Donna wasn't in a parallel universe.

We know this for several reasons. One is that the author said so. *Doctor Who Confidential* had Russell T Davies state it unequivocally. Another is that the script's internal logic requires the Beetle to feed off a personal timeline that was altered, rather than have it expend eye-watering amounts of energy travelling. A third is that the dying TARDIS can assist UNIT in making a time-travel backpack work, whereas travelling to the one parallel universe we know about nearly destroyed it (X2.4, "Rise of the Cybermen"). As you may recall from the essay with "Utopia" (X3.11), Davies was conscientious on getting the pop-science cosmology right enough not to have ten-year-olds writing in and complaining, so we can safely assume that he knew whereof he spoke in this instance. His solicitude in getting the distinction across is right and proper, so this gives us a chance to look at how these apparently similar ideas have been used over the decades.

We have these two terms, "parallel universe" and "alternate universe", which the Doctor and his chums use interchangeably. Mickey introduces both in the same breath in "Rise of the Cybermen" and the Doctor never gets around to correcting him, using both himself to describe Pete's World. The implication is that Lumic is at work in a variation of history from ours, and the Doctor fell into it through a glitch in the Vortex caused by the Void Ship popping up in 80s Docklands. We've been inundated recently with variations on the Many Worlds hypothesis, speculated upon by philosophers in the 1920s but given quantum physics legitimacy in the 1950s as a possible work-around for the Copenhagen Interpretation (see, amongst others, **The Big Picture** entry on X3.10, "Blink"). That idea took until the late 1990s to seep into pop culture via SF novels from the 80s and a few comics. For most purposes, the term "alternate" is used for when history has changed – which presupposes a "main" universe and then an infinite supply of variations from it, plus variations from the variations and so on.

However, from the late 1960s, astrophysicists were struggling with the conundrum of space being potentially infinite and bent in imperceptible dimensions (imperceptible to us, that is), but the amount of stuff that can be in our universe being, of necessity, finite. If the limit of what we can observe is material from the first couple of million years after the Big Bang – ancient galaxies and quasars whose light has taken 13 billion years to get here – is that the same as the limit of what else could be there?

This idea never really went away. The observable region of spacetime is, from our perspective, all receding from us at near lightspeed; in orthodox three-dimensional measurements, it can be considered to be a sphere of about 30 billion light years in diameter. That's the limit of how far we could possibly travel (even assuming a constant expansion at the same speed and some sort of magic faster-than-light engine as we're dealing in more than three dimensions). Much more mass/energy in such a noösphere and gravity will scrunch it all up into one dimension. But if space is genuinely unlimited, there might be any number of other observable regions – observable to anyone inside one, if not to us. Any number, including infinity.

Whilst there are so many quantum fluctuations going on in a space that's something like $4/3 (\pi \times 13 \text{ billion})^3$, there are, logically, an infinite variety of physical conditions including an infinite number of universes exactly like this one, an infinite number identical except for one tiny detail, an infinite number identical except a couple of details, an infinite supply of universes with Earths like ours but a small change in a different galaxy, an infinity of universes where the Weak Force was a tiny bit stronger and our 80 billion light-year diameter sphere is the size of a Volvo... and so on ad infinitum. This includes all the options that have been selected for fictional alternate timelines and others where physical laws vary, to say nothing of all

continued on Page 195...

seemed to the Rose who took a message about car-keys and dustbins (X4.1, "Partners in Crime").

[Yet comparing Rose here to how she reacts in the next two episodes, it seems as if either she forgets all of this and becomes just an unemployed shop-assistant with a big gun looking for her ex – or (and this is something we'll take up in this story's essay) the Rose who tells Donna to contact the Doctor is as different from the Rose who reunites with him next week as the Donna who moves to Leeds is from the one who visited Shan Shen. This story's Rose has foreknowledge of the *Titanic* and the stars going out, something that, logically, the Rose who met Donna outside Adipose Industries in "Partners in Crime" cannot have had. That Rose didn't seem to know who Donna was. Yet this clearly is Rose and not the Bad Wolf, as her powers are limited to a bit of foreknowledge and a technologically-assisted ability to pop in on Donna from another universe.]

UNIT/Torchwood In this timeline, it takes both to keep up with a Doctor-less cosmos, and even then with only moderate success. [Private Harris (X4.4, "The Sontaran Stratagem") pops up to tell us the worst after the Empress attacks, so he was likely working for UNIT by this point even in the proper timeline. He's 'Greyhound 15' and knows about regeneration, so it must be part of basic training.] When they find the Doctor dead by the Thames barrier, they load him in an ambulance to bring to the UNIT hospital. The leader at Donna's exit is Captain Magambo, a brisk woman very much after the Bambera model [26.1, "Battlefield"; we'll see "our" Magambo in X4.15, "Planet of the Dead"].

Jack and the Cardiff mob defeat the Sontarans; unlike the many questions we had concerning the Doctorless victories against endless invasions of Pete's World [consider 13.3, "Pyramids of Mars" or 17.2, "City of Death"], we have here a detailed account of why there's still a human race, mainly including the off-screen deaths of familiar characters. Mysteriously, Rose knows the names of all the Torchwood personnel in Cardiff. [Equally mysteriously, she won't recognise them in a fortnight's time (X4.13, "Journey's End") when they appear on the TARDIS scanner.

[The designers were explicitly making the props for the time-travel experiment sequences to look like the product of both organisations' technology, which suggests Jack was working more closely with UNIT by the time the Sontarans showed up.]

The Supporting Cast (Evil)

• *The Trickster's Brigade.* The Doctor explains that they're capable of changing people's lives in small ways. It appears this would normally only alter that individual's timeline, but in Donna's case the effect was so tremendous as to create an entire parallel universe. The Time Beetles live off changes in timelines [qv. The Weeping Angels, X3.10, "Blink" et seq.].

Planet Notes

• *Shan Shen.* We're not given that many details, but it seems to be a planet-sized Chinatown. [The set dressing more resembles the Hollywood idea of New York's Chinatown than, say, the London ones in Limehouse or Gerrard's Street.] It has low-flying spaceships and appears to be near three other celestial bodies, one of which has a ring-system. They have bargain-price Shukina and some better-than-usual Peshwami, plus drinks that look suspiciously like Coke floats [see **The Lore** for their true nature].

[They may or may not have fortune tellers in the normal course of events; this one seems to have been on the lookout for Donna.]

History

• *Dating.* For the Shan Shen sequence, we could be at any time in any galaxy. [The eighty-fifth century was cited in one of those BBC coffee-table books, *The Time Traveller's Almanac*, but with no substantiating evidence on screen or in the production notes. For this story to work at all the Doctor must, after this incident, not have been involved in any Earth-saving activities between Christmas 2007 and September 2009 (cf. X5.1, "The Eleventh Hour").]

Alt-History

• *Dating.* [Rose says in the script that the key moment of the intervention is one minute past ten in the morning on Monday the 25th. This applies to a day in June for 2007 (and February and August in 2008, and May 2009 while we're at it.) The 2007 date works with her having been at HC Clements for six months by Christmas that year. Sylvia's car has a registration number that would make it new-ish, but not ostentatiously freshly-bought by then.]

How is This Not a Parallel Universe?

continued from Page 193...

possible worlds in any work of fiction ever devised.

Nonetheless, in any given universe, there are only a finite (if still bloody enormous) number of options that can follow the first possible state-of-being, and once we get from the fizzy imperceptible quantum fluctuations to changes that can be seen, the available options diminish with time. Once we move from the quantum realm to the coarser-grained deterministic level, causality takes effect; even with exotic universes that departed from how things went here, the number of possible sequences of events is, in one widely-credited estimate, ten to the power 10150 – don't try to imagine such a number, you'll get a nosebleed – which is big but finite. These are, however, options: nothing prevents them being possible, but nothing guarantees their existence.

As the name implies, a "parallel" continuum isn't a branching-off (parallel lines never meet, after all), but is instead a totally different universe that was created in its very own Big Bang – and then, for story purposes, progressed practically identically to ours (or the Doctor's) except in a few particulars. There is a snag with using these for stories, namely that each observable region is only observable from within. The same physics of vacuum inflation that we encountered when discussing the end of time (**Why Hide Here?** under X3.11, "Utopia") makes these other versions inevitable, but sends them receding from ours as space itself expands.

Yes, there is somewhere physically distant an Earth where the BBC franchised *Doctor Who* and the CBS version outlasted the original, but that knowledge is of no practical use to us. We are within an event horizon as absolute as any black hole's. So are all the other universes. This isn't entirely bad news as, unlike the Many Worlds hypothesis, there are at least ways to observe, within our purview, the sort of events that underpin the theoretical grounds for believing this – and, so far, the whole hypothesis holds water.

Some models even have the expansionary phase we appear to be in slowing and halting eventually, potentially allowing someone with a TARDIS to travel towards the end of our universe and out into others that may be newer. This seems to be what happens in X6.4, "The Doctor's Wife". That's what seems to have happened in *The Sarah Jane Adventures* (specifically "The Secrets of the Stars"), the *New Adventures* books (see **Are All These 'Gods' Related?** under 26.3, "The Curse of Fenric", and the Doctor's explanation of Fenric) and 20.4, "Terminus" suggests that the Doctor is in one caused by such a process.

[NB: although we have now established a clear distinction between the terms "Alternate Timeline" and "Parallel Universe", we will continue to use the slightly inaccurate term "Evil Parallel Universe" to denote or ridicule use of the cliché even when the less euphonious "Evil Alternate Timeline" is more appropriate.]

With the *gran turismo* of a time-space machine, access to alternate timelines is easier than leaving the universe – traveling back to before a decisive moment allows someone with time-sensitivity (a Time Lord, a suitably-equipped Dalek, a Tharil, a Graske or Donna with a beetle on her back) to manipulate events and observe the changes then travel into the revised future. That, we were led to believe, was what the Time War was, a lot of these changes back and forth to give one side or the other a final advantage. This ended with the Doctor stealing the Moment (X4.13, "Journey's End"; X4.18, "The End of Time Part Two"; X7.15, "The Day of the Doctor") and the Time War was, apparently "sealed" (see **How Can Anyone Know There was a Time War?** under "Journey's End").

Travel to parallel universes was also possible when the universe was "kinder" and there were Time Lords. This was also a period when the TARDIS could cheerfully travel "sideways" and duck in and out of different time-lines, and they could come to visit us (26.1, "Battlefield"). Then, apparently, the ability to do either was lost to everyone except the Bad Wolf. The "walls of reality" were as impermeable to the Doctor as to anyone else. Except when they weren't.

Because no sooner do we come to terms with all of this than, we get Fixed Points and flux thrown at us. Agatha Christie could die in 1926 and create a minor ruction in history (X4.7, "The Unicorn and the Wasp"). Anything not a Fixed Point is amenable to erasure or alteration and even Bowie Base One can be changed, albeit with as-yet-unspecified consequences. Over in *The Sarah Jane Adventures*, we have time and mortality rewritten about twice a year.

Now, here's where it gets messy, because when they do mess about and erase Sarah from history, she lands up in a blank white void exactly like the ones we used to get when people were stuck between realities in places with zero co-ordinates

continued on Page 197...

Harold Saxon wasn't all that necessary for the big Army guns after all; he's obviously not around, so Professor Yana must have lived and died in the future without ever realising who he was. [See X3.11, "Utopia". In one of the script's cleverest moments, it's noted that there is a range of satellites around the Earth; they're called Guinevere, not Archangel.] Logically, the whole idea of life-after-death never caught on among humans [X8.11, "Dark Water"].

Nevertheless, in this reality the Doctor kills the Empress ["The Runaway Bride"] before she teleports away. At any rate, the Thames is closed off [for all we know, this happened in the regular reality as well]. All the people at the Royal Hope Hospital die of oxygen starvation on the moon [X3.1, "Smith and Jones"]. Sarah Jane Smith had been investigating the hospital and managed to stop the MRI from being used – at the cost of her own life and Maria Jackson's. In the meantime, Martha died heroically giving Oliver Morgenstern the last oxygen bottle. That Christmas, a falling spaceship rendered the whole of Southern England uninhabitable [X4.0, "Voyage of the Damned"]. At this point, it appears that an Emergency Government declares martial law. [This is entirely in keeping with what we'll assume is the same government in Torchwood: Children of Earth, meaning Brian Green was PM in all three versions of Britain.]

With Great Britain a wreck after the Titanic crash, the Adipose decide to set up shop in America [why they didn't do this in the proper timeline anyway is a matter for speculation]. Sixty million Americans die in the fallout. ["Partners in Crime" indicated that deaths in the process were caused specifically by the Matron's decision to pull out before higher authorities came along, which rather suggests that whoever it was handling aliens in America bungled the job. We expect it was President Winters (X3.12, "The Sound of Drums").] This puts the kibosh on the £50 billion in financial aid that would have gone to the UK.

In the meantime, someone else must have built the ATMOS devices [maybe some Chinese genius was feted by the Sontarans instead]. The Torchwood team takes over; Gwen Cooper and Ianto Jones end up dead, while Jack Harkness is shipped off to the Sontaran homeworld. [The non-disappearance of Jack after Abbadon trashes Cardiff (TW 1.13, "End of Days") may well have led to a more efficient organisation than we saw in

Series 2 of the spin-off, but his moodiness, if he hadn't gone to 100 trillion AD and spent a year chained up and eating mashed swede, might have got more of his team killed. Martha was certainly not around, so maybe the incident that led to Owen's first death was forestalled. There's no word on Toshiko or Owen here, so their deaths in TW: "Exit Wounds" perhaps still happened even though "Utopia" never did. The dates given in the Torchwood episode suggest that this was in 2008 and on-screen evidence suggests the run-up to Christmas.] Much of the planet gets choked. Three weeks later, the emergency government starts shipping foreigners to concentration camps. Then the stars start going out, across all Universes [let's assume this is the same date as next episode].

The Analysis

The Big Picture "Overhead, without any fuss, one by one the stars were going out". We saw in "Logopolis" (18.7) how the famous last line of Arthur C Clarke's story "The Nine Billion Names of God" provided an arresting image and a threat big enough to conquer Tom Baker's almost omnipotent Doctor. It was also the prototype of the year-long build up to a grand finale with hints and plot-developments feeding into it, the model now accepted as standard for Doctor Who. That's about to happen again, as the umpteen running clues this year feed into a two-part episode of sufficient scale to require every BBC Wales-era companion or recurring character (except Pete Tyler).

Before all that started, Davies had been playing with a What If? storyline about a Doctorless world since Donna was still called Penny (see X4.1, "Partners in Crime"). The idea of simply driving right instead of left having such big consequences came before any of the rest, but even this has a distinguished pedigree. We saw under "Inferno" (7.4) how long people have been running history with slight changes and wondering about the consequences of decisions by Great Men and mighty armies, but as the idea lost its novelty value, it became more democratic.

Perhaps the most famous ordinary-person-makes-a-difference scenario is It's a Wonderful Life (a film valorised by a generation of Americans as part of How Christmas Should Be, but not really that popular in the UK until Gremlins). Post-war novelists were making Big Important Statements about choice and free will as part of the general

How is This Not a Parallel Universe?

continued from Page 195...

(6.2, "The Mind Robber"; 9.5, "The Time Monster"; 18.5, "Warriors' Gate"). As one of these events has the Doctor showing up (A7, "The Wedding of Sarah Jane Smith"), we have to take it into account. What we have to ask now is which set of rules each individual changed-Earth story is following, and whether Rose materialising inside an aberrant Doctorless history created around Donna is violating one set of rules or two.

Apart from a few throwaway mentions in black and white stories, mainly in scripts by David Whitaker (or amended by him) where the older use of "universe" to mean "galaxy" seems to be in play, the first time we're looking at this concept is "Inferno" (7.4). Exactly what's going on here is confused, partly because the Doctor himself seems unsure if he's flipped across dimensions to a totally new universe containing an exact mirror-image of Britain that went much the same way until the 1930s, then didn't pull back from potential fascism, or the same physical universe that took a different track at around 1938. It is a matter of whether each universe has an immutable (or largely immutable) timeline, and one differs from the other merely in this one cosmically-insignificant detail, or whether the timeline has been adjusted at a critical moment.

In all the slightly anti-climactic stuff at the beginning of episode seven, the Doctor mutters to himself about free will not being an illusion. This chimes with what he later tells Lawrence Scarman in "Pyramids of Mars" (13.3), but what's odd is that it comes as news to the Doctor in the earlier story. Admittedly this phase of the series posited a Doctor with chunks of his memory gone, but one would have thought that this information was as basic as time travel even being possible. The conception of the Doctor being able to choose futures even when he has foreknowledge has been part of the story since "The Space Museum" (2.7), where a garbled pseudo-science rationale, one we can now we can interpret as a variety of Many Worlds theory if we squint and hold our noses, was offered. In this specific instance, two overlapping alternative sets of consequences of the TARDIS landing on Xeros that day played out – one leading to their capture and death, then being effectively stuffed and mounted in cases, the other not.

This looks as if we're strictly limited to alternate timelines, but there's a catch. More by luck than judgement, the majority of such instances we encounter are the same length of time from the decisive alteration. In "Inferno", the same length of time after the Republic either happened or didn't has elapsed in both versions of England the Doctor encounters, and it's the same day in both universes. "Rise of the Cybermen" happens on the same day in Pete's World that Mickey says he left on in his native continuum. Even though the space-time vortex has gone, the TARDIS gets them to that planet on that day and even the same city. That's handy! The Doctor and Rose also manage to return (without a prezzie for Jackie) the same day, it seems. From what little we can glean of the mechanisms at play in "Battlefield", Mordred opens a gateway between realities that has the same amount of time from Arthur's death on both sides.

This has stopped looking like coincidence and seems to be how things work. Rose's ability to pick and choose which planet and day to arrive in when looking for the Doctor is the exception. But perhaps this is itself a symptom of how things have changed since the Time War. According to her sources, the Void, the interdimensional medium, is "dead". Considering that it was described as being more nothing-ish than space first time we heard about it, this is extraordinary.

There are also a lot of unexplained features of this version of Earth, not the least of which is how they can jaunt between dimensions, so much more easily than the TARDIS, using only medallions. We first saw this when the Void Ship made a rupture between these Londons – an event that "killed" the TARDIS, and only allowed Cybermen to make a crossing after two months of practice-runs. The second time, there was a cataclysm destroying all realities and Rose had a mission-control with a Dimension Cannon, whatever one of those is.

We're coming to an alarming conclusion: perhaps the only genuinely parallel world we've ever seen in *Doctor Who* is Pete's World. It isn't a divergence from our history, but an entirely separate history that ran very like ours, to the extent of there being a Cuba Gooding Jr, Renault making long wheel-base vans and Rose's phone being compatible with the Cybus network. Yet the Doctor, berating Rose for thinking she's any better than the public who have Cybus ear-pods, says it's not so different, "only parallel". If, by this, he means it's a mere alternate timeline, we might default to the position we were encouraged to take at first

continued on Page 199...

ABOUT TIME 2008-2009

groundswell of interest in Existentialism, so that an apparently orthodox Victorian pastiche, *The French Lieutenant's Woman*, had multiple endings and a lot of talk about Darwin and teleology – whilst more playful French writers, notably Raymond Queneau, raised the issues of chance and infinity. The ideas were around in science and philosophy, but it took the post-1960s surge of interest in Latin American writing to push Jorge Luis Borges to the top of every sixth-former's must-read list and making "The Garden of Forking Paths" the touchstone for all conversations on this topic. (We examined the background to this trend in the notes for 2.7, "The Space Museum"; 17.1, "Destiny of the Daleks" and 19.1, "Castrovalva". If you missed Volume 7, the whole Multiverse notion within twenty-first century pop-culture was given a good seeing-to when we discussed X2.5, "Rise of the Cybermen".)

The increasing popularity of parallel/alternate universe stories in 90s pop culture made the idea of everyone's life consisting of thousands of small decisions that could have made big differences made the notion of euchronia (see "Rise of the Cybermen") almost as mainstream an idea as utopia. By the time a run-of-the-mill rom-com set in a weird, ethnically-cleansed London like that of Richard Curtis films, but without even his ability to surprise, came out (*Sliding Doors*, 1998), it didn't need anyone explaining the notion or excusing it with technobabble.[41]

Davies used the film as a shorthand for the idea in his emails, but someone being selected to go back and fix a wrong choice he or she had made had already replaced "and then he woke up" as a way out of worst-case-scenario episodes. If *Futurama* has done it more than once, it's officially a well-worn cliché. (See X7.11, "Journey to the Centre of the Tardis".) It's especially suggestive that *Buffy the Vampire Slayer* had provided more domesticated versions of the world as it would have been if the hero hadn't shown up at a critical moment: we examined the influence of the episodes "The Wish" and "Doppelgangland" in passing when discussing "Rise of the Cybermen", but one significant aspect of the former is that the person responsible for the change – the waspish Cordelia who made the wish – is herself killed and the altered timeline carries on without her.[42] Similarly, with both "Father's Day" (X1.8) and *The Sarah Jane Adventures* honouring the tradition founded by Harlan Ellison in *Star Trek* that aber-

rant timelines must be dissolved by a loved one having a fatal traffic accident, the ending for "Turn Left" was pretty much a given.

However, this is the latest in a set of episodes where Davies has shown how thin a thread binds Britain together, and allows things to get increasingly bad until pressing a reset button. "Last of the Time Lords" (X3.13) provided a sneak preview of this, and the Tone Meeting had the key phrase "Life During Wartime". This is his solution to one of the problems we identified with stories set in present-day Britain (**Was Yeti-in-the-Loo the Worst Idea Ever?** under 5.5, "The Web of Fear"), that a big enough disaster to make a story makes any subsequent adventure set in that slightly-altered version of our everyday world impossible (see also **Why Does Everyone Forget About the Aliens?** under "Smith and Jones").

The viewers know the nature of the reset button, but – for the person who has to die – it's still a bit of a shock. That person is an altered version of a regular character, rather like John Smith was ("Human Nature"), so the focus is on how a person reacts to the news that he or she is a failed version of a character from a long-running TV show. This is the element that worried Davies when the script for "Forest of the Dead" (X4.9) came in. In both cases, such humour as there was came from the fact that Donna wasn't *entirely* different.

Doctor Who has shown London being emptied several times. The two most detailed accounts, "The Web of Fear" and "Invasion of the Dinosaurs" (11.2), depict martial law run from secret bases in tube stations and allude to an off-screen government in exile (in Harrogate according to the latter). The logistics of hurriedly getting everyone away from London are a fascinating topic, one that fan fiction and articles over the decades have discussed, but with the new series having mooted the topic a few times now (X1.9, "The Empty Child", Wilf's first appearance in "Voyage of the Damned" and *The Sarah Jane Adventures*), it's only natural that the practical details were brought to the fore.

What seems odd to British viewers over 40 is the way that the ephemeral details seem to be travelling backwards in time as each disaster strikes. Donna's laid off by Chowdry because of an economic downturn that, at the time of broadcast, looked like the sort of thing consigned to the 1990s (see our comment on Sylvia's statement

How is This Not a Parallel Universe?

continued from Page 197...

broadcast – this is how things would have turned out if Queen Victoria instigated (or prevented) the Empire of the Wolf. It doesn't look quite as advertised, and there's a President rather than an Emperor. The 2007 that might have followed steam-powered spaceships could have turned out like the 2018 of 5.4, "The Enemy of the World" (especially if, lacking a World War I, there's still an Austro-Hungarian power-base), but there's no way it could have been so precisely like what viewers in 2006 were shown as almost their own world but with Cybermen.

It was always the assumption that the Doctor was a one-off. Barry Letts and Terrance Dicks, when planning "Inferno", were clear that there was no local equivalent. There are lots of reasons why the absence of the Doctor in any other history means there's no way the world could be so like ours. (We planned a jokey essay for "Army of Ghosts" suggesting all the ways that humans alone could have dealt with Sutekh, the Autons, Scaroth, Azal and the Great Intelligence. Then we dropped it, because it was stupid and any Doctorless timeline for Earth has humans wiped out before they evolve.)

All the conversations on altered personal timelines since 2005 seem to confirm the hypothesis we put forward in **He Remembers This *How*?** under X1.5, "World War Three" and refined in **Is Arthur the Horse a Companion?** under X2.4, "The Girl in the Fireplace". A TARDIS traveller's memory is copy-protected and, as we saw in X6.0, "A Christmas Carol", someone whose past is being rewritten by the Doctor can recall both versions equally clearly. In short, instead of splitting off two different Doctors or Amys or Kazrans, we get both overlapping in the same body and mind. Whichever timeline the Doctor and the TARDIS are in is the "official" one and every deviation becomes a branched-off alternate universe. The only way to get a variant Doctor would seem to be if he went back and changed his own past significantly, and his fear of doing that even in X9.4, "Before the Flood" indicates that Reapers (X1.8, "Father's Day") are still a threat.

If Pete's World is a full-blown parallel universe, does it have alternates of its own? Logically, it ought to. We could posit this as a solution to the weird anomaly at the end of Series 4, where Rose knows useful stuff when on her own hunting for Donna – but as soon as that timeline is closed off

from the "main" one, we encounter a Rose who needs the basics explained to her. Perhaps the Rose in "Turn Left" is an alternate version of the Rose in "Partners in Crime", "The Stolen Earth" and "Journey's End". The "Turn Left" Rose can pick and choose her entry-points in Donna's personal timeline, and can even pop back to before it all started in the "main" chronology and give dying not-real Donna a cryptic message. Davros's taunts to Rose in "Journey's End" could be interpreted as exactly this – that she has crossed not just physical universes, but many of the alternate versions of these (or at least one).

This brings up the vexed issue of bubble universes, Branes and so forth. These are created within our universe, but might have different physics. Access to these is as difficult as getting in and out of a time-bubble (eg. 17.2, "City of Death"; X7.16, "The Time of the Doctor"), which has been shown as tricky but just about possible. The double-talk for why the TARDIS can't do much travel between these (X7.9, "Hide") also makes the opening up of a doorway between them impossible as shown, but that sort of thing is in the same category as moving 27 stolen planets a second out of phase with the rest of the universe (X4.12, "The Stolen Earth") or losing Gallifrey down the back of the settee ("The Day of the Doctor"). The only one that's just a long way away is in "The Doctor's Wife"; the majority are "within" ours like Russian Dolls (17.4, "Nightmare of Eden" and also the mention of "pin galaxies" in 22.4, "The Two Doctors").

The main problem with the "Hide" scenario is that opening a gateway to a smaller, more energetic dimension – rather as the Logopolitans were doing with the Charged Vacuum Emboitment in Season Eighteen – isn't something you do in a drawing-room. Due to the Second Law of Thermodynamics, a small universe with all its energy in ferment would evaporate Earth and most of the galaxy when evening itself out with a larger, cooler, more spaced-out universe such as ours. Nonetheless, *Doctor Who* has shown us many compact, bijou cosmoses over the years, many of them white and cloudy but with air and a floor (e.g. "The Mind Robber", "Warriors' Gate", *SJA*: "The Wedding of Sarah Jane Smith" and earlier *Sarah Jane Adventures* yarns. See also **Where's Susan?** under "The End of Time Part Two".) Some of these are more like the scar-tissue protecting these universes from each other (a spectacular version of

continued on Page 201...

that "nobody's unemployed any more" in "Partners in Crime"). When the *Titanic* strikes, we seem to head back to the 1970s. The bus in which Sylvia and Donna are travelling is a 1960s model, and everyone's packed into a terraced street of the type most councils started demolishing in the era of high rise estates.

We see TV aerials, but no satellite dishes. The billeting system is a bit like Butlins (24.3, "Delta and the Bannermen"; 4.7, "The Macra Terror"), but uses rubber stamps and buff foolscap envelopes like an office in a "Kitchen Sink" drama. No computers, no photo-ID, just chits. Then the Adipose assault on America apparently cuts off the electricity in Yorkshire, and we have candle-lit singsongs like the early 70s miners' strikes and secondary picketing (see, for example, 9.2, "The Curse of Peladon" or **Who's Running the Country?** under 10.5, "The Green Death") while everyone talks about the Blitz. Then Britain, like Bosnia a few years before, implements ethnic cleansing policies and anyone with a non-local accent suddenly gets sent away, so the country only has white people with the "appropriate" accents, just like the 1950s. (Then Magambo and electricity come into the story as the turning-point.)

There were, apparently, discussions about yet another spin-off, *Rose Tyler: Earth Defender*. Just not many of them.

English Lessons

• *£23,000*: That's a much better than average yearly salary for a PA, and a little over $30,000 per annum. (Martha, as a junior doctor, would have got £400 a year less than this, Clara might get a bit more if Coal Hill School is in inner London, but everywhere else she'd've got £750 p.a. less in 2015 than Donna was offered in 2008. Then again, nothing else about Coal Hill resembles a real London school, so Clara being able to afford that flat is possible if she's paid well over the odds despite her lack of qualifications.)

• *Vera Duckworth* (n.) A *Coronation Street* character, half of a couple whose 50-year marriage was characterised by bickering[40]. Vera, played by Liz Dawn, was written out of the series in early 2008 after 34 years (but came back as a hallucination/ghost when husband Jack died in 2010). Typically, Donna doesn't distinguish between a fictional Lancashire and real Yorkshire, despite centuries of enmity between the two counties either side of the

Pennines. (You will recall that Rose described the Eccleston Doctor as sounding like he came from "the North".) This London-centric set of clichés also explains...

• *Whippets* (n.pl.): racing dogs, like greyhounds, traditionally kept as pets by folks Oop North, 'appen, bah 'eck (etc.). According to these stereotypes, in addition to flat cloth caps and trousers held up by string (for the men) or pinnies and mob-caps or headscarves covering hair-curlers (for the women), everyone also keeps racing pigeons and wears...

• *Clogs* (n. pl.): Wooden shoes that clatter against the cobbles that they have instead of tarmac in endless 1970s dramas about trouble at t'mill (see 22.3, "The Mark of the Rani"; 15.1, "Horror of Fang Rock"; X7.12, "The Crimson Terror") or the Ridley Scott-directed Hovis advert. However, the compound verb 'to pop one's clogs' is a euphemism for dying so Donna's jibe is more malicious than usual.

• *Rota* (n.) A schedule or duty-roster. House-shares have them for washing-up, but in the 70s they were published for when your street would have a power-cut in 1971-2 or which areas would have stand-pipes during the drought of 1975-6.

• *Wetherby* (n.) It's a town near Leeds. Both are in the West Riding of Yorkshire (being such a big county, it has traditionally been divided into three Ridings). Wetherby was a significant way-station en route from London to Scotland, but the Industrial Revolution made Leeds grow faster.

• *Ken Livingstone* (n.): the first elected Mayor of London. He had hitherto been the last leader of the Greater London Council, a body summarily ended by the Thatcher government in 1984 (see the essay with "The Sound of Drums"), and in both terms of his mayoralty, he sought to continue the populist policies on transport and housing that had antagonised the Tories and their supporters in the local press. By the time of the episode's broadcast, the efforts of those newspapers had engineered his replacement by shambolic Tory grandee Boris Johnson (aided by Livingston's inability to be tactful or admit mis-speaking). The assumption that he had spent millions on a spaceship for Christmas is the sort of thing that the *Evening Standard* was reporting as news prior to a Russian oligarch buying it.

• *The Boat Show* (n.): Note the definite article. This is an annual event at the vast Olympia complex at Earl's Court, as are the Motor Show and the

How is This Not a Parallel Universe?

continued from Page 199...

this idea is in X11.9, "It Takes You Away", but "Warriors' Gate" makes a lot more sense if the Gateway is a cordon sanitaire).

The physics, or at least the pop-science version available to TV writers, indicates that the conditions for making this happen are relatively commonplace in our universe – but we can't, by definition, measure any results, just as the people who built Terminus couldn't know that they had made our universe by dumping excess fuel. Each one we've seen in the series has had only slight variations to the laws of local physics, such as space being green when the effects team remembers (18.3, "Full Circle" et seq), but they open up possibilities for a lot more variety.

We also have to account for a pair of anti-matter universes impinging on ours in the mid-70s (10.1, "The Three Doctors" and 13.2, "Planet of Evil"), but we've tried to reconcile what was thought when those stories were written, what's thought now and how they fit with other stories in the essays with those tales. They seem to occupy the same spatial dimensions as ours but not interact, almost as described in the Doctor's whimsical ramblings in "The Mutants" (9.4) and the dimensional misalignment in "The Space Museum". These can also be considered as more or less inaccessible aspects of our own cosmos, rather than parallel in the sense we discussed above or alternate in the history-changing sense.

If you recall the far-off days of Volume 5, especially the essay **How Can the Universe Have a Centre?** under "Terminus", you'll know that the attempts to re-tell old stories using space-as-we-understand-it-now instead of abstract notions is a minefield. If you recall **Is This the *Star Trek* Universe?** earlier in this very book, you will recall that it's become common to use "universe" and "storyline" almost interchangeably. Well, the end of "Turn Left" takes this a step further and suggests that CAL's consensual hallucination was a "universe" of Donna's making, and that she's somehow created or accessed one of those parallel universes that have been shut off since the Time Lords ceased trading. The first of these we can pretty much dismiss as hyperbole, but the idea that Donna has been to a parallel universe is more complicated than it seems. Yes, she's been involved in a whole 'nother timeline that follows on from the Doctor's death at HC Clements, but that's not quite the same as a parallel universe. Popular cul-

ture and actual science are almost in synch on this, but there's a catch and it makes a big difference to what stories are possible.

So the question we're left with concerning "Turn Left" is whether A) it all happened but in a different physical space, or B) Donna was "merely" psychically transported into a different personal time-line, remembering it all in sequence as if it was happening in real time over a few years. That Rose seems to have little idea who Donna is when they meet in "The Stolen Earth" (X4.12) might indicate that the entire history only happened to alt-Donna, and real-Donna recalls bits of it because she's a TARDIS traveller and has bonus memory for altered events. Had Donna merely been dreaming the Doctorless chronology, there would be no reason for her to have encountered Rose.

When this version of events is changed back, Donna is back in the booth with a dead beetle – but, somehow, earlier time-sensitive observers comment on her having "something on her back" as if "our" Donna is just a guest in the orthodox universe. Had this been the case, though, none of the false-memory stuff inside the CAL mainframe would have happened. If the TARDIS had let her aboard at all – a questionable enough proposition given that Dalek-Caan-as-Bad-Wolf manipulated her fate – it should have prevented her from being transmatted into a digital daytime TV world (however that happened). The Doctor's attempt to link a consensual hallucination with an altered time-line, however much it avoids viewers thinking "hang on, they just did this story", confuses the issue.

However, in both cases, what seems like a rewriting of Donna's memory is presented to us (and her) as her physically going to a place where a different sequence of events from her recent past is unfolding. In both cases, a mysterious woman we recognise comes to tell her it's a fake but – while Miss Evangelista gets to stay put in a revised version where she is clever and pretty at the same time – we seem to get two different versions of Rose Tyler, one for each reality, with no means to communicate with each other except via Donna's hazy memory.

What's really puzzling with this is that people in the "correct" time-line can perceive Donna's connection with the Trickster. All the people who claim "you have something on your back" seem aware of the alternate version. Two of these, the

continued on Page 203...

Ideal Homes Exhibition. Few of the vast numbers who attend can afford any of the items on display, but that's part of the ritual. It's less of an event these days, and Olympia is being redeveloped.

• *Wizard* (adj.): a very dated superlative, like "ripping" or "top hole". The last known unironic use was by Christopher H Bidmead in 1983.

• *Earl Mountbatten* (n.): Second-cousin of the present Queen and uncle of her husband, killed by an IRA bomb in 1979, but controversial enough for them not to have been the immediate suspects. After becoming an Admiral in World War II, he was hastily made Viceroy of India to supervise the process of Partition. Nobody could have done a good job of this, but many in India and Pakistan believe he made things worse. He was also implicated in an apparent right wing coup plot in the mid-60s, one which may have influenced Harold Wilson's abrupt resignation as Prime Minister some time later.

• *Chippy* (adj.): Insolent, insubordinate, surly, etcetera. Not to be confused with...

• *Chippy* (n.): which is either a carpenter or a fish and chip shop (Donna is heading for the latter when Rose returns), or *chipper* (op cit, X3.8, "Human Nature").

Oh, Isn't That...?

• *Joseph Long* (newsagent, shares home with the Noble family) is often cast as Italian Londoners (as his ancestors were one or both of these). You can see him in the 1989 magic-realist heartwarmer *Queen of Hearts*, as the café owner in *Ashes to Ashes* and any long-running drama that needs someone to serve spaghetti and/or relationship advice. If you want to see him do something else, check out the film about the making of *Citizen Kane*, the 1999 *RKO 281*, where he plays studio boss Harry Cohn. Or try the Van Damme vehicle *Legionnaire*, where he does a French accent, and several 80s things where he's assorted dodgy Eastern types. If you are a really keen follower of *Who*-related television, you might spot him in the same episode of *Magnum PI* that has Peter Davison, or the unscreened pilot episode of *Sherlock* (he's Italian in that, for a change). He was back in 2017 as the Pope (X10.6, "Extremis"), a surprise for anyone thinking that the story was set in our world.

• *Chipo Chung* (Fortune Teller) was Chantho last year ("Utopia") and had been doing voice-overs and small roles in films fairly constantly.

Things That Don't Make Sense

A problem that vexes the season's big storyarc: how does Rose know so much about Donna's timeline? More strangely, she uses the term "Bad Wolf", even though she doesn't yet know that the Daleks are behind the star-snuffing. If, on the other hand, she simply wants to tell the Doctor "Hi, I'm back!" why spend a whole episode not telling anyone that she's the supposedly-dead Rose Tyler?

It's probably easiest to go with the straightforward interpretation, and accept that the Trickster's Brigade routinely alter their victims' histories with no consequence to history, but through Blind Luck one of them happened – in all of time and space! – to target one Donna Noble of Chiswick, all-important companion of the tenth Doctor. Otherwise, we'd have to ask why the Doctor wasn't targeted – would he have been too rich a temporal feast? Once you've established the one weak point in a time-travel show where disasters can happen, it's difficult to see why they don't happen continuously. If a villain can bring unravel the Doctor's casual nexus with a reality misstep, thus killing him and causing Earth's destruction, why doesn't this sort of thing happen every other Tuesday?

We should also assume that when Donna makes herself Turn Left, it resets almost everything, temporally speaking. Otherwise, it's funny that Donna and her family never hear about how her doppelgänger died in London. All right, perhaps she wasn't carrying any identification, but her fingerprints, or a canvassing of the local residents, would identify her as one Donna Noble of Chiswick. (And quite why it's bright and sunny half a mile away from where the "real" Donna is in a car in persistent drizzle is a bit of a puzzle – even in London.)

In the alt-version of "The Runaway Bride", the Doctor seems to have decided, for no good reason, to pop into the basement of HC Clements and blow holes to allow the Thames to flood in, despite the absence of a strange woman materialising aboard the TARDIS. We're invited to conjecture on a totally *different* chain of circumstances, in which he and the Racnoss Empress nonetheless followed almost exactly the same methodology on the same day. Even assuming that Lance dosed Nerys (or someone) with Huon particles and then copied the procedure we saw with Donna, right down to marrying her on Christmas Eve, we have to wonder how Nerys (or whoever) might have

How is This Not a Parallel Universe?

continued from Page 201...

seers in "The Fires of Pompeii" (X4.2), gained their prophetic powers from a different altered future, one where Donna would never be born. This resembles the confusion over the alternate "Empire of the Wolf" thwarted – we are led to believe – by the Doctor in 1862, but oddly unlike the other-other future with Pete Tyler rich and successful. It's as if all aberrant time-lines are one and the same rather than an infinite branching out from each decision or random event.

Nonetheless, all of Donna's life between the metacrisis and materialising aboard the TARDIS in a wedding-dress resonates backwards from the moment of her becoming part Time Lord, and has this impending transformation resounding around her for the Ood, the Shadow Acolyte and the competing clairvoyants of Pompeii to detect. (What exactly the Ood are sensing is a matter for a couple of later essays.)

influenced the progression of events and the outcome. How does draining the Thames make businesses other than boat-trips go bust?

Why is there a Chiswick *at all*, if the Doctor died before stopping the Pyrovillians from enslaving Earth, and rendering it all to ashes in 72 AD?

Donna's having drinks in Chiswick and runs to Woolwich. Apart from her stamina (and doing a half marathon in those shoes is doubly impressive), what made her decide to run towards an attacking spaceship? Never mind that if it's Christmas Eve, the Tube network would be heaving – getting onto the Jubilee line from Chiswick is a bit of a palavah, so she has to cross the (suddenly absent) Thames. Running 15 miles amid streets full of people gawping at the Racnoss ship is probably as fast a way as she can muster. But at the episode's end, running half a mile in four minutes is beyond her.

In this reality, the *Titanic* didn't wipe out all life in a nuclear winter (the Doctor was adamant that would happen in "Voyage of the Damned"). Perhaps the dust cloud of the *Titanic's* impact will eventually make humanity go the way of the dinosaurs (19.6, "Earthshock"), but the immediate effect, it seems, is radiation making southern England uninhabitable. Except that it's likely worse than that – the resulting electromagnetic pulse would have caused far more global disruption, and affected military signals. Submarine commanders faced with abrupt loss of contact were advised to listen to Radio 4 Long Wave, and if *that* wasn't on, they were instructed to assume war had broken out, and open the safe with the Prime Minister's sealed orders concerning which targets to launch nuclear missiles at. (The Navy would specifically be listening for the morning news marathon *Today*, but it seems only right and proper that the End of the World is presaged by *The Archers* going off-air.)

In fact, with an EMP pulse and a huge object showing up on everyone's radar, why *hasn't* war broken out? The seemingly-ludicrous story about a ship from 1912 falling on Buckingham Palace wouldn't have stopped NATO or the Pentagon assuming that Putin was up to something, and the magnetic wave would seem a very effective form of cyber-attack.

Come to think of it, how does the falling *Titanic* make a downwards-dopplering sound as it approaches at high speed?

Bilingual people aren't stupid. What's the point of telling a guest they have something on their back in a language they clearly don't understand? Why is a hotel of this kind employing Spanish-speaking maids rather than the more familiar Polish or Welsh ones?

The photocopy supply company is going bust because the Thames has been drained and most of their customers are south of the river. Because removing all the water apparently makes all the bridges go away. And the tube lines. And the Blackwall Tunnel.

If the Royal Hope Hospital was returned, and an incident with the MRI scanner occurred, then "Smith and Jones" played out almost unchanged, albeit with a different Smith. In which case, Sarah Jane had alien blood that the Judoon could detect when Florence Finnegan drank from her. If not, the Judoon would have kept the Hospital in detention, and continued their fruitless search for the extraterrestrial.

The £50 billion in US aid to Britain that Wilf mentions is... generous, to say the very least. For the last 40 years total, US foreign aid has been in $20 to 30 billion dollars per-year territory – in 2004, it went up to $44 billion, but much of that was military War on Terror stuff. For reference, the entire Marshall Plan was only $13 billion dollars over four years (in current money, only about

$30 billion dollars). Then again, the figure he quotes is in sterling, and the exchange rate might be lower pre-*Titanic*.

Something about this story that seems intuitively right, until you think about it in context: London's obliterated and everyone else stops watching television. In an actual emergency, there's a selected group of sitcoms, documentaries and trusted broadcasters chosen to maintain morale and let people know what is likely to happen. The week after Diana, Princess of Wales died was a sneak preview of the swaddlingly wholesome entertainment and solemn news coverage we could expect in a war or national catastrophe. There would be upbeat messages with Elgar-ish music telling us *Britain can take it*. (The spoof in the 1994 satire *The Day Today* looked ridiculous until 2001, when something almost identical but real was used when the Queen Mother died.) Apart from Trinity Wells telling us that the Adipose have wrecked America's economy, there's no hint of people being desperate for news or the nation being "healed" by three showings a week of *Free Willy* or *To the Manor Born*.

The way the episode's shot, it sometimes looks as if the electricity's gone, and everyone's eating out of cans and sitting in candle-light. Why? Even if London is devastated, they have generating facilities all around the country, and the wires are still up.

That's another thing: why has London getting nuked made all the vehicles revert to the 1960s? Did the EMP make all the later models with central locking seize up? Did it remove all supplies of unleaded petrol? And as with the Sontaran two-parter this year, we're greeted with the idiocy of soldiers thinking they can seal off car exhausts by shooting them.

Donna apparently thinks Leeds is a better bet than staying another three months in a hostel. Her priority is getting work. As an experienced temp, her qualifications are almost irrelevant (apart from 100wpm, almost guaranteed to get her a gig in no time, especially with computers suddenly vanishing), but surely the place for someone like her to get paid employment is the swamped, understaffed office where she's having that very argument. Moving that many people around would require a lot of admin staff, especially those who could drive (fewer people in London can than the national average). And yet, she's not qualified to work for the army pay corps – who, even in our

reality, have aptitude tests rather than formal interviews with CVs.

Why is Leeds more suitable for taking London's refugees (i.e. all those thousands of people – apparently – who were out of the city at Christmas and yet have nowhere to stay) than anywhere further north, with whole streets nearly empty? And what's happened to Cardiff on that map in the office?

Miraculously, Wilf has no sooner arrived in a new city under martial law than he gets an allotment just like the one in Chiswick. Even under normal circumstances, there's a formidable waiting-list (two years, on average, more in big cities). If the story wants us to think things are heading backwards to the Blitz, Wilf's allotment is a potential gold-mine. So why's he thinking of flogging his telescope, when growing tomatoes ought to have made him a king-pin on the underground fruit'n'veg circuit? (Has he got that pistol we see in X4.17, "The End of Time Part One"? He'll need it, if there are spud-rustlers about.)

Perhaps Davies planted it there deliberately to cheer up older fans, but... how can the constellation Orion vanish in one go, when others are still visible? Orion is only a pattern as seen from Earth (a basic fact that eluded everyone involved with X9.4, "Before the Flood"), the individual stars are all different distances away, so they wouldn't disappear at the same time *unless* the Daleks were systematically picking off stars across the galaxy, just to confuse and intimidate observers on this specific planet. Except that next week, we discover it's not the stars vanishing, it's Earth being transported to a place where no stars are visible, so they'd all go at once. (Unless Wilf is watching the Reality Bomb destroy stars one by one – which he can't, because the planet he's on is, apparently, the vital last component.)

If Wilf's such an experienced stargazer, why has he got a blazing log fire right under his telescope, making heat-haze, soot and light-pollution?

Critique You know the cliché about Graeme Harper always demanding "energy" and "pace"? He's got other strings to his bow.

Consider Sylvia's last scene here. She is in the foreground, in focus, impassive, as Donna finally wrings a confession that Sylvia wanted a different daughter. An earlier two-handed scene with Catherine Tate and Jacqueline King has them lying on the kitchen floor wondering about people they'd known (or not) in Chiswick, then transforms into a comedy scene with the sing-song before abruptly ending with machine-gun fire. In both cases, the script has been given room to breathe.

This is interesting, because it's the script that clips along briskly, not the directing. Partly as a result of having been written so rapidly, partly because it has to cover a lot of ground and partly because we've already seen a lot of the set-piece sequences, this story hurtles from disaster to disaster, through the prism of a family we sort-of know. Donna here isn't the one we've had for the last few stories. Sylvia is a more subdued, less truculent edition of her usual self. An economical script gives the cast just enough clues to develop their performances in slightly different ways from the regular patterns. The real beneficiary here is Billie Piper, freed from having to be the nation's girl-next-door and making a convincing development from the Rose we remember. It's a shame the next episode makes her squander this. As we saw later (X7.15, "Day of the Doctor"), she can handle exposition and the technical stuff as well as anyone cast as the Doctor, and sells the idea that she's not happy making even the "wrong" Donna undergo this journey.

(To get ahead of ourselves for a moment, this is the start of the problem with the season climax: this model of Rose is, as Jackie foresaw in X2.12, "Army of Ghosts", becoming more like the Doctor. Davies may have intuited that the logical next step was for her to become part-Time Lord, but he'd painted himself into a corner with the "One of them will die" thing he'd already set up, and needed to save Donna while writing her out of the series.)

It's all down to the performances, the dialogue and the directing because – let's be honest – this is about the most obvious story they'd not yet done. Once Penny had turned into Donna, all the options open to Davies about which Doctorless disasters would happen – and how they affect each other – are there for the audience to anticipate. We can almost join in with it, right up to the traffic-accident that makes everything all right and the prospect of Evil Parallel Britain opening concentration camps for foreigners. Here, in fact, the budget restraints help the story because it's almost all told in close-up, small details limning this altered world.

Or, rather, altered *Britain*, because this story's version of events still deals with the global threats

from the last couple of years (apart from the Adipose, for some reason, affecting America without any obvious side-effects). That parochialism is deliberate, to offset the idea that, whatever happens, Britain is special and can cope with things that would flatten other countries. The plan was to show how easily we could become like countries we see on the news. Paradoxically, it's messed up because Sarah Jane Smith and Torchwood fix the global problems.

Tonally, however, with the echoes of 70s power-cuts and troops on the streets in Northern Ireland, it's disturbingly familiar for older UK viewers. The fact that technology seems to go into reverse, and they use literal rubber stamps and forms – plus vehicles from the 1960s – is a subliminal self-congratulatory note of how far we've come, and what they don't show is as significant as what they do. If this had been purely intended to show how close contemporary (2007) Britain was to Nazi Germany or 90s Serbia, a familiar character – Sylvia, perhaps – would have been shown sliding into collaboration and getting a job with the Austerity government. We haven't had a Klaus Barbie in a Loo in Tooting Bec since "Inferno" showed an alternative Brigadier and we don't get it here, we get Wilf making a stand. Yet even then, Donna applies for a job with the army but (against all reason) doesn't get it, and we glide over this and back into the routine time-paradox malarkey.

Even with Bernard Cribbins as the voice of common decency and Joseph Long as a likeable foreigner caught up in the new regime's opportunistic policies, it still seems slightly out of tune. "Leeds" looks weirdly white, as if it had already been ethnically cleansed or had reverted to 1965; this, coupled with the grating Shan Shen sequence (even the BBC1 continuity announcer thought it was supposed to be Imperial China) rather weakens the story's argument. London is contemporary, everywhere else is stuck in caricatures from black and white adverts. Spanish housemaids are all clairvoyant, Rocco is just a shade away from Topo Gigio and America is full of fat, rich people unable to cope with even the slightest setback, unlike us. The story manifests exactly the kind of Anglo-Exceptionalism it sought to debunk.

But that's a fairly technical, theoretical quibble in the face of an episode that, once again, gets to the core of what *Doctor Who* was supposed to do without getting bogged down in what happened in a Tom Baker episode, or how impressive a computer-generated space-battle they can do now.

As with last week's "Midnight", the exigencies of production schedule and budget have forced Davies to raise his game. Unlike that story, this one is robust enough to withstand advert breaks, indeed works with the jump-cut nature of story-telling this imposes rather than trying to resist it. Yes, it has to use very broad strokes, because it's a whole story in one episode and hasn't got space or time for subtlety or detail. It still stands up to repeated watching, and is more fun along the way than the more abstractly-admirable "Midnight".

Unlike the previous season, when an argument could be made for thinking of the last three episodes as a three-part finale, it does neither "Turn Left" nor the subsequent two-parter any good to think of them as part of a greater whole. It'd quite possibly have been better all round to have an episode or two in the middle. Rose's characterisation is the worst casualty; here she's reasonably adult and obviously knows more than she's letting on to Donna, but once the Doctor shows up next week, she turns into a lovelorn schoolgirl and barely does anything in the episode after that.

The Lore

Written by Russell T Davies. Directed by Graeme Harper. (BBC1) 7.0 million, (BBC3 repeats) 0.91 million, with an AI of 88%.

Repeats and overseas promotion *Reise Rückwärts*, *Le Choix du Donna*.

Alternate versions BBC America trims five minutes off the 50-minute running time without too much plot-damage: the main casualties are the Noble family arriving at the hotel, Donna and Sylvia wondering about the fate of the woman at the newsagent's and the sing-song before the machine-guns fire at the ATMOS rigs.

Production

• Davies had been planning a "what-if" story about Penny never having met the Doctor, and instead staying in a tense relationship with Moira – her mum – right from the first discussions of Series 4. Once Penny had become Donna, the idea caught fire as – unlike a complete newcomer – Donna had met the Doctor before several big Earth-saving incidents. The altered timeline because increasingly grim as the un-prevented catastrophes now included London's destruction and America's economic and social collapse. Writing for the original versions of Donna and Sylvia lightened the tone slightly.

• A story-element not used in the final version: one of Donna's workmates was aware of the Beetle, but was ignored because she was from another culture and (according to one source) had restricted English. It's been suggested that a reason for this was a desire to use an undisguised Chipo Chung ("Utopia"), but instead the subplot was reworked for the oddly-named Alice Coltrane. Chung was in the final cast as the Fortune Teller, although it's unclear if the decision to have Shan Shen as a planet of Chinoiserie was taken before this casting was confirmed. A series of diseases presaged The End of the World, one of which was approaching Yorkshire as Penny and her Dad (then Donna and Geoff, then Donna and Wilf) were planting crops in a work-camp.

• It was always hoped that Billie Piper would return as Rose, but her success made timetabling this difficult. *The Secret Diary of a Call Girl* was an instant hit and the second series was commissioned, but it left Piper a window of opportunity in December and January. While everyone was publicly denying it – and with the other high-profile projects making Piper's unavailability plausible grounds for not doing it – Rose's mission to our dimension began to take shape. A small glitch came when Piper announced her wedding plans for New Year's Day and a honeymoon in January. Other returning or guest artists had been booked on the understanding that this was the only time that the episodes could be recorded.

A more significant problem was that the full extent of Howard Attfield's illness was only realised late on. As we discussed with earlier episodes, the plan to rewrite the stories with Bernard Cribbins as Donna's grandad was formed during recording of "Partners in Crime" and while "Voyage of the Damned" was being edited. Cribbins initially thought he'd be travelling in the TARDIS (he got his wish in X4.17, "The End of Time Part One"), and this took a couple of calls to resolve. In the process, the newspaper-vendor was renamed "Wilf Mott" instead of "Stan", the place-holder for the un-named character in the Christmas episode, and the number of coincidences around Donna's reunion with the Doctor became a plot-point.

• With the Doctor's absence such a critical feature of the story, it made sense to double-bank it, and the idea for what became "Midnight" evolved. That was written very quickly and proper work on "Turn Left" only began once the casting and broad shape of the season finale were in place. Davies properly began just as Steven Moffat formally accepted the role of executive producer for Series 5 onwards, and Piers Wenger was announced as Julie Gardner's replacement.

• The submission-date was under a week later, on 2nd November. He got the first 20 pages (about a third of the finished script) in on time. Piper was pleased by what she saw, but intimidated by the difficulty she was having recapturing Rose. Davies, meanwhile, was trimming the story to keep it cheap: mass graves, riots and explosions were removed and almost all of the special effects were reworkings of things that The Mill had on their hard-drives (e.g. Starship *Titanic* hitting Buckingham Palace instead of missing by a few metres).

• The episode was designated as Block Seven and given to Graeme Harper to direct and Susie Liggat to produce. Shooting was to begin in earnest on 26th and the read-through for this and "Midnight" was at Bloomsbury Baptist Church on 23rd. This is usually a propitious day for *Doctor Who*, but the news had broken of Verity Lambert's death the previous afternoon. Davies had been asked to hand her an award, but it became obvious that the cancer for which she'd been receiving treatment had returned.

• In fact, the first bits recorded were before the read-through, as Lachele Charles delivered the grim tidings to AMNN's fictitious viewers in the BBC Wales News studio C2 on the 22nd. Tate's first scenes were at the Bay Chambers in Bute Town; the majority of this was the location for Mr Chowdry's office, but a nearby room was used for some of the Housing Office scenes. The night of the 26th, in a fenced-off bit of Hamadryad Street, Billie Piper's not-as-secret-as-hoped return started with her genuinely surprising appearance in "Partners in Crime". The scenes of the dead Doctor (usual stand-in Colum Samson-Regan playing the corpse – we'll see more of the back of his head in two episodes' time) were, to Davies's relief, kept from prying eyes. Tate recalls bonding with Piper over the odd catering arrangements for night-shoots (especially the aplomb with which Piper extracted a baked bean from her coffee).

• Donna's time-travel anorak got its first outing as she materialised in Clearwater Parade next day,

which was also when the few scenes at the Noble house were shot. For the sequences at the T-junction, the police obligingly blocked Court Road, Gwan Tredon; Tate never learned to drive, so Marianne Hemming doubled for her in some shots. That night, at the allotments on Lady Mary Road, the scenes from "Partners in Crime" made with Howard Attfield were reshot with Cribbins, then new scenes supposedly in Leeds were added.

• In keeping with BBC guidelines on showing methods of suicide, the script made it clear that Donna's fatal crash was an accident. It was shot at St Isan Road and, as was his wont, Harper used a quad bike for some tracking shots (see "Utopia"; 8.4, "Colony in Space"). The police had also helped keep this junction clear and Bill Davey was the stunt-driver. November ended with a trip to Upper Boat for the "dead" TARDIS interior and the inside of the Fortune Teller's booth (erected in the Torchwood Hub). This was the day the Trickster's servant was revealed and the giant roach was made by Neill Gorton's team. The head was animatronic, but one shot of a leg on Donna's clothing was a more old-fashioned stick-puppet (could you tell?).

• The planet Shan Shen was a car-park and an alley, near Cardiff Royal Infirmary (using the same Maltings site we saw in "Gridlock"). Many of the extras had come in response to a Facebook posting that seemed to offer £700 for the day: it was actually £70, and people who'd shut down their businesses for this drifted off later in the day. Tate had a Black Cow, a coke float with vanilla ice-cream, to drink from a gourd. After all this, Tate and Tennant were back in the booth interior and BBC News reports were faked by Catherine York (getting the most from her BBC News brolly) and Ben Righton as Oliver Morgenstern.

• The swanky hotel was Egerton Grey Country House (earlier the convent in *The Sarah Jane Adventures* romp "The Eye of the Gorgon"), but en route to this was the desolate-looking road on which the old coach took the Nobles to Leeds. The street in the Yorkshire town was, predictably, in Wales (specifically Penarth, Machen Street); the cast had a guide-recording for *The Wild Rover* and *Bohemian Rhapsody* in case they'd never heard either.

• In addition to her scenes with Tate, Piper had popped into the studio to record Rose screaming "Doc-Torr" silently on monitors, as part of "Midnight" but reallocated to "The Poison Sky" as well. The first Thursday in December is a tradi-

207

tional peak-time for office Christmas parties in pubs so, appropriately, production moved to the Conway, on Conway Road, Portcanna. By now, Tate's prolonged spells in Welsh December rain had caused her to get flu, so the open-air location originally picked for this was abandoned in favour of the more sheltered Sophia Gardens. A green-screen was erected for the smog exploding into clear skies.

• The main shoot ended at Panteg, at a steel foundry, for two nights, for the UNIT base. Some of the design-logic here was that, with Torchwood gone, UNIT inherited a lot of alien tech and combined it with their own, creating a hybrid "look".

• Julie Gardner was keen to have more banners and posters reworded as "Bad Wolf", so some additional shots were added on 18th January and again on 24th, when some extra dialogue was added to the Doctor's comments in the Fortune Teller's booth. On the last day of that month, Jason Mohammed added to his tally of cameos with some BBC News bulletins about Sarah Jane Smith and other disasters. Finally, some extra TARDIS scenes were completed on 20th March, in between those for the two-part finale and some additional work on the Library passages and CAL's living room for "Silence in the Library"/"Forest of the Dead".

• By the time of broadcast, Rose's return was no secret, so the Radio Times gave it a cover (one of six that year given to the series). The episode was allowed a 50-minute slot but, due to an international football match, a slightly earlier start-time. It was still the fourth most-watched thing on that week, almost a record. The BBC3 repeat was delayed due to Glastonbury, and it got a double-bill with the next episode.

Noel Clarke had a film out that week (Adulthood, sequel to his directorial debut, Kidulthood), so was on the chat-show circuit and was allowed to reveal that Mickey would be back soon. By now, news of Moffat inheriting the series and Tennant's impending RSC stint were fuelling rumours of a regeneration, and this fed into the wild speculation about how this year's series would end (see the essay with next episode). Bookies were listing the usual suspects (Alan Davies, Richard E Grant) and, at 8/1 favourite, Robert Carlyle (because he's thin and Scottish).

X4.12: "The Stolen Earth"

(28th June, 2008)

Which One is This? "Dimensions in Time" with a budget. Rose is back! And Martha! And her mum! And Jack! And Sarah Jane! And Harriet! And Davros! And the Judoon! And Dalek Caan! And a lot of planets we'd heard had gone missing! But not the bees.

Firsts and Lasts The Daleks kill Harriet Jones, former Prime Minister. However, Penelope Wilton is one of the returning cast who has to be credited over the action, because there are so many ex-companions to fit into the title-sequence. Not even the 1996 TV Movie had to do this.

A mere 45 years after their debut, the Daleks on the Crucible get more practical hands, resembling giant shower-taps. We also get a big red Dalek Supreme with what looks like a wheel-clamp on his dome. (Yes, a red Dalek. Contrary to what Terry Nation told us in the 60s, the other Daleks can see him.)

Sarah Jane Adventures fans might like to know that this is the first time we're told Mr Smith has a "booting up" fanfare that people in the attic can actually hear, instead of just a theme on the soundtrack.

A poignant moment for older fans comes at the start when – probably as late as this is feasible – they use a milkman on his rounds as the signifier for suburban normality. (See 26.4, "Survival"; 25.1, "Remembrance of the Daleks"; 11.2, "Invasion of the Dinosaurs"; 8.2, "The Mind of Evil"; 7.1, "Spearhead from Space"; 3.10, "The War Machines" and most spectacularly 10.5, "The Green Death".)

At the end, we get big silver blocky letters in the space-time vortex slamming up, saying "To. Be. Continued."

Watch Out For...

• Yes, six people need giant steel name-tags to spin out of the vortex in the time it usually takes for two and the all-star cast spills over into the post-credits scene to include the Torchwood gang, Francine and Harriet. And, this being Episode 12, there are more celebs to come as we channel-zap for reactions to Earth's unexpected removal from its customary place.

• There's a lot of conversation for benefit of

casual viewers who only watch the primary series, and haven't bothered with *Torchwood* or *The Sarah Jane Adventures*. A lot of it is also Davies getting only his second chance to write for those characters after the pilot of each series, and commenting on things that look a bit silly. Why else should Sarah only now realise that Mr Smith's boot-up fanfare is a bit overblown, or UNIT's leader comment on Martha's membership of two rival organisations?

• The "Children of Time" (the collective term for the Doctor's core companions and associates) get a mid-90s-style theme that seems as though Gary Glitter's 1972 hit "Rock and Roll Part 2" is getting a bit of junglin' bashment. It's probably as close as they can legally get to the KLF chart-topper "Doctorin' the Tardis" (see Volume 6), right down to the *Hoo-Hah!* vocal. This almost makes the sequence of Gwen and Ianto doing a bit of plumbing as sparks fly seem as exciting as they want it to. (The two Welsh members of Torchwood get a whole subplot where they don't encounter the rest of the cast.)

• In an episode that nonchalantly has Dalek saucers trashing Broadway and downing *Valiant* in a suspiciously familiar manner, the most interesting effect is a simple shot of paint frying on a Dalek's eye-stalk. Bernard Cribbins partly improvised the paintball sequence after he'd made some suggestions for the scene to Davies. It prompts the Dalek to do something everyone does in this episode, mess with a catch-phrase: *my vision is unimpaired.* (See also Harriet Jones identifying herself as "former Prime Minister" and everyone – even the Daleks – replying "we know who you are"; the Shadow Acolyte telling Donna "there was something on your back", shortly after the Doctor's habit of talking fast extends to Judoon; the Daleks chanting "The Daleks are the Masters of Earth" over and over per 2.2, "The Dalek Invasion of Earth"; and Sarah Jane wimping out in front of Daleks and shouting "I'm sorry!")

• There's a cliffhanger, where the Doctor's been semi-exterminated and regenerates. If you've not seen it, guess how he gets out of that…

The Continuity

The Doctor is fond of Saturdays.

He's chuffed to find out Rose is back, even with the impediment of reality collapsing around him. When he and Donna lose the trail to the missing Earth, he slumps into a "Vengeance on Varos"-type despair [22.2, if you care to look]. He can speak Judoon, and warns Donna 'don't' with Captain Jack. A glancing shot from a Dalek triggers his regeneration [see the next episode].

• *Background.* As the age of 90 (which he thinks of as 'just a kid'), he travelled to the Medusa Cascade, the centre of a time-space rift. [The Master seemingly recalled the same incident in X3.13, "The Last of the Time Lords"; if so, it must have been a significant moment for the cosmos at large as well as for the young Gallifreyan. Evelina (X4.2, The Fires of Pompeii") picked on this as being linked to the Doctor's hidden name. Insert your own fannish theory.]

The Doctor believed that Davros died in the first year of the Time War at the Gates of Elysium, when his command ship flew 'into the jaws of the Nightmare Child'. The Doctor tried to save him and failed. Until Dalek Caan's Wild Ride, the Time War was 'time-locked' and couldn't be entered by time travellers after it had ended. [See next episode's essay for what this might mean.]

• *Ethics.* When the Shadow Proclamation demands in the bluntest way possible that he lead their forces into battle, he makes a run for it.

• *Inventory: Other.* He's carrying a stethoscope. [The shooting script didn't include this item, so perhaps it was ad-libbed.] Whether owing to Dalek interference, or the fact that the worlds in the Medusa Cascade are one second out of synch with the universe, those within cannot connect with the Doctor and Donna through their Magic Phones.

The TARDIS Rather sensibly [given how often he yanks the door open into vacuum], the Doctor's installed an automatic cut-in to keep the console room pressurised. Of course a time/space machine can handle a split screen video conference-call. Davros can hack into this whenever he feels like a quick taunt.

The Supporting Cast

• *Donna.* At the Shadow Proclamation, she starts hearing an odd heartbeat sound [see next episode]. One of the staff says she is sorry for Donna's forthcoming loss. [We can only presume that the Shadow Proclamation keeps psychics on staff; this one freaks Donna out by mentioning something on her back; X4.11, "Turn Left"]. She still thinks of herself as a temp [albeit one with 100 wpm]. She's puzzled by the term 'cold cases' [suggesting she's never seen any cop shows, not even the top-rated *Waking the Dead* with that nice Trevor Eve].

• *Martha* [joining us after X4.6, "The Doctor's Daughter"]. Promoted by UNIT and transferred to New York, where she's Medical Director on Project Indigo. The commanding general in NY sufficiently trusts her that she's given not only the teleport to road-test, but the Earth-destorying Osterhagen Key. Her first reaction when Earth moves is to try to call the Doctor.

She's on good terms with Jack [who keeps up the 'nightingale' riff from *Torchwood* Series 2]. When Project Indigo taps into her mind, she first wants to go home to mum.

• *Jack* [joining us after *Torchwood* Series 2, alongside the surviving Torchwood members Ianto Jones and Gwen Cooper]. His first reaction on hearing 'Exterminate' is to kiss both his colleagues goodbye, just in case.

He's been keeping tabs on Sarah Jane's work, including her stopping the Slitheen plan to switch off the Sun [*SJA*: "Revenge of the Slitheen"]. He digs up his old Dalek-killing defabricator gun from the Game Station [X1.12, "Bad Wolf"; he must have kept it somewhere for a solid century, and we've not seen him use it elsewhere]. When Project Indigo actually works, he borrows a trick from it to fix his own teleport. In the process, he exits with the only Dalek-slaying gun available to find the Doctor, leaving Ianto and Gwen behind with useless weaponry and Daleks on the way.

• *Rose* has been chasing Donna and the Noble family ["Turn Left"] because she can't find the Doctor himself. [The adverts suggest she arrives on our Earth in Camden but eventually she gets to Chiswick.] There are some hints she's been through even more than the one parallel universe we saw last story; she totes a big gun and wisecracks about it to anyone who'll ask. [There is an apparent subtext of Rose being jealous of Martha in particular; her snarkiest comments in an online conversation respond to what Martha's just said.]

After her omniscience last week, she here doesn't recognise Martha and forgets a great deal of what she told alt-Donna. [By next week, it'll seem as if she's borrowed some of Jack's retcon capsules.]

• *Wilf* assumes that all aliens are green and they always take the women first. He strives to defend his planet with, as needs must, a cricket-bat. He attempts to blind a Dalek with his paint gun. [It's not his fault that a half-century of jokes suddenly

goes wrong when the Dalek boils the paint away.] He couldn't get a webcam, because Sylvia thinks they're "naughty". The last time he talked to Donna, it was during the trip to Midnight [X4.10, "Midnight"]. To Sylvia's dismay, he voted for Harriet Jones as PM.

• *Sylvia* is startled to find out her daughter has been running amok across the universe with an alien. Wilf says that what with different planets and nebula in the sky, Sylvia can hardly keep denying the strange alien occurrences now. Conversely, she allows a random blonde to come into their house and commandeer their computer without complaining.

• *Sarah Jane* [joining us after *The Sarah Jane Adventures* Series 2]. She's aware of Torchwood, and stays away from them as they use too many guns, although Jack's flirtatiousness elicits a positive reaction. Last she knew, Davros had been killed [12.4, "Genesis of the Daleks"].

She has a co-ordinates setup with Mr Smith. As with her own series [but unlike X2.3, "School Reunion"], she drives a right-hand drive limited edition Spring 1991 model pistachio green Nissan Figaro and has a whole three-story house in Ealing [so is clearly making a bundle].

• *Harriet Jones*. After being deposed [X2.0, "The Christmas Invasion"], she went into cahoots with the Mr. Copper Foundation [see X4.0, "Voyage of the Damned"] to create the Subwave Network – 'sentient' software designed to seek out anyone who has information on contacting the Doctor. [And turn on the closest computer to them, it seems. It's simplest if we assume that Harriet's network only picks up companions of the incarnation with whom Harriet and Mr. Copper are familiar, ignoring other Earth-based companions. A shame, because if you're looking for a former capital-c Companion with a good tally of dead Daleks then Ace, Ian and even Jo Grant are safer bets than a man who was exterminated within ten minutes. Barbara's cardigan scores higher than Captain Jack at this point. And where's the Brigadier? Did Peru not have Daleks?]

Harriet is well informed about Jack being a Captain and Sarah Jane living at Bannerman Road. [Jones was, of course, acquainted with Torchwood in "The Christmas Invasion".] She knows about the Osterhagen Key, but Captain Jack doesn't.

Just before the Daleks attack her home and shoot her, Harriet transfers control of the software to Torchwood. [No one at UNIT UK even regis-

What Were the Strangest Online Theories?

In many ways, the cliffhanger of "The Stolen Earth" was a welcome return to how older fans used to watch, with a week between episodes to speculate on what would happen next. We had already had something of this when River Song showed up a month earlier.

What was different from school playgrounds in 70s Britain was that the internet allowed anyone with a theory to play along, across the globe, regardless of whether they had any of the context 70s kids had (or teachers and parents who remembered earlier episodes or the stories being ripped-off) to assess probability. A thousand flowers bloomed. By the end of Series 4, that division between the British public and fandom was as slim as it had ever been. Meanwhile, other series had taken the whole process of foreshadowing and story-arcs into the mainstream so anything, no matter how slight or oblique, was legitimately a clue. This was the era of *Heroes* and *Lost* getting convoluted after their initial splash, *The Wire* getting all the headlines, people filleting *The Sopranos* for tiny clues they'd missed and the *Battlestar Galactica* reboot being treated as suitable for adults. It wasn't just possible to spin a tenuous theory on minute pieces of apparent evidence, it was expected.

Online fandom had hitherto given hours of harmless amusement to the wider public (and more experienced fans) with the Eccleston's abrupt departure – the much-quoted "*Doctor Who* died today" line was used as an excuse not to take any notice of these people. Nonetheless, in this climate of speculation-as-the-preferred-method-of-engagement, it seemed as though any wild notion was as plausible as any other. With bookmakers taking odds on what "Bad Wolf" would eventually mean, and so many apparently ludicrous ideas actually happening on screen, nothing the public thought might come to pass seemed as silly as the climax of "Last of the Time Lords" (X3.13) or the Macra coming back. A bold and self-confident BBC Wales production team had already made things work that few similarly-budgeted Cardiff-based series could have attempted, so it looked as if money and resources were no object and no development was too fannish.

As the end-credits of "The Stolen Earth" rolled, the Doctor was in mid-regeneration, with the bathetic apparent dying words "I'm regenerating", Donna is the nexus of a lot of weird coincidences, Davros is back and all possible universes are under threat. *What would happen next?*

Here are some of the mysteriously un-used suggestions. They were all seriously offered online that week…

Everybody Female is the Rani

Considering that *Doctor Who* was supposedly taken off the air in 1985 because it was costing more than the ratings and AIs justified, and was generally considered to be a bit naff and only watched by anoraks, an amazing number of people remembered the Rani with great affection. It might be hard for even the most loyal fans – the ones who persevered in the mid-80s despite the episodes being made then – to find anything good to say about the scripts or production of Kate O'Mara's two legitimate outings in the role of the Doctor's old school chum and psychotic biologist rival, still less her semi-official 1993 appearance in "Dimensions in Time", but there it is.

So until Steven Moffat granted their wish in 2014, the online crowd were keen to see a female version of the Master, and looked for signs of her return in any strong woman suddenly in the story for no reason. A female hand with red nail-varnish picks up the Master's ring? That'll be her. The Doctor abruptly turns on Harriet Jones, and she responds by magically getting computer skills beyond those of mortal man? Slam-dunk. Someone with an Indian-sounding name (Shobu Kapoor) is credited in next week's *Radio Times* as "Scared Woman"? Kerchinggggg!

That last one's odd, because it's someone who did five solid years in *EastEnders* playing an apparently throwaway part with one whole line of dialogue. At least two-thirds of the first-night UK audience would know the face – possibly more than could pick Richard Dawkins out of a police line-up. Kapoor being just cannon-fodder was a genuinely unexpected development, if you knew who she was and what she'd done. If you didn't, then the idea of someone like that being a random member of the public took a bit of getting used to. Everyone in London wears a bowler-hat, after all.

Plus, the online poop (take that as you will) said that Maria Jackson was being written out of *The Sarah Jane Adventures* and replaced by someone called… "Rani". It cannot be any other than an Evil Time Lord. But the Sacred Woman definitely wasn't the Rani, she was just some scared woman. Ah,

continued on Page 213…

211

ABOUT TIME 2008-2009

ters, perhaps because all the candidates from X4.4, "The Sontaran Stratagem," etc. are all dead. It uses a four-beat callsign, so it might be repurposed Archangel tech – or she was a big fan of *V: The Miniseries*, which is more likely given that she guessed the Slitheen wanted Earth's water (X1.5, "World War Three").]

She's wondered about her actions in "The Christmas Invasion", but believes them justified, since the Doctor was bound to not show up one of these days. She had the *Spitting Image* board-game.

• *The Shadow Proclamation.* This agency, it seems, is based on a space-station with three long prongs jutting out from a central crystalline castle. [It has a passing resemblance to the Enlighteners' Palace in 20.5, "Enlightenment", if anyone wants to make anything of that.] The interior resembles the foyer of a conference centre. They dish out glowing water in earthenware bowls; it 'purifies', apparently. The Shadow Architect, who acts as if she is in charge, uses terms such as 'holy writ' to justify decisions [so they may be related to the Church Militant of the Moffat years (e.g. X6.7, "A Good Man Goes to War"), but probably not].

The Proclamation members themselves are [disappointingly] humanoid and soothsayerish; they have tight blond curls and red eyes, and dwell in marble halls. They employ the Judoon as shock-troops.

The Shadow Proclamation is broadly familiar with the concept of Time Lords, but only in the sense that the Higher Species have legends of them. [Unlike their next appearance (X9.1, "The Magician's Apprentice"), the Proclamation members don't believe their eyes when a TARDIS appears with a Time Lord in it and, seemingly, know nothing about Daleks, Davros or the Time War.] They have strictures that allow them to seize the technology and person of anyone they feel they need when faced with cosmic threats.

UNIT have a base somewhere near central Manhattan [probably Hoboken, from the exterior shots of Dalek saucers attacking], but it's confirmed that ultimate authority for the organization stems from Geneva. [Just like the old days. In "Last of the Time Lords", Geneva HQ asked what was going on when time wound backwards, but we had no proof that this was the global centre of operations.]

One of their current interests is Project Indigo,

a rudimentary teleport system salvaged from the Sontarans [after "The Poison Sky" (X4.5)]; it works telepathically, sending Martha from New York to her mother's house in London. Despite Indigo being massively top-secret, Jack Harkness claims to have learned about it from a soldier at a bar. 'Code Red' as given from Geneva sends everyone into battle-stations, 'Ultimate Code Red' signals the onset of war [presumably against an alien threat].

The Daleks shoot down the *Valiant* over London. [It's back in X8.12, "Death in Heaven".] The Daleks know about UNIT and target it by name [sensible on reflection, but odd if you recall 9.1, "Day of the Daleks"].

Torchwood are now based in Cardiff, under the fountain in Plas Roald Dahl (which can act as a transmitter). They have three members but Jack teleports into battle, leaving Gwen Cooper and Ianto Jones to face a Dalek with conventional weapons.

The Supporting Cast (Evil)

• *Davros.* Upon his return from the Time War, Davros started making Daleks out of his own flesh, to achieve what he considers to be truly pure Daleks – he refers to these as his 'children'. The genetic extraction process has, it appears, left his ribcage exposed under his tunic. His left hand has been replaced with a metallic prosthetic that resembles claws but he's apparently regrown his torso and arm [25.1, "Remembrance of the Daleks"]. He cautions the Supreme Dalek against hubris [so he's acquired some sense since the old days]. He's proud of Caan for being able to breach the seal around the Time War, something no other being could manage.

He is thoroughly unsurprised to see that the Doctor has regenerated yet again and insists he can recognise the arrogance of any Doctor's voice.

The Non-Humans

• *Bees.* Some, but not all, of Earth's bee population were immigrants from Melissa Majoria [the natural home of alien space bees, as any classicist could have told you] and have fled the impending catastrophe. [We presume they did a wiggle-dance that translates as *so long and thanks for all the pollen.*] They use something measured on the Tandocca Scale, a series of wavelengths, to travel.

• *Daleks.* As part of their Big Plan, they've tele-

What Were the Strangest Online Theories?

continued from Page 211...

well, next time we see a mysterious woman, it's bound to be her. Law of averages...

Obviously, Donna was also in the frame. Then, later, Clara. Then Mrs Gillyflower in X7.13, "The Crimson Horror" (because you don't cast Dame Diana Rigg in a faffy little role like a Victorian factory owner), then Missy... and that has probably killed off this line of speculation for a while.

The wider point is that almost all of these speculations, even up to Series 10, are about things from the old series coming back. No matter how trivial or unlikely that character was, there's someone out there who will identify any enigmatic character or piece of Big Name casting as a revival rather than a genuinely new idea. As often as not they are right – so Harold Saxon *was* the Master, as was Derek Jacobi, and the killer Snowmen were operated by the Great Intelligence (or something with the same name, at least). But a lot of the ideas floating around the net are similar but wrong, such as Patrick Stewart (or whoever's in the news as possibly being in the series) as the Meddling Monk, Drax or Borusa.

Harriet is the Master, and you will obey her

It stands to reason: she's female, so she wears nail-varnish, so it was her picking up that ring at the end of "Last of the Time Lords". In order to create the conditions for Saxon's reign, Harriet Jones had to become Prime Minister against the odds then abruptly, improbably, fall from grace. The Subwave network opened up with a four-beat call-sign, and is clearly way beyond the average ex-politician's abilities. And Sarah addressed her as "Harry" in the conference-call (and she's better than most at spotting aliens and trickery).

To add fuel to this, the BBC's website followed the broadcast of "The Stolen Earth" with a page showing Rose and a Dalek with the title "Master Plan". Alternatively, if Harriet isn't a big enough fish for the Master to use as an avatar, there's that peculiar ring Donna's been wearing...

Harriet of the Daleks

We never saw Harriet Jones die, we just had a sound-effect of a Dalek gun and the screen went to static, exactly the way webcam feeds don't. We know that the Daleks have adapted the bodies and genes of suitable candidates as a recruitment policy, so maybe there will be a big twist where one of the Daleks has a rush of guilt and duty and starts shooting her new colleagues.

There are two objections to this. One is that the previous episode established that Davros has made his new army from only the finest, purest ingredients, i.e. his chest-muscles and skin. Contamination by the "stink of humanity" (as the Doctor put it when the Emperor's army were brewed from reconditioned gameshow runners-up in X1.13, "The Parting of the Ways") is not possible. The Doctor says as much when he, Donna, Jack and Rose are stuck in a disabled TARDIS (a scene removed from some overseas transmissions), and that this lot are the cream of the crop compared to the tainted mad ones they defeated when Jack first got killed.

The other objection is that they'd already done this idea with Yvonne Hartmann in X2.13, "Doomsday". This isn't to say that the idea couldn't come back every so often, e.g. X7.1, "Asylum of the Daleks" with Clara-as-Oswin, X8.12, "Death in Heaven" with Danny and then Cyber-Brig or indeed the very next episode after "Journey's End", where it's a CyberKing being suborned by Miss Hartigan exactly like Miss Pendragon did in *Dark Season* by Russell T Davies.

And talking of "The Next Doctor" (X4.14)...

David Morrissey is the Doctor

What do we know about the near-future run of episodes? Well, they're taking a year out to do a few Specials rather than a proper series. David Tennant's off to do *Hamlet*. David Morrissey is in the first Special, entitled "The Next Doctor". Tennant's been seen recording scenes for that, but it's a series about time travel. Plus, there were snaps of Cybermen at a snowy Victorian funeral in the snow.

Had they really pulled off a surprise regeneration and recasting? They'd managed to keep Rose's return a secret, so almost anything was possible. As we're going to see in that story's write-up, a lot of people were enthusiastic about both such a versatile and popular actor being in the series and the return to a "proper" Victorian-style Time Lord. However, a lot of others were cautious – surely, this was a bit too obvious for Davies.

Yes, of course it was.

Paul McGann is the Doctor

More from wishful thinking than any coherent evidence, a number of people thought that McGann was unfairly sidelined after the TV Movie

continued on Page 215...

ported 27 planets into the Medusa Cascade, while maintaining their atmospheres and heat. [Presumably, Davros was working out the Reality Bomb program before the Nightmare Child incident and none of the Time War Daleks could follow up on it until now. In one of his rants in 17.1, "Destiny of the Daleks", he outlines a similar scheme. The Doctor notes how 'someone tried to move the Earth once before' – almost certainly a reference to "The Dalek Invasion of Earth", hinting that the whole mining-in-Bedfordshire business was an early attempt (from the Daleks' point of view) at this.]

They also send 200 saucers down to Earth to kill everything manually. [We assume that Clom, Pyrovillia et all are also subjugated this way, yet nobody from those worlds is used as guinea-pigs next episode. Perhaps experience has taught the Daleks and Davros to contain humanity first.]

These Time War-enhanced Daleks have a new 'maximum extermination' setting that obliterates whole buildings in seconds. Their mother-ship is called the 'Crucible'. It looks like a spherical building the size of a planet, with two struts pushed through the equator. [Perhaps even the Daleks, here in 2009, fear George Lucas and his lawyers. Incidentally, the Time War's turning-point was the Daleks capturing something called the 'Cruciform'. Is this the same object? That name suggests a cross-shaped something, rather than a melting-pot for metallurgy or alchemy. Or maybe they just like snooker.[43]] The Supreme Dalek thinks it's in charge, though it tolerates Davros. It talks like the Emperor. [See 4.9, "The Evil of the Daleks"; X1.13, "The Parting of the Ways". If Davros can be redeemed, so can the old Supreme but the title may have been transferred to a new, equally stroppy Davros-sceptic.]

A temporal shift got Caan [following X3.5, "Evolution of the Daleks"] into the Time War, where he achieved the feat of liberating Davros's ship from it. The Supreme Dalek thinks Caan's insane; Davros respects him and trusts his warnings. Caan's casing has been melted open with the dome and front missing, leaving the mutant exposed to open air. He's developed a peculiar sing-song voice and prophesizes that the Threefold God, who's been dancing in the lonely places, will soon show up. [He notes also that when he went into the Time War, he 'danced and died a thousand times'. We doubt 'danced' means what Steven Moffat thinks it means.]

At some prior point, Caan told Davros that the Children of Time would oppose the Daleks. [He came up with useful, testable prophecies earlier, we suppose.] He also claims that everlasting death awaits the Doctor's most faithful companion.

They're hiding their planetary shenanigans by putting the Medusa Cascade a second forward in time.

Planet Notes

• *Earth, Callufrax Minor* [16.2, "The Pirate Planet"], *Jahoo, Shallacatop, Woman Wept* [X1.11, "Boom Town"], *Clom* [X2.10, "Love & Monsters"], *Pyrovillia* [X4.2, "The Fires of Pompeii"], *the Adipose Breeding Planet (Adipose 3)* [X4.1, "Partners in Crime"], *the Lost Moon of Poosh* [X4.10, "Midnight"] and 18 other planets have all gone missing – stolen as part of the Daleks' scheme. Most of these have disappeared from the same point in time relative to the Shadow Proclamation, Earth's twenty-first century. The rest, oddly enough, went missing at points in history. [Donna noticed them – we will see later that this is not a coincidence.]

Callufrax Minor was presumably orbiting Callufrax [itself now within Zanak after a similar scheme (see "The Pirate Planet" and **The Big Picture**)]. It is, according to the readout, unpopulated, with a 27% OLB atmosphere, and is 62137 kelixes big and weighs 100 297.5 gaafs. Jahoo is only 41293 kelixes but 500 835.3 gaafs. It's also got a population of zero.

[Whether the removal of its twin planet, Clom, adversely affected the orbit of Raxacoricofallapatorius is unclear. The Blatherean, cousins to the Slitheen, came to Earth shortly thereafter in *The Sarah Jane Adventures*, but didn't mention anything about this.]

History

• *Dating.* It's a Saturday. The Daleks abscond with Earth at 8.00am, when it's light outside. [In light of the spin-offs, it's after Tosh and Owen died (*TW*: "Exit Wounds"), but before Maria Jackson left for America. This puts it in the school summer holidays – but, from the ephemeral evidence of how people are dressed, leaves on trees and so on, possibly right at the end, so perhaps the first week of September.

[In the alternate world of "Turn Left", the stars vanished when it was late enough for Wilf to have a bonfire, and so probably after he'd grown every-

What Were the Strangest Online Theories?

continued from Page 213...

and deserved a second, proper go at the part.

Quite how this would be achieved, and whether he would be followed by Sylvester McCoy, was unclear. McCoy had been in the previous *Doctor Who Confidential* wearing a polar-exploring jumper, which looked like a clue.

On the other hand, *Doctor Who* was now as big as they hoped it would become in 1996, and McGann wasn't really doing much at the time. He did eventually return to the fold for the 50th anniversary. Meanwhile, bookmakers were accepting odds on Robert Carlyle, Alan Davies and James Nesbitt as the new Doctor, despite Tennant and Morrissey having already been out on location for "The Next Doctor". Some online ideas even handled that, with the Doctor regenerating for half an episode then de-regenerating back into Tennant as the reset button is pressed (see below). Some posited that the "Threefold Man" was three different incarnations of the Doctor superimposed. It made more sense than what we got, but it was a bit too *Babylon 5* even for Davies.

Davros is the Doctor

Oh, the irony! The Doctor's greatest foes were created by an evil future Doctor, who behaves in this way because his personal time-line says he must. No wonder the Daleks were so easy to adapt into time-sensitive warriors, if they took his DNA as their baseline.

That this storyline had already furnished us with the Valeyard from Season Twenty-Three is no matter – all futures of the Doctor are contingent. However, we've now seen young Davros (X9.1, "The Magician's Apprentice") and (probably) a young Doctor (X8.4, "Listen"), and they weren't the same kid.

Donna is the Doctor's Mum and so is Rose

Anyone female, benign and mysterious will at some point be guessed to be the Doctor's mother. It's the law.

Although the majority of daft notions about the possible future developments start in the *New Adventures*, the biggest continuity-change they made is the one BBC Wales emphatically junked: the idea of Time Lords being born grown-up via a genetic roulette-wheel called the Loom. No, Time Lords have – or had – the TV series tells us, babies and childhoods and parents. The Doctor mentions being a kid of 90 in "The Stolen Earth", after a meet-

ing with an unorthodox daughter showed up, so maybe we were being set up for exactly this. Even though many recent episodes had contradicted the TV movie, it wasn't officially erased (certainly not while there were copies of the DVD unsold), so the Spock-like "half human, on my mother's side" gag could still be in play. So where is she? Maybe "Donna" Is short for "Madonna".

Donna seems to have some affinity with the TARDIS and is the focal-point of a lot of curious coincidences. On the other hand, Jackie commented in "Army of Ghosts" (X2.12) that Rose was becoming more like the Doctor and, in "Turn Left" (X4.11), she pretty much did his job. Why else bring her back?

As it turns out, Rose's contribution to the story was getting the Doctor shot, asking continuity questions then disposing of an extra Doctor... but come the big Golden Jubilee episode, Billie played a coquettish piece of Gallifreyan technology based loosely on Rose/Bad Wolf. In the same shed where this took place, we saw someone who may have been the Doctor as a child and two people who seem like parents (that was in "Listen"). More to the point, we have someone widely thought to have been the Doctor's mother in a later Davies episode, but we'll come to that in X4.17, "The End of Time Part One").

Donna is a TARDIS

We've seen already that ideas and entire plots from the 90s *New Adventures* line were being reallocated as and where the programme's bosses thought appropriate. If *Human Nature* could be remade with *TV Comic* scarecrows, anything was licit. Why not grab an idea from the BBC Books follow-ons from the *NAs* and have a companion become an embryonic TARDIS that can walk?

No, really, they did that. Compassion, AKA Laura Tobin (actually the real name of a real Met Office / BBC weather forecaster, amusingly), was introduced in *Interference*, a two-volume novel by one Lawrence Miles (we're guessing *About Time* readers will be acquainted with him), as a citizen of a culture that absorbed a cultural matrix telepathically (or something), as part of a splinter group of a cult called Faction Paradox. They'd been mentioned earlier in a Miles novel, *Alien Bodies*, wherein the assembled Higher Powers were attending an auction of the future Doctor's corpse (so not a bit like X7.14, "The Name of the Doctor" then), and

continued on Page 217...

thing that was going to grow there. Assuming that the date is the same across all universes, the best way to avoid discrepancies between series is to have Maria leave at the end of the holidays and Rani to arrive at half-term in late October – but then why wait for a new headmaster until then? A camping holiday in Cornwall for the Jacksons when preparing to move to a new country is perverse, but emotionally comprehensible.]

Richard Dawkins is alive, well and willing to go into TV studios at a moment's notice to point out very obvious facts about the universe. [Business as usual for him, but more realistically a job for Sir Patrick Moore (X5.1, "The Eleventh Hour").]

This Dalek incursion of Earth is very much out in the open. Their flying battleships strafe New York and their ground forces round up humans on the street, willing to annihilate entire buildings when people resist them. Contact with the Prime Minister's plane is lost amid the fighting.

The Analysis

The Big Picture ("The Stolen Earth" and "Journey's End") It's a team-up story, pure and simple. You have now got two spin-off dramas from *Doctor Who*, explicitly targeted at different audiences, so they need to be tactfully introduced for anyone who has only seen *Who* or is loyal to one spin-off but not the other. (Sort of: the advent of Martha as a *Torchwood* regular meant that they had special child-friendly re-edits of the episodes on BBC2 at 6.00pm, the day after the sweary, gory originals.)

Just as *Holby City* did crossovers with *Casualty* and *Angel* had guest appearances from the *Buffy* regulars, just as Worf showed up on the USS *Enterprise* in *Star Trek: First Contact* despite being a regular on *Deep Space Nine*, just as Steve Austin and Jaime Summers had to each donate an episode of their own series to a three-part story called "Kill Oscar" (in which fembots abduct the head of the OSI) and Detective John Munch has now been in a dozen or so US television series, so the three series being made at Upper Boat and Executive Produced by Davies needed to combine for a (temporary) grand finale.

Davies had negotiated a break. He'd been micro-managing every detail of not just *Doctor Who* but *Torchwood* and *The Sarah Jane Adventures*, to the extent of substantially rewriting all the scripts (except Steven Moffat's and Stephen

Greenhorn's apparently), supervising the edits and dubs and signing off on design features. He was also writing his own scripts and being an impresario, while single-handedly banging the drum for fantasy television in Britain, gay drama, children's television, Welsh writing and the entire history of *Doctor Who* before he arrived.

Doing this for one series is difficult enough. Two at once, as Moffat found with *Sherlock*, is a nightmare. A third is beyond anything any television writer ought to be expected to do. Ted Willis, who still holds the record for the number of hours of British TV drama written (at time of going to press) only really had two big series on the go at any one time, and *Dixon of Dock Green* pretty much wrote itself in the early days. Dennis Potter did things as big and ambitious as Davies was doing, but years apart and with the full support of one or more network. Davies had persuaded the BBC to allow him a few months off after the first four years – we'll discuss this in more detail when we get onto the Specials – and was contemplating his own future. It appears from the bumper book of emails, *The Writer's Tale*, that his health was suffering and he had virtually no social life. So four seasons in rapid succession, a few big-event hourlong special episodes and out.

To encapsulate everything that had happened so far (and the original plans had practically every major alien devised for BBC Wales to date), Davies needed a strong plot involving the Time War and the Daleks – but bigger than anything they had done to date. That many ex-companions and agencies (UNIT, the Shadow Proclamation, our Torchwood *and* that of Pete's World) demanded a big-enough threat. Unsurprisingly, the main source is old *Doctor Who* ideas done with 2008's effects and budget. Lots of them, all at once.

This is a mixed blessing. On the one hand, many of these concepts and images were strong enough to capture the public imagination all over again yet, for many viewers, the way they'd done it the first time around (if it existed in the archives at all) would be a bit underwhelming. On the other hand, with the public interest in the series piqued and peaking, a proportion of the viewers would investigate the first iterations of each notion and possibly conclude that the writers had run out of fresh ideas – or, worse, that there is a limit to the potential of *Doctor Who*. Remaking sequences that older fans recall with current techniques and budget is one thing, but redoing con-

What Were the Strangest Online Theories?

continued from Page 215...

another Time Lord had a Type 105 TARDIS that could adopt a human form and walk around and talk, behaving like a person instead of a massively superior Chameleon Circuit (a bit like Melkur in 18.6, "The Keeper of Traken").

However, as BBC Books's story-arc got into a Time War (of sorts), ending with the Doctor destroying Gallifrey (don't worry, it recovered so he could do it again in a different Time War on telly) against some capital-E Enemy or other, but only after the Doctor lost his own TARDIS and fled to fairy-land (see below), whereupon Compassion fully transformed into a TARDIS. Afterward, the Doctor and his misconceived male sidekick Fitz spent the next few books travelling inside her.

Whatever you're thinking about how they got in and out, it's probably right because they didn't spend long talking about it.

Anyway, this whole thing was given a fresh airing when someone noticed that Kylie Minogue's one-story character in "Voyage of the Damned" (X4.0) was called "Astrid". Obviously, that *has* to be an anagram, because nobody would be so crass as to give a space-girl a name that means "star". Except that it wasn't, Davies was and Astrid was just a cocktail waitress from Space. But surely that means that the next companion along has to be a TARDIS, because this idea's too good not to use?

Given the evidence in the previous two episodes and the level of coincidence surrounding Donna, it's as plausible in this context as it ever could be. There is a small detail of how a superior TARDIS is left abandoned when there are a kerjillion Daleks out there looking to destroy them all, but that could be why she was hidden in such an ordinary job and a dull family in Chiswick. And how else did she walk to Strathclyde aged five?

Of course, you can see the obvious flaw in this theory. If you put a TARDIS inside another TARDIS, they land up inside each other in an infinite regression and can barely take off. It happened twice in the past (9.5, "The Time Monster" and 18.7, "Logopolis"), so it must still be true. Besides, if any companion is "obviously" a walking TARDIS, it's Martha. She can walk around the Earth in a year, survive a journey of a hundred trillion years in the Vortex, operate Indigo without any training, steering it with pinpoint precision first go, and use the Psychic Paper – which she'd never seen work properly – to do things the Doctor couldn't (X3.5, "Evolution of the Daleks").

Donna is Romana and Wilf has a Very Special Watch

We last saw Romana, the Doctor's very special distaff Time Lord chum, she took K9 Mk II with her into a tiny pocket universe on the edge of a slightly larger one, to help free time-sensitive lionmen who'd incautiously got themselves enslaved despite clairvoyance and physical strength (18.5, "Warriors' Gate"). K9 said he had specs of the TARDIS, if she had an afternoon free to build one. With the barriers between universes collapsing, perhaps getting out of E-Space became easier.

In the books, she'd come back and become President of the Time Lords, regenerated into a Flapper and now was utterly cynical and anti-Doctor. (It was to escape her conniving that the Doctor blew up the TARDIS and travelled to Avalon, which is a *totally different* Arthurian alternate universe from the one in 26.1, "Battlefield", and with the Brigadier, Fitz and Compassion.) But if the Romana we saw on telly was back, in a different body, how did the Doctor not know?

Obviously, there was a Chameleon Arch involved and Sylvia isn't really Donna's mother. That's why there's such antipathy between them. It's not an unreasonable theory, but it ignores the elephant in the room – everyone knows that Catherine Tate is massively busy and will be leaving next week. On the one hand, we'd been told that one of the Doctor's posse would die, and that Donna would undergo a huge loss. On the other hand, we could confidently predict that Davies wouldn't bump off a popular character, so a regeneration could send the series off in a new direction as and when it returns.

Crucible = Cruciform and there's a Time Lord on each of 27 planets

The Doctor didn't mentally feel any Time Lords other than himself (X1.6, "Dalek"), because they were on planets stolen by the Daleks. This is evidently why those planets, and only those, were taken and why the Doctor's TARDIS arriving was the cue for Earth to go. The Daleks want closure, and that means hunting down any Time Lord they can find. That two planets are shown on screen to be uninhabited need not concern us.

It's also odd that we heard of a piece of Time Lord ordnance called the "Cruciform" last year (X3.12, "The Sound of Drums"), and now we have a "Crucible". Could they be one and the same?

continued on Page 219...

cepts simply to make pretty pictures that look like Great Moments in *Doctor Who* but serve no other purpose is petty. It can look as though the current executive producer is getting territorial. This time around, they get away with it by the skin of their teeth.

The fan theory that the hexagonal TARDIS console was intended for six operators (mentioned in one of Gareth Roberts's *New Adventures* novels) was one of Ed Thomas's guiding principles when redesigning it in 2004 (even though Peter Brachaki apparently intended the exact opposite, and tried to make it ergonomic for one person). We saw last time that the main image of the stars winking out was a reworking of Tom Baker's last episode (18.7, "Logopolis"), but here we have a re-visit of the idea behind "The Dalek Invasion of Earth" combined with the central concept of "The Pirate Planet". In the former, the Daleks were drilling to the centre of an enslaved Earth, to extract the core and replace it with a giant engine; in the latter, a hollow world with a warp-engine engulfs entire planets, and mines out their wealth before they're compressed and set in gravitational alignment to create a time-eddy. The last victim of this scheme was the planet Callufrax, so Davies has tipped us the wink (unlike X11.10, "The Battle of Ranskor Av Kolos"). Another Douglas Adams quote comes in the way the bees fled Earth's imminent destruction, just as the dolphins did in *The Hitchhiker's Guide to the Galaxy*. Yet another Adams-related detail is the plan to destroy all matter, which Davros apparently outlines in "Destiny of the Daleks".

Davros himself is now allowed back into the series. The problem had been that he got all the good lines, reducing the Daleks to repeating catch-phrases and being cannon-fodder. Davies had made every effort to restore them to their former brilliance and make each individual Dalek an unstoppable threat. In this story, he was the necessary component of the Daleks' return to power but not trusted by them one inch – a situation we had seen in 21.4, "Resurrection of the Daleks" and 22.6, "Revelation of the Daleks" (in which Davros lost his remaining hand, hence the claw we see here). He had then led one of two separate Dalek races from within a carapace (25.1, Remembrance of the Daleks"), but this story seems to have been an opening salvo in the Time War, so they could afford to restore Davros to his iconic original appearance (more or less).

The Daleks move Earth a second forward in time: this odd concealment tactic stems from "The Face of Evil" (14.4), but has an earlier provenance – it's in a 50s SF novel, *Stepsons of Terra* by Robert Silverberg. It's a plot device that Davies is very fond of himself; it's a crucial detail in his *New Adventures* book, *Damaged Goods* and was how the Sontarans hid the true mechanism of ATMOS (X4.4, "The Sontaran Stratagem"). The sequence of the TARDIS being transferred to the Crucible looks enough like the start of Season Twenty-Three (23.1, "The Mysterious Planet") to be plausibly a reference. The Shadow Proclamation resemble the Oracles from *Angel* Season One, except that they don't live under the Post Office. Their HQ looks like a Narn Listening Post in Quadrant 14 in *Babylon 5*, but both seem to derive from a 70s Roger Dean poster.

As many people noted, growing a second Doctor from a severed hand with the aid of some freaky energy closely resembles the sequence in *Carry On Screaming* where Jon Pertwee, as Scotland Yard's scientific advisor Doctor Fettle, places the finger the prehistoric giant Oddbod dropped inside a tesla coil and creates Oddbod Junior (who then does origami on the hapless boffin). If you're British and over 30, you can practically recite sections of this film; if not, just note that the plot is recycled as X7.12, "The Crimson Horror".

Oh, Isn't That...?

• *Richard Dawkins* (himself). Known to most older *Doctor Who* fans as Lalla Ward's husband (at least, at time of broadcast), but he's also professor of Public Comprehension of Science. He is reliably controversial when theologians get his goat (which is almost hourly). What exactly an evolutionary biologist is doing on a talk show arguing about astrophysics isn't clear.

• *Paul O'Grady* (himself). Afternoon talk show host, comedian and former drag queen. He is usually funnier than this. He used to be "Lily Savage", and as such hosted a revival of notoriously naff gameshow *Blankety Blank*.

• *Michael Brandon* (General Sanchez). Dempsey of *Dempsey and Makepeace*. Some reports say he was considered to play Van Statten in X1.6, "Dalek".

• *Julian Bleach* (Davros). He was in *TW*: "From Out of the Rain". Before that, he had been the Monster in the ITV adaptation of *Frankenstein*.

What Were the Strangest Online Theories?

continued from Page 217...

The Crucible is Shada and John Major's in it.

On the analogy of the Daleks using stolen Time Lord technology – specifically a PoW camp resembling a bottle bank – as their weapon in "Doomsday" (X2.13), it was suggested in some quarters that the Crucible might actually be the mysterious Time Lord penal colony Shada, from the famously unfinished Douglas Adams story from Season Seventeen. This is where the High Council kept all the worst criminals in history in stasis. Its location was kept hidden by a method a bit baroque even by their usual standards: a sacred book that over-rides a TARDIS when the pages are turned within its temporal field.

On the face of it, with all the offstage Time Lord weaponry we've been hearing about (and more to come) and the peculiar arsenal with which the seventh Doctor availed himself in Season Twenty-Five, this isn't too silly an idea. Where it got alarming was when one home theorist decided that one of the cosmic miscreants at large in this ship might be Meglos, the Last Zolpha-Thuran.

For those of you who unaccountably skipped Season Eighteen's lowest ebb, Meglos is a modulated light-beam that has a rest-state of a large cactus but can – with a suitable host – transmogrify into any form. It spent two episodes being played by Tom Baker, with occasional green skin and spines, in order to steal a... well, we won't dwell on the full stupidity of the plot, but it was possessing a bank-manager from England in order to wear the Doctor's new waistcoat and jacket. The nerdy Human host, called "George" in the novelisation, was, with hindsight, a dead ringer for future Prime Minister (and former bank-manager) John Major. Meglos making a comeback was a fan-joke for decades, especially after the Macra popped up in "Gridlock" (X3.3), and – as we'll see – it almost happened in "The Lodger" (X5.11).

Leaving xerophyte shenanigans aside, "The Stolen Earth" was about recruiting a team of former companions and their associates, so it makes an aesthetic sense that Davros would counter them with a Legion of Super-Baddies, like the 70s Top Trumps cards that had Annie Oakley and Sherlock Holmes against Omega and the Giant Spiders of Metebelis III. The ACTT union had denied us a season finale of the Doctor's mental force against Genghis Khan, a Wirrn, a Zygon and Lucrezia Borgia back in March 1980, but it could still work!

Osterhagen Anagrams

People had fun working out where the name "Osterhagen" came from. One bright spark pointed out that it was a combination of two Nobel laureates, Carl Richard Hagen, co-discoverer of Higgs Boson, and George Oster, Mathematical Biologist at Berkeley (who had the Oster Lab named after him). Somehow, therefore, high energy particle physics and Game Theory as applied to birdsong were combined to make some kind of UNIT super-weapon. Others were more taken with the fact that the letters E, O, R and S are in it and attempted anagrams involving "Rose". There aren't many that make sense. Other, non-Rose anagrams include "ghost rage" (maybe the Cybermen will come back, or the Gelth).

In fact, this wasn't a fruitless line of inquiry as apparently Davies made the name from "Earth's gone". At least one person guessed this but asked what use it was as a clue, since we already knew it was gone.

The Reset Button

"Turn Left" ended with everything having gone as wrong as it could possibly go, but Donna nabbing a Do-Over by travelling back in time and getting hit by a lorry. The previous season finale ended with time running backwards to exactly a year before, just before everything started going as wrong as it could possibly go, but in a different way.

Surely, with a situation where everyone on Earth knows about aliens and the massed might of UNIT failed against the Daleks, the only possible option for future stories where the general public don't know about all this is another such cop-out. Doctor Who without Yeti-in-the-loo stories is unthinkable, yet if everyone knows to call UNIT or Torchwood or the Shadow Proclamation or the Alliance of Shades or the Doctor's mobile phone, there's no point in having secretive aliens attempting sly takeovers of an unwary populace. There's going to be a reset button somewhere.

So what would it be? Maybe the whole last few episodes are a bad dream and Donna's still inside the CAL mainframe (X4.9, "Forest of the Dead"). Perhaps, with Dalek Caan having rescued Davros from a time-locked Time War, he and all his Daleks will be sucked back into it if the Doctor reverses the polarity or something. What if the Osterhagen Key is a rewind? Surely they couldn't be planning

continued on Page 221...

X4.13: "Journey's End"

(5th July, 2008)

Which One is This? Justice League of Penarth. The big companion team-up continues as Mickey and, er, Jackie show up to help save the multiverse and Donna acquires super-powers.

Firsts and Lasts Exit Donna as a companion. And (it appeared) Davros as a villain. And the Spare Doctor as something in the middle. It's not a good day to have a name beginning with D, is it?

It's chronologically the last we see of Rose and Jackie. Yes, we see them in the opening minutes of 2005 just before this Doctor regenerates (X4.18, "The End of Time Part Two"), and Billie Piper will be back in a different role for the big birthday bash of 2013 (X7.15, "The Day of the Doctor"), but here's where the story ends. It's also the last *Doctor Who* appearance for Ianto Jones and Gwen Cooper. Weirdly enough, it's the first time we witness a Time Lord experience a regeneration but emerge with the same body and persona.

This is the very last episode produced by Phil Collinson. From now on, we'll witness a giddying flurry of producers and even the executive producer credits will start getting complicated.

It's also the last time to date that the Daleks have a good old rampage. Under the next showrunner they'll be reduced to offering tea, lying around dying, milling about not doing a great deal, being washed away in a tidal-wave of sewage and getting shot by Movellans as a puddle argues with them. In fact, apart from Matt Smith's last two stories (where they are almost completely incidental to the plots but periodically get to fly around blowing up masonry and yelling at the Doctor), this is pretty much it for a decade (X11.11, "Resolution" had one doing its forlorn best to make up for lost time).

Former *EastEnders* regular Shobu Kapoor was in "Dimensions in Time" and then in *Doctor Who*, rather than the other way around, which is novel. And, although everyone seems to have forgotten this of late, we get our first female Doctor.

Watch Out For...

• The apparent cop-out of the regeneration-that-wasn't allows for the story's ending to make what sense it finally manages, *and* allows the grand finale of Matt Smith's tenure – but in a way

that contradicts this and "The End of Time" (X4.17/18). The Doctor wastes a regeneration so he can land up apparently unchanged, which is what less-observant viewers thought was happening with Romana in 17.1, "Destiny of the Daleks".

• Everyone's come to the party with an anti-Dalek weapon, and they all go wrong. Instead, the day is saved by Donna's 100 wpm typing. This gives this unwieldy cast something to do and – by virtue of the newly-forged Donna-Doctor getting all the doubletalk – allows Jackie to take over the comic relief undercutting at the end.

• Freema Agyeman does an excellent job with the small, understated moment where she realises that the girl on the screen is the elusive Rose that the Doctor kept banging on about. Likewise, Noel Clarke has perhaps the most practice of anyone on board in making the most of a supposedly-important-but-small part and consequently does very well with his meagre ration of lines.

The Continuity

The Doctor He actually undergoes a regeneration per the fatal Dalek shot from last episode, but uses the regeneration energy to 'heal' himself, at which point he physically dumps the excess regenerational pixie-dust energy into a matching 'bio-receptacle': his still-alive hand in a jar, severed in "The Christmas Invasion" (X2.0) and returned by Captain Jack at the end of Series 3. [So is the whole "changing bodies and minds" bit about regeneration at all necessary? The idea here is that it patches up a Time Lord's mortally wounded body and only *then* switches them into a new form. Why, under normal circumstances, bother with the latter if it's avoidable? Rose's sudden reappearance has nothing at all to do with the Tennant Doctor wanting to keep his mind and looks, we presume. See **The Supporting Cast** for what becomes of the hand.]

The proper Doctor doesn't think he ever needs to say aloud his last sentence to Rose on the beach [X2.13, "Doomsday"], but this is admittedly when he's persuading Rose and Doctor #2 to pair off.

• *Background.* Davros levels at the Doctor the accusation that 'You take ordinary people and you fashion them into weapons'. [Donna brought up the same in X4.4, "The Sontaran Stratagem". While the Doctor doesn't have any easy answers on this score, he experiences a long Donna-esque flashback to everyone who's ever been killed on

What Were the Strangest Online Theories?

continued from Page 219...

to fly really fast around the Earth to make time go backwards?

As it turned out, there wasn't a reset until the entire universe fell into Amy's crack, so "Planet of the Dead" (X4.15) and *The Sarah Jane Adventures* take place in an England where everyone remembered the Daleks and the 26 planets showing up on our doorstep. But then, everyone sort of forgot, even in *Torchwood*'s later iterations. Sadly, flying around the world really fast to make a breach in spacetime will return to haunt us in the aforementioned Easter episode. And Steven Moffat ended every almost season with a reset (the exception, Series 8, had a Christmas coda to fix everything).

his behalf, at least in the new series... There's Harriet (last week); Jabe, (X1.2, "New Earth"); Pete Tyler (X1.8, "Father's Day"); the Controller (X1.12, "Bad Wolf"); Lynda (X1.13, "The Parting of the Ways"); Sir Robert (X2.2, "Tooth and Claw"); Mrs Moore (X2.6, "The Age of Steel"); the Abzorbaloff faces of Mr Skinner, Bridget and Ursula (X2.10, "Love & Monsters", even though Ursula lived); The Face of Boe (X3.3, "Gridlock", although that's a bum rap); Dalek Sec (X3.5, "Evolution of the Daleks"); Chantho (X3.11, "Utopia", another slight slur); Astrid (X.0, "Voyage of the Damned"); Luke (X4.5, "The Poison Sky", definitely not the Doctor's doing); Jenny (X4.6, The Doctor's Daughter" – well, he wasn't to know); River Song (X4.9, "Forest of the Dead" – ditto) and the Hostess (X4.10, "Midnight").]

The Doctor knows before all this starts that a Human-Time Lord metacrisis is a biological impossibility. Consequently, Donna-Doctor knows it as well.

• *Ethics.* When it looks as if either Sarah's Warp Star or Martha's Osterhagen Key might save the universe, at the expense of destroying Earth, he asks his friends to wait and consider alternatives – causing enough of a delay for the Daleks to thwart both plans. The original Doctor risks his own life to have a very good go at saving Davros.

The original Doctor becomes so appalled by Doctor #2's decision to utterly wipe out the Dalek Empire seen here, the blue-suited Doctor is sent off to live in the alternative dimension with Rose forever [this, to him, is a punishment?].

He doesn't ask Donna whether she would rather die as a Time Lord metacrisis or live as a mindwiped human; he assumes the latter has to be better and makes that happen when Donna's mind falters, even though she's pleading with him not to.

• *Inventory: Sonic Screwdriver.* Used to wheel-clamp Jack's teleport yet again [X3.13, "Last of the Time Lords"].

The TARDIS The weaponry developed by this 'Dalek Empire' can depower the TARDIS and literally turn the door into ordinary wood. [We last saw something like this in X1.8, "Father's Day" and that involved the world nearly being destroyed into the bargain.] They refer to this process as a temporal prison; the Doctor indicates it's a chronon loop. Both the Daleks and the Doctor believe that immersion in the Crucible's heart of Z-Neutrino Energy will rip the Ship's dimensions apart if the defences are down.

The effects bear this out; several of the roundels break and the console room starts catching fire. [The door is still closed at this point, so what exactly is happening to the dimensional interface is a matter for speculation. Nevertheless, whatever Z-Neutrino energy is, it's sufficiently destructive to melt through dimensional barriers. Presuming the Doctor remembered to leave it on, whatever technology the Daleks are using overrides the HADS (6.4, "The Krotons", etc.).] Mind you, none of this stops Doctor #2 from dematerialising and repairing the Ship good as new in about five minutes.

The TARDIS has basecode numerals; extracting them would normally take some time. Fortunately, they've been loaded into K-9.

Here the Doctor uses the TARDIS to literally tow Earth across space, with a tractor beam of sorts, to return it to its rightful place. In doing so, we're given confirmation of an old fandom theory that a TARDIS should have six pilots, one for each side of the hexagon. The Doctor gleefully assigns Sarah, Mickey, Rose, Jack, and Martha to five sides, and keeps the last for his new other self.

[A famous missing scene had the Doctor give his human self a chunk of TARDIS coral to grow another one. Donna-Doctor even suggests a way to speed up the process, by shatterfrying the plasmic shell and modifying the dimensional stabiliser to a foldback harmonic of 36.3, which accelerates growth by the power of 59. There was some question about whether it should be portrayed as so simple to make another TARDIS; the sequence was filmed but cut for time.]

The economy-pack Doctor makes an anti-Dalek device from odds and ends left over from fixing the TARDIS.

The Supporting Cast

• *Doctor #2.* [Yes, that really is his official name from Davies's scripts.]

The excess energy siphoned into the Doctor's severed hand, combined with some Donna-ness when she touches its container, creates a new individual who grows from the hand out. [Of course it does.] In enthusiastic defiance of every previous Doctor-doppelgänger story, the duplicate Doctor hasn't any clothes on when created. [See, for example, 15.2, "The Invisible Enemy"; 2.8, "The Chase"; or, heaven help us, 18.2, "Meglos".] Fortunately, the Doctor's blue suit is on hand [with a maroon T-shirt under it, as originally planned for X3.1, "Smith and Jones"].

He's such a 'complicated event in time and space', Donna heard his recurring heartbeat before he was "born" [last episode]. One of the consequences of his "birth" is that Doctor #2 has some of Donna's characteristics; this manifests itself in shouting "Oi!" rather a lot and doing the neck thing. [The genocide maniac part, it seems, isn't inherently human or Time Lord, but the choice of this blue-suited individual.] As such, #2's body looks like David Tennant and is human, at least to the extent of having only one heart. This icks him out. It's expected he'll age per human norm.

He seems reasonably happy to be packed off with Rose at the end, and whispers something in her ear that delights her. The proper Doctor thinks that his genocidal actions are Very Naughty Indeed; Doctor #2 doesn't seem worried about it.

• *Donna.* Quite fancies the idea of being hugged by Captain Jack. She's taken aback by the sight of a nude Doctor, though not absurdly so.

The Ood Doctor/Donna prophecy [X4.3, "Planet of the Ood"] foretold Donna's transformation into the Doctor-Donna. [It's strongly suggested that Dalek Caan manipulated the timelines to bring Donna and the Doctor closer together, although we're not told what *exactly* this means, save for vague hints that it wasn't a coincidence that Donna sought the Doctor out after "The Runaway Bride", or even where precisely she parked her car in "Partners in Crime". Either way, it would seem that owing to Dalek Caan's schemes,

Donna becomes...]

• *Doctor-Donna*: a fusion of a Time Lord mind with human instinct and insights, as created when Donna touched the Doctor's severed hand and absorbed some of its latent regeneration energy. This is catalysed when Davros electrocutes her synapses [so he finally manages to 'kill' someone the Doctor cares about, while bringing about his own destruction but good]. Transformed into a 'human biological metacrisis', the Donna-Doctor can make connections the normal Doctor could never have imagined. Her Gallifreyan tech-savvy, combined with 100 words-per-minute, results in a virtuoso display of button-pushing, making the Daleks behave like remote-controlled toys.

As such a metacrisis isn't meant to exist, Donna's mind starts giving out while she's pondering ways to fix the chameleon circuit. She thinks it'd be rather fun to meet Charlie Chaplin.

In possibly the most terrifying companion ending since "The War Games" (6.7), the Doctor saves Donna's life by walling off her memories of him, the TARDIS and their adventures – forcibly reversing her back to the Donna we see in "The Runaway Bride" [or rather the parody version that Lance claimed her to be], only interested in cheap lager and blokes. The Doctor leaves Donna with Wilf and Sylvia, with a stern warning that they can never reveal the truth to Donna for fear that she'll 'burn', and after giving Sylvia an earful about her shameful treatment of her daughter.

• *Rose.* When the stars started dying around Pete's World, owing to the Dalek gambit seen here, Rose and company developed a Dimensional Canon that's enabled her to cross back to our reality. Eventually, the proper Doctor asks her to keep track of Doctor #2. After a moment of reluctance, she accepts (i.e. snogs) the blue-suited version and waves off the TARDIS.

• *Martha.* Still with the Medical division; her serial number is 56671. She heads off with Jack at the end, chatting – on his suggestion – about plans for continuing to keep Earth safe.

She knows enough German to be shaken when the custodian of the Schloss thinks she's worse than the Daleks for planning to use the Key. [Alternatively, this is a residual TARDIS translation facility. Something like that must be at work for Vicki, Steven or Nyssa to get by in their new lives after leaving the Doctor. Unless they didn't.]

• *Jack.* His immortality [X3.11, "Utopia"] lets him recover from a Dalek blast. He salutes Sarah

How Can Anyone Know About the Time War?

Once, there was a Time War, the last and greatest. So immense was it that beings unable to stand outside it were part of all that was changed and knew naught of it – but others, more powerful or just ancient and strange, knew of it while it raged. ... at least, that was the story we were told. Some of that was from the same sources that prefigured what we saw and heard in the official account, so it was given credence. One such chronicle was related by a bard from Abertawe in a book of tales for children to be told at the midwinter feast. It tells, in part, of two earlier Time Wars, if such a term obtains, one between the Halldons and the Eternals and another named the Omnicraven Uprising; both ended by the suzerains of Gallifrey. It relates how President Romana sought peace and did negotiate a truce with the Daleks yet this was shattered by the Etra Prime Incident. The tale, though the details were but few, indicated that the Lesser Species were oblivious whilst Higher Species intuited and divined that matters of great moment had altered reality again and again in eternal strife between Harmony and Purity. It became a tale for feast and fire, though the embers of the war itself were cold; men spoke of where giants had walked the stars, and everything sounded like the start of *Noggin the Nog*.

If you go looking for anything about this stuff on telly, you're up a gumtree. The stuff in the 2006 *Doctor Who* annual wasn't overtly contradicted on screen (although the re-use of "What I Did in My Holidays by Sally Sparrow" puts it in doubt as a canonical source) until 2013. We got a reference from the Shadow Architect that the Time Lords only linger in the "myths and whispers of the Higher Species" (X4.12, "The Stolen Earth") and Jabe couldn't believe that the Doctor was real (X1.2, "The End of the World"). That's about it. The Time War's main impact has been in the Doctor's apparently *ex cathedra* assertions that certain types of story we used to get (especially in the 90s books) are off the menu, or, to put it less contentiously, that the nature of reality has been shaken up and settled into a new alignment less "kind", less conducive to the Doctor's former modus operandi and ensuring that Parallel Universes can't be visited.

We've been presented with a new normal that includes a Time War in the Doctor's past and all sorts of novel features, such as the Shadow Proclamation, Fixed Points and beings that feed off aborted timelines. (The Trickster's malign Time Beetle in X4.11, "Turn Left" or the Weeping Angels

would have been conceptually bold in 1989, but both in rapid succession is remarkable, even without the Reapers from X1.8, "Father's Day" showing up as well.) The natural tendency among viewers has been to assume cause and effect, that the Time War and how it ended summoned these changes into being. It seemed logical, as this is how all previous Time War stories had panned out (including the one in the BBC Books version of the Doctor destroying Gallifrey to save the outside universe). Once forever stopped changing, it seemed to these beings as though the past had always been the way it was.

Not much that's said or shown to us flatly contradicts this. As a self-consistent account of what happened, it remains available even after the less-interesting depiction of bombs and zap-guns aimed at Arcadia. Actual, incontrovertible support for this account is – of necessity – hard to find and much of what the Doctor tells us when Davies is putting words into his mouth is deliberately cryptic and vague, with evocative Neil Gaiman-ish names of unbroadcastable horrors such as the Nightmare Child, the Never-Weres and the Neither-Nor.

This description of Weirdmageddon would, inevitably, look wrong on television, if not laughable or disappointing. The nature of reality altering is less immediately gripping than children fleeing masonry and laser-bolts. The two are not incompatible, but the recent decision to show the effect of it on Gallifrey has tended towards the latter. Oddly, for a writer who talks a good fight about using time-paradoxes as a first resort, Steven Moffat's version of the Time War was more akin to *Star Wars* across history than what Russell T Davies seemed to have had in mind, a war *for* time using altered history as a weapon.

Any attempt to reconcile the version of the end of the Time War we've had throughout this book and the last with any of that or what we saw and were told in X7.15, "The Day of the Doctor" and X9.12, "Hell Bent" is going to be provisional at best. Maybe it was a deliberate choice to make the off-screen adventures between the end of the old series and the resumption in Cardiff literally unimaginable, bleak and conceptually boggling but these books are all about making such anomalies manageable.

At this stage in the Doctor's story, we are able to ask a few pointed questions with some hope of

continued on Page 225...

223

upon meeting her. He and Mickey have a teasing banter going [completely unlike their last on-screen meeting in "Boom Town", as if they've met more often than we ever saw]. Somewhere along the line, he's learned to recognise a Warp Star. He doesn't trust UNIT anymore [we don't know if it was the Key or if he's been dubious for a while].

His mind wanders slightly at the prospect of three Doctors...

• *Wilf.* He's deeply unhappy about Donna's mindwipe, plaintively saying that she was better with the Doctor. He doesn't blame the Doctor for what happened, promising that he'll look after her. He salutes the Time Lord from his doorstep [and next appears in X4.17, "The End of Time Part One"].

• *Sarah Jane Smith.* She and Davros recognise one another from when the Daleks were first created [12.4, "Genesis of the Daleks"], but she's oddly silent when Davros calls the Doctor a genocidal monster. [She witnessed the Doctor having doubts about blowing up the Dalek hatchery; if anything, she was advocating that he not hesitate.]

Despite expressing a dislike of Torchwood's use of guns last episode, Sarah Jane here has no problem giving Jack a Warp Star – which she brought along – and standing by as he threatens to destroy the entire Crucible with it. A Verron soothsayer gave her the item. [They seem to have got along quite well; this is presumably the same one who gave her the puzzle box from *SJA:* "Whatever Happened to Sarah Jane?".] Said Warp Star is a warpfold conjugation trapped in a carbonised shell. She claims her adopted son, Luke, is 'only 14' [figuratively speaking; he's only months old].

She knows, somehow, that Daleks shoot anyone carrying a gun.

• *Mickey* [reappearing after "Doomsday"]. His alternative universe gran died peacefully in a comfortable mansion [probably bought by Pete], so takes this opportunity to leave Pete's World for our reality. Certainly, Rose isn't a reason for him to stay there. He's sadder about leaving Jackie than anything else. [In light of what happens when we next see him in "The End of Time Part Two", it might be significant that he departs the TARDIS in close proximity to Martha.]

Mickey and Jackie are both equipped with the Dimensional Jump devices used by the Pete's World crew; Rose refers to their projection unit as a Dimensional Cannon. Either way, they're only working right now because of Davros's reality

bomb. The outer design hasn't changed very much [since "Doomsday"], although the Cybus Industries logo style isn't so evident. They have a half-hour recharge in between uses. [No such limitations hindered Jackie and Rose before, but these gadgets don't seem to need an external power source. Given that X2.5, "Rise of the Cybermen" established that energy doesn't work consistently in the two universes, it must be that very differential that powers them.]

Mickey says that they work by ripping a hole in the fabric of spacetime [though whether this refers to their power source or the transport mode is up for debate]. Jackie's device can, apparently, home in on Mickey's one.

• *Jackie* [back from "Doomsday"]. Has reached the point where cross-dimensional travel and toting a hefty zap-gun appears routine rather than bewildering. Her son [she was pregnant with him in "Doomsday"] is named Tony. She makes no mention of Pete. Her main complaint is being stuck on a beach in Norway when it's her day to do the school run.

• *K-9* [joining us from *SJA:* "Invasion of the Bane"]. He's briefly released from his task of sealing off a black hole so it doesn't destroy Earth, then goes back again.

UNIT is responsible for the Osterhagen Key, an emergency suicide device (criteria: if the expected suffering of the human race from alien invasion outweighs survival) for destroying the entire planet from five stations scattered across the globe. Station One for the Key is German, 60 miles from Nuremberg. There's another in Argentina. Station Four is in Liberia, and Station Five is in China. [In terms of geographic dispersal, it would seem practical to have a station somewhere in Oceania, but we can't help thinking of the zeeeee bomb placed at the South Pole in 1986 – 4.2, "The Tenth Planet" – and what an odd place this was to deposit a hefty nuke.]

Inserting the keys into three stations explodes a series of 25 nuclear warheads scattered through the Earth's crust. UNIT protocol says that once three stations are online, they ought to detonate the warheads immediately; nevertheless, Martha first contacts the Daleks to demand their surrender. [The one time we can really imagine UNIT contemplating using this was during the Year That Never Was – but, it might not have been set up yet. Perhaps Martha's report on this year to

How Can Anyone Know About the Time War?

continued from Page 223...

getting answers. The main feature of the account we're going to try to piece together here is that all the conjecture and supposition we'll allow is from what is said or shown on screen, not fan-lore, astrophysics or comparison with the many other Time Wars in earlier fiction. The version in the 2006 Panini *Doctor Who* annual is there, available as a guide to how we could piece this story together, but even this attempt falls apart.

We'll also impinge on things that need whole essays to themselves but, to keep this one under novel-length, we're going to have to rely on the Eric Saward-era standby of promising to "explain later". The anomalies between what was the stated case in 2009 and later stories *will* be vigorously examined and partially resolved, but to settle what Davies stories said on the question we're asking now we'll have to just flag up problems concerning mutually-exclusive Rassilons, Daleks from Vulcan and Clara's school being put into Special Measures, then move on.

There is, therefore, a discrete section of the Doctor's past called "The Time War" and it had consequences for him but not the universe at large (at least, when we rejoined his adventures in 2005). We're told that the Time War has been sealed off and "time-locked" (X4.12, "The Stolen Earth", reiterated in "The Day of the Doctor"), making the final version of the chronology inaccessible. The death of Davros in the first year of combat was a given, unalterable by anyone from outside (until it wasn't). What does "time-locked" mean? Is it the same as being sealed off from the rest of the universe?

The Doctor finally addresses this in X4.18, "The End of Time Part Two" when explaining to Wilf how a magic diamond can leave a dimension that is inaccessible from ours and home in on the noises in the Master's head. His account is that the Time War is like a bubble and only things that were already outside the bubble (or inside, it isn't clear) can get in (or out) and that the Master's Morse-code "V" signal was somehow implanted by the President retroactively to allow the High Council (inside the bubble) to get out by way of the Master's head (outside) and send a White Point Star. This is so confusing that the drastic rethink at the end of "The Day of the Doctor" has overwritten it in most people's minds but it's still there, unresolved. Yet both the Doctor and at least one Dalek were at large in the normal *Doctor Who*

continuum as Series 1 began. Moreover, right from the start of this phase of the series, we had beings such as the Nestene (X1.1, "Rose") and Jabe aware of what the Doctor was and why this was remarkable.

Because the Doctor is (altogether now) the Last of the Time Lords. They aren't there any more. No more parallel universes (except by fiat of the Bad Wolf), no mental traces for the Doctor to pick up on, no protection from Reapers and Time Rifts... they aren't just preoccupied or not answering calls because they've got a war they're still fighting, they are no more. Well, all right, we now know that they aren't *really* extinct, but even the most powerful beings around believe what the Doctor believes at this stage – and if this later turns out to be erroneous, they would always-already have known, being time-sensitive (or friends of such beings). The *one thing* anyone who knows about the Time Lords at all knows is that they are in the past tense.

Calling whatever the decisive weapon was "the Moment" seemed to hint that it was a time-related entity rather than just a big bomb that impersonated Billie Piper. As we find out that it was never used we have no way of knowing which it was but given what we know of Omega's other toys (25.1, "Remembrance of the Daleks") and that the Doctor spends the best part of three lives thinking that he has destroyed his home world, and that this was the one as-yet-unused weapon the Time Lords hadn't tried, this wasn't just an explosive. (A name like that suggests that it does something to time, like the hypothetical prevention of all time travel ever again or something weirder. That's not quite what we're led to believe was about to happen – or cease to happen – in that barn on the Last Day.) Nonetheless, its effects seem limited to the immediate vicinity of Gallifrey as the Doctor sincerely believes he used it, and yet the universe is still a going concern after he regenerates. So, more curiously, is he.

Spatial metaphors seem unavoidable when people discuss this topic. Even the High Council of Time Lords, whose technical vocabulary might be expected to have more fluidity, make some odd statements in the opening sequence of X4.18, "The End of Time Part Two". The last day of the War is spoken of as the "far edge" and the people who, from their perspective, were half a billion years dead were discussed in the present tense as being

continued on Page 227...

Geneva when she enlisted convinced them to build it. Alternatively, such a development might have been why the Brigadier quit in 1976 (20.3, "Mawdryn Undead"). We'll pick up on this in **What Happened in 1972?** under A8, "Dreamland".]

Martha promises the Doctor to figure out how to get rid of the Osterhagen Key, somehow. [The Key was teleported from her hand and presumably destroyed when the Crucible blew up, but there's still a load of nuclear bombs to disarm.]

Torchwood Before Tosh died [*TW*: "Exit Wounds"], she developed a Time Lock to seal off the Torchwood Hub from the rest of the universe, in case of overwhelming attack. It automatically activates when a Dalek enters the Hub but doesn't survive the force of one exploding. [If that's all it takes to break a Time Lock, maybe Caan's shell got damaged rescuing Davros by the same method.]

The Doctor recognises Gwen Cooper's features [a gag about Eve Myles playing Gwyneth in X1.3, "The Unquiet Dead"] and writes the similarity off as 'spatial genetic multiplicity'. [Davies calls it "an echo and repetition of physical traits across a Time Rift", whatever that may mean. Perhaps it's like Clara jumping into the Doctor's time-line (X7.14, "The Name of the Doctor"). Perhaps someone looking like Terry Walsh did it, which would explain why the same face recurs across 1970s stories in various galaxies and time-periods.]

The Supporting Cast (Evil)
• *Dalek Caan*. After rescuing Davros from the Time Lock, he's been planning a Dalek downfall. Seeing so much of the timelines made Caan realise what the Daleks did 'throughout time and space', and he's [somehow] manipulated events to bring about the Doctor-Donna. [See **Bad Wolf: What, Why and How?** for the extent to which Caan can be considered an extension of the Bad Wolf – which in turn explains the bizarre ending of X4.11, "Turn Left".] He keeps predicting the Doctor's "most faithful companion will die". He denies being solely responsible for the coincidences [see "The End of Time Part Two"].

• *Davros*. Here Davros levels the Doctor with the accusation that *he's* the one who keeps turning innocent people into weapons, and that *he* is in fact 'the Destroyer of Worlds'. [Well, whose fault is that? Who made the Daleks and caused a Time War? Davros used to be better at debating than

this.] Dalek Caan told him quite a bit about Rose, but not Martha.

Planet Notes
• *Felspoon*. It has mountains that sway in the breeze.

The Non-Humans
• *Daleks*. Oh look, rels!

Their/Davros's big plan this time is the Reality Bomb: essentially a big device to destroy everything ever, save the Daleks insulated from it. The 27 planet alignment flattens Z-Neutrino Energy into a compressed 'single-string', although even the Doctor can't keep up with the technobabble after that.

Briefly, it works by cancelling electro-magnetic fields. Funnelling it through the Rift will send the destructive signal to every universe ever. [With hindsight, this appears to be the plan Davros mentions in passing when he's brought up to speed after his "death"; "Destiny of the Daleks".] Happily, Donna scotches the plan by closing all the Z-Neutrino relay loops with an internalised synchronous back-feed reversal loop.

The Crucible is the Dalek command ship, powered by Z-Neutrino Energy. [These engines visually resemble the nuclear storm drive from "Voyage of the Damned".] They call thier teleport system a 'transmat'. [The standard *Doctor Who* term since 12.2, "The Ark in Space" and popular across the cosmos (e.g. 22.4, "The Two Doctors".]

The Supreme Dalek can order a temporal prison – some sort of chronon loop, which looks like a blue circle of light – that can hold a TARDIS. When paired with a quivery tunnel, it physically moves the TARDIS through space [see the start of 23.1, "The Mysterious Planet" for something so similar, it must be a decision by the production team to echo it]. It also powers down the console room [this must be an overall effect, as Jack's teleport goes down as well] and turns the police box interface into ordinary wood. Similarly, they have holding cells with forcefields that look like vertical shafts of white light. The Supreme knows that Time Lords are connected to their Ships.

In Germany, the Daleks shout "Exterminieren". [Maybe they used Babelfish rather than learning German.]

Dalek weaponry can be blocked by 'Phwor. Macrotransmission of a K-filter wavelength in a self-replicated energy blindfold matrix'. You can

How Can Anyone Know About the Time War?

continued from Page 225...

in the "core". What's curious about this entire exchange is the way the people in charge of deciding how history is supposed to have gone seem so powerless to alter the past or future of their own race. (That said, they always were, hence the Matrix in 14.3, "The Deadly Assassin".) It's one big Fixed Point and is always happening "now" for them.

Fixed Points, from what we know of them, are the tent-poles of all other causality. It is only once the Doctor has dared to interfere with one that Gallifrey is able to leave its stalemate and start moving forward in its own history and, more to the point, materialise near Earth. The former change is indicative of the idea we're going to be discussing of "read-only" chronology, the latter of the "separate continuum" concept of the Time War. Just to muddy things further, we got a throwaway line in "The Day of the Doctor" suggesting that the contretemps between the Narrator and the Advocate is taking place just before the General starts grumbling about 13 Doctors showing up and arranging for the planet to duck the Dalek firepower and skip dimensions – a completely different direction to what we see in the skies over Chiswick. In fact the Soothsayer talks about the Doctor stealing the Moment as a recent event, ten minutes ago or so, so we can insert "The End of Time Part Two" inside the Gallifrey sections of "The Day of the Doctor".

If we're going with the idea that there was a war that had, in earlier iterations, entailed rewriting history but that somehow all they landed up breaking it so that no further revisions were possible, we have a reason why both sides ended up launching plans to destroy the entire universe and relocate. Faced with living like the rest of us, with immutable pasts, they have one option to make the future different and live without this literally interminable war. What this fails to explain is why either or both, when freed from time-lock, carry on with such apocalyptic schemes. And then decide not to.

The history in "Hell Bent" seems very different from that in "The End of Time". If both Donald Sumpter and Timothy Dalton were playing the same character as Richard Mathews in "The Five Doctors" (20.7), we have to suppose that the plan to destroy the universe and ascend to a higher plane of consciousness was abruptly abandoned after whatever happened to free them from their temporal prison, and Rassilon regenerated after dying of embarrassment at getting everyone's hopes up. Or something. This is harder to account for than the changes in the outside universe. There is one way it could have happened and that's the rewriting that first the Great Intelligence and then Clara did on the Doctor's timeline (X7.14, "The Name of the Doctor", which stops short of showing anything from this period). It could include the Time War, but running into a hitherto-undisclosed Doctor in a cave was as much of a surprise to her as to viewers. She didn't summon him into being, however tempting an explanation this might be, because if so then the Doctor's past before the rewrite had the Time War unstopped and, therefore, still running (or everything else ended). The Moment can bring back two future Doctors to intervene in their past, but that intervention was always what had happened, they just misremembered it because of a regeneration and the usual post-multi-Doctor-story amnesia (cf. **Why Not Mention The War?** under X3.13a, "Time Crash"). If the later Doctors' participation in this grim incident was *always* part of it, then we have a lot of contradictions. If not, we're in a hell of a mess. (See **What Just Happened?** under "The Day of the Doctor".)

Whatever the case, the Doctor doesn't dare amend a Fixed Point event on Mars until after the time-lock has been ruptured by Dalek Caan ("after" both chronologically and within his own time-line, so for once we don't have to ask which is more significant). This move also broke down the barriers between alternate timelines, allowing Rose, Jackie and a lot of Cybermen to slip in. Although the boundaries seem to heal up, it's hard to account for Gallifrey and a diamond making guest appearances in our universe unless saving Adelaide somehow ripped the sticking-plaster off the wound. Was such a move even possible for him prior to Davros being hauled out of his apparently settled fate? It's hard to say, as the Doctor's decision to intervene on Mars comes out of nowhere with only the precedent of Caecilius ("The Fires of Pompeii"; X9.5, "The Girl Who Died").

Davros praises Caan for doing what no other entity could have managed, entering the Time War from outside and freeing him from his inescapable death at Elysium. As we have conjectured and supported with on-screen evidence, Caan became a Bad Wolf to do this, something the Doctor fears.

continued on Page 229...

ABOUT TIME 2008-2009

freeze them on the spot and make them go round in circles by using the biofeedback shielding to exacerbate the Dalekanium interface, thus inculcating a trip-stitch circuit-breaker in the psychokinetic threshold manipulator. [We promise that this is the silliest that Davies's technobabble ever gets.]

History Charlie Brown is apparently definitely fictional in the *Doctor Who* universe [see X7.8, "The Rings of Akhaten" for The Great Pumpkin].

Here, humanity is made to witness as planet Earth is towed back into its proper place in time and space, with a whole lotta of shaking along the way.

The Analysis

English Lessons
• *Topping* (Adj.): Another 1920s superlative, like "wizard" (op cit), although the Donna-Doctor seems less sarcastic in using it than her usual self.
• *Charlie Chester* (n.): wartime comedian ("Cheerful Charlie") turned Radio 2 DJ in the 70s and 80s. He did slightly embarrassing topical doggerel and the radio equivalent of small ads.

German Lessons
• *Albtraum* (n.): Nightmare
• *Zur Hölle mit dir*: to hell with you.

Oh, Isn't That...?
• *Shobu Kapoor* (Scared Woman). Was Gita (pron. "Gee-ah" wiv a glottal stop) in *EastEnders* for five years in the 90s (and, therefore, "Dimensions in Time" – poor dear). Gita and Sanjay had a clothing business that wasn't going so well, and she sort-of became a kept woman of local big-shot Richard Cole (or, to us, the Chief Clown from 25.4, "The Greatest Show in the Galaxy", Ian Reddington). Then it got complicated as only a Walford family can, and the business declined into a market stall. But you may have seen Shobu Kapoor in *Bend It Like Beckham* or, more recently, her biggest role as the put-upon wife in the global hit *Citizen Khan*. (See also the essay with last episode for loopy theories attaching themselves to her.)

Things That Don't Make Sense ("The Stolen Earth" and "Journey's End") Let's agree that the big blue-white concentric circles emanating from

that Cardiff fountain across the cosmos are a narrative convention (otherwise, we'd have to ask how something travelling at about 30mph is reaching the TARDIS). As advanced science can look like magic, we'll assume there's a good reason why two dozen of the planets in the Reality Bomb are from 2009, but three others are from the rest of history.

We can forgive the "coincidence" of the Daleks using Earth as the last vital component of their Reality Bomb, because they're showy like that. We'll presume that with all the technology we've seen the Adipose, Abzorbaloff and Pyroviles muster, they've formed anti-Dalek cadres on their worlds that we simply don't hear about. We'll accept that although the Doctor-Donna (either of them) is a very plausible candidate for the Hybrid that everyone freaks out about in Series 9, the Doctor/s just kept that childhood terror to themselves. That Harriet being cut off results in a screen full of static, even though it's a computer and not a television broadcast, is also no matter – Daleks and static sort of belong together.

But many puzzles remain, such as why it's very clearly established that we start on Saturday, just before 8.00am GMT, and yet *The Paul O'Grady Show* is on. That went out Monday to Friday at 5.00pm.

Richard Dawkins, evolutionary biologist, isn't the obvious choice to explain astrophysics to the public at large in our universe but, as Professor Dawkins pontificates about stars in a totally different timeline as well (X5.13, "The Big Bang"), maybe this is a systemic change, like teddy bears replacing golliwogs. But how can he, or anyone, see stars with all those big luminous planets in the way?

Torchwood agent Gwen Cooper can't identify the hostile aliens croaking "Exterminate!" Quite aside from the small matter of them contributing to Torchwood London's downfall (while Ianto worked there), has she really been investigating aliens for this long without hearing about the Daleks? Her not knowing what the Doctor looks like is only marginally less daft (he's why the agency was formed, and Jack is obsessed with him). And after 130 years of collecting alien tech, the best anti-Dalek strategy they can think of is Kalashnikovs and gurning?

Luke Smith says Earth's transference into the Medusa Cascade "felt like some sort of cross-dimensional spatial transference". He know what

How Can Anyone Know About the Time War?

continued from Page 227...

Not even the Master dared to absorb the vortex. Caan died several times and landed up insane. (See **Bad Wolf – What, Why and How?** under X1.13,"The Parting of the Ways"). If this is the scale of mental and cosmic force needed to get in, how much effort was required to seal it off in the first place? If we're including Gallifrey in the Time War, as "The End of Time" indicates we must, this is impossible unless there are other Time Lord-like beings. The whole point of them is that they're unique. As with Omega (10.1,"The Three Doctors") and the Master of the Land of Fiction (6.2, "The Mind Robber"), it would be impossible for anyone sealing the War off from within to escape. The main precedent is the Time Lords impounding planets within Time Loops (15.3, "Image of the Fendahl"; 15.6, "The Invasion of Time"), but they did so while outside the target area.

Who from outside has that sort of ability? Not the Shadow Proclamation, for certain, as they even think the TARDIS is something out of a myth. The Eternals? We haven't seen them in the new series and – if they are the same ones from 20.5, "Enlightenment", which is only an assumption – this is more responsibility than they might be expected to carry. We have heard nothing about the Guardians this century (but see **Should the Trickster Have a Dead Bird on His Head?** under A7,"The Wedding of Sarah Jane Smith" and **What Do The Guardians Do?** under 16.1, "The Ribos Operation"). No, as with the Fixed Points and the Reapers, it looks as if the way things are now is just the way things are, a side-effect of the laws of physics rather than someone's imposed rules.

Continuing in this vein, the fact that the Doctor uses the passive mode ("The entire War is time-locked") makes responsibility for the process of locking as vague as possible. We might surmise that he uses "time-locked" as an adjective, like "the sink is blocked" or "the lake is frozen" and that this is a state of nature, a way spacetime behaves after a lot of abuse, rather as we were suggesting that the much-discussed "Fixed Points" were that way as part of how time behaves under certain conditions irrespective of the events that happen therein and the possible consequences. We'll assume you've recently read **What Constitutes A Fixed Point?** under X4.2,"The Fires of Pompeii".

The bubble metaphor is suggestive but the Doctor almost immediately denies that it's that simple. In every conversation on this topic the description is of that aspect of the Time War that is most relevant at the time, not a complete technical exegesis. "The End of Time Part Two" seems to imply that Gallifrey is already in a different, locked-off dimension and re-enters our continuum near to Earth. That's obviously not what happened in "The Day of the Doctor" and if it could just teleport without a baker's dozen time-vessels, it could have been a short war. If we take both accounts at face value. then the War was a bubble universe and then Gallifrey hid inside another bubble within that. A lot of the Doctor's activities after he finds that he didn't wipe out his folks seem contradictory. He spends some time after X8.12, "Death in Heaven" trying to "find" Gallifrey simply by punching in 10-0-11-0-0 x 02, even though he spent a thousand years on Trenzalore babysitting an interdimensional crack that might have let the planet back into this dimension.

If it's in a pocket universe it's not in ours, by definition, but it might be within it: Romana quipped that the people who invented Matroishka dolls unwittingly made a model of the cosmos (17.4, "Nightmare of Eden"), so the Gallifrey-universe might be embedded within ours but not materially part of it (and by "ours" we mean the Doctor's, if not exactly that of people who watch his adventures on telly). If even conventional planets could be undetectable to the TARDIS by being shoved a second out of phase ("The Stolen Earth"), then locating an entirely different reality would be hard. Just as well, or the Daleks would have done it. However, the conditions on Gallifrey within this bubble haven't changed, it would appear. The normal Gallifreyans are all frozen in time, living the same instant.

The Time Lords, who may well be aware of the change, can't do anything (except one, who sends out a message to stage-whisper "Doctor Who" through a handy crack in reality, and then replies to Clara asking Santa for a new Doctor by whooshing through some Orange Sparkly Pixie Dust). If the Time War is itself a bubble, from the perspective of the Doctor who survived it, then this bonus package of regenerations has traversed two such barriers - assuming the Russian Doll model. But if whatever they did with 13 TARDISes and a few archive clips took the planet not just further "in" but altogether outside, it would be just as accessible/inaccessible from any version of the cosmos. That's good, because the crack would work just as

continued on Page 231...

one of those feels like, would he? He was grown in a jar and, apart from one transmat journey to an orbital Laser-Quest game (using quantum entanglement that caused Rice Krispies to fall from the sky), he's not been anywhere beyond Ealing.

Years on, Harriet Jones is convinced she was right about the Sycorax because aliens might one day invade when the Doctor is absent. To guard against that, she spends much time and trouble to create a last-ditch safeguard... by helping Mr. Copper put together a subwave network to, er, track down the Doctor. Is that really the best idea's she's got?

The Doctor hazily recalls that someone tried to move Earth "once before". Actually, it was twice, if you count the Time Lords doing it in "The Trial of a Time Lord" (Season Twenty-Three), and the Daleks doing it in "The Dalek Invasion of Earth" (2.2). He is getting forgetful in his old age.

Earth has been moved a second out-of-phase and into the Medusa Cascade. The plan to Dial-a-Doctor is to shove phone messages out into all of space and time using the Cardiff Rift, and hope that only the Doctor can receive them. But if Martha's SuperPhone – the one that can call anywhere in time and space – can't reach him, how is this more likely to succeed? And although the Cracks in Time from Series 5 (X5.3, "Victory of the Daleks", etc.) might have removed both this and the next story from history, there remains a long period and three whole seasons of *The Sarah Jane Adventures* where everyone on the planet has the Doctor's number logged in their phones. The number is listed as belonging to "the Doctor", so he's going to get inundated with calls to book appointments or renew prescriptions.

Sake of argument, we can accept that 27 planets will form a Reality-Destroying Machine when combined. But, what kind of software has the Shadow Proclamation got, if it can figure that out without anyone having programmed it in? And why does it not consider the "cold cases" until someone suggests it? How does anyone know that it'll end with the 27th planet going AWOL? (And the computer has a glitch, unless it really is "CALUFRAX MINORr".)

The vista from Martha's window and the next shot of Daleks over Manhattan are curious. The view she has is that from Hoboken, New Jersey. However, unlike the most likely site of UNIT HQ, the Sheraton, this window has a lot of roads

between it and the Empire State Building – as if they have paved over or dammed the Hudson River, and built a lot of new offices and roads. (Before you ask, we checked: it's not the view from the UNO building on FDR Avenue, which might have worked.) The UNIT general gives Martha a Navy salute while in an Army uniform. Jack does too, while wearing an Air Force coat.

Project Indigo, a Sontaran device, has a readout that produces numbers from 0 to 9. Jack needs to know the two alternating digits in the fourth column to activate his Vortex Manipulator – they are 4 and 9. Sontarans have three digits on each hand, so why are they using Base 10?

It's left unclear how much knowledge carries over from erased timelines, as Donna remembered Rose's "Bad Wolf" warning for the Doctor, but Rose here boggles to learn that Jack can be killed and resurrected, that Martha Jones exists, that the Daleks are behind the stars going out and that Dalek Caan/Bad Wolf is behind everything. She knew all of this and more in "Turn Left".

The music gets all Richard Clayderman, the Doctor and Rose run towards each other, then she sees a Dalek and everything goes slo-mo. Rose completely forgets to use the dirty great anti-Dalek gun she's been hefting across the dimensions. The whole regeneration brouhaha, however, only occurs because Rose distracts the Doctor just long enough for the worst shot in the history of the Dalek race to zap him at point-blank range and only wing him, triggering the regeneration that causes The Undoing of the Daleks. Caan's fiendish plan hinges on there being a cross-eyed Dalek on that street at that moment.

We now know that with some spare regeneration energy and a handy body part (i.e. a "bio-matching receptacle"), you can grow a duplicate Time Lord, but – in a show that keeps bemoaning the Doctor being the last of his race – this option never gets mentioned before or since. (This facility would also have made the backstory and plot of 13.5, "The Brain of Morbius" very different. A leg in a fishtank would have worked just as well, and only looked slightly sillier.) What with this and "The Doctor's Daughter" (X4.6), the "Last of the Time Lords" could easily make friends.

Tosh's time bubble seems clever, but if it's really sealed off from the rest of the universe, then no time should pass either for Gwen and Ianto with respect to the outside world. (Or vice versa – the dialogue isn't clear on which way around it works.

How Can Anyone Know About the Time War?

continued from Page 229...

well for Daleks. Or, at least, some of them.

Caan redeemed Davros from the Time War's enclosure and thereby causes all the subsequent Dalek stories we see, but it isn't counted as part of the Time War. This is partly because no other Time Lords are at large, partly because they always lose (except X5.3, "Victory of the Daleks"), but even with their constant returns to overwhelming force they never make any big inroads and apparently never make any attempt to rewrite the past. It may be that they can't move in time the same way the Time War model ones could (see **What's Happened to the Daleks?** under X1.6, "Dalek"). The generation of Daleks we see now seem to be derived from the "pure" ones who formed the New Paradigm, even though these templates have apparently gone: the impurities these ones wanted gone might include the refinements introduced to their gene-code for Time War purposes.

Let's examine all the things we *know* escaped from within this allegedly sealed off, time-locked War. There's the Doctor and his TARDIS, obviously; they were permitted (or condemned) to survive the end of the war by the Moment, as far as we can tell. There are a few of the peculiar time-slice paintings, including one depicting/preserving the Fall of Arcadia; these came into the hands of the enigmatic Curator, who "acquired it in remarkable circumstances" (which we are invited to interpret as the Doctor grabbing them in a future life but let's not bet on it). There was the Metaltron, the Dalek that survived the end of the Time War and landed up in a collection (X1.6, "Dalek"). There was a Void Ship full of arrested Daleks and the Cult of Skaro (X2.12, "Army of Ghosts"). There's Davros, rescued by Dalek Caan ("The Stolen Earth"). Skaro was, apparently, rescued (X7.1, "Asylum of the Daleks") then, for some reason, rebuilt (X9.1, "The Magician's Apprentice"). Oh, and there was the Sisterhood of Karn (13.5, "The Brain of Morbius", A16, "The Night of the Doctor", "The Magician's Apprentice" and X9.12, "Hell Bent") who were eyewitnesses to the war and persist in the neighbourhood, visitable by Colony Sarf but popping in on the High Council when they feel like it. And there's Gallifrey and Rassilon's magic bling.

We were led to believe that the time-locked war was inside a bubble and inaccessible because it was in another dimension. Suppose, for a moment that the lock, however it is applied, means that no subsequent rewriting of the war is possible after

this. The Doctor's reluctance to save his people by intervening in his personal past is simply because it's physically impossible. This being the case, the Time War might be a patch of spacetime where nobody, even a Time Lord, can make a difference to events (see **How Does Time Work, How Did It Use to Work and What Changed?** under 9.1, "Day of the Daleks"). Rather than being a separate continuum, as is usually assumed, it might just be a selection of "read-only" moments. These moments seem to be happening in normal space and noticeable to less-advanced space-travellers (this is the basic assumption of "The Night of the Doctor"), but mainly consist of conventional warfare (as we saw in "The Day of the Doctor").

In these circumstances, the Doctor (and presumably all Time Lords) are no better off than any non-Gallifreyan time traveller and can participate in events in the past but not alter them. This accounts for the war being directed by a Narrator and a Soothsayer. And yet, at a crucial moment, the Narrator can chuck jewellery at a handy patch of wasteground near where the Master has mass-produced himself and this isn't as impossible as any other intervention. In many ways, the Narrator's actions in that episode are puzzling, just as the War Doctor's are in his one proper appearance. They are unable to alter anything except when they can. The Narrator can send the *Doctor Who* theme through the vortex as a meme to bug the Master-to-be for all his lives but, it turns out, this was always the case so nothing has changed. (Apparently. Missy neglects to mention anything about it and a later version of the earlier incarnation of the Master claims that his "little problem" is gone after he escapes from Gallifrey; X10.12, "The Doctor Falls".)

The idea of the Time War as set in concrete even for the Doctor would have worked until the Doctor just happened to bump into the Clambake Kid at the start of "The Magician's Apprentice". If such a change to (or at least participation in) this kid's journey away from the Dark Side by a Doctor who wasn't supposed to exist can happen, then surely all points in the Time War are amenable to change. If he's only making sure that it all happens as it "should" in the set-in-stone timeline, how could there have been a Time War at all? (This also applies to visiting Skaro at the start of "Asylum". Even just witnessing events made the Daleks expend energy and change position in combat.)

continued on Page 233...

We're assuming a variation on the Kerensky device from 17.2, "City of Death".) How the light's getting in is another matter – if time slows down a lot *inside* the bubble, the light's wavelength ought to red-shift towards being heat. If time goes syrupy *outside* the bubble, they'll get microwaved by sped-up visible light. Or perhaps the Hub moves into interstitial time (9.5, "The Time Monster"), "the gap between *now* and *now*", in which case there ought to be no light unless there's a passing Chronovore.

"Exterminieren" isn't quite the correct German for "Exterminate" in the imperative. And, as we've been very good and not grumbled about it for 13 straight episodes, there is rather an overabundance of explanations for bees disappearing than the opposite, mostly involving destructive agricultural pesticides and mite parasites. Turning genuine ecological concerns into comedy is something the show's been doing since "Planet of the Giants" (2.1), but it still grates.

How is Jackie Tyler, that's *Jackie Tyler*, able to fine-tune a device that sends people across the immeasurable gulf between realities, so that she can jump 30 feet into the next room? (Perhaps it was keyed to Mickey's gadget; if so, she reprogrammed it in a hurry). And with the End of All Possible Universes impending and Jackie hurtling across dimensions, where's Pete? Jackie and Jack never met on screen, but they don't bother introducing themselves.

The Daleks are testing their Reality Bomb. It either works or it doesn't, and – like the Manhattan Project – the only way to test it is to use it. As it destroys all matter, there isn't a second go. So why are they zapping people in groups of 20? And the Daleks fail to notice Jackie's escape from that, so their security is no better than in 11.3, "Death to the Daleks" (when one lone Dalek on guard self-destructed in shame when Sarah escaped, leaving nobody watching the remaining humanoids). Besides, if they set it off inside the Medusa Cascade a second removed from everything, won't it just destroy the Medusa Cascade and 27 planets?

Davros proudly displays his gaping pecs as proof that he bred the new Daleks out of his own tissues, making them "pure" Daleks. Let's pretend for a moment that the events of "Genesis of the Daleks" have been altered, and Davros *isn't* the result of chemical warfare or atomic discharge, that the Daleks *aren't* supposed to be bespoke

genetic adaptations to a post-war environment when the Thal weapons have made Skaro uninhabitable for Kaleds – and that Daleks *aren't* motivated by hatred of all genes that aren't the ones designed for them.

Even then, the scheme for making a race of Daleks cell-by-cell from his own body wasn't going to happen overnight. Smaller samples could have been biopsied and the Daleks bred the old-fashioned way: in vitro. There is no reason for that much of his chest to still be missing, unless he did it specifically to intimidate the Doctor with how hard he is. Remember, he's twice boasted that he had medical equipment for tissue regeneration ("Destiny of the Daleks"; 21.4, "Resurrection of the Daleks"). As far as we can tell, Dalek Caan rescued Davros (and Davros alone) from whatever pickle he was in with the Nightmare Child, so did the two of them get the Crucible, a new Dalek race and an enormous fleet from the Argos Catalogue?

Nonetheless, Davros has created his Dalek army and the Crucible – well done – and sincerely believes that peace will occur when the only living beings left are Daleks. Has he forgotten *every single Dalek story ever*? We know from "Dalek" (X1.6) that one Dalek can literally start a fight in an empty room, now they're all united in following a loopy plan just because Dalek Caan says so. Dalek Caan, whom they all hate. Dalek Caan, whose prophesies aren't all that much cop – he keeps repeating "one of [the Doctor's companions] will die", even though if the Reality Bomb works, *all* of them will. As it turns out, none of them physically die. Why do the Daleks bother listening to him?

Moreover, the shock twist in the plot is that Dalek Caan has engineered the defeat of his own race, because he has "seen the truth of us" and thinks they are generally a bad thing. Like Sec (X3.5, "Evolution of the Daleks"), another member of the Cult of Skaro, he's decided the universe would be better off without the Daleks at all. To that end he, er, rescued Davros and had him create billions more of them, then manipulated events to destroy them all.

The TARDIS loses all its power in a Z-neutrino cauldron, but the spare Doctor fixes this by pressing one button – while naked. Where does the energy come from? And the newly-made Doctor in the blue suit (a human-Time Lord metacrisis) won't have a meltdown the way Donna-Doctor (a

How Can Anyone Know About the Time War?

continued from Page 231...

The wider point is that the Tennant Doctor told us that such day-trips were impossible.

This brings up the other question we've never really had answered: what are the parameters? If we are to believe the Doctor and Jack (X1.13, "The Parting of the Ways"), all the Daleks left history-as-we-know-it to go and fight somewhere else. If the Time Agency don't know what happened to the Daleks, it must have been immense – Jack's Vortex Manipulator can ferry people a hundred trillion years. It's a big universe, and it lasts a long time, but something as devastating as a Dalek fleet fighting a war for time itself would be hard to miss. The Sontarans were aware of it (X4.4, "The Sontaran Stratagem") and, although they seem to be fairly rudimentary soldiers, they had dealings with Gallifrey (11.1, "The Time Warrior") before invading it (15.6, "The Invasion of Time") and playing the major powers of the cosmos against each other (22.4, "The Two Doctors").

That last incident is intriguing because the cover-story is that the Time Lords destroyed a research station because it threatened them – and the Doctor buys it, at first. The station is described as being run by "Third Zone" governments – who the other two zones might be is a good question, with one obvious pair of answers we'll come to in a bit. (For the rest of it, see **Has the Time War Started?** under 12.4, "Genesis of the Daleks".) The Sontarans have time technology – they can use it for the banal purpose of hiding the ATMOS mechanism – but aren't fully time-sensitive, hence all that Kartz-Reimer malarkey. Like the Daleks in 80s stories, they can visit the past but not alter it; they may not have the ability to recall previous timelines.

The main metaphor that gets used a lot is writing, a tradition begun in the very earliest days of the series (see **Can You Rewrite History, Even One Line?** under 1.6, "The Aztecs"). If, as we have been assuming, any revised chronology creates a branched-off separate reality that also exists in a mysterious *somewhere* that – for want of a better term – we call an alternate universe, is this what happened to the Time War? This was the basic assumption among quite a few fans in the early days of the BBC Wales episodes. The universe where Rose lived wasn't the one where the Time Lords had been active, and the Doctor was cursed with being the only survivor of all that in this new-made timeline. It allowed people to remove other old features of the series and start afresh... until Sarah Jane Smith wandered in and started talking continuity (X2.3, "School Reunion").

Now, it seems, not only are all the old stories back in play as part of this universe's past (and future), but even ones we were told had been erased, such as all Dalek stories prior to "Genesis", (if you're the type of person who thinks the Doctor's intervention there upended his previous Dalek encounters) were around to be alluded to, riffed on and sampled. Although not all of them are described quite as we saw them: in "Asylum of the Daleks" we hear about insane survivors of the incidents on Vulcan and Exxilon – 4.3, "The Power of the Daleks"; 11.3, "Death to the Daleks" – even though there were absolutely no survivors, unless reports of a lone shattered Dalek at the end of "Power" feebly raising an eye-stalk to watch the TARDIS leave are correct. Whether the account Davros and Sarah give of "Genesis" in "X4.13, "Journey's End" matches what was broadcast is moot as we now know that Davros had CCTV and was recording the Doctor's angst to play back and motivate the plot of X9.2, "The Witch's Familiar".)

If we take comments in "Victory of the Daleks" at face value, then the invasion in X4.12, "The Stolen Earth" has been erased from history and not replaced when whatever happened at the end of X5.13, "The Big Bang" took place. Yet Davros is free. This only works if the Time Sensitive survivors are able to take refuge in "our" universe with their memories and abilities intact.

So let's consider who, apart from beings we saw the Doctor explain it all to at various stages, knew about all this. The Nestenes, the Gelth and Jabe were the first to give us hints, back in the Eccleston months, but the next comment was a Krillitane ("School Reunion") who spoke as if he knew lots about the Time Lords but nothing of what had happened to them. Then, apart from sulky Sontarans, not much until everyone shows up at Stonehenge (well, almost everyone) and a similar pile-up at Trenzalore (X5.12, "The Pandorica Opens" and X7.16, "The Time of the Doctor"). It's mentioned in passing that this is what has made the Zygons show up on Earth ("The Day of the Doctor"; X9.7, "The Zygon Invasion"). Then, most recently, the Fisher King (X9.4, "Before the Flood"). One suggestive common feature to these races is a technology, or natural ability, that has no need of complex machinery.

continued on Page 235...

human-Time Lord metacrisis) did, because...

Nonetheless, he's a psychopath who needs Rose to cure him all over again, even though he remembers being the person whom Rose supposedly cured of all that. To defeat the Daleks present, Junior sends some kind of energy pulse back through the Dalekanium shells. Ergo, he doesn't actually kill those Daleks, he just makes their clothes fall off. This somehow destroys all their spaceships (which, fair enough, is likely to kill a lot of the nude Daleks, but see X11.11, "Resolution"). And that's somehow deemed worse than the genuine Doctor making everyone converted into a Cyberman explode when they get their emotions back (X2.6, "The Age of Steel"), barbecuing a schoolful of Krillitane (X2.3, "School Reunion"), sucking millions of conscious beings into the inter-dimensional Void ("Doomsday") or so many other less-than-humane things we could mention while Rose was still with him.

We'll grudgingly accept that Earth is pulled clear across the Universe in normal space in under an afternoon by the TARDIS's lasso of truth, but how is there sunlight on the planet when they're in interstellar space?

The original Doctor announces that they're taking one last trip to Darlig Ulv Stranden, but Rose doesn't work out that he means he's dropping her and Jackie and his spare self off until she steps out onto the beach. A beach whose name she told him originally. It's not as if that place would have slipped her mind, is it?

#

Finally, let's take a look at where Donna ends up. At story's end, she cannot be coaxed (intentionally or otherwise) into remembering her time with the Doctor, or her brain will be toast. Casually spotting the Doctor (here and in "The End of Time Part Two") is okay, but anything reminiscent of their adventures together is a risk. Ultimately, she's triggered in "The End of Time Part One" upon seeing the multiple Masters, just because it's *weird*, not something she remembers. Here are a few of the things Sylvia and Wilf have to prevent Donna from thinking about ever again:

Bees; wasps; any drama set in Rome; anything to do with Pompeii or volcanoes generally; weddings; spiders; Agatha Christie adaptations (so, not having a telly at all in Britain); libraries; diaries; kids called "Josh" or "Ella"; water-pistols; snow; the Thames

Barrier; Cardiff; Buckingham Palace; large beetles; diet pills; satnavs and car engines; garden centres (especially those that smell of bougainvillea); the word "midnight"; Health and Safety; shadows; chicken drumsticks; Linda Evangelista; Evita; albums by Donovan or Dennis Wilson; stars; The Lavender Hill Mob (and indeed any old British film with a police box in it); anyone on Earth who now knows about Daleks; any news footage of that time Earth was hauled through space; films or pop videos where girls do gymnastics to avoid tripping security lasers; squid; Persil balls; Lux flakes; Converse All-Stars; window-cleaners in cradles; Chinese food; rivers; songs...

... and all doctors. Good luck!

We'll assume that all dramas starring David Tennant, Freema Agyeman, Billie Piper, Felicity Kendal or Peter Capaldi, absolutely any of the umpteen Saturday Night shows with John Barrowman and reruns of *ER* are exempt, under the usual rule that stops anyone encountering the third Doctor and mistaking him for popular entertainer Jon Pertwee. This may also be how the Doctor could meet Astrid, McDonnell or Ashildr and not mention their resemblances to performers whose careers he's already mentioned.

We also assume that the frequent materialisations of the TARDIS outside 30 Oak Street, Chiswick, home of Artie and Angie and therefore of Clara Oswald, happen while Donna's off enjoying her newfound wealth. Wilf must tell the Silver Cloak ("The End of Time Part One") to keep quiet about it.

Critique ("The Stolen Earth" and "Journey's End")
And it was all going so well...

This was the Big One, the Season Finale to beat them all. As such, it's aged better than more recent attempts to top this story in scale and clout. We've used the term "high-water mark" a lot in this volume and that's how it seems now, the last time the series had this much money and public goodwill, this much momentum and "institutional charisma" (the term used for NASA in the 60s seems like the best way to explain how the two words "Doctor" and "Who" opened doors within the BBC and Britain in general). There are so many ways that the attention to detail makes this feel special even by the standards of Davies productions before or after. It's bolder, more felicitous and cheekier than even "The Sound of Drums". Technically, as a spectacle and a fast-paced depiction of what the world does when killer aliens

How Can Anyone Know About the Time War?

continued from Page 233...

Beings with this sort of genetic heritage are, therefore, able to know about events in a totally different dimension. Most, like Jabe, know of it as more than a legend but less than a possible experience. Plausibly, if the Doctor went around time and space whinging about his lost world, word would have got out eventually, but then he went around removing all gossip about him (A15, "The Inforarium"). There was a long time between these when the reports of his activities was one of his most potent weapons. Our usual assumption in these matters, which we unpacked in **He Remembers This** *How?* under X1.5, "World War Three", is that some beings can recall events from timelines that were amended out of existence. The majority of the ones we've met have been in the TARDIS at some stage, but it's not exclusively their prerogative. The Doctor subsequently unpicking his reputation from history might not matter to such time-sensitive entities.

So what if the Third Zone was an alliance of these Higher Species who were non-aligned in the Time War? Calling it a "Zone" makes it sound more like a region or place than an ideology. That's not unprecedented. (Think of the Cold War, with "East" and "West" applied, often geographically inaccurately, to countries affiliated to one side or another. Australia isn't "West" of China. If we've got space and time roughly interchangeable from some vaster perspective, it could even be like the "1917 Zone" or "Civil War Zone" in 6.7, "The War Games".) Putting "The Two Doctors" in the heart of the Time War makes a degree of sense, but changes the way we think of the whole category. With this in mind, the continued existence of the Sisterhood of Karn might be more significant than it appears. The Doctor and Colony Sarf are equally (un)welcome, officially, but Ohila is on the Doctor's side against Rassilon the Resurrected. She as good as created the War Doctor specifically to end the Time War ("The Night of the Doctor").

The Moment selected two models of the Doctor from after the time lock had been breached and the Fixed Point altered. This tells us a couple of things: first that the Moment itself, despite seemingly limitless power, can't reach out of a seemingly closed-off war (except as John Hurt's imaginary friend); second, that Doctors who are outside the War but whose time-line extends into it can be reached. These facts, and the persistence of the paintings, the TARDIS and the Doctor, tell us that

the time-seal wasn't put in place by anyone or anything within its purlieu. To do so would be to remove the possibility of ever doing anything "free", not prescribed and pre-ordained, which would make the Doctor's decision to end the Time War something the Time Lords and Daleks alike knew was coming. Perhaps, within the boundaries of the War-that-is-now-the-case, they do and are powerless to do other than what they remember they have to do, but the Doctor would also be fated (at least whilst he was a participant). If he imposed the time-lock as part of his actions on that last day, then he would be within its influence forever.

What we're left with is a messy but just-about viable sequence of events. The Moment settles upon a course of action that requires two future Doctors – casualties of the end of the Time War that's about to come – to intervene and offer an alternative course of action. This ploy results in Gallifrey being frozen in an instant, just before the High Council started their scheme to obliterate reality. One of the two future Doctors has just ruptured time by altering a Fixed Point at Bowie Base One, possibly the trigger that allows Gallifrey back into coterminous time. Shortly thereafter (in his personal time-line), he participates in the salvation plan and then, as luck would have it, gets a tip-off from the Ood that the Master's back. (That tip-off seems to be the result of manipulation by a double-agent on the High Council who is also leaving cryptic messages for Wilf).

The Master is Rassilon's personal cat-flap into real spacetime and, unwittingly, makes a splash by amplifying his inbuilt homing-signal (da-da-da-dum, da-da-da-dum) by a factor of six billion. The entire planet escapes its bubble and pops around for Christmas Dinner. This unfreezes the rest of Gallifrey but the Master severs the link and the Doctor dies, with the traditional post-regenerative block on any information that might lead his next incarnation into paradoxes. That Doctor is blighted by cracks in the walls of the universe, caused by the Kovarian Schism trying to prevent Gallifrey from making a proper full-time return by blowing up the TARDIS.

Most such ruptures are healed but the big one has a lot of force behind it to keep it open, as it's Gallifrey asking if it's all right to come out now. This request is sent across space and time, so we get all the cosmic baddies who attended PandoricaCon

continued on Page 237...

arrive en masse, it begins well and sustains the first episode better than the last two season-finale first-halves. As with "Turn Left", the absence of the Doctor forces the issue and the spread of story-lines across the world never gets diffuse or uninvolving.

Then, about ten minutes into the second episode, the cork's left out of the bottle a bit too long and the fizz goes. It's still fast-moving – it's Graeme Harper, for heaven's sake! – but the script seems to mistake movement for action. Things explode and people teleport, but it's all marking time. Too much of the episode is people locked in rooms, talking. There are far too many flashback montages. For whatever reason, nobody – even those able to swallow the idea of Earth being teleported into the Medusa Cascade and moved a second forward in time to become invisible – can take the Magic Lasso scene seriously, it seems.

This is the last straw for many, but others find their patience drained by the over-long "I will show you your soul" material. It's 2008: we'd had four years of the tortured, lonesome Doctor stuff by now. The public mood, especially among teenagers, was changing. Emo was *so* 2005. Of course, a decade on it looks, retrospectively, a lot more assured and nuanced than subsequent attempts to mine this played-out stratum.

Nobody can fault Davies's intentions. He wanted to make a menace so big that a team-up episode was needed and then have each sub-group's plan to thwart Davros come unstuck, leaving it to the temp from Chiswick to save the universe. He needed something big enough to cause Donna to have to leave but without killing her. He needed a threat so epic that Rose had to be sent back. He needed it to be more than just a lot of Daleks again. He needed to top his first season finale, where the Doctor was spared a terrible dilemma by a companion becoming supernaturally powerful. He needed to top the second, where the cost of saving Earth was forcing his companion to live with her family and never see him again. He needed to top the third, where mobile phones allowed everyone on Earth to join together and help him. So he did all of the above.

The criticism made of so many stories from the 80s or before was that all the effort and thought went into crafting cliffhangers, making the rest of the episodes slightly perfunctory. Something similar can be said here. The build up at the end of X4.11, "Turn Left" promises slightly more than any two-parter can deliver and certainly more than we get. The running strands of "something on your back", "your song is ending", "she is returning" and bees never amount to much. Adding "one of them will die" doesn't help, especially as none of them does in the finished script.

Then we get what looked like a surprise cliffhanger which was resolved by a clever twist, but which sends the subsequent episode down a side-alley. The Daleks come back, with the characters who've met them all messing themselves in blind panic, but they just mill about in suburban streets as if contractually obliged to invade a world they've already conquered. The Doctor's chums all have brilliant plans to save the Earth by destroying it, but get thwarted. All of this is resolved by the Doctor pulling a few levers, the twist being that there are three of him doing it.

The Threefold Man subplot is tonally all over the place. It looks as if we're going to get a new Doctor with some of Donna's mannerisms (and Tennant sells that very well) but then it turns out, when the plot needs a twist and some explosions, that he's half-human and therefore a psychopath. Once that's done with, he stays weirdly quiet when his other two selves somehow take him to Pete's World without him realising. And Rose is supposed to cure him of this because she's human and therefore not a psychopath. Or something.

By now Donna's become part-Doctor and – mercifully – refrains from the whole "wow, I'm female" aspect of that to do something that's written as a comic turn but performed as an audition to replace Tennant. Again, Tate's easily up to the challenge. Both of these new Doctors defer to the original in all things, which seems oddly out-of-character for Donna-with-superpowers or a newly-mortal Tennant Doctor. Many other ex-regulars go similarly awry: Sarah Jane Smith decides that the way to handle Daleks is to throw her hands over her eyes and yell "I'm sorry!" That's not the character of the spin-off series nor the one from the 1970s. As for gun-totin' Jackie Tyler, her one moment of proper Jackie-ness is apologising to Gita (or whatever her name was) before escaping.

But this is Russell T Davies, the man who stopped *Doctor Who* from being thought of as all nerdy and cold. He's supposed to be the king of character-driven spectacle. Just as we're now all supposed to find the earlier series' set-design and special effects risible, we're encouraged to judge the dialogue and motivation of the people in the

How Can Anyone Know About the Time War?

continued from Page 235...

and their friends amassing on a planet from all over history and laying siege to the world for upwards of 800 years. Then they all go away again, as does Gallifrey when Clara asks them to go (because somehow this General takes more notice of her than of the Doctor) and the remaining Daleks are scattered by a show-offy regeneration.

Then the Time Lords take it into their heads to torture the Doctor for information on some terror-weapon he heard about as a kid, but never thought to use before or even mention during the Time War, and this leads them to start intervening in Earth's history. (The script for "Hell Bent" almost perversely makes a point of not asking how Gallifrey unfroze.) They then move their world to the "end" of time, albeit apparently before the Face of Boe dies (see **When (And Where) Was Gallifrey?** under 13.3, "Pyramids of Mars"). By the

end of Series 9, we're almost back to 20.1, "Arc of Infinity". The Time Lords are talking to the mayor of a small colony of exiled aliens in twenty-first century London and the Sisterhood of Karn, who are also talking to Davros's right-hand snake, who is also talking to the Shadow Proclamation and Maldovar (see **How Involved Were the Time Lords?** Under 15.5, "Underworld"). The Doctor can almost nonchalantly take Bill to the middle of a battle between Daleks and Movellans, implied to be part of the Time War, in order to evade a persistent puddle (X10.1, "The Pilot").

That being the case, the real mysteries are (a) how anyone could *not* know there had been a Time War and (b) why it's considered to have ended. Gallifrey avoided the time-lock by not being there when it was imposed, Skaro by Dalek Caan's spaced odyssey. Neither of these developments seems to have over-written the earlier state-of-play.

story by higher standards than, say, "Nightmare of Eden" (17.4) or "Galaxy 4" (3.1). This story doesn't match those expectations. After the previous two episodes, also by Davies, this is especially aggravating. Rose here is a plausible development of the character we left two years ago – albeit a totally different plausible development from the one last week – but she spends most of her time with the Doctor just standing around. Once she's caused the cliffhanger, she's surplus to requirements until they have a spare Doctor to dispose of. It's not just a waste, it's not even merely frustrating, it's a kick in the teeth for all the people who wanted to see her back. (If you are in the minority and *didn't* want her back it's annoying but could have been worse). But it's considered enough that we get to see the Doctor and Rose together, without them doing anything much.

Sylvia never gets her comeuppance. The Doctor goads her a tiny bit but – if this had been intended as closure on a year's worth of episodes about Donna finding her true strength – viewers (especially young, female viewers, the target audience in this phase) needed a more definite rejection of this awful woman from Wilf or Donna. The real problem with the ending is that Donna isn't suffering but everyone around her is feeling bad about what's happened to her. The reason the character came back was at least partly because people enjoyed the original idea of the character, a reluctant participant in the Doctor's adventures

and one who is amusingly oblivious to all the epic stuff routinely happening when he's on this planet. One of the reasons "Turn Left" worked so well was that we got her back for one episode. Resetting the character to this and leaving her might be upsetting for the Doctor, briefly, but the person most affected is Wilf. The problem is partially resolved by bringing these characters back 18 months later and showing that things have moved on but, on first broadcast, we were simply being manipulated into thinking of this as a tragedy by Bernard Cribbins crying.

Cribbins is easily the best thing about this story. It's odd, with so many ex-companions around, that so much of the story assumes that the viewer-identification figure is the ancient, mysterious Time Lord – but for at least some of the story's best moments, it's Wilf who is our eyes and ears. He earns our interest and sympathy rather than just having it conferred upon him for services rendered in earlier seasons. It's obvious Davies loves writing for him and takes Cribbins's suggestions on board. So much else was cut or refashioned but all of Wilf's scenes were kept. In five appearances he's become the soul of *Doctor Who*.

In a Christmas Special, you can just about get away with soul and no brain. This story needs to avoid cheating people who've become invested in the various mysteries they've been carefully seeding for a dozen episodes and it has to make it seem as if the whole enterprise was worth attempting. A team-up story such as this in two episodes, even if both are distended, is too ambitious to do without compromises. Once a certain proportion of the former regulars are in, it gets to the point where it would seem weird that such-and-such is absent and we get insubstantial cameos from Adjoa Andoh and K9 for the sake of completism. It's like Pokemon – gotta catch 'em all.

So, yes, it's a mess, but it's a *unique* mess. They won't get another chance to do anything like this and, now that it's been tried and not-quite worked, nothing quite like it can be attempted until next time they have to cold-start the series after a 16-year gap. The resources aren't there for another story like this, but neither is the level of public indulgence. Only the 50th anniversary story came close, but that had other ambitions. Davies never again had to put the emphasis so firmly on plot rather than character, or expedience over plot and, despite the fanwank levels reaching critical, it's his least self-indulgent script for the series. It's as of-its-time (in production and television grammar, as well as where *Doctor Who* was that year and what Britain was like) as "The Ambassadors of Death" or "Battlefield". We shall not gaze upon its like again.

The Lore

Written by Russell T Davies. Directed by Graeme Harper. Viewing Figures ("The Stolen Earth"): (BBC1) 8.8 million, (BBC3 repeats) 1.0, 0.7, 1.6 million. Viewing Figures ("Journey's End"): (BBC1) 10.6 million, (BBC3 repeats) 1.2, 0.6, 2.7 million. This is the story that got AIs of 91% for both episodes, rising to 92% on the BBC3 repeats.

Repeats and Overseas Promotion *La Terre Volée* (meaning "stolen" or "flying"), *La Fin du Voyage; Die Gestohlene Erde, Das Ende der Reise.*

Alternate Versions In BBC America's efforts to get the second episode down to 42 minutes so they can show more trailers for *Copper*, everything from "Exterminieren" to the TARDIS "you were brilliant" scene goes and Supreme's denial of locking Donna in, then the other Doctor's explanation of why Donna is special (with all the flashbacks), the German woman's rant against Martha, Dalek Caan's last prophesy of the Doctor's soul, the Doctor and Rose speculating on Gwen's ancestry,

the global fireworks display and party and, mercifully, Rose's guess-the-end-of-the-sentence quiz on Daaleg Ulf Stranden disappear (they cut straight from "I could spend it with you, if you want" to the snog). The "Songs of Donna Noble" scene is drastically slashed and the episode ends on Wilf's salute.

Production

• The Series 4 season finale had a lot of functions to perform. It had to tie up the threads not only of the previous 11 episodes, but of the whole series since "Rose" (X1.1). It had to be bigger and have a more substantial threat than before. It had to leave the series on a high so that there would be enough goodwill for the public to stick around for a year with just some specials before the new team took over in Series 5. It had to justify so many returning characters and give them enough to do. But, above all, it had to be doable with the resources available and the time remaining.

Davies battled various illnesses and endless other calls on his time to get this all into two episodes and delivered a first draft that he knew would have to be cut. The Daleks arrived in a space armada that destroyed Parliament, despite new Prime Minister Aubrey Fairchild's attempt to reason with them (as per the priest in the 50s *War of the Worlds* and Solomon in X3.5, "Evolution of the Daleks"). This became people in Cardiff, Ealing and an office in New York looking at screens and hearing Nick Briggs say "exterminate". (The PM's name was reallocated.) Davros got a whole backstory of him in a World War I-style MASH unit resolving to heal his people and getting injured – apparently fatally – in the process. This would, of course, have been prompted by Rose showing compassion for this damaged genius and the conversation about what was said on Bad Wolf Bay originally happened here, to make Davros note how much more intimate this war-veteran Doctor is.

It was a toss-up whether it would be Rose or Penny/Donna who activated the Metacrisis and grew a new Doctor; the hand absorbing regeneration energy was an idea that had been in the back of Davies's mind since "The Christmas Invasion" and might have been how the dying Doctor (and departing showrunner) said a final farewell to Rose, but that was a throwaway idea and bringing it forward a year gave the new-minted Doctor something to do. As the availability of the guest-cast became more complicated various options were in play for if, for example, Billie Piper could only commit to one day, if they could get Catherine Tate to appear as Donna (this was back when Penny was the companion) and so on. Freema Agyeman was pretty much a given, as was John Barrowman, because *Torchwood* Series 2 was being made and the idea for the third series was for Mickey Smith, hardened after several years in Pete's World, to take over from whichever of the regulars would be killed.

The biggest casualty of the budgetary restrictions was the one most people, especially the effects crews, had been itching to do: a multi-alien team-up at Shadow Proclamation HQ. Work had progressed to the point of having Annette Badland record a voice-over as a baby Margaret Slitheen. This version of the scene where the Doctor learns the scale of the crisis was more like the first half of "A Good Man Goes to War" (X6.7), as the Shadow Proclamation were more akin to the Church Militant/Papal Mainframe and had a multi-species army coping with refugees and a long queue of people registering missing planets. The Doctor and Donna were to have been asked to take a number and wait among the aliens (the film version of *The Hitchhiker's Guide to the Galaxy* is the irresistible comparison, but it's fairly universal) until one of the Shadow Soldiers trying to prevent rioting is revealed to be Midshipman Alonso Frame (X4.0, "Voyage of the Damned"), who lets the Doctor jump the queue because he's the Doctor.

Davies found writing convincing dialogue for the Proclamation boss hard, because it was just numbers and made-up words: oddly, though, the version he landed up writing is like what Donna jokingly suggests she was expecting something called "the Shadow Proclamation" to be like (the Doctor replies that the Brotherhood of Darkened Time are the accountants). Removing the Krillitanes, Gelth, Vespiforms, Isolus-spores, Sycorax, Slitheen and "Sisters of the Wicker Place-Mats" (the ones from X1.2, "The End of the World" and X5.12, "The Pandorica Opens") cut hundreds of man-hours and thousands of pounds from the accounting; Russell Tovey's busy schedule did the rest (Alonso was to be the "one of them" who died in some versions). Even fairly late on, the Shadow Proclamation were to have been a more substantial force and the plan for the newly-created Doctor was to slip out of the time-bubble

and get the cavalry in the second episode, building up expectations of a major battle, rather than just him rushing out of the TARDIS and getting zapped.

Davies was given a delivery date of 7th January for the scripts and the Christmas Special was expected a couple of weeks after this. It was increasingly obvious that this was vastly optimistic and there was even talk of scrapping the Special. By mid-December, Davies was getting snarled up in the launch for "Voyage of the Damned" (and the final edits), but was still taking suggestions. Bernard Cribbins mentioned the paint-ball idea in a phone call; Benjamin Cook offered the idea of casting Richard Dawkins as the expert on telly in one of his many emails.

A lot of backstage changes were happening, with indomitable line-producer Tracie Simpson leaving, Julie Gardner starting a slow handover of her various responsibilities to Piers Wenger, Phil Collinson going to BBC Manchester and Steven Moffat agreeing to take over from Davies from Series 5. Plus, on 15th December, Catherine Tate mentioned in passing on Jonathan Ross's chat-show that Tennant wasn't going to do another series after Series 4. In the press confusion that followed, Davies was asked, at the launch of the 2007 Christmas Special on 19th, who ought to be the next Doctor and answered "Hitler". Such was his prestige at the time, he sort of got away with that one. Over Christmas, with a filthy cold, he was trying to finish at least the first episode and opted to cry-off Piper's wedding the next week.

By mid-January, he was on the second episode and still struggling to resolve the ending without adding even more exposition. Permission had been given for this to be an hour-long episode if necessary – Jane Tranter had loved what she'd read so far – but it wasn't entirely finished for the Tone Meeting on 23rd. The end was in place, and copies had been distributed prior to the read-through on 15th February. Davies had to miss that because of chickenpox (and Tennant filled in for Alexander Armstrong as Mr Smith) and was shown a recording made by the *Confidential* team. Seeing this prompted the removal of the Davros flashback. The ending had gone through every possible permutation of Donna and Rose and Doctor 2, with Rose needing to stay in Pete's World because it would be fatal to stay (an idea nixed by the need for Mickey to stay), both women being in the TARDIS when Donna creates a new Doctor or Rose getting that subplot and

ABOUT TIME 2008-2009

Donna being in the Crucible with the Doctor asking Davros what went wrong with his life. An extra week was added to the schedule for Block Nine. Davies used the notoriously wonky online translator Babelfish for the Dalek dialogue.

• The recording started at the Upper Boat on 18th February, with most of the Episode 12 scenes in the TARDIS, before another three days there using the Torchwood Hub set (although on 20th, there was also a revised TARDIS scene for "Turn Left") then a day of both. 21st was the day of the Dalek, and (as was now usual) armourer Faujja Singh was on hand for the gunfire for the big fight. Eve Myles claimed in an interview to have made her performance as Gwen a little less nuanced than in *Torchwood* – we're sure you all noticed the difference. By now, the second series of the spin-off was on BBC2 on Wednesdays and Martha was about to join the team.

Over the weekend Cribbins, interviewed by Alan Titchmarsh about the impending Christmas episode, announced that he'd been asked back to do a bit more *Who*. The last day of TARDISing for a while was the big team-up on 25th and any fears Davies had nursed about the various ex-regulars not getting on were scotched. Fuelled by chocolate Easter eggs (the big ones you get in Britain), the cast got giggly. Tate and Barrowman had devised a bit of business about the Donna-Doctor fancying Jack (some of which made it to the screen). On 26th, the team relocated to Nant Fawr Road for the first of two days inside the Noble house, then on 28th and 29th they were back in the TARDIS set (the latter day was also when the Upper Boat was used as the exterior of the Rattigan Academy in the Sontaran two-parter).

On 28th, Tennant had to lie, cold and nearly naked, on the sharp slats of the Console Room floor as Doctor 2 (the cast took the hint from the costumes and called them "Blue Man" and "Brown Man"). This was followed by Tate's big scene as Donna-Doctor in meltdown. The first take was considered perfect, but she opted for a second and improved it. Next day was a relatively straightforward procedure of setting fire to the TARDIS. This was 29th, the day *The Sun* blurted out the plot of "Silence in the Library".

Meanwhile, the story's principle new character was presented to the producers and cast. Collinson had seen Julian Bleach in a performance of *Shock Headed Peter* (see X10.3, "Thin Ice") and thought that if they ever needed a Davros, he was a slam-

dunk. Davies had similar thoughts when supervising the *Torchwood* episode with Bleach as the Ghostmaker ["From Out of the Rain"]. Neill Gorton had worked with him making the ITV *Frankenstein*. The return of this arch-villain was kept as quiet as possible, with the team referring to "Dave" when they thought anyone might overhear something. However, with Tennant, Collinson and many other older fans taking selfies with Bleach in his buggy, it was hard to keep a perfect lockdown.

• The cast took the weekend off after that, then, on 3rd March the Upper Boat became the vault of the Crucible, with a brief refresher course the day before for the usual four Dalek operators and a first go with the new action-grip hands. The Dalek Supreme was unoccupied, but the lights and head-motions were operated by radio-control. Tate was slightly bewildered to find that not every Dalek worked that way. However, all eyes were on Davros. Bleach found, like his predecessors in the role, that people often forgot there was an actor inside the make-up and lights. Briggs, meanwhile, was having to provide four separate Dalek voices, with a new Top Dalek and the insane, giggly Caan. A second day of this ended with Bleach getting a round of applause for his ranting and countdown.

• The team took 5th to leave the studio and head for Bad Wolf Bay. With tides and daylight hours to negotiate they only had a few hours to get it all set up and done. Most of the long shots came early, so that the cast and crew could stand on boards and not sink into damp sand during close-ups. This scene was the first to use multiple Doctors and a lot of time was spent on getting Tennant and his double lined up properly for the post-production split-screen. On the 6th, Tate performed her wire-work and had a double for the scene of Donna banging her head on the Console.

• The 7th was so hectic that, the DVD commentaries say, someone forgot to remove the back of the TARDIS prop and they literally tried to get eight people into a police box. By now, with all the costume changes for Brown and Blue Doctors, a second double had been called in. Tate also elicited applause for getting the bafflegab speech right first go. Briggs pre-recorded the Judoon dialogue that night, watched by a bemused Piper.

On 8th, Cardiff University's School of Optometry and Visual Sciences became the HQ for the Shadow Proclamation. This sequence had been the biggest casualty of budgetary restraint and actor-availability and casting the Shadow Architect had been one of the trickier assignments. On 11th, *Blue Peter* presenter Gethin Jones took over from Dave Hankinson as one of the Daleks.

• The exterior scenes at the Noble household were, unusually, shot in Hawthorne Road, Pontypridd and later that night the "Camden" location for rioting and Rose's raid on the electrical goods shop was Market Street. The biggest event of the location shoot was on 13th in Penarth. The TARDIS arrived at High Street, Rose arrived at Queen's Road and ran toward the Doctor as Graeme Harper, a driver and a camera operator rode in a Quad Bike – of course – and later a Dalek appeared at the junction of Paget Road. Jack materialised on Arcot Street, which was also where Jackie and Mickey surrendered to the Daleks.

More material of Dalek mayhem was shot the next night at Brook Street, Cardiff, with the paintball scene shot at Plantagenet Road. Wilf's "wanna swap?" was ad-libbed by Cribbins. As might be imagined, Daleks blowing up a house in a street was especially tricky to negotiate and the sightseers were kept well away for their own safety as much as anything. It was, of course, the school Easter holidays, so kids were allowed to stay up a bit later than normal to watch. Over at Castell Coch, pretending to be Osterhagen Station 1, Agyeman struggled to get the German pronunciation right (and was slightly intimidated by the fact that Briggs had nailed it as a Dalek at the read-through).

• UNIT's HQ in New York was, in fact, the Traffic Management complex in Coryton. It had previously appeared as a version of itself in the first episode of *Torchwood*. Permission to shoot there on the night of 16th (Sunday) had been granted conditional on the BBC crew leaving if an emergency arose, as indeed happened, so the night was slightly tense – they could have been evicted at any moment. The next night was where the Dalek tested their ultimate weapon; the Test Area was Alpha Street in Newport, at what's now Mir Steel.

• On 18th, the scenes of Harriet's Last Stand were shot at Michaelstone-le-Pit, near Dinas Powys, a small village of upmarket cottages. Phil Collinson spent much of the night thinking up ways for Harriet to escape; with the entire story subsequently stated in Moffat episodes not to have

happened, Davies now suggests that she is, in fact, still around. Penelope Wilton's busy schedule meant that contingency plans had been laid and there might have been a version of this thread with Elton Pope (X2.10, "Love & Monsters") uniting the Doctor's team (or, worst case scenario, Mr Copper from "Voyage of the Damned").

As one unit finished scenes in the Library and CAL's living room at Upper Boat, this story's recording continued on 19th with the big farewell in the Park (it was Morgan Jones Park), then off to Barry Island to use the Museum of Wales's Collections Centre at Parc Nantgawr for the UNIT vault with the Indigo space-parachute. The deadline approached for the end of the shoot as Harper tried to grab all the remaining shots in this set, finally ending with Rose reacting to Jack's apparent extermination. Friday 21st was Tate's last official day and was spent with a second unit shooting some of her solo TARDIS shots. She and Collinson both left and got a wrap party that evening.

• On the night of Easter Monday (24t,) two sets of exteriors were shot: Sarah's drive to find the Doctor was on Clinton Road while Martha was stopping off at her mum's (Cwrt-Y-Vil road, Penarth) for the first of two nights. The usual exterior for Bannerman Road, Clinton Road, Penarth, was used for Sarah driving away and nearby Robinswood Crescent was where she was stopped by Daleks and rescued by visitors from beyond space (Jackie and Mickey). Abbi Collins did the stunt-driving in the rain.

With Sladen and Agyeman slotting this in with work on separate spin-off series their work playing heroic ex-companions was almost the last part of the jigsaw and each continued the following week. Sarah Jane's attic was already built and these scenes were begun on the 27th (along with some of the extra green screen material); the next two days had more of these two.

Mat Irvine, the Danny Hargreaves of the 70s, came back to operate K9 on 28th and the interview with Richard Dawkins got more people excited than even Kylie. And that was almost it – on Monday 31st Paul O'Grady recorded a clip during work on his teatime chat-show (at Riverside Studios, where *Doctor Who* was made in its second year – see Volume 1). Gardner went along and watched from the gallery, her first experience of live television made that way. There was a plan to have the story end on a cliffhanger of the TARDIS being infiltrated by two Cybermen who pin the Doctor to the Console, leading into the Christmas episode, but this was abandoned as a bit trite. A new TARDIS scene of a forlorn Doctor setting off on his own again was shot on 1st May in the middle of making that Special.

• Even granted an hour for the last episode, there needed to be cuts. A sequence of the Donna-Doctor explaining how a piece of the coral-like infrastructure could grow a new TARDIS for the spare Doctor and Rose was removed, as it seemed to spoil the air of doom and futility of Bad Wolf Bay. One final shot of Donna hearing the TARDIS engines was removed because some people seeing a rough edit thought it meant she was about to die. "The Stolen Earth" didn't have a "next time" sequence, but "Journey's End" had one that made the original cliffhanger ending doubly redundant (photos of Cybermen at a snowy Victorian funeral had done the rounds by this point). As we saw in last episode's essay, the online speculation and garbled leaks from "insiders" led to some curious expectations of how the series would develop.

X4.14: "The Next Doctor"

(25th December, 2008)

Which One is This? Cybermen in Victorian London build Mecha-Godzilla. The Doctor can't stop them solo, but David Morrissey's on hand to do the sort of performance we used to get when episodes were 25 minutes long – thus letting the first-night audience think this might be Tennant's second multi-Doctor story.

Firsts and Lasts It's the first Christmas Special not to feature a Murray Gold Christmas ditty (one was scripted but got lost; they appear irregularly after this). Depending how you count, this is the start of the 2009 Specials-only run or the pause in Series 4. It's the episode made before Tennant took time out to do *Hamlet* and *Richard II*.

Pedants will say that John Smith's diary counts, but this is the first time Davies has gone for the old JN-T trick of rerunning footage of all the previous Doctors. It is admittedly characteristic of Cybermen and/or Daleks to do these video montages for no good reason (cf. 19.6, "Earthshock"; 21.4, "Resurrection of the Daleks"). Paul McGann's in it, John Hurt isn't.

Watch Out For...

• On first broadcast, the emphasis was on the identity of this mysterious newcomer. On subsequent viewings, the story's balance and timing seems really lopsided. (If you don't already know The Secret, stop reading, avoid all spoilers and watch it now, because you'll never be able to see it as intended after you read **The Continuity**.)

• This is the sort of story in which almost an entire hour of screen-time is spent building up to the money-shot: a 200 foot steampunk Cyberman stomping around Victorian London. To do The Mill justice, they seem to have given Davies precisely what he asked for. (Plus a bridge that shouldn't exist.)

• As in their first appearance (4.2, "The Tenth Planet"), the Cybermen look impressive striding through snow. Unlike a more recent appearance (X8.12, "Death in Heaven"), they march around a cemetery with a clear sense of purpose rather than just mooching about like bored Goths. They are killing Victorian workhouse-owners, so it's possible – just this once – to cheer them on as they rampage, and marvel at the so-wrong-it's-right spectacle of Lumic-model Cybermen trashing a Dickensian Christmas.

• … whereas their new attack-dogs, the Cyber Shades, are so wrong they're Wrong Beyond Words. They resemble shag-pile carpets with copper kettles glued to them and – even when performing the notionally cool feat of climbing up a sheer wall – look like nothing so much as the Taran Wood Beast (16.4, "The Androids of Tara"). Then again, with a choir singing "God Rest Ye Merry, Gentlemen", one suspects that a Venusian Lullaby is serenading Aggedor (9.2, "The Curse of Peladon").

• As in Tom Baker's time, the alien menace has a human front-person to deal with other humans and taunt the Doctor. Mercy Hartigan is a vampish Victorian of, shall we say, independent means (this being *Doctor Who* and Christmas, they can't elaborate) who chucks out innuendoes thick and fast. The mysterious new Doctor's companion, Rosita, seems to be in the same line of business but gets fewer decent lines. So both the speaking-part female characters in this story are prostitutes – how festive!

Miss H does gets a good line: when told that "the CyberKing will rise", she repeats the line and adds: *how like a man.* (Unless you're watching on BBC America, of course.)

• "Do you have your legs on silent?" It's a Christmas episode, so the Doctor can point out plot inconsistencies in earlier stories, in this case Mrs Moore's death in X2.6, "The Age of Steel".

The Continuity

The Doctor He's curious to meet someone he thinks *might* be a later incarnation [if we go with X7.16, "The Time of the Doctor", it'd be his last throw of the dice] and uses all sorts of recall-tripping ploys to try to jog the other's memory [in X7.15, "The Day of the Doctor", he seems more confident about ridiculing his next self – as if disappointed that his final body doesn't resemble Jackson Lake]. He absent-mindedly cracks that tripping over a brick might not be the worst way to die, depending on what sort of brick it is [he once regenerated after clonking his head on an exercise bike, so he knows whereof he speaks: see 24.1, "Time and the Rani", if you feel it's that urgent].

He refrains from comment when Jackson says it's natural for Time Lords to have bad dreams. When he finds the info-stamp with his profile, he's careful not to look at anything that might come after the pictures of him. [So this video *could* involve future versions; it stays active long enough for the Matt Smith version to appear, at least.]

He says he doesn't travel with companions anymore, because 'I suppose in the end, they break my heart'. [It seems he took the events of X4.13 "Journey's End" very hard, and sticks to this resolution for the next three-and-a-bit episodes.]

• *Background.* The Doctor knows all about the CyberKing and the mechanism of a Cyber Dreadnought ship. [It's a puzzle exactly when he learned this. Either the proper Cybermen did this, and the Lumic models used the same technical attacks by some freakish set of coincidences, or Pete Tyler gave him an amazingly comprehensive briefing back in X2.13, "Doomsday." In "Army of Ghosts" (X2.12), Mickey speculated on there being a 'Cyber-king' inside the Void Ship, which could support the latter.]

He temporarily thinks that Jackson might have concealed his memories in a watch. [X3.8, "Human Nature", implying that a Chameleon Arch isn't required to conceal *all* of a Time Lord's personality. If he'd programmed it more carefully back then, he could have saved Martha a lot of bother.]

• *The Time War.* The Daleks who hid in the Void

during the Time War had a lot of information on data-stamps that were, somehow, compatible with Lumic-model Cybermen. This info includes all of the Doctors. [The clips, by the way, involve a Doctor who came after the Daleks holed up in the literal middle of nowhere, but not the Doctor we now know was their greatest enemy, as portrayed by John Hurt; X7.15, "The Day of the Doctor".] They also filed away stuff about Shakespeare and maps of London, so the decision to make their return through a catflap a thousand feet over Docklands is less capricious than it seemed.

• *Ethics.* As we've seen in most of the earlier Christmas Specials, he gives the opposition one chance for life, offering to move the entire CyberKing somewhere besides Earth. When this doesn't work, he essentially blasts it to oblivion. Nevertheless, individual Cybermen are treated as fair game now. [We don't know if he bought the kids hot pies as promised.]

• *Inventory: Sonic Screwdriver.* Here used to scan for Cybertech, and open various Victorian locks. He considers using it to shut off the ear-pods [so he's changed his mind about that since X2.6 "The Age of Steel", only saying that it might hurt Mr Cole a bit]. At some point, he presumably uses it to revamp the info-stamps that he points at Miss Hartigan at the end. [They have a completely different effect there than the "make Cybermen explode" that Jackson's been using them for.]

• *Inventory: Other.* We have the stethoscope. Mr Lake only has one heart.

The Supporting Cast

• *Jackson Lake.* For half of the story, he's convinced he's the Doctor, albeit an amnesiac one. As such he's outfitted himself with appropriate paraphernalia: one standard-issue screwdriver, a T.A.R.D.I.S. (Tethered Aerial Release Developed In Style) gas balloon. He's even got a companion, Rosita. In this fugue-state heroic mould, he quotes Robert Burns [compare X2.2, "Tooth and Claw"].

Three weeks before Christmas, he was a well-off Maths teacher moving from Sussex to take up a position at university. At some point he and his family discovered the Cybermen; they killed his wife Caroline and kidnapped his son Frederick, at which point he retreated into a fugue state; when a data-stamp starring the Doctor went off, he adopted that identity. He's been hunting the Cybershades for a fortnight and building a balloon besides. [It seems not to have occurred to him to call in the authorities.] The T.A.R.D.I.S

ABOUT TIME 2008-2009

isn't home for him.

At the end, he intends to stay in London [presumably to take up that university position] and intends to give Rosita a position as Frederic's nursemaid.

The Supporting Cast (Evil)

• *Mercy Hartigan.* [The episode dances around the rather awkward situation of Davies scripting a prostitute as his lead villain, then only alluding to this fact in the vaguest of terms (he referred to her as "damaged" in interviews, and indicates that her child torture is the result of deep psychic scarring.)] As matters stand, she's found a way to cut through Victorian disempowerment, by assisting/directing the Cybermen to stomp it all out. While reasonably savvy, she seems to honestly believe the Cybermen would honour their bargain, and screams for mercy when they plug her in to be the CyberKing. Instead, her mind is powerful enough to override the conversion technology; it suits her after all. Accessing their information, she's fascinated by intel on the Time Vortex [possibly indicative of these Cybermen's time travel technology, but she only speaks of taking over the Empire].

The Non-Humans

• *The Cybermen.* [The idea seems to be that this group of Pete's World Cybermen ducked in before the universes closed off in X4.13, "Journey's End" (a complicated story; see **How Many Cyber-Races are There?** under X2.6, "The Age of Steel").] For some reason, they go along with Mercy Hartigan's plan to use workhouse children as muscle. [They must keep her on hand because they think she'll make good CyberKing material. That's the best explanation for the Cybermen going along with a scheme even more complicated and incoherent than they usually invent on their own.]

The data-stamps have a cyclo-Steinham core, which spurts out raw energy when the safety is removed. These clip directly into the C of the Cybus Industries logo on the Cybermen's chests, and can be used like dongles to store and retrieve data. [This and the ring-pull operation indicates that the Cybermen designed them for their own use, and they only contain bootlegged Dalek documentation (otherwise the **Things That Don't Make Sense** for this story would be twice as big).] The Doctor jury-rigs one to project images onto a wall. One malfunctioned and downloaded facts about the Doctor into Jackson Lake's mind.

Here the Doctor dispatches the Cybermen with a variety of methods, including data-stamp hacking, and hitting one unconvincingly with a cutlass.

• *Cyber Shades.* Some fairly common types of London animal [cats and dogs, probably] can be converted into a creature with a Cyberman's face, made of brass with bolts and rivets, but a body composed of shaggy black cloak. They have an ape-like gait, alternating between bipedal and quadrupedal, but can climb sheer brick walls and are formidably strong. [They run a bit like Peter Capaldi, loping low to the ground with arms flailing around.] They seem not to have hands or feet, but can hold a whip and reins when driving a carriage.

• *The CyberKing.* Actually a ship of the Dreadnought class, and towers over St Paul's Cathedral. [That's 111 metres high, because Wren wanted a building 365 feet tall for astronomical reasons, and it was the tallest building in London until the Post Office Tower (3.10, "The War Machines") in 1965. The effects team seem uncertain as to the King's height; in one shot it's approximately twice the height of St Paul's, and another soon after it's bigger. Let's say 250 metres or 800 feet.] A Cyberfactory in its chest can convert 'millions'.

The term "King" [confusingly] also refers to the individual who is plugged into the main control centre, which is in the giant's mouth within a head the size of an average church. The control mechanism is a throne-like creation with wrist straps. Miss Hartigan herself isn't visibly converted [the dress might cover it], and the only physical alteration comes when her eyes turn completely black. Despite this, the CyberKing is meant to be unimaginative – when Hartigan maintains her personality even after being plugged into the system, the Cybermen deem this a system failure.

The machine walks at a slight incline and the entire torso and head can revolve 180 degrees. It fires plasma-bolts from the wrists, but the chest has a visible steam-piston mechanism and cogs. The shoulders contain several smoking chimneys.

Forcibly severing the connection of a CyberKing to the main body causes feedback that explodes the ship. [We think: it's ambiguous what's actually going on. Davies himself has publicly lamented the ending, just about the most negative he's ever

Should *Doctor Who* be Appointment Television?

The single-most interesting thing about "The Next Doctor" is one that can never now be recaptured. The hype teased us with the idea that David Morrissey's character was indeed the forthcoming incarnation – David Tennant had already announced his departure, but the BBC were tight-lipped about his replacement. Nobody, at any time after 8.00pm on 25th December 2008, can see the episode the same way as anyone watching the premiere on BBC1 did.

In a lot of ways, this is how it should be. Russell T Davies was charged with making a series that would entice the whole family to watch around the front-room telly, like they used to in the 70s. The emphasis was firmly on each new episode as a shared experience: a one-off, one night only event, and all subsequent transmissions and the DVD were subsidiary. In moving from 7.00pm on Saturdays during Series 3, the steady ratings for David Tennant's earlier episodes wobbled. By the time of "The Next Doctor", the iPlayer catch-up service was a year old (see X4.0, "Voyage of the Damned"), but the broadcast was the "real thing" still. Davies was much exercised by a statistic that fewer than 10% of people who watched any one *Doctor Who* episode watched all of them in a series.

To some extent, each episode Davies produced is intentionally self-contained, with copious flashbacks and expository conversations for new viewers just joining. Major events on a Saturday in spring, such as London's Gay Pride march, would arrange for giant screens to show the new episode – nobody needed to miss the experience of seeing it when the whole country did. Meanwhile, after the shambolic first year, the security around forthcoming events became increasingly neurotic and almost an end in itself. They kept some impressive secrets, notably Billie Piper's return in Series 4. The teasing and hints about each year's Big Bad made more sense after the fact, but were less interesting once the cat was out of the bag. Just to make sure we were all on the same page, and understood the potential risk to this vogueish storytelling technique from premature elucidation, River Song showed up to disseminate the concept of "spoilers" to anyone not hitherto a cult-TV fan.

And yet, when the transmission times of Series 8 were messed around with to give a new start-time of 8.30pm, the BBC put out a statement saying that this wasn't a problem for younger viewers, because they all watched it on catch-up services far more than older ones. Steven Moffat's complex and obscure web of hints and disclosures was something to discuss online, not face to face as the end-credits roll. Had the entire nation's tele-viewing habits changed that much in five years? Well, yes and no.

The BBC Wales episodes were, and are, in constant rerun somewhere on British screens and across the world. As we have discussed, overseas transmissions are less methodical in their scheduling and often skip key episodes, especially the ones over the orthodox length. Adopting an American model of production and distribution was never entirely practicable, especially with the BBC's ways of funding drama and a mere 14 episodes a year (if that), but in one crucial respect, the situation after 2005 was unprecedented in BBC drama – or, indeed, in what was still then termed "terrestrial" broadcasting. The BBC Wales episodes were made and shown on the understanding that they would be repeated in Britain somewhere, not least on another BBC channel. They were also made with a halo of behind-the-scenes and associated material; the DVD "extras" were fitted as standard.

Although it was rare for BBC1, the programme's home, to repeat any episode after the first week even when Tennant was the Doctor (Christmas Specials were the main exception), BBC3 and some digital affiliates (notably Dave, a channel partly funded by BBC Worldwide and partly by advertising) would rerun entire seasons, usually in sequence. (There was also the messed-up online archive and BBC Shop, but we'll get to that in the essay with X5.3, "Victory of the Daleks".)

For most of the programme's history, the idea of ever seeing a particular episode again was never part of the BBC viewer's perception of *Doctor Who* – not least because once the lead actor was recast, the entire run of that Doctor's episodes was consigned to history. With two freakish exceptions, no repeats were sanctioned in the 1960s (see 1.1, "An Unearthly Child" and 4.9, "The Evil of the Daleks" for those anomalies). We've told parts of this story in more detail elsewhere in *About Time*, but the point we keep returning to is that one episode a week, with little prospect of seeing it again, formed the baseline for how the series was made to be watched. Every episode was an unrepeatable event (literally, once they'd destroyed any remaining copies they could find). The waiting

continued on Page 247...

been about a script. Apparently, he realised after production that the Doctor could have talked Miss Hartigan into disintegrating the CyberKing of her own accord, thus negating the awkward Dimensional Vault get-out.]

History

• *Dating.* Well, we're told it's Christmas Eve, 1851 and that this is London. The Doctor stays around long enough to have Christmas dinner with Jackson the next day. The Cybermen arrived two months earlier.

The Analysis

The Big Picture As promised, this is the *They Might be Giants* episode (the 1971 film – nobody watching this is thinking *Here Comes Science*.) Just as George C Scott had a trauma in the movie and believed he was Sherlock Holmes, so Jackson Lake copes with bereavement (and almost unimaginable information poured into his head) by becoming the Doctor. It's a scenario re-used in *The Fisher King* with Robin Williams chasing a dragon through New York.

As Scott's character mentions in the film, the archetype of this is Don Quixote. Almost any long-running television series after the film did this, usually with Holmes (even in *Magnum PI*, for heaven's sake) and Steven Moffat did it with the Doctor, sort of, in *Press Gang*. We mentioned when discussing "The Doctor's Daughter" (X4.6) that there are a number of such set-pieces, and Davies often identified in *Doctor Who Confidential* when he was doing one. "School Reunion" (X2.3) was explicitly The One Where The Girlfriend Meets The Ex, for example, and "Human Nature" (X3.8) was the amnesia/giving-it-all-up-for-a-normal-life story, but without any Paul Gauguin-esque Tahitian girl or penny-whistles (*Star Trek* did one per captain). They kept the "hero is mortally wounded and in danger, but is distracted by flashbacks about how the team met" and "someone accidentally becomes telepathic for a week" episodes for *Torchwood*.

In a wider sense, though, Davies's entire project for *Doctor Who* is to show people trying to live up to the Doctor's standards and, thereby, becoming better people. This has been a theme from the *New Adventures* books that was, if anything, ramped up in the first year of the returning series, most noticeably in "The Parting of the Ways"

(X1.13). The doomed occupants of the Game Station try to live up to the Doctor's lead even as he falters; Jack comes out and says that the Doctor's example has led him to inevitable self-sacrifice. Then Rose sits in a dingy café in her estate and tells Jackie what *Doctor Who* is about (according to the author) and gets her ex and her mum to start stepping up their performance, which lands up with the regeneration and Jack's immortality.

This thread gets picked up by LINDA in "Love & Monsters" (X2.10) and many other heroic moments, many of them people listed as casualties of the Doctor's callous heroism when Davros taunted the Time Lord last episode. Steven Moffat emphasised that side of it, with many speeches about what a menace the Doctor is for inspiring fatal or near-fatal bids to impress him. Even Davies has questioned it, most pertinently the Master ridiculing the Doctor's choice of name – *the man who makes people better* (X3.12, "The Sound of Drums").

It was always a trade-off for writers of the earlier series between making the Doctor someone who could set an example real viewers could follow and making him alien and superhuman, so that he survives things that ought to end the series. These days, we rarely see the Doctor work things out from first principles and available evidence (and when he does it's mindbogglingly stupid, such as X8.7, "Kill the Moon" or X8.10, "In The Forest of the Night"), but this was always at the series's core. Davies reiterated it, in a muffled and curious way, when writing his only solo episode of *The Sarah Jane Adventures* (A9, "Death of the Doctor"), and ending with the strong hint that every former companion still on Earth is, in some way, saving the world.

What's curious about this version of the idea is that, for once, fatherhood is shown to be more important. Once Jackson recalls and retrieves his son, his role as an agent in the story is over; instead, he's a chorus character cheering on the Doctor. However, even this is compromised as it's the Doctor who saves Frederick, not Jackson. The nuclear family isn't quite restored, as Rosita is given a paid post as governess (the only other option for single women in Victorian fiction), but as usual in books set at this time, motherhood is an ideal best exemplified by what happens in the absence of "the Angel of the House". Mrs Lake is only important as a lack – we hear that she was

Should *Doctor Who* be Appointment Television?

continued from Page 245...

between episodes was really what made it work.

Once domestic video became an option, the recently-shown episodes were more available than ever before, but releases of BBC video cassettes were constricted to the remaining older episodes on a somewhat haphazard release schedule. The videos, DVDs and sporadic reruns were like showing an old sporting event – an opportunity for reminiscence rather than an edge-of-the-seat anticipation of what might happen next. The 1966 World Cup Final may still inflame passions among football fans, but everyone not American knows the result (however much German fans dispute it). The 1981 Ashes series is remarkable for many things (not least the haircuts), but anyone who's chosen to watch has a pretty good idea of how it turns out. The end of "Earthshock" (19.6) may still brighten the day of anyone who saw it first time, but it won't stun anyone.

Get older UK viewers in a room together, and the conversation will eventually get to comparing scars on what inconsiderate parents made kids do that required not seeing a particular episode. Then, it will go into the other programmes of the same era, particularly what else BBC1 was putting out on Saturday evenings. That part has changed less than one might have hoped over the centuries. The shared experience of *Doctor Who* in Britain has been that it exists in a context of deeply peculiar programming that seemed to BBC executives and – until we stop and reflect – the general public to "belong" around a family adventure serial that wandered between costume-drama and space-opera.

The programmes bookending it tell the story. Seen again now, offerings such as *The Telegoons* or *Lamb Chop* are jawdroppingly bonkers, just as the things BBC Wales had to contend with already look. Many of the programmes on before and after Moffat-era *Who* seem like the results of bets. Indeed, working on *Don't Scare the Hare* might well have been the forfeit everyone involved had to do after losing a drinking game. As we will see in the next volume, Series 5 went out as BBC1 tried to make its Saturday night a seamless whole by dripping animated trailers into the end of the just-ending programme (notoriously in X5.4, "The Time of Angels"). The first and last episodes of a series are promoted as "events" and trailed extensively, as is the Christmas offering, but BBC1 treats rou-

tine episodes as part of the promotional material around whichever "shiny floor" talent-show is currently favourite to combat ITV. Series 8 was bookended by trailers for dramas they thought would win industry awards. Series 9 was sometimes less watched (on first broadcast, and even with the iPlayer catch-ups) than Season Twenty-Six, but got the whole "we make quality dramas as well" swaddling.

Under Davies, however, this context fed into the episodes themselves, nowhere more spectacularly than in "Bad Wolf" (X1.12). This, if you've forgotten, inserted parodies of other then-current terrestrial hits into the narrative, with the voices of the real Davina MacCall and Anne Robinson. On a few occasions in the past, there might have been guest appearances by monsters in whatever Light Entertainment show followed *Doctor Who* – but here, and with diminishing effect on subsequent Episode Twelves, normal Saturday night telly bled into the story. The alarming, exhilarating *wrongness* of these cameos fades with each repeat and passing year. Over a dozen years on, this episode seems as quaint as British astronauts using shillings (7.3, "The Ambassadors of Death"). The episode remains peculiar as ever if you've never seen the series being parodied, but you're missing the shock-value of first broadcast, *in situ*.

What is odd – and remains odd however much it's become an inescapable fact – is that anyone *other* than BBC1 viewers in the week of first broadcast gets anything out of any episode. A sliver of television drama made to be watched on a specific Saturday (or not, if it was the 80s), laced with (or constructed around) so many culturally-specific and topical allusions that we have to write these books just to scratch the surface, somehow makes some kind of sense to people not born at the time (or in countries where Ken Dodd isn't a household name). It's just not always the same *kind* of sense as it made to the first-night audience.

Even episodes made this century become so difficult to explain – to be fair, even *we* have difficulty grasping why Derek Acorah ever had a career (X2.12, "Army of Ghosts") – that it's alarming that they show the episodes without at least ten minutes of footnotes in other territories. Few of the jokes, which are what UK viewers think of as the reason the series is different from umpteen fantasy-adventure franchises, make the transition when the episodes are dubbed into other lan-

continued on Page 249...

called "Caroline" almost in passing.

[Apropos of names, Davies has, since at least *Casanova*, taken to having vital, earthy characters called "Jack" or something similar, so we can excuse the slight oddness of the name. He is a Victorian, and they did use maternal surnames as Christian names, but "Jackson" as a first name sounds as if he's a hepcat and street kids are getting fresh in a 40s chase-the-blues musical. "Rosita" was chosen to sound a bit like "Rose" and cast to look vaguely like Martha, a bit, sort of, but accounting for someone with an accent like that, a name like that and skin-colour like that all at once suggest a more interesting story than what we got. Instead, the character stands in as a purely decorative companion-esque Londoner.]

Around this, we have a Mulligan Stew of bits from 60s British children's books, especially the ones adapted for 70s editions of *Jackanory*. In the early 1960s and until the mid-80s, there was a boom in paperbacks for children beyond even the current YA me-too flurry, and the two publishers most reliably producing ones that would last were Scholastic in New York and Puffin, the junior imprint of Penguin, in London. For example, under editor Kaye Webb, Puffin found Roald Dahl's new niche after his adult thrillers had run out of steam. Webb launched literally hundreds of writers, and often found the appropriate artists with whom their work was most associated. Other imprints followed this lead.

British kids (and parents) often first encountered these in school libraries, or clubs set up by the publishers and run within the class – or on *Jackanory* on BBC1 at 4.15. This was a beautifully simple format: a good actor, an autocue, a few illustrations with a rostrum camera running over it occasionally, 15 minute episodes and a suitable book. Series creator Joy Whitby, Anna Home (production assistant and eventually long-serving producer) and maybe one or two other production assistants read anything they thought would work and, for the first decade, something like a third of those they selected were recent publications, a large percentage of these Puffin and most others Scholastic (which usually handled UK distribution of Puffin and vice versa – *A Wizard of Earthsea* was a Puffin here). The actor who did the largest number of editions was Bernard Cribbins, who was later the star of Russell T Davies's conscious re-re-reboot of the format, *Old Jack's Tales*.[44] (What were we saying about "Jack" just now?)

If you worked out the statistical average of all *Jackanory* produced in the early 70s, you would get *Harry Potter*. However, if you removed anything that Rowling had by then pilfered, the average of the remainder would be "The Next Doctor". We have a pseudo-Dickensian setting reminiscent of... well, Dickens, but also Leon Garfield. (Rosita is more like the sort of girl-who-adopts-the-street-urchin-hero in a Garfield book than she's like Nancy in *Oliver!*) In this is a bizarre alternate-universe workhouse run by a witchy madwoman for reasons of her own, such as in Joan Aiken's series of books that started with *The Wolves of Willoughby Chase*. Davies seems to remember the film version from the 80s rather than the novel[45]; in his rendition the wolves are replaced by Cyber-wolves that can climb walls, but lack the "don't leave the building" function integral to the novel's gothic stylings. By contrast, Sarah Dollard's two scripts for *Doctor Who* to date (X9.10, "Face the Raven" and more especially X10.3, "Thin Ice") are wholesale pastiches – check out Frost-Fair shenanigans at the end of *Black Hearts in Battersea,* for example.

"The Next Doctor" takes this fantasy version of London as the baseline-normal and then messes with it. Davies cited *Chitty Chitty Bang Bang* as the model for how the scared children had been put to work (the Dick Van Dyke film, not Ian Fleming's books; Roald Dahl did the screenplay). Philip Pullman revisited that sort of thing in *The Northern Lights* (then in cinemas as *The Golden Compass*, a rather botched adaptation but with the kids-in-an-exploding-factory scene: see X2.13, "Doomsday" for Davies taking what he needed from the books), and *Ruby in the Smoke* (the 2006 TV version starring Billie Piper, with Matt Smith).

The production of this episode seeks to emulate the *Jackanory* version of nineteenth-century London and the filmed dramas derived from them (often produced by Anna Home and usually on Wednesdays at around 5.00pm) rather than actual Victorian conditions or any novels written then. Even the sewers seem antiseptic. There's a giant mechanical man trashing London, rather like Ted Hughes's *The Iron Man* (an animated version of this was renamed *The Iron Giant,* because Marvel think they own everything). When that was on *Jackanory*, it was a rare 80s television appearance by Tom Baker, but the book had been a hit in schools a decade or more earlier. It was unavoidable for anyone of Davies's generation.

Should *Doctor Who* be Appointment Television?

continued from Page 247...

guages. The first casualties of BBC America's editing are the bits that casual UK viewers still remember when the plots fade. Still, the overseas revenue is handy (if not available in full to the programme-makers), so the after-life of any given episode is considered while they're making it.

In many ways, the latter half of Davies's reign was the equipoise between attempting to make something like 1970s *Doctor Who* (based on the premise that any episode would only be aired once), and making a *Buffy*-style series with pre-planned "arcs" and artfully-placed prolepses. The "Next Time On..." sequences, edited to suggest more than they revealed, are proof of this. There had been trailers before, sometimes specifically for *Doctor Who* that week or clips within a sampler of the night's viewing on BBC1 (these give the real flavour of the bizarre contexts in which it was shown, especially during Peter Davison's stint). On very rare occasions, bespoke pieces were made as part of the production, but not as part of an actual episode. (See 17.1, "Destiny of the Daleks"; 5.3, "The Ice Warriors"; 5.5, "The Web of Fear" and indeed the radio trailers for 1.1, "An Unearthly Child" and X1.1, "Rose".)

Now, though, the combination of topicality (in both its usual sense of "being about current matters of interest", and the more literal one of being tied to a specific place and moment, like a topical salve) and drip-fed hints of a definite forthcoming development, on a specified date, made being in front of a set for the dénouement the preferred method of watching. Moffat developed this in his own way – even when we got an "answer", it deferred a complete explanation of the storyline-in-progress and opened up more hints of further developments. For Davies, repeatability was an "extra" once the episode had made its initial splash; for Moffat, the whole point of making long-running stories was to keep them going, not resolve anything on a definite date. Viewers were expected to be able to go back and check details.

On the face of it, this is odd. Davies has a background in soaps, Moffat in tight half-hour farces. This might incline Davies to keep storylines going for decades, and Moffat to go for punch-lines and pay-offs. In fact, there are good reasons why these two writers tended towards the narratives they used. British Soaps have "event" episodes, sometimes tied to anniversaries or public holidays, sometimes ruthlessly aimed at knocking a rival's

ratings. Returns of popular characters, or the introduction of a star or a significant relative of a long-running household, are trailed for weeks ahead of transmission. Soaps tend not to have trailers except for when a simmering storyline is about to come to a head, or when they want you to know of a new arrival (the latter don't include clips, just a mood-piece culminating in the former star's face and a few in-character words to the camera).

More to the point, the context in which episodes are broadcast is addressed – either by inserting rapidly-made new material to episodes recorded months back, where characters react to a major news event, or by making storylines include a known forthcoming event[46]. The *EastEnders* Christmas episodes are proverbially catastrophic (for the characters, if not the ratings), to the extent that a happy one is too freakish to be memorable (2010's doesn't linger in the memory like the previous year's murder of Archie) unless it's that other soap attention-getter, a wedding. Only in soaps and Davies-era *Who* does anyone add the stress of Christmas to the stress of a wedding (X3.0, "The Runaway Bride", c.f. 2003's *EastEnders* with Alfie and Kat).

Repeat, out-of-sequence showings of soap episodes are not in anyone's game-plan. British soaps don't really export well. The original BBC Wales production team used this model for the relaunched *Doctor Who*. After all, the only previous occasions when the transmission-date was specifically and explicitly linked to an episode's content were 25.3, "Silver Nemesis" (the constant harping on about it being 23rd November, 1988 was another embarrassing glitch in one of the most summery episodes ever) and "The Feast of Steven" (episode seven of 3.4, "The Daleks' Master Plan"). That was considered an anomaly even when scripted, as it had no connection to episodes either side. It was omitted when the remaining 11 episodes were sold overseas. International sale of modern BBC output is a routine fact, as we saw in an earlier essay, but is rarely the primary concern. For Davies it was a bonus, just as getting a bit of money when US producers took the format of *Queer as Folk* and made in effect a new series was tidy but not essential.

Moffat's view was more complex, perhaps as a result of having to talk things up whenever the BBC hierarchy moved the goalposts on him. His public ire at "spoilers" would seem to indicate that

continued on Page 251...

ABOUT TIME 2008-2009

In Volume 7, we had a fairly thorough look into the origins of the Steampunk fad, so we needn't labour the point here (look at X2.5, "Rise of the Cybermen" for Zeppelins, Multiversal shenanigans), but industrial Britain's iconography and the dauntless ambition and technical prowess of the age is appealing. Why else set this story in 1851, the year of the Great Exhibition (see 19.7, "Time-Flight"), even though a later sequence requires there to be sewers built ten years ahead of time?

In making the CyberKing look like other iterations of the Hollywood idea of Brunel-era London, there is a conscious decision to make it functional and obviously so, revealing the workings in as much detail as the digital artists can muster in so short a time. A genuine one, had such a thing been built – or a real T.A.R.D.I.S. balloon for that matter – would have been painted pillar-box red and British Racing Green, but that doesn't chime with the notion of raw power and simplistic metalwork with no circuitry or plastic. Functionality as an end in itself isn't how Victorians did things, but for some reason the Cybermen have met them half-way on the design. There is no logical reason why a Cybermen-designed ship would have giant pistons and gears, runs on coal and yet fires plasma-bolts. Yet the Steampunk aesthetic demands this sort of hybridity – and that is, after all, the point of having Cybermen in a Dickensian Christmas story.

In a 1980s edition of what was then *The Official Doctor Who Magazine*, there was a wonky timeline for the Cybermen that claimed – with no foundation – that the ones in the Death Zone in "The Five Doctors" (20.7) were taken from Victorian London. A great many fanzines picked up on the hint, and wrote articles about whether the series ought to go in the then-fashionable direction of *The Difference Engine* or *The Anubis Gates*. Then again, the image of Cybermen in sewers was hardly new (6.3, "The Invasion", 22.1; "Attack of the Cybermen"), nor was the image of them stomping past St Paul's Cathedral (again, "The Invasion", repeated less iconically in X8.13, "Death in Heaven" along with this story's graveyard imagery).

We alluded to the similarity of this story's climax to Toho Studios's cash-cow (if that's the beast we want), the *Kaiju* films such as *Mothra* and *Godzilla*. It's not unprecedented for *Doctor Who* to attempt this, and however hard it is to take the third cliffhanger to 12.1, "Robot" or the second

from 13.1, "Terror of the Zygons" seriously, they are clearly in this idiom and surely no more daft. The difference is that the giant monster trampling on people and smashing things is an incident along the way in those two stories while, for this one and the 60s films, it's the entire point and everything up to then is stalling.

In more recent years, there was the big relaunch of the 80s *Transformers* franchise (with the UK comics putting more thought put into it than any of the TV shows or toys they promoted). In the wake of this, there were a lot of jokes and spoofs, notably the adverts for the Citroen C4 (which began shortly before the Michael Bay flicks, but not before news of them had got out). In this, the tedious city-trashing stuff was replaced by disco dancing, then speed-skating. There had also been the curiously uninvolving *Sky Captain and the World of Tomorrow*, attempting to make a 1930s-style version.

The turning-point is an ambitious woman finding a pre-existing machine, and seeking to use it for her own ends, but getting into a mental battle with it once she's in the hot-seat. We've already mentioned the similarity of Miss Hartigan to Miss Pendragon in Davies's first solo TV commission, *Dark Season*. The end of that didn't make sense either. Eyes going totally black when possessed by evil is a pretty off-the-shelf 90s television shorthand: see, for example, Lyta Alexander in *Babylon 5* or Willow in *Buffy the Vampire Slayer*. And the name "Aubrey Fairchild" was left over from the Prime Minister who tried to stand up to the Daleks in early versions of the last story. "Scoones" seems to denote the effect designer from the 1970s, Ian Scoones.

But, of course, the obvious thing about "The Next Doctor" is that they've gone for the one Christmas setting they've avoided so far: the Dickensian, snow-capped London. (Yes, they did it in X1.3, "The Unquiet Dead", but not on Christmas Day.) This is a sure-fire hit with audiences, especially in America, and advertisers have tapped into it as ruthlessly as Perry Como or *The Black and White Minstrel Show* ever did.

In particular, the iconography is familiar for families who'd be handing around a tin of Quality Street chocolates with pictures on the lid closely resembling the opening sequence. Light Entertainment specials of the 1970s would take turns using the BBC's log-fire props and big flouncy dresses (most of these were recorded in

Should *Doctor Who* be Appointment Television?

continued from Page 249...

he believed the revelation of a significant plot-twist is to be timed precisely for optimum effect. Yet he also claimed that the viewers may prefer to digest television in box-sets rather than weekly episodes and – on the strength of the half-series bursts and the sporadic release of *Sherlock* – he factored this into his storytelling. Nonetheless, the "Netflix Generation" seems not to give a monkey's about spoilers and, in fact, prefer a sense that a story is going somewhere to apparently noodling along self-indulgently. His overarching plans each lasted one series and then the next arc – which he started before the previous one ended, despite them being mutually-exclusive – relied on nobody remembering last year.

What's interesting is that the self-contained episodes – the ones where the production and writers could try things out – were less self-contained than under Davies. Even something as apparently inconsequential as "The Curse of the Black Spot" (X6.3) had a brief interlude connecting it to the year's main plot about Madame Kovarian and got a call-back four episodes later. A completely "arc"-free episode, such as Moffat's contributions to Series 2 and 3, wasn't an option (until the first spurt of Series 7, which had two "arc" stories by him, two by Chris Chibnall that only related to each other and online material – that's interesting with hindsight - and a forgettable Western).

However, Davies pulled the biggest such switch on us with a seemingly throwaway episode providing the missing piece of a puzzle (X1.7, "The Long Game"). It was written by the head honcho, and thus always likely to be more significant than it seemed. The next apparently lightweight piece of fluff was "Boom Town" (X1.11), which set up the whole of *Torchwood* and the handy space-surf-board that got the Doctor out of two tight spots. Davies used a relatively light touch when seeding clues in scripts attributed to other writers, whereas Moffat seems to have substantially rewritten "The Rings of Akhaten" (X7.8) to set up the whole element of Clara's Leaf.

When Moffat deliberately sought to provoke interest, it sometimes backfired. Selling "A Good Man Goes to War" (X6.7) as a "game-changer" of unprecedented proportions was later seen as a mistake, especially as it follows a series where the whole Universe blew up. What we *got* was confirmation of the least interesting of many theories doing the rounds and an underwhelming cliff-hanger. This, after a fair amount of over-egging within the story, including River declaring, "This is... the Doctor's darkest hour. He'll rise higher than ever before, and then fall so much further," when in fact he pretty much dusts himself off and leaves with a song in his hearts for parts unknown. The series was split into two, for reasons still being resolved at time of going to press, but the return four months later didn't answer the majority of the questions viewers were supposedly asking. BBC internal politics made this half-series and the one that followed less cohesive and more repetitive, but spinning the half-time pause as an "event" failed to make the content any more special.

Series 7 was the one where every episode was given a fake movie poster. Fewer episodes per year make *any* episode an event and 2012 had five "normal" ones and the Christmas thing. The BBC's attitude at this stage was that each episode is worthy of a big, teasing build-up, and only then a volley of behind-the-scenes material online. The BBC1 publicity machine so loves promoting a new series start – and the deployment of the first transmission – as a weapon in a ratings war against various bewilderingly-popular Simon Cowell projects that its attempts at mystery-generation are an integral part of the broadcast. Each episode was sold on spectacle, but just six in one calendar year isn't enough to gather momentum. What was lost in this was any sense of the weekly ritual of settling in front of the telly for each new episode. If we are absolutely honest, this aspect is what anyone in Britain who fondly remembers the London-made stories has most affection for, and any specific incidents that arose along the way were heightened moments amid a general Saturday-night-ness.[47]

The 1980s experiments with two episodes a week on different days each year, then 45-minute episodes, then after *Wogan* opposite *Coronation Street*, all removed the habit of watching the series regardless of whether anyone was especially committed to it. Most households had other things to do than watch telly on weekday evenings and made anything they *did* watch fit in around their lives even before home recording. We discussed this in Volume 5 (**What Difference Does a Day Make?** under 19.1, "Castrovalva") but it effectively made *Doctor Who* less of a link in a chain than grouting behind the tiles.

This was a big change from the norm. Mealtimes

continued on Page 253...

August and booking the studios and facial-hair was almost like a military operation), but it was when the big supermarkets started their ad campaigns that you started to wish Charles Dickens had been drowned at birth. (Mercifully, Woolworths went bust over Christmas 2008, so we were spared theirs for ever more.) The other use the BBC had for Dickens at Christmas was, of course, spooky stories – see Volume 4 – but they avoid trying that this time around. And, as everyone pointed out at the time, the first time we saw Cybermen, they were marching through snow (4.2, "The Tenth Planet").

Oh, Isn't That...?

• *David Morrissey* (Jackson Lake). Although he'd been around for decades, in such films as *Drowning By Numbers* (1988), his eruption into the public eye was with a TV movie, *The Deal*, in which he played Gordon Brown to Michael Sheen's Tony Blair. There were many other projects (such as the underwhelming *Basic Instinct II*), but the series either side of this episode are noteworthy: *Blackpool*, in which he starred, had him singing and occasionally dancing with Sarah Parish and David Tennant (X3.0, "The Runaway Bride"), then the *Red Riding* trilogy: a 70's set grim police procedural murder in three TV movies that were *Life on Mars* for grown-ups (X3.4, "Daleks in Manhattan"). He'd been in the version of *Our Mutual Friend* (the Dickens novel about the coming of railways and the corrupt business behind it) produced by Susie Liggatt. Latterly, he's been the Governor in *The Walking Dead* and Borlu in the recent adaptation of *The City & the City*.

• *Dervla Kerwan* (Miss Hartigan) had a habit of quitting hit shows before the writers could remove the character, so in both *Goodnight, Sweetheart* and *Ballykissangel*, she was hastily replaced and everyone unfavourably compared the stand-in to her. This ploy seems to have backfired, as no more long-running series were offered to her for a while. At the time this episode was broadcast, she was known for doing sultry voice-overs for Marks & Spencer's "food porn" adverts (*This is not just food...*), and had been Casanova's mum in, um, *Casanova*. If there's a four-part drama made in the UK, chances are she's in it somewhere.

• *Velile Tshabalala* (Rosita Farisis) was in the most BBC3 thing ever, a sketch-show called *Tittybangbang* and CBBC kid-entrepreneur sitcom *Kerching!*

Things That Don't Make Sense The Daleks' database on the Doctor includes his habit of saying "allons-y", even though he'd only just adopted that when the Cybermen were cast into the Void with them. As the Daleks inside the Genesis Ark were POWs from the Time War, they have no way of knowing that he'd regenerate into the last two faces we see in this clips compilation. (And if the Cybermen updated it, Eccleston is still a bit of a problem, epistemologically. So's the lack of John Hurt, but we'll let them off this time.) It's worse if you're aware of all the stories whence the footage came, and wonder how and why Daleks or Cybermen would have acquired clips of Peter Davison panicking in "Arc of Infinity" or Colin Baker yelling at Sagacity in "The Trial of a Time Lord", but that way madness (i.e. X9.12, "Hell Bent") lies.

If you're the Cybermen, the first thing you do, upon arrival in a strange time, is locate a mad woman who runs an orphanage. Don't bother to convert her or anything, just play on her incoherent desire to avenge the wrongs done to women by, um, making little girls work in factories.

Nonetheless, you have to construct a huge machine in a hurry. You have an army of Cybermen from an alternate twenty-first century at your disposal. Do you employ these technologically-adept alien cyborgs to bump-start the thing they need to have so *desperately* by themselves or do you team up with a mad woman who runs an orphanage, on the grounds that malnourished Victorian street-urchins have proven expertise in micro-electronics and large-scale foundry-work? Despite Cybermen being tireless machine-men, you need a lot of muscle to power up the CyberKing. You've established your base right next to the Docks, where all those hunky stevedores and sailors congregate. So, obviously, you would abduct... children who've not eaten recently. At midnight.

In fact, the whole timing of this yarn's a bit wonky. The CyberKing has to be ready by dawn of Christmas Day, to appeal to Miss Hartigan's sense of dramatic irony. However, the abduction of the children only gets under way at 2.00pm on Christmas Eve. To effect this, Miss Hartigan bumps off Reverend Fairchild and must have stage-managed his funeral. Even though this enterprise began long enough ago for Lake to have constructed a balloon, it all seems a bit rushed.

In all that time, the baddies have failed to find

Should *Doctor Who* be Appointment Television?

continued from Page 251...

had traditionally been arranged around particular all-family shows, which were themselves scheduled for optimum matching with the majority of mealtimes. Although there is that collective, public, clichéd memory of hiding behind the sofa when watching as a child, ask individual members of the British public about it. Like as not, you will have eating your tea off your lap offered as the genuine recollection of what it was like watching *Doctor Who*. Chris Chibnall tried valiantly to evoke this when "selling" the idea of *Doctor Who* being on Sunday nights in 2018, with a press-release pitching it as part of the routine of getting ready for the school week. (Oddly, he inherited the old *Songs of Praise* slot rather than one associated with drama.) This ritual element, the way an episode of *Doctor Who* slots into the week, was more powerful than the contents of any one episode. This sense of the rightness of things, and the potentially limitless storytelling possibilities, is why the title-sequences are so evocative even compared to the rest of any older episode. You didn't know what was going to happen, but you knew where you were, what time it was, what day and what was for tea.

Don't go thinking that this was an accidental extra. That initial memo from Alice Frick and Sydney Newman's plan for what became *Doctor Who* was explicitly and calculatedly geared towards filling a specific slot in the weekly broadcast schedules. It was a drama version of *Six-Five Special*, a programme for the family in the blank spot before the evening line-up, to make sure that audiences didn't drift away after the sports coverage and Pools results of *Grandstand*. Some episodes commented on their place in the plan. (We've mentioned "The Feast of Steven", but look at the end of 5.7, "The Wheel in Space", a scripted excuse for a rare re-run of an earlier story, or the in-story trailer when the Doctor shows us a Macra claw at the end of 4.6, "The Moonbase".) It was an exercise in what they called 'flow', a familiar drip-feed of episodes from week to week and *Doctor Who* in a niche among other, varied, shows of interest to most of the family across Saturday's schedule.

Britain's most rigorously-timetabled family mealtime is on Christmas Day. The Christmas episodes' entire *raison d'etre* was to be on screen for the family to slump near. Moffat was almost dismissive of this ritual: his comments about what

can be done in a Christmas edition indicate that a drunk, sated, bleary audience don't want clever plots or intricate continuity so much as pretty pictures. Yet even he played along, making each festive extravaganza more larded with tinsel and paper-snow than ever before. By 2014, he was even putting snow and sleigh-bells into the title-sequence.

With the obvious exception of the supposed resolution and ending of Matt Smith's storyline on a planet called "Christmas" and a subplot about a turkey, these episodes are made to function independently of the ongoing storylines. There are good reasons for that, as we've mentioned elsewhere, to do with who is watching and what they can be expected to know, but there is a bonus that – even when it isn't Christmas – these episodes can be shown in isolation. For any other broadcaster, who might be filling a 45-minute "hour" hole with a cheap import, these longer episodes have to be promoted separately as Specials. They might do a theme-night of all the David Tennant Christmases (and Easter and, um, Remembrance Sunday – X4.16, "The Waters of Mars"), or save such episodes for when there is a live sporting event that may or may not over-run, and cause a 75-minute gap in the planned *Midsomer Murders* marathon. They may be doing a telethon, and need a longer-than-usual episode that hasn't been shown yet.

Moffat, of course, was in charge during the single-most elaborate "event" episode in the series's history: the 50th anniversary special. The BBC had foisted 3D on this project, the plot had an Eccleston-shaped hole that needed an entirely new, hitherto unmentioned incarnation to have happened and been forgotten, this in turn needed a season-finale set-up, and the whole thing was simultaneously broadcast in a-hundred-and-umpteen countries, plus a cinema release for anyone who hadn't bought a 3D set (which was everyone, hence the BBC dropping the whole project). Even the title, "The Day of the Doctor" (X7.15), was about the broadcast's circumstances rather than the episode's content. This was the occasion for a publicity blitz and tie-in chocolate bars, but a month later came another biggie: the Christmas/Regeneration episode that was supposed to resolve the on-running storylines.

The interviews around this time were interesting, as people got the two blockbusters muddled

continued on Page 255...

and stop this rather noticeable chap and side-kick, even though he's been going around shouting "I am the Doctor" like he was Colin Baker. Conversely, Jackson Lake "died" three weeks ago, and since then has been heroically trying and failing to untangle the Cybermen plot. Fair enough if it's just been a night or two, but doing this for weeks puts everyone's competence into question.

How come a vicar gets buried on Christmas Eve? He'd have contacts in the trade, of course, but the availability of another vicar at such short notice must be a problem. On this of all days, he'd be too busy. And why is a lady at a funeral so "debatable"? Even if she seems to be a prostitute, the salvation of such a sinner is precisely the sort of memorial a Victorian man of God would want (think of William Gladstone). Her dress isn't *that* inappropriate, compared to keeping your top hat on at the graveside like all these respectable men do. Even weirder, this is the only time the Victorian characters *do* wear hats, after that opening sequence with the cheeky urchin.

What kind of alternate-universe 1851 London is this? One where the Cybermen fell from the sky in a blinding flash and nobody noticed. One Workhouse-owner with an Irish surname going uncommented-upon two years after the Potato Famine we can just about believe, if we hold our breath and screw our eyes really tight shut. Two of them? Mercy, herself conspicuously Hibernian, ignores this.

This must be both the coldest day on record, as all the powdery snow stays put despite all the activity around, and one of the warmest Decembers ever, as Rosita and Miss Hartigan lack gooseflesh despite not having shawls, bonnets or the statutory furry muffs beloved of Dickensian Christmases-for-export and smuttily-minded schoolboys. It's just about plausible that someone could dress like that and not die in daytime – but at night, in the snow, it's just not on.

So, 2.00pm, a massacre at a funeral. By the time the Doctor and Jackson meet Rosita at the balloon it's dark – for once, they got this bit of Christmas in London right – then, next thing we know, it's striking midnight. It's about two in the morning of Christmas Day 1851 when the CyberKing is activated, so why are all those people wandering around whichever bit of London this is supposed to be? Why are none of them police officers? Why are factory chimneys still smoking? Cutlasses on the vicar's wall is sense itself by comparison.

The Doctor recognises the CyberKing as "dreadnought" class, which means it exists elsewhere, but do all Dreadnought ships seriously look like steampunk cosplayers? Do all space-vessels designed by the Lumic-model Cybermen burn coal? And why do Cybermen make a point of calling something a "Dreadnought"? Do they secretly still dread things? And what is that huge metal ball with the spikes doing swinging from the ceiling? Is that really how you generate electricity?

Do info-stamps with damaged cores make Cybermen's heads explode because of an energy discharge, or because they release all of their facts and figures in one go? If the latter, we can put "reading very fast" at the top of the list of Stupidest Weaknesses of the Cybermen ahead of jazz or nail-varnish remover (at least, for now: just wait until X6.12, "Closing Time"). We have to assume that the stamps were of Cyberman design; otherwise, how did the Daleks use them? This just makes their use as anti-Cybermen weapons a spectacular own-goal.

Quite by chance, you've had a lot of biographical data about The One They Call Doc-Tor downloaded into your head. Do you wonder how many hearts you ought to have? Especially after someone's literally pulled out a stethoscope and examined your chest? When the stamps trigger Jackson's first flashback, of the night he allegedly regenerated, he sees himself with overlays of Tennant looking worried. So Jackson thinks his previous self looked *exactly* like the mysterious stranger who's been running around with him but, all the same, accepts "John Smith".

Jackson Lake is a Maths teacher. One of those flamboyant, wealthy maths teachers you all remember from school. He was going to be a University lecturer, but hadn't started work yet. So in the middle of moving house and setting up in London beforehand, he loses his marbles and starts building a balloon. None of his neighbours, who've seen him move in, notice. Nobody from the University went to Latimer Street to knock on the door and ask after him – neither (again) did the Cybermen, who are busy chasing him. And if Jackson's so well-off, why is he living close to the river during the era of the Great Stink?

Lake's T.A.R.D.I.S. is a balloon with no flame under it. He says that he gets gas cheap from the Mutton Street Gasworks. That's fine, sort of, only a Victorian gasworks would be processing coal

Should *Doctor Who* be Appointment Television?

continued from Page 253...

up. Jenna Coleman occasionally tried to avoid spoilers for an episode that had already gone out. The 3D thing is more significant than it appeared, as much of the plot revolved around the mysterious time-paintings (themselves a way to show off the technique) and the whole publicity build-up started with an elaborate trailer emphasising this gimmick (and looking like a computer-game ad as much as a contrived means of using clips from the whole half-century), plus the hashtag "Save the Day".

Those cinema showings, and the global TV simulcast, highlighted a technical problem that thwarts all the pronouncements about how people watch television now. Not everyone has the quality of TV set to make the most of the sound and picture as transmitted. Television professionals seem to assume every viewer is in their income bracket, and cares as much about the image fidelity as they do. Many viewers still have old CRT, 4:3 ratio tellies souped up with digi-boxes. Meanwhile, the BBC's marketing strategy assumes that everyone in the UK has broadband of comparable quality: some bits of Scotland and Wales don't have it at all, while even London is patchy and subject to drop-outs during light drizzle. (Viewers with satellite dishes are more vulnerable to heavier rain, which fills the dishes rather than blocking microwaves. You'd think British engineers would have thought of this but it's a fact of life for the more affluent viewers.)

Moffat's public pronouncements on this are, alas, self-contradictory and rebarbative. On the one hand, the episodes are purposefully made more "cinematic". It's assumed that everyone has the optimum size of screen, and can adjust to the right aspect-ratio. On the other hand, when the ratings slump, everyone calmly states that the series is being watched on people's phones and tablets, so don't panic! The episodes are purposely designed to have big set-piece effects and moody, tense sequences in near-darkness, but nobody watching on a bus with a screen the size of a *TV Comic* panel is missing out, apparently. That's a big change from the 70s. Even when colour was first introduced, the set-designers and so forth were advised to take the majority of viewers seeing the episodes in black-and-white into consideration. A lurid story such as "The Mutants" (9.4) was made to "read" in monochrome. Now, with the picture quality more manipulable than ever before, the

directors and executives are making episodes that some viewers simply can't follow and are doing so by choice. Murk is cool.

However, the return to a continuous run of episodes on Saturdays in autumn wasn't as much of a slam-dunk as many expected. While the feature-length debut of the new Doctor on the Saturday before August Bank Holiday was a hit (X0.1, "Deep Breath" reached 12 million), subsequent episodes were less-watched on first transmission. This is still a drastic improvement on the Saturday evenings a year earlier. *That Puppet Game Show* and *I Love My Country* were spectacular flops, axed after sliding to a barely-registerable 1.2 million viewers. The semi-series shown in September 2012 got *Doctor Who* into hitherto unimaginable positions in the Most Watched stakes, relative to other programmes on at the same time, but the ratings were also high. Series 8's overnight figures (the crude TV-watching estimate without iPlayer or BBC reruns) were wayward, but with none of the fake-poster hoo-hah, just routine trailers. Even at the lowest, it did better than the most popular series of *Robin Hood*. It was looking like the resumption of 1970s-style "normality": autumn debuts with no *Confidential* or *Totally*, and no attempt to make any episode more special than any other bar the new Doctor's introduction.

Yet the fall in overnight ratings to just over eight million between "Deep Breath" and "Into the Dalek" (X8.2) was greeted with something like panic by the BBC, who later moved the start-time to a record late start of 8.30pm. Who but a hard-core fan eats their tea at that hour? What's the point of a family adventure show that goes out after the kids are in bed? Nonetheless, this had no impact on the viewing figures for the rest of the year. The 2015 series had worse problems with the overnight statistics – worse than the "disastrous" ones for Sylvester McCoy's episodes – but nobody correlated this to an 8.35 start-time during a major sporting event lasting a month. By the time Series 10 started, it had been four years since families had all been able to watch together and a whole generation of children had failed to get into the series. The proportion of viewers under 18 was down to 8% (i.e. fewer than half a million children) at exactly the point where the production team had decided to skip complexity and aim for child-friendly content (sort of).

Even in this, the pattern is more complicated in

continued on Page 257...

ABOUT TIME 2008-2009

into town-gas, which is heavier than air. (Yes, it's 50% hydrogen, but with a lot of methane and there's CO_2 in there. Splitting them up would require a process that was undiscovered then, or electrolysis. Passing a current through that lot is a good way to blow up London.) After getting it into the air regardless, the Doctor steers it towards the CyberKing – despite the obvious fact that the breeze would be pushing him in the opposite direction, towards somewhere that isn't on fire.

And if they have a gasworks, they have gas. It had been used across London for a quarter-century by 1851. So why are the street-lights all big candles in glass cases on top of the normal-looking (i.e. gas-powered) lamp-posts? Why are they on in broad daylight?

It's London. It's Russell T Davies. Of *course* there are geographical cock-ups. Our in-house Diamond Geezer pointed out pages of them, but here are the highlights. A whole new bridge seems to have been built between St Paul's Cathedral and Southwark. It's on exactly the same spot as the Millennium Bridge which, as the name suggests, was opened 150 years later. We're told it's 1851 and somewhere around Ludgate. (Fortunately, the corrupted data-stamps have the same wrong information about London that the production team are using. It also suggests factories near the Old Bailey and a smelly gasworks in upmarket Clerkenwell.) Somehow, the Thames just west of Blackfriars' Bridge is deep enough for a giant killer robot to be built there without affecting shipping on the busiest stretch of river in the Empire. Indeed, quite why the baddies have set up base camp in what was then the busiest part of London is another matter for another day. (London might offer some availability of spare parts for alien technology, but even then we're in a pickle. No two manufacturers made the same gauge screws – a problem which beset Babbage's Difference Engine. Birmingham would have been a better bet.)

As every British schoolkid knows, the sewers we see in this story weren't built for another ten years, as part of Joseph Bazagette's programme of Cholera-prevention. As the site seems to be right under Fleet Street, the press would have noticed something that big being constructed in three weeks. The CyberKing marches north from the Thames near St Paul's (why do they love this building so?) and zaps ahead of it. One blast hits Jackson's house as he, Frederick and Rosita are there. So they ran from more-or-less Blackfriars to what looks like Smithfield in five minutes.

Assorted anachronistic oddities: they have loofahs on sale in market-stalls rather than chestnuts, oranges or the proverbially popular hot cakes, but the electrically-lit Christmas tree and pre-Crimean War facial-hair are way off. Jackson Lake-as-the-Doctor speaks of "some advanced form of electrocution" as though the word "electrocution" were common in 1851 (*maybe* that's from the Info-stamp). As you may recall from Volume 8, "fob-watch" is the wrong term for what Jackson has in his waistcoat. "Silly" didn't mean what Jackson uses it to mean, unless he thinks that the TARDIS is feeble or pitiful. Miss Hartigan, as CyberKing, uses *faux*-regal dialogue from before the Civil War ("this I would see', "What do you make of me, sir, an idiot?") as if she's Elizabeth I. And a lot of people are wearing clothes dyed chemically, ahead of the invention of Mauve. She also owns the only two horses in the whole city. Even Fairchild's hearse seems not to have any.

Doesn't the Doctor's brilliant plan to sweep the CyberKing under the carpet, dimensionally speaking, also result in bits of London being consigned to the Void? (The only way to avoid this is if the Cybermen and all their kit and caboodle are infested with the "background radiation" so handy for pulling them back last time. This suggests that they carried steam-engines, pressure-gauges and vast quantities of coal and steel with them between dimensions, on the off-chance that they'd be stuck in the past.)

Amazingly, we've come this far without mentioning the Cyber-Shades. The basic idea is intriguing. Cybernetically-enhanced cats and dogs driving horse-drawn coaches is a bit more of a stretch. How do they hold the reins, or the whip? Why not just make Cyber-horses? Plus, while altered humans doing all the things we've seen Cybermen do is just about imaginable, it's peculiar to believe that altered pets could overcome millions of years of quadrupedal walking so that they can move like the Pantomime Cat in a production of *Dick Whittington*. They also have to adjust to not having tails; odd, for an ex-cat at anything above street-level. Dock a cat's tail, and it loses balance. How do you train them to climb up walls?

We also have no information about what happens to them, beyond the two evaporated when Miss H yells herself to death. The script drops them as if embarrassed by them even before seeing the televised result so, for all we know, they're

Should *Doctor Who* be Appointment Television?

continued from Page 255...

detail. Some parents, alarmed by what was broadcast in the first two Capaldi seasons, took to "auditing" the episodes ahead of watching a time-shifted replay with the children. It's the exact opposite of what Davies intended when he resumed production. He cited communal experiences of *The Lion King* as his model for what the series was for, why it should return. Some viewers get an additional charge out of imagining – or watching – how other people are reacting to the same thing going out now, today, on air at this moment. Watching alone on DVD after the event isn't enough for everyone.

Series 11 squared the circle. The first episode had more promotion (posters on bus shelters, magazine covers and teasers, to say nothing of the free publicity from outraged bigots) than anything

since 2005, plus a three-week gap between the season finale and the one-off special for New Year. The start-time moved around a bit, but in only ten weeks it seems that they'd invented a new habit, making the season as a whole an event.

It was the public's reaction to Series 8 overall that provides the biggest argument against "Event" episodes. Looking at the websites of newspapers, or listening in to conversations on public transport, indicates that everyone remembers the Master's funeral in X3.13, "The Last of the Time Lords", but nobody remembered anything about X4.17, "The End of Time Part One". The ratings suggest the opposite would be the case. But no, in 2014, the general public appeared to believe that Missy would be the person who took the Master's ring from the ashes, a "mystery" resolved in front of 12 million people on Christmas Day 2009.

still in London. (Maybe, as with the Santa-faced Roboforms in "The Runaway Bride", they became licenced cab-drivers.).

And as even the test-screen kids at the BBC noticed… why isn't it a Cyber-Queen? All right, so it's "Cybermen" rather than "Cyberpeople", but Miss Hartigan, of all people, would make the point. And 1851 is "a bit dull" according to the same time traveller who thought it would make the ideal destination for a cheer-up treat after Adric died (19.7, "Time-Flight").

Critique Nobody watching this now enjoys the same *frisson* that – despite any cynicism we might have had about the motives of all concerned – they might not be kidding, and David Morrissey might be the literal Next Doctor. That was a one-off, only good for one ride on one day.

The residue, once that tease is discharged, is often gorgeous and refers back to a lot of fondly-remembered things. It does something new with the Cybermen, and something unprecedented with Victorian London. They are given a spokes-model whose characterisation is cryptic, and frustratingly close to making sense on its own terms. It's not entirely shy of the grubbier side of mid-nineteenth century Britain, a refreshing change from the usual Christmastide Dickensian kitsch, but it's still mainly primary colours and suspiciously-clean snow. That's what people want, apparently. Above all, it has a barnstorming, nuanced performance at its core that threatens to

eclipse the ostensible star for the first 40 minutes or so. Had this been an old-style four-parter, the first three episodes were fine… then it all fell apart and started talking about the least interesting things in the story (so, sort of like 14.2, "The Hand of Fear" or 9.2, "The Curse of Peladon").

The fizz goes away at exactly the point when Rosita thumps Miss Hartigan, losing all agency thereafter. Jackson Lake lets the Doctor rescue his son and resigns himself to info-dumping. After half an hour or more of Lake displaying heroism and inventive responses to threats, he becomes an extra in his own story and the episode just strings together special effects and technobabble. Miss Hartigan has long since stopped being interesting as a person, and has become an odd phenomenon for the Cybermen and the Doctor to deal with. Her death is perfunctory.

All the things we'd been told for nearly five years that the new *Doctor Who* would be better at – and the reasons it was different from the derided old series – have ground to a halt. This has become exactly the sort of thing Davies told us he hated about other shows with aliens and spaceships in. Yet it lacks the things that appeal to the audiences of those series, the internal logic and sense of people who live in this world reacting to new situations plausibly. After such a good opening and interesting development, it's turned into 22.3, "The Mark of the Rani" as Michael Bay would have made it.

Actually, it's not even as satisfying as either mid-

80s Pip & Jane Baker or Hollywood toy-adverts-with-explosions, because you go into those knowing what to expect. "The Mark of the Rani" got most of the period details right, and never forgot that we needed to see the bitchy villainess defeated properly. Autobots and Decepticons have reasons for trashing cities beyond ending a story that ran out of steam (sorry) ten minutes earlier. Nobody signs up for either expecting any depth or subtlety. Distinguished actors used to do *Doctor Who* for their kids or for the Richard Briers Exemption: a chance to stop worrying about subtext or authenticity and play with broad strokes, like in Panto. Audiences came to expect that in the 60s and 70s, and dread it in the 80s.

In 2004-5, we were sold a new, improved series where that wasn't going to happen and, for much of this episode, they try but then it goes into exactly the same mix of children's television acting and "presents for the fans" that got the series cancelled. We've been told, if not ordered at gunpoint, to expect better now. Just last Christmas, we had a potentially interesting cross-pollination of 70s Disaster Movie and twenty-first-century television drama protocols chucked away in the last act, in favour of the sort of thing that works in the *DWM* comic strip but not as television for the over-tens. This year, we see a lot of time, money, software and care misapplied to something monumentally stupid after a much better build-up.

This is British television's most lauded writer, Russell T Davies – a man whose emails got published as hefty books in time for Christmas. He gets interviewed on BBC4 by Mark Lawson and Charlie Brooker. This is what's become BBC drama's most high-profile flagship series. Viewers feel cheated if it's not only failing to live up to the heightened expectations of 2008, but not even doing giant robot rampage malarkey as entertainingly as the notoriously inept finale of "Robot" (12.1) in 1975. There, the thing stomping on soldiers and firing an energy-gun was a character with a valid point of view; resolving the situation upset Sarah and a lot of the viewers. It might seem stupid talking about the motives of a 200-foot killer robot, but this laser-gun carnage in 1851/ Series 4 is pointless and just there for its own sake, ticking a box.

Almost all of the anachronisms and flaws mentioned in **Things That Don't Make Sense** occurred to people (including children) during the first transmission. The woman whose quest for vengeance led her to take charge of a potential instrument of justice might have followed through on the Hollywood vibe and smashed up the half-built Houses of Parliament. She gets precisely one conversation with the Doctor before being semi-converted. A potentially fascinating story about a brilliant mind trapped in Victorian expectations and getting revenge is chucked away, and we never find out why the Cybermen chose her rather than, say, Ada Lovelace. The man who's set himself up as the defender of London Town against aliens and injustice might have involved himself more, tripped the thing up with chains from a railway yard or something. After the first half of the story got us invested in these characters, some kind of pay-off might have been nice. We deserve it for having gritted our teeth when the Cyber Shades appeared.

But no, the Doctor's feeling sorry for himself (again) and so he risks his life to ride in a pretty balloon and point shiny ray-guns at the big nasty robot. It's as if, once the story had reached the cellar in Latimer Road, Davies went off clubbing in Manchester and let Eric Saward take over the script. Except Saward would have been more excited about writing for Cybermen and a big effects budget. (There is an "Excellent" in the dialogue when Miss Hartigan talks to the Cyberleader, as it happens.)

As you may recall from Volumes 5 and 6, Saward – as script editor in the mid-80s – tended to dispatch characters once their plot-functions were over in a particularly uninvolved and uninvolving manner. The ends of stories were almost like accounting exercises, removing anyone left from each faction until the Doctor and his chum(s) were the last speaking-roles standing. Miss Hartigan's departure from the story recalls those dark days. Rosita's whittling down from exposition to onlooker is similarly dispiriting.

It might have been nice if someone had sat director Andy Goddard down in front of the 40s David Lean Dickens adaptations – but, as we've said, we're in the advertisers' idea of nineteenth-century Christmas, aimed at people for whom "Victorian" is one homogenous, unchanging lump. It gives an impression of the time, as people who don't know it think of it, before wrecking it with Cybermen.

And yet, so much of this production is *so nearly right*, the disappointment hurts more than a piece of Saward-edited clockwork storytelling (e.g. 21.1, "Warriors of the Deep") ever could. People are paying attention to a lot of the peripherals – from hanging orange-slices on the Christmas tree to finding the right posters for the walls, and sourcing clips from the TV Movie and old episodes. Ludicrous and occasionally anachronistic as it is, nothing about the CG set-piece at the end looks inept. Dervla Kerwan, as Miss Hartigan, doesn't chew the scenery. David Morrissey starts as a convincing retro-style Doctor, then develops into a credible damaged man. Velile Tshabalala, as Rosita, does as much with an utterly thankless role as anyone could. They all seem to be listening to each other.

Even if we don't go along with Steven Moffat's statements that Christmas episodes should be exempt from usual standards and just accepted as pretty pictures and feelgood vibes watched in the haze of a drunken hour, a lot in the first half of this adventure is better than it needs to be even for an orthodox *Doctor Who* yarn. Indeed, it's way beyond the standards of anything else made for yuletide family viewing (except the production-number adverts for John Lewis or Marks and Sparks). But that's not how it seems as a whole – or in retrospect – and on first broadcast, the first half had an added ingredient that will never be recoverable. This episode centred on a surprise, a much-anticipated Christmas present. Seeing it now is like playing with the box it came in; traditionally something a lot of kids prefer. If you weren't fooled by the coy attempts to kid us that Jackson Lake was actually the Doctor, it wasn't much of a surprise anyway – but then, the gifts and jokes inside Christmas crackers aren't much cop. The episode we have now is gaudy, empty and slightly embarrassing, like a vast pile of *Quality Street* wrappers on Boxing Day.

A lot of the time, reviewing *Doctor Who* requires listening to one's inner eight-year-old. When that eight-year-old, on Christmas Day, is saying *I'm bored* when a giant robot is trashing Victorian London, something has gone very badly wrong. It just sort of happened and then got lost in the shuffle, like the Tritovores next episode.

But if you think *we're* being harsh, check out the end of "Vampires in Venice" (X5.6). This and the two-part season finale immediately before it are the first *Doctor Who* stories ever to be explicitly removed from the canon, on screen, by the Doctor. "The Web Planet" (2.5), "The Horns of Nimon" (17.5) and "Time-Flight" all persist and get acknowledged, but not this one.

The Lore

Written by Russell T Davies. Directed by Andy Goddard. Viewing Figures: (BBC1) 13.1 million, (BBC3 repeat) 2.27 million (this was on BBC1 on New Year's Day, still just under a week from first broadcast). It had AIs of 86% first time, and 88% 'pon de rewind.

Repeats and Overseas Promotion *Der Andere Doktor* ("The Other Doctor"), *Cybernoël*.

Alternate Versions *Children in Need* provided a first glimpse of the pre-credits sequence during the telethon on 14th November. BBC America lose the "how like a man" line (several more in similar vein) and ends with "Bravo, Sir!"

Production

• Almost a year ahead, Davies checked with the BBC Drama heads about whether there would be a Dickens adaptation or similar over Christmas 2008. *Little Dorrit* would be finished weeks before, and the next major Victorian-set Christmas project was a *Cranford* spin-off over 2009. The idea of Cybermen and a man who thinks he's the Doctor came fairly easily, but Davies only had time to pick at it in between drastic rethinks on how to make Series 4's last two episodes work. Other possible festive ideas – a Tudor-era adventure or something involving JK Rowling and a Time-Beetle (X4.11, "Turn Left") – were kicked around, but everyone preferred a Dickensian *Quality Street* Christmas with a giant Cyberman, a variation on the Little Match Girl, and a story where the real Doctor plays companion to someone claiming to be him. The Cyber Shades were conceived as more wraith-like variants on the Cybermats. The end of "Journey's End" (X4.13) was to have been Cybermen materialising aboard the TARDIS and grabbing the Doctor, before all parties spin through the Vortex and land in 1850s London.

• The precise nature of 2009's *Doctor Who* output was still being worked out. It had been public knowledge since September 2007 that that specials would fill in a gap between proper series, but the press couldn't determine whether the 2008 Christmas episode would count as part of this or not. Tennant was signed up for a stint at the Royal Shakespeare Company, touring in July 2008. Davies had a few ideas for how the regeneration ought to work (on the assumption that the star would leave when the executive producer did), but everything was still up in the air.

• By Easter, when the new series began transmission, Davies's workload expanded after Chris Chibnall left *Torchwood* for *Law & Order: UK*, and the projected third series of the Cardiff *Ghostbusters* was rethought as a five-part miniseries. A drawback of the decision to do a year of *Doctor Who* hour-long specials was that funding for longer episodes (harder to timetable and very difficult to sell overseas) wasn't available unless Davies were named as author. This now applied to the hour-long episodes of *Torchwood: Children of Earth*, and Davies had to provide a template for the rethought series and scripts for entire episodes. The BBC were worried about the plan to make three, four or five special episodes of *Doctor Who* rather than a 13-part series; the budgets for these were generally less per minute of air time, and there was less chance of amortising the costs over time than in a proper series.

• Meanwhile, the BBC was under the cosh from the tabloids and back-benchers after a silly dispute over a documentary about the Queen, a clumsily-improvised solution to a problem with a poll on *Blue Peter*, and a hoo-hah about Jonathan Ross's salary all led to the resignation of Peter Fincham, BBC1's head. His replacement was Jay Hunt, beginning in January 2008, so Davies became less inclined to rock the boat. Even when offered a chance to skip the Christmas Special or – at Julie Gardner's suggestion – put production of the entire series on hold for a week to allow time to write the Special properly, Davies stuck to the original plan. He knew that Moffat was already at work on Series 5.

• With rewrites and rethinks of the season finale continuing up to the wire, Davies picked away at the Special for most of spring. He delivered a script on 17th March, two weeks after work had officially started on the episode (you'll recall from last story, this was the period of chickenpox and almost continual last-minute calls on his time). He had plumped for the Victorian feel, and locations were scouted out for a start just under a month later. Tennant had a deadline that made the usual July start to a season impractical, so this was appended to the end of Series 4 rather than being the start of Series 4A or whatever. (All subsequent episodes are considered part of Series 4, even though there's a nine-month gap in produc-

tion after this one and the last, X4.18, "The End of Time Part Two", was broadcast 18 months after the ostensible season finale X4.13, "Journey's End".)

• Susie Liggatt returned as producer after "Turn Left" and the director was a *Torchwood* veteran, Andy Goddard. Plans to render the Cyber Shades in CG were abandoned, and Julie Gardner expanded the proposed Info-Stamp projection of the Doctor into a full-blown flashback of all previous Doctors. (Davies suggested the BBC series *The Hanging Gale* as a source of long-haired Paul McGann images, believing that the confusing ownership of the TV Movie would lead to royalties costs and legal wrangles.)

By 31st March, the script was issued to the cast ahead of a read-through on 4th – although on April Fool's Day, the *NME* had "leaked" news that, after Kylie last Christmas, it would be Amy Winehouse that year. (With online fandom getting the wrong Morrissey through the grapevine, this was only the second-funniest pop-star-related rumour doing the rounds about the episode.) The climax of the episode was reworked after this: the original ending, with an Info-Stamp pointed at the control nexus of the CyberKing, was to all intents and purposes the Doctor shooting a gun at a woman strapped into an electric chair. The eventual solution was considered the least-bad alternative.

• Shooting began on Monday, 7th April, with two days at Fonmon Castle (out in Rhoose, about ten miles west of Barry Island), which was Fairchild's town-house. On the 9th, the big set-piece attack on the funeral was shot at St Woolas's Cemetery. Photos of this leaked, so the Cybermen's return was effectively teased without need of a closing tag-scene in "Journey's End". The first day was the Cybermen stomping through smoke and snow; there was zero chance of that staying secret.

For some of these scenes, small trampolines were secreted behind fake gravestones, or patches of green screen cloth were used to conceal wires in post-production. A SteadiCam was hired for this sequence. Tennant wasn't needed for this material. (He was contemplating a proposal from Steven Moffat to stay on as the Doctor for another year, and smooth over the transition from Davies. He'd been given the weekend to make a decision.) Lambeth Palace granted permission for the older version of the Book of Common Prayer to be used in entertainment. (The BBC has a department for such clearances, and matters to do with Royalty – after the Fincham incident, nobody was taking chances.)

• Sunday 13th was the start of a two-day return to a familiar location, the Maltings (which we last saw as Shan Shen in "Turn Left" and before that as downtown New New York in X3.3, "Gridlock"). This time, it was the courtyard where the pre-credit sequence ends. This done, the location was rigged up for next day's set-piece, the abseiling up the factory wall. Morrissey was coached in lasso-throwing, and this shot was completed before the flying-harness unpleasantness began. On the Tuesday, the team moved to a warehouse (Building 568) that was part of a disused Ministry of Defence complex in Caldicott for a day of sliding around on hidden trolleys. As was becoming usual, the camera was mounted on a quad bike for some shots, with another to drag the two lead actors. (Whether this experience was the final confirmation that Tennant needed to help him decide is unclear, but he met Moffat and Piers Wenger to discuss what a Series 5 would be like, and decided that he'd rather watch it all as a fan than be in it.)

• Another often-used location, Tredegar House, had an outhouse and stables that were useful for the Doctor's reveal of Jackson's identity. The team had assembled both a montage of previous Doctors and a history of London from 1066 to 1851, which were shone onto the walls at the start of the day's work. The tunnels, shot on Friday 18th, were those of Hensol Castle (used since X1.4, "Aliens of London"). The day ended with Tennant's 38th birthday party.

• During this week, Davies had been busy having his photo taken for the cover of *The Writer's Tale* (the first edition, the one where it looks like he'd got a glowing *Doctor Who* codpiece), and rethinking his plan for the Specials now that Tennant was definitely exiting. It was looking as if the next Christmas Special would be the finale and one option, Christmas on Mars, was briefly the front-runner. They knew that a sunny, upbeat story had to come before the *sturm und drag* of the regeneration episode, so Gareth Roberts's desert-planet story was pencilled in for Easter Sunday. There was an option on the table to make the regeneration story a two-parter, but precisely when to show the episode that wasn't on Christmas Day was unclear.

• On Sunday evening, after the services, Gloucester Cathedral became the main location for this story. For four days the back of it, Miller's Green, was used for assorted streets, alleys, docks and the main marketplace. By now, *Doctor Who Confidential*'s popularity had given practical effects supervisor Danny Hargreaves his own cult following, and was causing Liggatt problems. The whole city, it seemed, had come to watch. Fortunately, much of the action was scheduled to happen overnight and school was back after Easter, but there were concerns about the safety of the crowd and spoilers. It was also a problem getting child actors to work such hours, so most days began with their input.

• With *Torchwood* not in production again until July, the Hub set was used for the Factory interior over the last six days of recording. As before, the children were first in the queue, then a trial for Miss Hartigan as the CyberKing tested the contact lenses (she went to SpecSavers, apparently) and a first-attempt helmet (it looked too much like the one in *TW*: "Cyberwoman" – apparently nobody wanted reminders of that episode). Much of the next day was stunts and flying harnesses. (Morrissey's wife, Esther Freud – 22.1, "Attack of the Cybermen" – showed up for this.) On Thursday, 1st May Morrissey finally got to shoot a scene aboard the TARDIS and Graeme Harper recorded the new last shots of "Journey's End".

• The last day, 3rd May, was also the day Tennant and Jimmy Vee made their contribution to the Proms (see A6, "Music of the Spheres"). And that was that for Tennant until January (barring a lot of promotional work). "The Poison Sky" was broadcast that night.

• … then the producers and other interested parties met for a long talk about what should happen next. That was on the 8th, and included an extended conference call between Davies, Wenger and Gardner in Cardiff and Moffat, Tennant and Jane Tranter. Moffat was expected to get a BAFTA craft award for "Blink" on 12th May, so the timetable was to start with the news about the change of executive producers, then discuss Tennant's time off for Shakespeare. With so many eye-witnesses confirming Tennant being in the Christmas episode, they thought that the wilder speculation would be curtailed.

As we've seen in the essay under "The Stolen Earth", it still got pretty silly. The news about Moffat was released on the 20th and – to begin with – this took the sting out (although Phil Collinson, watching TV at the gym with headphones on, saw Davies's face and thought they

ABOUT TIME 2008-2009

were announcing his death). Davies was busy putting out fires with *Torchwood* Series 3 and boggling that he was being considered for the Birthday Honours. Tennant talked up the future on chat shows as Series 4 continued, but the speculation was mounting, mainly on the grounds that he'd said "three years" when he took on the role.

• The fake regeneration at the end of "The Stolen Earth" fuelled the press and internet for another week of this sort of thing, after which Tennant went to the RSC and Morrissey got a lot of practice at teasing interviewers. He briefed his children on how to avoid answers. *Doctor Who* stayed in the news all summer, with Moffat's decision to follow his childhood dream rather than commit to doing a sequel to the Spielberg/Jackson *Tintin* film amusing the tabloids prior to him getting another Hugo for "Blink". The Proms kept Tennant's Doctor in the public eye in late July, and his *Hamlet* opened in August. September was the start of TV awards season, with Catherine Tate and Tennant getting *TV Quick* wins (Tennant was busy on stage, so Bernard Cribbins picked it up and got the biggest cheer of the night).

• By mid-September, when Davies started laying plans for Tennant's big announcement (sardonically named "Operation COBRA", after the incident room used by the Cabinet for national emergencies), everything seemed to be under control. The plan was that Tennant would be addressing the nation at the National Television Awards in late October. In answer to the obvious rhetorical question, what could go wrong was that Tennant, nominated for an award, might not get it (he was running against Catherine Tate); that the awards were announced live; that Tennant would be on stage with Patrick Stewart and a skull at the time the show went out; that someone might blow the gaffe first (Tate was especially loose-lipped), and there was no way to foresee what else would be happening in media that day. That last point was the first hurdle, as a scandal raged on the tabloids' front pages concerning then-fashionable presenter Russell Brand.

Davies also had a small tour promoting a book of the emails between him and *DWM*'s Benjamin Cook – so if the announcement went as planned, a lot of local radio people would line up for a chat anyway. As things turned out, "Brandgate" came to a head just as this was starting, and everyone was trying to distance *Doctor Who* from the BBC's latest controversy. The day of the NTA ceremony,

29th October, was also the day Cook and Davies were interviewed by Richard and Judy (a husband-and-wife team who'd started on the ITV mid-morning show, but moved to a smaller digital station to run a more relaxed and bookish operation), but their sections were recorded before the broadcast (scheduled for after the big reveal).

Hours before the planned bombshell, the BBC suspended Russell Brand (who immediately quit and went to Hollywood) and Jonathan Ross. As we now know, the announcement went without a hitch – Tennant was in the interval of *Hamlet* when his win was announced and, flanked by actors who played guards in the play, he accepted the award and broke the silence. The audience in the Royal Albert Hall were shocked, but not as much as the press, who'd been wrong-footed.

Tennant flanked by actors playing guards in the production, during the intermission of *Hamlet*. He quipped that leaving now was the only way he'd ever give up the part ("you'll be wheeling me out of the TARDIS in my bath-chair" otherwise). This tied in with Davies and Benjamin Cook promoting *The Writer's Tale* and the re-opening of the Cardiff *Doctor Who* exhibition during school half-term, so the series remained visible during a production hiatus. By now the pattern for the Specials was worked out in some detail – there would be four more episodes made after this, and this Doctor's story was knowingly being drawn to a climax.

After the *Children in Need* preview of the pre-credit sequence, this became a self-feeding story. People reported on the speculation, and others wondered why it was so important, then different reporters checked with the bookmakers to see who was the fancied choice. Morrissey refused to rule things out, taking on the bulk of the chat-shows in the weeks before Christmas. Paterson Joseph (X1.12, "Bad Wolf") was the bookies' favourite for a while and joked about it when promoting his new series, a revival of Terry Nation's *Survivors* (also featuring Freema Agyeman). The press warmed over Davies's comments about Russell Tovey, as well as the same old names as the last two times (Bill Nighy, Richard E Grant, James Nesbitt), some newcomers (Chiwetel Ejiofor, David Walliams) and predictable topical jokes. (The BBC had sacked Russell Brand after a tabloid tantrum, so he was cited. Catherine Tate got so used to phone calls from the press, she wondered if she'd been cast without anyone getting clearance to tell her.) The betting on who'd be the real next Doctor intensified after the episode was shown.

On the morning of the special BBC1 edition of *Doctor Who Confidential*, the news broke that betting had been suspended after a sudden interest in an unknown outsider, Matt Smith. On the evening of 3rd January, 6.3 million viewers tuned in and received confirmation that what one wag called "the Work-Experience Doctor" would be taking over in 2010.

X4.15: "Planet of the Dead"

(11th April, 2009)

Which One is This? Get on board with the double-deckers and see… sand. Lots and lots of sand. And a one-off companion more irksome than Mel, Dodo and Adric combined.

Firsts and Lasts *Doctor Who* officially moves over to transmission in HD, after a trial-run with the Proms. It's part of a long tradition of the BBC testing new technical advances on *Who* before using it on anything that matters, like news or *Strictly* (see 17.1, "Destiny of the Daleks"; 18.2, "Meglos"; A3, "Dimensions in Time"; X7.15, "The Day of the Doctor"). Consequently, the story was broadcast on BBCHD at the same time as its BBC1 airing. As practically no other drama made in HD existed as yet, it scooped top ratings for the new channel.

This was the first time the show had filmed outside Europe (unless you count 15 seconds' worth of establishing shots, heavily processed in post, for New York in X3.4, "Daleks in Manhattan"). Dubai, home of all those amazing futuristic buildings ideal for an extraterrestrial *Doctor Who* story, was used as Generic Desert Location. (Presumably the usual Spanish locations were booked and Namibia was reluctant, after *Lexx* and the dreadful reworking of *The Prisoner*.)

The official guest-star, in the titles and everything, is Michelle Ryan. Lady Christina de Souza is the first of a strange new type of sidekick for the Doctor, one who is so obviously companion material as to be downright suspicious (see Amy Pond, Clara Oswald, Ashildr, River Song, Bill Potts…) This happened in the tie-in books and comics, sort of, but apart from Turlough (clearly a rotter from the outset, see Volume 5), this was a bit of a departure for telly *Who*.

The other guest-star is Lee Evans, playing

Malcolm: the first UNIT scientist to be a gushing, socially maladroit geek who adores the Doctor. Unlike Osgood (X8.12, "Death in Heaven") or O'Donnell (X9.4, "Before the Flood"), he isn't horribly killed as soon as he gets fannish.

In a sneak preview of the forthcoming Doctor, we have the first use of "Geronimo", as the name of the pizza delivery company with a number one digit different from UNIT HQ. (This looks like a throwaway joke, but Jubilee Pizza was next door to Torchwood's base in Cardiff…) We also get "He will knock four times" for the first time. And, it's the first episode written after the public knows for certain that Tennant is on his way out.

It's purely subjective, of course, but it's widely accepted that this is the first story to be less entertaining than the attached *Confidential* episode. The making-of story is more edge-of-the-seat exciting and the location, before they turned it into an alien planet, looks a lot more exotic.

Watch Out For…

• It's the first time in 35 years that the Doctor's called in UNIT to help. It might be a coincidence that this iteration is the most reminiscent of the silliest days of the Pertwee era, complete with absurd guest scientist, embarrassing regional accents and the gun-wielders generally not having a clue. And a Rhondium Detector.

• They spent a fortune to shoot this in Dubai. It still looks like a quarry in Dorset, but they took a double-decker bus with them, the long way around.

• We have some scary CG aliens and some comedy cannon-fodder aliens. The former don't get a name, and are just space-locusts. The latter are called "Tritovores". If you can work out the derivation and aren't concerned that it ought to be "tritophages", fine; if not they are, just for a change, Paul Kasey and Ruari Mears in orange boiler-suits wearing animal-masks and gloves. This time, they're being house-flies. The aliens make chittering noises like the Foamasi (18.1, "The Leisure Hive"), and before they appear in full, they're watching the Doctor on a monitor screen, which they stroke lovingly the way old-school monsters did prior to the first cliffhanger. You know, when they appeared in full for the first time (e.g. 12.3, "The Sontaran Experiment"; 13.1, "Terror of the Zygons").

• There's a woman on the bus who's a bit psychic, and offers prophesies of doom when the plot's sagging a bit. To the surprise of nobody who watches US fantasy shows or reads Stephen King, she's black and middle-aged, and is excused any heavy lifting or acts of heroism. She just sits there being spooky, setting up plot-developments for later. Her last jeremiad is: "It is returning... he will knock four times." Under normal circumstances this stereotype would have been the most irritating character in the story. However...

• Michelle Ryan left *EastEnders* to do more varied things, and so had gone to America to star in yet another "gritty", "dark" reboot of a 70s fantasy show with all the charm removed (as was the vogue on US telly in 2003-2008). To nobody's surprise, *The Bionic Woman* was a massive flop, so she was free to dress up as Modesty Blaise and try to talk like Joanna Lumley. For much of this episode, Christina seems to think this is *X Factor* for companions and is just stopping short of mouthing to the viewers "pick me", miming a phone with her thumb and pinkie.

Nonetheless, she is only the *second*-most-annoying character in this story, as they've given us a scientist with a duff Welsh accent. Guess what? He's gauche and clumsy as well.

• In among the apparent cannon-fodder is a future Academy Award nominee. If you found it hard to spot any Oscar potential in X4.7, "The Unicorn and the Wasp", you'll *really* be up a gum-tree here. (HINT: if you're a fan of BBC sketch-shows, think "Parking Patowayo"…)

The Continuity

The Doctor Fond of his current incarnation's teeth, so avoids too much sugar. He tastes the sand to try to determine its constitution.

Surprisingly, he's much better at handling isolated groups of panicky people. [See X4.10, "Midnight". If anything, the absence of a human companion seems to have upped his people-skills – compare this to, for example, X2.11, "Fear Her" or X3.11, "Utopia". Perhaps having human friends makes him stop even trying with others.]

He still isn't thrilled about being saluted [but takes it with better grace from Magambo than we might have observed before "Journey's End" (X4.13)]. He speaks 'every language' – handy with the Tritovores, when the TARDIS is out of range.

• *Background.* He claims to rarely do Easter, because he has trouble finding a moveable feast [we'll write off a hint that he showed up at the original as a gag]. He's memorised the public

UNIT number. [Possibly by a mnemonic about a favourite pizza delivery but it might be in the phone book, since the first option on the menu is for anyone who's made a UFO sighting.] Of all the UNIT stories he might bring up, he mentions the one with the giant robot [12.1, "Robot", surprisingly].

He mentions Donna in passing and a number of adventures: World War One, the creation of the universe [19.1, "Castrovalva"], the end of the universe ["Utopia"], 'the' war between China and Japan [there's many], and the Court of King Athelstan in 924 AD. He's seen *Monty Python's The Meaning of Life* [unless he just thinks that machines that go "ping" are intrinsically funny].

• *Ethics.* He facilitates Christina's escape upon her arrest, so that she can fly off with the alien-enhanced double-decker. [Maybe he thinks he owes her one, or just doesn't want to explain what he did to £18 million-worth of antique cup.] He does, however, refuse to bring her along in the TARDIS, claiming that he doesn't want anyone to be hurt by travelling with him. [That's more or less consistent with the Specials arc. It's open to interpretation whether her questionable ethics are a deal-breaker, but he doesn't seem impressed by her lifestyle.]

• *Inventory: Sonic Screwdriver.* It can superspeed a winch. It also adds the superphone enhancement to Barclay's mobile, opens handcuffs at 30 paces and turns the Doctor's glasses into a pair of shades. [He takes them off before using ultrasound on them, as pointing the screwdriver at his eyes would give him a splitting headache. Nobody involved in Series 9 or 10 seems to have thought of this.] It can somehow open the doors of a bus, despite the lack of pneumatic pressure [otherwise he'd use the buttons like anyone else].

• *Inventory: Psychic Paper.* As we've seen before, it works on Oyster card readers. It also identifies him to UNIT personnel.

• *Inventory: Other.* Another wacky alien-detection device alerted him to the gestating wormhole problem. [It seems to be a version of the doo-hickey he built in 11.1, "The Time Warrior" – that device was a rhondium sensor that detected delta particles using a lump of rhondium, to alert him to any space-time matter-transmitter shenanigans. This new gizmo detects rhondium particles, to alert him to any wormhole shenanigans. Yes, maybe you need rhondium – whatever that is – in solid form to detect the particles and, yes, maybe

What Difference Did Field-Removed Video Make?

First off, we should pause to explain the tense in the title question. *Doctor Who* was made in the then-standard field-removed format between 2005 (X1.1, "Rose") and 2008 (X4.14, "The Next Doctor"). The next episode, "Planet of the Dead" (X4.15), was the first to have been shot in the new High Definition format, a fact trumpeted loudly in the publicity material. If you didn't notice any difference after this, you're not alone – but you're probably either advanced in years, or not in Britain. Or you've not bought a new television this century, which is environmentally prudent, but increasingly strange. The overseas broadcasts are often degraded back to SD format (standard definition, or "normal" as older people think of it), so people there watching on phones aren't losing out compared to people watching on vast plasma sets. Even if you are now accustomed to HD, and find going back a bit of a lurch, it's not such a big change as earlier ones. The gulf between film and 625-line video tape is far bigger, as was the wrenching change between orthodox video-tape and Field-Removed VT.

If you can't see the difference between the picture-quality in "Rose" and "Survival" (26.4), there are two possible explanations: Either you're one of those strange people mentioned in the first edition version of **Which is Better, Film or Video?** under 12.3, "The Sontaran Experiment", or you have only ever seen *Doctor Who* on imported, standard-converted copies (such as were used in American broadcasts of British shows until relatively recently) and/or only ever used an LCD or plasma screen. For about half of the original first-night audience, buying a new set to catch up with all the changes in picture-format was an ambition for the medium-term future; about half of *them* were still watching in 4:3 ratio. (See **Why is Trinity Wells on Jackie's Telly?** under X1.4, "Aliens of London" for a lot more on this.) They were watching the then-standard 625-line, 50i, colour transmissions as had been possible since 1967, compulsory since 1974 and the broadcast standard since November 1969.

The "50i" bit is the important one here. What appears on a television screen is never a whole picture. In Britain, the standard has been to have alternate halves of the whole image broadcast, decoded and scanned onto the screen at home with a refresh-cycle that effectively means 25 entire images per second. Not that the eye can perceive even these but the rapidity of overlapping half-images, 50 in a second, makes for a smooth and natural-looking picture.

In America, they have been using 60 half-images (the correct term is "fields"), or 30 frames a second if it had been whole pictures. Cinema uses 24 frames per second, as does most telecine equipment. Conveniently, both the US NTSC and UK's PAL can readily be adjusted to almost this (although US digital copies of filmed series from the past occasionally judder as people move across the screen). For decades, many viewers have known that a TV screening of a feature film, with no adverts, is fractionally shorter than seeing it at a cinema. (It's about 4% for PAL, so Bank Holiday showings of *Around the World in Eighty Days* are shorter than sitting through it at the pictures, by the length of time that end-credit animated summary of what you've already seen takes.) It's 50 in the UK and 60 in the US, simply because that's the cycle-rate of the alternating current coming out of the socket. Britain always used to have 50Hz, 240 Volt, 13 amp power (now it's 220v to harmonise a bit better with EU supply and, in theory, sell more machinery overseas).

Older *Doctor Who* fans will know the next bit only too well: film copies of 50i video lose detail and look jerky and cold. What the BBC called "telerecordings" and America calls "Kinescopes" were the main way of preserving broadcasts if the tape was re-used or unusable. The technicians pointed a 16mm camera at a top-quality monitor and filmed the pictures off the screen, 24 frames a second, to flog overseas. About half the picture-information is lost. Even after the conventional picture-restoration, the VHS releases of Hartnell and Troughton stories seemed to have been made in the 1940s.

Then came the digital jiggery-pokery we've come to know as vidFIRE. This is, to put it at its crudest, a way of getting a computer to guess what the fields between frames of film ought to have been like, interpolating them between fields made up of the film-frames, and making a result that resembles (as far as anyone ever will know) the original VT. For anyone who saw the originals on first broadcast, the result is semi-magical. For those raised on the telerecordings, it's a bit of a shame that the "Nowhere" in 6.2, "The Mind Robber" is now obviously a television studio. We touched on this in **How Does This Play In Pyongyang?** under X4.1, "Partners in Crime", but it's worth bearing in mind for what is to follow.

continued on Page 267...

265

Linx was using a wormhole instead of a simple time-scoop – whatever "simple" means here – but we ought to note this distinction in case anyone thinks we're slacking. Neither should be confused with *rhodium* detectors, used in real-life nuclear reactors to measure neutron flux.]

The TARDIS. The Doctor as good as says the Queen lets him park at Buckingham Palace. [We know from "Voyage of the Damned" (X4.0) that there's some kind of understanding there (see also 23.1, "The Mysterious Planet").] He implies that he can influence the wormhole's opening to direct the stingrays towards uninhabited planets.

The Supporting Cast

• *Lady Christina de Souza.* She is an aristocrat whose family has fallen on hard times, but this seems like a flimsy pretext for daring robberies and general louche behaviour. She is shamelessly arrogant and puts herself in charge of any situation. She planned an escape with an accomplice, Dmitry, but abandons him when the police catch him first. Despite this ruthlessness, there's no sign of a good backup plan; she spectacularly fails to remember what London public transport cards are called. At the end, she's very keen on travelling with the Doctor; more than he is on her coming along. However, the Doctor lets her leave in the No. 200 double-decker bus, which has been modified for flight.

UNIT It's only UNIT this time [it's a small-sized threat, in London, so there's no reason for the Cardiff kids to involve themselves]. The "proper" version of Captain Erisa Magambo is just as calm, responsible, and no-nonsense as her parallel self [X4.11, "Turn Left"]. According to her, everyone wants to meet the Doctor, but fears the circumstances under which this is possible. She appoints a Sgt Calhoon to keep order and deal with the press and public.

UNIT also has a new scientific advisor: Malcolm Taylor, a Welsh fanboy who loves homages to *Quatermass*. [He named the unit of spacetime flux after himself, but 100 malcolms = one bernard. See **Is This the Quatermass Continuum?** under 15.3, "Image of the Fendahl", plus 25.1, "Remembrance of the Daleks" and X2.0, "The Christmas Invasion". Non-SI units take a while to be accepted and need three separate experimental verifications for the *mise en practique* to be agreed,

which raises worrying issues of what else involved something measurable in bernards.]

When the area commanding officer authorises it, UNIT has a shoot-to-kill policy. The policy for handling civilians caught in the middle of an incident involves Geiger counters, screening and debriefing. The Doctor's name still carries a goodish amount of weight and he can recommend random civilians for recruitment. The UNIT phone is set up so that if you press zero, it'll transfer you to a live operative.

Planet Notes

• *San Helios.* A planet in the Scorpion Nebula, halfway across the universe from Earth. The system has three suns. It had a population of one hundred billion a year before.

The Non-Humans

• *Tritovore.* As the name suggests, they are dung-eaters and so, appropriately if unimaginatively, look like giant house-flies in boiler-suits [cf. A5, "The Infinite Quest" and the Mantasphids]. For some reason, their translation technology isn't working both ways [c.f. the Hath (X4.6, "The Doctor's Daughter") and the Sycorax (X2.0, "The Christmas Invasion"), not to mention the Foamasi (18.1, "The Leisure Hive") and Erato (17.3, "The Creature From the Pit" – all beings with no larynx or jawbone as we understand them, except the Sycorax, who were just rude].

They have some reasonably sophisticated spaceships, powered by a crystal nucleus that runs on dry filaments. This has to be supported by anti-grav clamps. Captains don't leave their ships.

• *Stingrays.* Even less interesting. They're massive metallic flying stingrays, who eat the easily accessible organic and metallic content of planets. Their shells allow them to generate electrical fields [and we have a laborious explanation of Faraday Cages to get the message across, although it's more deft than the one in X9.3, "Under the Lake"]. They travel by flying around planets so fast, they rip a hole in spacetime towards another planet. The Doctor doesn't think they're sentient.

History

• *Dating.* The bus driver confirms that it's April. [It might as well be Easter Sunday, but with the buses apparently running as normal and a lot of traffic. So which Easter was it? It could be the day

What Difference Did Field-Removed Video Make?

continued from Page 265...

As we saw in that essay in Volume 4, there is an innate prejudice against VT as a medium among people raised to think of it as a cheap substitute for the "real thing". For those people, the look of Field-Removed Video is desirable as an end in itself. Field-removed video is, as the name suggests, a sort of reverse vidFIRE where the fields of a VT image are bundled together into 24 faked-up frames every second, the intermediate half-frames dropped and the result messed with in post-production so that it looks like film. A bit.

[Side note to say... "Film-look", the less-technical term for field-removed video, is a misnomer as anyone who has seen all the different ways film can look will have noticed. If you want to revisit the Series 1 trailer, which really *was* made on 35mm film, you'll see how odd it looks compared to Series 1. However, specific adjustments to a digitally-sourced image need to be made if they are attempting to make the end-result approximate the actual look of film, as we will now see. Field-removal isn't just to fake film, as it can help with standards conversion and processing old films for broadcast.]

Take a look at the cut scenes from Series 4's DVD to see what the unprocessed feed from the cameras looks like. Those of you still with cathode-ray tube sets that can take a DVD feed can see it in its full strangeness. It's obviously video, but lit weirdly. There are a number of reasons for this to do with the amount of available light an individual pixel on a CCD (charged coupling device, the video-camera equivalent of the film negative) requires, relative to how much light film needs. If the end-product is going to resemble film as much as possible, the sets or locations need to be lit like film – even though the reasons for film-lighting being so lurid are to do with shutter-speed and depth-of-field, film emulsion's less linear response to the number of candles per square centimetre ("candles" as a unit of light-intensity, not real ones) and the human eye's logarithmic response to intensity. None of these except the last really applies to video – a pixel getting twice as much light gives out twice as much energy, therefore the aperture doesn't need to be completely re-adjusted just because a different focus is applied.

["Aperture"? The iris-like mechanism that makes a hole for the light to get through, and which used to be the main way to determine how light or dark a picture you'd record on film emulsion. If you're undercranking a film to speed up the playback pictures, you need to tighten the aperture to amend for having each frame of film exposed a little longer than the usual 1/24th second. It also comes into play when you are trying to get a lot of different planes, i.e. things at different distance from the camera, into focus or not. This matters more if you are using physically smaller film-frames, 16mm or 8mm, or using colour film instead of black and white.]

The majority of film used for television before practically everyone went over to so-called "film-look" video was 16mm – for which coloured lighting was sometimes needed in every plane of the image, so that it didn't all look like it was made inside a cupboard. (One of the many paradoxes at work here is that the lenses for video cameras were better at capturing sharp images in lower lighting, and gave pictures comparable to the superior 35mm film. However, the industry-standard had shifted to 16mm, so programme-makers opted for a degraded video image to make it look more "classy", i.e. more like what people subconsciously interpreted as being more expensive per minute.)

Much of the film used for 1970s television was the cheap, fast colour-reversal negatives. These had the virtue of not needing an intermediate step; news footage could be processed within a day, and on screen within hours if the camera was in the same country. However, the blue layer of the film faded faster than the red or green (pigment using those three rather than the red, yellow and blue of light in a video camera). Or the stock that did need reversing from negatives was sometimes mistimed and came out faded in some hues. Or the telecines machines used (Rank Cintels more often than not) had a damaged tube. So we have inherited a myth that the 1970s were a sea of browns and beiges.

It's slightly different regarding *Doctor Who*, as the film used is within a video-taped broadcast and so retains the original colours, albeit not *quite* the same way that they appear with the same props or costumes in the studio. (Tom Baker's first velvet jacket is a clear example; it looks brown on location and near-black purple at Television Centre.) Nobody is entirely sure what life-expectancy digital media have. Video-tape from the 60s is already as fragile as 1920s celluloid, relying as it

continued on Page 269...

ABOUT TIME 2008-2009

after transmission, 12th April, 2009. Or, maintaining the whole Year Ahead of Broadcast paradigm would make it 4th April, 2010. The bus passengers discuss the whole "planets in the sky" thing from X4.12-4.13, "The Stolen Earth"/"Journey's End", and Carmen vaguely forecasts Gallifrey's return ('it is returning') in X4.17-4.18 "The End of Time". For what it's worth, *SJA*: "Mona Lisa's Revenge" refers back to this story, so it can't be any later than that – nothing rules out that the Doctor's bus ride was, in calendar time, after Sarah's wedding, which he crashed in an earlier *SJA* story we'll look at in the Appendix.]

Christina's father lost his fortune in the Icelandic banking crisis [late 2008 in our world, the effects really manifesting in Britain in mid-2009]. The mobile phone advertising on the bus refers to the company run by Josiah Naismith [see a few episodes down the line, and **The Lore** for a near-miss with lawyers on that front].

Athelstan gave a jewelled gold cup to Hywel, King of Wales. It survived, unsullied, until the Doctor bashed it out of shape.

The Doctor isn't at all surprised to run into a casual psychic whose abilities are enhanced by alien surroundings. [This would explain a lot about the way psychic abilities manifest in the *Doctor Who* universe; see 15.3, "Image of the Fendahl".]

The Analysis

The Big Picture The two accredited authors each had earlier versions of the two big ideas here. The swarm of aliens flooding through a wormhole into present-day London was the first-thought idea of the problem that would get Penny into the Doctor's life – or, later, Donna back in (X4.1, "Partners in Crime"). This idea was also the occasion for Davies's misprision of "tribophysics" (the science of lubrication) and "triobiphysics" (the science of making doorways appear by waving your hands about, as per 13.3, "Pyramids of Mars") in *Damaged Goods*, his *New Adventures* contribution. The busful of people whisked across the galaxy was handled in more detail in Gareth Roberts's first novel, *The Highest Science* (except it was a train and the aliens were like the Ice Warriors, but quadrupeds – see **Wot? No Chelonians?** under X5.12, "The Pandorica Opens").

That idea was a version of the supposedly-

common commuter daydream about which of the strangers you're travelling with would be friends or enemies, which would crack up, which would be romantically-involved and so on should the train, bus or tram be ambushed by aliens or whatever. It was in the public eye again as the US series *Lost* began and Davies's former mentor Paul Abbott was talking up the first episode as a textbook example of modern television writing. Difficult as it may be to believe now, *Lost* Season 1 was being talked up in the broadsheets as a new kind of TV drama, one where the small details were in fact clues to planned developments and the eventual final mystery.

The late 2000s was a peak time for this form of narrative – common in the kinds of "cult" shows posh critics didn't watch for decades before, but now offered to mainstream audiences. (The pompous reboot of *Battlestar Galactica*, the much-hyped first series of *Heroes*, the child-friendly *Smallville*, the less-watched *The Sarah Connor Chronicles* and *Eureka* and Davies's *Doctor Who* were all the subjects of think-pieces on how it was now officially "cool" to like this sort of thing, all ignoring the simple fact that *Buffy the Vampire Slayer* and, before that, *Babylon 5* had done it *despite* studio interference rather than at the networks' urging. And woe betide anyone bringing up the subject of *Blakes 7* inadvertently beating them all to the punch by decades or old-style *Doctor Who* sort-of doing it with Metebelis Crystals in the early 70s.)

Carmen's proleptic fits are as obvious a period detail for 2009 as bad CSO for 1974, Linn-drums and emulators for 1987, or one of the regulars taking an episode to sleep off a gas-attack in 1968. Whatever qualms we might have about the predictable combination of ethnicity, sex, age and lack of any other plot-function or character at all (and this is almost a decade after Spike Lee gave the cliché a bad name), a character is needed to drop unhelpful-but-tantalising hints of the forthcoming plot.

Shortly after Roberts submitted his book proposal, the allegedly universal daydream was the focus of dismal ITV fantasy-drama *The Last Train*, in which a train in a tunnel was the only place immune from a gas attack that emptied Britain. (Roberts approached the idea of two people stuck on an otherwise abandoned Earth in *The Sarah Jane Adventures,* but that version of the idea was even more frequently-used from the 1970s on, as

What Difference Did Field-Removed Video Make?

continued from Page 267...

does on whale-oil to bind the magnetic oxide to the plastic strip.

Nonetheless, one production-aspect is now much more like film that older-format television production. The majority of shoots, either on location or in a studio, just use one camera and take multiple angles of the same scene, one after the other. For each line-up, the lighting has to be rearranged and practical effects reset. This automatically pushes up costs and reduces the potential amount of footage shot per day. Again, though, this is not unlike the production of the all-VT location work that characterised Sylvester McCoy's term as the Doctor. There is less of a gulf between "Survival" and "Rose" than between either and the last story to be made at Television Centre, 26.2, "Ghost Light".

In the latter, although there are many cutaways and inserts along the way, the bulk of the screen-time entails long takes shot on three cameras, all directed from a studio gallery far overhead. The actors, most of whom have theatre experience, have to respond to each other in real time rather than speak lines to a camera in response to an off-screen floor-manager reading the cue-lines, as might happen on location or a movie. This affects the intensity of the performances. Directors trained in the three-camera studio have to be good with actors, first and foremost, but adept at the split-second timing of camera-changes. And it all needs a lot of rehearsal, something now thought of as a luxury. Three weeks in a church-hall or bespoke rehearsal-room tied up fewer resources when there was a rapid turnaround of studios for everything the BBC did. Perhaps the biggest change that the one-camera system needed, and caused, was a purpose-built complex just for Doctor Who (after a lot of "guerilla" shooting in the first two years; see Volume 7).

Incidentally, don't run away with the idea that faux-film production techniques have completely replaced the older style of television production in Britain. The majority of British-made soaps and continuing dramas are still made in this way. When, on occasion, some hot-shot new producer comes along and decides to "upgrade" to "film-look", the result is a drop in ratings and a huge outcry, whereupon it's quietly dropped. (Or, if the hot-shot is one of a number of increasingly desperate measures to arrest a decline in a long-running series, the shift to the gimmicky new format,

bringing back old characters and a new regular time every month all combine to sound the show's death-knell.) Viewers like dramas to look as if they are really happening in real time. Similarly, the news isn't tinkered with to anywhere near the same extent as it could be, at least as far as picture-quality goes. (We're speaking as if all field-removed images take a while to do, but there is a version that can be applied to live broadcasts. An experimental Top of the Pops from 1991 was roundly condemned for attempting to mess with the familiar formula.)

Nonetheless, the relative low cost of re-usable tape as against film, which needs to be printed, developed and returned before anyone knows what they did on the day, affords a degree of redo-ability denied the three-camera studios. As you will recall from Volumes 1 to 3, each 25-minute episode was allocated enough time to re-do one recording-block (if the video machine would rewind, which wasn't always certain) from the last time they paused the recording, anything up to ten minutes before. Even into the 1980s, fluffed deliveries were kept because there wasn't time to retake.

Yet with so much of the BBC Wales version being shot on locations that had a best-before date, up to and including the building being scheduled for demolition, the new model isn't as luxuriantly relaxed as it might appear. The production is working to a deadline, and that includes the pre-arranged broadcast dates. Even when the episode is finally in the can (and that can take ages, as witnessed by X3.1, "Smith and Jones" or X2.1, "New Earth"), there's a mountain of post-production to do, starting with converting the image to the field-removed format.

It's in post-production that the most obvious benefits of field-removed come to the fore. Film-stock has been evolving over decades, and now comes with an inherent bias close to that of the human eye. Video records faithfully what is put in front of it. While film printed from untreated negatives can look flat and has disproportionate responses to light-levels at different intensities, this is slightly compensated for by the simple fact that half the time you are watching film projected on a screen, the whole screen is dark as the frame moves on. Thus, in video post-production there is a whole science of grading the image. Any aspect, colour, contrast, grain (or the equivalent) and the

continued on Page 271...

ABOUT TIME 2008-2009

we saw with 12.3, "The Sontaran Experiment".) However, as we've already mentioned *Lost,* you can join the dots for yourselves. The flying sting-rays setting up a space-time flaw is sufficiently like the Zamp-loops in Roberts's last *New Adventures* yarn, *Zamper,* to be worth a mention.

One aspect of the story that's got a slightly more curious past is the link made between Faraday cages and ESP. Here we get into the murky world of Theosophists, MKULTRA and Mesmerism (which, as you'll recall from 4.9, "The Evil of the Daleks", was posited as a literal magnetic phenomenon; see **What Planet was David Whitaker On?** under 5.7, "The Wheel in Space"). From 1947 on, someone called Andrija Puharich was attempting to prove that neurons acted like radio antennae and, after 1953, got US military funding for it. He put subjects inside Faraday cages to block out local electromagnetic disturbances (including, according to the theory, Earth's own magnetosphere) and claimed that this would enhance receptivity. Before Uncle Sam footed the bill, he had received money from a body he and his wealthy subjects set up: the Round Table Foundation of Electrobiology, whose members included Henry A Wallace (former US Vice-President and agricultural reformer, supposedly responsible for the eye in the pyramid on the $1 bill) and Arthur M Young (of Bell helicopter fame). And the CIA was somewhere in there, apparently.

The idea resurfaced in the 1970s when Stanford Research Institute in (where else) California used it as a means to prove that no trickery was possible – blocking off hidden radios – as well as supposedly enhancing remote viewing of top secret Kremlin papers or whatever. Their published papers in *Nature* have been roundly ridiculed and unpicked for dodgy methodology, but it gave a veneer of objectivity and science probity to tests on Uri Geller (see 11.5, "Planet of the Spiders" and our comments on the Hieronymus Device).

Before all this, and largely unknown to the US, the Soviets had developed similar ideas since the 1920s, mainly under the influence of an Italian neurologist called Cazzamalli, and one Vladimir Bekhterev had supposedly shown that "mental radio" was the true secret of hypnotism by placing mesmerised subjects in a Faraday cage, whereupon the spell broke and they were themselves again. The connection between Faraday cages and supposedly serious research into the paranormal

was confirmed in the public imagination in a 1957 episode of *Perry Mason* ("The Case of the Missing Medium"). In the 1970s, it was a known part of the sales pitch for the "ESP episode" of any long-running TV series, along with Zener Cards and water-tanks (or, if they could afford it or get the right stock footage, submarines). We'll see this association of ideas again in X9.3-9.4, "Under the Lake"/"Before the Flood".

Although the whole heist and police chase aspect is played for laughs, the shots of police and military vehicles at a road tunnel have a familiar look. In the wake of the 7th July bus and tube bombs, there were frequent exercises for how the armed forces and emergency services would react to various contingencies. More by luck than judgement, the wrecked double-decker (see **The Lore**) landed up looking like the news footage of the overground aftermath, when one of the would-be "martyrs" missed the tube and had to self-immolate on a bus. (One of the most striking images, used by *The Sun* whenever they wanted to stoke up islamophobia, was of John Tulloch, co-author of *Doctor Who: The Unfolding Text.* He successfully sued the Murdoch tabloid for a border-line hate-crime in his name.) But those photos went around the world and struck chords with people because it was a red double-decker, as emblematic of London's tourist idea as the Houses of Parliament, Tower Bridge or the Changing of the Guard. Or the red phone boxes replaced everywhere that tourists don't go.

In particular, it's how overseas film companies try to sell London-ness to people when they are cashing in on the city's appeal. Thus whenever a UK-based production tries to go for a global hit, the double-deckers are pushed front and centre. In 1963, the first bid to make Cliff Richard an international star was a film about him and his usual co-stars driving one across Europe – with a token American girl as the love-interest, because they honestly thought *Summer Holiday* would appeal. (Lauri Peters vanished without trace, but everyone remembers Una Stubbs.) Endless US-financed "Swinging London" films brandished the things. *Kaleidoscope, Sebastian, Modesty Blaise* (see below), *Casino Royale* – the entertaining 60s one – *Blow Up,* even *Thirty is a Dangerous Age, Cynthia...* any time the object of the exercise was to flog the flick to the Yanks, out came the red Routemasters.[48]

An attempted Anglo-American franchise, *Here*

What Difference Did Field-Removed Video Make?

continued from Page 269...

smoothness of a tracking-shot can be altered digitally. The eye notices more distinctions between darker tones that are fairly close in intensity than between two higher-intensity shots that are far further apart (e.g. 10 candles per square centimetre looks more different from 20 cd/cm2 than 200 looks from 400).

The graph of input to output across all intensities is a reasonably straight incline for video, whereas for film there are kinks, the "toe", "knee" and "shoulder", where it needs more change in the light to cause a change in the recorded intensity. A video camera shoots what's there, but reality has to be made more "realistic", more how human eyes and brains perceive and interpret it. It can also be made *less* like what was happening on the day of the shoot, so grey skies and heavy rain can be magically brightened, sunsets created with a twist of a knob or fields of barley turned purple. It's no more effort to do this than to render the image "normal"-looking. In the end-credits of most US television, you'll see the credit "Color Timer": that's a holdover from the era when film was chemically developed. These days, it's the job-title of the person in charge of the digital grading.

Again, we're not so far away from what was being done in the last days of the older series; the advent of Paintbox and HARRY allowed the episodes made after the 18-month suspension to integrate digital malarkey seamlessly (by the standards of the time). The generation of cameras in use in 2005 had different baseline responses than before (and we'll come to that in a while), but the techniques are almost unchanged. While for some purposes the idea is to make the video look like old-style video, as with news, even the majority of feature films for theatrical release are originated (sic) on video cameras and get adjusted to mimic 35mm film. Few multiplexes show actual celluloid films now, it's almost all digital projection. Some neurologists and cineastes reckon that this makes modern films less memorable.

Hard as it is to imagine now, if you didn't experience it at the time, the majority of news coverage in the 1960s and 70s was on film. Often the colour-reversal stock that could be processed more rapidly – although overseas stories often entailed a three day time-lag between hearing about an event and seeing it. Thus the *faux* news reports in, for example, 9.1, "Day of the Daleks" looked almost like a real news report in a way that Trinity Wells or Kirstie Wark in a real newsroom, but on field-removed footage, can't. In later instances, the image was degraded further by pointing a camera at a television set conveying these jeremiads, so that we were told subconsciously that someone in the story was watching television (the individual pixels or phosphor dots were visible, and the newsreader's whole face was only briefly shown before a close-up of her mouth). The *frisson* that accompanied Kenneth Kendall doing a bulletin about rogue robots on a killing-spree in London (3.10, "The War Machines") is gone. The news doesn't want to be mistaken for a feature film.

Material originated on VT and processed to look like film didn't always mean "quality drama" the way some commentators seem to believe. The earliest imports of *Star Trek: The Next Generation* were in a format that looked shockingly bad when shown on UK screens, even in the year of manufacture. (BBC2 viewers had a four-year delay because of the satellite television bottleneck we outlined in Volume 7.) NTSC conversions approached UK broadcast standards in the 1990s (although the gag about it standing for "Never twice same colour" remained valid), but it was mainly the lower echelons of imported television drama that used it. (Imports on video-tape from electronic studios were even more derided. Such series were used as fillers until 1977, when *Soap* surprised everyone by being genuinely funny, and changing UK perceptions of US sitcoms. Even then, most were shoved on in the gap between kid's shows and the news. When *Dallas* adopted this format, everyone knew the former hit was on borrowed time. It looked "Cult".) Series made this way were the sorts of programmes more likely to have actors with latex masks, digitally-modelled spaceships and guest appearances by Brad Dourif, so posh critics failed to spot the shift.

However, a lot of the mainstream soaps from abroad, and any new ones starting on British television, used field-removed as standard – and soon so did dramas that you were allowed to admit to watching. Similarly, sitcoms trying to ape US models jumped on the bandwagon. Steven Moffat's *Coupling* looked a bit weird at first, pretending to be on film and consequently having odd-coloured sets, but this was accepted as part of the BBCs bid to replicate *Friends* in every detail, even the picture-quality. By 2002, the centre of gravity had shifted so that orthodox video seemed perverse.

continued on Page 273...

Come the Double Deckers, had an ostensible lead from America and some terribly English kids hanging out in one in a junk-yard, with Melvyn Hayes (from *Summer Holiday*) as their token adult chum (see also 2.7, "The Space Museum" and "The Sontaran Experiment" for that programme's pedigree). The decision to make a story about a red London bus (not a Routemaster any more, even the 159 from Brixton had stopped running them in 2005) whisked to another planet made for a publicity still guaranteed to make the overseas markets bite.

We can't say that this is unprecedented: one of these icons of London-ness, abruptly wrenched from context and left in a desolate wilderness, makes as arresting an image as a police-box in a blasted heath at the end of the very first episode (1.1, "An Unearthly Child"). One of them flying over the heads of police and soldiers is as improbable and cosily English as a Ford Anglia flying over the countryside in *Harry Potter*. If a Hollywood producer were trying to invent a franchise along these lines, it's difficult to see anyone doing better than what we got, but it would be laughed at in Blighty as too crassly obvious. (The only way to top this would entail Concorde landing in Prehistoric times with a crashed alien ship and an Arabian Nights sorcerer, but that way madness lies – 19.7, "Time-Flight" being as good a definition of "madness" as any in this context.)

It's hardly a coincidence that "Planet of the Dead", a stand-alone "special" made in the new HD format, leaves so little to chance. Davies's name on the credits was almost the only thing that got this made (regardless of whether he really did any more than other Gareth Roberts episodes) and, without a proper series to help sell it, this one needed to be all pitch and no novelty. It doesn't have the "here comes the regeneration…" buzz, neither is it Christmas, so an hour-long piece needs all the help it can get. Davies wasn't about to install the first available American in the guest-star role but, instead, got someone known to US "Cult" audiences to play the other reliable Yank-bait, Posh Totty.

The obvious starting-points for this story's guest-companion are Emma Peel and Modesty Blaise, 1960s assertive women with a penchant for clingy catsuits and breaking-and-entering. Mrs Peel, in particular, combined the athleticism and polymath skill-set with a vaguely aristocratic savoir faire (she mixed with lords a lot, as if she'd

known them for a while). Her main characteristic was the ability to keep cool and quipping when captured, shot at or worse.

These traits, plus a lot of Indiana Jones, fed into the computer-game icon Lara Croft, from the *Tomb Raider* franchise. It's hard now to recall how omnipresent this cluster of pixels was in the late 90s, but what's worth noting is that the first-person player-proxy in the games themselves detached from the version in advertising and media fairly early – that version became the protagonist in the wretched film franchise with Angelina Jolie. With Jolie's personal life feeding into the film's script (we can hardly call it a "story" – the writer and director called it "post-narrative cinema", which is a generous description of this mess), Lara acquired daddy-issues to go with her terrible taste in music and habit of trashing World Heritage Sites.

If nothing else, Jolie did sound like an English aristo, except when she sounded like Sandi Toksvig. So when we see someone in a tight black ensemble, with a handy backpack of ladders and gadgets, we're encouraged to think of Lady Christina as the latest version of this, rather than what the casting directors did when Sophie Aldred hung up on them (see Volume 6 for Ace). That Lady C is doing this to help her allegedly-impoverished dad, and chooses to steal an ancient artefact rather than diamonds or state secrets, just rams it home. That she does it with a harness like in the original 1962 film *The Pink Panther* (itself riffing on *Rififi*) and slightly updated by the 1996 *Mission Impossible* film (see 7.3, "The Ambassadors of Death") is as inevitable as Jenny flip-flapping past lasers (X4.6, "The Doctor's Daughter").

Some of the tabloids made rather a thing of old Season Twenty-Seven plans (outlined in **What Would Season 27 Have Been Like?** under 26.4, "Survival") that would have involved the Doctor's new companion, Raine, being a lady catburglar – albeit a fairly young one groomed for a life of crime by her father. Some of the hard-core fans made rather a thing of Iris Wildthyme, a perky, middle-aged Time Lord claiming to be the Doctor's ex (played by Katy Manning in the Big Finish audios, but she was from the BBC Books originally), the point being that she owned a double-decker (a 22, via Chelsea) and that the presence of a bus in this story was one of the first bits of info to escape the publicity machine. (We'd already seen a Wildthyme-analogue in the series, X4.8,

What Difference Did Field-Removed Video Make?

continued from Page 271...

In fact, looking over the schedules for the period 1999-2004, what's striking is that the dramas and comedies with incidental music tended to be made in field-removed, whilst the supposedly "honest" ones – the main soaps and the quasi-factual *Casualty* – had neither. It's tempting to put a gender or class spin on this, that, say, *Linda Green* or *Hollyoaks* were intended for a predominantly female audience, while *Queer as Folk* or *State of Play* assumed a sort of heightened state but were aimed at TV critics as much as affluent viewers. These viewers had spent much of the 90s being courted with two-hour-long filmed whodunits set in rural, regional locales, or hour-long semi-soaps in the same areas and Range-Rovers-across-cattle-grids.

For the ITV companies, such aesthetics almost guaranteed advertisers and overseas sales. Filmed dramas had a patina of "quality" even when, as in the cases of *Born and Bred* or *The Last Train*, they were almost unwatchable. Even when such productions switched to field-removed video, they could pretend they had money spent on them, even when the same capital outlay produced almost half as much broadcastable material again as when made on real film. BBC Wales's drama output had been almost all field-removed, even their long-running soap *Pobol Y Cwm*. However big the ratings for *Coronation Street* or *EastEnders*, most drama wanted to look as unlike that as possible.

The logic of switching from something that looks analogous to news footage to something that looks like fictional television almost entirely owes to a generational debate. Older viewers think of drama done on "pure" VT as cheap and fake, because they remember the days when filmed drama got kudos simply because of the overheads, and because so much of it was imported. For a younger viewer, however, it seems patently obvious that *Doctor Who* is a kid's show because it's on fake-film, whereas all the other Saturday Night fixtures, from *Strictly Come Dancing* to *Casualty*, are live or live-looking. Even when the story inserts fake news reports from real newsreaders or journalists, it's manifestly a wind-up. Maybe it's connected with the fall-out from *GhostWatch* (see X2.12, "Army of Ghosts"), but *Doctor Who* no longer looks contiguous with other BBC1 output. The immediacy is removed.

Nonetheless, it's on video and the ability to insert computer-generated effects into a video image without a lot of messing about with mattes is a big help. In the past, optical printing allowed film to be placed in film while the wonders of CSO, and before that more straightforward inlay, allowed video images to be mixed. Attempts to mix the two were never entirely successful and often laughable. You can find your own favourite examples from the 1970s *Doctor Who* efforts, but a clearer one (because the BBC spent a fortune on it, and – worse – made a whole documentary in a grown-up slot about how it was done) is the 1985 production of *The Box of Delights*, where filmed animation sat uneasily with Quantel and three-camera electronic studio material. These days, it's possible to inlay a real-looking alien or flying saucer in unprocessed news footage, but viewers have become accustomed to only seeing such things in productions where the attempt to replicate film clearly labels the picture THIS IS A FAKE (17.2, "City of Death"). Even small children can tell the difference.[49]

Therefore television drama now has need of cinematographers, something never considered necessary when actual film was used. They'd send out experienced camera-operators such as AA Englander or Fred Hamilton to do location work and the director would ask what was doable, then the cameraman would do it. They'd often claim it wasn't doable without a lot more money. Of necessity, they hardly took any other staff, except on night-shoots. A certain amount of guerrilla filming took place in the 1970s, something barely possible once the basic crew-size grew. Compared to something like 11.2, "Invasion of the Dinosaurs" or the hare-brained scheme to make "City of Death" on the fly over a weekend with three cast-members and three technical staff, a BBC Wales shoot is like the circus coming to town.

On the other hand, the abrupt lurch from *this is in a studio* to *this is on location* has gone. Even in the 1970s, there were many – including directors and critics – who were unhappy with "piebald" productions. To many viewers now, these vintage dramas and comedies seem odd. In the past, making entire shows on VT, including the location work, was a logistical problem and an aesthetic compromise. Now it's standard. This allows the use of locations as sets, so that starship engine-rooms are often abandoned warehouses or factories (e.g. X3.7, "42"), whereas factories are now castles (X6.5,

continued on Page 275...

ABOUT TIME 2008-2009

"Silence in the Library", so it was more plausible than not, but the tabloids scored rather better on this one.)

There was a spurious list in *Doctor Who Magazine* claiming that the next episode after "The Next Doctor" (X4.14) would be the 200th story made. That list gerrymandered somewhat ("The Trial of a Time Lord" was counted as one story, as was X3.11-3.13, "Utopia"/"The Sound of Drums"/"Last of the Time Lords", but X4.11, "Turn Left" was tallied separate from "The Stolen Earth" and "Journey's End"), but the "Mighty 200" references in the episode were an allusion to that (and the then-recent *300*). After, so to speak, missing the bus with the Crusader 50 (X4.10, "Midnight"), they went for it in the face of facts, as a lot of this story is in dialogue with that and X4.0, "Voyage of the Damned" about how humans respond to such events.

But at the core of this story is an idea they tried in 1976, giving the Doctor a new one-off companion every story (see 14.3, "The Deadly Assassin" et seq. – it didn't work then, either), added to a desire to do a straightforward adventure romp before all the "heavy" stuff to write out the Doctor.

English Lessons

• *Lover* (n. coll.): what Christina calls her nabbed getaway driver. People from the West of England often use the term simply to mean the same as "buddy" or "mate" (or, more usually, "I'm not going to admit I've forgotten your name"). The name "Christina de Souza" sounds as if she comes from Portugal, but her accent is supposedly refined, via a posh school, so she could be from anywhere in England.

• *Oyster Card* (n.) A pre-pay card for electronic readers on any public transport in the London area. Since 2013, the buses within Central London have been cashless and only take these or one-day travelcards. There's a plan to phase them out in favour of contactless bank-cards, but not everyone in the UK trusts those.

• *Easter Egg* (n): The thing the Doctor's eating at the end of the pre-credit sequence is what everyone in the UK eats on Easter Sunday (yes, there are sugar-free, gluten-free and lactose-free ones). That German stuff with rabbits never really caught on with us, any more than the French thing about bells or the hunting down of small plastic eggs (although, like the US Halloween and "Prom" dances, that last one's spread because of the bombardment of American films). The chocolate eggs are engineered to stay solid until you break in and often contain smaller sweets. In some cases, there are mugs enclosed in the packaging or small toys. There are, inevitably, *Doctor Who* ones on sale, often with marshmallow Daleks or similar. Although the sale of Cadbury's has compromised some of their brands, the type of chocolate needed to keep the egg egg-shaped is a very specific recipe, so even they can't mess it up too badly.

• *NVQ* (n.) National Vocational Qualifications. Professional qualifications graded to reflect level of proficiency, starting with the basic level for people who didn't do so well academically at school, but at the higher levels they're an entrance qualification for skilled work.

• *Hold tight, ding ding* is a memory of when double-deckers had proper bus conductors who'd advise passengers when the bus was about to start, then ring the bell twice to advise the driver that everyone was aboard. (See also 25.4, "The Greatest Show in the Galaxy".)

• *The Honourable* (prefix): In the UK or Commonwealth, it's a courtesy title for the children of Viscounts or Barons and the younger children of Earls (so not the direct heir to the title). It can also be used if the daughter of such a noble has married someone without a title. So you can't really be "the Honourable Lady" anyone; it's either-or. The Doctor is extracting the micturition somewhat.

• *Aythangyow* (interj.): "I thank you" as said by "Big Hearted" Arthur Askey on *Band Waggon* (sic), on BBC radio in the 1930s. One of the first catchphrases of the media age.

• *A Dickie Bird* (n. coll.): A sound, or a word (it's a rudimentary rhyming-slang), usually in the negative. In this specific case, it's odd that Christina uses this and not the more appropriate "not a sausage", as if she was expecting noises rather than motion or light.

• *Brixton* (n.): A suburb of south London, the last stop on the Victoria Line tube. For most of the last half century, it's been known as one of the focal points of Britain's Afro-Caribbean population (we mentioned it in the essay with X3.2, "The Shakespeare Code"), but more recently it's been a bit gentrified. A fair amount of Eddie Grant fans seem to need telling that this is where Electric Avenue is. (See also 16.6, "The Armageddon Factor") There's a bus depot there.

• *Icelandic Banks* (n.): Unsurprisingly, banks in

What Difference Did Field-Removed Video Make?

continued from Page 273...

"The Rebel Flesh").The scale of the shoots and settings has grown year by year, even if available locations in south Wales aren't always the most logical places to do drama. The fannish gag "beaches are the new quarries" reflects that this century's attempts at alien worlds became as formulaic as the earlier ones (see also **What are the Most Over-Familiar Locations?** under "Army of Ghosts") until they gave in and started shooting everything in Spain. Nonetheless, if they had tried to make "42" in a normal-sized television studio, it would have looked like, er, 13.2, "Planet of Evil", but not as good.

There was, of course, more BBC politics at work than even Julie Gardner's bid for total world domination. It was widely accepted that before long, all broadcast television in Britain would be available in digital transmission, and the government would sell the old analogue frequencies to wi-fi and phone companies. The date was eventually fixed as May 2012, just ahead of the Olympics, and most broadcasters started pushing HD as the next step. With so much of the revived *Doctor Who*'s strategy relying on repeatability and overseas sales, the new series badly needed to start off from Day One as future-proofed. This, as we've seen, is a prudent precaution.

However, it does all look much of a muchness. It's often hard to tell where or when a programme was made. Time was when a reasonably experienced viewer could date an old film to within five years, and take a stab at any old television not already over-familiar with reruns in the post-Ted Turner era. Without paying close attention or knowing in advance, it would be hard to identify the country or year of origin of, say, *Murdoch Mysteries*, *Miss Fisher Investigates* or *Commissaire Magellan* (Canadian, Australian and French). The old certainty of a BBC series looking BBC, an American show being either brassy-looking film or chalky-looking VT, and a French-made film series having great production values and lousy picture-quality because of the dodgy film-stock have long passed.

Twenty-first-century *Doctor Who* looks at home on any screen in the world, even if it no longer looked entirely comfortable on BBC1 on Saturdays at teatime. The HD era has exacerbated this tendency, but that's another story for another time (see **Working for the Yankee Dollar?** under X7.5, "The Angels Take Manhattan"). Field-Removed and HD send out the message *we think this is good enough for export.*

Things have moved on a bit since 1965, and a camera's inbuilt tendency to make anyone not somewhat pallid seem to be drawn in crayon is no longer deemed advisable. It may make grass look like seaweed if not actively adjusted, and make set designers tend towards the notorious orange-and-teal combination. It might make buildings look like porridge unless care is taken to make exteriors less gloomy and oily, but it no longer automatically skews the picture-quality in one direction. It has to be thought about case by case. Paradoxically, a lot of the simplest things to do in the 405/625 style of electronic production are fiendishly difficult now. We commented on how the relatively straightforward matting-in of electric sparks has been replaced by laborious computer-generated fake lightning (X3.5, "Evolution of the Daleks"), but the routinely-used bright white sets – as per the TARDIS console room or various labs, bases or spaceships of the 70s and 80s – are now a nightmare to light. The facsimile Hartnell TARDIS used in *An Adventure in Space and Time* and then X9.12, "Hell Bent" and X10.13, "Twice Upon a Time" was frustratingly hard, and landed up looking strange and grey.

[Talking of which, in one regard, the shift to field-removed has been an enormous step forwards. If you've ever bought Kodak film in Japan, you'll know that the layers of pigmentation in film made for the Asian market are in a different proportion from reels bought in Europe or the US. The base-line assumption of skin-tone is different. Similarly, the early Technicolor and Eastmancolor processes needed adjustment to work in the UK, let alone India. This also applied to video cameras. The BBC, when moving to colour, adjusted the EMI Plumbicon tubes to work best with very pale Caucasian skin. Even visiting Hollywood stars looked like burnt meat. As the name suggests, the Plumbicon system used lead in the array, tending the picture towards reds, since the majority of people they expected to be pointing cameras at were pinkish.]

Thus, the BBC would have asked any new drama project for a compelling reason *not* to make it in the new industry-standard format. This also applies to the shift from 4:3 aspect-ratio to the preferred 14:9 or 16:9 "letterbox" proportions. As before, we have to note that not everyone had

continued on Page 277...

275

Iceland. The financial services sector was the tiny country's main source of income after tourism, Björk albums and stealing cod from British waters and many of the banks offered generous interest on savings. Thus several private individuals and British public institutions (notably county councils) placed their assets in these banks and therefore lost devastating amounts when these failed in the whole 2008 sub-prime lending debacle.

Oh, Isn't That...?

• *Michelle Ryan* (Lady Christina). She'd worked with Steven Moffat on *Jekyll*, but the most notorious role she'd had recently was the lead in *Bionic Woman*, a hilariously inept "dark" reboot of, er, *The Bionic Woman*. Prior to this, she was another alumna of *EastEnders* (as Zoe Slater), which is why her talking posh was so widely ridiculed (even though that's really how she sounds off-screen). Apart from these and *Merlin*, this episode was about as good as it got.

• *Lee Evans* (UNIT scientific advisor Malcolm Taylor). Once upon a time, he was a stand-up who combined mime with observational humour, then he got film roles. *Funny Bones* had him co-starring with Jerry Lewis in a film set in Blackpool; *Mousehunt* was more bizarre than the child-friendly promotion made out. You can also see him in *The Fifth Element* and *There's Something About Mary*. But in Britain he's still thought of as a Norman Wisdom tribute act – not entirely accurately, although his sitcom *So Now What?* had many moments where the similarity was inescapable. *Doctor Who* seems to have been his TV swan-song, as he took on the role of Leo Bloom in the West End production of *The Producers*, then resumed his (astonishingly lucrative) stand-up tours before retiring in 2014 to move to America, where his daughter was studying, then returning to "legitimate" theatre. His stand-up, incidentally, included a misfit character called "Malcolm".

• *Ellen Thomas* (Carmen, a psychic) has a varied career. These day's she's best known as the passive-aggressive parishioner Adoha in *Rev*, but her past includes a semi-regular gig in the ill-fated *OTT*, pouring custard over herself.

• *Daniel Kaluuya* (Barclay, a bus passenger) got an Oscar nomination for Best Actor in *Get Out*, but before that and *Black Panther* (where he rode an armoured rhino), he was mainly a fixture in sketch-shows (*Ruddy Hell! It's Harry and Paul* at least gave him a catch-phrase) after starting his TV career as "Posh Kenneth" in the last series of *Skins*. The hinge-point in his career was an episode of *Black Mirror*.

Things That Don't Make Sense Things to not do if you wish to avert a heist of your £18 million historical artefact: erect a laser defence system without any covering on top at all; make sure your four armed guards face away from it; put it under a cupola with openable windows. Things not to do when stealing this item: assume that the security staff are all deaf as posts and can't hear winches whirring *right behind them*; unmask while still on the premises (in bright light, for the benefit of CCTV); look surprised that you've been rumbled because of the squeaky toy that you deliberately planted for the heck of it; use a back door that should be alarmed and locked; try to con a bus-driver while on CCTV on a bus. Oh, and try paying your bus-fare with diamond-stud earrings. Any bus, anywhere. Just try.

Even granted that the stingrays can construct a space-time tunnel from one planet to another, there's no indication that this swarm has any navigation when making holes in the cosmos. With San Helios being halfway across the universe, having Earth as the next victim just because it's a planet, and they like planets, is implausible. If it's affected by gravity-wells, then stars or bigger planets would be more likely destinations.

The current UNIT Scientific Advisor is played for laughs but, let's face it... by not immediately closing the wormhole, Malcolm runs a good chance of getting quite a lot of Londoners killed out of sheer stubbornness and devotion to his beloved Doctor. Who thought that putting this bloke in the field was a good idea? The other problem with the Magambo/Malcolm story is this: the Doctor's unable to analyse the wormhole because he hasn't got the TARDIS; he needs to fly a bus through a wormhole that has to be shut *right away* to defend London because he hasn't got the TARDIS... and UNIT's got the TARDIS right there on a flatbed truck next to their mobile HQ. They have could shoved it through at any time. At least two thirds of this story is a waste of time because Erisa forgot to mention this.

# # #

[Here we're going to diverge onto geography issues, which we'll freely admit is of more interest to UK read-

What Difference Did Field-Removed Video Make?

continued from Page 275...

traded in perfectly functional 80s or 90s sets, so the majority of programmes were made to work in either ratio. Everyone with the DVD of X2.13, "Doomsday" can see a CG Cyberman falling from a gantry on the far right of the picture, an effect that must have cost as much as a whole Hartnell episode, but it was invisible to anyone watching the broadcast on an old set. With BBC Wales tooled up for taking on more drama, and the *Doctor Who* team desperate to avoid comparison with what older viewers remembered *Doctor Who* being like (accurately or not), making it in the currently modish proportions and picture-quality was a no-brainer.

As with the shift to 45-minute episodes with plot-beats timed for US advert breaks, the move to season-long arcs with Big Bads, and the pseudo-orchestral Hans Zimmer stylings of Murray Gold, there is a sense that making *Doctor Who* in field-removed video was bowing to the inevitable, taking the path of least resistance and assuming *Star Trek: Voyager* to be the base-line of normal television. It didn't need to be this way. Had the entire world adopted 625-line 50i PAL as the industry-standard, and had it had the snob-value of fake movie aesthetics, maybe everyone would be falling over themselves to make feature films that resemble *I, Claudius*. To some extent, Peter Jackson and James Cameron's recent experiments in 50

frames-per-second are exactly that. They both proclaimed this to be a superior picture-quality format, more immersive and better for 3D. If as much effort had been put into this as has been applied to inflicting 3D on cineplexes, perhaps field-removed VT will become as creaky and obsolete – as embarrassing to the next generation of viewers – as 405-line monochrome.

We have now left this phase of production behind us. Today we have series shot in HD: 1250 lines in the picture instead of 625. The picture-quality is more amenable to manipulation than ever before, although the majority of directors seem to have decided to make everything look like sump-oil. Rather than grading the image and applying mist-filters to resemble comedy-dramas such as *Cold Feet* or *Linda Green*, the Moffat era wanted us to think it was Christopher Nolan or Michael Winterbottom. The 1980 scenes in X9.4, "Before the Flood" were manifestly shot in bright sunlight, but they contrived to make it look murky and uninviting. When Spain impersonated an alien planet ("Hell Bent"; X10.2, "Smile"), things looked oddly like 26.4, "Survival". The warmth of the Davies stories, even when dealing with grim subjects, was replaced by a sombre brutalist picture-quality even when they were aiming for "chirpy" (X8.13, "Last Christmas" for example). The era of field-removed video as used for the bulk of the Davies era of *Doctor Who* is a snapshot of British television and culture as it was.

---

ers. Overseas folks can put themselves in our shoes (one at a time, please) for a bit... if a story took place in Omaha, and claimed you could look out the window and see the Principal Tower some 135 miles away in Des Moines, you'd sit up and go "Hang on a minute..." too, wouldn't you?]

Let's pretend that the International Gallery is in the same place as the National Gallery, in Trafalgar Square, and that they really are headed for Brixton (south of the Thames). It's the 3 they want, not the 200 (a local service around Wimbledon and Mitcham, not even a double-decker), and it goes all the way to Crystal Palace. If they're going via Victoria, then it's the 2 from Marble Arch, the terminus for which is Tulse Hill, not Brixton. Either way, the bus states the destination is Victoria, a completely different bit of London (between Buckingham Palace and Chelsea), so why does the Doctor even mention Brixton?

But the police tell us, several times, that they're

travelling north in the tunnel, from the South entrance. (Gareth Roberts lived in South London: he lacks the excuse that Davies has for his odd ideas of where Chiswick and Greenwich are.) It might *almost* work if the International Gallery is where Battersea Power Station ought to be (X2.6, "The Age of Steel" is just the most recent cameo by this landmark) and if there's a local service to Victoria via, um, the Blackwall Tunnel. (US readers: think Jersey City to your own-brand Chelsea via the New Jersey Turnpike.) No buses would go through either of the big tunnels out east to get to Victoria, and any location near them we can imagine for this big a place is too far from built-up areas. (And the exterior seen in *SJA* is Victorian, not a famous 1930s power-station converted into an art gallery along Tate Modern lines.)

So wherever the International Gallery is, and whichever bus it is, the route heads towards either Victoria or Brixton by way of a major museum and is running on Easter Sunday – but, despite the restricted service for Sundays and Bank Holidays, there's hardly anyone on it. Wherever these people have been, they were passing a museum after closing hours and after dark in April (9.00pm at the earliest), so the bus would be one of only two per hour on a major route, just after practically everything to do in London on Easter Sunday shuts. There'd be a lot more people aboard. (If this were a Night Bus, apart from the lack of an N before the spurious number, it would be heaving with clubbers and/or shift workers even with Easter Monday to come.) Most London attractions, and we can take the National Gallery as an example here too, are open on Easter Sunday and Easter Monday – in fact, these are peak days.

#

The whole principle of a Faraday cage is that it's an enclosed system, so a ripped-open bus isn't going to cut it. (This made more sense during scripting: see **The Lore**.) The wormhole's circumference grows to ten miles (16 km), but UNIT's entire force is in a tunnel, and both the bus and the stingrays come out there. Why do only things like buses or exploding drivers cause ripples in the invisible doorway? There's a lot of loose sand and a strong wind.

Photafine steel, apparently, is a metal that inverts the temperatures on the outside, making it nice and warm when travelling in vacuum. But if a desert makes the humanoids' breath mist, entering a planet's atmosphere would freeze the crew solid. It's not a very practical design for life-support, even if the Tritovores are impervious to extremes of heat and cold. Or, a spaceship that freezes in a desert would be unbearably hot if you fly it anywhere in space (at almost Absolute Zero). It can't just be an inversion of, say, one degree Kelvin upwards inside the ship for every degree lower the exterior gets, hinging around 300K (room temperature). Not the least of the problems with that is where the energy would come from to heat a ship in space, when entropy is taking all the energy and spreading it around – hence the Absolute Zero-ness. (So, all right, one way what we see and what's described could match is if the metal acts as a heat storage bank and releases previously-captured energy once the interior goes below 300K and retains it when they go drasti-

cally above that. How does it make the switch? For the hole in the side to be making the steel misbehave it has to have changed the molecular structure of the entire ship just by hitting it with a planet. That's a design flaw and a half.) The Tritovores' internal comms seem designed for humans. How do Tritovores wear them?

Buses don't have height controls fitted on the off-chance that someone refits one to levitate. How could either the Doctor or, more puzzlingly, Christina, steer in three dimensions? And if the fuel's used up, why is there any electricity for the lights and hydraulics? Batteries can only do so much and they've already run theirs flat.

Critique We'll start with the positives: there are quite a few.

Captain Magambo's back, for real this time, and she's got a competent UNIT with her. They genuinely seem as if they could defend Earth. This is the version we've been waiting for since, for some people, 1970. Definitely since 2005, when the plot of "Aliens of London" (X1.4) hinged on removing the ones with a clue. It's not the cosy, annoying "family" of "The Claws of Axos" (8.3) and after, nor the amateurish cannon-fodder of "The Poison Sky" (X4.5), nor yet the Guantanamo-inspired sinister black ops outfit in *Torchwood*. It's not even the sub-*Men in Black* collectors of alien tech led by Kate Stewart in the Moffat stories. Instead, we have an agency letting the science lead but only as far as the determination of threat-level; able to negotiate and communicate but, faced with silent predators, able to use effective firepower once every other option is ruled out.

They have an arms-length relationship with the Doctor – admiring him, but not just there as his backing-band. This tension is one that allows for more different types of story, shades of grey between the two poles of Yeti-in-the Loo and Doctor-against-the-World. It's certainly more plausible than the comic-relief police in this story, although this aspect isn't as bad as it could have been. Compared to "Logopolis" (18.7), the cops in this are tenable. (When has *Doctor Who* ever depicted the police as anything but comedic or sinister? Even *Torchwood* uses them as drab functionaries unable to grasp the basics, and our supposed identification-figure was WPC Gwen Cooper.)

Over on the alien world, we've got a crashed spaceship and – in our first glimpse of it – we get a 70s paperback cover come to life. The flashback to what San Helios was like before is similarly enticing. Neither is exactly a cliché, but they hint at something beyond even the unprecedented budgets of the Davies era. The crew may be disappointingly prosaic and the interior is yet another abandoned factory in Cardiff, but the fragments and ruins help the viewer imagine how things were before the disaster. There's a suggestion of a bigger world just out-of-view, something *Doctor Who* always used to be best at. Christina has a life beyond the episode, even if nobody else gives that impression.

After nine months on stage, Tennant's enthusiastic enough to overcome – for the duration of the episode – the knowledge that he's making his farewell tour. We don't get any new aspects to his Doctor, but the run-through of the character's defining-points propels the episode for an hour of screen-time. As a production, it was (sometimes literally) unfamiliar territory, so his energy and ebullience were at a premium on the shoot. We needed one last uncomplicatedly "up" story where the Doctor is in control, and Tennant is brimming with zest, ahead of everything unravelling. His curiosity about the metallic aliens is of a piece with the general comic-book vibe here (it's a bit Reed-Richards-Meets-Galactus, if you want a specific comparison, but also vaguely like a French *bande desinée*). Tritovores sort of fit that, although perhaps they ought to have been a background detail to keep that feel. All that in a story that *starts* with a heist that otherwise would have climaxed most productions.

Ranged against him is a conceptually-simple alien threat; not a spoiled billionaire or xenophobic tyrant, but pure appetite like a swarm of locusts or the Warner Bros version of the Tasmanian Devil. The design is how the Cybermats *could* have been, like a wildlife documentary, but also appealingly 1930s Deco. They generate wormholes somehow (like Superman flying really fast to make time go backwards, a daft idea we'd had recently in X3.13, "Last of the Time Lords"), but with all the talk about Faraday Cages, the word "wormhole" sounds sciencey enough to get nodded through. So we can find things to praise, even if most of them are pats on the back for business-as-usual and not getting the basics wrong, or as wrong as earlier stories. It's intended to be fun, and *Doctor Who* ought always to be fun, or else why bother?

Now the bad news… The first broadcast made it plausible that all the smug "we're such a great team" stuff was setting us up for another supposedly-tragic loss (X4.0, "Voyage of the Damned"), but she survives. So Christina's just annoying, even if Michelle Ryan did most of her own stunts and did her best with the material. So is the contractual-obligation foreshadowing stuff with Carmen, the sort-of spooky hint of future plot developments that come fitted as standard in shows with "arcs" and time-paradoxes. Back in 2009, this had become the norm for imported series that the posh papers claimed were better than mere cult shows (see **Is Kylie from Planet Zog?** under "Voyage of the Damned"), but these days we know that no revelation ever really delivers or lives up to these hints. Davies and Roberts don't give Carmen any more character than this. She never even gets off the bus until the end.

But never mind all that – look, they've gone to Dubai! *Doctor Who* is now a Global Brand! Everything in any episode has to justify a lot of pre-selling and, when there isn't a whole series to back it up, a stand-alone "Special" has to be, well… special. This isn't. As far as content's concerned, this is a season-opener stretched beyond the appropriate length, and without as much effort put into "selling" the series and its concepts to any newcomers. It coasts on the assumption that everyone watching is (if you'll forgive the phrase) on board.

You can do that if the new character will be along for the ride, but they've decided that the Doctor is (to use the annoying phrase common in online fandom back then) "the lonely god". An actual season-opener is allowed a lot of leeway by hinting at things to come, and having another 12 (or 11, or now none) weeks' worth of stories explaining these. This one tries valiantly to intrigue us about the regeneration, but we went in knowing that there were nine months to wait and only one other Special to come before the pay-off. This episode craves our indulgence without earning it, and just limps along for longer than a normal one, for no good reason. All of this is therefore subordinate to telling an already enthusiastic audience: "Look! Sand!" So we looked and, yup, there was sand. And more sand. So we all looked at the sand for a bit and asked: now what?

The single worst thing to say about the desert material is that the very next story did a more convincing job using a Welsh quarry (X4.16, "The Waters of Mars"). As we'll see in **The Lore**, they had a lot of things working against them, but they

ABOUT TIME 2008-2009

made a rod for their own backs putting faith in Dubai as a solution to a problem of their own devising. Spain would have worked and been logistically easier. The fabled "BBC Quarry in Dorset" of 1970s/80s stories wouldn't have looked much different. The problem isn't sandstorms or a wrecked bus, it's the script needing a selling-point beyond "people cut off on an alien world". If they were worried about unfavourable comparisons to "Midnight" (X4.10), they shouldn't have started. Biff, Val and Jethro in that story have more solid characterisation, even though they're from another planet; this story uses the broadest brush possible and seems to want a round of applause for it. The two lads who are pimped to UNIT at the end are presented as a double-act despite not having any connection, as if there is a composite "Nathan 'n' Barclay", either half of which can do what the other does at any moment. The Tritovores were better differentiated than that.

And the stick-figure passengers don't get a chance to develop beyond the trite one-line ideas of "home" they all deliver because – well – this isn't "Midnight", it's a string of detachable set-pieces, as if they thought that any five-minute section could be put on as part of *Children in Need* to sell the rest. Even when they leave the desert, we get a shedload of heavy artillery – as if that's also an end in itself, and what looks like the start of yet-another spin-off series about a criminally-minded posh bird and her flying bus. It even has the rumpitty-tumpitty music appropriate for a cheap CGI-heavy 90s adaptation of a children's fantasy novel – one that some ailing film company got the rights for and rushed out between *Potter* flicks.

As a character-concept, Malcolm is a bit weird: he's prepared to die for someone he's never met and has only just spoken to by phone for the first time 20 minutes before. Apart from being the irritating geek, he's an exaggerated version of the sort of relationship UNIT staff were usually given with the Doctor in Davies stories and shows up how silly that idea was. Even without the slapstick, the iffy accent and the glasses, he's the sort of figure best used sparingly (see also Osgood – either the one in 8.5, "The Daemons" or the cosplay caricature in "The Day of the Doctor"). Of Lee Evans, the best we can say is that, compared to Wilf, we can confirm that 100 Malcolms equals one Bernard.

The whole episode is as gaudy, over-sugared

and hollow as a supermarket own-brand chocolate Easter Egg (the empty ones without even marshmallow or Cadbury buttons inside). It has no ambition as far as storytelling is concerned, while being hubristically ambitious as a production. Even at its most cinematic, BBC Wales's production has given us stories that were *about* something more than being entertaining or spectacular. The only "what if" here is "imagine what a Hollywood feature film of *Doctor Who* would be like" and – as we saw with the 1996 TV Movie debacle – the result is trite and insubstantial. It's not as continuity-clogged and misguided as that, and it looks more expensive at about a fifteenth of the cost, but it shares a lot of that misfire's flaws.

The Lore

Written by Russell T Davies and Gareth Roberts. Directed by James Strong. 9.54 million on the first BBC1 broadcast, but it was simultaneously shown on BBC HD (0.21 million, because hardly anyone could get it then), the following day (Easter Sunday) BBC3 showed it and got 0.91 million viewers. On Easter Monday (a Bank Holiday in the UK), BBC1 and BBC HD showed it *again* and got 2.04 million and an extra 0.56 million came from BBC3 that Friday, so these days we'd consider that a "consolidated" rating of 13.26 million over the week, not counting unrecorded iPlayer streaming. AIs were 88% first time, fluctuating between 89 and 87 for those repeats. HD and BBC3 showed it a further nine times in the next year.

Repeats and overseas promotion Planet Der Toten, Planète Morte.

Alternate versions BBC America has to remove a whopping 15 minutes, because arthritis medicines and dating websites don't sell themselves. All of Carmen's spooky stuff is cut, as is everything about Magambo pulling a gun on Malcolm and him standing firm. Nor do we hear what the Tritovores eat. Generally speaking, though, this edit is a less annoying version than what was originally broadcast.

Production

• With Tennant taking six months out to play Hamlet, the production team thought they had a breather. There was a Christmas Special in the can, a plan to make the third series of *Torchwood* as a five-part serial and *The Sarah Jane Adventures* was ticking along nicely.

The only obvious cloud on the horizon was that the scheme to cover 2009 with hour-long Specials was harder to finance. The global distribution body, BBC Worldwide, sold the series around the world as multiples of 42-minute episodes (i.e. an hour when advert breaks are added), but stand-alone pieces, needing a longer time-slot, were less popular with buyers and thus got less per minute from the BBC's production budget. In a series, you can potentially offset a costly episode with a cheaper one, but making each hour as a one-off meant they were inherently more talky, with a smaller ratio of costly CGI effects to (relatively) cheap practical ones (explosions, mainly). Five of these, spaced out over a year (as opposed to the Monday-Friday stripping of *Torchwood: Children of Earth*), was a tough sell.

• Russell T Davies was advised that all forthcoming scripts had to bear his name, regardless of his actual input, simply to get any interest from the usual overseas networks. (Such that remained: Japan, confused that what they thought was a horror show was too child-friendly to put on in the conventional midnight slots, had dropped the series. CBC, one of the first on board with the relaunch, and formerly credited at the end for their financial assistance, had also bailed.)

His plan had been to farm out the two Specials following "The Next Doctor" to reliable specialists: Gareth Roberts to do the sort of goofy space-opera pastiches he'd honed in the 90s *New Adventures,* and Phil Ford to provide a more conventional space-adventure. Both were regular writers for *The Sarah Jane Adventures,* so were as in-house as anyone could get without a title and salary. With the Doctor probably regenerating at the end of the Specials, it was thought that the first adventure needed to be fun. The plot of Roberts's debut book, *The Highest Science*, was a selection of strangers on a train whisked across the galaxy and dropped into the middle of a galactic war – so this was the starting-point for his proposed story. Davies was toying with an idea of the sort of story Steven Moffat was famous for writing, involving a deserted hotel (see X6.11, "The God Complex"),

and offered it as a possible component for the Roberts adventure.

• Another thread of the Specials was how far off the rails the Doctor could go without a full-time human companion, so there was to be a one-off character for each. Roberts thought of someone who undervalued herself, possibly a bit chubby and in a dead-end job, along the lines of Ricki Lake's character in *Hairspray* (or Nikki Blonsky in the remake, then just out on DVD). One possible ending was a parody of a space-dogfight from umpteen *Star Wars* knock-offs, with the Doctor disabling all the weapons. This was in part a legacy of a wild idea to do a crossover with a big US franchise – although the obvious one, *Star Trek*, had gone belly-up on TV around the time *Doctor Who* returned.

• With Tennant on stage for much of the summer, the logistics of producing this spread of episodes forced changes. A train, or bus, in space would need a protective bubble to stop the air escaping, but that required the aliens involved to notice the humans and give a toss what happened to them. Sending them to a deserted space hotel wasn't quite right either; the obvious solution was arriving on a planet with breathable air. If the episode was to be shot in January, this meant a foreign location, which meant expense – and that ate the effects budget. (Well, they *could* have plonked a bus on a beach near Mumbles Pier and made a joke about it.) If it's a desert location, actors dressed in tortoise costumes would die, so the Chelonians (from *The Highest Science* et al) were replaced by humanoid flies.

An idea first floated for what became "Partners in Crime" – of a wormhole opening in London and thousands of alien predators flying through – was reworked to provide a rationale for the bus disappearing and a climactic invasion-of-Earth threat. By the end of July, the story was distilling itself into something like what was broadcast, with the companion-of-the-day changing into a slinky jewel-thief called "Hermione". The vehicle was to be a double-decker bus, even though London was in a phase of using single-decker Mercedes "Bendy" buses.

Roberts accepted these changes with apparent enthusiasm, although the name "Hermione" had to change. At the same meeting (1st August), Ford was told that his Mars adventure wasn't quite to Davies's taste. (See next story's write-up for more on this and X10.9, "The Empress of Mars", and the Disney dud *John Carter* for what the first version was to have been like.) Davies let them get on with it, as he had fires to put out.

• Although Moffat briefly courted Tennant about staying for a year to ease the new production-team in, the star had decided to leave in the last Special – but the announcement had to be handled carefully. Davies was keen to give Tennant the initiative and control of the timing. The fevered speculation in the week before "Journey's End" had been a foretaste of what could happen. Obviously, casting the replacement was not his problem, but Davies didn't wish to make it worse.

Meanwhile, he was contemplating his next move: a fresh start in Hollywood seemed like the only way for whatever came next not to be reported as a let-down. As the summer wore on, the global economy went into a tailspin, making the BBC more cautious about future spending plans – as well as getting paranoid about the tabloid coverage of its every decision. Davies, as high-profile an executive as they had, was forced to be circumspect. Worse yet, the Torchwood scripts weren't working and both Freema Agyeman and Noel Clarke had got other parts, so needed to be written out. The relative ease of Roberts's drafts, and the news that former production manager for the series, Tracie Simpson, would be producer for this and the final Specials, were welcome.

• Roberts had renamed the burglar "Christina de Souza", but was on alert for a change – casting such a character was going to be tricky, so if needed they could fall back on the "ordinary" character, provisionally called "Eileen". Simpson and production designer Ed Thomas had responsibility for finding two suitable buses, one for the location shoot overseas (Dubai was selected early on, partly because it had a good bit of desert 20 minutes from a reasonable-sized road and town) and one to be used in Cardiff, either on the road or in a studio mock-up of the desert world. A couple of 1980 Bristol VRs (a marque not manufactured since 1981 but in service in some parts of the UK today – it's the same model Meat Loaf drove in Spice World) had their journey to the scrap yard interrupted. James Strong, after doing Hustle and the un-loved Bonekickers, returned to the fold to direct.

• By now, the 2008 Credit Crunch was beginning to bite, and the deal between BBC Worldwide and Woolworths (commercially releasing programmes on DVD via a company called 2Entertain) was in jeopardy. Funding for even a high-profile

international success such as Doctor Who had become more tentative, and a real chance existed that one of the proposed Specials would have to be sacrificed. Worldwide was donating monies for the Specials as a lump-sum, regardless of how many reached the screen. "Planet of the Dead" had been committed to already, and had its first Tone Meeting (key-word: "Joyous") on 20th November. This revealed a few script glitches, the streamlining of which eventually led to an under-run of a few minutes. (If you think the broadcast version was Pertwee-lite, the communication with the Tritovores was apparently to have been rather more like the Pictograms used in 8.4, "Colony in Space".) Casting "Eileens" had been difficult so they went with Christina.

A more ominous potential problem was that the deal to make the episode in HD was under threat, which would cost the episode money already allocated for computer effects – a quick estimate suggested that 90 effects days would be lost. Julie Gardner swiftly dealt with the problem, but it was a sobering reminder that now not even Doctor Who was sacrosanct.

• By Christmas the team had cast Christina, decorated a bus in adverts for a fictional mobile phone network (a hint for the later episodes), put it on a pallet and shipped it, carefully avoiding four or five war-zones between Cardiff and Jebel Ali. A bus was too heavy to put on even a RAF transporter, so the sea route seemed safe and practical. Davies, Tennant and various other interested parties contributed to a Doctor Who Confidential special about the casting of the real next Doctor, as the press launch for the Christmas episode gave the first public hints about the Easter Special. "The Next Doctor" was broadcast, feeding the public appetite for daft guesses, and Davies noted the BBC1 idents of Wallace and Gromit as a possible idea for next year. Once Matt Smith was announced, the team expected something like normality to resume and preparations for the shoot neared completion. The bus was due to be offloaded at the docks in the small hours of Monday, 5th January.

Unfortunately, someone swung an 18-tonne crate into the unprotected bus. In among all the insurance and logistical implications, there was an unusual problem of The Mill having started work on scenes with a bus flying. The version Davies gave the press was that he laughed immoderately, and then stated that this is what happens to buses when they fly through wormholes, no rewrites necessary. Privately, he was less sanguine. Plan A, sending the second bus to Dubai and buying a third junker of the same make for Cardiff use turned out not to be practical. Plan B was to secure the damaged vehicle and inflict identical damage on a third, non-functional bus to preserve continuity, copying The Mill in on detailed photos of what the bus now looked like. The pranged double-decker couldn't be driven to the location, so they had to rent a low-loader.

• By the time of the read-through, on 14th, the situation seemed to be in hand. Tennant watched old episodes to get back into character, while Ryan finally got to see some Doctor Who. Lee Evans was the last to be cast. Davies added a few new scenes with Malcolm to make up the missing three and a half minutes of screen-time, and tightened up the rest with small cost-cutting changes. (During filming, as Malcolm, Evans spent a lot of time proposing comedy business. About one suggestion in five was used; one vetoed straight off was comedy dentures.)

• The recording itself began the following Monday, 19th, at the Welsh National Museum, in Cathays Park, Cardiff, for the pre-credits heist scene. Lee Sheward supervised the stunts, with Bob Schofield operating the wires and Ryan doing some of the shots, the rest being a double (Kim McGarrity). The night ended with the working bus and a black cab driving past the exterior of the building for establishing shots.

Another nearby location, the Bute Town Tunnel on the A4232, was scheduled for resurfacing and maintenance, and the production team negotiated night shooting on the closed road. On the night of the 20th, they began at the exit. During the day, there had been a quick refresher course for Keith Parry, a qualified coach-driver cast as the anonymous bus-driver, plus a demo of the skeleton model falling to the floor and smouldering. Adam James, as the cop (mis-identified by the unit make-up artist as "Dai McMillan"), had worked with Tennant at the Royal Court and with Strong on Hustle.

• Monday evening started with the bus driving around Cardiff; just for a change, St Mary's Street doubled for central London. It was recorded in reverse order, with the Doctor's gadget reacting, then him joining the passengers, then Christina trying to blag her way on, then her evading McMillan. Tuesday was back on the tunnel exit location, with UNIT shooting at flying stingrays and a bus flying overhead (both added later) in a torrential downpour (not seen in the finished version – even HD cameras don't register raindrops).

• The bus-prang incident made the papers; some questioned whether the Sultanate of Dubai was an appropriate location for a series about a champion of the oppressed. Others reported it as a serious disaster that triggered drastic rewrites. As if to disprove this, some of Tennant's video diary entries from the previous week were cleared for inclusion on the BBC's Doctor Who website.

• The main activity of Thursday was recording bus scenes in Upper Boat 6, using a translight (basically a giant photo blow-up of the location lit from behind, and surrounding the bus) to simulate the desert world exterior. Prior to this, there had been an experimental session with the Tritovore prostheses – insect movement by Ailsa Berk. Word of this got out, and the BBC pre-emptively released pictures. As might be expected, Danny Hargreaves was on hand to blow stuff up, this time soft transparent silicon in a "woofer" mortar for the windows shattering as the bus sustained damage between dimensions (as if an 18-tonne crate had dropped on it).

• The steel plant used as the Dalek test-chamber in "Journey's End" became a Tritovore spaceship for four days. Snow had made the location so cold, Ryan and Tennant couldn't speak without their breath misting – so the line about "Photafine Steel" turning cold when it's hot was added, and the stingray being revived by body heat came in. So did snow, through a hole in the roof. Ryan was called upon to dive into the mis-named "gravity well", but only about a metre, onto green crash-mats onto which a tunnel could be matted in post.

• The team had a recce at a deserted spot in Margham, the location for the bus, on 11th, preparing for proper shooting the next day. The area had to be defoliated and combed to make the sandscape pristine. The bus with Tennant and some of the crew was stopped by armed police, and made to stand around in the desert in the dark while the driver talked his way out of a fine for some small infraction. Another bus, with the sound recordist, took a wrong turn and almost landed up in Oman.

• It was colder than expected, and the hotel seemed slightly dubious. The team had to be up by 5.30am but, being recently arrived from Cardiff, five hours behind, this wasn't as arduous as it could have been. On the 12th, the work properly began – in what the locals described as the worst February weather for years. Some footage was shot, but it looked disappointingly like Britain. The weather worsened in mid-morning, with a sandstorm reducing visibility and making the security tape rustle. (The cast and crew were prescribed areas they could go to avoid making footprints and messing up continuity. In the event, this was moot on that day.)

Sand got into the cameras, stuck to Simpson's make up and Tennant's hair-gel – Daniel Kaluuya called him "Barry Manilow" – and was very visible in HD. Associate producer Debbi Slater went into town and bought lots of Arabic headscarves – this kept most of the crew from abrasion, but made it harder to tell anyone apart. The shoot was abandoned for the day and the team returned to the hotel, convinced that they would have to make up the lost time on a beach in Wales. Friday 13th was luckier, despite interruptions from local quad-bike enthusiasts, and as the skies brightened they were almost back on target, even allowing for reshoots.

• There had been a snag with Mears and Kasey getting a flight – British Airways was happy to oblige *Doctor Who* even after "Time-Flight" (19.7) – but other than that, the main problem was Tennant dressed in a big coat for some shots. As it turned out, the animatronic insect-heads were cooler than not wearing anything on their heads, especially with the detachable eye-covers removed for ventilation between shots. Finally, the crew returned to the hotel and packed, relaxed or watched an England-Wales rugby match. After a pick-up day in Cardiff, all that remained was post-production – but with under two months to go until Easter, this was a tighter schedule than usual.

• Five days later, Tennant was on Mars (well, Taffs Wells quarry). The first few edits over-ran by almost five minutes, but very little dialogue (mostly technobabbly with Tritovores) was trimmed. About 70 of the desert shots needed to have footprints digitally removed (ironically, the better weather on 14th made shadows sharper, so the prints were more visible in the good takes). Most of the digital effects were agreed "blind", i.e. incomplete at the time of the official lock on the edit in early March. It was still being fine-tuned nearly a month later.

As a result, the usual press screenings and build-up were curtailed; instead of the formal screening a week or so beforehand, there was a debut in selected cinemas in the Cardiff area on Good Friday, the day before broadcast, with tickets allocated by lucky dip. Tennant, Strong and Gardner did the DVD commentary on a nearly-finished edit on 2nd April, just over a week before transmission.

• Any thought that the apparent curse on this episode was over was dispelled on the 5th, when the adverts for Naismith's fictional "Neon" 3G network rang an alarm bell – just after filming the desert scenes was completed, AT&T announced a link-up with LG called "Neon", which meant that the BBC's guidelines against advertising real products were potentially being breached by accident. Nonetheless, this – and a potential worry that the 6.45 timeslot made the driver's death too gory to transmit – resolved with a few phone calls and the edit was finished that night.

On Easter Saturday, the episode went out opposite the hapless ITV bandwagon-jumper *Primeval* and got about three times as many viewers. It picked up two million more on Easter Monday (a Bank Holiday in the UK) in a double-bill with the only other HD production the series had to offer, *Doctor Who at the Proms* (see Appendix 6).

• Michelle Ryan's career never quite perked up again, despite the well-received *Cockneys vs Zombies* (in which she hotwires a red double-decker). In 2018, she starred in a *Lady Christina* box set from Big Finish.

X4.16: "The Waters of Mars"

(15th November, 2009)

Which One is This? It's *The Martian* for people who like Disco. Sort of.

Actually, as befits a moderately-well-researched story of a British-led international crew setting up the first colony on Mars, it's midway between *Scott of the Antarctic* and *The Good Life* – at least, until the killer water-zombies start chasing people up and down corridors. Then the Doctor decides he's god (but largely forgets his transgressions against the Nature of Reality by next episode). On the plus side, Liverpool's started manufacturing space equipment.

Firsts and Lasts It's, er, the first time that *Doctor Who* has had a Thanksgiving Special. (Unless you somehow count 20.7, "The Five Doctors"; X7.15, "The Day of the Doctor"; or A3, "Dimensions in

Time", which were aimed at the programme's anniversary, or X1.13½ "Pudsey Cutaway" and X3.13a, "Time Crash", which were *Children in Need* orientated.) Without a need to release "The Waters of Mars" on any particular day between Easter Sunday and Christmas Day, the BBC put it on late on a November Sunday when there weren't any other big drama series running. It suits BBC America to think it was done for their benefit.

It's the last story directed by Graeme Harper, who'd been behind the cameras in one capacity or another since the Pertwee days and was now finally getting awards from professional bodies.

Watch Out For...

• The first episode broadcast after Barry Letts's death was dedicated to his memory. It does, in fact, resemble what *Moonbase 3* was supposed to have been like and, as we hinted, echoes his most famous film role (see **The Big Picture**).

• They have their cake and eat it, incorporating an annoying cutesy robot into the plot, and having the Doctor channel his inner eight-year-old *and* comment upon the habitual television science-fiction use of cutesy robots. Oddly, Gadget wasn't in our shops at Christmas this year, and there are no recorded instances of kids saying "gadget-gadget" in school playgrounds.

• Plenty of stories took place in botanical gardens and greenhouses, but the bird-filled greenery here is about as good as it gets. There's a good solid plot reason for the scene and the idea of the first colonists on Mars going to such pains to grow carrots for Christmas Dinner is almost self-parodically British while being entirely accurate. They retained enough of the original "Christmas on Mars" premise to make it more useful as a festive Special than most of the increasingly desperate tie-in attempts to come. Of all the birds the Astronauts could have brought from Earth, it's *Erithacus rubecula*, the European robin from all the cards and songs.

• For the first 45 minutes, this seems like almost a textbook example of the Base-Under-Siege format of *Doctor Who* perfected when Patrick Troughton was the star, mixed with the look-but-don't-touch approach towards historical events from the show's first two years (especially 1.6, "The Aztecs").

Then the whole thing shifts gear, and it goes from being about the colonists' response to a water-zombie virus to the Doctor's decision to transgress all the laws he tried to follow. The intention was to push this Doctor into a new area, showing hubris and slight madness that would inevitably lead to his regeneration – but, to an unsympathetic viewer, Tennant's performance here as a fast-talking wide-boy with delusions of godhood is pretty much how he always played the part. The *real* change is that his blonde co-star this time is multi-award-winning Lindsay Duncan; she doesn't simper adoringly like Billie Piper did as Rose and literally kills herself to rebuke him. It's not that the Doctor has changed, it's that he isn't indulged any more.

The Continuity

The Doctor Knowing that the Bowie Base One crew must die in accordance with history, he attempts to leave, several times, but seems drawn back to the action by his own curiosity. [And, perhaps to a lesser degree, to ensure that he won't become a zombified Time Lord roaming the cosmos.] With the base on the threshold of destruction, he saves Captain Brooke and the two surviving crewmen, announces he's the 'Time Lord Victorious' and allows himself to be every bit as smug as the Master, until Adelaide's death shocks him out of it and he admits that he's 'gone too far'. He twice acknowledges the validity of the 'he will knock four times' prophecy from last episode.

• *Background.* He's steeped in the backgrounds of everyone who went on this expedition. He brings up the Pompeii incident [X4.2, "The Fires of Pompeii"] when he's trying to tell Adelaide about fixed points. He also mentions Ice Warriors in an off-handed, but respectful, sort of way.

• *Ethics.* His long running survivor's guilt concerning the Time War bursts out in unexpected fashion as he feverishly explains to Adelaide that he 'won' it and is now entitled to carry out whatever changes to time he fancies. After convincing himself that he *can* save the crew from rather nasty deaths, he does so in a churlish and patronising fashion. After getting a wallop from the forces of the universe, he realises he did rather go too far.

His objection to deliberately 'funny' and 'cut' robots seems to be grounded in the dignity of the machines themselves. [After the Heavenly Host of X4.0, "Voyage of the Damned", this is understandable. It's analogous to contemporary views on performing animals or minstrel shows.]

• *Inventory: Sonic Screwdriver:* It really is a magic wand by now; one wave and a 2mph cargo hauler turns into a DeLorean. As a final indignity to Adelaide, he uses it to flick open her door and turn on her lights.

• *Inventory: Other.* The Doctor's modified it slightly, but he's wearing essentially the same orange space suit he borrowed in X2.8, "The Impossible Planet". [Presumably there wasn't much call to give it back.]

The TARDIS The Cloister Bell tolls in the final moment, despite the lack of mechanical faults. [See the next episode for the possible causes of this. Or, perhaps, it stems from the Ship's indignity of being dematerialised and rematerialised on split-second timing by a jumped-up toy robot.]

UNIT/Torchwood [All right, you'd reckon that UNIT would have had a few words with a team heading off to Mars. Even if we leave out the incompatibility of 7.3, "The Ambassadors of Death" with anything else – see this story's essay – there's the comment in X2.0, "The Christmas Invasion" that Martians do exist. Perhaps there were some clandestine negotiations, although that raises the disturbing possibility that the native Martians suggested this glacier site quite on purpose. If we take the hint from X2.9, "The Satan Pit", a "Torchwood Legacy" agency was active in space exploration. That would explain the number of English accents on this 'international' crew.]

The Non-Humans
• *The Flood* [identified as such in a cut scene]. A virus that understands Ancient North Martian. There's some signs of minimal intelligence, enough to communicate with people and carry off rudimentary deceptions, but it infiltrates its human hosts with impressive speed. [Imprudent haste, actually – the colonists would have probably headed back home regardless, so taking them over that fast before it's infiltrated the systems thoroughly is a big risk.]

[It's tempting to think of the Flood as an Ice Warrior invention; creating a way for organic beings to generate water has obvious applications on a liquid-starved planet. If it proved to have the same effect on *them* as on humans, it would be understandable if they buried it and abandoned the planet – except that plunking it under a glacier is a very serious sacrifice of valuable resources just to rid themselves of a bioengineering experiment gone wrong. Perhaps the Bowie Base crew

were just unlucky enough to land on the equivalent of a weapons-dump. Or, perhaps the glacier is made of water generated by this peculiar virus, which would explain the concentration of water near the surface on an otherwise arid world. That makes it a lousy place to build a farmstead but ideal for an unmanned probe.]

Planet Notes
• *Mars.* Pretty much as advertised: a very thin atmosphere, so pressure-suits and breathing apparatus are needed for surface travel. [The gravity seems more like the 1/3 g we might expect, although flames and mushroom clouds behave as though a thicker, oxygen-rich atmosphere is present.] Humans found an underground glacier in Gusev Crater [a real place]. There was an Ancient North Martian language [so presumably there were others as well].

History
• *Dating.* It's 21st November, 2059. The Doctor returns the three Bowie Base One survivors – Adelaide Brooke, Yuri Kerenski and Mia Bennett – to Earth the same day. There haven't been Martian flowers in ten thousand years, the Doctor says [underestimating by a factor of 50 million percent by current estimates – see X7.9, "Cold War" and X10.9, "The Empress of Mars" for more Areology-fail].

Adelaide Brooke's bio says she was born in 1999. Between her childhood and now, there's been problems with the climate, ozone, and the "oil apocalypse". [Adelaide specifies '40 long years', which means it gets nasty around 2018 (more in accord with 5.4, "The Enemy of the World" than X9.7, "Kill The Moon").] It nearly killed the human race, and the bios say that Andy's on the rocket because he developed groundbreaking solutions for nurturing particularly arid soil on Earth. [Odd hints about Adelaide's captaining aside, the fact that the colonists have started farming this fast hints that people are interested in Martian terraforming potential.]

There's something called the World State now [see "The Enemy of the World" again], but there's lots of independent states as well. Spain and the Philippines are both possible candidates for launching an independent space programme; the former might be working on a "Spacelink" project, while the latter's credited with working on a traditional rocket. The Branson Inheritance [Richard

Was There a Martian Time-Slip?

Back in 2005, it was possible to suppose that the reason the Nestenes tried to invade contemporary England with shop dummies again was that they'd never tried it before. The Time War, one could imagine, wiped the slate clean and all earlier adventures were vague memories for the Doctor and some of the viewers. We could watch "Rose" (X1.1) as though "Spearhead from Space" (7.1) had never happened.

This was fine and dandy, except for throwaway references to the Doctor's past involvement with UNIT (X1.4, "Aliens of London") and a hint in "Dalek" (X1.6), confirmed by the online support-material, that the UN was involved in alien-suppression. Then came a new Doctor, whose first act was to undo a historical development he'd already explained to us (X2.0, "The Christmas Invasion" and see **He Remembers This *How*?** under X1.5, "World War Three") and suddenly the world inside the story started resembling the world inside the older, pre-1990 stories. Sarah Jane Smith shows up "School Reunion" (X2.3) and talks about old times, bringing K9 with her to confirm that this isn't just an alternate-universe Sarah who remembers travelling with some iteration of the Doctor we never saw. This is *the* Sarah we can watch on DVD and – alas – 18.7a, "K9 & Company" really happened. Subsequent developments left us in no doubt that this version of *Doctor Who* was contiguous with the other series of the same name rather than being a reboot, re-imagining or any other Hollywood term for selling people things they already had.

Then things got complicated. Sarah got her own show. In this, we had a lot of on-screen confirmation that she was from roughly our time and that, therefore, the UNIT stories were roughly in the 1970s when she was in her early 20s. Actually, it's even more specific than that. *SJA:* "Whatever Happened to Sarah Jane?" establishes that Sarah was born in 1951, a fact doubtless calibrated to coincide with her being "23" in "Invasion of the Dinosaurs", so aligning that story to occur in its broadcast year of 1974. The scales of the UNIT Dating controversy began to tip heavily to one side as the cumulative evidence in the new episodes of both series added to the circumstantial, but overwhelming, on-screen data that sets 7.2, "Doctor Who and the Silurians" in the late 1960s (February 1971 at the very latest), and "K9 & Company" definitely at 21st December, 1981.

However, a line in *SJA:* "Warriors of Kudlak" suggested that the young lad she'd just saved might

be inspired to become "the first human man" on Mars. This is the same Sarah Jane Smith who reported on the disappearance of Guy Crayford (13.4, "The Android Invasion"), an English astronaut who got lost en route to Jupiter in what's blatantly 1975. That story continues a future-history that had the British Space Programme landing men on Mars when the police rode Mk II Jaguars with bells instead of sirens (7.3, "The Ambassadors of Death"). In both stories, UNIT handling the security at Mission Control and/or Devesham as a matter of routine – the same UNIT, even the same Sergeant Benton, we've seen in all the other adventures that get talked about in twenty-first century stories.

Devesham, we have a problem.

"The Ambassadors of Death" was always hard to reconcile with orthodox UNIT stories set in a more recognisably contemporary location. "The Android Invasion" also strained to incorporate pseudo-documentary fidelity to the daily lives of the viewers with a story about a man returning from Jupiter, to a village with a pub that served McEwan's Export. It matched the "Ambassadors" world fairly exactly – as befits a story that Barry Letts, the director of the story, reconstituted from Terry Nation's script to resemble Letts's first full story as series producer (see Volume 3 for the complex backstory for "Ambassadors") with bits of his first off-the-books script collaboration (8.5, "The Daemons").

The hints of an England that was just-around-the-corner include so many very easily dateable details in that little shop where robo-Sarah tries to trick the Doctor, it's arguable that the team included this scene specifically to cram in as much 1975-ness as possible. This was a studio set, not a location, so these posters and comics are all there on purpose. The scene's almost redundant in plot terms, and most of what it covers could have been done in any of the locations already established, so there are good budgetary reasons to not have that sequence. We're being told, in effect: *look at this, it's happening in your world about now.* (Well, it's not, it's the planet Oseidon and the shop is reconstituted from Crayford's memories of two years before – but that just makes it weirder that they bothered with jars of boiled sweets, easily-datable comics and packaging for cakes and soap drawn from the contemporary consumer world.) Even if we swallow whole the stupid line from

continued on Page 289...

ABOUT TIME 2008-2009

Branson's heirs, surely] are interested in space travel. [Virgin Galactic was set up in 2004, and there was a big unveiling of their light-aircraft-like Space Ship Two less than a fortnight after this episode was broadcast. Apart from a fatal crash in 2014, there has been less progress than advertised – typical Branson. So we can piece together that Bowie Base was the product of the World State's Space Agency.]

It took Brooke's crew two years to reach Mars; they set up base in the Gusev Crater on 1st July, 2058. [In keeping with the general Troughton-era vibe, this version of the twenty-first century seems to lack any significant input from the USA (see **Whatever Happened to the United States?** under 4.6, "The Moonbase").] The most reliable space technology is manufactured in Liverpool: Hardinger seals are the last word for airlocks. [If, as widely anticipated, the city's largely underwater by 2040, this would make sense.]

The news page of bbc.co.uk [or something very like it] is a going concern for decades after, recognisable with the red masthead and Gill Sans font.

We're given to believe that Adelaide's death is a Fixed Point because of a Dalek deliberately sparing her life during events in X4.13, "Journey's End". [There's no implication that the events of that episode are themselves a Fixed Point (quite the opposite if anything – see X5.3, "Victory of the Daleks" and **What Constitutes a Fixed Point?** under X4.2, "The Fires of Pompeii"). Which leaves this version of the future, with no serious interplanetary travel until mid-century but interstellar travel a generation after, available for any later producers (even though it slightly clashes with X8.7, "Kill the Moon").]

Thirty years after this episode, Adelaide's granddaughter Susie Fontana Brooke pilots the first lightspeed ship to Proxima Centauri. Her descendants remain an integral part of the space effort for years, travelling to the Dragon Star, the Celestial Belt of the Winter Queen, and others then mapping the Water Snake Wormhole. At some point, a Brooke falls in love with a Tandonian prince, 'and that's the start of a whole new species'.

The Analysis

The Big Picture The clue is the date this is all set and the date they expected this to go out. Had this been shown the following Saturday, it would have been broadcast 50 years to the day

before it's supposed to be happening. The track-record of *Doctor Who* for second-guessing future developments within the expected lifetime of the audience isn't great, and Davies played safe by setting most future episodes in Umpty-Zillion AD (but with everyone looking human and dressing at Top Shop), but now he's on his way out, so they can finally play the same game as "The Ambassadors of Death" or "The Moonbase".

Phil Ford's recent past included the 2005 CG re-working of *Captain Scarlet*, which had a back-story similar to the (presumed) collective future-history of Gerry Anderson shows, but tweaked slightly for character arc potential and plausibility. His Mysterons were from a Mars that closely resembled the one we can all look up on Google Mars, mapped by satellites and littered with probes (see "The Christmas Invasion"). Similarly, Ford had been working on *The Sarah Jane Adventures,* and so had factored in NASA's probe-buggies as part of what kids would know about. (Admittedly, his *Scarlet* Mars has active volcanoes spewing lava when they need a cliffhanger.)

Mars had been having something of a resurgence of interest. Once the 60s Mariner probes had killed off the idea of canals, lost cities, princesses and BEMS, there was a move away from stories using it as an all-purpose Arabian Nights setting, but the more detailed analysis made the neighbouring planet seem almost like real-estate. For the last half-century or so, human settlements on Mars have always been about 30 years away.

The mid-1990s was the turning-point, as Kim Stanley Robinson's multi-layered trilogy, beginning with *Red Mars,* re-opened the idea of a different-but-knowable planet to serious consideration as a setting. There was a spate of me-too books and a few earnest and ponderous films coming out between 1999 and 2001 (debate rages to this day if the Gary Sinese one is really worse than the Val Kilmer career-ending dud).

In the meantime, there was a huge surge of interest after the examination of a rock found in Antarctica (Allen Hills 84001) led to rumours of microbial life. Bill Clinton did a press conference and everything. The US sent robots, notably the plucky and indefatigable Spirit and Opportunity, as the rest of the world sent orbiters (and despite Beagle II's failed parachute, the Mars Express that took it is going strong – "The Christmas Invasion"). By 2008, it was possible to name specific sites on Mars that would support a manned landing, and

Was There a Martian Time-Slip?

continued from Page 287...

"Pyramids of Mars" (13.3), where Sarah claims to be from "1980" in the face of all the evidence, that still leaves Guy Crayford's jaunt beyond Jupiter firmly in the past as seen from 2007.

The other UNIT story that's proved intractable for anyone trying to make sense of the dates is "Battlefield" (26.1). That's set in a mid/late 1990s that never happened and that, even in 1989, was looking dodgy. The alternate universe with Ornithopters and sorcery is slightly more plausible than a Cold War-era nuclear arsenal in Cornwall, a king on the throne, landline phones that respond to voice commands and men over 40 wearing corduroy pedal-pushers. However, the portrait of Brigadier Lethbridge-Stewart that his daughter has on board Boat One is of him in UNIT combat gear from that story. "Battlefield" had therefore happened in the timeline that has "Death in Heaven" (X8.12) in it.

For better or worse, we're stuck with these three anomalous stories and while we have General Carrington going to Mars some time before the Space Shuttle was commissioned, we also have Bowie Base One as the first people on Mars in 2059 in "The Waters of Mars" (X4.16). It would be nice to pick and choose, but the UNIT stories – especially the 1970s ones with the "family" – are a period of the programme's history in which people have a lot invested as a linked, unified series of incidents. The people making the series then put a lot of effort and thought into making them consistent and continuous, to the extent that the Doctor makes sour comments about the Brigadier's genocidal attack on the Silurians at the start of "Ambassadors", very explicitly saying that this story happened soon after that. The people making the series after 2004 grew up on this and made sure that they referred to favourite incidents from their childhoods. Unpicking these three stories, *and only these*, from the internal referential continuity of early 1970s *Doctor Who* is well-nigh impossible.

But, as Carrington would say, it's our moral duty. So cut us a bit of slack while we try.

The first option is that *all* UNIT continuity has been changed while we weren't looking, and that only TARDIS travellers remember the ones we saw broadcast after *Grandstand*. The incidents on file to which later officers refer aren't what we think they are, but similar ones several years later. Hypothetically, if the past was changed, and only those who'd been on the TARDIS remembered

what things used to be like, it would explain why so many of that cohort found themselves in a UNIT that didn't make sense to them and left to sell cars, teach maths or develop anti-Zygon viruses (20.3, "Mawdryn Undead"; X9.8, "The Zygon Inversion") in the late 1970s while the Doctor was elsewhere.

This would account for a great deal: although we saw flashbacks to the stories we know when Sarah and Jo remembered the Doctor (*SJA*, "The Death of the Doctor") and the Master reminisced about Axons (X3.12, "The Sound of Drums"; X3.13, "Last of the Time Lords"; and of course 8.3, "The Claws of Axos"), the only clips sequence we've had of past invasions is the deeply weird one at the end of X5.1, "The Eleventh Hour" in which the Hath (X4.6, "The Doctor's Daughter"), the Ood (X2.8, "The Impossible Planet" et seq) and the skeletal remains of sixth-millennium archaeologists in spacesuits (X4.9, "Forest of the Dead") menaced Earth at some time in the past alongside the Sea Devils (9.3, "The Sea Devils", would you believe) and various Tennant-era nasties (and Linx from 11.1, "The Time Warrior" rather than the more recent Sontarans most viewers would recall). An invasion by the Hath is one UNIT could handle without the Doctor's help – unless they thought to use bullet-proof glass for their breathing apparatus, these are the least menacing aliens possible. Perhaps, therefore, Colonel Mace (X4.4, "The Sontaran Stratagem") has a dossier detailing all of the times the Doctor saved Earth from second-rate invaders too inept to get screen time, probably while doing something else.

While a Bandril onslaught might have been amusing to watch, and a definite victory for even the somewhat *Dad's Army* UNIT of 9.5, "The Time Monster", there have been too many authenticated call-backs to broadcast 70s incidents for us to sweep all of this under the carpet. The Silurians alone make up a fairly big chunk of recent continuity (X5.8-5.9, "The Hungry Earth"/"Cold Blood"; X5.12 and on for quite some time plus, less obviously, X8.7, "Kill the Moon" and – we'll be arguing in the next volume – possibly X5.2, "The Beast Below" and therefore all fifty-first century shenanigans and thus Captain Jack, River Song, the Silence and all the Doctor's lives after Trenzalore.)

Nonetheless, there is a fairly hefty change to the core continuity of UNIT that we've all observed lately. The origin-story for almost all then-contem-

continued on Page 291...

write about them with as much authority as someone who'd not been to an inaccessible part of this planet could describe the physical features, and research how people might live there even if nobody does. Davies and Ford had been talking about doing something along these lines since the early days of *Sarah Jane,* but the announcement of clear indications that the Martian surface had water relatively recently (first announced in October 2006) made it a matter of "when" rather than "if" they would do this story.

Davies and Ford's approach is something that Barry Letts, Innes Lloyd, Graham Williams and Derrick Sherwin all claimed to be doing: taking *Doctor Who* away from borrowing from other series or films, and mixing in whimsical fantasy, and moving towards knowable science as a source of plot ideas. Most of New *Who* has been cosily derivative, mainly from other effects-led franchises, rather than made from scratch using fresh ingredients ("Hard SF" is the usual term for not reheating ready-made stuff). It was a traditional first move of an incoming producer, but here the outgoing executive producer (in so many ways) has opted to do it for very different reasons.

Ford's first go, if *The Writer's Tale* is any guide, was sword-and-sorcery Barsoom stuff with an alien Princess – the kind of thing Mark Gatiss later did with his characteristic broad strokes in Series 10 – and Davies reined it back, first to being about a human colony on Mars, and then to the very *first* colony. Everything had to be worked up from NASA plans (at least, that was the original scheme). He removed all hints of previous attempts to settle (algae tanks, terraforming and so on) to make the story about a historic, doomed group of pioneers in a set of pressurised sheds.

The obvious analogy is *Scott of the Antarctic,* the 1948 film of the 1912 expedition to the South Pole. The film emphasised the inspiring fortitude of the small party that set out for the Pole just ahead of the worst storms on record, rather than the more successful scientific base-camp who sent out the rescue/recovery party that found the diaries of the dead explorers. Scott's stoicism was perhaps in the minds of the *Doctor Who* team, because of Gatiss's 2007 dramatisation of *The Worst Journey in the World,* the account by Apsley Cherry-Garrard – one of the base team – with portions of the book read by Barry Letts (who had played the same role in the 1948 classic). Gatiss's version focuses on the survivor's guilt of "Cherry",

who led the recovery mission. One of Davies's changes to the second version of this episode was that the Russian leader became British and her "British pluck" (his words) was her defining feature. The 1948 film's emphasis on facing literally insurmountable odds in the hope that others might benefit struck a chord in post-war Britain, however much later dramas debunked it. Another topical connection was that Scott's tomb carries the last line of Tennyson's *Ulysses*: "to strive, to seek, to find and not to yield". These words had, impropitiously, been selected as a slogan for the forthcoming 2012 Olympic Games in London.

Why was Adelaide going to be Russian? They had a vague plan to ask Dame Helen Mirren to play a role not entirely unlike her part in the perfunctory film *2010: The Year We Make Contact.* In all stories of near-future space, the base-line assumption was that there would be a Soviet Union, a United States and A.N. Other, usually all of Europe. Ideas that China, India or Japan might have viable space-programmes were discounted even as late as 1987's *Star Cops.* The all-Europe base (space being a matter for governments and not bored billionaires) was usually third in a two-horse race, but allowed the BBC to claim to be "realistic" and hire actors who could do accents.

Letts and Terrance Dicks had gone down this path with the hapless *Moonbase 3* in 1973. After 1975, it wouldn't have been acceptable to present a UK-only space programme (as seen in "The Ambassadors of Death", and even then they opted at the last moment to give Bruno Taltalian an iffy French accent). "The Android Invasion" (13.4) failed to entirely sell the idea, even when smothering it in even sillier ones. Of course, *Doctor Who's* key text on this is "The Moonbase", which took its cue from the George Pal films of the early 50s and presented an "international" crew (lacking Russians or Asians of any kind – the BBC did at least have a non-white crewmember as cannon-fodder, unlike Universal Pictures).

Davies was scathing about that story and its semi-sequel, "The Wheel in Space" (5.7), for using the accents to distinguish otherwise interchangeable characters. It's notable, though, that his version doesn't spare time to do much better (a coltish German woman called "Steffi" – like Steffi Graf, y'see? – is hardly any more insightful than a Dane called "Nils"), and uses the videophone calls to families on Earth to do the heavy lifting. That's a trick used in Kubrick's *2001: A*

Was There a Martian Time-Slip?

continued from Page 289...

porary tales of alien incursion into Britain is "The Abominable Snowmen" (5.2). We've got an essay on the anomalies between this and its sequels, and that whole "Impossible Girl" thing, coming up in a couple of volumes (*The* **Great Intelligence or Just *a* Great Intelligence?** under "The Snowmen"), but a quick synopsis is that the latter half of Series 7 tries to over-write the Yeti with stories about literal killer snowmen, a less-literal web of fear (X7.7, "The Bells of Saint John") and creepy pale-faced Victorian undertakers ("The Name of the Doctor" rather than the ones in "Deep Breath" or X9.3, "Under the Lake"), even though this forgets that the set-up for the Yeti was four centuries earlier. This risks making the Brigadier never have happened. No "Abominable Snowmen" means no Travers and no "The Web of Fear" (5.5), therefore no Lethbridge-Stewart, no UNIT, no "The Invasion" (6.3), no "Spearhead from Space" and no "Doctor Who and the Silurians". This risks more paradoxes than before, especially if the Silurians aren't there either.

A bigger problem with using this to account for UNIT anomalies is that the anomalies were apparent before this alteration took place. Even if these newer stories in 14:9 format bulldozed over the old ones, they did so indiscriminately so we are back to square one. "The Talons of Weng-Chiang" (14.6), to name but one, is referred back to often enough for such erasure not to have happened. Besides, a large part of the plot of 2013's episodes was that Clara went back and put everything right. A change to history that amends three stories and leaves everything else *exactly* as it was is not something to be left to soufflé-obsessed amateurs. This requires finesse, and to have been effected at a specific point in the Doctor's life. It also, crucially, requires someone with that amount of control and power to have a good reason to do it that way. We'll examine two obvious suspects in a moment but first, there's another odd anomaly that might shed some light on it.

We've argued that, logically, all the activities of Torchwood must have been in play during the version of the 1970s we saw in the 1970s. The activities of Mr Chinn in "The Claws of Axos", Colonel Trenchard in "The Sea Devils" and Professor Brett in 3.10, "The War Machines" all make a lot more sense that way, as does the whole of 26.3, "The Curse of Fenric". (You can mark our homework in **All Right Then, Where Were Torchwood?**

under "The Sea Devils"). However, Torchwood itself makes less sense the more we look at it. If, as we are told (X2.12, "Army of Ghosts"), they exist to extend the British Empire and use alien technology to that end, and have been doing so since 1879, they've been spectacularly useless. Why was there even a First World War, let alone a sequel? How did the Empire collapse, especially as they have a Time Agent they don't trust, and who they can torture to death as often as they like to get the jump on Stalin, Hitler and Bezos? Neither the almost-familiar world where Jackie Tyler is convinced her dad's come back, nor the almost-familiar alternate world where Pete Tyler is still alive, come close to what such an organisation would have created.

However, there is also the almost-familiar world where they've been sending Englishmen to Mars so often that people have the telecasts on as background, and where the regulars at the Fleur de Lys are as blasé about having a space control centre as neighbours might be. You can draw a line from World War II to 5.4, "The Enemy of the World" and thence to 17.4, "Nightmare of Eden" and it goes through the Ralph Cornish/Guy Crayford version of the 1970s. It might, at a pinch, pass through 6.5, "The Seeds of Death" (by way of the TOMTIT gap a la "The Time Monster", a UNIT story some would like to see vanish as well).

What it *doesn't* pass through is the present-day of the early 1980s stories where Concorde is the last word in British technical prowess (19.7, "Time-Flight"), and the Walkman was cutting-edge even to space-scientists (18.7, "Logopolis"). The world of "The Ambassadors of Death" is almost the Torchwood version of utopian Albion, but it would have made all other present-day stories impossible if they had engineered this state of affairs. The dates of medium-range future stories also get trampled. "The Moonbase" (4.6) would have been set in the 1940s rather than 2070, and there would have been no other European nations involved. We'd certainly not have Hungary as a significant power in 2018 (see "The Enemy of the World", which has already missed the deadline for Ramon Salamander to have saved the world we inhabit with solar collectors and robot combine harvesters). We can discount Torchwood as culprits if we're looking for why these stories were removed, but not necessarily if we're asking how they came to happen at all. In that light, all stories that resemble our everyday experience are the anomalies,

continued on Page 293...

Space Odyssey, although there the sheer banality of the messages was part of the point. Here, it's got a remnant of the "Christmas on Mars" idea and is used to milk Steffi's death for pathos.

This is the most peculiar thing about the story: Ford wrote a tale about a heroic-but-doomed Mars colony and nonchalantly mentioned that the incident was a Fixed Point – as famous as Pompeii, but one that hasn't happened yet. The focus was on the colonists' heroism in trying to avoid a fate the Doctor knew to be pre-ordained, not the pre-ordination itself. Davies made that the whole crux of the story, and used it as the first act of a three-part tragedy ending with the Doctor's regeneration.

"Tragedy" is, in this case, the literal term. Davies has fallen back on Aristotle's *Poetics*, and made the Doctor's fate an inevitable consequence of a slight flaw in his character. The cockiness that was usually a slightly endearing quality of this Doctor – and made him regenerate into himself at the start of "Journey's End" – becomes an arrogance that makes him talk unabashedly of saving "little people". As Mr Cotton observed in "Voyage of the Damned" (X4.0), this makes him a monster. In the broadcast version of "The Waters of Mars", there's an understated hint that the string of small accidents that befall the Doctor once he's decided to intervene are Time trying to stop him, a sort of inertial force of events.

The Greek model continues until "The End of Time Part Two" (X4.18), and an evening of the balance by the Doctor's "death" following an act of humility saving a complete stranger (albeit compromised by making it Wilf instead). If you're really looking for a close match for Sophocles and that crowd, note that the climax of the three-part story is a god-like being who's been acting as narrator intervening directly in events in the material world (the words we're looking for are "Theophany" and our old chum "Deus ex Machina"). The idea seems to be that the Doctor's sin in saving three of the colonists and altering a Fixed Point directly causes time to go wrong, the Ood to develop prophetic abilities and Gallifrey to return, although quite *how* or *why* is never explained, and it's never even stated as causally related. It's just "wrong".

As we hinted in Volume 8, just as X3.7, "42" reached our screens, the film *Sunshine* (directed by Danny Boyle) came out and caused Davies a few headaches. This story resembles it in both tone and specifics. Both are set exactly 50 years in the future, both have multi-ethnic crews representing the most likely nations to have mature space programmes by then, both feature vast herbaria, claustrophobic living conditions and characters being picked off by a human contaminated by an environmental force. Boyle's decisions to clamp down on romantic relationships between the crew, and not cut back to conditions on Earth until the mission was over, are echoed in this episode. *Sunshine* wasn't the first collaboration between Boyle and Alex Garland; their second had been *28 Days Later*, in which a blood-borne virus turned people into rampaging killers, and people became infected by a single drop falling on them in slow motion, as happens to Roman here.

Again, the idea is that people are killed by sheer bad luck, not inexorable machinations of Fate. Davies, Ford and Harper have taken these images and used them more in a supernatural-horror patterning, as with *The Omen* or *Final Destination*, to suggest the impossibility of running away from a prescribed death. These can look, to anyone raised in 70s Britain, like a string of Public Information Films. The Hollywood version is, ultimately, rooted in Puritan ideas of Preterition and the Elect – that some people are "saved" from before birth and the rest are doomed, with nothing anyone can do on Earth affecting this lottery. As we've seen, this idea is generally thought in Britain to be the root of all evil. Way back in "Boom Town" (X1.11), the Doctor and Margaret Slitheen discuss whether a killer who arbitrarily decides someone ought to be spared because they "deserve" it is any less terrible.

More obvious cinematic borrowings – notably Gadget's conceptual similarity to *Wall-E* – ought to be noted in passing. The scorch-marks made by the souped-up robot are from *Back to the Future*; the dome, a genuine feature of the location, looks to have been inspired by *Silent Running;* and Flood victims walk in the now-traditional George A Romero zombie manner. One that didn't make the finished version was the CG water-creatures originally planned in Ford's early drafts, based loosely on the beings in *The Abyss* (an effect finally achieved in X10.13, "Twice Upon a Time"). A more widely-seen version of this was in the video for *Waterfalls* by TLC. And, although it's not said out loud, the Maggie's make-up is a close match for Alan Bennion as various Ice Lords (6.5, "The Seeds of Death"; 9.2, "The Curse of Peladon";

Was There a Martian Time-Slip?

continued from Page 291...

and the 70s UNIT stories should have all been set in a world of hover-bikes (driving on the left) and 3D TV (with Peter Bolgar or John Marsh doing the announcements). Once again, the change that Torchwood would bring is all-or-nothing rather than the piecemeal one we see.

So from the Doctor's point of view, which is ours as well, there may have been an amended edition of history that came into effect at a point in his life between "The Seeds of Doom" (13.6) and "Logopolis". As far as his on-screen exploits go, it's a period in which he's not only avoiding present-day Earth where possible but dodging the Black Guardian for a large chunk of the time. Admittedly, his bid to avoid the most likely places he'd be found lands up with the Randomiser taking him to Skaro, then 1979 Earth (but Paris, rather than London or Mummerset), but the intention was there.

We're used to thinking of the Time War as being an isolated incident, one that happened while the series is off-air, but there's a good case that the opening salvo between Gallifrey and Skaro was "Genesis of the Daleks" (12.4). There's also a lot of odd stuff happening in Season Twenty-Two, with half the stories being about illegal time experiments, and the Time Lords being more like the US State Department than the Secret Masters of the Universe they'd hitherto been. They are major players on the cosmic stage in ways that they themselves found distasteful when the Doctor was tried for small-scale interventions (6.7, "The War Games"). Since he became Lord President, there seems to have been a pressing need to get their hands dirty without using him as their agent (as they had done in "Genesis" and 13.5, "The Brain of Morbius", plus a few Pertwee stories).

He never mentions any other time wars and is on such unprecedentedly good terms with the Time Lords that word would have reached him. One fairly big change is that the material universe gets eroded by entropy ("Logopolis"), but this is – absurdly, perhaps – all supposed to happen in one day in 1981. Before that, however, we had a fairly substantial off-screen reboot of the cosmos at the end of Season Sixteen. In the opening sequence of "The Ribos Operation" (16.1), the Guardian tells the Doctor that the universe is out of whack and has to be reset by pressing "pause". When the Key to Time is assembled, the Doctor is confident that the White Guardian has done this while our atten-

tion was distracted by the Black Guardian (16.6, "The Armageddon Factor"). It's only after this that we see the Doctor become cautious again with regard to Earth history (19.4, "The Visitation"; 19.6, "Earthshock") and start to become a regular visitor to our time and place again – this, after a long spell seeing what else the universe has to offer. The Earth he visits is England in the early 1980s and it looks like the one with aerobics and Exocets.

One thing is certain: Earth in the early twenty-first century is, in the current configuration, a Level Five world. Had it not been, the Judoon would have simply killed everyone for harbouring a fugitive (X3.1, "Smith and Jones"), and most of the invasions the Doctor thwarts would have been straightforward military incursions without all the sneaky plots and subterfuges. The alarming prospect opens up that the Doctor *himself* sought to safeguard his favourite pied à terre by taking it off the menu and into the protective custody of the Shadow Proclamation, the Alliance of Shades or others.

The version of history with manned Mars landings before the Raleigh Chopper[50] is, as the Brigadier tells Liz at the start of "Spearhead", asking for trouble. It might have been a prudent policy to have Earth less dependent on him to fix things while he was on the run after Season Sixteen. Taking a detour to micro-manage one small part of the history of the mid-twentieth century, so that he could leave that bit of cosmic history to its own devices, might have been the most completely predictable move he could have made. Yet it's looking as if only he could have done it, and only realistically in that phase of his existence. This in turn means a major alteration to Earth's time-line while trying to avoid the Black Guardian's gaze, but with Romana in tow telling him not to do it (or how to do it properly) and the Time Lords taking a dim view of this.

Unless, of course, they ordered it. All we have to go on is that things were a bit messed-up after "The Invasion of Time" (15.6), so there may have been a bit of a power-struggle as the clean-up took place. We also know that the Sontarans were after Gallifrey, and that they had dealings with the enigmatic Third Zone who were sanctioning the Kartz-Reimer experiments (22.4, "The Two Doctors"), so we might add this to the list of lesser Time Wars implicit in the description of the big Dalek-Time Lord tussle as the "Last". Then the only

continued on Page 295...

11.4, "The Monster of Peladon"), and the material about the caves and ancient language is the sort of thing Benny Summerfield (see X4.8, "Silence in the Library") got excited by in the *New Adventures* books (notably *Transit* by Ben Aaronovitch).

English Lessons

• *Glacier Mints* (n.): Mint/menthol-flavoured boiled sweets (boiled sweets were an integral part of childhood around these parts, but "hard candy" covers most, but not all, of it for US translation purposes). It was almost pure sugar and mint, like a miniature Kendal Mint Cake, and made by a company called "Fox's" (not, as far as we can discern, the biscuit company), so the TV ads had a fox wondering why a polar bear got to be the brand icon. They were "glacier" mints because they were transparent. (Rachel Whiteread's controversial Fourth Plinth installation in Trafalgar Square brought them back into the public consciousness a few years before this episode went out.)

• *Bish Bash Bosh* (interj.): doing a simple job faster than necessary to grab the cash (as per Harry Enfield's "Loadsamoney" house-plasterer) and nonsensical magic-words for conjurers, also used interchangeably with "as easy as that", "Bob's your uncle" or "seemples". The technical term for this sort of jingle where the vowels change is "ablaut", a subset of "apophony" (the general heading that also includes "Oedipus Schmedipus" and "timey wimey").

Oh, Isn't That...?

• *Lindsay Duncan* (Captain Adelaide Brooke) now has a CBE and more industry awards than you can shake a stick at after a long career. She has tended towards theatre and the sort of television that gets serious prizes and critical acclaim rather than big audiences – *Shooting the Past*, *GBH*, *Traffik* – but you can see her in *Rome* and *Spooks*. Her TV debut was the 1975 *Up Pompeii!*. More recently, she appeared with Matt Smith in *Christopher and His Kind* (as his mum), and was in *Birdman*, *Sherlock* and the televised version of *Richard II* that gave Ben Whishaw's career such a boost. *Doctor Who* – even a glum episode such as this – was significantly more downmarket than much of her work (as was doing a robot voice in *The Phantom Menace*). Shortly before this episode, she had played Margaret Thatcher in a prestigious production, *Margaret*.

• *Peter O'Brien* (Ed Gold). O'Brien is the most prominent alumnus of Davies's breakthrough show *Queer as Folk* to make it to his most famous project (surprisingly, very few of the others scored even a cameo when *Doctor Who* came back). Nonetheless, for most people in Britain he was Shane Ramsey from the original run of *Neighbours*. He was also the token Australian in various 90s things, such as *The All-New Alexei Sayle Show* (but not in the same sketches as Peter Capaldi).

• *Sharon Duncan-Brewster* (Maggie Cain) had been in *Bad Girls* (a not-at-all-exploitative Women's Prison series, honest) and a stint in *EastEnders* before this. Now she's got *Rogue One* (as Senator Pamlo) and Russell T Davies's comeback show *Cucumber* under her belt, but best of all (at least financially) she was Scratchy in *Rastamouse*.

• *Gemma Chan* (Mia Bennett). After getting to the finals of *Project Catwalk*, she became a regular on *Secret Diary of a Call Girl* and Watson's girlfriend in the second episode of *Sherlock*. She was also Moss's date in the last episode of *The IT Crowd* and you could have seen her in *Humans* and *Fresh Meat*. *Transformers: Last Knight* and *Fantastic Beasts and Where to Find Them* followed. (Let's not dwell on *London Fields*.) Most obviously, she was in *Crazy Rich Asians* as Astrid, the character who's mainly there to set up the sequel.

• *Chook Sibtain* (Tarak Ital). Apart from a stint in *EastEnders* and *Doctors,* he was the slimy Mr Grantham in *SJA*: "Warriors of Kudlak".

• *Alan Ruscoe* (Andy Stone). You wouldn't recognise him, but we couldn't fit this gobbet in anywhere else: he was inside the Anne Droid in "Bad Wolf"/"The Parting of the Ways", as well as a few Autons and assorted aliens.

Things That Don't Make Sense According to the online bios, Gemma is from Dallas, Andy is from Iowa and Maggie is from Sheffield. No, no and no.

The most overt glitch, of course, is that the Doctor never considers that he could just whisk the Bowie Base survivors away to another time zone or planet completely removed from Earth, to live out their lives incognito. The base's nuclear obliteration would preclude anyone from counting the bodies, so – loss of family contact aside – everyone's a winner.

Well, to be fair, he could maybe do that for anyone but Adelaide. It's bizarre how the story treats her physical death as the Fixed Point, even

Was There a Martian Time-Slip?

continued from Page 293...

problem is why these were deemed to be less worth showing us than, say, 24.3, "Delta and the Bannermen".

This line on inquiry reveals something startling but, with hindsight, self-evident. There were no Fixed Points in the period of Earth's history that includes the Doctor's exile after the Time Lords caught him, nor apparently at any time between the eruption of Vesuvius and Easter Saturday 2011. That one (X6.1, "The Impossible Astronaut") was in a freshly-reconstituted universe that the Doctor made happen, so may not fall into the same category as the one on Mars 48 years later. We looked at this from one angle in **How and Why is the Doctor Exiled to Earth?** under 9.5, "The Time Monster", but in this light it seems as though the Doctor was being used as a walking, talking, Venusian-Karate-chopping Fixed Point himself, shoring up a planet and species that were going to be important later, but were especially vulnerable at this stage. It's a period the Doctor seems not to have revisited since leaving his involuntary berth (the one exception we can think of, assuming that our UNIT dates are right, is X2.10, "Love & Monsters" and Elton's first encounter with the Doctor around 1975).

If it's not the Doctor doing it, then who? The Daleks only really have the capability to make this precise an alteration, after their refit for the big Time War we all know about (see **What's Happened to the Daleks?** under, well, "Dalek"). That doesn't entirely rule it out, but they surely have bigger fish to fry than a few details of Earth's fledgling space programme. What does it profit them? They aren't especially fond of this planet, partly because of the whole magnetic field thing (2.2, "The Dalek Invasion of Earth"), generally because they have a bad track-record of encounters with the Doctor. In fact, almost all of their visits to Earth before the twenty-second century are to lay traps for him, or because he's laid one for *them* (4.9, "The Evil of the Daleks"; 25.1, "Remembrance of the Daleks"; 21,4, "Resurrection of the Daleks"; X4.12, "The Stolen Earth"; X5.3, "Victory of the Daleks").

Humans going to other planets is perhaps a problem they could nip in the bud, but the precision and relative mercy of this sort of intervention is out of character for them. Why not just nuke humanity back into the Stone Age? It's the surgical neatness of the changes made that make the Daleks seem unlikely agents. Other potential interventions are implausible, simply because the Time Lords exiled the Doctor to Earth, and any attempt to change his life and Earth's history up to the start of his UNIT tenure would have been circumvented by them, regardless of when (from their or his perspective) the intervention originated.

We floated a notion in Volume 6 that the Time Lords of the Doctor's era were locked into their own chronology (**Why Do Time Lords Always Meet in Sequence?** under 22.3, "The Mark of the Rani"), and that Time Lords from a later, contingent period could dip into the past and use earlier Doctors as agents. If anything went wrong, his subsequent impact on history was so great that other forces (including the Time Lords from his own time) would be forced to clean up their mess (**Was There a Season 6B?** under "The Two Doctors"). Is this what could be happening (or made to un-happen) in these cases? Well, the Mars Probe thing might be possible to make go away with few consequences, but the Crayford incident – evidently a consequence of the same set-up – is harder to wish away, as it's fairly clear that this is what led Sarah to meet the Doctor in the first place.

We know they met while she pretended to be her own aunt to sneak into the Brigadier's secure facility for elderly male scientists (in "The Time Monster"), but listen to all the things that aren't said later. When her photo shows up at the UNIT base in a school (11.2, "Invasion of the Dinosaurs"), Benton identifies her to the Brig. So they *both* know who she is, despite neither of them speaking to her in the earlier story, or even knowing she was on the premises. Mike Yates chats to her as though she were an old friend. In "Robot" (12.1) she knows Harry Sullivan – yes, she's been popping in to UNIT HQ for the last three months to check on the comatose Doctor but that just makes it weirder that she has such free access.

Then it turns out that two years before "The Android Invasion", she had covered the story of Crayford's disappearance and stayed long enough to remember the name of the landlord of the Fleur de Lys. Benton and Harry are on duty at Devesham as though this formed a regular part of UNIT activities. The most straightforward way to account for all of this is if, in order to get the Crayford story, she was already either on the UNIT

continued on Page 297...

ABOUT TIME 2008-2009

though the known context for it completely changes after the Doctor explains that the consequences of the Bowie Base *story* are the real issue. Surely, it's going to make a significant difference to history if, instead of heroically sacrificing her life and crew, possibly to protect humanity, she's inexplicably found on Earth, in her own house, self-zapped? It's like saying that if President John F. Kennedy hanged himself in the privacy of his own home, after being magically teleported there, rather than being assassinated in Dallas everyone would find him just as inspirational as before and history continues unchanged.

The news reports claim the two survivors exposed the Doctor as behind their miraculous survival – but won't that just trigger even more questions and uncertainty? Won't the public still be in the dark about why Adelaide blew her brains out? Won't disclosure of the enigmatic Doctor's involvement diminish her agency and legacy? (Remember: the Doctor only explained his presence at Bowie Base One to Adelaide.) It's also odd how a news item claims that the infected Bowie Base crew underwent a "metaphysical" change – they became angels?

# # #

So, the team have interplanetary Skype with their kids and partners, but communications with Earth are suspended owing to "solar flares". Mars hasn't got a magnetosphere (unlike Earth), so a solar flare is *really* bad news and they should go underground throughout the whole incident. Pretty much all of their electrical systems would be fried, and the radiation would sterilise any virus they've unearthed.

It's even weirder that the team is a mixed-bag of people in their 20s, grandparents, mums and people conducting long-distance relationships with partners on Earth. What criteria were they using for selection? The Apollo missions picked middle-aged test-pilots with PhDs who'd already had their children, so wouldn't inflict genetic mutations on their potential future offspring. The radiation in just a week-long trip to the Moon was thought to be risky. Nine months on a flight to Mars (that's NASA's guess, the script says two entire years) and then an indefinite stay on the surface – no magnetosphere, remember? – isn't a nice prospect for anyone hoping to return and raise a family, or indeed come back without can-

cer. The first mission is pretty much a one-way journey. (Nine months in weightlessness is tolerable with a medical team waiting for you but there's nobody on Mars yet. Did they send Gadget ahead to build floatation-tanks?)

Bringing back pioneers is mainly to examine the results of doing so and the publicity machine needs returnees to talk about it. So either Bowie Base One is intended as a long-term colony, or it's a relatively brief sojourn (Ed says it's a five-year mission) to see what it's really like. This story seems to suggest two different missions in alternate scenes. People in their 20s or 30s are there to raise kids on a new planet; not for the first-ever go, nor for any mission where they are planning to be back. (Then again, we've speculated about anti-radiation gloves… er, drugs as a major difference between the Pertwee UNIT era and our world before, so maybe that's less of a problem in this future.)

Either way, a "no relationships" rule is asking for trouble. It's strongly hinted that the base's destruction remains a mystery because the solar flares cut the live feed – but if there's one of those, surely viewers on Earth speculated about Mia and Yuri before now. (These are the first people on Mars, so they'd be scrutinised more avidly that even the first couple of series of *Big Brother*.) These people have presumably trained together for at least as long as the Apollo crews and will have been screened, profiled and matched to check that they all get along. Ed's beef with Adelaide would have been detected, and he would have been off the mission – or if she's adhering to this rule against relationships against his wishes, that would have been a red-flag issue in pre-flight training. Moreover, Ed claims he hated the job. For that matter, Andy's sister working for the Spacelink project ought to have debarred him from such a sensitive mission (unless the World State is less paranoid about politically-divisive and historically significant projects than Britain, the US or Russia now).

# # #

The Gusev crater has many interesting characteristics, including some of the strongest evidence for water having once existed on the surface. What it definitely isn't is a likely spot for a glacier. It's all the sillier since the polar ice caps have all the ice a colony would need. Plus, as a tip of the

Was There a Martian Time-Slip?

continued from Page 295...

payroll or known to them and allowed access fairly regularly before she met the Doctor. (It's worth noting that when he explains his part in the missing scientists caper, she asks "You're with UNIT?", obviously aware of their existence but unsure of the Doctor's status.) The casual references in *The Sarah Jane Adventures* confirm that she was always considered part of UNIT, and can call on their services and offer likely candidates interviews.

Moreover, her time with the Doctor (first time around) is marked by some pretty powerful cosmic forces; compared to – say – Zoe, she's faced big-league players such as Davros, Sutekh and Morbius, rather than penny-ante Space Pirates or Krotons. Her later career as a freelance alien-chaser gets her some upscale antagonists (see **Should the Trickster Have a Dead Bird on His Head?** under A7, "The Wedding of Sarah Jane Smith"). Anyone attempting to mess with the first time Sarah came into UNIT's purlieu is taking a big risk. Then again, one possibility is that Sarah herself was part of the alteration. We'll look into the most likely reason why a change might have been necessary in **What Happened in 1972?** under A8, "Dreamland", but we've already seen that, from a galactic perspective, the Earth's ambiguous status as a Level Five world with aliens showing up on global telecasts had to be fixed.

We'll come back to "who" in a moment, but we need to ask "how". How can these three incidents, and only these, be amended whilst leaving history untouched all around them? What kind of magic bullet can anyone use to make such specific changes without the knock-on effects creating an unrecognisable world? One obvious place to look is the United States. We've commented before on the relative absence of America from the 1960s version of the twenty-first century (**Whatever Happened to the USA?** under "The Moonbase"), and on the way BBC Wales has introduced the Yanks as more than just cities mentioned in a list (e.g. **How Come Britain's Got a President and America Hasn't?** under X3.12, "The Sound of Drums").

"The Ambassadors of Death" makes mention of some American space agency, but not NASA directly. They can send up a small unmanned probe, but Americans on Mars? Forget it! As late as "Delta and the Bannermen", it appears that the US is a bit behind in the space race – their first probe was launched in 1959 according to that story, even though "The Seeds of Doom" confirms Gagarin as the first human in space. Now, by "The Impossible Astronaut" (X6.1), things match our history and Neil Armstrong took one small step in 1969, but it's noticeable how little America's space research is mentioned. In fact, it's odd how little America shows up at all before 2005. We have General Cutler (4.2, "The Tenth Planet"); the American delegate assaulted by a cute pink dragon (8.2, "The Mind of Evil"); Bill Filer ("The Claws of Axos"); Peri (21.5, "Planet of Fire" et seq); Morton Dill, for crying out loud (2.8, "The Chase"); and that's about it for contemporary Americans. France is better-represented.

Removing the US from history is a little extreme even for the Pertwee Doctor, but it doesn't have to be that severe a tweak. One option that makes the "Ambassadors" history more plausible, without ruling out something as real-world verifiable as 10.5, "The Green Death", is making Harry Truman's presidency go away. America still gets to claim the spoils of World War II, but doesn't bust a gut sabotaging the Attlee government's plans for postwar Britain and the Empire. As we shift into the era of the Commonwealth and the Marshall Plan, the Labour government no longer has to choose which of the projects on the drawing-board they can develop fully.

One of Truman's first decisions was over the use of the atomic bomb: Einstein and others on the Manhattan Project had offered Roosevelt an option of destroying an uninhabited but visible island to demonstrate the weapon to the Axis powers, and end the Japanese war by intimidation rather than an attack on a civilian target. Whether this would have been enough to enforce a surrender and prevent another five years of conventional warfare (the usual justification for destroying Hiroshima is that Japan would not have acceded to anything less) is a matter for conjecture, but a less intense Cold War and more well-thought-out civilian use of atomic power seems to be a regular feature of the UNIT future stories.

It's also worth noting that no version of televised *Doctor Who* mentions of the state of Israel, so perhaps the enforced partition, one part of Truman's policies nobody expected, never happened and there was no need for Black September, the PLO or Mossad. (**How Plausible was the British Space Programme?** under "Ambassadors

continued on Page 299...

hat to *Moonbase 3*, we observe that building a large, heavy metal base on top of ice and then heating up the ice is rather like digging an escape tunnel from a prison ship. Or pitching a tent in a swamp.

The speculation about the Philippines separately sending someone to Mars seems weird too – it's a whole planet with a surface-area bigger than the US, so anyone visiting Gusev would have been seen coming a long way away. Let's not forget that, as the authors knew from their scant but relatively thorough research, Mars is being scrutinised from orbit in great detail even now. The people on it would know if they've got new neighbours. (And, there's a 'World State", but Spain and the Philippines haven't joined in?)

The first thing Adelaide does, upon being informed that an alien stranger has mysteriously appeared, is hold a gun on him. Was this really down in the contingency plans? Adelaide is packing a laser gun, yet there's a big bang when she shoots herself off-screen. There's all sorts of problems with having guns lying around in a pressurised environment with thin walls, but for whom were they intended? There weren't deer or rabbits in the biodome, so is the weaponry just to keep the bird population in check? Why not just, you know, bring a cat?

How birds cope with low atmospheric pressure and 1/3 Earth-normal gravity is best not investigated, as we'll have to ask about running, the weight of the Flood-zombies, how long it takes a drop of water to fall and so on. It's one of those space-bases where the gravity leaks out if you open the air-lock – see "Oxygen" (X10.5) for more stupidity on this front – but to gripe about this too much is to bring back memories of Graeme Harper's attempts to suggest different gravities in *Star Cops,* so we'll leave it aside.

An overloaded nuclear reactor would just send out superheated steam, hot and fast and copious so that the station would most likely be destroyed, but not in such a "we've set off a nuke" way. Would a mushroom cloud even form in such thin air?

The bio-dome has an air-lock that needs to be pressurised before the Doctor, Adelaide and Tarak can get in. As it's the source of most of their air, it's the one place not needing one. Then we see everyone's breath misting, even though it would logically need to be warmer. An environment with limited atmosphere and resources wouldn't design

great big rooms and long corridors full of wasted oxygen and heat. (X2.9, "The Satan Pit" got that bit right, so how hard can it be?)

But the single *weirdest* aspect of the whole story is that they've been there at least one Christmas already and yet only now have their first ever carrots. If they were serious about this base as a long-term prospect, they'd've started on the journey out, nine months with no home deliveries of air or food. If they were planning to live on what they brought with them for a five year-stint before all going home then seeds and soil are an unnecessary weight. Presuming they've got enough oxygen for a long stay without using plants to replenish it, which is daft.

It would be a major task establishing a biome from scratch, we have to assume that it was always part of the plan and Andy was selected for the mission for his expertise in generating soil from sewage and Martian rock. They were all presumably trained to look out for micro-organisms. Taking a bite out of a muddy carrot is risky enough on Earth, so why someone who'd devoted his life to inventing ways to grow things on a new world thinks to chomp on one is baffling.

We have a basic chemistry problem of where all the water comes from; the Flood-victims exude a mass greater than what can be present in their bodies. Even if 70% of human flesh is water, and assuming that Andy is 14 stone (terrestrial weight), he'd produce 79.5 litres tops, and that's with him turned to powder at the end. We see him gush out at least twice that. (We let off X3.2, "The Shakespeare Code" because that was Evil Since the Dawn of Time messing with the cosmic base-code. This is a virus.) Yet the Doctor states that this bug "creates" water. The atmosphere of the base is apparently Earth-normal (or else they'd be talking like Bart Simpson) so there's not much hydrogen around and changes in the amount or percentage of oxygen in the air would be the first thing that would set off alarms (it's a fire-risk apart from anything). The only available solution is that this infection allows the victim to teleport water from the glacier.

The shuttle explodes, causing flaming debris to fly around. The three things everyone knows about the atmosphere of Mars – it's too thin for anything like that; it's extremely cold; it's carbon dioxide, as used in fire-extinguishers. Then Gadget leaves tyre-tracks on the surface of Mars, flaming the way things can't. It's also not clever

Was There a Martian Time-Slip?

continued from Page 297...

of Death" details some of Truman's impact on the UK economy, as does the background material on X2.7, "The Idiot's Lantern".) The worst effects of his plan were ameliorated by Winston Churchill, who underwent a lecture tour of the US at the behest of the government which had ousted him from Number 10. In a notional revised version of this sequence of events, Churchill could have been an even more significant participant. On-screen accounts of the Doctor's engagement with this controversial premier were noticeably scant before Series 5. Apart from the Doctor's ability to forge his signature ("The Curse of Fenric"), it was mainly the spin-offs that played this card (see **Can They Do It Live?** under A6, "Music of the Spheres"). By the time we get to X5.3, "Victory of the Daleks", there is considerable history between them.

What if, therefore, the solution is the reverse of this: that the Doctor (or someone) stage-managed Truman's succession to the Presidency and unexpected victory in the 1948 election (the pollsters, notoriously, had Dewey comfortably ahead). He (or whoever) created the Cold War, crushed Britain's economy and shifted from the Empire to the Commonwealth. This would be a bittersweet victory for someone as anglophile as the Doctor, but it saves Earth from the attentions of aliens, sort of, even if it makes a nuclear war more probable. It does, however, sabotage Torchwood's plans – admittedly, the Doctor didn't know about them until just after he'd caused them. If it *was* him, it may have been after 17.4, "Nightmare of Eden", hence the rather optimistic dates for Galactic Salvage and Insurance.

However, the Troughton twenty-first century and the slightly utopian Mars programme paid for in shillings do seem to come from the *Dan Dare* future foreseen at the 1951 Festival of Britain so, perhaps, they occupy a timeline where Henry A Wallace (as mentioned *re* Faraday Cages in X4.15, "Planet of the Dead") became President and committed America to psychic research rather than ICBMs. However, all those World Peace Conferences UNIT had to police would have been less urgent with no risk of a nuclear holocaust, so it's perhaps an event caused by a subsequent (from the Doctor's perspective) change.

One thing changed between "Ambassadors" and "The Mind of Evil" – the Master showed up and found that the Doctor was handcuffed to 1970s Earth. That's tempting as a solution to the specificity of the changes – doing it to make his own plans easier to achieve and annoying his old rival – but it's a bit petty for this Master and there's no reason for his later self to pop back and make sure it all worked out for his short, dapper predecessor. (It might even explain why UNIT uniforms abruptly change to something like our real-world military and only the Doctor notices.) It's a slight problem that in the broadcast chronology his TARDIS is immobilised at the end of "Terror of the Autons", but we've talked about that; Season Eight makes more sense if it's told from the Master's point of view, chronologically speaking. It's also weird that he'd do that and then try to wreck it again in "The Mark of the Rani", but by this stage he's dressing as a scarecrow and hiding in a field just on the off-chance that the Doctor will pass by. The precision of the changes looks more like the result of two parties altering history, one making a big change and the other almost restoring the *status quo ante*.

If that's the mechanism, and it was the Doctor who did most of it, we still have problems with the reason for making such a specific change. In the case of "Battlefield", it may simply be that the future in which the later Doctors interfered with an alternate universe was closed off when Gallifrey's removal made travel between these impossible (as mentioned in X2.5, "Rise of the Cybermen"), but that doesn't of necessity make the consequent incidents in "our" history go away. (See, for example, 9.1, "Day of the Daleks" and the essay therewith.) If events in "Battlefield" are in flux both with regard to the possibility of later Doctors having caused them, and the possibility of the world in which these events unfold ever happening, we have to assume that stories set in a time of flux are "valid" because the Doctor and his chums remember them (as we discussed in Volume 7) and that unmotivated events are part of the normal life of a time-traveller.

As we'll discuss in the next volume, the unpicking of the disaster at Bowie Base One seems to have made flux even more common than before. (As far as the Doctor's personal time-line is concerned, the word "before" works here but other observers wouldn't be in any position to comment; see **Is Time Like Bolognese Sauce?** under X5.5, "Flesh and Stone".) Apart from its many other problems of continuity and aesthetics, "Kill the Moon" presents a snag in that its depressing view

continued on Page 301...

having an evacuation plan that takes nine hours to do properly. They must have brought all the rations via the ship, why aren't the bulk of them still there in case of emergency?

A repeat from "The Impossible Planet" (X2.8): it's a bit of a problem, having lights inside a space-helmet when walking around in near darkness.

Critique Once again, the snags inherent in making an "event" episode taint an otherwise exemplary story. Now we know the circumstances of the regeneration, all the effort put into making us curious is forlorn and the gulf between how this episode ends and the ones that follow is glaringly obvious. We said when reviewing "Planet of the Dead" (X4.15) that the prolepsis, all the prophesies and foreshadowing, seemed like contractual obligation. This story is no less a fashion-victim than that.

That said, it's aged better than a lot of the episodes a year either side of it. Everything up to the Doctor reluctantly leaving is vintage Graeme Harper, taking on Danny Boyle at his own game and winning (at a fraction of the cost of *Sunshine*). Our qualms about "Iowegian" Andy's Brummie accent aside, it's perfectly cast and even the smaller, thankless roles (the relatives on screen, young Adelaide) are filled with the right people doing the right things. Using the National Botanical Garden makes the episode look bigger and more lavish than most films of this kind. Our usual niggles about how it's Earth-normal gravity indoors and Mars-normal on the surface – how they've put in a cutesy robot and so on – are easier to set aside here than in "Oxygen" or "Kill the Moon", and Mars seems more Mars-like here than in X10.9, "The Empress of Mars".

People cared about the sense of *rightness* of the story. That said, definite decisions were made about the overall tone that limited this: it had to be "scary" so the local virus was an "infection" rather than a First Contact situation and made the victims want to smash things up without even hinting at a reason; it had to be about isolated pioneers, so nowhere in the script is it suggested that they might send a message – the solar flares ought to have sent them back to the safety of the ship straight away anyway. As a result it gets a bit generic, but within a sub-genre *Doctor Who* has shied away from since its return and ought to have been doing right from 2005. Twenty-first century cinematic SF has produced a lot of rea-

sonable near-future space stories using NASA resources as references, and that's been just lying there waiting for BBC Wales to apply their own spin. It's possible to get it very wrong, but deciding not to try was misguided.

Why do it *now*? Because the whole idea of Fixed Points is in need of a refresher – and not in a known bit of history. This is the story's heart, and relegates all of the Mars Exploration elements to background. That might have been a prudent precaution in the planning stages, in case they got it wrong or were unable to deliver a suitably plausible locale. But, it moves the story's centre of gravity to the running-up-and-down-corridors elements and makes these skilled, hand-picked specialists all look a bit silly. Having so many problems befall a crew when it was technologically-advanced antagonists making a planned incursion (as per "The Moonbase") is one thing, but this virus's teleological response is ridiculous. Unless we'd had more hints of possession by an alien intelligence, or a remarkable fluke that the best strategic thinkers on the base were taken over first (as per 15.2, "The Invisible Enemy"), it seems a bit strange.

A relatively "straight" story about a set of near-simultaneous glitches making the base uninhabitable would have been about as exciting, but it's been decided that *Doctor Who* needs an identifiable "baddie" even when the setting is as exotic and futuristic as this. The previous episode's flirtation with an opponent that's just an unintelligent life-form doing what it does has been dismissed as an "experiment" and we're back to a planet's native life resisting a human invasion and therefore being bad. The Doctor mumbles something about the Ice Warriors, then everyone changes the subject and we go back to lots of running. (Again, comparison with "Oxygen" or X10.2, "Smile" makes the lack of any allegory or subtext almost refreshing. The mouthfeel of this episode is of "what would it really be like?" rather than "does it make a point?")

This story doesn't seem to get any credit for this attempt at authenticity. A lot of that is that – with the bits not needing digital retouching getting released first – the build-up was all about how scary it was. There was talk of transmitting it later, at 8.00pm (they wisely opted not to), but nothing could have been sufficiently terrifying to live up to this hype *and* be transmitted on BBC1 before the watershed. It also relegates all other responses to

Was There a Martian Time-Slip?

continued from Page 299...

of near-future space exploration flatly contradicts the version we have in "The Waters of Mars" and we are told, in no uncertain terms, that the latter is a Fixed Point and incontrovertibly "true". (Inevitably, we point you towards **What Constitutes a Fixed Point?** under X4.2, "The Fires of Pompeii".)

If we are to take this line, then the whole of the Doctor's exile was in a phase of Earth's history that was provisional, and his memory of what "ought" to have happened was messed with. Later when he was operating a fully-functional TARDIS with a new, improved head, it became possible for him to strap history down more tightly so that it wouldn't change while he wasn't looking, and to prevent him from spending all his waking hours preventing invasion-of-the-week. Later still, he was forced to perform on the whole of creation something like what the BBC's Restoration Team managed with Chroma-Dot, and reconstitute the universe with the Pandorica and whatever he had in his pockets. A whole new set of revisions and Fixed Points came into being, until the universe was reset *again* the following year. However, in the phase of the Doctor's life covered in this volume and the last, the UNIT of the 1970s is more or less as it was when he was wearing velvet and beating up anyone who looked like a member of Havoc, with only a few slight changes.

being distractions, so all the wonder, excitement and curiosity this story evokes in its early stages are seen by people for whom "scary" is intrinsically good as wasting people's time. The other problem is that all of the story proper is now seen as preamble to the material about the Doctor's hubris and opening the door to his eventual death. Just as with 4.2, "The Tenth Planet" and 6.7, "The War Games", the tail wags the dog and the coda is seen, in some circles, as the whole point.

Within the narrower context of the episode-in-itself, the decision to return weakens an otherwise strong drama about the Doctor taking the time to get to know doomed people, just so someone can tell their story. It's a cop-out from what could have been this Doctor's defining moment. It could have taken his now almost kneejerk "I'm so sorry" into a more personal and moving examination of a Time Lord's routine assumption that everyone dies – has already died from some perspective – but is, in his or her point in history, alive and unaware of this. If the end credits had run as the Doctor walked away, hearing the screams on the radio in his helmet, it would have been a truly great episode.

Instead, and apparently for the benefit of the eight-year-olds watching, the Doctor becomes a more conventional hero and stages a rescue, then gets a bit cocky. Even here, the author's thumb is on the scale – it would've made more logical sense to take them somewhere far from contact, and let them have good lives in secret. Davies thinks that this is what the story is "about" and subordinates everything fresh about the episode to the Doctor's moment of hubris. The story is too overtly manipulative for this supposedly-fatal swagger to seem in-character, or even in keeping with what will actually cause this Doctor's end. Adelaide's suicide is arbitrary, anomalous after all her determination and hope. Even the idea that saving people from a Fixed Point would unravel the cosmos is weird after X4.2, "The Fires of Pompeii". Did they really think that after episodes centred on child-abuse (X2.11, "Fear Her"), mob-violence (X4.10, "Midnight") and a companion's suicide (X4.11, "Turn Left"), the nation's children were unable to cope with a downer? Kids are resilient and, as *The Sarah Jane Adventures* shows, the production team had a lot of faith in their ability to watch stories about difficult subjects. The child audience can handle the Doctor failing occasionally. What they can't take is being jerked around.

But the needs of the series-as-product overall prevailed, and the soap-operatics relegated this story to being a set-up for the main event rather than being especially "special". Paradoxically, the hour-long format makes it harder to schedule, so it's rarely shown. Very little of it is extraneous (compared to how "Planet of the Dead" can be trimmed with ease). It's been almost forgotten, unfairly overlooked and, on the evidence of "Kill the Moon", the alleged Fixed Point was removed from history anyway.

By falling between two stools, this story has vanished from the popular memory of the series, when many far worse episodes have stayed lodged in the public's mind. By making an unprecedentedly pacey and plausible near-future adventure worthy of Hollywood (but as only *Doctor Who* can do), then abruptly lurching into schlock and gimmicks, it's simultaneously the best and worst features of Davies's term all in one bundle.

The Lore

Written by Russell T Davies and Phil Ford. Directed by Graeme Harper. Viewing figures: 9.94 million (BBC1) and 0.38 million (BBC HD), to which BBC3 added 0.70 million three days later. Both that week's transmissions got 88% AIs.

Repeats and Overseas Promotion *Der Rote Garten, La Conquête du Mars*.

Production

• The precise nature of the year of Specials took ages to figure out. The regeneration story was probably going to be the Christmas episode, there was a fun romp with a bus before that and some kind of set-up for the finale. One option was a Christmas on Mars that led into a last episode early in 2010, ahead of whatever Steven Moffat had ready for Series 5.

As we mentioned last time, funding for however many Specials were being made was tricky to secure, and contingent on Russell T Davies being at least co-credited. Nonetheless, Davies had earmarked any Mars story for his *Sarah Jane Adventures* co-producer Phil Ford. While Davies was still keen on the empty hotel idea, he pitched it to Ford as a hook for a Mars Christmas idea and Ford did his best to comply, concocting an idea of an alien princess being brought to Earth for some ceremonial function (a marriage was one idea). This led into ideas of ancient Mars as an *Arabian Nights* world. Davies hated all that and asked Ford to try again, without the hotel or the princess.

Take Two was a tale of a settled community under threat, but Davies wanted pioneers and moved it to the earliest possible date for such a heroic endeavour, although script editor Gary Russell doubted that, even 50 years from broadcast, it would be realistically possible. A workable version, then called "Red Christmas", was thrashed out over August and September 2008, with Davies at first vetoing the idea of the TARDIS being summoned by remote control, then adding the idea of the cute robot. Graeme Harper was attached to the project in October, starting once he'd finished work on *Robin Hood*.

• By December, with Tennant's departure now public knowledge, the episode's *raison d'etre* had become to establish the Doctor's hubris – to make the regeneration a consequence of his transgres-

sion. Julie Gardner ensured the funding, but the precise slot for this episode was still unclear. By now, Christmas Day and New Year's Day had been earmarked for the final two-part story (a double-header on 25th December would have overloaded BBC1's schedulers). Ford's script had a leader called "Valentina" and there was vague talk of asking Dame Helen Mirren to play her. When Davies decided to make the character more Scott of the Antarctic-ish, Ford changed the name to "Grace" (but was advised that this brought unwelcome associations with the McGann TV Movie).

The plan was now to show this episode on the Saturday before Christmas, 19th December 2009, so it was set 50 years after this date (thus 51 years after Davies knuckled down to revise the script to cut costs and bring it into line with the finale). Adelaide's suicide ran into trouble with BBC guidelines, so the crew of the otherwise-realistic Bowie Base One ("Camp Bowie" was deemed too near the knuckle) were equipped with laser-pistols. With 2Entertain looking vulnerable and Japan cancelling the order for further episodes, the budgets were tightening. Davies realised how much his last two episodes would need computer-generated effects, and so the water-creatures became make-up and concealed hoses on the actors.

• The technical aspects took a lot of meetings to resolve. The sets needed to be big enough that water could flow without getting into the electrical systems, and to take the right amount of time for actors to cross for dramatic purposes, while looking authentically cramped and NASA-like. Gadget, the robot, needed to be practicable. Davies had seen the National Botanical Garden of Wales advertised on the back of a bus but it needed to be sounded out. So did the more famous Eden Project in Cornwall, cited in the script as a model for how the dome should look.

By late January, Neill Gorton's team had devised a prosthetic system for the Flood (as the infected humans were called) but the first few goes, including a wig concealing tubes that just poured into the actors' eyes, weren't quite right. Harper recalled that it took four goes to nail the design; Davies said it was the single-hardest thing to resolve in his time on *Doctor Who*. They were still fine-tuning it a week into shooting, when the rushes came in.

• Meanwhile, the BBC1 schedulers were less keen on 19th December, so the episode had to downplay the Christmas material. By 4th February, the second Tone Meeting, most of the problems had been identified and plans put in place. (*Confidential* recorded it, and it's interesting how uncertain Harper looks about Gadget. Note also how ebullient Davies seems compared to what *The Writer's Tale* would suggest.) The read-through was the last day of work on "Planet of the Dead". Lindsay Duncan had been cast as Adelaide: she had recently been on stage with Matt Smith in *That Face* at the Royal Court (and transferring to the West End).

• The shoot started on the evening of 23rd, a few minutes' drive from Upper Boat. The Cemex quarry at Taffs Wells made a reasonable facsimile of Mars. The radio-controlled robot proved as reliable as K9 but with additional tricks, including a hand that kept falling off (in one take, it reversed over its own hand). The following morning, the revised design for the water-zombies was approved, using contact-lenses, hair-gel (to make the clothing look consistently wet for long periods without giving the cast flu) and hoses near the mouth under the latex.

The second night was Tennant sort of solo, with Gordon Seed doing stunts as Bowie Base One exploded. The girder that fell near the Doctor was the same one that pinioned Davros nearly a year earlier. On Wednesday 23rd, the team relocated to the Botanic Garden in Llanarthne, Carmarthenshire (a bit more of a step from Cardiff than usual) for a night-shoot in the Dome. Davies was woken at 3.00am because of an unforeseen snag: the lights woke up the birds residing near all those nice juicy insects, so the dialogue was inaudible. Davies tweaked the scripts to account for the birds and their not being infected like the humans.

A second night in the Mediterranean flora dome had Ailsa Berk showing the afflicted Flood-victims how to run mechanically; the idea was to resemble the gait of the T2000 from *Terminator 2*. The water, as in most scenes of the Flood at work, was cold and heavily-chlorinated. Next morning, Davies reviewed the rushes and asked that in subsequent shots the make-up should be less alarming. (Note that Maggie's eyes never go the same way as Andy's.)

That evening's location was Victoria Street in Newport, originally intended as the site of the funeral procession in "The Next Doctor" and earmarked by Davies for this scene. Sixty or so onlookers braved the cold to watch but Davies wasn't happy, upon seeing the rushes, with the

eyelines for Ood Sigma or the Doctor's reaction-shots (these were remounted during the Powell Estate scenes in "The End of Time Part Two").

• During the location shoot for "Planet of the Ood", Harper had used the front of a computer firm in Newport. Now the interior – specifically a spectacularly long, straight corridor, a *Doctor Who* director's dream – was being used. On Monday, 2nd March, the four tunnels were in use for Doctor-Adelaide running, Ed sprinting, water-beings robotically moving and so on. Unsurprisingly, Harper used a quad bike for the tracking shots and Duncan occasionally had a body-double.

• As the Torchwood Hub had been blown up in *Children of Earth*, Studios 1 and 2 had room for a big set. The team would spend six days there, shooting in more or less chronological order, with a weekend off. On Friday 6th, they filmed the Doctor realising who these people were. A longer version of this was recorded, with the Doctor realising that Yuri and Mia were an item by how close they stood – and Adelaide announcing that now that it was out in the open, she was forced to order them not to work together. Tennant had by now received the scripts for his last episode and factored this in to his performance.

• Tuesday 10th had a test-run for Wednesday's key scene: the intercom conversation with the Doctor in the airlock. Davies wanted this to be shot by two cameras in real time, with Duncan and Tennant interacting via monitors. Attending the recording on Wednesday were *Confidential*, *Doctor Who Magazine*, someone from *The Observer*, Davies and a competition winner. Tennant's helmet was wired for sound, enabling him to perform to Duncan's image on a practical monitor in the airlock set.

After him, the deluge: Any Effects had rigged two large tankers of chlorinated water to rain-bars strategically placed, to avoid it seeming as if anyone would be splashed by accident, then released 15,000 litres into the set to show Steffi getting trapped. With water and electrical equipment in use, everything had to be thoroughly insulated and methodically sprayed. This meant a lot of individually-shot spurts and gushes, edited to look haphazard, and took ages. Friday 13th began with a return to Studio 5 as young Adelaide saw a Dalek in what's fairly recognisably Sarah Jane's attic lightly redressed.

The next two days were the climax of the story with the Doctor returning, taking command, operating Gadget and dodging water. One scene lost from this is Mia holding a gun to Adelaide's head to try to disarm the self-destruct just before the TARDIS arrived. Finally, on Friday 20th, the TARDIS materialised, followed by scenes of the Doctor refusing to accept his fate, Gadget operating the controls and a few pick-up shots. The following evening Tennant was at Blackwell's bookshop for the Jessica Hynes scenes of "The End of Time Part Two".

• BBC1's schedulers tried to find a spot for "The Waters of Mars" where ITV's headwinds wouldn't dent the ratings. (This was back when Simon Cowell was bafflingly popular. Weekends became a turf-war between *Strictly Come Dancing* and *X Factor*.) This hadn't yet been decided when a few scenes were shown at the end of "Planet of the Dead". Davies talked "The Waters of Mars" up as the scariest adventure yet, although he was more concerned with moving to Los Angeles and starting his career again (almost) from scratch.

• An early edit of the episode on 17th April revealed that Davies and Harper had different ideas on what aspect of the story was to be emphasised. Harper and the editor, Will Oswald, thought it was about the humans fighting the inevitable, Davies wanted the focus to be on the Doctor's moral dilemma. It was also over-running by five minutes and lacked web-pages for the whole crew, just Adelaide and Ed. Jennie Fava supervised the latter, making them look close enough to BBC's online news circa 2009 to convey a subliminal impression. Mia's surname was given as "Bennett", with a father called "Peter", as an in-joke about the incoming producer (guess his name, go on).

• A fresh edit was attempted on 19th, lacking only The Mill's contributions. By now the episode was announced as "The Waters of Mars". With the last effects shots sutured in, clips began to be released in July and a trailer was premiered at San Diego's Comic-Con and thereafter on the BBC website. Tennant, Davies and Gardner were by now spending most of their time in America but, as part of the collective farewell tour, the star and showrunner made strategically-timed returns for the rest of the year.

• The death of Barry Letts, who had reformed *Doctor Who* into exactly the sort of vehicle for a story of this kind, was acknowledged by the caption at the end and in interviews by Davies. The press got a look at the story two days before

Hallowe'en, just in time for Tennant's appearance on *The Sarah Jane Adventures*. The formal launch, at the Savoy, was the following day. The transmission date was only announced that week: it would go out on Sunday, 15th November, at 7.00pm, between top-rated hits *Countryfile* and *Antiques Roadshow*. ITV had nothing much planned for that night.

• The ratings were healthy – eventually becoming the most-watched thing that week in the UK – and the episode was followed by a trailer for "Dreamland". BBC4 did follow-up with a selection of documentaries about Mars, including an edition of *The Sky at Night* (see X5.1, "The Eleventh Hour"). BBC3's repeat offered a podcast commentary by Davies and Gardner, recorded in her LA flat. The episode also broke records for BBC America's broadcast a month later. The following summer saw Ford pick up a Hugo award for Best Dramatic Presentation (Short Form), beating Joss Whedon's *Dollhouse* and the previous two Specials.

• As was traditional whenever the series did anything bold, there were comments in the press about how the episode was unsuitable for children. In particular, the suicide of someone presented as heroic and admirable was, as Davies intuited when writing it, a cause for concern. The same critics failed to mention that *Countryfile* had, just the previous week, included a gruesome section on fox-hunting.

X4.17: "The End of Time Part One"

(25th December, 2009)

Which One is This? Wilfred Mott misses his Christmas Dinner. The Master eats everything in sight, and the Doctor pops in for tea with the Ood before getting goosed by June Whitfield. Then the Magic Sunbed of the Conker-People turns everyone into the Master.

Firsts and Lasts For the first time since "Survival" (26.4), we have a multi-episode story with the same name for all of its parts.

This was the first time a custom-made BBC1 station ident for Christmas (often a bit of a production-number) was *Doctor Who* themed. For three weeks, every programme on BBC1 was introduced with one of the "bumper" films of the

Doctor trudging through snow, meeting reindeer and taking the TARDIS for a loop-the-loop to make the circular emblem.

When President Barack Obama enters the room, it's the first time a living, named world leader has been impersonated instead of using an alternate-universe surrogate. (The corpse in X1.4, "Aliens of London" was probably supposed to be Tony Blair, but they avoided naming names.) Amazingly, we cannot think of a single precedent for the fake Obama, unless we count the two versions of the Queen (25.3, "Silver Nemesis"; X4.0, "Voyage of the Damned") or, stretching a point, Helen A (25.2, "The Happiness Patrol").

Watch Out For...
• The spooky woman stage-managing Wilf's coincidences (colloquially known as Spooky Claire, as she's played by Claire Bloom) is, with hindsight, remarkably like the Moment (X7.15, "The Day of the Doctor"), but the way she shows up on the telly during the Queen's Speech is unique to this episode.
• The Ood provide a handy info-dump, with the Doctor filling in the backstory about the Master (for them and any new viewers), and offer sneak-previews of the Doctor's forthcoming plight. So, that's the old woman on the bus (X4.15, "Planet of the Dead"), Spooky Claire *and* a hitherto-unseen Ood Priest giving supernatural warnings.

On top of that, we get another layer of portentous statements to which the Doctor isn't privy, from a character called "The Narrator", telling us that this is the Last Day of the Human Race (he audibly uses the capitals). You'll be amazed to hear that this is hyperbole, but at the time it seemed plausible. It's theoretically possible that some people watching hadn't heard that Tennant and Davies were leaving, but four separate prophesies is over-egging it.
• The mystery of who picked up the Master's ring from the pyre (X3.13, "Last of the Time Lords") is resolved. If you guessed that it would be a full-on reworking of *Prisoner: Cell Block H,* give yourself a mince pie.
• "The Silver Cloak": Wilfred Mott pulls together all his friends to go look for the Doctor, and they manage to track him down in a day. They're like fandom, but they all get on better. Had the this group been around to help Donna, she would have been on the TARDIS a year earlier.
• Wilf's less-than-whelmed reaction to entering

the TARDIS was long overdue. If travelling in the Ship is the qualification, Wilf is the second-oldest companion after Romana. (She was 125 or 140, depending which episode we're in. If you count Kamelion as a companion, then we have to confess to having no idea of the robot's age. Let's not worry about Madame Vastra.) Thrillingly, Bernard Cribbins gets the big metallic letters in the titles.

The Continuity

The Doctor He's moping about his impending regeneration, telling Wilf at length how he's going to die. [So he believes the psychic forecast from X4.14, "Planet of the Dead" and the Ood prophecy. In Tennant's first season, he insisted that any and all pronouncements about Rose's forthcoming death were lies. Admittedly, the events of X2.13, "Doomsday" and X3.11, "Utopia" might have soured him in this regard.]

This Doctor counts regeneration as a death – inasmuch as his consciousness will go whether or not a new Doctor emerges. [He seems bothered about being replaced by his swaggering future; this is markedly different from how later Doctors will see things.] As such, he's been avoiding going gentle into that goodnight with a selection of wild parties throughout history [cf. X9.1, "The Magician's Apprentice"].

He's almost out of his depth when the enthusiastic Silver Cloak treat him like a celebrity. It doesn't take much persuasion when Wilf insists on coming along in the TARDIS, even though he's been avoiding companions lately [perhaps it's as much to keep Donna safe; he's certainly curious about what coincidences have brought them together again].

This incarnation's fondness for unfunny anachronistic jokes leads us to the natural conclusion of the Doctor attempting to explain car alarms to an Ood. He knows an identity-concealing Shimmer when he sees one, and says 'Shimmer' in a 90s football-stand sort of way ["shee-aaaa-murrr" in an arpeggio].
• *Background.* He's experienced a lot of adventures since we last saw him, including getting married to Elizabeth I, self-censoring a comment about her nickname now being inoperative [see X7.15, "The Day of the Doctor"]; seeing the phosphorous carousel of the Great Magellan Gestalt; saving a planet from the Red Carnivorous Maw and naming a galaxy Alison. ["Dreamland" takes place in this gap as well and the script suggests

that the Doctor's lei is from Hawaii. "The Waters of Mars" (X4.16) seemed to be building to an immediate resolution, so it's peculiar for him to take off so much time in the middle. Yet the next Doctor does much the same in X7.12, "Closing Time").]

Wilf sees evidence of an unseen adventure: in the twelfth century, the Doctor showed up at a convent somewhere near present-day Chiswick. A demon [alien?] dropped out of the sky, the Doctor showed up and 'smote' it before vanishing in a blue box. Because of this legend, a stained glass window in a Victorian church includes the TARDIS. [This could, of course, be yet more 1138 AD antics along with the online preamble to "The Magician's Apprentice".]

Back in the distant past, the Doctor-to-be and the Master-in-waiting used to run across fields of red grass, yelling at the sky, on Mount Perdition. The Master's father owned vast estates. [This detail, and the later hints of the Doctor apparently spending his childhood in a barn, suggests a peculiar class dynamic to the Master's resentment of the Doctor. Constantly being outdone by a kid from the wrong side of the tracks would make this worse each time. See next episode for a different perspective on this when no less than the Lord President addresses them as 'Lord Master' and 'Lord Doctor'.]

• *Ethics.* Once he verifies that the Master really is at large, he takes it upon himself to handle the other Time Lord, and is horrified when guards with guns show up to take him. He doesn't blame Lucy Saxon for either her marriage or murder, saying only that the Master corrupted her.

• *Inventory: TARDIS key.* By waving this, he can lock and unlock the TARDIS remotely; the light on top winks with the central-locking noise. This is also how he time-slips the Ship to hide it [see **The TARDIS**].

• *Inventory: Other.* His glasses are in sonic-sun mode again [see "Planet of the Dead"], and he first exits the TARDIS wearing a pink lei and straw hat.

The TARDIS It's clearly unhappy when the Doctor puts it on overdrive to find the Master. [Both he and the Ship seem synched to the Master's timestream – despite his best efforts, the Doctor doesn't arrive until after his nemesis's escape. The Doctor says as much about staying relative to the Master within the casual nexus. Even without Gallifrey, they still run on Gallifreyan Mean Time

as speculated upon in Volume 6.]

The Doctor can put his Ship out-of-synch with the surrounding universe by a second. [See also X4.12, "The Stolen Earth"; 14.4, "Face of Evil" and Davies's New Adventures novel *Damaged Goods* – which he'd also recently recycled for *Torchwood: Children of Earth*.]

The Supporting Cast

• *Wilf* has organized some local pensioners into a Doctor-catching club. They call themselves 'The Silver Cloak'. Minnie uses the name like a cheerful catchphrase [so they've likely done other things before]. They even have code names (Wilf is Paratroop One, and Two seems to be the pensioners' bus they use as transport). His contacts include a bridge club, an old skiffle group and 'the Old Boys' [possibly the local school: Bobby is in charge of contacting whoever this is].

He's still hoping that the Doctor can cure Donna's memory-wipe [X4.13, "Journey's End"]. Later, he invites himself aboard the TARDIS, partly to look after the Doctor. Its size doesn't impress him.

He isn't fond of churches, saying they're too cold for him. Before gallivanting around with the Silver Cloak, he tells Sylvia he's off to the Lion for a snifter. His service revolver, never used in combat, has been kept in his pristine bedroom all these years. There's a certain ambivalence about the way he responds to the Woman when she notes he never killed anyone in the war.

• *Donna* has no recollection whatsoever of her time with the Doctor and just recalls being a temp in Chiswick [see "Journey's End"]. She's now engaged to a young man, Shaun Temple (Wilf says he's 'a bit of a dreamer'), and they plan to hyphenate their names (Temple-Noble rather than Noble-Temple). Neither's making much money, but they're planning to move into a small flat by themselves. [This is a step ahead of her plan to move Lance into her mother's upstairs in X3.0, "The Runaway Bride". Presumably they'll move out of Chiswick to get something affordable.]

She purchased Wilf a rubbish biography for Christmas, but it provides a hint where he and the Doctor need to go. The Doctor optimistically interprets this as a sign that Donna is still aware on some level.

She's the only person on Earth who can resist the Master's metamorphic wave by herself [presumably because she's still part Time Lord].

Where's Susan?

If – as we are led to believe – the Time War was prosecuted in its darkest phase by Time Lords endlessly resurrected to keep fighting, then the fates of any individual Gallifreyan we have ever met is open to debate. From a one-line remark in the climax of "The End of Time", we can guess whether the character identified as "the Narrator" and "Lord President" is the one and only truly original Rassilon. The President we see in X9.12, "Hell Bent" certainly doesn't live up to the original's reputation, however much he shouts that he is Rassilon the Resurrected. Is this the same person as the Narrator? Are they both *the* Rassilon?

If so, then the end of 20.7, "The Five Doctors" gets interesting. The Master's exculpation (by someone who's *definitely* Rassilon) for doing something very like what got Borusa and several others turned into hood ornaments for the bier (and all his other crimes, ever) is part of a plan that was hatched millions of years before, by someone who's known for all this time that Gallifrey wouldn't win. But the Master was also resurrected during the Time War (X3.11, "Utopia"). For all we know, so were all the other Time Lords. Borusa may have manned an ack-ack gun at Arcadia, brought back to fight alongside Pandak III, Co-ordinator Engin and Zorac. (Older British readers or those who take the hints in these books will now be imagining *Dad's Army* in velour robes and big collars, with George Pravda in an ARP helmet shouting "raddy ooli-gentz".)

The description given by the Partisan (widely assumed to be Chancellor Flavia) is spectacularly gruesome, in ways they could never have shown on screen; she says that "millions die every second" and that this continues as "time itself (is) resurrecting them". As we will see, this doesn't necessarily denote millions of Time Lords. In a situation this dire, the Time Lords must have had to use every asset, every possible recruit. This makes the seemingly permanent deaths of about 30 of them in a pocket universe more than slightly embarrassing, it is a calamity. How the situation in X6.4, "The Doctor's Wife" reflects this description is only part of the wider problem we've identified elsewhere in this book: the Davies-model off-screen Time War is more conceptually brutal and eldritch than the diet-decaf version Moffat has actually shown us.

Nonetheless, it's very likely that every Time Lord and ex-Time Lord we ever saw was on active duty (with the possible exceptions of Morbius and Omega, although we can't even put that past the High Council). If the Master was there despite several deaths and not being physically a Time Lord any more (18.6, "The Keeper of Traken"), then Drax, Goth and the Monk must be assumed to have been let off with a warning, then given a staser and dog-tags. If there's an available Time Lord, he or she must be assumed to have received call-up papers. The Doctor had, according to Clara (who's been up and down his time-line, except for a significant chunk when he looked like John Hurt), grandchildren. Plural. The only person who called him "grandfather" on screen was Susan who, as we now know from "The Five Doctors" and "The Name of the Doctor" (X7.14), left Gallifrey with him.

Susan's past was kept vague. She had travelled with the Doctor for a while and had psychic powers far in advance of his. Indeed, the one time they discussed returning home (1.7, "The Sensorites") was to see if these could be refined and trained. We can interpolate details we now know about Gallifrey (a planet she identifies on sight in "The Five Doctors") and the un-used ideas of the early scriptwriters (notably David Whitaker) until the cows come home, but it's undeniably true that the Doctor didn't know anything much about the Daleks when he first met them (1.2, "The Daleks"). Even if, as Whitaker still thought possible when drafting "The Power of the Daleks" (4.3), the Doctor and Susan fled a great war on his own world – one he either saw or foresaw – it wasn't necessarily *that* war.

What we've seen recently makes things look as though Susan was about the same age when they fled with a stolen TARDIS ("The Name of the Doctor") as when we first met them (1.1, "An Unearthly Child"), which means she would already have undergone the business with the Untempered Schism (X3.12, "The Sound of Drums" et seq). If that's the case, she was either accepted or rejected. If we're to believe the odd incident at the end of "Listen" (X8.4), the main alternative to training for Time Lordliness is becoming a soldier. There's room for doubt in this, of course, but that's clearly what we're meant to think and it connects to Series 8's shtick about the Doctor not liking soldiers. We're free to speculate on which fate would have been worse for her.

In case you've got this far without knowing, Susan finally left the TARDIS when the Doctor decided that she couldn't come back in – this, after she fell in love with a skinny Scottish bloke with big

continued on Page 309...

ABOUT TIME 2008-2009

Unfortunately, this activates all her hidden memories and she starts going into shock.

• *Sylvia.* Doesn't even pretend to like a present from Donna, but gets at least one naughty card.

• *The Woman in White* gives Wilf some vague and unhelpful prophecies, suggests coincidences don't exist and stays mum concerning her own identity. Wilf can't discuss her with the Doctor, she says, or the Time Lord will definitely die. Nonetheless, she encourages Wilf to go along with the Doctor, gun on hand. [She seems to find it easier to communicate with him in ceremonial situations. A miraculous appearance in a church, then hacking the Queen's Speech, is rather showy.]

• *Ood Sigma* [glimpsed last episode]. He's either running Ood society, or just in charge of handling the rogue Time Lord.

• *Lucy Saxon.* She's officially a goodie for about a minute and a half. Her trial [following "Last of the Time Lords"] was held in secret, with no jury [normally a wartime provision except when accused of treason, at least at time of broadcast]. Since then, she's been kept in solitary confinement. [It's indicated that the Master's past finally was investigated and found to be false, but that no one could work out who he really was, and Lucy wasn't forthcoming. Her treatment is consistent with the depiction of UNIT in *TW*: "Fragments".]

Trying to stay ahead of the Cult of Saxon, she's made arrangements with with her family to concoct a poison, which interrupts the Master's resurrection ceremony. [Is this the same stuff Martha was supposedly collecting in her year-long peregrination? The Master took it seriously enough to zap the vials then. Here, all the liquids we see resemble fabric conditioner.] She's MIA after the massive explosion that destroys the prison.

Torchwood Naismith picked up the Immortality Gate 'when Torchwood fell'. [What with this and "The Runaway Bride", one gets the impression that someone organised a fire-sale after the Battle of Canary Wharf. See *TW*: "Cyberwoman" for how shambolic this must have been. Alternatively, he could have plundered the Hub after *TW: Children of Earth*.]

The Supporting Cast (Evil)

• *The Master* is back [of course], having contrived a typically complicated emergency resurrection plan involving: an obsessive cult happy to carry out self-sacrifice; a woman who has his 'imprint'; a set of blue immortality potions; a ring still on his person when the Doctor set his corpse on fire; a maximum-security women's prison… [had it worked properly, there may also have been a cuddly toy and a fondue set, or at least a change of clothes]. This being one of the Master's plans, it all goes spectacularly wrong, when Lucy Saxon adulterates the home-brew.

The Master's ring appears to have been containing his essence [possibly with some kind of psychic field rendering it beneath the Doctor's notice (c.f. 13.5, "The Brain of Morbius" and the watches in X3.8, "Human Nature" and X3.11, "Utopia")].

Despite Lucy's interference, his physical appearance switches between his Harry Saxon identity and a neon, energy-laced skeleton. [The latter appears to be his "true" form, and people only see Saxon if he's concentrating. As scripted, the polarised visors worn by Naismith's guards reveal "Skeletor" as he is.]

With his resurrection sabotaged, his life-essence is leaking out, sometimes in controlled bursts of energy that allow him to fly and project energy bolts. He needs to eat frantically to stabilise his metabolism (he later devours a whole turkey in under 20 seconds) and can ingest the life-force of people who annoy him, leaving skeletons behind [as per 13.2, "Planet of Evil"; 17.5, "The Horns of Nimon"; 14.6, "The Talons of Weng-Chiang"].

He missed the drumming in his head [X3.12, "The Sound of Drums" – whatever has been happening while he's been technically dead, not even the Time Lord signal could reach him]. The Doctor, he knows, will be able to smell him; the Master also sniffs the air when the TARDIS arrives. When the Doctor begs for his help vis-à-vis all these prophesies he latches onto the 'something is returning' part and not the 'end of time' aspect.

• *Josiah Naismith.* A British billionaire who wants eternal life for the sake of his daughter Abigail [she's not even ill or something like that; they're just greedy]. He's a software/mobile phone magnate. [This might explain why he/his daughter heard odd rumours about Saxon's return and immortality. In light of the later News Corp scandals, it would be indecorous to ask how a major business executive can tap so much information.] His book, *Fighting the Future*, is on sale now. [We might guess it has something to do with his interest in biomedical treatments. The title is undoubtedly his, even if the rest was ghostwritten.]

Where's Susan?

continued from Page 307...

hair who'd led the resistance in London after the Dalek invasion in er, let's say 2164 (2.2, "The Dalek Invasion of Earth"). We are left to imagine that she helped David Campbell (or "Cameron" if it's the novelisation – the mind boggles) rebuilt Earth, and make the exciting future we got in earlier Hartnell stories come about (see **What Kind of Future Did We Expect?** under 2.3, "The Rescue"). The Daleks bombarded Earth in 2157 with meteors and plagues before invading and – seriously, this is their plan - mining the planet's core so that they could install an engine and make Earth a giant space aircraft-carrier. This plan failed, mainly because Earth has a magnetic field they'd forgotten about.

The Doctor never returned to check on his potential great grandkids, because in those days he couldn't steer the TARDIS. By the time he could, that version of history had been changed a few times. The first two were in 9.1, "Day of the Daleks", when first a peace conference in 1973 (yes it was, deal with it) failed, and Earth was plunged into a war that did the softening-up the Daleks needed for them. Then they let a time-corridor generator fall into human hands (why Daleks design machines that need fingers to operate them is another problem we discussed in Volume 3), and the Doctor un-revised this version, after some guerrillas set about causing the event they went back to try to prevent. Then the Doctor set back Dalek progress a thousand years (12.4, "Genesis of the Daleks") – so all earlier Dalek stories were, we thought, *sous rature* and never happened to anyone but the Doctor.

The Doctor didn't really have much of an idea what became of Susan even then. As early as "Genesis of the Daleks", he was misremembering the events of "The Dalek Invasion of Earth" as happening in "2000 AD". (Not the comic, we assume, but the year. As opposed to 2157 as specified in 3.4, "The Daleks' Master Plan" when discussing the Earth's last encounter with Daleks, by the same author as "The Dalek Invasion of Earth" and "Genesis of the Daleks".) By the time we get to "The Stolen Earth" (X4.12), the Doctor is so hazy on the topic that seeing Earth get whipped out of space-time to form part of a giant engine is only vaguely familiar as a concept. He might be old and forgetful, but this is his granddaughter and maybe her kids. And this version of the Doctor is all about how much he misses Gallifrey and all his chums

(until they start returning). Would such a self-pitying incarnation really miss out on the chance of some family and at least one other person who remembers Gallifrey as it used to be before it all went horrible?

A later version, less given to maudlin interludes, spent the best part of an episode happily chewing the fat with Davros (X9.2, "The Witch's Familiar"). That's peculiar because, as we've mentioned a lot in this volume, the events in "The Stolen Earth" and "Journey's End" were removed from the time-line. As usual, we last saw him in a life-threatening situation vowing vengeance on the Doctor, but he's back, safe and sound on a mock-up Skaro, in "The Magician's Apprentice" (X9.1), with archive recordings of all his previous encounters with the Doctor. (Except, for some reason, 17.1 "Destiny of the Daleks". Well, he wasn't looking his best and the most quotable line is "Spack Off!") His only hope of surviving that situation was if the story never happened, and he was still in a *different* fatal combat situation in the jaws of the Nightmare Child, but with the Time War still unsealed because of Dalek Caan's intervention during the run-up to the erased. He could then be rescued by any old Dalek, apparently (see **How Can Anyone Know About a Time War?** under "The Stolen Earth" for our attempts to figure this all out). But he's got "The Stolen Earth" on his monitors too, so scratch that. However, if he'd tinkered with his own body to give himself and his buggy the same abilities as the Cult of Skaro and various other Time War Daleks, he might be in the same position as a Gallifreyan teenager left stranded in a time-line that never happened.

Let's leave the Time War out of the equation for a moment. Instead, let's ponder what happens to a TARDIS traveller who is left out when history changes. Our best information comes from *The Sarah Jane Adventures*, where altering history to remove Sarah leaves her in a blank white void of the kind we recall from "The Mind Robber" (6.2) and "Warriors' Gate" (18.5). This also happens to Maria Jackson when she's tippexed out of the time-line, then to a whole hotel when the Trickster attempts to escape such a realm by marrying Sarah off, and thereby preventing some significant future event (A7, "The Wedding of Sarah Jane Smith"). This last one has the Doctor running around in the hotel, separated from the TARDIS, so it's not easy to break into one of these places.

continued on Page 311...

Planet Notes

• *Earth*. The entire population of Earth has been dreaming of the Master laughing hysterically. Although they largely forget about it in the daytime, it's close enough to the surface for everyone to look nervous when Wilf says it. The Master uses the Immortality Gate to turn the whole planet into duplicates of himself.

• *Gallifrey*. It exists. [Tune in next episode for the exciting conclusion.]

The Non-Humans

• *The Ood*. They've developed [or redeveloped] a civilisation with psychic Elders, who go in for grey robes, fire, and incense when they're really trying. The Elder we see has a less bulbous head, with brain-crevasses visible on the top. He has a voice of his own, without recourse to a bulb. They can reach back to the twenty-first century with sheer mental force. [We're not told whether Ood Sigma's appearance in the last story was physical time travel or a mental projection.]

Although the Ood-Sphere is still snowy and bleak [compare with X4.3, "Planet of the Ood"], there are now tall city-sized hive/tower structures and a cave system where the Elders dwell. The Doctor is stunned by this sudden growth spurt, and suggests that they're being unnaturally stimulated in some fashion. The Ood seem to agree, saying they can now see through time because it's 'bleeding' [they also use the metaphor of a veil], and that the End of Time itself is coming.

They explain that they're picking up on Earthling bad dreams. [The same everyone on Earth experiences of the Master. There's a line suggesting that the entire universe is also dreaming of him, but that's nonsensical. It's *almost* intimated that this ability, and the return of the Time Lords becoming possible, is all down to the Doctor disrupting a Fixed Point last episode; but, ultimately, we don't know.]

The Ood-eyes all turn red when they're discussing the temporal danger.

• *Vinvocci*. Spiky green aliens; the ones seen here, Rossiter and Addams, were sent to salvage a big sophisticated piece of their world's technology (AKA the Immortality Gate) that crashed into Mount Snowdon. A technology called a Shimmer lets them disguise themselves as human; it's like a low-intensity Perception Filter, and one wave of a sonic screwdriver dissipates it. Their Gate involves slots, harmonised shatterthreads, densified friable links, triplicated multiple overshots and something about a ratio foldback. They don't like being called cacti, and are disgruntled about being mistaken for the smaller, red-skinned Zocci [X4.0, "Voyage of the Damned"].

History

• *Dating*. [Earth is facing its greatest peril so, obviously, it's Christmas-time again. Barack Obama is President of America – he took office in January 2009, so let's assume it's the very day of broadcast: 25th December that same year. For the time-scale here to work, we might suggest that Wilf and the family have to have been watching the Queen's Speech at around 10.30am (technically illegal, but never mind) and Obama's glad tidings at about 8.00am Washington time (about 3.00pm GMT). The shot of Earth from space as the John Simm impersonation wave spreads seems to confirm this, but it's The Mill and a Christmas episode, so there's the traditional festive celestial dynamics cock-up about 20 minutes before this. Davies *intended* the Queen's Speech to be at 3.00pm and even had The Mill recolour the Nobles' turkey to make it look cooked. NB, in parts of London, the sight on cherry-blossom on trees in late December has become familiar enough for this apparent anomaly to be given a free pass.]

The Ood portion of the story takes place a hundred years after the Doctor last visited in "Planet of the Ood". [If it's a hundred terrestrial years (and they all talk as if Ood-Sphere has the same length of orbit), then that's 4226 or thereabouts.]

Back in the present, there's a recession on [cf. X4.1, "Partners in Crime"]. Obama is scheduled to announce his Cunning Plan to end it. [Obviously this didn't happen in reality, although such a dramatic announcement, if it happened, would have taken place around the time Davies was writing the script. We ultimately have no idea what it would have been, although there's a line about revolutionising the "nature of money itself", so maybe Bitcoin or equivalent was going to be the global currency, and trading overhauled to remove the kinds of fraud that the 2008 recession revealed. Maybe Lego was to replace the Gold Standard. Frankly, it's the least plausible Trinity Wells speech we've yet seen, and that includes *The Sarah Jane Adventures*.]

Where's Susan?

continued from Page 309...

Hypothetically, then, if the Dalek invasion of Earth is either prevented from happening, forestalled by a different Dalek invasion or happens differently because of the Time War, there's a risk that Susan might wake up and find she's in one of these paradoxical spaces. She's a former TARDIS traveller, and thus immune from being rewritten out of history (see Volume 7's many essays on this), yet she left the TARDIS for reasons that are no longer possible.

That doesn't seem so likely once we've seen her, all grown up, in "The Five Doctors". Other than identifying the Death Zone and saying "Gallifrey" out loud, she seems much as she was but mature, so we can assume that she was from 2184 or thereabouts, on a rebuilt Earth with a branch of John Lewis that sells 1980s couture. She doesn't pounce on the snacks Tegan and Turlough provide as though she's not seen a decent meal since Revolutionary France. The sequence of events in "The Dalek Invasion of Earth" is evidently still as it was, despite the Doctor's change to Dalek history in "Genesis of the Daleks". If setting Dalek history back a thousand years doesn't make any difference, what could?

This all sounds suspiciously as though the 2157 incident was a Fixed Point. This makes the "Day of" Daleks' plan to get a jump on the humans by invading in the 2070s after a century of war not just risky but a bit impossible. This might, in fact, be the specific incident that the Time Lords stuck the Doctor in 1970s England to deal with when they exiled him. That being the case, messing with his memory when they exiled him was extremely silly, unless there were things they didn't want the paradoxical future Daleks to find out.

The Time Lords' biggest secret is that they exist. The Daleks' freak-out upon finding that the person who steals their Honda trikes is the same Doc-torr who gave them all that grief on Vulcan and Skaro indicates this is news to them. They seem to still be thinking of him as a human with a time machine that's better than theirs, as they did in 2.8, "The Chase". They do a deal with the Master, which might change their view (10.3, "Frontier in Space"), but it's really the Doctor's chats with Davros that make the difference – after which point the relations between the two races changes. Nonetheless, the quest for full Time Travel with history-changing privileges occupies Davros for the rest of his appearances before the series goes off air, so the

Daleks can't do anything drastic to a Fixed Point unless the Doctor is present (which suggests the mess in "Day of the Daleks" is directly caused by the Time Lords exiling him in the first place).

"The Name of the Doctor" twice showed us Susan more or less as we first saw her and the Doctor largely as we first saw him. The evidence suggests that they stole the TARDIS (or, as she would say, the TARDIS stole the Doctor – "The Doctor's Wife") only a few months before meeting Ian and Barbara. Apart from all the messy continuity questions this creates when we list all the names the Doctor drops in the first year, before there is the slightest chance of any unscreened incidents between adventures, there's no way that Susan hasn't faced the Untempered Schism.

If Susan made the cut, then leaving her on Earth just as interstellar transport gets going is asking for trouble. For the Doctor, it means there's an obvious and traceable link to him for the Time Lords to use, if they seriously wanted to capture him. For the Time Lords, apart from all that, there's a security risk in leaving one of their own available for anyone looking to unlock their secrets (as per 6.7, "The War Games" or 22.4, "The Two Doctors"). She was probably invaluable when the Time War got going and retrieved by any means necessary – if that were at all possible.

And not just invaluable to the Time Lords. If the Daleks got hold of a leftover Time Lord, they could uncover the genetic tricks to unlimited time travel. Maybe leaving her on a planet to which Daleks seem allergic wasn't such a bad move. Even if she isn't a full-fledged Time Lord, or a trainee who skipped the exam and was sent off to become a soldier or work on a tea-plantation (because they definitely have tea there – 15.6, "The Invasion of Time"; X2.0, "The Christmas Invasion"; 16.1, "The Ribos Operation"; and above all 9.5, "The Time Monster") – she knows that Time Lords exist and has been to other planets and times, so is still a worry for the High Council and an asset for anyone who can grab her. However, she seems to have kept a low profile until Borusa recruited her for the Game of Rassilon. (He found her because he's President and has access to the Matrix. The Doctor had been President and, later, inside the Matrix after his apparent execution – 20.1, Arc of Infinity" – so Borusa had all the Doctor's memories except the How To Build a Demat Gun instructions Rassilon blocked off and, logically, the location of

continued on Page 313...

The Analysis

The Big Picture ("The End of Time" Part One and Part Two)

Let's wind back to the mid-nineties, when *Doctor Who* was as popular as Roger Whittaker. (Don't worry if you've not heard of him, just accept that he was confoundingly popular in the early 70s and then... not.)

Granada, one of the biggest ITV companies, had a number of young writers who were being given gigs on children's drama, then soaps (including the biggie, *Coronation Street*) and allowed to experiment. Thus Paul Abbott rose to prominence. He accumulated a loose collective of hungry young dramatists who all seemed to work on the same series. As you'll recall from Volume 7, Russell T Davies, Paul Cornell and Frank Cottrell Boyce were among these, and you can do a *Rock Family Trees* diagram of who worked with whom on what over a ten-year period. (See also **Why Weren't We Bovvered?** under "The Runaway Bride" and **Was Series 2 Supposed to be Like This?** under X2.11, "Fear Her".)

We discussed the amount of crossover between *Linda Green* and early BBC Wales *Doctor Who* in Volume 7, but we've a couple of Davies projects to mention now that weren't helpful to bring in then. One was the bonkers 1994 soap *Revelations*, created by Davies and so lurid that only three ITV companies showed it opposite *Newsnight* to make sure nobody saw it. (It was made by the notoriously naff Carlton Television, so the PR and publicity was predictably pathetic.) It was about a bishop's wife who goes on a killing-spree, but that doesn't really convey the full jawdropping daftness of the plot-twists. It *still* got better ratings that Abbott and Boyce's next project, *Springhill*, for which Davies wrote scripts.

This was, loosely, *The Omen* set in a Merseyside estate – but it did all the Magic Realist tricks you can't normally get away with in soaps (except *Telenovelas* or the last few months of a cancelled US daytime show). The storyliners for the second, final series were Cornell and Gareth Roberts and they wrote for it too. Those who stayed up until three in the morning the week before Christmas 1997 to watch it on Channel 4 will recall that one character attempts suicide and hallucinates messages from the telly, seeing the rest of the family carry on as normal after her death, walking straight through her.

As is so often the case when we discuss the deep background to *Doctor Who*, it's less about the detail and more about the overall mood, the mouthfeel, the "Structure of Feeling" as they used to call it. British soaps don't normally do things like this; it's more common in outright fantasy series (where, by using the label "fantasy" they are – paradoxically – positing a mechanism for this within the rules of that world and normalising it).

One of the aspects of Davies's *Doctor Who* we addressed in the last book (**Is Kylie from Planet Zog?** under X4.0, "Voyage of the Damned") was that he took the visual vocabulary from the umpteen imported science fiction franchises apologetically shoved into "Cult" slots on BBC2 and Channel 4, and brought them into a drama series watched by critics who ignored these shows – exactly like the way they had overlooked what had happened to British soaps other than *EastEnders* in the previous ten years. Just as *Springhill* took the conflict of Order and Chaos so common in space opera and domesticated it into a family split between a prim, maternal Northern matriarch who did the cleaning and a louche Irish temptress (called "Eva Morrigan", in case we missed the symbolism), so Davies's *Doctor Who* occupied a Venn diagram overlap between children's television, space opera, soap, costume drama, Hollywood blockbusters, shiny-floor talent shows and autobiography.

There's not a lot new about that: look back at earlier volumes of this series for ways in which the BBC used the series as a televisual Swiss Army Knife. The difference now is that there's a dedicated staff and facility in Wales, rather than anyone available at Television Centre being given a gig on *Doctor Who* in between whatever else they might have been asked to work on. In every other respect, this is how it's always been – the series taking on the colouring of the programmes around it, but with different programmes in 2005 than in 1989 or 1963.

There's always a peril in trying to explain how much the series is embedded in the rest of BBC1's output in any given year – it makes it seem as if we're saying *if you didn't see it, then you're not really seeing it* – but any attempt to consider it *purely* as a children's show, or *purely* a science fiction franchise, or *purely* as something made for box-sets or online binging misses the point. It's not "purely" anything, it's the most promiscuous programme around and it's most completely itself when it's mixing techniques and content from sources usu-

Where's Susan?

continued from Page 311...

the Hand of Omega. And the Nemesis statue. And Shada. And details of the Hybrid that not even Rassilon could find.)

Therefore, unless Susan was completely inaccessible, she was undoubtedly pressed into service at some level, or at the very least put on gardening-leave to stop the Daleks getting her. As we gather, even if she'd been killed, she would have been back on duty soon afterwards. Yet according to Clara (X8.12, "Death in Heaven"), all the Doctor's grandchildren are missing in action, presumed dead. (In 26.3, "The Curse of Fenric", the Doctor's uncertain about how much family he has.) Under the circumstances (trying to kid the Cybermen that she was the real Doctor), she'd give verifiable facts. They may have had the data-stamp things left over from "The Next Doctor" (X4.14), or they were using their mini-Matrix.

This is remarkably imprecise for either the Doctor or Clara (who knew more than *he* did about his life – he thought Jenny was dead at the end of X4.6, "The Doctor's Daughter" but Clara knew otherwise). Of course, Clara's journey up and down the Doctor's timeline omitted an entire incarnation active during the Time War. The Doctor might have mentioned it, though, especially once Clara got a job – somehow – at Coal Hill School. That whole business is peculiar in many ways, especially compared to the usual legal procedure for getting a teaching job, so many people have taken the hint from the sign outside the gate in "Day of the Doctor" and suggest that the Doctor had a word with the head of the Board of Governors, Ian Chesterton. That would have been a tricky conversation and the subject of Susan would have been unavoidable.

So if Susan was on the way to becoming a Time Lord when she left with the Doctor, she is very unlikely to have been permanently dead. If she was involved in the Time War, she was probably resurrected, maybe repeatedly. If not, she's stuck in a timeless void after history was pulled out from under her. Yet the Doctor seems to have given up on her. Perhaps the non-Time Lord Gallifreyans involved in the fighting were killed in the numbers the Partisan suggests. If it's only Time Lords being resurrected, this could account for the uncertainty over her fate. Despite her psychic abilities, she wasn't up to snuff.

There may be more than one other grandchild on active duty, but we don't see or hear anything

about them. Susan was the only one who left Gallifrey, apparently. (Much as we might enjoy the idea of John and Gillian from the *TV Comic* strips of the 60s being horribly killed time and again, Clara's story is the only mention on screen of any others and we don't get names.) Even if it's just Susan, we have a final problem remaining. The Doctor's farewell tour at the end of "The End of Time Part Two" (X4.18) is stated, in *SJA:* "Death of the Doctor", to have included Jo Grant and every other companion or near-miss ever. Even on-screen valedictions include the granddaughter of Joan Redfern. If Luke Smith warrants a visit, why does he not know where Susan is or if she's alive? Well, she could be inaccessible.

We know from "The Pilot" (X10.1), that he knows about her (there are just two pictures on his desk: Susan and River Song), so his memory's not been tampered with in this regard. We are left with one obvious possibility that could open up a lot of stories: she's back on Gallifrey under another name. There are two anonymous women who look after the Doctor in times of crisis. One is the enigmatic Woman in White. The nearest the Doctor comes to identifying her is when Wilf asks who she is and the Doctor glances at Donna, i.e. Wilf's granddaughter.

Not many people favour this explanation. Apart from the sentimental notion that Spooky Claire is the Doctor's mum, people have suggested that this Delphic oracle is Leela, Romana, Ace, the Rani – everybody female is the Rani until proven otherwise – the First Mrs Who (Susan must have at least one granny as well), Flavia and any other woman who may have washed up on Gallifrey. Nowadays, we might also propose that it could be Borusa, Engin or the War Chief.

Similarly, whoever it is who restores the Doctor after five billion years punching a diamond by pouring him a nice bowl of soup (X9.12, "Hell Bent") seems to have the keys to the family shed. (We'd like it if that was the mysterious "Granny Five" mentioned in X11.9, "It Takes You Away".) If the woman-in-the-shed *is* Susan, why not say so? Why not talk a bit more about old times? Why isn't she either all over him, or putting strychnine in the soup for leaving her on a derelict planet with someone whose only real enthusiasm is milking goats? Perhaps they said all there was to say during the endless battles we never got to see. (Of course, what we are shown in "Hell Bent" is only

continued on Page 315...

ally thought to be incompatible. This is easier to explain once the finished story is made than at any time in the development process, and easier for Davies to do in practice and contemplate later than to suggest to other writers. The common gripe about "shopping-list" stories is in part a result of him seeing the way disparate items could work in *Doctor Who* as nowhere else, but not always conveying this to others. (See **Are Credited Authors Just Hired Hands?** under X2.5, "Rise of the Cybermen" for an analysis of this complaint and its complexities.)

If anything, the clearest "source" for the material here is old *Doctor Who* stories. But even then, these are shaken up and put back together in a completely new configuration, and repackaged for a new audience. The most obvious is at the start of Part Two, when we get a scene straight out of a Davison-era *DWM* strip with the High Council of Time Lords, vast buildings with thin bridges and a crashed flying saucer outside the ruined Capitol. This is juxtaposed with stuff in a millionaire's mansion out in the stockbroker belt, the *locus classicus* of Tom Baker present-day stories but, until now, un-used in the revived series. Davies-issue standbys from previous Yeti-in-the-loo adventures are present and correct (a Chiswick street with a planet in the sky, Trinity Wells, a sort-of celebrity cameo, randy old ladies, helicopter shots of the Thames, comedy aliens, flashbacks…), and we get the standard signifiers of a Christmas Special (fake snow, Noddy Holder telling us *It's Chri-i-i-i-istma-a-a-a-as*, a new song by Murray Gold), but, again, mixed up and recontextualised.

Lurking behind the Gallifrey scenes is the idea that the 70s stories about Time Lords left things to the imagination for budgetary reasons, but now *here it all is*. Underlying the scene with Wilf in the café is frustration at perfunctory regenerations (obviously 24.1, "Time and the Rani", but also the nonchalant way Borusa was never the same actor twice, the lack of explanation about why Romana changed). With a large chunk of the British public now on-board, Davies could indulge himself in matters best avoided in his first two series, for fear of alienating the casual viewer. Looking at *The Writer's Tale*, it's odd how many blind-alleys Davies explored before coming to the obvious conclusion that the story would be the Master bringing back the Time Lords, unaware of how terrible they'd become. It's been ticking away ever

since we discovered that the Doctor had been forced to put the safety of the cosmos over loyalty to his own people.

What's interesting, and indicative, is that all the season finales have either featured the Master or the Daleks, and the raising of the stakes each time presented us with increasingly powerful figures behind these, culminating in Rassilon and Davros. Davies, like Moffat and Chibnall, is of the generation who believed that *Doctor Who* peaked under Philip Hinchcliffe, however much they as individuals dispute this. The story's overall shape is entirely in keeping with the programme's traditions from the 1970s but, like all the earlier producers, Davies is inserting elements from a wide range of popular culture. It's just that, in 2009, there's a wider array of that to choose from than, say, Innes Lloyd had available. Also, the technical facilities – and budget – made everything equally possible.

The Cult of Saxon, for example, seems awfully familiar to fans of naff 80s Australian soap *Prisoner: Cell Block H*. (We're using the UK title imposed by every ITV station who ran it in the small hours, just making sure nobody switched on expecting Patrick McGoohan to be involved. Amazingly, some American stations ran it too, under that name.) This was a lurid melodrama set in Wentworth Prison, which was (usually) all-female and had a higher horrible-deaths-per-hundred-residents tally than Moonbase Alpha, Midsomer or the USS *Enterprise*.

The series started violent and sordid, then ramped it up a few notches when a new officer, Joan "The Freak" Ferguson showed up in the 1982 season. She was a panto-villain, along the lines of JR Ewing, Servalan or Alexis Colby, but with sinister Nazi-interrogator black gloves. She was both a manipulative bully and a predatory lesbian, not above planting drugs as a pretext for a beating or an intimate search. Miss Trefusis (hardly a subtle hint – see 16.3, "The Stones of Blood" and **What Are the Gayest Things in Doctor Who Ever?** under 25.2, "The Happiness Patrol") is clearly and deliberately in the same mould. It's not nearly as glamorous or slick as *Orange is the New Black*. (There was a reboot called *Wentworth*, for which Pete McTighe, author of X11.7, "Kerblam!", won awards.) Unlike *Number 96* (a previous Reg Grundy soap), there wasn't ever a black mass in the laundry room, but a notorious storyline used a séance (organised by Zara

Where's Susan?

continued from Page 313...

the gaps in the Doctor's memory from that period when knowing that Clara existed was a threat to all creation. Giving him back those memories in X10.13, "Twice Upon a Time" isn't, apparently, any risk to anyone.)

There's also the General, broadly on his side and sent to ask "Doctor Who?" to see if it was all right to come out of hiding. It must be someone the Doctor trusts, and someone Clara has come to know during her million-lifetime stint as his guardian angel. In which case, shooting his grand-daughter – his one friend in the Time Lord hierarchy – and forcing him to regenerate back into a female body was as nasty a thing as we've ever seen the Doctor do, so let's just acknowledge the possibility and then sidle away slowly.

Gallifrey does seem to be the one place the Doctor can't just pop in and visit. Even once he's sure it still exists (as only happens rather later), he's not everyone's favourite person and he went and forgot where he put it. If the reasons for missing her are that she's incommunicado, rather than just embarrassment or guilt, this is as likely an explanation as we're likely to get. This is one of those issues that the series, and especially those writers who came up through fandom before 1990, know better than to discharge by giving definite answers – like the Doctor's name (see **Is His Name Really 'Who'?** under 3.10, "The War Machines" and X7.14, "The Name of the Doctor") and marital status (X7.15, "Day of the Doctor"; X10.0, "The Husbands of River Song"; X3.10, "Blink").

The other big question is whether, in either a repeatedly-rewritten Earth or a Time War where people died again and again endlessly, Susan would remember much of her own (original) past. We discussed in two essays in Volume 7 the way the memories of TARDIS travellers are seemingly "copy-protected" when the past is changed, but in stories such as "A Christmas Carol" (X6.0) and "Cold Blood" (X5.9), this has been shown to be more complicated. (See **He Remembers This How?** under X1.5, "World War Three"; **Is Arthur the Horse a Companion?** under X2.4, "The Girl in the Fireplace"; **Is Time Like Bolognese Sauce?** under X5.5, "Flesh and Stone".) In the meantime, Carole Ann Ford is apparently quite happy to do Big Finish audios, so the question may still be addressed on screen – but nobody's holding their breath.

Moonbeam, played by Ilona Rodgers of 1.8, "The Sensorites") as part of one of The Freak's ploys to oust "Queen" Bea, the prisoner who really ran the place. Combining this with *Raiders of the Lost Ark* effects as the cultists are consumed, putting them both on the same plane as raw material, is characteristic of the series and of Davies's work in general.

Davies had a running gag about aliens picking ill-fated names for spaceships ("Titanic" and, until a rethink caused by a film, "Icarus" in X3.7, "42"), and this time he plumped for "Hesperus", as in *The Wreck of the Schooner Hesperus* by Longfellow (one of those poems 70s schoolkids had to learn by heart, although half of them muddled it up with *Casabianca*). The imagery of the Master turning everyone into himself was a version of something that had become a commonplace in pop culture after *Being John Malkovich* and *The Matrix*, rooms full of the same head on different bodies. By the time of this episode, insurance adverts and music videos had used it. Also familiar from these were the CG metallic skeletons (the most overt and obvious was "Hey Girl, Hey Boy" by the Chemical Brothers ten years before). We could explain where the ideas of a spaceship in a WWII-style dogfight and a bar full of aliens came from, but you'd not thank us. The point is the people placed incongruously within each: Wilf and Alonzo.

Both were, from the author's account, intuitive choices made after the scenario was beginning to crystallise. In the case of Wilfred Mott, the idea of the character was evolving to fit both Bernard Cribbins's public persona and his off-screen manner. *Doctor Who* had reminded the viewers that he was an actor who did comedy and comic song, not a comedian per se, and his back-catalogue was being reassessed. Even before the character had a name, Wilf was given Cribbins's military background with a Para badge on his hat, so this aspect started to come in as a scripted detail (or semi-scripted, in the case of the paint-gun in X4.12, "The Stolen Earth"). Through conversations with Davies, other details filtered in, particularly the moment when Wilf sees Palestine from space and reminisces. (According to Davies, Cribbins described a literal blizzard, which seemed improbable, so it became bullets *like* a blizzard.)

Also in this scene is an idea curiously like the

ABOUT TIME 2008-2009

concept in X8.12, "Death in Heaven" of everyone who has died also being affected by the alien transformation. This fits with the notion earlier in the episode of the Time War being fought by troops who were endlessly dying and being resurrected to fight some more. Davies suggests that this and the Woman in White subplot emerged from a line in the moody intro to the otherwise up-tempo Chris Rea song "Road to Hell" (a hit around the time *Doctor Who* went off the air in late 1989). The narrator's late mother was on the roadside, so worried by what was about to happen as to be unable to rest.

There's a small in-joke in the "Reward" sequence: Tommy Knight is saved from oncoming traffic because Davies was annoyed. The road used on location is closed off by the police, so only vehicles in the story ever travel in-shot, so the cast got used to walking across Clinton Road without looking out for cars. Davies was aware of the responsibilities of writing for CBBC, so put this near-fatal collision in as a sly rebuke.

One final item to remind readers that even this episode isn't as fanwanky as some of the books and audios. A big part of the *New Adventures* version of Gallifrey, along with removing the need for mothers at all, was the Menti Celesti: effectively the gods of the Time Lords, incarnated as Death, Pain, Time and so forth. There was also the Celestis, Time Lords formerly of the Celestial Intervention Agency (14.3, "The Deadly Assassin") who went beyond the need for bodies and became conceptual entities (*Alien Bodies* by one Lawrence Miles). The starting-point for the former was Marc Platt's novel *Cat's Cradle: Time's Crucible*, but a glance at the more convoluted Big Finish storylines about Leela and Romana and all the stuff mentioned in **Did Cartmel Have Any Plan At All?** under 26.1, "Battlefield" might prove either illuminating or profoundly scary.

English Lessons

• *Governor* (n.) The person who runs a prison or remand centre. America calls it a "Warden"; that's a junior post in the UK or Australia.

• *Skiffle group* (n.) A group that plays skiffle, obviously. After the first giddy rush of rock and roll (1954-6), there was a bit of a lull. The BBC's first big Saturday teatime show, *6-5 Special*, capitalised on the rock scene when the commercial stations wouldn't touch it, but then they needed to find the Next Big Thing and found… jug-bands

playing Leadbelly songs. The thing about skiffle was that practically anyone could do it: three chords on an acoustic guitar, a washboard for percussion and a tea-chest and a broom-handle, plus a bit of string, for bass. Jazz performer Lonnie Donegan became a huge star and inspired the nation's 15-year-olds to get up and have a go. A few years and a bit of practice later, a large percentage of the nation's 19-year-olds were semi-pro musicians and four of them, after a sojourn in Hamburg, became the next Next Big Thing. So far, nobody's made a film about Donegan (although he's the climax of the feature film version of *6-5 Special*), but if they do, David Tennant ought to play him.

The thing is, although the original idea was that the character who became Wilf was in one, the dates we get here – and those of Bernard Cribbins in real life – mean he'd've been way too old for that sort of thing, and probably too busy with baby Sylvia.

• *Winston* (n.): Wilf's mate, as it happens, is given almost the most stereotypical name for someone of his age and race in Britain. If you think back to the account we gave in the essay with X3.2, "The Shakespeare Code", you'll know why there was a lot of immigration into Britain around the time Churchill was held to be the hero of World War II, and why so many new-born boys were either called "Winston" to their faces or – as with John Lennon – got it as a middle name. (It's like the whole trend for Ellis Island babies to get the most posh-sounding first names as part of the whole assimilation process, hence all the "Leonard"s "Melvin"s and "Irving"s who became famous in 1930s America.) The only way Wilf's wingman could be more of a cliché is with a Scottish surname. Davies's antennae for a propos names that sketch in age, background and aspirations were finely-tuned, even if the results occasionally got a bit repetitive.

• *August Bank Holiday* (n): When Minnie misbehaved in a police box, August Bank Holiday was the first Monday in August (in 1962, it was 6th). By the end of that decade, the government decided to put it on the last Monday. This means it's now the unofficial start of the wind-down of the school holidays, the seaside peak-time and – once upon a time – the cricket and tennis seasons. A week of haircuts and last-minute homework then follows, after which the term starts in the first week of September and we can all eat mashed potato again. (See **September or January?** under 13.1, "Terror of the Zygons" for more on what this meant and X8.1, "Deep Breath" for what happened last time they launched a new series that weekend.)

• *Queen's Speech* (n). The monarch's broadcast to the Commonwealth is now a pre-recorded video and shown several times during Christmas Day, but the big one is traditionally the 3.00pm transmission. It's ten minutes long (and apparently written by the Silence – X6.1, "The Impossible Astronaut" et seq. – as nobody can ever remember what she says). The entire country watches patiently so that they can eat their dinner and pull their crackers (see X2.0, "The Christmas Invasion" for details).

• *Mount Snowdon* (n): Wales's biggest mountain gave its name to one of the first National Parks (Snowdonia) and the Queen's brother-in-law. In *Doctor Who* lore, it's famous as where the Jathaar Sunglider crashed (X2.12, "Army of Ghosts") and the bigger UNIT base (*SJA*: "Death of the Doctor"). Snowdonia doubled for Tibet in 5.2, "The Abominable Snowmen", and the area became the Death Zone and Eye of Orion (20.7, "The Five Doctors"). Despite Snowdonia's many unearthly vistas, the Cardiff-based productions have preferred to go to Croatia, Spain and South Africa than shoot there because it's too fiddly a route to get articulated lorries to and from easily.

Oh, Isn't That...?

• *David Harewood* (billionaire Joshua Naismith) is now known in America for *Supergirl* (his character, the Martian Manhunter, is head of an agency that's like a competent version of Torchwood), *Homeland*, *The Night Manager* and – sorry to bring this up – *Selfie*. He was a counterintuitive Friar Tuck in *Robin Hood* (see the essay with X4.10, "Midnight") and, in similar vein, was a C of E Vicar in Victorian London (and his dodgy twin brother) in *Ruby in the Smoke* and back for the sequel.

• *Barry Howard* (pensioner Oliver Barnes) is best known for *Hi-De-Hi* (see 24.3, "Delta and the Bannermen") playing Barry Stuart-Hargreaves, half of a bitchy married couple who give dance lessons to the campers while waiting for the divorce laws to change. *Doctor Who* was his last TV appearance.

• *Sinead Keenan* (Addams, a Vinvocci) was Nina, the girlfriend of Russell Tovey's character in *Being Human*.

• *Brian Cox* (voice of the Ood Elder) later on was Sydney Newman in "An Adventure in Space and Time". He was the original Hannibal Lecter in *Manhunter* (1986), and was a bit of a fixture in historical epics in the mid-90s (*Rob Roy* and *Braveheart* in rapid succession, several feature-length episodes of *Sharpe*), but has popped in for small roles in unlikely series (*Red Dwarf, Frasier*) and narrated a great many other things. He was also in *Deadwood* and the 2016 *War and Peace*. In short, if you want a Scottish movie star who's game to try anything (*Adaptation, French and Saunders, Scooby Doo*), he's your go-to guy. (He's also credited as "David Tennant" in a film called *Shoot on Sight*, of which nobody's ever heard.)

• *Timothy Dalton* (Rassilon) made an impression as Heathcliffe in the 1970 *Wuthering Heights*, retained his dignity in Mae West's freakish *Sextette* (a film where Dom DeLuise and Keith Moon looked embarrassed), seemed at home as Prince Barin in the lurid *Flash Gordon*, made a couple of ahead-of-their-time James Bond flicks, and played something not unlike a Bond Villain in *Hot Fuzz*. In between this, he's kept working, so has a large number of interesting oddities and spectacular disasters on his CV. But yes, a former 007 is playing Rassilon. Strange days…

• *Claire Bloom* (the Woman) was launched to global by Charlie Chaplin when she was 21, and put in the lead role in *Limelight*. Before all that, she'd been one of the earliest television stars in Britain, and a mainstay of the Old Vic and Stratford Festival theatre companies in the immediate post-War years. After that, she shifted between Broadway, Hollywood, the West End and Television Centre. In between a much-discussed private life (marriages to Rod Steiger and Philip Roth and a candid autobiography, countered by Roth's novel I Married a Communist), she was Lady Marchmain in the 1981 *Brideshead Revisited* and Queen Mary in *The King's Speech* – but, keeping her hand in, has done episodes of *Midsomer Murders* and *The Bill* and a semi-regular role in *Doc Martin*.

• *June Whitfield* (pensioner Minnie Hooper) had been performing in comedies since the 1950s, first on radio (*Take It From Here*), then television (e.g. the nurse in the *Hancock* episode about blood donation), and eventually a set of slightly twee sitcoms playing women called "June" married to men called "Terry" (played by Terry Scott), notably, er, *Terry and June*. After decades of this, she got a whole new audience as the gran in *Absolutely*

Fabulous. Let's put it this way; even if the *real* Barack Obama had been in that episode, he'd only have been the second-most-talked-about piece of guest casting for British viewers. She was a Dame and died in late 2018.

X4.18: "The End of Time Part Two"

(1st January, 2010)

Which One is This? It's the long goodbye. Fifteen minutes of it. Before that, there's an episode full of stunts, explosions, space-dogfights and lots and lots of continuity-based arguments. For once, the Chinese Army really *do* all look alike, as do the entire world (except Donna). And they give us a good look at those prog-rock-style Time Lord collars out before putting them back in the toybox until the 50th birthday. Russell has just left the building, and therefore ramps up the CGI action scenes, fanwank and high camp, plus enough soap to scrub the comedy spaceship.

Firsts and Lasts It's a regeneration story. Consequently, it's David Tennant's last hurrah (but not the last thing he recorded as the Doctor). It's the last story by Russell T Davies, and the last one he produces. After 22 months, it's the end of Series 4.

This is, therefore, the last Russell T Davies finale – with all that that entails. He took the opportunity to do the biggest conclusion he could muster, so this is the last (barring the odd bit of archival footage) we see of Donna Noble, Sylvia Noble, Wilf, Rose Tyler, Jackie Tyler, Mickey Smith, Martha Jones, Captain Jack, Alonso Frame, the Adipose and the Judoon. Sarah Jane Smith and her adopted son Luke log their final appearances in *Doctor Who*, although they've got some time remaining on their own show. Billie Piper will be back, but as a totally different character who's chosen to look like Rose.

It's the last story producer Julie Gardner worked on, and director Euros Lyn's farewell to the series. This is also the end for the Series 4 reworking of the theme.

It's the first episode to debut on New Year's Day since "The Face of Evil" (14.4) and the first "Part Two" for 20 years, one month and a day. This is the first time we have a BBC1 continuity

announcement precede the episode with Tennant as the Doctor (and, obviously, the last as well). In fact, it's the first time any Doctor has done it.

It's the last time we see the "proper" space-time vortex effects in either the title sequence or the stories. Henceforth, we get things that resemble ads for antacid tablets (perhaps the vortex is afflicted by a threat mentioned in this episode). We'll elaborate on this in the next volume.

Matt Smith has his first go at playing the Doctor. It's a fun-packed minute or so that gives us a fair sample of what's in store for the next four years and ends with his first yell of "Geronimo!"

It's the new-series episode in which Time Lords other than the Master turn up, along with the planet Gallifrey itself; we've not seen either properly since 23.4, "The Ultimate Foe". (Well, all right, they briefly cropped up last week, but more as a tease than a plot-development.)

But, listen up: the Doctor seriously believes that he might have regenerated into a girl at first. That's going to come back a few times in the next decade, culminating in a near-identical crashing TARDIS scene just after a regeneration (X10.13, "Twice Upon a Time"; X11.1, "The Woman Who Fell to Earth").

Watch Out For...
• This episode opens with a CG shot of the Capitol on Gallifrey, with its glass bowl cracked and a crashed Dalek ship nearby. Then people in velveteen robes and pixy hats stride around and Timothy Dalton (as the Lord President) barks "What news of the Doctor?", whereupon we get earnest gibberish about how badly the Time War's going. It's like fan-fic come to life: the really convoluted continuity-choked type beloved of 13-year-olds, but drastically better than it has any right to be.
• The *Star Wars* dog-fight escapade is obviously derivative and ought to be embarrassing, but Bernard Cribbins does a remarkable job reminding us how surreal it ought to be. Ditto Captain Jack's farewell in a bar that's not Mos Eisley Cantina at *all*.
• The climax hinges on Wilf's revolver and the Doctor cocks the hammer rather too often. Somehow, the absurdity of this doesn't seem to matter.
• The part where Murray Gold gets an Ood choir to belt out "Flavia's Theme" is where you realise that the regeneration's finally coming, after

a *lot* of prevarication. Admittedly, the delay isn't an entire hour's worth of television set in four time-zones and two TARDISes ("Twice Upon a Time"), but if there's anything that can make anyone warm to that daft pre-credit scene from "Time and the Rani" (24.1), it's this.

And, as it happens, the farewell/whatever-happened-to sequence ends by coming full circle back to Rose and Jackie on the Powell Estate. Billie Piper and Davies do a reasonable job recapturing the girl who went off joy-riding with Eccleston in the first season, rather than the slightly irksome character she became. It's certainly the most dignified of the various cameos.

• … and then Matt Smith and Steven Moffat take complete possession of the series in just over a minute of screen time. They even trash the TARDIS set.

The Continuity

The Doctor He claims to be 906 on this, the day of his death. [The next Doctor along is '907' in X5.5, "Flesh and Stone".]

While tied to a trolley with the Earth at the Master's mercy, he attempts something we can only describe as a chat-up line, apparently in all sincerity. It puzzles him when the Master turns this down. [All right, it's a little more complicated; he butters up the Master as much as possible, and tries to show off his own joy in seeing the universe.]

He judges being carted down a flight of stairs while strapped down as the 'worst rescue ever' [compare with 22.3, "The Mark of the Rani"].

He throws a childish tantrum upon realising he'll have to sacrifice his own life to save Wilf [the message seemingly being, "I'll save your life, sir, but only after making you feel like crap about it"], then collects himself. When Wilf says the Doctor is better than him, the Doctor looks horrified and asks him to never ever say that. He finally accepts his fate by concluding that he's 'lived too long' [presumably meaning that specific version of him, who's all of six years old at this stage – three of those, apparently, spent flying on Caw in A5, "The Infinite Quest"].

Here we see the dying Doctor visit many old friends. [In fact, the *Sarah Jane Adventures* story "Death of the Doctor" suggests that the Doctor visited every single companion ever on the way out. This presents all sorts of issues, such as how a visit to Adric would have gone.] Among other

loose ends, he has a go at matchmaking Jack with Midshipman Frame [X4.0, "Voyage of the Damned"], can't resist a hint to Rose in early 2005 about her future and recruits the late Geoff Noble to fund a triple-rollover to give Donna a happy ending.

Falling a couple of dozen feet, and through a dome, doesn't set off the Doctor's regeneration. [Perhaps he used the muscle relaxant technique that was so helpful in "The Paradise of Death" but which he forgot in 18.7, "Logopolis". The thirteenth Doctor, similarly, both plummets to Earth and slams through a train roof – albeit directly after regenerating ("X11.1, "The Woman Who Fell to Earth").]

The radiation poisoning the Doctor incurs takes an excruciatingly long time to kick into gear [and resembles, aptly enough, his death in 11.5, "Planet of the Spiders"]. It's obviously a different kind of radiation from the one in X3.1, "Smith and Jones", or he'd just take off his shoes.] One of the first symptoms is the almost immediate healing of superficial damage on his face. Eventually, the standard Orange Sparkly Pixy Dust explosion kicks in.

Post-regeneration, the new Doctor does a quick examination of his anatomy – he's still disappointed he's not ginger ["The Christmas Invasion"], at first guesses (judging by his hair) that he's a girl, counts his legs, grudgingly accepts that he's 'had worse' noses, exclaims 'blimey' about his chin and then – in the most delighted way imaginable – notes that the TARDIS is crashing.

• *Background.* It's clear that he recognises the Woman in White and takes her unspoken hint about how to defeat the Time Lords without hesitation. He knows that the Time Lords were planning their Final Sanction during the War.

• *Ethics.* It's strongly implied that the Doctor now has a death wish, and feels guilty about the number of people who he's arranged to get killed one time and another. [The odd taunting Davros gave in X4.13, "Journey's End" seems to weigh on his conscience.]

When put to it, the Doctor insists that the consequences of allowing the Time Lords out of the time lock are too horrific to contemplate. And yet... he still won't kill the Master, even though it'll save the Earth and his own life. He seemingly considers shooting both the Lord President and the Master, before getting a prompt from the Woman in White, and just uses the weapon against an inanimate object.

319

• *Inventory: Sonic Screwdriver.* It wrecks up a spaceship, fixes a spaceship, breaks a teleport… but can't fix a Nuclear Bolt gone critical.

• *Inventory: Other.* The Doctor tells Wilf and Sylvia that he never carries money and borrowed a quid from Geoff [but he must have paid for the hardcover at Verity's book signing somehow].

The TARDIS The Doctor put her ahead a second in time last episode. While in this state, even an entire planet full of Masters don't find it. [It's suggested the Ship might come in handy for triangulating the Time Lords' signal, but this proves to be unnecessary.] The sheer explosive force of the Doctor's regeneration damages the console room [see also "Twice Upon a Time"].

Catchphrase Counter We dropped this feature after Volume 7, simply because there were so many prophesies, slogans, verbal tics, call-backs and stock phrases, it was getting like *Rentaghost*.

However, we can make a tally for the tenth Doctor and his chums, restricting ourselves to the biggies. Oddly, Eccleston's "Fantastic" shows up five times after he's gone, the last being the Master in this episode (whereupon the Doctor gives him the dirtiest look we've seen between the two of them in five episodes). We also have six "Molto Bene"s and five "nonononono don't don't don't do that"s for companions trying to do the local patter (and one that was cut, the Master telling off the US president-version of himself).

There are seven times when "Oh yes" comes out as "WorrYuss!". The word "Spoilers" crops up eight times in two episodes, with a lot more to come. (Incidentally, Professor Song only calls the Doctor "sweetie" once, whereas CAL's fictional dad uses it five times when reassuring his daughter.)

The big ones, though, are well into double figures. Various things are described as "burning", "burned" or "he/she/it burns": 17 in those forms, plus another 11 in X3.7, "42" when possessed people croak "burn with me". We're treated to 18 "Allons-y"s, with increasing levels of self-conscious "lets make this a catchphrase"-ness (see "I should like a hat like that" in Volume 2 and "Brave heart, Tegan" in Volume 5, plus "Geronimo" to come). Someone, usually the Doctor, telling someone else "I'm sorry, so sorry" (or a slight variation thereupon) happens 21 times. The Cybermen burble "Delete" 27 times (and 12 "upgrade"s).

Oddly, the Daleks don't say "Exterminate" *at all* in X3.4, "Daleks in Manhattan". They say "Exterminieren" five times in X4.13, "Journey's End", when Davros gets to use the catch-phrase once. Across the six Tennant episodes with Daleks in, however, they say it 86 times. Forty-eight of these are in "The Stolen Earth"; all six parts of "The Power of the Daleks" (4.3) only had 47, and that includes the Doctor saying it. There are as many (four) in the last minute of X2.12, "Army of Ghosts" as in the Dalek Civil War in episode seven of "The Evil of the Daleks" (4.9).

The Supporting Cast

• *Wilf.* He knows perfectly well that the Doctor doesn't do weapons, but ventures to suggest it anyhow, and downright *orders* it after the Doctor admits that everyone would go back to normal if the Master died. Almost instinctively, he saves a frightened technician, setting off an unfortunate chain of events. As the Doctor explains that the radiation compartment will kill whoever is inside, he begs the Doctor just to leave him to die. He sees the Time Lord off to his regeneration with a salute and blows a kiss.

In 1948, Wilf was assigned to the Mandate in Palestine. Minnie makes a cheeky suggestion about a bouquet; he laughingly tells her off. Sylvia's house is somewhere very close to Wessex Lane.

• *Donna* marries Shaun Temple. The Doctor gives her a winning lottery ticket as a present [we're left to infer that she and Shaun live happily ever after]. She gets on as well with Nerys as she ever manages. It turns out that the mental safety protocols the Doctor left for her work perfectly well, resulting in some sort of psychic blast that simultaneously wipes her memory and stuns all the Masters chasing her.

• *The Woman in White.* She appears in the flesh as one of the Time Lords who opposed breaking the Time Lock. To Wilf, she'll say only that she was 'lost, so very long ago'. The Doctor doesn't answer Wilf's question about who she is directly but, perhaps significantly, glances at Donna.

[Here we'll throw out a bonkers idea… what if the Woman in White is a Watcher-style avatar (see 11.5, "Planet of the Spiders"; 18.7, "Logopolis"; and, maybe, 17.1, "Destiny of the Daleks" and Season Twenty-Three) between full incarnations? It's not the Doctor, though, it's Rassilon. Just as the Watcher acted as a causal sheepdog, making sure everyone did as they ought in order that entropy is stopped and the Doctor turns into Peter Davison, so the only way the Rassilon who's the Narrator can be talked out of ending all matter and stopping time is if his next persona, the Diamond Geezer from "Hell Bent" (X9.12), sends an intermediate stage as an intermediary to make sure that his future/past happens just so. Thus, the freakish coincidences aren't coincidences at all. This also explains how the Woman in White can escape the Time Lock and pester Wilf, because – like the message inside the Master's head – she's rooted in something from after the Final Day and out in the wider universe. Assuming that Gallifrey *is* out in real spacetime in the Capaldi Era.]

• *Rose Tyler.* Here we briefly see the sensible 2005 iteration. She was already dating Mickey at the New Year, and thinks her mother's current boyfriend ('Jimbo') is useless. Oddly, it appears that Jackie went out partying for the rest of the night while Rose went home.

• *Mickey Smith* and *Martha Jones* married, and are going in dark leather around fighting aliens with Mickey-style big guns. Martha says she's gone freelance. [So, presumably, they're operating independent of UNIT and Torchwood. She's credited as 'Martha Smith-Jones' at the end.] She's had her hair braided; he's got a beard.

• *Captain Jack.* Currently recovering from events in *Torchwood: Children of Earth* by sulking in alien bars. He looks a little perkier when the Doctor passes him a note setting him up with Alonso [X4.0, "Voyage of the Damned"].

• *Sarah Jane* covered up the entire planet-turning-into-the-Master business single-handedly, by putting out a story about wi-fi giving people mass hallucinations. [From here, she goes on to Series 3 of her own show.]

• *Verity Newman* is the spitting image of her great-grandmother, Joan Redfern [X3.8, "Human Nature"]. It turns out Joan kept her own diary to journal the events of 1913, and tucked it in the loft; Verity retrieved and published it a century later. The Doctor asks whether Joan was ultimately happy; the one time he smiles in the whole farewell tour sequence is when Verity says yes.

• *Joseph Naismith.* Arrested and jailed, along with his daughter, for crimes undisclosed.

UNIT UNIT Geneva has tech that can track down a spaceship and coordinate NATO defence to shoot one down with missiles.

The Supporting Cast (Evil)

• *The Master.* There's several billion of him now. They all accept the goals and decisions of the prime version, and can all link with him psychically [or not, when there's an opportunity for a good sight gag].

He explains to Wilf that he was brought to the Untempered Schism as a child, looked into time, and promptly acquired a pounding headache. [It's confirmation, in every detail, of the "legend" the Doctor told Martha and Jack in X3.12, "The Sound of Drums". A deleted line cites the Master's birthday as the Eve of Cold Lamentation, whatever that might be.] The four-beat drumming in his head is so constant, he's not sure what he'd be like without its sound. He briefly seems to listen to the Doctor's "road trip across the universe" offer, then realises that the four-beat is a signal from the End of Time, and promptly resumes threatening everyone.

The whole business of the Time Lords having set up an agonising paradox that's haunted his entire life doesn't seem to bother him, until Rassilon ostentatiously rejects him as 'diseased'.

Having his spur-of-the-moment plan to impose himself into all the human race deleted doesn't overly bother him and he *claims* to go along with whatever Rassilon has planned – up to and including the apotheosis gambit. Matters between them fray, however, and he lets his frustration about the years of insane drumming spill out into a very good go at killing the Lord President. We last see this Master disappearing into the Time Lock. [He next appears, healed, in X10.11, "World Enough and Time".]

The Time Lords They're currently led by a Lord President, someone the Doctor identifies as 'Rassilon'. [Surely, in a script written by Russell T Davies, and script-edited by Gary Russell, he's intended as the same being who petrified people back in 20.7, "The Five Doctors". We might imagine that it's a name used as a title (the way "Caesar" became a job-description rather than a surname), but there's no evidence of that, and it's not an established tradition among Time Lord presidents before now. A later President calls himself 'Rassilon the Resurrected' ("Hell Bent").

[It's never explained why, strangely, this version of Rassilon is less powerful than when he was a corpse (see "The Five Doctors" for his posthumous potency and "Hell Bent" for his regeneration into an East End hard-case). If he's lost his knack for "immmmmmmmortality" and needed to transform from 007 to Mad Frankie Frazer, then something weird's happened. That's "weird" where all of humanity looking like John Simm is baseline-normality.]

The Lord President possesses a gauntlet that can vaporise his opponents and, with a gesture, cancel out the Master's transformation of everyone on Earth into himself.

The High Council is, once again, just senior figures around a desk ["The Five Doctors"]; the Lord President and the Visionary, the Partisan, the Chancellor and some bloke with a beard, plus non-speaking ones. Rassilon seems to exert absolute or near-absolute authority over the group – when the Partisan suggests an end to the Time War, he disintegrates her. A formal vote, however, is taken to leave the Time Lock [as if it were within their power to do so].

They still use the word 'Contact' for the initiation of mental communications [10.1, "The Three Doctors"].

Rassilon and the Council take advice from the Visionary, an elderly henna-tattooed woman who mutters and sketches the circles that are Gallifreyan language. She forecasts Gallifrey being done for, but suggests breaking out of the Time Lock with a white-point star, which the President just happens to carry atop his curly-straw staff.

Here the Time Lords vote to initiate the Final Sanction – a scheme they were working on during the War [see **History**]. Only two of those present vote no – one of these is the Woman in White; we learn absolutely nothing about the other. Rassilon shames the dissenters by making them cover their faces with their hands, 'like the Weeping Angels of old' [so the Angels feature into Gallifreyan history/ mythology].

The Doctor's fighting with the Master remains a byword for catfighting, and even Rassilon knows about it [he did seem familiar with them in "The Five Doctors"]. By this point in the War, no one objects to setting up a temporal paradox: the planting of a signal in the Master's mind, via the drumming that drove him mad, that will let Gallifrey return to reality. [Effect seems to be muddled with cause as it is. Time Lord history now records that the Master always heard the four-beat, even though that's set up here.

[The decision to leave the Time Lock suggests that the combatants in the Time War have imposed that lock themselves. Other discussions

about it, especially in X4.12, "The Stolen Earth", indicated that the lock resulted from how the War ended and was a natural effect, like Fixed Points. It's only the Master and the Doctor having lives after the end, out in the material universe, that gives Rassilon the option of tuning in to the Master's drumming. See **How Can Anyone Know About the Time War?** under X4.13, "Journey's End".]

Both the Master and the Doctor think that exposure to the Untempered Schism is traumatic and painful.

Planet Notes

• *Gallifrey* is noticeably much larger than Earth [it almost seems swollen] and seems to have no atmosphere or oceans, with a surface covered in fires/lava eruptions that can be seen from orbit.

It's the only place to get white-point stars in the universe. Properly configured, with a power source like a Nuclear Bolt putting out 500,000 rads, the diamond can shift an entire planet through time, either by opening a way for it to emerge under its own power or actively drawing the planet. [It look as though the Doctor shoots out the machinery surrounding it rather than the diamond itself.]

The High Council sit around a small table, apparently made of burnished wood, but with a built-in projector for what seem to be real openings in spacetime [the President chucks a diamond through it to Earth and sends a Morse Code 'V' into the Master's childhood via the Untempered Schism], but look like Hollywood holograms. All but one speaking-role has a title (the Chancellor, etc…) and there are eight members, including three who don't get any dialogue. Apart from the Lord President, the male Councillors wear hats.

There's more racial diversity on Gallifrey than before, but not in the speaking-role characters – just one female Councillor and one of the President's guard. At the head of the table sits the Lord President. The Visionary sits facing him, the others along the long sides of the oval table. The full Council stand in a conical chamber, each higher row bigger than the ones at the base, with the Lord President at the apex. There are hundreds of them, all in scarlet robes with gold collars. [So are they all Prydonians now? See 14.3, "The Deadly Assassin".]

The Non-Humans

• *Vinvocci.* Rossiter says that calling them 'cacti' is racist [but they do immediately bring to mind 18.2, "Meglos"]. They have rather snazzy asteroid lasers with automatic tracking. [A cut scene gives the real names of the pair seen here as 'Shanshay' and 'Shanshay' – the Doctor can hear a difference in pronunciation, but neither we nor Wilf could.]

• *The Ood.* Once more, they either have time travel, or can mentally project an image for the Doctor across several centuries [X4.16, "The Waters of Mars"]. They think it's very important to sing the Doctor through his regeneration, then disappear.

History

• *Dating.* The story begins on Christmas Eve; it's Boxing Day when the Doctor confronts Rassilon. Sarah Jane and Luke's bit is, apparently, later that same day. [Quite a few of the scenes with the dying Doctor visiting his friends could take place any time – though they're all probably not long after events here. Jack's story happens after *Children of Earth,* for him, but he's got a Vortex Manipulator so it could be any time when Alonso Frame's that young.]

There are 6,727,949,038 copies of the Master. [Add two more for Donna and her grandfather, and this is presumably the current human population of Earth (cf. X5.11, "The Lodger"). Our best guess is that the world turned into bottle-blond Mancunian wide-boys for 18 hours: it's still light when the wave hits humanity (Davies was careful to time the Queen's Speech and Donna's turkey for just before sunset); Wilf sees Earth from orbit just as the sun's rising over western Ireland (so, around 9.30am GMT) and Rassilon cures everyone of Simmness about an hour later.]

The Master seems only to be interested in the military potential of the Northern hemisphere, China and Europe in particular.

Thanks to Sarah Jane, the entire turning-the-world-into-Masters is written off as a technological misfire that 'gave everyone hallucinations'. [Is that remotely plausible? Surely there's droves of digital evidence proving otherwise. *SJA*: "Goodbye, Sarah Jane Smith" has her cover up a crisis by claiming that a 3D game promotion caused humanity to think a meteor was coming straight at them. It's a wonder there hasn't been more of a movement against tech in the Davies universe.]

Rassilon says that Gallifrey's history is a 'billion years' old. [Possibly hyperbole – "Hell Bent" looks

like this, but contradicts it in the dialogue, so we've no idea.]

• *The Time War.* The episode opens on a wartorn version of the world we saw in "The Sound of Drums". The Citadel's spherical barrier has been shattered, Dalek spaceships are embedded in the ground and, as seen from space, Gallifrey has been burned black.

The Doctor cites a number of entities in the War besides the Daleks: Skaro Degradations, the Horde of Travesties, the Nightmare Child, the Couldhavebeen King with his Army of Meanwhiles and Neverweres. [It's not clear which side these were all on.]

The war was so horrific that the Doctor obtained the Moment, an item able to stop both Time Lords and Daleks. [Here, it's implied that the Council gave it to him for safekeeping. "The Day of the Doctor" (X7.15) contradicts this and much else in this episode, but we have good reasons to believe that his entire timeline was altered *twice* in "The Name of the Doctor" (X7.14), allowing a whole extra incarnation he didn't recall in the episode before that. What little we hear of the Moment here suggests something more than just Billie Piper re-enacting the end of *Dark Star.*] In the War's heart, the temporal effects are killing and resurrecting millions of people every second.

The last prophecy of the War speaks of two children of Gallifrey outside the Time Lock [a fact upon which Rassilon capitalises], bound in the Enmity of Ages, and the word 'Earth' repeating many times.

Presumably, it isn't possible to initiate the Final Sanction from within the Time Lock. It entails the destruction of the Time Vortex, while the remaining Time Lords will lose physical form and become pure consciousness in a different cosmos. The Doctor wrecks/dislodges the white-point star, severing Gallifrey's link with reality and causing it to fall back into the Time Lock. [We'll next see the planet in "The Day of the Doctor" and – after some looking for it under the cushions – X9.11, "Heaven Sent."]

English Lessons

• *Triple rollover* (n.) the Lotto, formerly the National Lottery, was originally only run on Saturdays, then a midweek Wednesday one began. If nobody wins for three consecutive draws, the total amounts for all four are in the pot for one last go. It's usually won on the last go by multiple entrants who receive a split of the prize.

ABOUT TIME 2008-2009

The most any one ticket has won is £22 million, for a consortium (see X1.1, "Rose"), and the most an individual has won is £20m. Euromillions, a Friday lottery across the EU, provided a Scottish couple with £161 million about a year after this episode was broadcast.

Oh, Isn't That...?

• *Matt Smith* was, at this stage, vaguely known for *Party Animals* (sort of *This Life* for Spads), a cut scene from *In Bruges* where he beheads a police inspector in bad CGI, and the two Philip Pullman adaptations with Billie Piper as Sally Lockhart. He's got a higher profile now (you can guess why) and is mainly playing real people (Prince Phillip, Charles Manson, Robert Mapplethorpe, that sort of thing) despite not looking like any of them – or anyone else.

Things That Don't Make Sense ("The End of Time" Part One and Part Two)

Any accurate plot-summary of this story that you have read, or will ever read.

Oh all right. Let's instead begin with an oddity that several people noticed: who builds a radiation-containment compartment with the controls *inside* the venting chamber, meaning that if there's a crisis, it'll kill the operator?

For that matter, Wilf ended the first episode inside one of these booths, so he knows how they work. He has also heard about the "knock four times" thing twice. He's not normally forgetful, so changing the end of the story this way makes him look like a right git. Perhaps that's why the Doctor's such a prick about saving him.

Why did the Doctor regenerating at the end of "The Parting of the Ways" (X1.13) and "The Stolen Earth" just result in Rose looking a bit glum but here, and in "Twice Upon a Time" (X10.13), it's a TARDIS-wrecker? Has the Doctor got an inbuilt "innocent bystander" cut-out for turning into a firework display? (It's been suggested that the explosiveness of a regeneration is connected to how long the Doctor tries to hold it back, and that the Tennant and Capaldi incarnations simply fought the oncoming change for too long. That's possible, except that – following what we see in "Twice Upon a Time" – Ben and Polly ought to have been toasted in 4.2, "The Tenth Planet".)

# # #

Another "so huge you can't ignore it" snag, and one that requires some space to game it out... the Doctor becomes alarmed that Ood society has advanced to an unnatural degree, indicating history is out of whack. The cause of this is never revealed. We might infer that it's related to his tinkering with a Fixed Point at Bowie Base One, but that isn't said. (At least, not in the episode: Davies made sure that all the interviews included the idea that saving Adelaide caused this Doctor's death.) The aberrant society seems to survive at story's end, since its members sing the Doctor unto death, and the Ood remain time-sensitive in every subsequent appearance, so what, from their perspective, is the problem? What was the Doctor's crime that caused Ood Sigma to pop up in 2059?

And yet, the whole story seems to hinge on Ood Sigma's comment that the Doctor delayed too long in coming to fix this situation. This means the Doctor's timeline is synched with the Master's directly... well and good, but, unless being stored as data in the ring is counted towards his lifespan and exactly as long has elapsed while the Cult of Saxon dithered about as has elapsed for everything the Doctor has done since the *Titanic* crashed into the Console Room, there's no reason for this to matter. And if it does, then rupturing a Fixed Point is irrelevant.

Really, the only way that the Doctor's antics have any bearing on the time-line for the Ood is if the nightmares about Saxon began as a consequence of the preparations the Cult underwent in the days prior to the ritual. If so, for the Doctor, all that stuff with the Red Carnivorous Maw, Viperox Hordes, the Phosphorus Carousel, getting locked in the Tower of London with his past and future selves, meeting the Trickster, negotiating a peace-treaty between UNIT and the Zygons and changing his suit twice took place in (for him) an action-packed 18 hours after the Ood summoned him. (Maybe the Moment removes the events of "The Day of the Doctor" from the log, but it's still an absurd amount to squeeze in.)

Either way, the Doctor and Ood Sigma agree that the new Ood civilisation isn't more than a hundred years old. Siggy's in good shape himself, so Ood must have a long lifespan. (The economics of slavery make this slightly improbable, but never mind.) Their best psychic is called an "Elder", so he must be older than Ood Sigma. So where was he when the Ood were being enslaved or liberated (X4.3 "Planet of the Ood")? "Elder" could be a title (like the LDS, who have "Elders" who've barely started shaving), but he's also physically different. He'd have been culled, unless an unmentioned resistance movement hid him out in the tundra.

# # #

Another colossal problem to wrestle with...

The closing scene of Part One intimates that the Narrator, played by Timothy Dalton (i.e. the Lord President), has just given a version of the story we've been watching to the Gallifreyan High Council. Why would he do this? Why should events on Earth matter to them, prior to him and his council of creeps deciding that Earth is going to matter? Besides, the only people listening already know all of this anyway. Logically, he could only relate these events when they're stuck in amber in a miniature cosmos and he's about to start regenerating into Diamond Geezer ("Hell Bent") because the Master shot fireballs at him. And you thought Peter Capaldi's death-scene was verbose and protracted.

But then, something *weird* needs to have happened for the Time War to be happening live and direct, with the High Council worried about losing while sealed away from orthodox spacetime, yet also for the conflict to be long-finished. (That's despite the whole planet being frozen in time and hidden inside a *different* pocket-universe, per "The Day of the Doctor", minutes after the end of this story. Then someone from inside this perpetually-frozen Grecian Urn of a planet asks the Doctor if it can come out and play; X7.16, "The Time of the Doctor".)

... which is to say: the General's problem with one Doctor stealing the Moment is simultaneous with Beardy Guy telling Spitty Rassilon that the Doctor's done stole the Moment. Rather than act on this, he gets news of what the Doctor's going to do after the War's over, and opts to take advantage of Gallifrey being destroyed in order to, er, save Gallifrey. (He doesn't know anything about the "Cup-a-Soup" gambit and neither, oddly, does the Visionary. This presumably means that, somewhere, there's a rather embarrassed soothsayer. No wonder the General thinks that the High Council are idiots.) This only begins to make sense if the Master getting all Doctor Doomy on Rassilon's assilon somehow makes the entire eisteddfod of Time Lords abruptly and simultaneously go off the whole subliming-to-become-

beings-of-pure mind idea. And then time stops for them until they (somehow) come out of stasis and wonder where the universe – and all those Dalek warships – went.

# # #

A round of trivial details: snow on New Year's Day 2005 in London; Wilf suddenly knowing the word "metacrisis" despite never having heard it. When Spooky Claire shows up in the Queen's Speech, she somehow makes the recording of the "God Save the Queen" turn into "My County 'Tis of Thee". There's an extra note in the last bar that grates on the ears of anyone who hears it. (Generations of Commonwealth citizens have grumbled when this happens in overseas sporting events anyone from Britain wins. The BBC made Her Majesty's Message to the Commonwealth – as it's formally called – until they committed a transgression far less ghastly than this.) Wilf does the washing-up on what we'll agree is Christmas Eve, and there's a thunderstorm outside. Minutes later, the whole of London is bone-dry and delicate blossom is on the trees.

It's again questionable (X3.1, "Smith and Jones") that snogging a Time Lord would leave an indelible DNA print, but it's bonkers to resurrect one from this and not get any of the animals or plants used in her lipstick thrown into the mix. Harold Saxon is more likely to be reborn as a bee than his old self.

The Master has the Doctor confirm the drumming is real via forcible telepathy through the medium of a head-butt (at last, casting a Scotsman as the Doctor makes sense). Okay, but why didn't he try that during the Year That Wasn't (X3.12, "The Sound of Drums"; X3.13, "Last of the Time Lords")? A stealth-helicopter sneaks up on the wasteground and Naismith's goons abduct the Master – except that whatever muffling-device they use doesn't work when you're directly underneath.

Naismith, a billionaire with connections to Torchwood, and who must also have anticipated the Cult of Saxon, identifies the Master as the perfect candidate to repair an immortality device – but utterly fails to consider that "Saxon" would have his own use for the alien tech.

We probably shouldn't question the Master's motives for turning everyone on Earth into himself – it's the Master we're talking about, after all – but it's remarkable that the human-Masters all defer to the Master-prime. (To be fair, a few cut scenes addressed this, but it's not quite the *Gremlins* scenario one might expect.) Actually, if the Master replicates himself into humanity, why don't they *all* become glowing skeletons who fire energy bolts? And what happened to those guards who stood ready to shoot him at the drop of a hat?

Logically, as it's different times of day all around the world (although The Mill never got the hang of that, and have shown Beijing in broad daylight), people will have been doing different things when transformed. A small but significant percentage will have been having sex or giving birth, several hundred would have been undergoing surgery, almost a billion would have been under five years old and about a quarter would have been out of the loop on whatever cover-story Mr Smith devised simply through not having phones or tellies. But neither this nor a planet popping up on the same day has any lasting consequences on human society. Sarah Jane's cover story is cute, but daft.

Obama's at the White House on Christmas Day. Not Hawaii, not Camp David, he's the first President since FDR to stick around. Did he get Congressional approval for whatever economic rabbit he's going to pull from a hat? What *was* his plan? Trinity Wells thinks it's something huge to do with the very nature of commerce. America was apparently going to do it unilaterally, expecting the rest of the world to follow although it relies on them knowing about it. The United States adopting show-tunes as currency (or whatever) is pointless if nobody else plays along.

What exactly is going on with the Vinvocci that they need a device capable of rewriting the biology of entire planets, especially since this one hasn't, it seems, gone missing in a war? Rossiter and Addams are scavengers, not frontline personnel. Is this some kind of racial purity thing? Side note to say that the Doctor failed to identify the Vinvocci on sight in the first episode, but accurately attests to the radiation-absorbing potential of their glass in the second.

Triumphant, Rassilon appears at Naismith's pad accompanied by just four people, two of whom are the only dissenters to his scheme left alive. This decision forms the key to the Woman in White's plan – so she, at least, saw it coming. Even a couple of Chancellery Guards with Patrol Stasers ("The Deadly Assassin"; 15.6, "The Invasion of Time" and others) would have added some extra pomp and stopped the Master.

How does Spooky Claire contact Wilf? She's inside the Time Lock, although contacting the outside world requires several paradoxes and prophecies, yet she wanders in and out of Wilf's consciousness as she pleases. And what *was* her goal, exactly? Was her purpose all along just to ensure that the Doctor would have a revolver on hand to destroy the white-point star with? If so, how did she know he'd need to do that? She starts chatting to Wilf about the importance of being armed before the Visionary tells Rassilon that the solution lies in his bling.

The scenes of Gallifrey from space don't match the CGI shots of it from Earth at all. This being a Christmas episode, The Mill have screwed up celestial dynamics more than normal. Just before our first sight of The Narrator, there's a shot where the sun moves behind the Earth and the stars stay still. That's right, we're in a Geocentric worldview, as if the last 500 years never happened.

Hrm, Gallifrey seen above Earth... no matter whether the Doctor restores the correct orbit, the effect of a mass at least as big as Earth's coming that close is pretty Old Testament. It's been suggested often enough that Gallifrey's gravity is the same as Earth's (Romana talks about "Earth-normal" gravity, and Leela's knees don't buckle or anything). So we'll assume that, despite its size and the fact that there's a thumping great black hole under the Panopticon set (all together now) "in an eternally dynamic equation against the mass of the planet" ("The Deadly Assassin"), it has the same mass as Earth. The least you'd expect is unusually high tides. The most likely outcome is that Gallifrey and Earth would orbit a common centre of mass, and spin around facing each other in a captured rotation.

Yes, but when Gallifrey goes away just as suddenly, Earth would whizz off in whatever direction it happened to be travelling in – into the Sun, away from the Sun, off the plane of the ecliptic entirely (if Gallifrey arrived above or below that plane) and henceforth the length of a year would change. Gallifrey is, apparently, there for about 20 minutes, during which time it is always shown moving rapidly across Earth's sky (which, from Chiswick, is always sunny even when in eclipse from its new neighbour) – yet when both worlds are seen from space, Earth is always between Gallifrey and the Sun and it's night-time in Europe.

[Back-of-envelope time: if Earth orbits the Sun at 107,000 km/h, then in that 20 minutes, it was whipping around that common axis in an arc almost a third of its own diameter. That's enough to make a big impact on the orbit. Not as damaging as lugging it from the Medusa Cascade in normal space, but bad enough for people to start thinking about long-term solutions such as "sibbernetic" surgery a la 4.2, "The Tenth Planet" or hiding in caves for millions of years per 7.2, "Doctor Who and the Silurians". We'll assume that the TARDIS put it back, as one of many scenes in the "reward" sequence we don't see.]

Of course, Earth is close to Perihelion on Boxing Day – we usually get closest to the Sun around 3rd January – so there's a remote possibility that this abrupt change in angular momentum might be damped down to acceptable levels, if such a thing exists. Even so, they could just rip each other apart with tidal forces, and both become part of a new asteroid belt with the Moon as the biggest single lump. (Oh yes, the Moon might well have been flung into deep space. That's a bit of a continuity worry too.)

Nobody questions that a WWII service revolver can kill a Time Lord, even one famous for his tenacity and terrifying power when dead for ten million years. Everyone seems to think that the Doctor only has one bullet in the revolver. And the one *everyone* mentioned at the time: how many times does he cock the gun without ever firing it? Moreover, it takes the Master ages to figure out that shooting a diamond will easily fix everything and he doesn't do it himself with his mysteriously-restored zapping powers.

Remember that massive list of things under **Things That Don't Make Sense** in "Journey's End") that Donna can't think about, lest she knock over everyone in the vicinity with a forceblast? At her wedding here, how do they avoid anyone (especially Nerys) mentioning the bizarre events of her first attempt? And, this last time, the Doctor and the TARDIS are in her line of sight.

Verity Newman's book got into print despite UNIT, Torchwood, the Alliance of Shades, Sarah Jane Smith and Martha Smith-Jones having reason to stop it. But, good on her, she succeeded, then seems surprised when someone comes along and wants it signed to "the Doctor".

Critique ("The End of Time" Part One and Part Two) At the time it was easy to criticise this story, to pull apart the topical and then-fashionable elements, the writer's tendencies and the way the production had to "perform" within the BBC's overall strategy. Above all, the way a number of features that were fresh and exciting in 2005 (then expected, then comforting, then confining) were here taking a bow made it easy to give a functional account of the two and a quarter hours of television, and how people responded to it in 2009/10. Now, it's not so clear-cut. We have a relic, an object left behind, that looks increasingly bizarre and, frankly, "special" in as many senses as the word supports.

The things that were singular and commented upon at the time are still remarkable. This story has a cast like no other. Many of these are in significant roles, rather than being frittered away in cameos-for-their-own-sake. The nearest to a throwaway is June Whitfield as Minnie, and even this is an aspect of what the story did most spectacularly right: placing Wilf at the drama's core. The entire nation loves Bernard Cribbins, but this was a reminder that he'd earned that over for decades by playing vulnerable men as well as voicing puppets and performing comic songs. (Non-British viewers might find it easier to accept him in a straight, unsympathetic role, but his turn in Hitchcock's *Frenzy* seems almost blasphemous to us.) If anything, this story cashes a cheque written in 1970, when he was Mr Perkins in *The Railway Children* – another humble man with wounded pride. He is the ideal identification figure here, because his own daughter infantilises him (the red hat was another point where children took to him as one of their own), and he was denied military glory but he could, even now, step up and be a hero.

This is partially undermined by the late decision to make Wilf, not a "rando" technician, the one trapped in the radioactive chamber. The original idea, the Doctor atoning for his comments about "little people" when saving Adelaide Brooks, was better. Hubris, as demonstrated in the Doctor's sin against time, is resolved by sacrificing himself for someone he didn't even know. The quasi-mythic way in which this Doctor's end has been presented to us – with prophesies left, right and centre, powerful beings setting up bizarre coincidences and the whole cosmos having the same nightmare – demanded more contrition.

The narrative presents the Doctor's transgression on Mars and eventual regeneration as causally related, with all the peculiar events in between as symptoms of time going wrong. Yet there is no logical link, just aesthetic associations. We have a procession of incidents, increasingly weird and abruptly shifting in tone, that feels like storytelling but needs outrageous nudges (dreams, hallucinations, improbable choices of book, Wilf's comically unlikely success in finding the Doctor, psychic "smelling" of Time Lords…) to move the Doctor from place to place without him exerting himself to find things out.

Those incidents, though, are the most remarkable collision of the various things *Doctor Who* can do we've seen since "Planet of the Spiders". Somehow, nothing in this story seems out of place, even when they slam together Gallifrey and Chiswick with such merry abandon. Bringing back the villain's mansion locale for the first time since, um, "K9 & Company" (18.7a) or, more legitimately, "The Stones of Blood" (16.3) 30 years earlier was, like the near-future setting of the previous story, a way to refresh the series. Infusing the old settings within the types of thing that were not possible back then was reassuring to older fans, but a revelation to anyone who'd joined since 2005. Only fleeting moments of fanwankery cropped up before the end of Series 3, but Davies became increasingly shameless once he knew that the public were with him. The use of old *Doctor Who* as one more ingredient among the Hollywood blockbusters, soap opera set-pieces and topical commentary hadn't alienated the viewers – a high-street chain of second-hand media and electronics had a poster of Davros rocking out with an iPod – but he knew how far to go too far.

He also knew how to use these images in the service of character-development. Even if we have qualms about the plot-mechanics, as a way to round off the progression of various semi-regulars, this story's processes do exactly as required. Most alarming, if welcome, is the Donna-Sylvia dynamic: Donna never got to stand up to her domineering mother on screen, but Sylvia has gone from hectoring to protecting her daughter and, in an unforeseen turn of events, actually seems to be praying to the Doctor when Gallifrey materialises overhead. Donna gets a legitimate happy ending, Wilf gets to ride in the TARDIS, Martha and Mickey get the life they might have got if the actors had been available for *Torchwood* and so on. Whatever our reaction to the "reward" sequence, it's rooted inside the everyday (for most of the characters).

We've seen the same thing attempted again and

executed far less well, so it's less irksome to those it irked on New Year's Day 2010. For anyone who wasn't grinding their teeth on first broadcast, this sequence is a reminder of when practically everyone in Britain knew the names of all these characters and most of the actors. Similarly, the Ood sequences are superfluous and a bit hokey but, for Joe Public (especially the kids), it's great to see them back. For anyone who had – mysteriously – never seen *Doctor Who* before, or wasn't up to speed on the story so far, this sequence is a necessary info-dump, but done with more style than it needed. Their use as all-purpose sight-gag aliens in later stories might have taken the shine off them, but at the time it was right and proper.

With Tennant's departure such big news, anything less than epic would have been frustrating. Closing the storyline of the Time War, allowing the Master a moment of heroism, rounding-off the stories of former companions and indicating that time itself has gone wrong are what we expected. The unexpected parts are what stand out now: the Silver Cloak, the Master becoming everyone and "Obama" all look, with hindsight, in keeping with the farting fatties in 10 Downing Street or the Titanic colliding with Buckingham Palace.

That bravura cheekiness, more akin to a CBBC series than any of the imported US superheroes or space-opera shows, all seems to belong in the same story as Rassilon and the Untempered Schism. This is much harder than it looks. If the balance is off, favouring fannish "scenes we would like to see" or domestic/invasion silliness and celebrity cameos, it can all come crashing down. Davies risked that here more than at any time since Eccleston, and just about got away with it. The result has improved with age, unlike any other Christmas Special.

The Lore

Written by Russell T Davies. Directed by Euros Lyn. Viewing figures for Part One: (BBC1) 11.57 million, (HD) 0.47 million, (BBC3) 1.18 million, (BBC1 repeat ahead of Part Two) 2.24 million. Viewing figures for Part Two: (BBC1) 11.79 million, (HD) 0.48 million, (BBC3) 1.21 million. AIs 87% and 89% (first transmission), 89% (both episodes on BBC3 first time), 90% and 89% (second BBC1 run).

These two were shown again in mid-January on BBC3 (after the one-week window that got them added to the consolidated ratings back then), and again on BBC1 just ahead of Series 5's start. There were also 1.3 million hits for both episodes on iPlayer that week, itself a new record. The combined ratings for Part Two made it the most-watched thing that week, which was only the third time this had happened since 1963 (it'll become more common for a while over the next few years).

BBC America broke records with their first showings (on Boxing Day and 2nd January respectively) and the US iTunes store logged these two episodes as the top two bestsellers that week. Even Australia's ABC2 grabbed 0.8 million viewers opposite a cricket match (although Ross Noble knocked it out of the Top Thirty for that day, 15th February, 2010).

Repeats and Overseas Promotion *Das Ende Der Zeit, La Prophétie de Noël.*

Alternate versions When BBC America shows this at all, it's as a three-hour compilation with just slight – and odd – trims coming out of advert breaks. The most obvious is the start of Part Two, with the crashed Dalek spaceship at the base of the Capitol, and that shot of the Narrator walking along a bridge in the blackness gone (a bit of a shame as more time, money and thought went into them than into whole Colin Baker stories). We also lose Lucy's lipstick-wiping as part of the resurrection of the Master. They cut straight from Wilf's Tommy Cooper impression and "Oh blimey!" to him wandering the ship and finding Spooky Claire. France4 has, on occasion, run one episode or the other in the middle of Matt Smith reruns apparently at random, usually in the same edits as the original but saying things like *je ne veux pas mon renée* ("I don't want my rebirth").

Production

• David Tennant was the most popular Doctor since Tom Baker. Russell T Davies was the biggest thing to happen to *Doctor Who* since Sydney Newman. Leaving quietly, in either case, wasn't on the menu. Davies was relying on his usual mix of half-formed thoughts from years (or decades) back and last-minute inspiration to provide a compelling narrative. He had seeded ideas well in advance, such as the Master's ring, without any coherent plan or even any confidence that it would be him using these as plot-devices. The

Time Lords returning as villains was inherent in the well-established concept that the Doctor had destroyed Gallifrey during the Time War, but needed teasing out. However, Davies was adamant that detailing the horrors of this war would be unacceptably dark for a family series and remove some of the potency of the semi-legendary final combat.

• Another key idea, one he'd nursed from the start, was that this Doctor would die saving relatively insignificant people. From this, the whole notion of hubris causing the Doctor into this position developed, adding a layer to what became "The Waters of Mars". Who those people would be changed over the course of six months. A family of alien refugees in a beaten-up spaceship, possibly escaping a brush-war elsewhere in the galaxy, seems to have been front-runner for a while. Elements of this remain in the Vinvocci storyline, although their similarity to Bannakaffalatta (X4.0, "Voyage of the Damned") was a late addition, once the old idea of the melty-face aliens (also in the gestation of what became X4.1, "Partners in Crime") was abandoned.

Instead, an otherwise overlooked member of the cast would be trapped in the final conflagration and the Doctor would save him or her and be forced to regenerate. This led to the Nuclear Bolt concept. "Keith", the technician stuck in the booth, would knock four times to be let out. However, when checking on the availability of former regulars for the "reward" scenes, it became clear that Catherine Tate could do more than one scene, so Wilf became the obvious candidate both for the one-off companion role and the person whom the Doctor would save. This in turn meant that the original idea of him reuniting his old skiffle-band to hunt aliens on the sly came back as the Silver Cloak.

• Seeking a Doctor-sized problem to cause all of this led to a notion that the Time Lords and the Daleks were conspiring to destroy the Universe as the only way out of stalemate. This might have introduced the Dalek Parliament (see X7.1, "Asylum of the Daleks" for how this could have panned out), but as the previous season finales had almost all involved the Daleks, this was considered too obvious.

•The Master returning had legs (literally and figuratively), but this time he would have to be on the back foot. One notion, based on a scam in the documentary series *The Real Hustle*, was for the newly-reborn Master to dress as a waiter and steal

329

ABOUT TIME 2008-2009

someone's credit card. Had a new actor played the Master, this might have worked, but everyone was excited by the prospect of John Simm as a more desperate, feral Master. So, this plotline was repurposed for the third episode of *TW: Children of Earth* (although why a posh restaurant would have a waiter in trackie-dacks and a T-shirt is never questioned). Davies sounded Simm out on the prospect of a return, and warned him that hair-dye would be involved.

The Master's fight-back was envisaged as more like the Joker (as played by Heath Ledger) than a Bond-Villain, but the idea of him climbing back to power came with the idea of him subverting UNIT from within. This led to notions of Geneva as the location for the climax. One wild idea Davies floated in his emails to Benjamin Cook was Julie Andrews as a Bond villain. The conceit of the Master turning everyone on Earth into him was there long before the idea of bringing back Gallifrey; Davies thought of the Time Lords being brought out of limbo as a straight swap – Earth for Gallifrey – and as a temptation for the Doctor. Meanwhile, without saying so in as many words, Steven Moffat made it known that the Daleks' return in Series 5 (or "Series 1", as the BBC's publicity was calling it) would be better if they hadn't been on screen for a while.

• The start of Part Two would have included more detail of the various Masters adopting elements of the host-bodies' personalities; Abigail-Master (as designated in the script) would flirt with the original, Obama-Master would be told "no, don't do the accent, no" and so on. A number of scenes were trimmed lightly, to cut down on the effects budget. "The Waters of Mars" had undergone a similar process to release funds for this story, but Davies actively considered having all the original actors cast as Naismith, Danes, the UNIT general et al playing the Master – the mind installed, but the physical appearance unchanged.

By the time Part Two was submitted, line-producer Tracie Simpson had found that "Planet of the Dead" had underspent by £30,000, so some effects money could be spent (as well as on set-construction, extras and so on). The logistics of the former regulars returning for their cameos was another worry: the decision was made that if one couldn't make it, the whole lot would be ditched. Davies and Gardner wanted Euros Lyn to direct, but that required him to go straight from the five-part *Children of Earth* to this. It took a lot of sweet-

talk to get an agreement.

• The final Tone Meeting (key-note word: "The Best") was on 20th March, with Davies sardonically sporting his OBE and flashing the medal at people to pull rank. Five days later, the read-through marked the start of a two-month shoot, finally ending with pick-ups on 3rd June (by which time Davies and Gardner had upped sticks to LA). The shoot officially began on 30th March, but while the rewrites after the read-through were being collated, a scene was shot in Blackwell's, the University bookshop in Cardiff, on 21st. This was the sequence of Verity Newman signing copies of *Impossible Things*, brought forward to accommodate Jessica Hynes (who was flying to New York the following day to appear in the Broadway production of *The Norman Conquests*). *The Sun* got wind of this (hardly a secret) and conflated it with the idea of JK Rowling appearing (floated by Davies a couple of Christmases before) into a report that this was the whole of the two-part story. In fact, the sequence was such a small component, Lyn left it out of one of the original edits. Neither Davies nor Gardner noticed until he pointed it out to them.

• The shoot began properly in one of the very first locations used in 2004: Tredegar House (which doubled for 10 Downing Street in X1.4, "Aliens of London", the start of a long association with the series). For once, it was being used as an interior *and* exterior location, beginning with Wilf and the Doctor sneaking past guards and the TARDIS landing in the stables (the same ones where Jackson Lake acclimated to not being the Doctor after all).

The extras playing guards were (for obvious reasons) all the same height and build, but (for less obvious reasons) wore visors as part of the uniforms. A whole subplot about how polarised goggles or visors allowed people to see the Master's true form, his skeletal self, was excised; only a few shots of Simm turning into Skeletor remain. (These were laborious to record, as Simm's face was dotted with the silver balls used for cake-decoration – X2.11, "Fear Her" – to match the alignment of the computer-modelled skull. Removing these shots except where absolutely necessary sped up the storytelling, saving man-hours of modelling for the many other effects this story needed.) However, the visors helped to reduce the number of John Simms needed. Ed Thomas had designed wallpaper with the

Naismith crest in silver on black but, on seeing it, Davies opted not to have it in other scenes.

• The Vinvocci made their debut on Day Three, with a complicated make-up that took over two hours to add, but which subtly blended the green of the spikes with a more humanoid pink for the faces. This looked fine in close up, but long shots made it seem as if actors were wearing punk wigs, so the first scenes shot of the aliens in mufti were digitally altered to make them all-green. For some of the "worst escape ever", the Doctor was replaced by a latex dummy – even without his recent back surgery, Tennant was unlikely to want to spend multiple takes being jolted around in an odd position strapped to a glorified wheelbarrow. Gordon Seed, by now Tennant's regular stunt-double, was in the mix, and close-ups were the star, not entirely faking the wincing. In the basement (familiar as Cassandra's base from X2.1, "New Earth"), the Vinvocci transformation scenes were shot using an old-fashioned blue screen (the one drawback with green aliens).

• Noel Clarke was making films, and Freema Agyeman was in Chris Chibnall's *Law & Order: UK*, so there weren't many days when they were both free. On Saturday, 4th April, they were on hand to run around the slab yards of the Corus steelworks in Newport, Gwent. They, with Tennant and Dan Starkey (as a Sontaran named "Jask" in the script), were the only people not wearing hard hats, goggles and work-boots. Elsewhere on the complex, in a section moth-balled and due for redevelopment, scenes of the *Hesperus*'s engine-room were shot the same day. Claire Bloom's white suit had to be kept immaculate between takes. (Yes, Claire Bloom in a steel-works in Newport. And breathe.)

• The next week, the usual location of Nant Fawr Road was turned into Chiswick. While Tennant was in London (this was the week leading up to broadcast of "Planet of the Dead"), Simm came to the kitchen to shake his head and dress up as Donna's mum and boyfriend. His first few head-shakes were a little over-emphatic and caused him a bit of pain, but after trials the camera team had found the optimum number of frames to cut out. The various actors turning into the Master and Simm himself could move their heads fairly gently, and it would look violent. (The optimum was found to be to shoot four frames per second instead of 25.) Nonetheless, as Simm had to do more of it than anyone, he landed up needing a trip to an osteopath.

For the remainder of the day the interior scenes of the Silver Cloak's bus were shot, with tinsel inside the vehicle to cover for the fact that the streets weren't decorated and partially mask that it was a spring day with blossom on the trees. It was also handy for obscuring that the bus was simply driving around the block several times.

• On Good Friday, the team went to Penarth, starting in back-alleys for several Masters closing in on Donna (with stunt performers Sarah Frantzl and Paul Herbert taking the falls), then on a familiar part of Clinton Road for Luke Smith walking into traffic. The scene of the Masters approaching Donna is one of the few times they used the John Simm masks prepared by Millennium, other than in very long shots. On dummies they looked plausible, but very few actors have Simm's bone-structure. With the first Special being premiered in Cardiff and shown on Saturday, Tennant and Tate filled in for Jonathan Ross on his Radio Two weekend show (with special guest John Barrowman).

• Easter Monday was the occasion for a very public shoot at the Kardomah café in Swansea. Just in case the passers-by failed to spot anything unusual, the team had erected one of the London Credit Bank signs from Donna's first story and festooned the café with tinsel. Oh, and Catherine Tate was out in the street arguing with a Traffic Warden (June Campbell), very overdressed for the warm weather. This was her last shot in *Doctor Who*, and she returned to work on the Jack Black version of *Gulliver's Travels* in Greenwich.

• Tuesday the 14th was the day at Cardiff Docks, specifically a tract seen in X2.5, "Rise of the Cybermen" pretending to be London wasteland and several times since. Here is where the Silver Cloak interrupted the Doctor's pursuit of the Master. June Whitfield seems to have enjoyed the bum-fondling scene.

Meanwhile, a big announcement about Steven Moffat's team caused a slight blip in production of this story as Tracie Simpson – up until then producing this story day-to-day – left to set up Series 5. Eventually Peter Bennett came in, but in the interim Julie Gardner took over, retaining her executive producer status for post-production. She was already gearing up for her next job, running the Los Angeles office of BBC America. Her first day in the unexpected temporary job was on the same part of Taffs Wells Quarry that had been the surface of Mars in the previous episode, now painted white (as far as the camera

ABOUT TIME 2008-2009

showed) and festooned with paper snow. The next day, 17th April, was a night-shoot at Wookey Hole. This entailed a lot of equipment being moved by hand down narrow passages (as you will recall from 12.5, "Revenge of the Cybermen"), and it got very cold and stuffy, even with all the candles and incense-burners. The shoot went on for nearly nine hours, then Tennant emerged to celebrate his birthday.

Saturday night was another late start (without Tennant), this time at the same Traffic Management Centre used as UNIT HQ in "The Stolen Earth", but now staffed almost entirely by multiple Masters. The Simm masks were used sparingly here. The same complex was also Beijing SAC. On Monday night, the Doctor arrived too late at Broadfell Prison (not a million miles from the bit of Paget Road where a Dalek zapped him in "The Stolen Earth"); Tennant had been in the TARDIS during the day recording a Davies-scripted skit for John Barrowman's Saturday Night show *Tonight's the Night*.

The crew, with Cribbins and Bloom, recorded the pre-credit sequence that evening, starting in Penarth. St Augustine's Church has a very distinctive pattern of polychromatic brickwork, less recognisable in the shots used here. As it's a Grade 1 Listed Building the stained glass, also by William Butterfield, wasn't really altered to include a police box (The Mill did that). Back north-east a mile or two to Cardiff city centre (Wharton Street), for Wilf's shopping expedition, the brass band seems to have been the same local Salvation Army band who had re-recorded "God Rest Ye Merry, Gentleman" that afternoon. Murray Gold also hired a choir to sing a Latin valediction to the Doctor, set to a melody he had used for River Song's death in X4.9, "Forest of the Dead".

• Two more days of Simm yelling in waste ground followed. These were back at the Mir plant in Newport, at the smelting works in thick noxious dust. The first day, 21st April, started with a demonstration of how they'd spend the second – the elaborate helicopter scene was to be shot without a helicopter, but with a huge wind machine and actors in helmets. Everyone needed to see it in daylight without the fan before attempting it when nobody could hear or see anything. What was actually recorded that day was the Master gnawing on rags and bones, then the Doctor walking as the Master fired energy-bolts at him. Among the explosions going on

behind Tennant was a squib on his chest, wrecking one of the jackets he'd wore since the start of his Doctorate.

Day two also began at 7.00pm, with – among other things – the Doctor encountering the non-existent choppers. There were two cranes involved. One had a searchlight, a rotating red light on a pole and a wire-crew as used for the opening of "Tooth and Claw" (X2.2) in a cage. The other had a camera and swooped around getting helicopter POV shots. Off to the side, Hargreaves had the giant blower and operated the squibs for gunfire, Faulja Singh and Gary Georgiov supervised the firearms and Bob Schofield oversaw the wire-work. The people in the lighting cage were up for almost ten hours with one break. The most risky part was Paul Herbert, as the unconscious Master, held by the two men on wires but having to be limp.

• Another slightly inaccessible location was used on Monday 27th, when Caerphilly Castle doubled for HMP Broadfell. The vaulted ceiling they needed was in a gate-house with a spiral staircase as its only access. It was also draughty and damp on a miserable day. Simm's part of this was recorded the following day at Upper Boat; he needed to wear a wig that looked like his normal hair, which had to be kept on in the face of another huge wind-machine. A big event that day was the debut of the new Time Lord costumes, photographed against a black screen just outside the door of the TARDIS set.

• Back on April Fool's Day, the production team had told the press that President Obama was going to be in the Christmas episode. Nobody bought this story, but Roger Haynes – a reasonable facsimile – was at Cardiff City Hall on 28th for the cheeky press conference scene. After this, Julie Gardner directed a second unit of John Simm in 32 costumes (he hated the tights) over four hours while Lyn was at the familiar venue, Tiger Tiger, for the Zaggit Zaggoo scene. (You'll recall this bar from the start of this book, as well as a few *Torchwood* episodes.) For this, the team were joined by John Barrowman, Russell Tovey and Jimmy Vee, plus the Mears/Kasey combo and Ailsa Berk.

While everyone else was away the studio set-dressers had reconfigured the *Hesperus* set to make the flight deck, which is where the next day's work took place. The Doctor disabling the ship was the last time Tennant would use the sonic screwdriver until the 50th anniversary episode. The Tommy Cooper gesture when Wilf suggests a bit of "flim-flam" was improvised on set, as was Cribbins's dialogue during the gun-turret sequence. Cribbins and Lawry Lewin spent Saturday shooting down missiles. The gun-turrets worked almost as they seemed to and the actors operated the controls for the hydraulics. Cribbins ad-libbed the dialogue. Also that day the Doctor's jump from the ship was begun, with Gordon Seed in some shots. Tennant, after playing host to various family-members, returned briefly to London to record the first session of "Dreamland" on Bank Holiday Monday.

This was the first day on the vast Gate Room set, taking up Studio 6 of Upper Boat. This was Turkey Day, when the scripted snack for the Master turned into undercranked recording of Simm eating a whole roasted fowl, spitting each mouthful into a concealed bucket to save time and hiccups. The smell lingered as scenes of the Vinvocci in human disguises and the Naismiths drinking to their victory were taped.

• On Tuesday, 5th May, the Master freed himself from his straightjacket (with the aid of six off-screen technicians with wires) and vaulted into the Gate (impersonated by a tennis-ball on a stick for eyelines, with Peter Bennett supervising the shot). Matt Smith was along, to see what he'd let himself in for in between being measured for suit-adjustments, but Davies was in London getting a work visa at the American Embassy (he and Bennett spent the next day hosting the press launch of *Torchwood: Children of Earth*). On Thursday, Simm and Tennant joined Davies on the TARDIS set, to shoot the cover for the extended version of *The Writers' Tale*.

• A 12-hour session on Monday 11th began the eighth week of this marathon, with Tennant and Cribbins performing the intense scene of Wilf's release from the glass booth on a closed set. Other scenes were being shot elsewhere in the building; Gardner supervised the second unit. Meanwhile, some additional material was added, as Smith's first lines as the "New Man" were officially included in the script. Davies had just ended with a line about the New Man emerging, but Moffat had a whole scene and Lyn had some complex shots from above the Console to add to the general mayhem. Blocking the main event, the two-hander with the Doctor and Wilf, took a while and there were multiple angles from which to shoot it. The skeleton crew found it gruelling;

Tennant's video diary has him simply retreating to his trailer to recuperate from the emotion and physical effort. Over lunch, everyone in the production team took part in a video performing "(I'm Gonna Be) 500 Miles" for Tennant (now on YouTube).

• As if this hadn't been intense enough for Tennant, next morning he began regenerating. Lyn shot four versions of the last line, shifting between stoicism and self-pity, and selected the second. There was then the small matter of blowing up the Console Room, which required everyone else in safety gear, and Tennant to stand very still as flaming debris fell around his precisely-calculated mark. Just in case this wasn't weird enough, Timothy Dalton had come for a fitting and watched the shoot.

The set was cleared, everyone thinking that Matt Smith would need a bit of privacy to compose himself before making his debut. Unfortunately, this meant that everyone was milling around outside, on precisely the tarmac strip from his trailer to the set, so he walked a gauntlet of a few hundred people. One of these was Davies, who wanted to give the new star space, so made a point of not approaching him. Smith, on the other hand, wanted to introduce himself, so a slightly awkward conversation ensued where Davies claims he was mainly preoccupied by someone else being in Tennant's suit.

• As we mentioned, the Gate Room set was enormous. Only half of it was in Naismith's mansion (with the red flock wallpaper chosen instead of the original); the rest was the Cavernous White Void of Rassilon. On the 13th, Tennant and Simm greeted Dalton's arrival – in full regalia – by performing the James Bond theme, to which Dalton added "diddly-dum"s. This was the day when the Doctor crashed the reunion, so the floor was covered in rubbery shards of silica glass. Some of the fall was performed by Gordon Seed, some was Tennant on a small rostrum five feet over a crash-mat in the car-park. Dalton hadn't really watched *Doctor Who* since the Hartnell days, but had caught an episode of the BBC Wales version in LA and been impressed, then won over by the ambition and tone-shifts of the script for this story. Word of his casting, and Bloom's, was now out. Tennant was now confirmed as the new host of PBS's *Masterpiece Contemporary* slot for repackaged BBC, ITV and Channel 4 dramas.

• The team were in London for the next couple of days: on the Rodney Estate in Southwark.

Simm and various Simm-alikes shot the scenes of Winston's tower-block being over-run by Masters. They managed all of this without anyone noticing. Tennant, Davies, Gardner and Phil Collinson had a dinner at Claridge's. Collinson was to take over *Coronation Street* in Salford, the rest were leaving for America. The following night an exhausted Billie Piper took time out from Belle duties to reunite with Camille Coduri on the Powell Estate (as usual, the Brandon Estate in Kennington, but for the first time in nearly four years). The area needed to be filled with fake snow, to the now-familiar irritation of a few residents. One insisted on walking her Siberian Husky through a take, yelling "Bollocks to the lot of yer!" Davies was still making travel plans but getting texts from Coduri, and the atmosphere on location was, appropriately if improbably, festive. Needless to say, news of this "surprise" cameo broke quickly.

A weekend off and then back to Upper Boat to complete the White Void scenes from Monday (18th) for two and a bit days. Tuesday was a whole day of the Doctor pointing guns at people, which Tennant found unsettling. Wednesday, 20th May was Tennant's last official day as the Doctor. There was still *The Sarah Jane Adventures* to come, but he ended this story's work with some none-too-dignified green-screen work for the Doctor's plummet from the *Hesperus* "like an un-cool Spider-Man", as he put it. Then he walked off. Bennett called him back, on the pretext of a lighting set-up, to celebrate the Golden Wrap. Tennant tried to be stoic and British (claiming he'd changed his mind about leaving).

It didn't entirely end there. The following day had the team once again borrow the HTV studio at Culverhouse Cross (see Volume 7) to make use of their big black curtains for the High Council's deliberations. Tennant, in London, shot the BBC1 Christmas idents with a reindeer and, of course, paper-snow. A second and final day of black void shenanigans, 22nd, formally ended the shoot (barring a few pick-up shots on 3rd June). Davies was by now packing to move to Venice Beach.

The White Void set became the venue for the wrap party. (Some of which was recorded on special keepsake discs, including *The Ballad of Russell and Julie* – a parody piece, featuring Tennant, Tate and John Barrowman. It's available on YouTube.) Tennant got a sonic screwdriver prop, one of the six made. Later, he was allowed to have some keepsakes after the shoot: a brown suit; a blue suit; the tux; all in case he found himself coming back for a hypothetical Anniversary multi-Doctor story in four years. There was also a coveted gold *Blue Peter* badge. Cribbins received a picture commemorating his status as longest-serving companion (1966-2009). Simm kept one of the masks and Davies had a small Davros model. Photos of Dalton in Presidential regalia leaked from this bash.

• Neither was it entirely over *then*. On the following Monday, Tennant went on location to start work of *The Sarah Jane Adventures* (see A7, "The Wedding of Sarah Jane Smith"). As if to prove that the old order was changing, the next big news was Karen Gillan's casting (X4.2, "The Fires of Pompeii") as an as-yet-un-named companion for the new Doctor on 27th. On 3rd June, the TARDIS – no longer needed for *SJA* – took a bit more of a beating, including exterior shots of the windows smashing and some more flaming chaos inside. There were a few other insert shots (the Master's ring dropping into a chalice), but mainly this was helicopter day, when all the aerial shots of the Bristol Channel and Tredegar House were taken for the *Hesperus*'s wild ride.

By 11th of that month, a first edit of Part One (still called "The Final Day of Planet Earth", festively) was beamed across the Atlantic for Davies and Gardner to watch. Their departure had raised the usual press interest in a *Doctor Who* feature film, but would also, briefly, be the topic of a series of ten-minute podcasts for BBC Wales Radio. Just over a week later, Part Two was submitted for their approval in a 75-minute edit (lacking Verity). These still needed music and finished effects (the score would be recorded in October).

• Tennant's new life included a new wife, Georgia Moffett, and a more concerted effort to break in America. Davies was in talks with Starz, a US production company, about a co-production reworking of *Torchwood*. Cribbins was to receive a Children's BAFTA lifetime achievement award. Over the summer, Davies and Gardner appeared at US conventions and Tennant was interviewed about *Doctor Who*, but by mid-July attention was being paid to Smith's new costume, and the fact that the first post-Tennant story recorded had River Song and Weeping Angels in it (X5.4, "The Time of Angels"). The drip-feed of information about forthcoming episodes was about 50/50 Tennant and Smith.

• By October, with the start of the build-up, Davies and Tennant were back in Blighty doing interviews and recording features. Tennant and Tate did DVD commentaries and *Nan's Christmas Carol* (an extra online commentary for both was recorded in Gardner's LA living-room when Davies returned to his new home just before Thanksgiving). The sequence of the Doctor on Ood-Sphere was shown, without the credits, as part of *Children in Need* and netted 12 million viewers. With a touch of extra grading on the Doctor at the Powell Estate, to suggest that Rose never saw his face, the episodes were ready.

• On 1st December, the website launched the now-traditional "Adventure Calendar" with clips, messages and production designs. Simm, Whitfield and Tate had other projects to promote, but weren't averse to discussing what was allowed about the episodes. A press edit of Part One, ending before Dalton is revealed as a Time Lord, was issued and now both episodes had the same title, to add to the epicness.

• As we mentioned, the BBC1 station idents for that Christmas were the Doctor, some reindeer and the TARDIS. These started on 4th December, just as the bumper double issue of the *Radio Times* came out (a Christmas ritual and the most sought-after front cover in television), offering a choice of a *Strictly*-themed cover or a near-identical painting with Father Christmas winding up a clockwork Dalek. The issue covering that week's programming, which had come out before, had Tennant looking stern, the masthead *Death of a Doctor* and, um, a Sycorax (X2.0, "The Christmas Invasion").

This marked the next phase in the build-up, after the triple-whammy of "The Waters of Mars", "Dreamland" and "The Wedding of Sarah Jane Smith" over the previous month (and that year's *Children in Need* tie-in). Tennant had spent the months between finishing the episode and leaving for America recording interviews and guest-spots – he called it his "scorched-Earth campaign" – and these started to be broadcast now. Some estimates put it at 75 separate programmes with him in during this period, becoming more frequent as the first episode approached.

Highlights include: *Never Mind the Buzzcocks*, hosted by Tennant and with Tate and Cribbins on the opposing teams in the comedy pop-quiz (Cribbins, now 80, seems very at home there) recorded in early November; *QI* (especially the full-length edition, *QI-XL*, where Tennant boggles

as Bill Bailey – X7.0, "The Doctor, the Widow and the Wardrobe"– goes on an idiosyncratic riff about lesser-known Osmond brothers and Lee Mack speculates that one of these will be the tenth Doctor's final foe; two Radio Two shows, one Tennant and Tate for three hours on Boxing Day morning as before (X4.15, "Planet of the Dead"), another, on the Tuesday between episodes, was called *Who on Who*, with Tennant and Davies playing songs used in the series, a few Murray Gold tracks and a lot of reminiscing (Tennant back-announces "The Angel Put the Devil in Me" as performed by "Miranda Hart", which is a curious notion).

This and the ident before every programme or trailer for 28 solid days was a bit much for some people. A year on from the whole mess over *Blue Peter* and Russell Brand, Beeb-bashing had once again become the tabloids' favourite blood-sport. Nonetheless, coverage of the actual episodes was lukewarm-to-positive.

• Davies's next project, *Torchwood: Miracle Day*, didn't exactly set the world alight. (That the first episode's UK broadcast coincided with riots across Britain is coincidence, not criticism.) His partner's health problems meant that returning to Britain and the NHS took priority, and he delivered *Cucumber* (a series about middle-aged gay men, closer to what the BBC had originally approached him to do in 2000 than anything in these books) and an adaptation of *A Very British Scandal*. (It's a rather terse book about the Jeremy Thorpe scandal – see **Who's Running the Country?** under 10.5, "The Green Death" – that mysteriously omitted any mention of Peter Cook's parody of the judge's summation. Davies improved on it greatly.) Other projects for CBBC (*Wizards vs Aliens*) and CBeebies (*Old Jack's Boat*, starring Cribbins with Freema Agyeman and a few other familiar faces) came and went without much notice.

• As is traditional amongst new ex-Doctors, Tennant sloped off to Hollywood without immediately making an impact. There was a much-talked-about disastrous pilot for a TV series that wasn't, *Rex is Not Your Lawyer*. Whether his turn impersonating Russell Brand in the pointless remake of *Fright Night* is any worse than Eccleston's decent-ish performance in the wretched *GI Joe: The Rise of Cobra* (or his retrospectively amusing tweeds-and-bow-tie in *The Dark is Rising*), Smith's part in *Pride and Prejudice and Zombies* or Davison's stint on *Magnum PI* is for you to judge. There were also British-made films, some shot during the

Hamlet break, to keep his face in the papers (*St Trinian's 2: the Legend of Fritton's Gold* gives him another Jodie Whittaker connection).

He returned to Britain and re-established himself in *Broadchurch* (see X5.1, "The Eleventh Hour"), but then did the ill-advised US remake with a less convincing accent. *United* and the TV version of his RSC *Hamlet* did him more favours. As far as American telly goes, nothing worked until he took the Marvel shilling and played a manipulative villain (for which an English accent is mandatory) in *Jessica Jones*. A stage highlight was his playing the lead in *Don Juan in Soho* and he was latterly cast as the demon Crowley in Amazon's TV adaptation of the feted Neil Gaiman/ Terry Pratchett collaboration *Good Omens*. He is now the voice of Uncle Scrooge McDuck in *Duck Tales*, and can therefore be heard saying *Bless ma bagpipes* when you squeeze the doll.

A6: "Music of the Spheres"

(27th July, 2008/1st January, 2009)

Which One is This? Now they know how many Whos it takes to fill the Albert Hall. It's the six minutes everyone remembers from a two-hourlong concert of Murray Gold's Greatest Hits and Vaguely Appropriate Classics.

Firsts and Lasts Even by the standards of *Doctor Who* mini-episodes, this is an oddity. Davies was asked to do a story for the 2008 *Doctor Who at the Proms* that would combine pre-filmed *Doctor Who* footage with live-action interaction at the Royal Albert Hall, and which could be simultaneously broadcast by BBC Radio 3. There had been a *Doctor Who* Prom in 2007, but this time it had to be (to use the *Confidential* catch-phrase of the year) bigger and better. It would be challenging, then, to come up with any sort of coherent story.

The original broadcast was the first time this century that they used the Delia Derbyshire "realisation" of the theme for the end credits (the last consistent use of the "un-stung" one was 7.2, "Doctor Who and the Silurians"; the last time it was used outright was 17.5, "The Horns of Nimon"). Ostensibly, it was there as part of a 50th birthday celebration of the BBC Radiophonic Workshop. (They would get a Prom to themselves in 2013, including Dudley Simpson's "lost" soundtracks being recreated live.)

This is the start of the trend for live performances with monsters running around for scripted reasons, as opposed to static displays at Blackpool or Longleat. When Matt Smith became the Doctor, there were two much bigger events, with longer runs, and a third was planned for a US tour but never quite made it. There were also more *Doctor Who* Proms performances.

The full-length version included the UK premiere of "The Torino Scale" by Mark-Anthony Burnage – an event in itself, which showed a lot of faith in the open-ness of the child audience to new music.

And this is the first *Doctor Who* of any kind made to be shown in HD.

Where Does It Go? Let's assume that the original broadcast date is about in synch with other broadcast stories, so it could be just after X4.13, "Journey's End". However, if the wormhole doesn't have a time-shift and the TARDIS is running roughly concurrently with Earth time (as seems to be the working assumption for the series), then, for the Doctor, it's a year earlier in his life and he's just drained the Thames into a big hole (X3.0, "The Runaway Bride").

(Lurking behind our inability to commit to a date is a weird vacillation in the whole project: everyone knows that *Doctor Who* is a made-up show on telly, but everyone seems to accept that the Doctor is real. Freema Agyeman introduces herself as herself, but introduces "the man himself" as "the Doctor". The name "David Tennant" is never to be mentioned, except when he texts his mate Freema to tell us he's listening in.)

Watch Out For...
• A neat piece of stagecraft, when the on-screen Doctor chucks manuscript paper at the camera, and an imperceptible drop-box releases sheets of score over the orchestra's heads in the Albert Hall.
• Observe the audience reaction when the orchestra has obediently played the Doctor's little snippet. Applause, laughter and bewilderment vie for dominance.
• The Graske (*SJA*: "Whatever Happened to Sarah Jane?" et al) runs around the stage with a water-pistol, and one of the cellists uses the spike at the base of his instrument to defend himself. Don't try this at home.
• The whole event, apart from Tennant on a big screen, is hosted by Freema Agyeman (showing

Can They Do It Live?

Let's get one thing straight – no matter what those 80s guidebooks suggested, *Doctor Who* was never broadcast live. Video-recording was crude, editing haphazard and costly and the machinery broke down, but it was all pre-recorded, sometimes months in advance (usually three weeks ahead of transmission until 1970).

But live *Doctor Who* has been done. There have been stage performances for half a century. Audiences who enjoyed a brief burst of unreality disrupting their living-rooms every Saturday were sometimes reluctant to return the favour and visit a strange theatre to see monsters (usually Daleks) in their natural habitat: a make-believe world. Nonetheless, there's nothing that quite matches the *frisson* of something happening in front of you that you didn't think they could pull off, an effect more technically adept than the usual theatrical just-go-along-with-it. People kept trying to do space-opera in front of a live audience.

It seems odd but – despite their intimate connection – fantasy and the theatre don't seem like natural bedfellows unless it's in a traditionally-prescribed manner, such as musicals or panto. (By which, of course, we mean the convoluted mix of cross-dressing and Grimm's Tales that nobody in Britain can quite believe other countries don't do.) A completely new play with spaceships and monsters is a hard sell, but attaching it to a hit TV show can seem like a logical way to exploit all the things theatre can do that films and television can't, combined with things atypical for theatre.

It doesn't work like that, though. It took several blind alleys and near-misses to hit on a formula that works for children and avoids just being for indulgent fans...

The Curse of the Daleks

At precisely the same time that BBC1 was showing "The Daleks' Master Plan" (3.4), with a script largely credited to Terry Nation but somehow making 12 episodes from a few sheets of foolscap with notes on, original story editor David Whitaker was eking out Nation's ideas to make the first BBC-licensed stage production of *Doctor Who*. It was produced by John Gale, whose big hit *No Sex Please – We're British* was running somewhere in London for most of the 1970s and 80s[52], and publisher Ernest Hecht. Gillian Howell directed it.

It was a weird project in some ways. It only ran as matinees at Wyndham's Theatre between 21st December, 1965 and 15th January, 1966 – evenings were for *Maigret and the Lady*. That's less of a gulf as it might have been, as the Dalek play was itself a murder mystery of sorts. It is also Doctor-less, but capitalised on the ubiquity and extra-mural appeal of the Daleks during Panto season. As we outlined in **Are All Comics Fair Game?** under X4.7, "The Unicorn and the Wasp", Whitaker had been involved in the Dalek comic-strip in *TV21* (or whichever permutation of the name was being used), and been advisor on the big-screen Peter Cushing film. The posters for *The Curse of the Daleks* used the Greek-style lettering by now associated with the Daleks, even though it had never been seen in their TV adventures. As with the comics and "Mission to the Unknown" (3.2), it was part of Nation's attempt to give the Daleks legs, so to speak – to establish them as bigger than *Doctor Who* prior to launching a Dalek-only series.

The plot is familiar with hindsight. Humans, including two convicts being ferried back to Earth, stumble across a planet called Skaro and a lot of powered-down metal creatures called Daleks. They were inactive for 50 years after that business with the Thals and Fluid Links, but suddenly (and fatally), it seems someone's found a way to get them working and thinks that the Daleks would be grateful and compliant.

Whitaker used bits of this in "The Power of the Daleks" (4.3), and other elements pop up in "The Tomb of the Cybermen" (5.1). At one point, the quest for small crystal cubes involves the audience scrabbling under their seats for some that were secreted in the auditorium. Whitaker's Daleks were – as always – using human nature against itself, but the script had some oddities of its own: Dalek nursery-rhymes and humans who know the Daleks from history books, but make Doctor-ish pronouncements about their methodology. Revisions would be needed if anyone revived this story today – casual sexism aside, it's all a little obvious and most of the new abilities the Daleks acquired for the story worked their way back into the televised version. It seems, from the surviving documentation and some diligent sleuthing by Dalek design aficionados, that the five new Daleks needed for the production were built and paid for in collaboration with Aaru Productions (makers of the Peter Cushing Dalek films). For plot reasons, some of these Daleks needed unorthodox hand-attachments such as a blowtorch, a lamp and a claw-hand, so the film had all of these on view without any clear explanation for why.

continued on Page 339...

off her new hairdo), with Catherine Tate. It also has Sontarans, Judoon, Cybermen, a Dalek and, as mentioned, a Graske in the auditorium with the audience. Ben Foster, the orchestrator of most of the recent scores, conducts... but Murray Gold shows up at the end to play piano.

The Continuity

The Doctor He's having a go at writing a symphony, "Ode to the Universe", and seems to use Gallifreyan pictograms alongside regular stave-notation to sketch the notes. [Such graphic notation was more common in the 1950s and 1960s, when orthodox notation was inadequate. Some have exhibited as artworks. One pioneer was Daphne Oram, who left the BBC Radiophonic Workshop to plough her own furrow.] Still, the score is readable for terrestrial musicians. More or less; the orchestra plays about 30 seconds, and can't quite tell which way on the sheets is up, or who should get to play what and on which instrument – but the Doctor seems to think it sounds alright. Whether he has any idea how to conduct an orchestra is up to the viewer's discretion.

When the Graske asks him to explain the music of the spheres, he can't resist sitting down and doing an excited lecture, even though mere seconds ago he was ordering it to leave. Ultimately, he sends the Graske back to its point of origin.

• *Background.* He met Beethoven [cf. X3.6, "The Lazarus Experiment"; X9.4, "Before the Flood"]. He's been to the Albert Hall before, and is quite fond of the Proms as an institution, playing tuba at the first one in 1895.

He knows what Graskes are, and regards them as general nuisances. [Compare with their baddie role in The Sarah Jane Adventures, and remember that they first appeared in an online game released just after X2.0, "The Christmas Invasion".

[The interested reader may infer from the closing monologue that the Doctor admires John Cage. (Silence isn't the Doctor's thing, so it's less likely to be "4'33"" than "Sonata for Prepared Piano" or the "Imaginary Landscape" pieces for consumer electronics. Of course, the four and a half minutes of the orchestra not-playing inclines us to listen to everything else in the auditorium, for as many seconds as there are degrees Kelvin below freezing.)]

His audience call-and-response business seems to indicate that he's been to a few pantos in his time. [Overseas readers who don't "get" British traditional Christmas Panto will have a rough guide provided when we rework Volume 4. It's the missing link between Chaplin, Python, early 80s electro-pop and "alternative", plus a lot of what's great and terrible about 80s Doctor Who in particular and all of the series.]

• *Inventory: Sonic Screwdriver.* The Doctor employs it as a baton to conduct. Even at full stretch, it's a touch short for the job.

• *Inventory: Other.* When composing, he uses a quill and parchment-coloured paper. He's down one water pistol at the end of the story [maybe the same one he was waving around in X4.2, "The Fires of Pompeii"]. He has a music-stand, but does his writing on the floor of the console room.

The TARDIS The Doctor's developing a bad habit of leaving her shields down (this time to listen to the music of the universe), which is why the Graske can just teleport in. An irritating alarm warns of a teleport breach. There's a harmonic filter which, when tracing the gravitation paths of the universe's star systems and the orbit of every moving body in an expanding universe, renders them as music [it sounds like whale-song]. The Ship also has a music stand on hand, apparently made of rosewood with Gallifreyan Spirograph-writing on the back.

Weirdly, the screen says 'ALERT TELEPORT BREACH' in English.

The Non-Humans
• *The Graske.* It's trying to go to Earth for some reason, and pretends to warn the Doctor about a space portal that it then jumps through. Once there, it runs about waving a water pistol at people and attacks a cellist before the Doctor brings it back. The Graske can teleport interstellar distances, nd into a TARDIS if the pilot isn't paying attention.

History
• *Dating.* [It's fourth-wall bending and all that, but we can presume that they're still running the Proms in contemporary time in the Doctor's own universe. And that the BBC orchestra, at least, has noticed a lot of odd alien intrusions lately and just rolls with it. Pity Donna didn't ask them in between her first two encounters with the Doctor.

[The Doctor's in his blue suit. The space-time wormhole comes out at 27th July, 2008, but in a

Can They Do It Live?

continued from Page 337...

Kids and critics seemed to like it, but after that brief run it went away (until Big Finish remade it for CD in 2008, after a 90s attempt to make it with computer images). With Nation so keen to grab all exploitation rights and opportunities, it seems odd that this production didn't tour or return to the West End for a longer run the following year. Nonetheless, the point had been proved.

Seven Keys to Doomsday

With Jon Pertwee associated with a hit show, there had been renewed talk of a stage version of the series. It made sense, and personal appearances by Pertwee as the Doctor were always popular, especially if he came in costume and with monsters. Barry Letts was always keen to promote the series and Pertwee was always enthusiastic about promoting Jon Pertwee. So there were talks but, predictably, the putative star (and his agent) held out for more money than was on the table. There's a way to do a play of this kind without the Doctor but that needs the Daleks, and Terry Nation also wants dosh up front.

Then Pertwee left the series, and Letts began a phased withdrawal. The forthcoming Doctor was a relative unknown and wouldn't be seen until after Christmas 1974, so there was a slim window of opportunity for a play with *a* Doctor but not either of the television ones on offer. You can get around the audience acclimating to a new lead, because they're all doing that already. Impresarios Robert De Wynter and Anthony Pye-Leary got the rights to do a stage production over three weeks and recruited outgoing script editor Terrance Dicks to write it. He'd been keen to do something like this for a while, it seems, so it all came together fairly fast.

The fetch-quest plot he devised for *Seven Keys to Doomsday* involved power-crystals for a yet-another Dalek-designed Ultimate Weapon, allowing a number of smaller adventures in different locales (yes, pretty much like 1.5, "The Keys of Marinus"[53]) and most famously included giant spare-parts cyborg, the Clawrentular, that prefigured the Morbius monster (13.5, "The Brain of Morbius"). A child who won a contest in a newspaper suggested the beast's name, after the producers rejected Dicks's original suggestion, the Crocs. We mentioned "Brain of Morbius", and it's worth noting that one planet visited in this search was Karn. The Master of Karn was Simon Jones, best

known as Arthur Dent from *The Hitchhiker's Guide to the Galaxy*, and he was hidden inside a bulbous green head (rather like the Mekon from *Dan Dare*) and built into an inhumanly tall costume. He was on stilts. (Now we've seen the Sisterhood, it's probably as well he was prevented from dancing.) There were also white-haired humanoids in body-stockings, and what seem like white metal lederhosen.

But it was mainly about Daleks, which can slide around on a flat stage and sound impressive "in person", and a bespoke Doctor and Companions who were introduced in a curious way: an old man looking a bit like Pertwee staggers onto the stage, asks for volunteers from the audience and gets two who were ringers – one being "Jenny", played by erstwhile TARDIS traveller Wendy Padbury (see 5.7, "The Wheel in Space" et seq.), the other "Jimmy", a lad called James Mathews who wore a football scarf vaguely echoing what Tom Baker would put on during this play's run.

Then they put on a slide-show of earlier Doctors and, in a flash, the old man is "rejuvenated" and Trevor Martin, who'd been one of the Time Lords at the Doctor's trial (6.7, "The War Games"), is a sort of hybrid Hartnell/Troughton like the one in the Wall's Sky Ray cards. He was one of those actors who was never not working and had a television and theatre pedigree going back decades. As you may recall from earlier volumes, drama at the BBC had used a few actors well-versed in the difficulties of the infant medium in the 1950s (Roger Delgado, Patrick Troughton, Barry Letts, Paul Whitsun-Jones and a few other names you'll see a lot in the casts of early *Doctor Who*), so Martin's IMDb entry has a lot of stuff that went out live or was wiped long ago, as well as National Theatre productions.

Letts, still officially producer of *Doctor Who* when the play was being cast, oversaw the casting. They didn't use the regular Dalek voice-actors, which is hardly surprising as one of them (Michael Wisher) was just about to start rehearsing "Genesis of the Daleks" (12.4), which went into the studio two weeks after the play closed – indeed prefilming of stunts began the day after the last night of the play's run. (Nobody seems to know who was operating the pepperpots but, for similar reasons, it can't have been the usual posse of Cy Town and John Scott Martin. The pictures make them look like purpose-built, slightly taller casings, like the

continued on Page 341...

universe where Catherine Tate and Freema Agyeman are such big stars, Martha and Donna would always be dealing with people noting their resemblances. If we synch it to broadcasts then, for him, this is shortly before X4.12, "The Stolen Earth". (It's not quite got the same sense of crisis as the end of X4.11, "Turn Left", so let's assume that we're in the "holiday" phase and Donna's having a kip while the Doctor calms his nerves after X4.10, "Midnight". If not, it could be in that reckless phase after X4.16, "The Waters of Mars".]

The Analysis

The Big Picture American readers, quite understandably, might be confused by the word "Proms". It's nothing to do with Cissy Spacek getting drenched in blood, or Molly Ringwold helping Jon Cryer out of the closet[51]. Neither, despite the mildly grotesque spectacle of the Last Night (note caps), is it about jingoism or xenophobia.

What it's for is to democratise access to music that isn't commercially-orientated. The original idea, in the 1890s, was for a top-drawer orchestra to play in public and the attendees to promenade, possibly smoking or drinking wine. This plan needed reliable weather, so in 1895 Henry Wood organised indoor events with low-cost tickets only available at the door. This was to prevent advance booking and enable Joe Public to wander in out of curiosity.

The idea was that income shouldn't be the sole dimension of taste. If you were a street-sweeper or file clerk, but preferred Beethoven to Vesta Tilly or – scandalously – liked both equally, your choice and access wasn't limited by class or employment. It was an idea percolating across all forms of what came to be called "culture" in the late nineteenth century, in synch with the Municipal movement that made libraries and parks open to all for free. Ultimately, this idea led to the cluster of museums in South Kensington ("Albertopolis"), the Great Exhibition (19.7, "Time-Flight"), the Arts Council and the BBC itself (especially the post-war meritocratic, autodidactic generation's favourite, the Third Programme).

In fact, it now seems odd that the Proms were ever held anywhere but the Royal Albert Hall, or that the BBC didn't take over running the events until 1927. Despite recent developments and numerous experiments over the last century or so, the fundamentals remain the same: newly-commissioned avant-garde works, themes of specific composers (usually tied to anniversaries), noted performers or conductors and a few perennials.

If you managed to snag five tickets, you can present the stubs and be in the running for standing-room "seats" at the Last Night of the Proms (now usually in mid-September after eight weeks of concerts roughly corresponding to the school holidays). If you don't mind standing, you can get a spot on the night for about £10. (There is now online booking and you can get advance seats for most performances, but not the Last Night.) What's on could be anything from Alleghri to Zappa, Pierre Boulez to Philip Glass, Hildegarde of Bingen to world premieres, for the same cost as ticket for the current summer blockbuster at the pictures. Or you could tune in to Radio Three or watch BBC4, and get the same gig without the atmosphere but with specially-commissioned talks or features in the intermission.

Between 1950 and 1980, there was no shortage of Classical, Romantic (in the strict sense of post-Mozart, pre-Stravinsky) and "serious" Modern music for the punters. It was used as TV themes, in adverts and as an easy way to delineate character in dramas. If you asked a 70s British viewer to name a piece by Aram Katachurian, Carl Orfe or Gustav Holst, they had at least one of each handy. Then schools had budget cuts, Performance Rights law changed and the myth got about that interest in anything other than the Top 40 or Film themes was "elitist". It became cheaper to knock something out with a synth than take a pre-existing recording and use that. There were attempts made to make "good" music accessible, which may have scared more schoolkids off than anything else. Sitting still and listening to an orchestral piece was like eating your greens. Nonetheless, the BBC persevered in making fun events using orchestras and the spearhead of this – as with so many other "outreach" schemes – was *Blue Peter*.

You will recall from earlier volumes that this is a much better fit for the title of *Doctor Who*'s sister-series than *Torchwood* or *Blakes 7* ever could be (see **Did All the Puff *Totally* Change Things?** under X2.1, "New Earth" and **Cultural Primer: Why *Blue Peter*?** under 15.2, "The Invisible Enemy"). A Prom for kids, linked with and cross-promoted by the series that kick-started audience access in the 50s, was an obvious move. Making the tickets even cheaper was such a popular move, they needed remounts. This went on for a

Can They Do It Live?

continued from Page 339...

2010 model.) This big-voiced new Doctor and the chance to see live Daleks were publicised well in advance in the national press. Those people who went to see the production were impressed by Martin and the show overall, but there weren't enough of these.

The Adelphi theatre, on the Strand, is a 1930s rebuild, one of several on the same site since 1806, and specialises in musicals. (*Chicago* was based there for ages, and the next production after the Daleks had been sent packing was the London premiere of *A Little Night Music*.) It's big enough for the show-piece sets the play demanded, but it needs commensurate audiences. It took hundreds of thousands of pounds to put on a production on this scale and a mere few weeks, even in Panto season, was barely enough to recoup that. Even without the costly rights to the Daleks *and* the Allister Bowtell-built Clawrentulars *and* the on-stage effects for lasers *and* force-fields, it needed a lot of full houses just to rent the Adelphi. Even two performances a day for 17 days (16th December to 11th January, barring Christmas Day) had to have a lot of bums-on-seats. As it turned out, December 1974 was a lousy time to put on any kind of spectacular.

Three weeks earlier, on 21st November, 1974, three bombs in pubs in Birmingham killed 21 people and injured hundreds more. The IRA had been setting off a bomb on average once every three days in mainland Britain for the previous year, but usually gave tip-offs to the local papers – earlier bombs in Birmingham had been bigger, but were intended to disrupt and scare. This time the process broke down, so only a few minutes elapsed between the warning and the explosions. Within days, the IRA were officially proscribed and a new Prevention of Terrorism Act rushed through Parliament.

Predictably, the IRA tried to show that they were not cowed by the Government, so more bombings in London followed – one in Harrods three days before Christmas, but also one at Tottenham Court Road the day after the play opened. Pubs in Guildford and Woolwich, East London, had previously been targeted, but Christmas shopping and the West End were especially vulnerable. The first night of *Seven Keys to Doomsday* was disrupted by a suspect device at the Adelphi. No matter how keen your kids are on *Doctor Who*, it's not worth getting involved in another massacre to see it on stage with a stand-in Doctor.

So the original plan to take the show on the road – and end up at the Blackpool exhibition that had opened the previous April – was dropped as the first run ended up losing over £8,000 (this is just before the big inflation we mentioned in **Why Didn't They Just Spend More Money?** under 12.2, "The Ark in Space", so call it £60,000). Transport for the props and sets, plus the publicity for each new opening, would have been prohibitively expensive unless full houses were guaranteed.

But that wasn't the end of it. As the play was considered to have been unfortunately-timed rather than misconceived, there have been small revivals in New Zealand and Buxton, Derbyshire, c.1980. Big Finish did an audio adaptation (along with *The Curse of the Daleks* and *The Ultimate Adventure*) with Martin reprising his lead role and Padbury's daughter, Charlie Hayes, as Jenny. Plus, this time around the BBC's own Dalek voice, Nicholas Briggs, is on hand to help his Big Finish colleagues.

The Inheritors of Time

Roger Mueller is the Doctor! Except that he wasn't.

An American stage-play was an obvious move after the boom in US conventions in the 1980s, and the complex arrangements of which local stations ran which episodes when (see **How Does This Play in Pyongyang?** under X4.1, "Partners in Crime"). This was advertised in *DWM* and given a fair amount of build-up, but it just didn't happen. That the writer-impresario John Ostrander wanted $500,000 to make the TARDIS materialise seven different ways may have been a factor. Oddly, there are details of the plot that closely resemble X4.12, "The Stolen Earth" and X4.18, "The End of Time Part Two" (someone wants to make Earth the new Gallifrey; someone else removed Earth from spacetime), but you'd only know that from reading 80s New Zealand fanzines.

Recall UNIT (or The Great Tea-Bag Mystery)

Ah. This is going to take a bit of explaining.

First off, the Edinburgh Fringe. Every August, artsy types invade the Scottish capital for the Edinburgh International Festival (terribly worthy highbrow stuff that seems increasingly under-reported and almost irrelevant) and thousands of struggling actors with one-man/one-woman

continued on Page 343...

341

decade after 1997 (a notable Proms season for many reasons, not least the reaction to Princess Diana's death curtailing the usual flag-waving faff at the Last Night), but the BBC had a Cunning Plan and moved all bespoke children's programming to a pair of purpose-built digital stations before everyone had digital access (see **Why is Trinity Wells on Jackie's Telly?** under X1.4, "Aliens of London"). There was only one universally-accessible BBC series with a lot of child viewers and near-total public affection left. A *Doctor Who* Prom in 2008 was as much a no-brainer as casting Catherine Tate as Donna, or playing "Land of Hope and Glory" at the Last Night.

In his notes for the event, Russell T Davies claimed that his intent was to add this to the ways previous Doctors had been musical (he seems to have forgotten X3.6, "The Lazarus Experiment", perhaps understandably). His list of instances is slightly spurious (playing a lyre for Nero is proof that the original Doctor wasn't even slightly gifted; 2.4, "The Romans"). In *Doctor Who Magazine*, on the other hand, he cited attempts by his school to get kids interested – notably an apparently duff performance of *Peter and the Wolf* – as everything he was trying to avoid.

His solution was to integrate a mini-episode on screen, address the live audience, then send monsters into the auditorium and thus the template for some of the live spectaculars of Matt Smith's tenure was born. The music surrounding this event was all themed around space, either re-using Murray Gold's orchestral cues from old episodes, or using popular bits of "monster" or "space" music. Making the entire event an "experience" rather than "shut up and listen" was in keeping with the way museums had tried to make school visits accessible (see 22.3, "The Mark of the Rani"). At the core of this is something we've been stressing throughout *About Time*, especially in the new-series volumes: the British public think of *Doctor Who* as primarily a family show, but specifically a child-friendly one with a few scares. Anyone who'd encountered the series via BBC America or online forums would be nonplussed by the make-up of the audience in the Albert Hall on that day.

As for the concept of the Music of the Spheres, we direct you to the notes for 18.6, "The Keeper of Traken" and **What Planet was David Whitaker On?** under 5.7, "The Wheel in Space". If you lack these, the Doctor explains it to the Graske.

Things That Don't Make Sense The Doctor seems to think that the first Prom was at the Albert Hall.

It seems peculiar for the Graske to hitch a lift via the Doctor's TARDIS, when there's easier ways to do it. It might be less effort, like jumping on a passing lorry rather than walking to another city, but there's no way to guarantee the destination.

When exactly the Graske jumps through the hole is unclear.

Critique There's no substitute for being in the presence of a real orchestra. No matter how familiar a piece is from use in soundtracks or on record/CD/radio, the visceral impact of that amount of sound and the performance's unrepeatability is something all children should know. If *Doctor Who* is the conduit, so be it.

But unrepeatability is the reason that reviewing the event as a whole is pointless. Instead, the bit that warrants inclusion in this book – the six minutes of David Tennant on a screen – is what we have to consider, almost in isolation. We've tried to give the context – the Proms is one BBC event bigger than *Doctor Who*, even at the programme's saturation-point in Tennant's time – but this situation-specific clip just about functions as a mini-episode regardless. Given the question "what would you do with an orchestra?", the Doctor comes up with an unexpected answer. There wasn't much choice, if you think about it, as any conventional piece would fall short of what people think the Doctor ought to be capable of devising. What's impressive is that the tricky brief of catering to three separate audiences, and making a work for the live audience in the Albert Hall that works on radio and television, is only obvious with a lot of hindsight.

Reverse-engineering like this only makes it more admirable – but the thing is, on first viewing (and it wasn't intended to be pored over), it's fun. It connects kids and the BBC Symphony Orchestra in an unpatronising, entertaining way. It works as well as any of the *Comic Relief* or *Children in Need* bespoke clips (actually, better than some).

The Lore

Written by Russell T Davies. Directed by Euros Lyn. Viewing figures: 1.70 million on New Year's Day on BBC1, 0.2 million on BBCHD the following day. The 1st January showing had AIs of 86.

Can They Do It Live?

continued from Page 341...

shows; small, strange plays by strange, small-time playwrights; up-and-coming comedy troupes; or stand-up performers and old-timers using the Fringe's informality and lowered expectations to re-invent themselves (or just talk about their lives in a pub or small hall.) The whole thing started in the 1940s, but really took off when Cambridge Footlights performers Peter Cook, Dudley Moore, Alan Bennett and Jonathan Miller made a splash, then took it to London and New York as *Beyond the Fringe*. It's been the start of many long and successful careers, and makes being in a pub in London in August much more tolerable. Yet for every League of Gentlemen, Tom Stoppard or Derek Jacobi there must, of necessity, be at least a hundred no-marks who don't make it and a lot of misfiring projects that fail to catch anyone's imagination. It's a turkey-shoot, in many senses.

It's 1984 and Richard Franklin – formerly Captain Yates – hasn't been in *Doctor Who* for a while, nor much of anything else. He's been on the convention circuit, though, and met some of his former colleagues. John Levine and John Scott Martin are both free for the summer and, until fairly late on in the planning, so was Nicholas Courtney. Franklin thus devised a strange meta-fictional play riffing on the lives of resting actors, the Pertwee-era UNIT stories and current events. Sort of.

So in the story, Franklin and Levine and someone who's supposed to be Courtney are all recruited to put on a play for an assembly of politicians in the Falkland Islands by a mysterious Swedish impresario, Ms Bergbo. As things get strange, the three find that they are, in reality, Captain Mike Yates, Sergeant Benton and the Brigadier's aide, Major Molesworth, and the Master's up to no good. Following this, they learn that the Dalek Supreme is also there (played by John Scott Martin, of course) and a race of lizards, the Dragoids, who all look like Margaret Thatcher. Of course. So our heroes hotwire the TARDIS and go to the Falklands, infiltrating a panto – Yates and Benton drag up to play Ugly Sisters and perform "Daddy Wouldn't Buy Me a Bow-Wow" – before saving the world and discovering that the real Mrs T has been shrunk by the Master's Tissue Compression Eliminator and hidden inside a teapot, hence the subtitle.

Let's just remind ourselves that Levine had refused to come back as Benton for a cameo in "The Five Doctors" a year earlier, as he thought that it would be an insult to the memory of such a popular character...

There was a pre-recorded insert from Courtney and some talk of Jon Pertwee himself making a guest appearance in one of the performances over the five-day run. Some of the Dragoids were local fans – as were, to be frank, the majority of the people in the Moray House Theatre.

Unlike the previous two plays, little of this made it into broadcast episodes, but Franklin's engagement with fandom resulted in a small sub-group, Franklin's Bow-Wows. Opinions and accounts vary on what this lot got up to – and we don't want to get sued – but there was some fundraising for good causes along the way. The idea of UNIT putting on a panto was mentioned in some of Paul Cornell's early *New Adventures* novels. However, putting in a song was an idea that came back to haunt us...

The Ultimate Adventure

At last, we get the Doctor, the Daleks, the Cybermen, Thatcher, a Vervoid, a Draconian and the TARDIS. And it's a musical!

That last bit is what most people comment on if they recall it. Ask anyone in the know, and they'll shudder at the memory of "Business is Business". Then comes the discussion of which Doctor they got, Jon Pertwee, Colin Baker or David Banks. Banks, best known as the Cyberleader in 80s stories, mainly played the Space Mercenary Karl, but replaced Pertwee in a couple of performances as a new Doctor in a designer suit and a Greenpeace T-shirt. (Sort of like then-current script editor Andrew Cartmel, in fact. This was written by an earlier one, Terrance Dicks.) Pertwee, now in his late 60s, was the focal point of the excitement and spectacle around him. He took the play for the first half of its run, barring those two nights. Baker finally had the chance to go for broke on a part that had been taken from him, and those who saw it tend to say this is his finest hour as the Doctor.

Err, yes, talking of "finest hours", there's a scene where the Doctor takes credit for Churchill's speech. It's one of two that take place in 10 Downing Street; the first, introducing the Doctor, is the one with Margaret Thatcher (this is from 1989). This retro feel also extends to the nightclub sequence that introduces Jason (not, as it turned out, played by Jason Donovan as some people seemed to have hoped) and Crystal, the other new

continued on Page 345...

Repeats and Overseas Promotion There was a trimmed version, with just the *Doctor Who* bits, shown just before the re-run of "The Next Doctor" (X4.14) in the early afternoon of New Year's Day. At time of broadcast, the BBC website put up the story for viewing temporarily. It was webcast again as part of the rest of a Proms Highlights night, also on 1st January, 2009. (Two days later, the casting of the real next Doctor was announced, after days of headline-grabbing bets, so it was a hectic week for viewers even with only this on air.)

Alternate Versions Unless you were there, all versions are "alternate". The Radio Three live broadcast had a talk in the intermission by SF writer Justina Robson. The event was shown on television a few days later in a 94-minute version, skipping the preamble and half-time break.

The version that made it to DVD (both as an extra for "The Next Doctor" and as part of the Complete 2009 Specials, interestingly enough) lost half an hour from what was aired at the Royal Albert Hall. The opening and closing credits, including the Derbyshire closing theme, were omitted as was all non-*Who* music. Other bits of the same concert were included as "Music and Monsters" on the disc with "The Runaway Bride".

Production

• In reconfiguring the *Blue Peter Prom* for *Doctor Who*, there were two obvious precedents: a 2005 Space-themed Prom in which a Dalek had introduced the *Doctor Who* theme, and a 2006 *Children in Need* fundraiser at the Millennium Stadium in Cardiff. In the latter, Ben Foster conducted Murray Gold's music for the series in front of a live audience, including a sneak preview of the Motorway chase from "The Runaway Bride".

Julie Gardner discussed the possibility of another live orchestral event, and this led to talks with the Controller of BBC Radio 3, Roger Wright. Radio 3 was a development of the post-war Third Programme and had been on air since the big reshuffle of 30th September, 1967 (the same day as BBC2 started colour television transmissions and BBC1 began transmitting programmes in 625-line UHF; see 5.2, "The Abominable Snowmen"). Its remit was less-commercial music, originally just classical, ecclesiastical and avant garde (although since 1997, Wright had increased coverage of jazz and World Music) as well as scholarly talks.

Wright's job had been amalgamated with that of being Director of the Proms in 2007, and he was concerned to evade the accusation that his network was elitist. (A commercial station, "Classic FM", specialised in making orchestral music into a form of easy-listening, only playing the famous bits of symphonies, and peppering the arias and catchy allegros people knew how to hum with recent film themes by the likes of Jerry Goldsmith and James Horner. Radio 3's efforts to avoid sliding downmarket to compete made them an easy target for faux-populist tabloids.)

Gardner, similarly, wasn't prepared to just do an evening of space-movie themes, but wanted something about the links between music and "Doctorishness". A programme of pieces was put together combining a cross-section of Murray Gold's cues from the episodes made so far, some reasonably well-known pieces connected with those episodes, some slightly more recondite bits and an interactive section involving the Doctor on a screen and monsters in the Albert Hall.

An obvious choice was the unofficial Series 3 theme, "All the Strange, Strange Creatures", written for X3.7, "42", but used again in a lot of later episodes and underscoring the series trailers in Spring 2007. Equally obvious was having Melanie Pappenheim perform vocals on known crowd-pleasers "The Doctor's Theme", "Song of Freedom" and "Doomsday". Dotted in between these were pieces tenuously connected to the series, to space or to the theme of "love of humanity". Aaron Copland's *Fanfare for the Common Man*, Wagner's *The Ride of the Valkyries*, Prokofiev's *March of the Knights* and Holst's *Jupiter* from *The Planets*. The most interesting choice was a work by opera composer Mark-Anthony Turnage, *The Torino Scale* (named after the calibration of the strength of meteor-strikes). Turnage was in the audience. His interest in giving children something slightly challenging is evident from his last opera to date, *Coraline*, based on the Neil Gaiman book. (He's also got a track-record for nudging the boundaries of subject-matter for adult works, as in *Greeks*, *Three Screaming Popes* and *Anna Nicole*, based on Steven Berkoff's reworked *Oedipus Rex*, a Francis Bacon painting and the life of Anna Nicole Smith respectively.)

Within this context, the interactivity with the (predominantly) child audience was paramount. Apart from the monsters roaming among the

---

Can They Do It Live?

continued from Page 343...

companion, who sings in a club unlike anything anyone had been to since before Pertwee's shirts were in fashion. An audience familiar with 80s Rave culture or *The Hitman and Her* just had to accept this curious version of the normal world before the space stuff kicked in. Jason, a fugitive from the French Revolution, is a Hartnell-style male sidekick for action scenes, although Pertwee's old stunt-double and (literal) sparring-partner Terry Walsh is on hand for fights, so it's not so very unlike a 70s episode. It has laser displays, for space-time flights and information readouts, but combined with old-fashioned stage magic (in a nod to another set-piece of 70s scripts, the Doctor states that in fact Houdini studied under him rather than vice versa).

The plot is as clear as you can get, given that it has to have time, space and contemporary London and both of the famous monsters in it, plus songs and stuff. The Daleks have laid a trap using a threat to yet another World Peace Conference (as per 8.2, "The Mind of Evil" and 9.1, "Day of the Daleks"), so Mrs Thatcher sends for the Doctor and briefs him that MI5 have discovered aliens at a night-club. So off he pops, with Jason in tow, and there's a raid on the club just after Crystal sings (polite of them). The trail leads to Altair III (a planet with flying insects, as per 2.5, "The Web Planet"), where the Cybermen are waiting for the Doctor. The Cybermen, not really involved except as a token cameo, have been reduced to hiring Space Mercenaries so, predictably, there's a sleazy bar with all sorts of aliens – all together now, a *wretched hive of scum and villainy* – run by Madame Delilah (the same performer who was Thatcher) who, as you've guessed, sings about how cynical she is.

Here the TARDIS crew adopts her barman, Zog, who is the Taran Wood Beast with a female voice (16.4, "The Androids of Tara") and not a cash-in on the Ewoks, gracious no. The mask for Zog was the work of Susan Moore, who'd made monster-masks for Sylvester McCoy stories, so it looks very like Eric from 24.4, "Dragonfire". The Daleks capture Our Heroes, but the Doctor escapes by seemingly activating the conscience of their human stooge, Karl, but – while a Dalek scientist was investigating the TARDIS – he (again, all together now) Reversed the Polarity of the Neutron Flow, so that rather than take evasive action, the Ship went to very dangerous bits of history, starting with Paris in 1789. (The Bicentennial celebration made this almost topical.)

They don't have enough sets and costumes to keep this up, so the TARDIS returns to Delilah's to get the price off the Doctor's head. There's a shoot-out and the Daleks kill Delilah, but Karl seems to be conflicted. Back on Skaro, the Daleks seem to have won, but one of them is really Zog inside a shell (the Doctor has a Dalek voice-changer – bear this in mind). Nonetheless, Our Heroes find the US Peace Envoy (remember him?) on whom the fate of Earth depends, trapped inside a force-field (that laser again) and not even the sonic screwdriver will get him out. The Doctor finds the off-switch in time for the laser to be used as a space-time tunnel (the pendant Crystal was wearing can soak up TARDIS energy) to get the Envoy home, but the others are caught.

With a recording he made of the Emperor Dalek gloating, the Doctor persuades the Cybermen and Space Mercenaries that they have been used by the Daleks and shouldn't really have trusted them (how do such alliances ever get started?) and a fight breaks out – but, luckily, nobody sings. Then back in Downing Street, the Doctor gets his voice-changer out to uncover the Daleks' brainwashing of the Envoy, then deprogrammes him with a Venusian Lullaby (go on, guess which one) disabling the Dalekanium Neutronic Bomb inside Thatcher's teapot (what is it with Thatcher, tea and the Pertwee era?). All that in two hours, with two days' rehearsal.

The show began with a moderately successful run at the Wimbledon Theatre in south London, then hit the road, zipping across Britain apparently at random, starting with a trip to Aberdeen. At the Alexandra Theatre, Birmingham on 29th April, Pertwee collapsed minutes into the show. This was the day Banks stood in. Later performances with Colin Baker were tweaked to make it less Pertwee-indulgent and the Doctor more affable and physically active. His costume was adapted to use the colours left out for CSO reasons back in 1984. The play was a big spectacle with enough fannish touches (the Dalek Emperor is a version of the "Evil" one from 4.9, "The Evil of the Daleks", and they have a huge screen for inserts and info-dumps), but as the run continued, the audience numbers dwindled. 1989 was a famously hot summer and *Doctor Who* was about the least popular it has even been. So the planned stage play by Ben

continued on Page 346...

Can They Do It Live?

continued from Page 345...

Aaronovitch and Andrew Cartmel, the one for which they created the Metatraxi (see **What Would Season 27 Have Been Like?** under 26.4, "Survival") never got off the ground.

Hellblossom

For most of the 1990s, fan productions were home-made videotaped productions of varying quality. Some of these became the successful BBV projects and their ilk, even including characters they couldn't call "Doctor" but played by Colin Baker or Sylvester McCoy. Watching a lot of these, one may wonder exactly how many children the Brigadier had and why so many people across time and space look like Sophie Aldred (the exception being Ace in Jon Blum's "Time Rift").

One fan drama made it to the stage – three times, at least – and had a *DWM* write-up. Ian Wheeler's play Hellblossom (supposedly part of a trilogy) was first performed in 2000 and, therefore, had a ninth Doctor in velvet, a belligerent future female companion and that year's must-have Steampunk accessory, Spring-Heeled Jack. It was very fannish, which might have limited its appeal, but very Letts/Hinchcliffe, which would have broadened it. This was at the New Theatre Royal, Portsmouth (film buffs may know this as the location for Ken Russell's film of *The Boy Friend*), which will seem logical after the next entry. A revived production in 2010 in South London sparked curiosity (it's currently on YouTube in shaky-cam), mainly about how they got clearance. The BBC's now very protective of its rights and most of the recent stage events have been commissioned by BBC Worldwide, the semi-autonomous commercial wing of the corporation.

It wasn't always that way. Back in the 1990s, *Doctor Who* was as popular as chest-hair and considered just as much a throwback. We told a lot of this story in **What's All This Stuff About Anoraks?** under 24.1, "Time and the Rani", but the rest of Volume 6 tells the wider story of how little regard the BBC had for what had once been one of their most popular series. As this play was first performed in a period when different bits of the BBC were tripping each other up about exploitation rights for *Who*-adjacent projects (see A5, "The Infinite Quest" and associated essay), a revival was in a legal limbo. Perhaps this is why it's under everyone's radar. Only the Australian production seems to have prompted anyone not involved to

comment online, except to ask who's in it. We can't even get a consensus on whether the title is one word or two.

It would be a shame if our writing about it here alerts the Corporation's lawyers: from the script and the clips it seems about as good as anything Big Finish managed and as interesting as the similar stuff about the Paternoster Gang in subsequent broadcast episodes.

Remounts

As we mentioned, a student company has successfully adapted "Midnight" (X4.10) for stage. That wasn't the first time a broadcast episode had been adapted, although it might be the last for a while. The rights for stage adaptations were a lot easier to negotiate in the 90s, because nobody within the BBC was fighting for them, and the company that did most to put old episodes on stage picked ones written by people who had sicced lawyers on the Corporation. You may recall from X1.6, "Dalek", that Terry Nation's estate – especially their legal representative at the time, Roger Hancock – had zealously and jealously fought the BBC and others over misuse of the Daleks. You may also remember that Mervyn Haisman and Henry Lincoln had sued the BBC and sought an injunction to prevent broadcast of 6.1, "The Dominators", causing ructions over use of things from their other scripts for the series. You may also remember how many of the black and white episodes were then in the BBC's archives – and what percentage weren't any more. It was relatively easy (note, "relatively") to arrange for a lost story to be re-enacted and amended for stage when the BBC thought only a handful of people would bother to go and see it.

So when a small amateur theatre group reworked Haisman and Lincoln's story "The Web of Fear" (5.5) for a space with two small stages, it was almost beneath the BBC's radar. The story starts a couple of years before, in 1996, when it was becoming obvious that the Paul McGann TV Movie wasn't going to launch a series. Actor Nick Scovell wrote and starred in an original *Doctor Who* play *Planet of Storms* (not the uncompleted Philip Martin script with Sil and the Ice Warriors, but something about the Terrible Zodin – yes, again; 20.7, "The Five Doctors"; 22.1, "Attack of the Cybermen" – and some gold-skinned aliens).

That went down well with a small audience and one of them, Rob Thrush, was making a semi-pro fan video "The Millennium Trap". Scovell's

Can They Do It Live?

Troughton/McCoy hybrid performance of the Doctor was a hit, and the video was popular on the convention circuit, so Thrush proposed remounting "The Web of Fear" as a stage production in 2000. Although directed by one of the most assertively cinematic directors of the early episodes, Douglas Camfield (**Who Were the *Auteur* Directors?** under 18.5, "Warriors' Gate"), the story was mainly focussed on one base, a series of tunnels and a few one-off locations (notably the TARDIS and a couple of Tube platforms). Much of the story's appeal was (and is, now we can see it again) the claustrophobia and paranoid uncertainty about who is on which side. On stage, in the Portsmouth Arts Centre, the physicality of the huge Yeti with glowing eyes was, apparently, even more impressive (although photos don't really convey this). The show sold out almost immediately and extra performances were added. Some pre-recorded sequences were relayed on monitors, so the only real amendment to the broadcast version was that the lead wasn't taking a week off (Troughton was absent for episode two).

On the back of this, the team set to adapting the next story, also missing from the archives, "Fury from the Deep". Whereas the televised original (5.6) featured helicopters and extensive location filming, this was tweaked for stage to pull the focus to the base and the tunnels, as with "Web". This was staged in the three days leading to Easter 2002 at the New Theatre Royal, Portsmouth. Again, it proved a big success, not just with older fans, but as a theatrical experience for kids.

By Summer 2004, with the BBC preparing to relaunch the series on television, Scovell and Thrush went for the big prize and secured the rights to "The Evil of the Daleks" (4.9)… eventually. With the Nation estate dragging its feet over the BBC's rights to use the Daleks (see X1.6, "Dalek"; **What Might Series 2 Have Been Like?** under X2.11, "Fear Her"; and X3.12, "The Sound of Drums"), this production was in jeopardy until a lot of phone calls were made after the cast had been hired and the theatre booked.

Halving the running-time meant removing large amounts of episodes one, three, four and six. With this done, and Kemel removed, it became possible to relocate the Skaro scenes to Maxtible's house and reveal the Dalek Emperor as a fixture (within the fireplace). This *coup de theatre* was the main substantive change, but the characters' motivations altered slightly. The Daleks were now desperate, attempting to close off a future they

had seen/experienced in which they were defeated utterly. Maxtible, under the influence of Season Twenty-Six, became a troubled clergyman. With Daleks borrowed from the fan-video *Devious* and the *Comic Relief* special "The Curse of Fatal Death" (A4), the production was another hit and paved the way for one last ambitious project.

With the series back on television and as popular as it had ever been, the team in November 2007 took on the big one: 3.4, "The Daleks' Master Plan". If whittling seven episodes down to 90 minutes had been tricky, this required extensive streamlining. All the time-travel/escape material in episodes seven to ten was removed, including the Monk, and the nature of the Time Destructor altered to allow for a cast without any freaky-looking aliens at the conference (see **Which Sodding Delegate Was Which?** under that story, although we still hadn't quite got it right even then). Instead, all the galaxies were populated by post-human adaptations from the original Earth-resident stock, and the Daleks were collecting DNA from each to make them all vulnerable to the Time Destructor (which, in this version, was rigged not to affect Daleks). The story still crossed the galaxies, albeit suggested by the re-positioning of two rectangular pillars, one face of which was Dalek control-panelling.

The story also ends differently as the Doctor (as has happened on screen and in *DWM* recently) absorbed the power of the space-time energy and regenerated. (Scovell sort of played the Doctor again, as the motion-reference for the animated Patrick Troughton and a few others when 4.3, "The Power of the Daleks" was animated in 2016.) For this last scene they had a coup as, unlike before, the Dalek voices were now provided by Nicholas Briggs and, again, as in *DWM*'s strip, he emerged from the TARDIS as a regenerated Doctor in a tux. (The play ends with him seeing his bald head reflected in a Dalek dome and saying: "At least I'm not ginger!")

This grand finale ended with a day in which a mini-convention took place on stage: Briggs, Scovell and Thrush, "Dalek" author Robert Shearman and TV Dalek operator Barnaby Edwards answered questions from the audience and told anecdotes, some for the first time. With a month to go before X4.0, "Voyage of the Damned", this was the last time the BBC OK'd any fan-based project. But not the end of *Doctor Who* on stage…

continued on Page 348...

Can They Do It Live?

continued from Page 347...

Doctor Who Live – The Monsters are Coming!

Just as Russell T Davies and Steven Moffat can't go five minutes without a call-back to when Philip Hinchcliffe was producer, so Gareth Roberts can't let the Pertwee era alone. What flavour toothpaste do you want? Venusian Spearmint, obviously (X3.2, "The Shakespeare Code"). You want a space-age metal for a Cyber-ship to be made of? "Molectic-bonded disilium" fits the bill (X6.12, "Closing Time"). In fact, 10.2, "Carnival of Monsters" provides a template for many of Roberts's early novels and audio plays.

Brilliant though that story was, however, the only slight blemish is the name (Robert Holmes wanted to call it "Peepshow"), partly for the clumsy way the dialogue alludes to it, but mainly because there isn't actually a carnival of any sort. Kids who'd seen the new Saturday morning filler *Outa-Space!* on the morning of episode three were perfectly happy to watch just a parade of odd things, dodgy effects and retro clips without any plot or sequential logic. "Carnival of Monsters" was more like a lot of old men in funny make-up arguing, with occasional glimpses of monsters and some groovy set-design and pretty girls. Nobody felt especially short-changed, but who wouldn't love a lot of scary creatures on carnival floats?

When BBC Worldwide asked Steven Moffat about a stadium show, he and Roberts supervised the scenario, and Roberts did the script with impresario Will Brenton to oversee production. They immediately thought to base it on the Holmes story, with a hint of *Jurassic Park*, and make it an actual carnival. The main object of the exercise was to have the music from the BBC Wales series and a lot of familiar aliens stomping about on stage; plot and character are optional extras. Ben Foster, who conducted and arranged Murray Gold's material, and was more actively involved after Gold became based in the US, got to rearrange pieces originally written for specific incidents as concert pieces. Nonetheless, there was more to it than a simple pretext for extras in fancy dress and pre-recorded messages from Matt Smith. Brenton's previous extravaganzas included *Thomas the Tank Engine Live* – the world's biggest model train set. This was an even bigger deal.

There's a "Minimiser" (basically the MiniScope from 1973) containing live aliens which escape their artificially-maintained cages. Each one struts its stuff in front of cheering crowds with a slightly shambolic showman emceeing. They even called Nigel Planer's character "Vorgenson", to keep the connection to Leslie Dwyer's "Vorg". The key point to remember here is that this is the O2 Arena, originally built to house the Millennium Experience and now the venue for huge rock concerts and the farewell *Monty Python* show. The spectacle had to be immersive, using the projecting T-shaped stage and the vast audience space to do a theatre-in-the-round with escaping Cybermen and Judoon as well as a gigantic projector-screen.

The music was entirely performed live. Foster, already well-established as composer for *Torchwood* and arranger on big films, with extensive experience of working on stadium tours, was undaunted by the Dome's scale. He had been Murray Gold's ministry on Earth in the 2008 *Doctor Who Proms*. Practical effects were supervised and devised by Paul and Gary Hardy-Brown (who brandished their fan-credentials by not only referring to "CSO" when discussing green-screen, but displaying a photo of themselves as kids visiting the location of 17.1, "Destiny of the Daleks", where their dad was on the film crew). They made Daleks fly over the heads of the audience. These brothers were experienced stage-illusion engineers. Planer, despite still being best-known in Britain as Neil from *The Young Ones*, had spent several years in the cast of *We Will Rock You*, so was a clever choice for a lightly-plotted run-through of "greatest hits" with special effects.

Above all, the production was one where the illusionists, music-arranger and impresario worked out what was possible and would excite audiences, then got a script together that made it all work as *Doctor Who*. Thus the plot twist was that Vorgenson had allowed things to go wrong, engineering a crisis so that people would be endangered and the Doctor would have to come – and thus Vorgenson could meet his hero. As with "Music of the Spheres", there was a pre-recorded video link-up with the current Doctor, but this time it was the resolution of the crisis rather than just an interlude.

The Crash of the Elysium

In the 60s, there was a lot of talk about "Environmental Theatre". It was a methodology based on taking a real-world location, using its properties and quirks and staging a piece there, often without telling passers-by that it was a play.

Can They Do It Live?

The name to bandy about was Jerzy Grotowski, whose book *Towards a Poor Theatre* was influential, but it could be argued that Mickey Rooney and Judy Garland started it by saying *Let's do the show right here!* in umpteen 30s musicals. One extreme of this was performing a situation in a public space and seeing if people who weren't the cast responded, got involved or walked past. (There was a gent on the London underground who used to get his umbrella stuck in a tube-train's doors and let the slapstick and social observations evolve from how helpful people were.) You would hear tell of "Happenings" in New York, Hampstead or Buenos Aires that began as couples noisily breaking up in restaurants, and were only revealed as theatre-works when the hat went around for contributions at the end. Sometimes the police or proprietors were told in advance, usually not. It was part of a Utopian period where the artificial hierarchy of "practitioners" and "audience" was being nibbled at, of a piece with Scratch Orchestras and Oral History projects.

The modern twist on this is Immersive Theatre, where a selected small group (picked by lot, or by only advertising for a few hours) is taken to a purpose-built set, minutely detailed to lock the visitor in the world-view of the piece, and allowed to engage with something midway between theatre-in-the-round and a guided tour. London's Punchdrunk company is at the forefront of this. Recently there was a problem with their rethink of *Macbeth*, called *Sleep No More*, where the audience/guests were hazy on the difference between "participation" and "sexual assault", but most of what you'll hear about them is positive. Some of their work is now on the school GCSE syllabus. Of late, they've been looking at how to work with primary-schools using a fake village called "Fallow Cross" as a sort of hands-on Sims. Felix Barrett and Peter Higgin, the core of the team, met at Exeter University in the 80s and try to retain the student zeal for experimentation as an end in itself.

In June 2011, the team put on their most well-publicised event to date: *The Crash of the Elysium*. It was for children, although one adult could accompany any invited participant, and formed part of the BBC's contribution to the Manchester International Festival (the bulk of non-fiction, non-news television was now being moved to a facility in Salford, on the outskirts of the city). The previous year had seen a collaboration between them and documentary-maker extraordinaire Adam Curtis with music by Damon Albarn and the Kronos Quartet. It was an Event.

Nobody was sure how they could top that, but what they came up with was more unexpected than anything they'd done to date. It was, in effect, LARPing a *Doctor Who* story, like generations of British eight-year-olds did, but with professional adult intervention and a purpose-built site. And special effects. Everyone had to put on protective suits to explore a steam ship that had been wrecked under mysterious circumstances in 1888, led by actors also in decontamination suits or military garb. It starts as something more or less like a laser-tag, until the Weeping Angels show up. Tom McRae wrote the scripted elements from a scenario Steven Moffat devised (sort of like X5.4-5.5, "The Time of Angels"/"Flesh and Stone"). In most performances, the Doctor came through on a video-screen with helpful hints.

Not every performance, though: the session/performance on 16th July, 2011 had the Doctor there in person. Matt Smith, primarily a theatre actor before getting cast as the Doctor, had been to previous Punchdrunk events. So, with a free day in the peculiarly complex shooting schedule of Series 6, he made a house-call. It made headlines, but was never repeated – theatre should always be slightly unrepeatable. Nonetheless, the event was restaged again a year later in Ipswich as part of the "Cultural Olympiad" and they even bowed to public pressure to do adult-only shows (not rude or anything, just allowing grown-ups to go in if they weren't accompanied by a child). Barratt said he was slightly saddened by this, as the idea of a unique event that adults only hear about when a kid tells them was one of his starting-points.

The only downside to this is that any subsequent theatrical event tied to *Doctor Who* will have to somehow deal with this one's impact. At time of going to press, it's been eight long years and the nearest we've had is cinemas used to show TV episodes (or reconstructions thereof) – hardly the same thing.

audience, Davros and the Daleks claimed to have gone back in time and abducted Henry Wood, ensuring that only Dalek music would ever be heard. The Graske tormented the string section of the orchestra, and former cast-members made unannounced appearances.

However, the main audience-engaging section was the Doctor's mini-adventure, some of which was happening on a number of screens around the auditorium. This was carefully scripted to make sense to anyone in the Albert Hall, anyone watching it on television or DVD, and anyone listening on Radio 3.

The insert for the concert was the last item recorded for Series 4. It was appended to the studio session for "The Next Doctor" on 3rd May 2008. Euros Lyn directed the six-hour session. Tennant amended the line about reversing the polarity, added to make sense of the action to radio-listeners, to the full Pertwee/Davison "reverse the polarity of the neutron flow" (see 9.3, "The Sea Devils", etc.). Jimmy Vee had been back in the Graske costume for *The Sarah Jane Adventures* after his last *Doctor Who* appearance as Bannakaffalatta (X4.0, "Voyage of the Damned"), so knew what he was doing. He was redubbed in post by Philip Hurd-Wood as usual. Tennant was offered use of an autocue, but managed without one. Vee, on the other hand, had to synch what happened in the studio with his activities in the Albert Hall seven weeks later.

• Came the day, Sunday 27th July, and the auditorium was decorated with a police box, BAD WOLF graffiti and the various screens (the big one concealing a woofer for when the score is lobbed at the orchestra). The presold tickets had been massively in demand – commanding a lot of bids on eBay – and there was a queue from 5.00am for the 500 held-back £5 tickets for first-comers. The hall held six thousand people, and it was full early. At .11.00am, the event began with Freema Agyeman greeted like a rock star. The Doctor's six-minute appearance was at 11.40, just before the intermission (a Cyberman telling the audience that anyone returning late would be deleted).

Part two had Camille Coduri and Noel Clarke welcoming people back, the Daleks being less cordial and Catherine Tate introducing a section of the ladies in the Doctor's life. (She claimed later to have mistaken the Judoon for a very tall Sontaran.) Toward the end, Murray Gold came on stage to play keyboards and Tim Phillips sang

"Song for Ten" (X2.0, "The Christmas Invasion"). Then, finally, the "Voyage of the Damned" arrangement of the *Doctor Who* theme.

• Immediate press reaction was hugely favourable, but later commentators bewailed the dumbing-down of culture and accused Radio 3 of playing the Classic FM game. A subsequent Prom in 2013 celebrated the work of Dudley Simpson and the BBC Radiophonic Workshop and had one of Matt Smith's last performances as the Doctor (minus his hair because of a film role; see X7.16, "The Time of the Doctor").

A7: "The Wedding of Sarah Jane Smith"

(29th - 30th, October 2009)

Which One is This? Well, apart from the title and the event to which this alludes, it's the one where the Doctor shows up – that's why it's in this book.

Where Does It Go? It's clearly a while after "Journey's End" (X4.13). Maria's long gone, Rani's part of the gang and everyone else in the previous three stories knew all about the Daleks. For the Doctor, it's probably just before X4.16, "The Waters of Mars" (broadcast a month later).

Firsts and Lasts This is the last thing David Tennant did as the Doctor until coming back for the 50th anniversary. His last line (in recording order) was "Spit-spot".

It's the first time the Doctor shows up in *The Sarah Jane Adventures*. A year later, he'll be late for his own funeral. It's therefore the first time the Doctor is formally a supporting character in someone else's series.

Hidden in the dialogue is the first substantive hint about how this Doctor's song will end: "the Gate is waiting for you".

Watch Out For...
• Obviously, in a two-part story, the cliffhanger will entail the Doctor showing up. With that title, you know exactly what will be happening when he does. The trick is to avoid everything before then seeming like stalling. If you're a regular viewer of *The Sarah Jane Adventures,* they did this by focussing on how Sarah's adopted son Luke and their partners-in-saving-the-world Clyde and

Rani, react to their chum getting a boyf, with detours along the way about keeping their peculiar lifestyle from him. It's pitched, unsurprisingly, between *Buffy* and *Brookside*, if either had included a CG slug-Mogwai and a sort of cybernetic version of *Vicious* with K9 and Mr Smith.

But if you tuned in just for David Tennant, then it's pretty much stalling.

• The other big-name guest has to be the kind of man that would finally win Sarah's heart, after decades of her putting Earth-saving first and hoping the Doctor would come back into her life.

For the children for whom this was primarily intended, the main thought was *how is he good enough for her?*

For the ones clued-up on *Who*-Lore, it was *Doesn't he look like Jon Pertwee?*

But for most people in Britain, it was: *Bloody hell! Nigel Havers on a kid's show!*

• Actually, the flashback to his death looks oddly like a daytime advert for a personal injuries lawyer. *Fatally injured in a trip or fall? Call Trickster Direct – part of Black Guardian Royal Exchange.*

• Devout *Sarah Jane Adventures* viewers will find this all very familiar, in that it's the *third* time the Trickster has menaced Sarah and company, always in stories written by Gareth Roberts. The beats remain the same, in that the Trickster derails time through a Faustian pact, a problem Sarah solves by convincing someone to tear up the contract by obligingly committing suicide. In *SJA*: "Whatever Happened to Sarah Jane?", it was a school chum; in *SJA*: "The Temptation of Sarah Jane Smith", it was her own parents. Here, it's her husband-to-be.

• As you know, since 1970 all benign alien energy has been either blue or orange (the last three Pertwee season-finales have looked like battles between those colours, with humans and the odd giant invertebrate standing around in the middle of it). Since 2005, all Time Lord energy or mysterious technology has been Orange Sparkly Pixie Dust. We also know that when the TARDIS is travelling forward in the space-time Vortex prior to 2010, there's a blue time-tunnel; backwards, it goes reddish. So when Clyde gets dosed up on Artron Energy from the semi-materialised TARDIS, it's blue and sparkly. Bear this in mind for later (a whole Doctor later and in the next Volume).

The Continuity

• *Sarah* has been seeing Peter Dalton secretly for over a month before the kids investigate why she's been sneaking out so often. In under a week from this, she's of her own volition agreed to marry him. The engagement ring Dalton immediately slips on her finger, as connected to the Trickster, influences her mind – enough that she seems to swear off this whole "protecting the Earth" thing, and opts to deactivate Mr Smith.

The wedding is scheduled for a fortnight after that. By this time she's found all the dresses in her wardrobe and is wearing them again. [Perhaps she bought them new, but even the lemon frock doesn't quite look right for the period. As a middle-aged woman routinely seen in Size Zero jeans, she's obviously proud of being able to get into such things again.] She has a Margherita when they go out for pizza, with dry white wine.

When confronted over chucking in her entire lifestyle for someone she barely knows, she becomes defensive and complains about how little she's allowed herself to enjoy a normal life.

She and Mr Smith monitor eBay for alien artefacts and stray life-forms.

• *Background.* Rani and Clyde worry, incorrectly, that Dalton is after Sarah's wealth, including all the money she gained 'from her aunt'. [This must be Aunt Lavinia (11.1, "The Time Warrior"; 18.7a, "K9 & Company"). She was – all together now – an 'eminent virologist' and owned a mansion in Gloucestershire. There's no mention of any other family, suggesting that something terrible has happened to Brendan. What a shame.]

• *Inventory.* Sarah forgets which lipstick is which and almost unscrews her face. There's a hexagonal blue tracking device that can attach itself to cars: Luke here uses it to track Sarah's movements. A gasmask is hanging up in the attic.

The Supporting Cast

• *The Doctor.* [This incarnation previously met Sarah in X2.3, "School Reunion" and X4.12-4.13, "The Stolen Earth"/"Journey's End"; he saw Luke over video in the latter.] He's wearing his blue suit. He knows Clyde and Rani by reputation. All the old favourites are here: 'Allons Y', a 'nononono', 'I'll explain later', an Eric Morecambe cheek-slap for Luke and 'I'm so sorry' to Peter. [He'll see Sarah and Luke one last time, in X4.18, "The End of Time Part Two".]

• *Background.* He knows about the Pantheon of Discord from childhood, but doesn't seem to have encountered the Trickster directly before now [cf X4.11, "Turn Left"]. He knows more about the futures of the Bannerman Road gang than he's willing to let on.

• *Inventory: Sonic Screwdriver.* He whips it out to take measurements of some kind. [In the first draft, this would have cued the kids in as to the identity of this wedding-crasher.] It bleeps when used as a tracker.

• *Inventory: Other.* He's got an old-fashioned football rattle handy for stopping rows [see 14.1, "The Masque of Mandragora"].

• *Clyde.* Has enough experience with adventuring that when he's stuck in a time-loop, it doesn't surprise him that a spatial anomaly goes with it. He wears a pinstripe suit, dark blue tie and white plimsolls [this may be why the TARDIS takes a shine to him]. He dislikes 'lame' excuses and people over 22 snogging in public. He rapidly figures out how to use an accidental infusion of Artron energy to poleaxe the Trickster.

At the end, Sarah forbids the kids from travelling in the TARDIS, as the Judoon previously forbade Clyde and Rani from leaving Earth. [*SJA:* "Prisoner of the Judoon". A later story, *SJA:* "The Empty Planet", establishes that this "grounding" extends to teleports, so it may be concern for the TARDIS rather than just strict parenting.]

• *Rani.* Likes being a bridesmaid but, as always, spends this story anticipating her mother's unwelcome interventions. She can order Clyde around with a scowl and a pointed finger.

• *Luke* is slightly awkward about giving his mum away and has trouble saying anything about Rani's fuchsia above-the-knee dress.

• *Mr Smith.* Sarah's supercomputer has got something like a quiet mode for boot-ups, without the fanfare. It's still a bit showbiz. With the aid of a big lever in the wall, Sarah can shut him down, but only does so after instructing him to initiate a 'Protocol Five' closedown procedure.

• *K9* doesn't get on with Mr Smith. It's as tense as supposedly-unemotional machines can get.

Stairs pose less of a problem for K9, as he announces 'activating stair-negotiation: hover-mode' when leaving the driveway for the attic. He can scan people surreptitiously. He can also detect 'veracity level' when he suspects that Sarah is lying and registers that she fancies Dalton based upon her 'heightened emotional state. Alpha waves

high, heartbeat fast, increased serotonin.'

UNIT The Brigadier is unable to attend Sarah's wedding, as he's back in Peru. [4.4, "The Sontaran Stratagem". Maybe he's investigating talking bears who eat marmalade.]

The Non-Humans

• *The Trickster* has taken to wearing white when pretending to be an angel, but reverts to basic black when revealed. Despite his ability to manipulate time, he acts as if he's on a deadline vis-à-vis the Bannerman Road massive's part in some forthcoming event he wants to prevent.

• *Travas Polong* seems to be the name of a resident of Polungus who was stuck on Earth. While he was in his dormant phase, someone sold him on eBay. While inside a cardboard box, Travas seemed like the Warner Bros Tasmanian Devil – but was revealed to be a ciliate slug with four eyes on stalks, roughly a metre long at full stretch, and capable of moving faster than walking-speed. It's a sort of salmon pink on its dorsal surface. The Polongus government arrange a transmat home via Mr Smith. [This may be the same beastie wandering around a hospital a year or so earlier; Sarah chased something very similar in *SJA:* "Mark of the Berserker".]

History

• *Dating.* The Doctor knows Luke from their teleconferencing session ["Journey's End"], so it's after that. Sarah had met Peter five times in a month before the story starts; we get on-screen captions 'Two Days Later' and 'Three Days Later' and the wedding's two weeks after that. It looks like spring. [Another story that season, *SJA:* "Mona Lisa's Revenge" refers back to X4.15, "Planet of the Dead" but with the Doctor on the lam from Destiny/Ood Sigma, he might not be playing by the usual rules as far as sequential meetings go.]

The Analysis

The Big Picture In the beginning (1999, 2000), the BBC approached hot young writer Russell T Davies and asked him if there were any pet projects he wanted to do on the back of *Queer as Folk.* They were expecting something cutting-edge about drugs, gay men and gay men doing drugs, but he insisted on *Doctor Who.*

Should the Trickster Have a Dead Bird on His Head?

This is a book explicitly about *Doctor Who* but specifically, in this volume, about episodes made and shown when the majority of viewers would be familiar with one or both of the spin-off dramas. However, the intended readership might not have seen either of these. More to the point, the official viewership of *The Sarah Jane Adventures* weren't expected to be familiar with *Doctor Who* stories from the era when Sarah Jane Smith travelled in the TARDIS. The people writing the allegedly juvenile part of the franchise sure as hell were, though.

In the interests of getting everyone onto the same page, therefore, we ought to set this two-part Tennant-Sladen summit-meeting in its wider context… or contexts. This isn't Sarah's first on-screen run-in with this entity – or, rather, these entities, as it's a walking "Pantheon of Discord". It's sort of like the City of Pandaemonium dressed as Yartek, Leader of the Alien Voord impersonating Arbitan (1.5, "The Keys of Marinus") and finally speaking whole sentences this week. But when the Doctor harangues the Trickster, his comments make more sense to older viewers, or at least a *different* sense.

For these purposes, our story begins with a game made available to viewers with digital television, computers or suitable phones: *Attack of the Graske*. The eponymous adversary was a literal little green man (you can guess from this that Jimmy Vee was our guest star), and the new Doctor (this came out immediately after X2.0, "The Christmas Invasion") talked the player through rescuing a family that had been abducted and replaced by doppelgangers. The Graske had tentacles growing from his head. So far, so generic.

But once they'd shelled out for all that latex, it was wasteful not to re-use this design; that's a large part of what *The Sarah Jane Adventures* was made to do, after all. The Graske showed up in *SJA* as the agent of an entity called the Trickster or, more accurately, a bond-servant. In *SJA*: "Whatever Happened to Sarah Jane?", things were changed around so that Sarah drowned in 1963 and her best friend from school (who had died in the usual chronology) had always lived in Bannerman Road. An alien artefact protects Maria, the kid next door, from the historical alterations, so the Graske is dispatched with his time-space Taser to zap her, and send her to the same limbo where Sarah has been languishing. However, once this is all resolved, the big problem is that Maria's dad has found out what goes on in Sarah Jane's attic. He's

out of the series, as is Maria, when the Trickster tries again in *SJA*: "The Temptation of Sarah Jane Smith", and messes with chronology when Sarah is a baby in 1951.

However, apart from the now-traditional need for a relative to die in a traffic-accident to reset the timeline (her parents), and meeting loved ones in reduced circumstances in an Evil Parallel Universe (Rani's parents), the situation is resolved by persuading/allowing the Graske to quit. In both of these, and *SJA*: "The Wedding of Sarah Jane Smith", the hinge-point is the Trickster asking someone who's about to die if they'd prefer to live, then leveraging this to pre-emptively remove the *SJA* regulars from a more significant hinge-point where Earth is fairly doomed without them.

For the purported main audience for *SJA*, therefore, "The Wedding of Sarah Jane Smith" finished a trilogy of stories where the Trickster tried to neutralise Sarah ahead of some enormous contribution she was going to make to establishing order and harmony. Significantly, once this storyline was dropped a new semi-regular character – an enigmatic shopkeeper with a parrot – started giving her team odd tasks (one involving three separate junction-points in history; *SJA*: "Lost in Time"). This seemed almost as if he was auditioning Sarah, Luke, Clyde and Rani for some future role (a hint reinforced by his off-stage manipulation of a second Magic Alien Baby, AKA Sky, for Miss Smith to raise once Luke had gone to Oxford). The Doctor as good as says that the Bannerman Road team holds a future importance beyond even the repeated world-saving stuff in the series's first three seasons. Whoever the Trickster might be, the chances to thwart this future seemed to be running out.

The Trickster, or his Brigade, is mentioned outside Sarah Jane's show. The most significant happens when a Time Beetle takes Donna's past and twists it into a whole different dimension (X4.11, "Turn Left") – it was merely trying to feed off the altered timeline of an individual, unaware of this individual's true power. (Another creature turns up in *Torchwood: Miracle Day*, but the stuff about FDR's hat isn't of any use to us here.) It was stated to be one of the Trickster's "pets", which suggests that there are others. But, with the marked similarity of feeding-habits between the Beetle and the Weeping Angels (X3.10, "Blink" and many others), it would also seem as if the Angels were part of

continued on Page 355…

So they asked him for a low-cost relaunch, and he pitched them a series about teenagers finding that the daffy old woman down the street who told them stories about time travel, monsters and alien worlds wasn't making it up. The name "Judi Dench" was floated, rather optimistically. Then other bits of the BBC gave the world *Death Comes to Time* and *Scream of the Shalka,* and the project withered on the vine.

A few years later, Davies was asked again and gave the same answer. You know the rest (if not, look out **Why Now? Why Wales?** under X1.1, "Rose"). That was BBC1's big hit, and BBC Wales's, so other bits of the BBC asked for their own piece of the pie. BBC3, the network that gave us *Swiss Toni* and *Snog, Marry, Avoid,* got *Torchwood* to play with (until that series got too successful). Children's television, formerly distributed among the "proper" channels (BBC1, est.1936, and BBC2 – even in the digital-only era, two of the three that most people watch) was in the process of being hived off into two ghetto channels, CBeebies (for toddlers) and CBBC (then for eight to 15 year olds) and the latter wanted a fantasy drama from Davies.

Well, what they *wanted* was a *Harry Potter*-like series about the Doctor as a teenager at Gallifrey Academy, but Davies told them where to shove that (and then *Merlyn* happened, see **What Were the Daftest Knock-Off Series?** under X4.10, "Midnight"). Then he pitched them a series about teenagers finding that the daffy old woman down the street who told them stories about time travel, monsters and alien worlds wasn't making it up. Starring Elisabeth Sladen, as seen in X2.3, "School Reunion".

Just to step back a bit and unpack something we've just touched on, the existence of a purpose-built BBC channel for eight to 15 year olds is part of the biggest change the Corporation had undergone since the advent of ITV in 1955. Owing to political pressure from the Blair and Thatcher governments, everything the BBC did was being evaluated on simplistic cost-benefit terms, as well as the more sophisticated and nebulous "quality" and "public service" criteria. Financial considerations were a key reason the government was now imposing a move from a mix of analogue, digital free-to-air and subscription services to an all-digital television landscape (albeit with Rupert Murdoch's channels – the ones with the Premiership football, Test cricket and US-made

Fox programming – hidden behind paywalls for first-run transmission).

The switch-off of analogue services was coming in mid-2012, just ahead of the Olympics. People were now obliged to buy set-top boxes or complicated cable subscriptions to watch things that formerly came with their TV licence. Streaming was also supposedly coming, but ITV never really got behind this. (To date, they still think of it as a way to front-load more adverts – see the complaints to Ofcom about the 2018 World Cup coverage on a system still based on Flash.)

The situation in 2009 was, therefore, that most people were sticking with analogue unless they'd gone the whole hog with a satellite dish (see **Why is Trinity Wells on Jackie's Telly?** under X1.4, "Aliens of London"). Parents with small children were more inclined to get a set-top box than most, because some well-meaning legislation aimed at curtailing the amount of junk-food advertised during ITV's children's output prompted ITV to stop broadcasting children's programming on analogue. The BBC didn't go that far, as they got public money specifically because they were there to do the less-commercial stuff.

With ITV now substantially homogenised into one agency, production houses had less need to differentiate themselves. ITV had always been ambivalent about children's television, as it lost them money for every minute shown but, with the BBC making all the running and keeping expectations higher than the undisciplined market would have done, the small regional companies had historically been coining it in exports of better-quality stuff to other countries. That aspect of ITV's output was heavily regulated, as part of the initial 1950s agreements to allow commercial television in Britain in the first place, and forced them to spend a bit of money. However, in the era of Nickelodeon, it now looked like a smart way to position themselves globally.

Which is, of course, the rub. Many families that had access to the CITV digital station also had Disney, Nick Jr, Cartoon Network and umpteen others, all paid for by shrill adverts for bits of pink plastic that made noises. The BBC's move to take their trusted and loved brand to a pair of digital, commercial-free channels was to help them survive the impending shake-up but, at the point we're talking about now (2005-10), the 70-year tradition of an hour or two of children's programming on BBC1 before the 6.00pm news was still

Should the Trickster Have a Dead Bird on His Head?

continued from Page 353...

the Pantheon of Discord, or at least a subsidiary (a Sticker-Album of Strife?), however much their actions seem to increase the amount of order and pattern in the cosmos. (Or, at least, keep the level of entropy constant above a very localised turbulence, as we'll see shortly.)

For older, or simply genned-up, viewers, there's another interpretation. This Trickster bloke, a being from beyond the Universe with a vested interest in chaos for its own sake, sounds *very* like the Black Guardian from the original run of *Doctor Who*. Which makes his counterpart, the White Guardian, the bloke with the parrot. Is this really be the case?

The available information on the Guardians comes from a few stray (and wilfully cryptic) comments in half a dozen stories, plus some notes in a BBC document proposing the idea. We elaborate on the overall conception of this fresh set of bosses for the Doctor to pretend to ignore in **What Do the Guardians Do?** under 16.1, "The Ribos Operation". In that story, we had the initial set-up... there's a Guardian of Light in Time (the White Guardian, for short) who seeks to preserve balance and order, and an opposite number who's all about chaos. They need each other to define themselves.

It's the same old binary opposition: Signal and Noise; Structure and Entropy; Sterility and Riot... either, followed to extreme, ends in death and/or meaninglessness but we're tacitly encouraged to think of Good and Evil, with Black as the latter. The Doctor annoys the Black Guardian, who some time later recruits Turlough as an assassin (20.3, "Mawdryn Undead"). To get Turlough's aid, he appears to the lad just after a near-fatal car-crash, and offering him a Faustian pact: his life and escape from his miserable existence at a minor public school in return for the small favour of murdering the Doctor. It's exactly the methodology the Trickster uses three times in a row.

The last we saw of them (in that configuration) was the climax of 20.5, "Enlightenment", where they delayed the "shock" revelation that the Doctor wasn't dead by discussing their bookend-like co-dependent relationship. The White Guardian, whose previous appearance had been giving the Doctor his marching orders at the start of Season Sixteen whilst dressed as a plantation-owner, had a hat made from a dove; the Black Guardian was dressed as he had been for the previous 11 episodes, in a black doublet and a

raven-like hat. Both were played by the usual actors (Cyril Luckham and Valentine Dyall respectively), although there is a school of thought that the chap at the start of "The Ribos Operation" was also the Black Guardian setting up his trap. The Guardians can take any form, including posing as Borusa and each other: the Black Guardian posed as White in "The Armageddon Factor" (16.6) to get the Key to Time from the Doctor.

In that final appearance in "Enlightenment", they were jointly judging a race conducted by the Eternals, who exist outside time and – if such a term applies here – pre-date it. There is a delphic comment about the Black Guardian's apparent demise being a sham as the White Guardian is still in business "until we are no longer needed", whatever that was supposed to mean. Other than that, we had a few hints in 16.3, "The Stones of Blood" that ravens are somehow the agents of the Black Guardian and a very odd set of circumstances in arguably the dullest *Doctor Who* story ever broadcast, 20.4, "Terminus" (wherein the Black Guardian knows that the Universe was created by a leaky sump-tank on a spaceship and uses this knowledge to try to make the Doctor accidentally end everything). But that's it. Setting aside various Big Finish audios, you now have all the data on the Guardians that anyone who saw every single episode has, without the need to endure Dyall's gurgly *Nyarr Har Harrrrrs*.

It's therefore possible to make this connection if you don't look too carefully, but the details don't entirely stack up. This isn't entirely unprecedented in the three-series cluster (see **Must All Three Series Correlate?** under X4.4, "The Sontaran Stratagem") and it's far from the biggest anomaly in Sarah's differing pasts (see **Was There a Martian Time-Slip?** under X4.16, "The Water of Mars"). Nonetheless, let's pay attention to these gaps and contradictions and see what other information they reveal.

The Trickster speaks of the Doctor as a story he's heard. He talks in vaguely awed terms of how the Last of the Time Lords once held the Key to Time in his hand. (The Black Guardian, as an eye-witness and agent in the climax of "The Armageddon Factor", would know that this is a slight exaggeration. The Doctor once completed the sacred object on his coffee-table, but never actually held it as a complete artefact.) The Doctor's met the Black Guardian, the Trickster's not met the Doctor.

continued on Page 357...

sacrosanct. (See **What Was Children's Telly Like Back Then?** under 3.7, "The Celestial Toymaker" and **Cultural Primer: Why *Blue Peter*?** under 15.2, "The Invisible Enemy" for the background, then **Did All the Puff and Hype *Totally* Change Things?** under X2.1, "New Earth" for how we got to here.)

The most noticeable thing about watching recordings of the 2009-vintage BBC1 slot for CBBC programmes is how much it looks like an extended shop-window for the stuff over on the digital channel. *The Sarah Jane Adventures* was a textbook example, as they timetabled the BBC1 reruns of last week's new episodes to end just before the broadcast of the next one over on the other channel. (The dates we've given for this story are the BBC1 debut, a week after the CBBC channel had shown it.) The BBC1 timeslot and the digital channel had the same branding and jingles, but different hosts. (At this stage, there was a puppet of a cactus with a monobrow… there was a good reason for this once, apparently.)

In other ways, though, *The Sarah Jane Adventures* was a glaring anomaly. The people commissioning the programmes generally relied on research (usually by educational psychologists or people investigating a "sure-fire" hit that failed), which led them to believe that a series such as this – if pitched by anyone else and at any other time – wouldn't be worth doing. It's about an old woman. Other parents and adults are largely comic figures, or obstacles, but Sarah Jane is the prime mover and instigator of the majority of the plots. A number of episodes concern her difficulties with adjusting to change, while the kids around her have smaller transitions to negotiate. The teenagers aren't as desexualised as in any other series. In the first year, single-parenthood was the norm and the parents all had lives of their own. When a stable married couple come in, they're written as "Northern" first, "clueless" second and British-Asian barely at all.

Above all, it's aimed at the older end of the CBBC target audience, an age-range they later ruled out when commissioning programmes on the grounds that – their research told them – nobody over 12 watched television until they hit middle age. There is now no BBC programming aimed specifically at 12-16 year-olds and the 16-25 channel, BBC3, went off-air just ahead of another *Doctor Who* spin-off targeted at them. (*Class* had other problems, but demoting the

channel for which it was made onto online-only, just after the show was announced, wasn't helpful.) When Davies later tried a CBBC series not linked to a pre-existing hit, the hapless *Wizards vs Aliens*, he was constrained by these guidelines. That series didn't exactly set the world on fire.

So what we have in these two episodes is a bit of BBC politics. Other hit CBBC shows were getting attention and a mixed adult/child viewership (*Horrible Histories* for example), but none that could pull off such a high-profile crossover episode. In the same period, the big attention-grabbing pre-teen shows were *High School Musical, Spongebob Squarepants* and *Hannah Montana* (plus the unwelcome tabloid attention directed to *Zoey 101*) – but, in the UK, these were only available on certain subscription packages. BBC1 was in every home.

However, the move away from showing children's programming on BBC1 had already begun, and there was talk of relocating *Blue Peter* to digital-only, as part of moving production away from Television Centre. (There was a weird period when the series was done live from inside the Blue Peter Garden at TVC, inside a greenhouse when it rained. Moving non-news non-fiction to Salford, while keeping news in London but selling off Television Centre to a consortium of property developers – including Michael Grade – was another cost-benefit calculation. It was based on a faulty premise, but they were committed to it.) Grabbing headlines and ratings by finally bringing the TARDIS to Bannerman Road was a tactical move, but one that came at a critical moment.

As with many *Sarah Jane Adventures* stories, this gives us a worked example of one of the regulars dealing with a common emotional difficulty faced in adolescence, pitched up a few notches by aliens, but finally presses the reset button so that the next story can start from scratch on a different form of teen-angst. The ostensible target audience were too young to remember *Buffy the Vampire Slayer*, and *Charmed* was on Channel 5 (which nobody willingly watched). Most of the comparable US imports such as *Roswell High* (called *Roswell* in the US), *Smallville* et al were over by 2008 or on unappealing niche digital channels in the UK. They were, of course, foreign and thus slightly incomprehensible – so, for the British public, *Doctor Who* and its derivatives were both more accessible physically (even if they could receive them, so few people ventured onto the

Should the Trickster Have a Dead Bird on His Head?

continued from Page 355...

Assuming some kind of synch or meshing of the Time Lord's personal timeline with the cosmos as a whole and malign entities at work within it, this makes it unlikely that the two similar nefarious agencies are the same. We're led to believe that the Guardians see all of time in a synoptic fashion (one hesitates to use the word "Panopticon", but perceiving every event as simultaneous and inter-linked seems to be part of what they do). We can't really rely on a timey-wimey cop-out that this is the Black Guardian in embryo, before he became the gravel-voiced embodiment of evil with terrible taste in headwear.

The motives of beings like this are never exactly clear. Sutekh loftily said "your evil is my good", and that was as much as we needed or got ("Pyramids of Mars" again). Davros started out having a comprehensible reason for keeping his race alive in any form, by any means necessary – but by Series 4, he was reduced to destroying the universe because that's what baddies do (see also X4.18, "The End of Time Part Two"). However, in SJA: "The Temptation of Sarah Jane Smith", the Trickster is trying to use the breach in history to escape the Limbo Dimension where he's been stuck (more on this in a tick), and then… trash Earth to build rockets and spread destruction across the galaxy.

This is something of a come-down, if this really is the Black Guardian. A spot of vandalism isn't really the same as the sort of grand scheme of cosmic dissonance we would expect from Chaos Incarnate. However, it seems to connect to the overall thread of disrupting how history ought to go. Humans become big players in the future (indeed, under Russell T Davies, the only significant ones), and removing this from the pattern might be a significant contribution to destabilising the cosmic order. But that's not how the Trickster pitches it. This disordered version of 2009 is somehow necessary for the Trickster to stay out of Limbo. So it's worth asking whether he/it/they feed on alterations to time, as the Time Beetles and Weeping Angels do, and as the werewolf in X2.2, "Tooth and Claw" hinted was his sole purpose.

There was an earlier encounter with something that fed on lifespans rather than life, the unloved "The Time Monster" (9.5). In this we saw Kronos, a Chronovore, ingest Stuart Hyde's expected lifespan, ageing him half a century in a heartbeat. If the Trickster were somehow related to these, even

as some sort of idiot cousin they don't talk about, the Doctor might have mentioned it. Given the way the SJA writers littered the dialogue with references back to the 70s episodes, it seems odd that they didn't identify the Trickster or the guy with the parrot as any kind of continuity reference. Conversely, it also seems odd that no effort was made to deny that these two were old characters in new drag, on the assumption that about half the audience were thinking it.

As SJA unfolded, it became increasingly obvious that its cosmology differs slightly from what the new iteration of Doctor Who after 2005, but conforms to a lot of the inferences from the older iteration that were current in the 1990s. SJA: "Secrets of the Stars" posits powers from a previous universe where the laws of nature were subtly different, allowing astrology to work in a way almost like the actions of the Mandragora Helix (14.1, "The Masque of Mandragora"). This is also the basis for the dénouement of "The Infinite Quest", another tale of a ship from the Dawn of Time imbued with eldritch powers (but with rather better acting than "Terminus"). We saw in **Are All These 'Gods' Related?** under "The Curse of Fenric" (26.3) how this idea, combined with warmed-over HP Lovecraft and regurgitated Michael Moorcock, dominated the Virgin Books. If the writers' past performances could be relied upon, we would have heard if these two new characters been old ones reformatted. Admittedly, The Sarah Jane Adventures ended rather more abruptly than anyone hoped, but a few more clues yea or nay weren't out of the question.

Let's assume for the moment that neither of these manipulative entities was anything we'd heard about in any form of Doctor Who. It's interesting that the Doctor identifies the Trickster to Donna as the culprit behind "Turn Left" as if she ought to know who or what that means, but then he encounters this being – apparently the first time for either party – and acts as if he can easily stop it with a screwdriver. That's not at all in keeping with any comparable old series malign forces of comparable abilities. The Black Guardian is never overcome, just obstructed; Kronos is annihilated, then comes back and amuses itself by pressing a reset button to spare the Doctor, the Master and Jo; the Eternals (as identified) simply end their game and leave our dimension – the games of the possible Eternals in "The Celestial Toymaker" (3.7),

continued on Page 359...

ABOUT TIME 2008-2009

digital channels without an experienced guide) and conceptually.

Within the programme's context, this story has a fairly linear plan underlying it. On two previous instances, the Trickster has found someone in Sarah's past who died and offers that person a chance to live, conditional on other changes that happen as a result. First time it was a school friend who fell from a pier in 1963; she lives and Sarah died, but only Sarah's friend Maria knows the difference. Second, it was Sarah's parents, in 1951, and she is forced to stand by and let them be killed in a car crash. These incidents were juxtaposed with the consequences: first an impending meteor-strike wiping out all life on Earth, because there's no Mr Smith to stop it, second a dystopian present where Rani's mum is one of the few surviving humans, enslaved.

So far, these followed the template established by Harlan Ellison in 1966 and refined by Paul Cornell in 2005 (X1.8, "Father's Day") by way of "Mawdryn Undead" (20.3) and the Black Guardian's deal with Turlough. This new story adds to the mix the *Last Temptation* thread of "Human Nature" (X3.8) by offering Sarah a normal life with a straightforward marriage. In the earlier versions, this was offset by focusing on Clyde's difficulty in adjusting to the gang splitting up; the Brigadier is on hand to give away the bride and compares it to the UNIT family going their separate ways. (This would have been the one on-screen use of the word "family" to describe the 70s stories' line-up.) Thus the story's focus was on the team needing each other, just as the previous story (*SJA*: "The Madwoman in the Attic") hinged on Rani's sense of being a spare wheel and the next year's season opener, *SJA*: "The Nightmare Man", explored Luke's anxiety about leaving, Clyde's worry about not being special enough and Rani's dread of not measuring up to her ambitions.

A further indication of this programme's anomalous status within BBC drama is that a lot of the guest-cast were known to viewers over 30 for other things. Appearing in something ostensibly for children allows them to evade type-casting – the supposed viewers wouldn't be familiar with Russ Abbott, Cheryl Campbell or Peter Bowles, but the parents watching alongside would. The extent to which this is aimed at parents, especially those who remember Sarah Jane Smith from her TARDIS days, was made clear when Jo Grant popped back the following year (*SJA*: "Death of

the Doctor").

Deploying Nigel Havers for the spin-off's most visible story yet was less calculated than it might seem, if you'd not seen earlier episodes. He had appeared in a Big Finish audio (*No More Lies*) shortly before, so the production team knew he was out there and not fantasy-averse, but his role here is within what the casual (adult) viewer would think of as his comfort-zone. A more alarming casting-against-type, as with Bradley Walsh in multiple guises as a child-stealing demon (yes, this happened – he was the first antagonist Rani faced, in *SJA*: "Day of the Clown"), would have been risky in a story intended as a showcase for the series, but aimed at people who wouldn't otherwise watch. The press reaction to Walsh being in *Law & Order UK* and *Doctor Who* Series 11 indicates that not everyone was watching *SJA* when Tennant wasn't in it.

English Lessons

• *Gob on you!* (interj.): not an intention to spit phlegmatically: there ought to have been a definite article at the start, as in "you have a big mouth". It's as northern as Rani gets, despite her parents. (Accent-spotters will have picked up that Anjli Mohindra's from the East Midlands rather than Lancashire).

• *Buckaroo!* (n.): a game popular in the early 70s. Jon Pertwee did the voice-over for the UK adverts. It's the original one-trick pony, a spring-loaded plastic mule that you take turns loading up with mining equipment (think California 1849 rather than Rhondda Valley pre-1984), until something triggers a tricky cog and the thing flips all of it across the room. Made by MB games, so Hasbro now.

• *London W4* (n.): Chiswick. The posh bit. Just as well Luke didn't go with Clyde and Rani to investigate Peter's gaff; Donna might have remembered him.

• *Brussels* (n.): Capital of Belgium and rather a pretty Baroque/Beaux Arts city with an exciting post-war overlay (and that giant iron molecule with restaurants built for the 1958 World's Fair). Nonetheless, for people who've not been there, it's famous for sprouts and the EU, so as a romantic honeymoon destination it's slightly counter-intuitive. It's thus exactly what Haresh would pick, and precisely the sort of thing Gita would bring up.

• *Our* (adj.): Gita refers to "our Rani" in a specifically northern way, emphasising the odd class-

Should the Trickster Have a Dead Bird on His Head?

continued from Page 357...

"The Curse of Fenric", "The Greatest Show in the Galaxy" (25.4) and "The Mind Robber" (6.2) end with the Doctor out-cheating a cheating semi-deity.

So even allowing for the tenth Doctor's turbo-charged screwdriver, the quality of the game being played is different here from any of these. Why, then, have we never encountered these beings before, and why does the Universe need (or allow) such duplication of cosmic manipulators? As we've not heard a dickie-bird about the Guardians in the new series – despite one expecting they'd have a keen interest in the Time War, if only as umpires – this silence is palpable and probably deliberate. Logically, if the White Guardian sides with order, then he would have been rooting for the Daleks in the Time War – eliminating all other species and imposing iron rule on the inanimate matter left after the carnage is almost the definition of order. Davros and Rassilon planning to make matter revert to chaos is, by contrast, doing the Black Guardian's job for him.

The Time War can't have destroyed the Guardians, but they may have withdrawn for a while. The War's end may also have allowed other lesser (but still immeasurably puissant) beings to stand in for them in everyday affairs. Perhaps the Pantheon and the Parrot are symptoms of the Time War rather than instigators or agents. Of course, when it comes to the space-time vortex arranging things in favour of either order or destruction, we *have* seen a matched pair of entities: the Bad Wolf twins, manifesting as Rose-with-superpowers, and the coincidence-arranging Dalek Caan (see **Bad Wolf – What Why and How?** under X1.13, "The Parting of the Ways").

So, this Limbo Dimension thing, then. It's remarkably like the ones we saw in "The Mind Robber" and "Warriors' Gate" (18.5) and is a repository for beings removed from time by the Trickster's machinations. But, as we discover later, it's also where the Trickster is imprisoned, pending getting its altering history to gain a toe-hold in our reality. It speaks about this as if it draws energy from such disorder and bruised time. Moreover, Artron Energy (blue this time around) seems to repel it.

In the two old-series stories (and, arguably, in 6.7, "The War Games" as a barrier between time-zones), that white misty void thing was a symbol

of being on a threshold between realities, the TARDIS co-ordinates reading zero in both cases. This is a different thing from being a pocket universe in and of itself (see, for example, X6.4, "The Doctor's Wife", X7.10, "Hide" and **How is This Not a Parallel Universe?** under "Turn Left"). So whatever this misty nowhere is, it can't be considered a different universe spatially, but more a side-effect of sheared-off timelines. It seems to stem from the laws of this universe as regards time-paradoxes, not a different one with different laws. Perhaps, then, the Trickster is a manifestation of such a temporal holding-bay seeking to preserve or expand itself by creating wrongnesses. If this were the case, the Black Guardian might have common cause with it, or – seeing that it subsists from damage to this reality rather than utterly destroying it as the Guardian seems to desire – see it as a parasite, almost as indebted to the White Guardian for preserving the order it needs to poison.

We have, within the new *Doctor Who*, a rough analogue: House from "The Doctor's Wife" is a consciousness embodied as a pocket-universe. It feeds on TARDISes, yet seems oblivious to the Time War and the sudden end to its food-supply. Moreover, the Doctor hasn't heard of it – and neither, apparently, had the 20-odd Time Lords killed by it. For the Trickster to be a conscious pocket-universe and at large within our cosmos seems strange, but mainly because there aren't others equally active. Then again, as we have said in earlier volumes, the curious thing about the Doctor's travels is how small a slice of the known cosmos he ever visits (**How Many Significant Galaxies are There?** under 2.5, "The Web Planet").

For what it's worth, the early scripts for this story name-check the Guardians as part of the Pantheon, alongside the Trickster and his shadows, the Reapers (X1.8, "Father's Day") and the Graske. This makes the Guardians a bit less ultimate than advertised. However, the broadcast version see the Trickster almost star-struck by the Doctor – something the Guardians never were, so presenting them as equals isn't going to wash. We seem to be looking at a chain of middle-management (of *EVIL*), from Fenric and/or the Guardians to the Pantheon and the bloke with the parrot to the Graske and Sarah's chums. The Graske wasn't entirely chuffed to be indentured to the Trickster, and rebelled when given the chance. The Bannerman Road Mob were at least given the

continued on Page 361...

ABOUT TIME 2008-2009

divide in that marriage. She's not above beginning sentences with "Ee". The use of "our" as a prefix usually suggests affection or familiarity, but can be a put-down for anyone who fled that background and tried to make something of themselves.

Oh, Isn't That...?

• *Ace Bhatti* (Haresh Chandra, Rani's dad) had been in *The Second Coming* as best mate to Steve, the Messiah (Christopher Eccleston). He'd been in both *Casualty* and *Holby City* (as the same character in each) and in *Bend It Like Beckham*. His breakthrough role was in *Cardiac Arrest,* but the biggie so far is nefarious Yusef in *EastEnders*.

• *Mina Anwar* (Gita Chandra, Rani's mum) first came to people's notice in Rowan Atkinson vehicle *The Thin Blue Line*. She was in *The Bill* for a while, and popped up hither and yon in the usual cop-shows and soaps and *House of Anubis*. You may have seen her in "Smile" (X10.2) as "Goodthing".

• *Anjli Mohindra* (Rani) was recently in *The Bodyguard*, the other BBC1 Sunday Night drama people were obsessing over in Autumn 2018.

• *Zienia Merton* (Registrar). Oh, look, it's Ping-Cho. Since her TV debut in "Marco Polo" (1.4), she was most prominent in *Space: 1999*. Lots of small film and telly parts (often uncredited), but other highlights include playing "Zenia" in the *Jason King* episode of the same name and Christina in the Dennis Potter *Casanova*. She died in 2018, her reading of the "Marco Polo" novelisation released posthumously.

• *Nigel Havers* (Peter Dalton) is now mainly famous for being Nigel Havers. He cornered the market in suave bachelors with slightly guilty consciences, to the extent of getting the lead in a drama called *The Charmer*. After a slew of starring roles in costume dramas (e.g. *Upstairs, Downstairs, Nicholas Nickelby* and most notably *A Horseman Riding By* on Sundays in 1978) and a hit sitcom (*Don't Wait Up*), he was, by 1990, almost a professional self-parody. This made his twenty-first century role in *Coronation Street* almost perversely inevitable. Ditto 1990s drama *Sleepers*, in which he and Warren Clarke are chalk-and-cheese *spesnatz* agents who went native: Havers as a playboy stockbroker, Clarke as a union leader. Inevitably, he landed up in *Downton Abbey*. In film, he's got a tranche of 80s period dramas to his name, especially *Chariots of Fire* and *Empire of the Sun*. His dad was Attorney General.

Things That Don't Make Sense [Here we'll assume that the lurid red glow of the ring when controlling Sarah's mind is a narrative conceit, and not visible to the various people who would normally ask "why's your ring doing that?".]

Isn't "Pantheon of Discord" sort of like "Hermits United"? Does the discord extend to their inability to get on with each other, or is it just outsiders they want to turn against everyone else? And it's not a logical or factual flaw, but still... with Gita usually so inquisitive about Sarah's life and affairs (and able to name her hairdresser and ex-editor and recognise her accountant), isn't it a bit odd that she never mentions the abrupt disappearance of the dishy fiancé again?

Sarah gets back to the attic and changed before the kids return. They're still in wedding togs. Did she cadge a lift in the roller, and leave the rest to go home in Gita's flower-van?

Critique It is, as football commentators like to say, a game of two halves. The second episode has all the brio and sparkle we came to expect when Tennant is playing the Doctor, plus a reminder that the kids we've been following for all the adventures so far haven't actually seen the TARDIS, but it's a bit fannish.

The first half, however, has warmth and wit of a different kind. The core of that episode is a small scene of Peter and Luke giggling over Sarah's habitual curiosity, just after the *Men in Black* slapstick of getting an alien millipede off the planet without people noticing. Even though the situation is increasingly bizarre, it's grounded in character-humour and observation. This earns the more frantic latter episode the right to be mainly people running up and down corridors spouting continuity and technobabble. So long as you hadn't tuned in specifically to see the Doctor, the first half grounds the second and justifies it.

The story's secret weapon is Nigel Havers. He's almost the last person one would have expected to see in a children's television spin-off of *Doctor Who*, but he sells the climax and seems completely at home. It seems criminally unjust that Peter doesn't get a happy ending, or that Sarah can't save him. Older viewers and hardened fans would have seen the ending coming a mile off, not least because they've done it before in this series and recent *Who* – but, while you're watching, this barely matters. The performances make it seem fresh at that moment.

Should the Trickster Have a Dead Bird on His Head?

continued from Page 359...

choice. Maybe the ultimate battle of Light and Darkness is run like a Ponzi scheme. It's a familiar idea from many faiths, but doesn't quite match what we see in these stories. Moreover, the absence of the Guardians from any conversation about this, even when the Eternals have been dropped into the dialogue rather nonchalantly, seems strange.

The Trickster, when the Doctor finally explains, is from "beyond" time and space, attempting to manifest fully in our dimension. This seems a stark contrast from being, as the Guardians are implied to be, themselves embodiments of our universe's natural laws. However, our main evidence for thinking this of the Guardians is what Graham Williams wrote in his memo, not anything explic-

itly stated on screen. They define each other, are "needed" and each have reasons to want the Key to Time assembled, but are they local?

What if, just as the Ood seem to be developing to replace the Time Lords, the Trickster and the Parrot (in some scenes, the Shopkeeper apparently took orders from the bird rather than just confided in it) are a Guardian tribute-act caused or recruited by the cosmic order needing beings of that sort to replace the long-lost originals? This implies a lot more weirdness, not least some event so cataclysmic that it destroys the final arbiters of order and chaos. The Time War doesn't cut it. If anything, the Time War would have consolidated their positions. Perhaps such an event is, from our perspective, yet to occur. Maybe it's the very thing the Trickster wants to stop Sarah and her Scooby Gang from influencing.

Not that the regulars are at all shabby, but we'd come to expect that. It's become a set of double-acts; Luke and Sarah Jane, Clyde and Rani, Haresh and Gita and now Mr Smith and K9. The writers and directors had picked up on this and were working with it, but the fact that Peter didn't immediately disrupt the dynamic was part of the story's subtlety. Making Luke resentful would have been easy and a bit cheap. Making Peter obviously a hypnotist or con-man would have deflated the whole story. Showing Clyde to be concerned about how Peter would react to the whole Earth-saving aspect of their lives, rather than thinking of him as a threat per se, then getting nosy, then concerned, was more in-character and allowed Rani to be the voice of moderation for once. Even if it was forced on them by circumstances (see **The Lore**), it's indicative of how much care went into the series.

The drawback to all of this is the way Sladen becomes almost an afterthought in her own show. In the first episode, this isn't so obvious. She's having to negotiate a smooth transition from the cheery Series 3 version of Sarah Jane Smith to a defensive, outraged aspect, more like how she was in Series 1 but embittered. Over the 15 previous stories, the character had altered and mellowed, overcoming the regrets that formed the core of "School Reunion". Whatever the female equivalent of "avuncular" is, she's it, not maternal – even with Luke it's never quite that – but giving us a character who's enjoying the peculiar life she leads

and not initially willing to give it up. It's entirely plausible that being made to choose between that and happy-ever-after would be a wrench. The script makes this hard to convey, because the timescale is so telescoped. Then in the second episode, the Doctor and Clyde are making most of the running and Sarah's nearly sidelined. These sections of the story are made a lot more effective by Sladen and Havers seeming to have a genuine rapport.

But we have to wonder what anyone unfamiliar with the series made of it, even if they had been diligently watching *Doctor Who* and knew about the attic, K9, Mr Smith and Luke. Would they have wondered why Rani's parents were so prominent in the story? Would Sarah wearing dresses have flummoxed them or seemed like a warning sign? It's probably a good thing that the story made no more concessions to a hypothetical novice viewer than usual. However, it's hard to avoid the sense that anyone just watching for the Doctor was missing the *real* story and lost a lot of the flavour. They were probably entertained, but may have wondered why. It's really Clyde's story and – if you don't know him or how far he's come – this might make it seem a bit perfunctory.

The Lore

Written by Gareth Roberts. Directed by Joss Agnew. BBC1 figures 1.6 million, 1.5 million (not bad for the 4.35 pm slot), AIs 87%, 89%.

Production

• Having the Doctor, especially the Tennant version, pop in on Sarah Jane Smith within her own series was always the ambition. Timetabling the schedules of the three series in production at Upper Boat was a bit tricky (as we saw when Freema Agyeman went straight from *Doctor Who* Series 3 to *Torchwood*, but the publicity needed to be handled deftly). At the end of the second series, Nicholas Courtney had appeared as Sir Alistair Lethbridge Stewart – apparently a last-minute move when Agyeman was unavailable to play Martha, a character more children would have known about – and bringing the Brigadier back to meet the current Doctor was universally agreed to be right and proper. Eventually, it became clear that Tennant would appear in a two-episode story of *The Sarah Jane Adventures* as soon as his other commitments allowed.

• The obvious choice to write it was Gareth Roberts, who had by now notched up three broadcast scripts for this Doctor and two stories for *SJA*. The latter had been about attempts by the Trickster to rewrite the past and trap Sarah before she could prevent a catastrophe. Roberts submitted a script in January 2009 in which Clyde was narrating from the limbo dimension. This version featured the Brigadier and Doris (26.1, "Battlefield"), a different alien delivered by post and more details about the Pantheon of Discord (see this story's essay).

However, the production of *Doctor Who*'s last two episodes was a marathon, and the only available slot was in late May, after the wrap on "The End of Time", after which Tennant had other plans – many of them involving Hollywood – and would not be around in July as originally hoped. The small snag that this would clash with Tommy Knight's exams could be handled with careful scheduling. (They'd had similar problems with Yasmin Paige, hence Maria's easing out of the series.) Unlike Daniel Anthony (Clyde) and Anjli Mohindra (Rani), Knight (Luke) was genuinely still at school and sitting GCSEs. Making this story the mid-season boost rather than the season finale meant shifting K9's return to the second story, thus swapping around the running-order and putting K9 in some later episodes. On the plus side, this put *SJA*: "The Eternity Trap" (their version of a ghost story) on air on CBBC at Hallowe'en.

• A bigger problem then arose: Courtney suffered a stroke and was unable to appear. This caused significant rewrites at short notice, and meant that Luke would have to give away the bride, which in turn meant careful planning to allow Knight his exam leave. Luke also identified the Doctor, something the Brigadier surmised in the first draft. The scripts were issued on 13th April, two days ahead of the read-through. (Knight was hitherto unaware that Tennant has a Scottish accent in real life.) Havers had yet to be confirmed and wasn't at the read-through. Small rewrites added more of the Travast Polon and the pizza restaurant scene, with Luke and Peter bonding the following week.

• Although this was made as Block Three of the series, the first parts shot were in Block One, also directed by Joss Agnew. Luke's dialogue was recorded first to release Knight for revision (a double, Christian Byard, deputised for some later shots). There was a weekend off, then three days on Block Two with Alice Troughton directing, while Tennant finished his TARDIS scenes for "The End of Time". The crew did a few recces while this was happening, but the first location used was the familiar Clifton Street exterior posing as Bannerman Road. On this day, Mat Irvine showed what the latest rebuild of K9 could and couldn't do, and Nigel Havers joined the production. (Some of the regulars had video cameras, and the results can still be seen on the CBBC website if you're quick.)

• The week beginning 25th May (Bank Holiday) was Tennant Week. After the *sturm und drang* of the regeneration, it was fun for the guest star to be playing the chirpy Doctor of old again. A lot of the first day was stunt-work, with Abbi Collins supervising – Tennant was surprised that he was given less leeway to fall over than he had been in *Doctor Who*. The TARDIS arrived in the attic (courtesy of an experienced construction crew), then the regulars joined Tennant in the hastily-rebuilt TARDIS set in Studio 2. (Even though it was only briefly seen, in ruins, in the pre-credits scene of X5.1, "The Eleventh Hour", the set was mothballed for use in X6.4, "The Doctor's Wife", which was on the blocks for Series 5 at this stage.) By now, it was hard to keep the secret, so the press were told about Tennant's appearance in the spin-off.

• As we noted in "The End of Time", this story's transmission and pre-publicity was the start for what Tennant called his "scorched earth" publicity blitz. There was a sneak preview at a cinema in

Liverpool on Saturday, 24th October, five days before the debut transmission. Knight, Mohindra and Anthony were in attendance, and the *Radio Times* used it, with a photo of Sladen in the wedding dress, as the hook for a feature on children's drama. Other listings magazines are available, and it made the front cover of one of them, *Total TV Guide,* a week before.

A8: "Dreamland"

(5th December, 2009/24th December, 2009)

Which One is This? The *Indiana Jones* ripoff that hasn't got Matt Smith in it. Or, in terms of the medium used, the animated serial made with kind-of the software they later used in the online games, but a whole Doctor earlier.

Where Does It Go? According to Phil Ford, this story is meant to occur at some point after "The Waters of Mars" (X4.16); he worked on both, so ought to know. To anyone confused as to how this light-hearted story follows on from that ending, see also X7.15, "The Day of the Doctor".

Firsts and Lasts Other than a fleeting reference in "Dalek" (X1.6), this is the first time *Doctor Who* has tackled Area 51.

It's also worth noting that as of publication, this has been the last attempt at animated *Doctor Who* on UK television (even though Matt Smith's face seems made for the format, and both Peter Capaldi and Jodie Whittaker can be sketched in very easily). Under Moffat, animation was strictly the province of video games, some of which have been officially designated canon, but that's a matter for later (see **What are the Worst Merchandising Disasters of the Twenty-First Century?** under X5.3, "Victory of the Daleks" and **What were the Best Online Extras?** under X4.9, "Forest of the Dead").

Connected to this, we have here the first broadcast *Doctor Who* with Piers Wenger credited as an executive producer.

Watch Out For...
• Georgia Moffett and Tim Howar here give voice to temporary companions Cassie Rice and Jimmy Stalkingwolf. One of those actors is featured in the opening credits, one isn't. One of them had already appeared in the show and was dating the star at the time, and one isn't. We think

you can guess which is which.
• The opening animation, featuring a crashing spaceship, is an obvious money-shot and looks smashing. So they use it twice. There's also a dogfight with USAF jet fighters. Oddly, though, when a full-blown CG rendering of the same ship appears in *The Sarah Jane Adventures,* it looks rather less impressive.
• Much of this story's feel was reused for X6.1, "The Impossible Astronaut" (and, to a lesser extent, X9.12, "Hell Bent"); the roadside truck stop diner opening, the Doctor's bewildering attempt to latch on to a chunk of American culture (Tennant spends less time trying to fake an American accent than Matt Smith spends in his hat) and the whole business of stereotypically-shaped aliens straight out of UFO mythology with the inevitable "surprise" twist about the nature of the Men in Black. (In **The Lore,** we'll see that the resemblance could have been closer).
• On the other hand, this story has consequences for the Bannerman Road Massive, as the author revisits both the spaceship and the Alliance of Shades in *The Sarah Jane Adventures,* and links those to the Judoon and the Dalek theft of 27 planets. There is even a physical Ionic Fusion Bar somewhere in a cupboard in Cardiff.
• During the climax, the animators take advantage of the opportunity to portray the console room through the TARDIS door. It's more realistic than anyone's teeth or walk in this story.

The Continuity

The Doctor He seems to have an abiding fondness for bobby socks, and certainly likes chilli, though he wanders off in search of a Chinese takeaway at the end. He doesn't like being called 'Doc', and his tolerance for salutes is low. He skirts the question of whether he's 'Briddish'. Counting one's steps back to the entrance strikes him as a useful piece of life advice.

He also seems to be matchmaking again at the end, even though Cassie and Jimmy have displayed all the chemistry of Argon and broccoli. [But, it saves him the trouble of inviting either of them along in the TARDIS.]

• *Background.* He knows more about Manchester United than he ever let on to Mickey. Whether the same goes for his viewing of *Alien, Aliens, Die Hard* and *Die Hard 2: Die Harder* is another matter [see X4.0. "Voyage of the Damned" for a paraphrase that suggests that he has].

Once again, the Doctor insists he's 900. He insists, seemingly with foreknowledge, that the Varnox will be a better species in future. [One gets the impression he went off and met Houdini once just so he could dine out on the anecdote for the rest of his lives; the magician's muscle-relaxation technique comes up when he's handcuffed. Should we even mention 11.5, "Planet of the Spiders" by this stage?]

• *Inventory: Sonic Screwdriver.* Still enjoy "the sonic screwdriver taps into a sound system to explosive effect" gag? This time it's with a juke box. Then he does the exact same thing in the finale with an alien shooty machine.

The TARDIS Something's gone funny with the temporal sat-nav. The TARDIS's sound system is terrific – with enough welly in the amplification, it can drive away an entire alien invasion when the right attachment is plugged in.

The Supporting Cast

• *Cassie Rice.* The waitress and owner of a small diner, which she's run ever since her mother vanished. As decoration, she has a piece of alien equipment whose characteristics she hasn't fully understood. She and Jimmy are apparently friends even before the ruckus starts, and finish the story as a couple.

• *Jimmy Stalkingwolf.* A Native American-cum-cattle rancher, he goes in for a peculiar mixture of native and contemporary dress. [We infer that Jimmy's native culture are the Shoshone, going by the pained reference to the Bear River Massacre (different state and different tribe, but they would have spoken the same language).]

His grandfather, Night Eagle, is the leader of his local tribe. We're given a half-baked excuse as to why Jimmy doesn't know that his grandfather has been hiding an alien in a cave for years. Nevertheless, he suspects aliens have been around anyway and stealing cattle. Despite the Doctor's increasingly frustrated attempts to make him stop, Jimmy insists on calling him "Doc". He also owns a truck.

Planet Notes

• *Earth.* There really are alien artefacts at Area 51. [Anyone surprised? See X1.6, "Dalek" for sidelights on this, and X6.13, "The Wedding of River Song" for Area 52.]

The Non-Humans

• *The Time Lords.* The Doctor says humans look "Time Lord" [see also X4.15, "Planet of the Dead"].

• *The Alliance of Shades* [see also *SJA*: "The Vault of Secrets"]. It's been working to hide alien secrets from humanity, using a selection of androids that look like the popular conception of the Men in Black. They aren't brilliantly programmed; for one, their bland pseudonyms and unimaginative suit disguises give them away, and for another it's possible to reprogramme them to do the opposite of their intentions. Something as simple as an arrow can disable them.

In 1972, the organisation behind these machines shut down the majority of their operations on Earth. [See the accompanying essay.]

• *Grey Aliens.* They look just like the America idea of the Roswell aliens [see **The Big Picture** for all that malarkey]. They're rather badly losing a war with the Viperox [and this story does nothing to reverse that]. They sent an ambassador to the Viperox, Seruba Velak, to try to negotiate peace; she was shot down by "pirates" [not the Viperox, so far as we know] on the way and crashed on Earth in 1947. The US military has held her there ever since; we're not told what's been going on with her home planet since then.

• *Viperox.* A blue-green stalk-eyed insect species with excellent hearing. Like longbowmen, they seem to have problems attacking anything at too close a range. Archery kills them quite effectively, and they're vulnerable to specific high-pitched sounds that don't affect anything else. Here they're led by Lord Azlok.

Their method of interstellar attack is to send a Queen a target world, so that it can lay an army's worth of Battle Drone eggs. [The process must not take very long, as they haven't been on Earth for more than a year when the Doctor shows up. It's ambiguous whether Lord Azlok is invading Earth because he's chasing after the Viperox, or because he feels like ruining Earth for kicks.]

They have a biological caste system composed of drones and Lords; inevitably, the latter plan the invasion proper. Unlike the drones, their Lords can fly. Their spaceships are more or less flying-saucer shaped, and appear to be part organic.

• *Skorpius Flies.* A not-overly bright hive mind of small glowing blue flies. They like eating and apparently not much else. Hiding under a crate keeps the Doctor and Cassie safe from them.

What Happened in 1972?

When we published the first version of *About Time* Volume 3, there were some who disputed our UNIT dates. Then, helpfully for our cause, BBC Wales started broadcasting new episodes and making spin-off series. *Doctor Who* itself has confirmed almost all of the suppositions we made, except one that was an anomaly even in the year it was shown (7.3, "The Ambassadors of Death") and two apparent sequels, and we've got an essay on all that in this book (**Was There a Martian Time-Slip?** under X4.16, "The Waters of Mars"). There are, apart from that, only two real matters that BBC Wales has complicated. There's the existence of Torchwood from 1879 to *Torchwood: Children of Earth* (set in 2009), but we comprehensively accounted for that in **So Where Were Torchwood?** under 9.3, "The Sea Devils" and **The Great Powell Estate Date Debate** under X2.3, "School Reunion" and address it from a different angle in this book.

However, we still have to resolve one peculiar anomaly that has arisen due to the handover of production team, and the multiplicity of side-projects towards the end of David Tennant's doctorate. Apparently, between 1968 and 1972, there were *three* different agencies handling alien incursions and tripping each other up. On top of all the trouble UNIT were having with Cybermen, Silurians, etc., and whatever Torchwood was up to, an elite team of androids was going around wiping memories and confiscating spaceships. The Alliance of Shades was active in the Ealing area while the Master was becoming a vicar for a few weeks, and somehow missed shop dummies going on a killing-spree in Ealing Broadway.

For those of you not up-to-speed with *The Sarah Jane Adventures*, the story you need is "The Vault of Secrets". It begins, appropriately, with Sarah and Mr Smith sabotaging the feed from the Mars Rover so that NASA don't see any pyramids. Well, not quite: it began a year earlier with "Prisoner of the Judoon", when the Galactic plods showed up in Ealing to hunt an alien war-criminal called Androvax of the Veil. He escaped from a crashed Judoon spaceship, and commandeered local technology to build a getaway car based on one kept in Area 51. The Judoon let themselves be seen, so in "The Vault of Secrets", Rani's parents join a support-group for people who've encountered aliens (British UFO Research and Paranormal Studies Society, or if you prefer BURPPS). This would be a tiresome children's TV subplot and not worth our notice, except that the founder, Ocean Waters, has the key to the eponymous vault and has been running BURPPS as therapy because of the gaps in her memory.

Here's the thing: Ocean encountered Mr Dread (leader of what look suspiciously like Men in Black) in 1972, shortly before he and his fellow androids retired from scavenging alien tech and became custodians of a hyperspatial garage of spaceships inside a disused mental hospital in Ealing. The dying Androvax's attempt at redemption (by repossessing the ship with the gene-bank of his lost race and taking it to a new world) re-activates the Alliance of Shades for one last mission, after which Mr Dread wipes Gita Chandra's memory and deactivates himself, the gateway to the Hermetic Garage sealed from inside forever.

"Prisoner of the Judoon", "Dreamland" and "The Vault of Secrets" are all by Phil Ford. They refer to each other, to *Doctor Who* both from the 70s and the new series. We can't wish them away just because BBC America hasn't shown them. The Alliance of Shades were active when UNIT and Torchwood were also nominally in charge of dealing with the countless invasions of the Home Counties, back in the era of *The Liver Birds* and *Jonathan Livingston Seagull* lunch-boxes. What changed and why?

Leaving aside all that malarkey with Mars Probe 7, UNIT seems to have established themselves fairly thoroughly. President Winters tells us (X3.12, "The Sound of Drums") that since 1968, UNIT has been accorded responsibility for any First Contact situations, hostile or otherwise. If (as we all presumed from the novelisation of 5.5, "The Web of Fear"), UNIT was launched as a direct result of the Yeti incursion, then we can slot the dates together with ease. Exactly how secret or celebrated they are changes from story to story, as it always had under Lethbridge-Stewart. By the time we get to "The Vault of Secrets", the past has changed again. The Alliance of Shades was active between 1953 and 1972, from a base in West London as well as, or maybe instead of, New Mexico. Mr Dread, apart from a major reboot and a change of hair-colour, moved from the US to the UK some time between 1958 and 1972. From the newspaper clippings in their bunker, it appears that the Alliance robots were active in Britain for some time before shutdown. Yet their decommission is almost the first thing we learn about them; within moments of the Doctor being confronted with Mr Dread and

continued on Page 367...

ABOUT TIME 2008-2009

[They seem to run by the Ravenous Bugblatter Beast principle; if you can't see them, they can't see you.]

History

• *Dating*. The opening scene is, of course, 13th June, 1947. We're told that the Doctor arrives 11 years later and it's nice and sunny. [So let's call it June, 1958. "All I Have to Do is Dream" had been released in April, but hit the top of the charts in May and stayed there for a month, so that timing works out nicely.] The American government admitted to the existence of Area 51 in 1994.

Something goes horrifically wrong with American chili around 1962, in the Doctor's opinion. [We can darkly speculate that it's the advent of Taco Bell in that same year.] The US government in 1958 makes use of an amnesia gas, but it appears to be of limited use, as the Doctor says that human race doesn't develop a good amnesia drug for about 50 years after this story. [In other words, approximately when Torchwood develops it for dishing out to sundry Cardiff residents.]

The Analysis

The Big Picture Why do so many people think that aliens look like spooky pale Teletubbies? A lot of this was the fault of horror writer Whitley Streiber, whose novel-that-claimed-not-to-be-one, *Communion*, described his abduction, in 1985, by beings noticeably similar to creatures from his earlier fiction. His subsequent work on the alleged cover-up, *Majestic*, gave the name to the fictional outfit in brief 90s US show *Dark Skies* and his podcast on alien matters is called (drumroll, please) *Dreamland*.

The cover to the Streiber book depicts one of the so-called "Grey", analogous to the purported abductors of Betty and Barney Hill in 1961, itself not unlike various BEMs in Hollywood product of the 1950s. Carlo Rimbaldi's design for *Close Encounters of the Third Kind* is the obvious starting-point for the modern iteration; these were explicitly made to look "wise" and vaguely oriental. In the mid-90s, what purported to be a clip of film of the passenger of a crashed flying saucer in Roswell, New Mexico half a century earlier, became a meme and it too had a doe-eyed, pot-bellied ET.

Science-fiction aficionados – well-versed in duff special effects, implausibly humanoid extra-terrestrials and picking holes in daft stories – didn't buy this for a second, but it was too good a story to leave alone. Every space-themed franchise does a Roswell story at some point, especially after the whole "Alien Autopsy" kerfuffle in the mid-1990s. As a plot-motor, it's as hackneyed as lizards in human-skin suits taking over the world, or someone experiencing a breakdown and thinking he's a fictional hero after seeing his wife die. As iconography, it's as tired as all spaceships having warp drives and teleports, all galactic empires being evil and run by English-accented Nazis and all Martians being green.

The Roswell fad was already a standing joke by the time *Futurama* pummelled it into the ground. Had *Doctor Who* been on air in the 1990s – properly, we mean – there would have been a whole lot of stories like this one. Even the botched TV movie had a strong hint of it, when Grace Holloway is encouraged to forget the strange patient with two hearts. *Torchwood* was little more than a late addition to the me-too rash of series based on this paranoid urban myth; American television produced them in industrial quantities in the late 90s and even adapted more overtly space-operatic shows to embrace it.

They even did a teen-drama, *Roswell*, that was like *Class* but less corny – and, of course, a whole year of *Buffy the Vampire Slayer* riffed on the governmental cover-up and bids to harness eldritch powers for Special Ops. Those of you following the bizarre careers of Ant and Dec (see 22.1, "Attack of the Cybermen" and comments on Russell T Davies's early career here and in the last two volumes) will know of the film *Alien Autopsy*. That tied together Crop Circles (X6.8, "Let's Kill Hitler") and the dodgy internet "footage" in a farce plot based on the real backstory to the entire imbroglio. It also had Lachele Carl as a US news-anchor. One thing the film made clear: the whole thing began as a joke and got too big to stop.

Twenty years on, it's almost impossible to comprehend how accepted this all was. It was an article of faith for anyone with any pretensions toward being an outsider, either as a signed-up member of the plaid-shirt-and-piercings crowd (who would never self-identify as a "slacker" – because that was, like, totally corporate), or the raw-meat-eating survivalist types with fishing-vests, oddly square beards and military clothing, that the government was lying about everything to do with space. The Moon Landing was a fake,

What Happened in 1972?

continued from Page 365...

his posse in the desert, he tells them about the 1972 Best Before date.

Let's get the time-line straight: the original saucer crashed in New Mexico in 1947 (after being shot down en route to a peace-conference that had, apparently, decided on genocide as the best means of securing a ceasefire). The US Army grabbed the pieces and survivors and built the Roswell base, and in 1953 sought to requisition the rescue mission that the aliens had sent.

This is where the Alliance of Shades intervened. Why they didn't respond to the initial crash is unclear, but 1953 is the stated date, in both series, for their arrival. Their mandate is to prevent anyone on Earth from knowing of the existence of life elsewhere. Unlike the fabled Men In Black, they have no connection to Earth's authorities and indeed see Roswell as an inconvenience. The Doctor visits Area 51 in 1958 and Mr Dread is shut down twice in a day, first by an arrow in his central processor and then by the Doctor's screwdriver. Area 51 is only publicly acknowledged to have existed in 1994 and the administrators before that had prevented successive presidents of the USA finding out about it. (Or, at least, "Dreamland" says they didn't tell Ike.)

Here's our first piece of handy ex-post-facto complicating data: since these adventures were broadcast, we have had a *completely different* alien conspiracy storyline involving totally different skinny men with tight suits who make people forget stuff. Series 6 has them in it a lot. The story (X6.1, "The Impossible Astronaut") begins with the Doctor helping President Richard M Nixon – and, as he leaves, advising the already notoriously paranoid leader to record all his phone calls. If the Alliance of Shades seeks to keep Earthlings in the dark about aliens, surely a broadcast message from one inserted into the most watched event in history counts as dereliction of duty. If the Silence infiltrated so much of Earth's past, how much back-up did the Alliance of Shades have to call upon? That's a bigger question than it sounds, because the most obvious candidates for their employer is the Shadow Proclamation – and they are so powerful, the Judoon aren't allowed to set foot on backwater planets like Earth except in dire emergencies.

Obviously, if the threat of sanctions from the Shadow Proclamation were enough to intimidate any advanced race from going to Earth voluntarily,

there would have been no need for UNIT, Torchwood, the Alliance of Shades or Sarah Jane Smith. A quarantine so strict that you can't even send your law-enforcement officers in is counter-productive, should anyone wish to break it. Half a dozen robots dressed as the Blues Brothers won't cut it. Either the Shadow Proclamation has mandated the Alliance of Shades to represent them, act in their interests and report back if a situation gets too big to handle, or these snappily-dressed Terminators are themselves in breach of Article Five of the Shadow Proclamation and constitute a hazard.

But so what if they are? It's not as if the Judoon can arrest them, unless they step off Earth for a few minutes. There's a further problem with the precise terms of the Alliance's brief and the Shadow Proclamation's definition of "natural development". Earth has been messed up by aliens so much, humans have developed as we see them today; every passing creature from the Jagaroth (17.2, "City of Death") to the Fendahl (15.3, "Image of the Fendahl"), the Daemons (8.5, "The Daemons"), the Exxilons (11.3, "Death to the Daleks" and the Osirians ("Pyramids of Mars") have stuck their oar in.

If, as we are clearly meant to assume, the creation of the Shadow Proclamation has the same relationship to the end of the Time War that the UN has to World War II, their policy is to keep things in a state of *status quo ante*, preventing any change from how things were pre-Time War (as far as they could tell, being themselves liable to change from temporal anomalies). If so, that's a problem, since alterations to Earth's future are happening all the time. Let's be honest, if there's any entity mucking up Earth's development, it's Torchwood – especially once they start drilling to the planet's centre and making everyone stop dying. Moreover, if the Alliance of Shades had been active in Britain in the mid-60s, as is implied, then the entire premise of *Torchwood: Children of Earth* (first contact with the 456 happens in 1965) is shot to pieces. There is clearly something else we aren't being told.

One big one is whether "Mr Dread" designates one specific robot or a rank, like commander or Super Voc (14.5, "The Robots of Death"). If the blond one in Arizona isn't the same one asleep in Ealing 50 years later, a lot of things become clearer. The one based at St Jude's Psychiatric Hospital has

continued on Page 369...

NASA was a fraud, but nonetheless covert organisations were rounding up alien infiltrators and anyone who knew about them (and a spaceship that had crashed near the site of the first nuclear tests in New Mexico).

That new-fangled interweb thing allowed people to see the autopsy photos of a stranded "Grey" (like the ones in that Whitley Streiber novel-that-pretended-it-wasn't-one) that *They* were trying to suppress. (And, yes, the whole AOL boom was the concatenation of ARPA's earlier military computer link-up and the World Wide Web developed at Cern, another uncomfortably science-ish international agency doing things the tinfoil-hat theorists couldn't understand and therefore suspected of being evil, plus the manifestly sinister Time-Warner. That didn't matter – information wants to be *free*, man.)

It was obvious: slanty-eyed homunculi were crossing the galaxies to perform anal probes on people in remote areas, simply because they didn't trust Bill Clinton. A diluted version of this crossed the Atlantic, so that you couldn't go to Camden Market or the Glastonbury Festival without people who thought that foam-rubber crowns and ginger dreadlocks went together promulgating this *X Files* baloney.

Ah, yes, *The X Files*. It may be hard for younger readers to fully gauge how popular this ludicrous hybrid of an anthology series of ghost-stories and a conspiracy thriller with an all-embracing plot-line *was* in the late 90s. Two FBI agents with nothing better to do investigated a string of mutually-exclusive bogie-men. The series toggled between reasonably stand-alone monster/witchcraft/human serial killer stories, and an ongoing Conspiracy storyline in which oh so many unclassified species or alien interventions were, apparently, part of a huge plan hinted at pseudonymous informants rather like Deep Throat in *All the President's Men* or the various people in Oliver Stone's *JFK*. It made the classic error of hinting that there was going to be an all-embracing "solution" to all the hares the Conspiracy stories set running, but forgetting quite a few of them, and teasing people for *too long* for anyone to care when the disappointingly garbled end finally came. Nonetheless, and despite the lousy feature films and revival(s) that fizzled out rather quickly, it's one of the most influential shows of the 1990s.

Belief in alien abductions went from a lunatic fringe to a commonly-held misapprehension during the mid-1970s, with even Jimmy Carter hinting that he'd seen something. Once American political life moved away from the Kennedy era's near-neurotic pursuit of reason and progress to gut-instinct and outright hogwash, anyone who doubted that "Greys" in Flying Saucers were coming for Midwestern sphincters was the freak. Millennial death-cultists called the Heaven's Gate sect died believing that mass suicide would get them a free ride on comet Hale-Bopp. This wasn't 1800, it was 1997.

The only other time we see the Alliance of Shades is in the *Sarah Jane* episode "Vault of Secrets". It would be easy to describe this as a pastiche of the *Men in Black* films, except that they, and the comic from which it was derived, were themselves parodies of a real urban myth about a sinister government agency covering up UFO sightings with amnesia-rays. The look of the MiBs was well-known enough for *The Blues Brothers* to incorporate it in 1980.

Consequently, from a *Doctor Who* point of view, Ford had plenty of room for a story. On the other hand, both the production and the in-universe dating were a year after *Indiana Jones and the Kingdom of the Crystal Skull* (2008). Not that the idea of a secret alien artefact warehouse in Nevada run by conspiracy-happy US soldiers, who want to use the little green men's technology against the Soviets, was exactly a new idea in the first place – but a story looking so derivative of a pastiche of earlier pastiches is simply unfortunate. 1958 was chosen partly to allow a gag about the guard on the door being Private Presley (his one line being a mumbled "thangyouverrimuch").

We would be remiss to overlook the prior usage of Area 51 in "Dreamland," the final story in the *Sarah Jane Smith* audio series. This was a Big Finish project from around 2004. There were two seasons, and more might have been planned, but "Dreamland" was released in April 2006 and thereafter the BBC had bigger plans for Elisabeth Sladen. David Bishop wrote a story combining a non-copyright version of the Mandragora Helix (14.1,"The Masque of Mandragora") with a cunningly disguised version of Virgin Galactic. The space tourist base is in Area 51, which is a complete red herring.

This story, by contrast, is by Phil Ford, who used diners in the desert (usually in Arizona) several times in the 2005 CG version of *Captain Scarlet*, often for hand-overs of stolen technology

What Happened in 1972?

continued from Page 367...

developed a very English sense of humour, sounding at times more like the Brigadier than Arnie. (There's one line at the end, "I need a holiday", that sounds like an anglicised version of a line from *Terminator II*, but he was deactivated in a sarcophagus when that film came out.) This Mr Dread drives a Ford Zephyr, the car allocated to police units in the early 1960s (the eponymous *Z Cars*) rather than whatever model would have been appropriate in 1972. (A Mk II Jaguar, as seen in "The Ambassadors of Death", driven by Benton and Tracy in 6.3, "The Invasion", and taken over cliffs in umpteen ITC adventure shows, perhaps.) The robots in "Dreamland" appear out of nowhere. If the Ealing Mr Dread could teleport, the story would have been over a lot sooner. If we posit a global network of robots scouring the world for people who've encountered aliens, their departure must be a recall from their masters.

A logical assumption is that the Shadow Proclamation knows about the potential temporal anomaly if UNIT's Scientific Advisor were shot while attempting to apprehend his old chum, the alien super-criminal who keeps bringing offworlders to Earth. We run into the old problem that if the Time Lords have been erased from this plane and "sealed off" somehow, then this must work retro-actively to include the Time Lords who exiled the Doctor here as well, so there is no possibility of these people informally advising the Shadow Proclamation of their plan. If, as we are assuming, the Alliance of Shades has more than a similar name to the Shadow Proclamation, then whatever caused the change in policy towards safeguarding Earth from being turned inside out during Grand Theft Spaceship is their own decision rather than a treaty agreement.

In fact, a lot of smaller anomalies occur when the logic of these agencies overlapping is examined. If there are robots with memory-wipes who want to prevent anyone on Earth knowing of aliens, and if these robots are active in New Mexico from 1953, then how is anyone at Roswell exempt? Mr Dread tracks down the crashed alien's husband, but in five years hasn't located the original ambassador/scientist. If a waitress has heard about this spooky government plan, then a robot with access to all local telecommunications would too. Colonel Stark interacts with two separate extraterrestrial cultures and gets out of the story with his memory intact. Indeed, he's been using a prototype amnesia drug on apprehended trespassers, so if the Alliance has sanctioned Pentagon sovereignty over this enclave, he might well have suggested refinements. The existence of Area 51 suggests that the Alliance of Shades has been in talks with the local authorities to clarify jurisdiction, so that J Edgar Hoover doesn't haul in any robots.

Mention of the FBI brings us to another hot topic of 70s fandom that's been revived lately: for whom does Bill Filer work? It's never actually stated in "Claws of Axos" (8.3) whether he is UNIT USA, CIA, FBI, UNCLE, Interpol or the Post Office. He's just "from Washington" – that would seem to rule out the FBI and CIA, but UNIT has an HQ in New York in X4.12, "The Stolen Earth". If we assume him to be UNIT (as the novelisation suggests), then Nixon's actions in "The Impossible Astronaut" make rather less sense. Even as aliens sabotage Nixon's (inherited) prestige project, he refuses to contact an agency with proven expertise in this field and instead goes for Canton Everett Delaware III, a disgraced ex-FBI agent.

Nixon, who was vice president under Eisenhower, seems unaware of the possibility of aliens, and after six months as president has no idea about UNIT – even though that agency has been in charge of several major international military interventions, and has responsibility for this sort of thing (something even "President-Elect" Winters knew). Perhaps Colonel Stark or Mr Dread wiped his memory. Nonetheless, even if Nixon has reasons to avoid using experts and coerce Delaware, there is an acknowledged global authority with whom the off-world MIBs can negotiate. This can't have taken four years, surely? It certainly can't have taken 15 years, during the peak period for alien intervention in Earth's affairs. The most logical solution is that there was an abrupt change in circumstances at some point between 1969 and 1972, followed by a sudden change in policy. Either circumstances on Earth shifted after nearly 20 years, or something went very awry on the cosmic scale.

The main things we know about in this period are on Earth, mainly southern England. This makes moving the Alliance's last outpost to one of the surprisingly high number of derelict complexes in the Ealing area a bit more sensible. Axos arriving with a distress signal on frequencies used by the terrestrial authorities seems to have legally cov-

continued on Page 371...

or data. Apart from looking exotic to anyone more familiar with Watford Gap Services or high street branches of Gregg's, they have the singular advantage of clean lines and repetitive design – meaning they're much easier to render as CG, as are straight roads in deserts. (See also the early episodes of *Lapins Cretins/Raving Rabbids*.)

The animated serial is, in a lot of ways, the most ambitious of the online "goodies" offered by the BBC's *Doctor Who* site before the devastation wrought by the BBC Trust. It originally ran as a serial in five-minute instalments, which explains a lot about the corkscrew plotting and grinding changes of gears whenever a cliffhanger was due. After this, almost all of the online computer-generated material was a bid to get a toehold in the games market and grab a slice of school IT lesson utility. Although it looks like a trial-run of the graphics needed for a game, this is a sequential narrative and runs without any input from the viewer. Precisely where they thought this would lead is unclear, as it was commissioned long after Tennant's resignation had been announced.

Oh, Isn't That...?

• *David Warner* (Lord Azlok). My, you *have* been sleeping soundly. He was one of that generation of actors who played misfits in 60s British films (the big-screen adaptation of *Morgan: A Suitable Case for Treatment* is a prime example), but he went to America and did three roles in *Tron*, then worked on umpteen franchises set on spaceships. So you'll maybe have seen him made up as a Cardassian torturing Captain Picard (after two turns in the big-screen *Star Trek* films, V and VI), looking for the Holy Grail on *Babylon 5* and doing odd things with gorillas and brains in jars in *The Man with Two Brains*. He also played an alternative version of the third Doctor for Big Finish – one who, after a slightly shaky start, got to take the Brigadier on joy rides across the universe while evading the Time Lords. (The Brigadier was, of course, played by Nicholas Courtney. Some things don't change.) Most recently, for our purposes, he was the New Romantic-obsessed archaeologist who defrosted an Ice Warrior in X7.9, "Cold War".

• *Clarke Peters* (Night Eagle) and the award for Weirdest CV of Any Actor goes to a New York native who's been in very British things (*Silver Dream Racer, Holby City, French and Saunders, Midsomer Murders*), very American things

(*Damages; Treme; Three Billboards Outside Ebbing, Missouri*), keeps getting cast as Nelson Mandela and did this story straight after *The Wire*.

• *Stuart Milligan* (Colonel Stark) will be back on our screens in "The Impossible Astronaut" as Richard Nixon. Before that, he was the annoying Blaine/Copperfield hybrid illusionist who employed the hero in *Jonathan Creek*.

• *Nicholas Rowe* (Rivesh Mantilax, a Gray). Shortly before this was broadcast, he played Malcolm Rifkind opposite Lindsay Duncan in *Margaret* (see X4.16, "The Waters of Mars") and was often cast as real-life ministers or dignitaries (e.g. *The Crown*). He may never live down his youthful break-out title role in *Young Sherlock Holmes*.

• *Lisa Bowerman* (Seruba Velak, another Gray). The main catgirl in 26.4, "Survival". She's better known to *Doctor Who* fans as the voice actress of Bernice Summerfield for Big Finish.

• *Georgia Moffett* (Cassie Rice). If you skipped X4.6, "The Doctor's Daughter"...

Things That Don't Make Sense The Doctor's reaction to seeing a big sign saying CAUTION BIOHAZARD is to say "I wonder what that is?" and press every button. He gets away with it.

But the most blatant error, actually, is why there's an entire room for the application of amnesia gas, and how it's attached to a ventilation shaft. Wouldn't that wipe the minds of the entire base personnel? For that matter, why flood an entire room with the gas, when they could just tie up their prisoners and overcome them with breathing masks?

We don't know the weird backstory by which the US military claimed an alien spaceship but its most critical component ended up on display in Cassie's diner. We can, however, marvel at how the Alliance of Shades are right on top of it *within seconds* as soon as the Doctor makes it function. Literally, seconds.

A situation in which aliens run roughshod in public, but are trying to stay out of the public gaze, is very hard to convey coherently. On the other hand, the production team deserves credit for avoiding stereotyping American soldiers as trigger-happy – even at the expense of their completely failing to shoot the Doctor and company at several points when it would have made sense.

The story's timescale is, er, problematic. Seruba crashes on Earth in 1947, Rivesh crashes the year

What Happened in 1972?

continued from Page 369...

ered the alien parasites. The biggest celestial player in this phase of human-alien relations is Azal. It might be that, far from having our best interests at heart, the *real* reason for anyone keeping Earth off the trade routes was to stop anyone getting their hands on Daemon technology. After this is removed, there might be grounds for thinking that humans were able to develop without supervision. Perhaps the Daemons were thought to be distorting influences that made Earth a potential threat to be cauterised if necessary. Either way, their removal from the stage after half a million years is the most significant change that anyone monitoring Earth over a similarly long period would notice.

So by 1972, there is an agreed global body with whom the Powers That Be can negotiate, grounds to believe that humanity can be trusted to develop unimpeded and an indigenous local procedure for keeping the populace unaware of the existence of offworlders. And, handily, there's a Time Lord on the premises who can supervise such a summit-meeting. There's at least one off-screen event of potentially cosmic significance that ought to have been conducted under the aegis of powerful entities – at the end of "The Daemons", the Master is apprehended, but by the time of "The Sea Devils", he's imprisoned in a stupidly low-security complex on Earth. The Time Lords haven't come for him, the representatives of the countless races he has damaged in his long criminal career don't want reparations and nobody's posted a reward for him anywhere in the universe. Earth's cordon sanitaire must be thoroughly established by now.

We can't surely be the only Level Five planet off the menu. If the rules prevent any other race making contact and humanity losing its innocence too soon, then the same rules must apply across the board. In which case, stories such as "Colony in Space" (8.4), "Kinda" (19.3) and "Planet of the Ood" (X4.3) are impossible, even though it's now Earth going around despoiling less-developed worlds.

---

after, and for the next ten years... er, not much happens. So that's a year for the Grey Aliens to be losing so badly, Rivesh thinks he needs a genocide-level weapon. Which he brings with him to Earth, where he's come to look for his wife, a high-ranked ambassador. To be fair, perhaps Rivesh wasn't that serious about the superweapon, and simply brought it with him to keep it away from everyone else – he certainly goes along with the Doctor's argument that they oughtn't to use it. Still, one does wonder why none of the other Greys, it seems, have similarly thought about tracking down their ambassador, nor the war-winning tech her husband possesses.

Who used the word "nuke" in 1958? Not waitresses, that's for sure. How does a Grey alien who's been in solitary since crashing know what a snail is? Why does the Doctor keep assuming that all of the USSR is Russia? (See 6.5, "The Seeds of Death".)

Critique Everything here is good except the humanoids.

Watching it in one lump is something of a drawback, given the need for frequent cliffhangers and plot-twists across a seven-part adventure. Still, this is at least a cure for longueurs – and, this once, they can make up for the bittiness by changing location frequently without constantly returning to the same sets. Where "The Infinite Quest" took advantage of this to showcase all the types of space-adventure *Doctor Who* can do, this one takes the Doctor's presence and inevitable alien threat as a pretext to tell all the kinds of 1958/Desert/Spaceship/Big Bug tales Jack Arnold used to make in one go. This is a story with a grin on its face, figuratively turning to the viewers and saying "we can do this now" the way such exuberant episodes as "Gridlock" (X3.3), "Remembrance of the Daleks" (25.1) or "The Christmas Invasion" (X2.0) did, and "The Pandorica Opens" (X5.12) and "The Day of the Doctor" (X7.15) will. Spaceships in dogfights with vintage USAF aircraft? No problem. Giant insects trash a town in Nevada? Almost an incidental detail. David Tennant and Georgia Moffett resuming the on-screen interaction that partially redeemed "The Doctor's Daughter" (X4.6)? Er...

The character animation and design is repellent. There's no other word for it. They all look like badly-painted wooden dolls and move like *Thunderbirds* puppets. No, worse, like Mike Mercury in *Supercar* (the Gerry Anderson show from the early 60s that never gets repeated). It's not just the lack of this Doctor's energy or grace, or that Cassie ought to be on the prow of a pirate ship, it's that the vocal performances don't match what we see. They got it right in "The Infinite Quest" – but this supposedly superior rendering lacks exactly the quality inherent in the word "animation". We see dead people. The colour-scheme imposed by the locale serves to further flatten the image, so that we've got less depth in this 3D cartoon than in the 2D one. Only set-pieces like the start or the machine-on-insect action really work visually.

Under this is characterisation that isn't quite right. Jimmy and Cassie are too modern, and Jimmy's occasional reminders about his people seem shoehorned in for bonus brownie-points. Colonel Stark is too clichéd to be taken seriously and the Doctor is just slightly out-of-key for this incarnation. Tennant's doing his best – and he's a veteran of this – but the rambling-on after people have asked him to explain twenty-first century references is the sort of thing Matt Smith would do better. It makes the Doctor seem merely eccentric rather than ironic and hip.

Thus, it's the insects who steal the show. Davies made several jokes in 2005 about how he'd never do anything like "The Web Planet" (2.5) but, then again, he said he'd not do anything like the start of "The End of Time Part Two" (X4.18). If you were watching on a big television as a family, or in episodes on a computer, this is the take-away image of the story. David Warner, still identifiable under all that distortion (sounding like the MCP from *Tron*, in fact) sells Lord Azlox as a character rather than as a mouthpiece for a slavering horde. As a spectacle to be watched supinely – as a viewer rather than moving the characters with a joystick – it's acceptable so long as none of the humanoids walk or try to smile. But the whole thing is like a walk-through video of a game.

The Lore

Written by Russell T Davies. Directed by James Strong. Viewing figures: (BBC1) 9.1 million (and an 88% AI), (BBC3 repeats) 1.4 (87% AI) and 0.7 million.

The BBC2 debut had 0.5 million viewers. Not bad for the Saturday Morning Kids slot shortly thereafter dumped in favour of cookery. On BBC1 on Christmas Eve, it did rather better: 0.73 million. The other BBC2 showing, the following February (15th) did half as well: 0.26 million.

Repeats and Overseas Promotion Technically speaking, the BBC2 transmission in December was a repeat as the story, in episodic form, was available to digital viewers a fortnight earlier. The 45-minute edit, as shown on BBC2 at 10.00am in between *What's New, Scooby Doo* and *ChuckleVision*, was released on DVD and is available on Region 1.

Alternate Versions This was shown in seven epi-sodes, each approximately six minutes long, on the BBC's digital-only "bonus" channel Red Button. These were in continuous rotation on 21st November, 2009, as well as being accessible on the *Doctor Who* web-page on bbc.co.uk (where they're still available, if you're in the UK and a licence-fee payer).

Production

• As with "The Infinite Quest" (A5), this was – for the cast and *Doctor Who* production team – more or less a Big Finish audio with pictures added. Gary Russell, who had directed many of these and supervised recording of that story, had been script-editing on *Doctor Who* and *The Sarah Jane Adventures*, so was on the staff and had worked with Phil Ford and David Tennant. Ford's background in CGI action-adventure series *The New Captain Scarlet* (where he wrote the first eight episodes and the bulk of the rest) made him ideal for the project. He had been working on *Sarah Jane*, but had just started work on X4.16, "The Waters of Mars".

Apart from that, this was a move towards the more complex 3D animation used in gaming. Other than a need to show it before Tennant's last episode (projected to be around Christmas 2009), there wasn't any limit to what could be done. Given the compromises forced on the team last time they did a story in America (X3.4-3.5, "Daleks in Manhattan"/"Evolution of the Daleks"), Ford grabbed the chance to do a story in Nevada, pastiching 50s paranoid Flying Saucer/giant insect films. The initial brief was for an hour's worth of adventure, so Ford contrived a plot to include a bit of every kind of story in that setting. An out-line of six ten-minute episodes was finalised in August 2008, with a one-off companion originally called "Jolene" (as in the Dolly Parton song) and her boyfriend Jimmy talking to his grandfather ("Limping Bear") in Shoshone.

• Littleloud, an animation studio in Brighton

that prior to this largely worked on computer games, did the animation. Some of their artists were Cosgrove Hall alumni. They had a background in interactive drama, so tended to make animation that responded in real-time, rather than taking up data-space with extraneous detail. They also made 2D animation for the equivalent of storyboards for the BBC team.

Incoming executive producer Piers Wenger, taking over from Julie Gardner as BBC Wales's Head of Drama, was increasingly the day-to-day liaison between the Davies/Gardner production team and Steven Moffat's "regency". He was interested in taking *Doctor Who* beyond television and into interactive gaming, available for free online in the UK (especially for schools as a resource for History teaching). We have touched upon some of the ways that the Corporation had been savagely removing some of the online support and facilities in the wake of internal paroxysms and drastic cost-cutting after mid-2008; this decision was a strong endorsement of *Doctor Who* as a continuing mainstay of the BBC's activities. We'll examine some of the consequences of this elsewhere (see **What are the Worst Merchandising Disasters of the Twenty-First Century?** under X5.3, "Victory of the Daleks"; **The Lore** for A5, "The Infinite Quest"; and **What were the Best Online Extras?** under X4.9, "Forest of the Dead").

• Ford delivered a first draft early in January 2009, still in the six ten-minute episode format, with slight tweaks to character-names and a different ending from what was made. (The Doctor banished all the Viperox with the "fusion-bar" genetic weapon without altering it to merely emit sounds; this looked a bit too much like genocide, if you weren't paying attention.) The escape in the mine-cart was added, after the fashion of *Indiana Jones and the Temple of Doom*, apparently because Davies had assumed that was why a mine-cart was in the story at all. The jukebox ploy was a later substitution for the Doctor making foodstuffs overheat (including eggs popping).

• Gary Russell assembled a cast mainly from people with whom he'd worked on Big Finish plays. This, of course, included Tennant and Georgia Moffett – her mum is Sandra Dickenson (so an American accent came fitted as standard), and she had worked on a Big Finish called "Red Dawn" ten years before. By now, she was dating Tennant. Casting the Shoshone characters was tricky, but Canadian actor Tim Howar is a quarter Native American. Clarke Peters was his grandfa-

ther – and the publicity played up the connection with *The Wire*, now belatedly showing on BBC2 and getting a lot of attention. The real coup, however, was David Warner, himself a Big Finish veteran. The other big player was Stuart Milligan, still best known then for *Jonathan Creek*. Of more interest to Big Finish fans was Lisa Bowerman, the audio incarnation of spin-off series protagonist Bernice Summerfield (see X4.8, "Silence in the Library").

• Before 2012, only a small proportion of BBC viewers had access to digital content. One of the enticements to make people invest in the technology ahead of the analogue switch-off was the Red Button, a sub-channel carrying additional content (sort of like a broadcast DVD extra). This was usually ten-minute clips in constant rotation for a limited time. "Dreamland" was premiered on this on 21st November, 2009 in episodic form; the plan was to have the next live-action episode at roughly the same time or, better yet, that very day. You will note that the action of "The Waters of Mars" (also predominantly by Ford) was set exactly 50 years later. The Red Button was also the venue for the commentary by Ford and Russell when the one-episode version was shown on BBC1 on Christmas Eve.

• As part of the build-up for this, the BBC's *Doctor Who* website ran a blog about the making of the story, with video messages, storyboards, script excerpts and Q&As. It also formed a small part of the website's Adventure Calendar, a December-long drip-feed of build-up to the Christmas Special. Doug Sinclair assembled the music, from cues by Murray Gold. Most of these were from Series 4 (with "Silence in the Library" especially prominent), although a few over-familiar moments were trimmed. As it turned out, the episode was launched online and on Red Button the weekend after "The Waters of Mars", got its analogue TV premiere on BBC2 amid routine children's television and finally reached BBC1 (not the sole criterion for things being canonical, but a big help) on the morning before the more widely-trumpeted "The End of Time Part One" (X4.17).

ABOUT TIME 2008-2009

1. A broadcast of *This is Spinal Tap* bleeped out the word "pump", for example. On the other hand, every showing of X5.3, "Victory of the Daleks" retains the line "Keep buggering on". BBC America started out trying to be like the real thing but anything too BBC-ish – such as *EastEnders*, *Snog Marry Avoid?*, reruns of *Dad's Army*, *Storyville* or rugby – were ignored or dropped and replaced with endless reruns of *Star Trek*, peppered with bursts of *CSI: Miami*.

2. No, really, it's a station formerly called "UKTVComedy" and, like all the former stations with the prefix "UKTV", it was partly-owned by the BBC and mainly ran 70s and 80s Beeb shows. A lot of these renamed themselves in 2008 and "Dave" was picked partly to reflect the blokey good-humour (it styles itself as "The home of witty banter", which means it reruns *QI* and *Never Mind the Buzzcocks* a lot), but mainly, it seems, because its big hit was repeats of *Red Dwarf*. Eventually it started making its own programmes, including a relaunch of *Red Dwarf*.

3. *CSI* gave us a *cri de ceur* on this topic in the episode "Space Oddity", written by former *Trek* writer and *FarScape* producer Naren Shankar. In this, the fans of a thinly-disguised *Star Trek* were up in arms about a "re-imagining" (itself a thinly-disguised *Battlestar Galactica*), but the murderer turned out to be a thinly-disguised Constance Penley (see **The Semiotic Thickness of What?** under 24.4, "Dragonfire"). Depicting any fan who objects to a drastic junking of all the things that made it worth watching as a potential psycho, in the season where Laurence Fishburne replaced William Peterson and a whole load of soapy stuff about the investigators' personal lives crept in, might have been a pre-emptive move. Nonetheless, it came in the era when old kitsch such as *Flash Gordon* and *The Bionic Woman* got the *Galactica* treatment (see X4.15, "Planet of the Dead"), for no very good reason.

4. The first *Doctor Who* story to win a Hugo, "The Empty Child"/"The Doctor Dances" (X1.9-10) admittedly wasn't against up much opposition, as the ballot included two episodes from the same series ("Father's Day" and "Dalek"), plus a *Battlestar Galactica* and, um, the awards ceremony from the previous year's Hugos. But the relevant category was a new one, and finalists from the first time this "Short Form" award was hived off from an overall Best Dramatic Presentation included Gollum's acceptance speech from the MTV Awards. The category seems almost to have been devised specifically for Joss Whedon after episodes of *Buffy* kept showing up amid feature films, so the revamped *Buffy*-lite *Doctor Who* dominated the awards after Whedon moved on to the less-popular *Dollhouse* – and *Enterprise* was canned.

5. The Finnish band "Nightwish" might have launched, or received, legal action over their track "Song of Myself" vis-à-vis Murray Gold's "I am the Doctor" had anyone in Finland bothered watching *Doctor Who*. The album whence the Finnish version came is a film-score called *Imaginaerum*, the CD release was in 2011 and the film on 23rd November, 2012. The 2004 album by Nightwish has a picture of a weeping angel on the cover... Gold's stirring accompaniment for Matt Smith yelling has also been used as the "Last Time" music for the French remake of BBC's biggest export, *The Great British Bake-Off*, broadcast under the title *Le Meilleur Patissier*.

6. Les frères Bogdanoff burst back into the public gaze twice in the early twenty-first century, first for their (disputed) authorship of Ph.D theses on topology and spacetime that posit a phase before the Big Bang, then for their somewhat extreme facelifts. British readers might want to imagine Gaz Top and Fred Dinage claiming to have cracked cold fusion and proved the existence of God, then being surgically altered to resemble *Spitting Image* puppets of themselves. We're struggling to think of a US equivalent – Svengoolie and Vampira working at the Large Hadron Collider is the closest we can come up with, but that's not quite bonkers enough. How about Hannah Hart, of *My Drunk Kitchen* and BBC America's *Doctor Who* promotion, performing a liver transplant?

7. As we mentioned in **What was Children's Television Like Back Then?** under 3.7, "The Celestial Toymaker", British kids in the 60s and 70s saw a lot of redubbed film series, often with the same handful of actors apparently stood in a cupboard in Dean Street to record the anglicised versions. Sometimes they just had a narrator talking over the (still-audible) original soundtrack. If you were lucky, they'd provide a cooler new theme-tune (as with *The Aeronauts* or *White*

Horses) or a whole new score (as with the achingly evocative and often-sampled *The Adventures of Robinson Crusoe*). By the 1990s, these were being ridiculed by *The Fast Show* and *On the Waterfront* (a 1990 kid's Saturday Morning show notable only for Russell T Davies-scripted re-redubbings of *The Flashing Blade* along the lines of *The Staggering Stories of Ferdinand de Bargos*), but the better ones got DVD releases this century. Part of the appeal is the slight sense of disbelief that something as, shall we say, "ambient" as *Belle and Sebastian* was about as good as it got for summer holiday viewing – there's a boy, a dog, some snow and that's about it. The recent French film version adds Nazis and Resistance and is in colour, but was somehow less mesmeric.

8. Chickens are often used as a way of "normalising" an unfamiliar setting. Sometimes, as with 18.5, "Warriors' Gate" or 1.5, "The Keys of Marinus", this flies in the face of reason, but as early as 1.4, "Marco Polo" and most obviously in 10.2, "Carnival of Monsters", this is how the TARDIS travellers start to feel at home in a historical period. In the 1970s, the Film School at Hollins University, Virginia, tried a radical rethink of its teaching methods and devised a study-programme entirely based on looking out for the chickens in any film. Compared to the Griemasian diagrams and Lacanian analysis to be found in *Screen* and other scholarly journals of the era, this is relatively sensible.

9. Trying to convey Frankie Howerd – yes, it was spelled that way – in print is a mug's game. His delivery was more vocal than verbal, with over-modulated "hmmm"s and "ooooh"s, arched eyebrows and use of "Missus" punctuating relatively routine innuendos. If you can bear it, the atrocious 1979 film *Sergeant Pepper's Lonely Heart's Club Band* has him mugging as Mean Mr Mustard, but to get the full impact try *The Ladykillers* (not the pointless Coen Brothers remake, but the original with Alec Guinness) or *Carry On Doctor* (see 5.3, "The Ice Warriors") or just listen to any film where Alan Rickman was playing for laughs. No kidding: *Dogma*, *Galaxy Quest* and *The Hitchhiker's Guide to the Galaxy* have Rickman doing the same Frankie Howerd impression every schoolboy in Britain used to attempt. Or you could try watching *Up Pompeii!* and marvel that this got better ratings than *Monty Python*, which started at the same time.

10. Anthea Bell, the English translator, did this in between translating Kafka, Freud and WG Sebald. Her dad more or less invented the cryptic crossword.

11. It really is an eye-opener. After his surprise hit with *Altered States*, the last thing anyone expected from Ken Russell was a deliberately cheap horror film based on a justly-forgotten Bram Stoker story. It was his last cinematic release, and he spent the remainder of his career trying to get funding to expand glorified home-movies made on video. That's what this looks like, although, with the exception of one badly-converted green-screen scene originated on VT, it's on film and made on location in Derbyshire. Imagine, if you will, a 90s BBV fan-video based on a hybrid of 20.2, "Snakedance"; 7.2, "Doctor Who and the Silurians"; and a bit of 19.7, "Time-Flight". Then chuck in Hugh Grant as near-as-dammit Captain Mike Yates of UNIT and Capaldi as a kilt-wearing character-we-can't-legally-call-the-Doctor. Let the two male leads have a floppy-hair stand-off, while their respective blonde love-interests compete for who can melt into the background fastest when the vamp's on screen (Amanda Donahoe, looking as if she knows exactly how bad a dent the film will make in her CV). And along the way, remind everyone of Russell's earlier, more accomplished works, notably *The Devils*. Stir in Catherine Oxenberg saying "Ooh, me spotted dick!" in a very bad Northern accent. Then it gets silly. We'll leave you to find out how bagpipes fit in, but be kind: everyone had to start somewhere and Neill Gorton's make-up effects improved a lot after 1985.

12. The attempted "explanation" in X7.16, "The Time of the Doctor" makes nonsense of the attempted resolution of Series 6, unless the Silence are monumentally stupid – or forget instructions given to them by another of their kind – and have unwittingly picked the worst possible place to pre-emptively close off an unwanted timeline. At time of writing, how many essays we'll need to fix all this is unclear. Every time-traveller we've encountered lately treats history as a place to visit and witness, except Krasko in X11.3, "Rosa".

13. Once again, Davies is disavowing his interest of That Kind of Series, but we can't help thinking of the Pak'Ma'Ra in *Babylon 5*, who were

squiddy and yukky and often used as comic-relief, but turned out to have a psychic song they performed as a ritual when they thought no other races were around. They used a hand-held glowing sphere to talk English. The series also made the public mistrust of human telepaths and the cynical exploitation of them as war-weapons a thread, with even an Underground Railroad (explicitly called that). The first half of Series 5 rammed home the Israel analogy with a massively dull storyline concerning what the irritating leader called "telepaaaaths" claiming asylum and causing trouble in the station's very own ghetto.

14. As you might expect, there's an equation to figure out how long it would take if you knew the mass of both bodies, the perigee, apogee and dissipation function of the moon and what's called the "Love number" – oddly, Steven Moffat omitted to give us any of these.

15. There's another possibility, that the planet we see is A) flipping enormous, B) very close to Trenzalore and C) orbiting the star at 45 degrees to the ecliptic plane. This is just about possible, but the effect of the nice stable orbit Trenzalore needs to have the set-up we see – and to get any of our hypothetical accounts for this working for more than a few local years – is too disruptive for the rest of what we see and hear.

16. A shop that vends the nation's other favourite post-pub fast-food, doner kebabs (X11.1, "The Woman Who Fell to Earth"). These aren't like shish kebabs. Confusingly, a form of these has caught on in some parts of America, but called "gyro", which means something else to us. If you've not encountered this, think of a spit-roast rotated 90 degrees to vertical, with a cone of laminated beef and mutton that is shaved off. These slices, usually two or three, go into a pitta bread "pocket" with a salad, chili sauce and perhaps a falafel. You may get US-style fries or, if you're lucky, proper chips. And Ayran, which is like a salty lassi.

17. The sheer number of similar organisations in television series from 1965-75 makes the head spin. That UNCLE was a template for UNIT is obvious from the first draft of "Spearhead From Space", in which Liz Shore (sic) is taken into a shabby run-down shop like Del Florio's tailors

and, just like The Man From UNCLE, it's a front for a swish complex with offices and uniformed secretaries. Something similar happened with the Harlington-Straker film company, conveniently based at Elstree Studios, which was the front for SHADO in UFO. Less subterfuge was used by the eponymous Department S, the Department for the Measurement of Scientific Work (Doomwatch) or BIPS, the pan-European version in the Franco-German Aux Frontieres du Possible. Add to this the independent alien-hunters such as Simon King (Counterstrike), David Vincent (The Invaders), Drew and Anne (Undermind) and even Steed and Mrs Peel when vegetation ran amok ("The Man-Eater of Surrey Green"; see 13.6, "The Seeds of Doom") and it's amazing aliens ever bother trying to invade. Or maybe the various extraterrestrials bumped into each other too often. Many of these series were in rerun after the initial run, so it was possible to see several secretive acronymic organizations hidden behind perfectly ordinary businesses in the space of a weekend c.1970. So perhaps it's all of these agencies that have been "unified".

18. The fictitious Kent seaside resort expecting to be Hitler's point of entry into England, but defended by elderly tradesmen in Dad's Army. This has as good a claim as any to be the most nearly perfect sitcom, mixing minutely-observed social nuance with outright slapstick and multiple catchphrases – in a situation where the stakes couldn't be higher, but petty personal rivalries still somehow come to the fore at the worst possible times. There was recently a film version for the US market, recast rather oddly. It came and went. The series ran at around the same time as the Pertwee-UNIT episodes and Monty Python, so they are all associated together by anyone watching at the time. Truth be told, Walmington-on-Sea Home Guard are a bit better-drilled than some of the extras playing UNIT troops, and some of the comedy explosions are more impressive than the supposedly serious ones in the "Action by Havoc" scenes in Doctor Who. As the UNIT era progressed, many of the writers gave the Brigadier some of Captain Mainwaring's mannerisms – 10.1, "The Three Doctors" is especially noticeable.

19. You read that right: the pilot episode, "The Cage", wasn't shown until 1992. "Miri" and "The Empath"; both got shelved (warranting a special

VHS release in 1985) because the BBC bosses thought it was primarily a children's show. They promoted it as such, with amusing consequences we address in the next essay. "Plato's Stepchildren" was considered too sadistic to be shown (and also, let's be honest, it's a bit crap even by Season Three *Trek* standards). The BBC had little idea what to do with the series and moved it all around the schedules, settling on Monday at 7.20 after a few experiments with putting it on in the *Doctor Who* slot of Saturdays at around 5.15, before Simon Dee or whoever and just after cartoons or puppets, but was later moved to Friday instead of *Nationwide*. It began in a completely arbitrary order, with "Where No Man Has Gone Before" and "Amok Time" (because people acting out-of-character is the best way to introduce everyone) then "City on the Edge of Forever", "A Taste of Armageddon", "Mudd's Women" and "Tomorrow is Yesterday". As we said in the notes to "The War Games" (6.7), the actual series, in black and white until BBC1 started colour transmissions, was disappointing compared to the comics, being just a lot of old men standing around talking on unconvincing desert sets. It's amazing the series caught on at all...

20. No doubt some idiot will now pipe up and mention the "Alice" robot in "Shore Leave" or the eponym in "The Squire of Gothos". These both score 4.5 on the Cheadle Scale – a metric named in honour of Don Cheadle's performance in the *Ocean's Eleven* series, which supplanted Dick Van Dyke as the SI unit of crap American attempts at sounding English. The nearest to an accent you'd hear anywhere in the UK was Joan Collins trying to pass for a New Yorker in "City on the Edge of Forever".

21. Something to throw to the nutters who contend that the whole Apollo Program was a fake done in a studio: the BBC's then state-of-the-art studio simulations were less good than the stuff in 7.3, "The Ambassadors of Death". Even then, because there are some real numpties out there, they flashed up a caption saying STUDIO SIMULATION. There may have been people who thought that *The Clangers* was a documentary but we suspect that rational adults can tell late 60s special effects when they see them. We needed these visual aids because, despite the thrillingly advanced technology involved, there were only satellites in low orbits for television feeds across

the Atlantic – so any live link-up, such as the Beatles doing "All You Need is Love" or the Mexico Olympics, were carefully timed for when the comsat was in sight. Therefore, James Burke and Patrick Moore – or Peter Fairley and Lew Gardiner on ITV – had to vamp furiously until we could see anything, and we had an on-screen countdown to when a live transmission would be available.

22. It has the same Utopian "internationalism" as *Trek* or "The Moonbase" (4.6), but this time everyone speaks German and it's obviously German actors playing characters with Japanese, Italian or English names. It has a starship and its crew enough like the almost-contemporary *Star Trek* to make it function as a prequel, or pre-emptive parody. Each hour-long episode of the German series had a budget almost what the BBC spent on Anneke Wills's hair the same year, but was endlessly ingenious in how to solve basic problems such as distracting the viewers during info-dumps with choreography and goldfish. Every single episode has the maverick hero Cliff Allister McLane being given orders, and him finding devious ways to avoid being caught disobeying them and thereby saving humanity – 1960s Germany had issues with people blindly obeying orders. Let's just say he gets through a lot of spaceships. It has a much better theme-tune than *Trek* and some freaky looking aliens and robots, but it was planned to only have seven episodes. However, the tie-in books kept the story going for 145 volumes, still selling well.

23. At press time, the Jane Austen note is still coming – see X8.6, "The Caretaker"; X9.1, "The Magician's Apprentice" and X9.10, "Face the Raven". Four hand-crafted £5 pound notes were issued by an art-gallery in 2016 with tiny engravings of Austen on them, each worth about £50,000, and a plastic tenner with her on will be issued shortly after this book. And there's a two-pound coin. Choosing a subject on our banknotes entails asking who makes us feel good about being British, but also how difficult the portrait is to forge. People with elaborate hairdos, facial hair or lots of lace are preferred, although at least a tenuous link to fiscal policy – Newton was head of the Royal Mint – is also a good move. Since you ask, Sir John Houblon owned a house in Threadneedle Street that became the Bank of England.

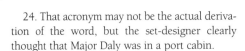

24. That acronym may not be the actual derivation of the word, but the set-designer clearly thought that Major Daly was in a port cabin.

25. Our sources for this include *Family and Kinship in East London*, Butterworth and Weir 1957, available in Penguin and a set-text for O-Level Sociology. Their dismay at the term's currency is palpable even as they strive for objectivity (pp 20-21). We could also cite various prissy relatives who blanched at the term.

26. Oh, lumme! Brucie was a staple of our television since the 50s and was, in 2008, main host of *Strictly Come Dancing* (retitled for umpteen overseas versions, notably *Dancing with the Stars*). He had a prominent chin, a string of catch-phrases and a slightly odd habit of pausing to think of his next quip by making an odd "zizz-zizz" sound. See Volumes 3 and 4 for more on his significance to *Doctor Who*.

27. The first pictorially-based merchandising was launched even before the return of the Daleks. Sweet cigarettes were candy sticks, made from cornstarch and sugar, in white cylinders with a pink tip on one end. On cold mornings, your breath-mist could complete the illusion that you were actually smoking one. They came in small boxes very like cigarette cartons and, like the real thing, had collectable illustrated cards of cricketers, sports cars, film stars or wildlife. The Cadet company launched a series of 50 illustrated episodes of a *Doctor Who* adventure in which the Doctor is caught up in a Dalek-Voord conflict over rare minerals in Earth's solar system. Giant mushrooms are involved, so it's possible Terry Nation was at least consulted on the story. For much of the adventure, the Doctor abandons his waistcoat and cloak and dresses like a member of Devo, the better to wrestle with Voord and put on diving gear. He negotiates a truce, so the Daleks lay on a banquet for him in the last card.

28. People who already know this are all looking up from their copies of this book and shouting *Die, hideous creature, DIE!*. Mad Norwegian extends its apologies to anyone sitting next to them on the bus. People who don't already know that this is what the Troughton Doctor is shouting when frying a giant robot spider with his laser-pistol are invited to read the 1967 strip "Master of Spiders" and consider that, on telly at the same time, he could have really used one of those against the Chameleons in 4.8, "The Faceless Ones".

29. It starts out like 8.4, "Colony in Space", with the Doctor "and his pretty assistant, Jo" popping off to the planet Quorus and seeing what they think is a Primitive, but is actually a dinosaur. Not a robot with claws, but a real-ish one (and slightly better than the ones in 11.2, "Invasion of the Dinosaurs"). They then stumble across the Master picking up blue crystals (11.5, "Planet of the Spiders"). Using a device like the one he built in 9.3, "The Sea Devils", he controls the beast and sets off towards Earth. As head of MacMaster Electronics, he infiltrates a power-station on the Yorkshire Moors (you know, like 7.2, "Doctor Who and the Silurians") and uses his Metebelis crystals and radio-control to make the dinosaur grow even bigger, trashing the reactor-plant. The police don't believe the Doctor's explanation of this, so he gets into Bessie (a copyright hassle-in-waiting) and sets off for London for permission (because having UNIT involved would cost Nestlé more money). Godzilla chases him until he flips a switch on Bessie and... well, we're not sure what it does, but the monster leaves him alone (so maybe the static Anti-Theft from 7.3, "The Ambassadors of Death"). As he returns to Yorkshire, the Master uses the crystals to teleport Godzilla to Trafalgar Square (possibly by means of TOMTIT; 9.5, "The Time Monster") and deploys his remote to conjure ultrasonic sounds and send it trashing more recognisable monuments. (Ultrasonic fear-control? That's 10.3, "Frontier in Space", that is.) Luckily, the Doctor has an ultrasonic whistle (the one he used for K9?) and interferes with the controls, until the monster walks into a power-line and dies. The Master shouts "Curses" (yes, really) and escapes, while Jo gets the entire army to the base and rounds up all his hypnotised goons. The end.

30. Anyone who doesn't know is now invited to guess what the Big Finish anniversary story-arc was. And, yes, it was the Master doing it this time too.

31. There are some who claim that because they have never encountered this idea, it cannot ever have existed. One of the present authors

grew up in a household partly paid for by television repairs, and the number of sets wrecked by children trying to feed the characters peas or sweets was alarming.

32. As Miranda Hart became so crucial to BBC1's elaborate plans, to the extent that Danny Cohen reportedly forbade her to be in *Doctor Who* – see X7.0, "The Doctor, the Widow and the Wardrobe" – we might be in trouble if we use the word *Hyperdrive* in conjunction with BBC planning and remind everyone that neither she nor the actor Kevin Eldon (X11.9, "It Takes You Away") is infallible. And we're definitely not going to use the term *Top Gear...*

33. Assorted has-beens and wannabes are carted off to the Australian outback, and the public votes them off depending on how game they were to undergo humiliation, usually involving being smothered in insects or made to eat marsupial offal. Baker's go at this coincided with the augmented reissue on DVD of 22.2, "Vengeance on Varos", in which a corrupt society votes to torture people through interactive television. The irony didn't go un-noticed.

34. The more fannish among us may, on first transmission, have found this behaviour familiar from Klieg in "The Tomb of the Cybermen" (5.1) and thought that Professor Song was to be a new arch-villain. It was only that leak in *The Sun* that prevented everyone online from pronouncing that she was the Rani, as happens with any unfamiliar female character. With a decade's perspective and Michelle Gomez playing the Master as a *different* loopy ex of the Doctor's, it's now hard not to see Anthony Ainley's version of the Doctor's nemesis as a trial run for River, embarrassing disguises and everything. Given that she's caused the Doctor, and thereby the entire universe, grief, misery and apocalyptic breakdowns on three successive season-finales, she's actually a more successful antagonist for him than even Davros. He only *threatened* to destroy all matter and time – see this season's finale – and rewrite the Doctor's timeline (12.4, "Genesis of the Daleks"). She really did all of these and personally murdered him twice in Series 6, looking him in the eye on both occasions.

35. We know that the statistics of how many Americans were in London for the 2012 Olympics in no way represent how few Americans anyone living in that bit of East London encountered during the fortnight. Museums and other attractions reported a drop in visitor numbers, having catered for an expected increase, so the Londoners who'd been put off by previous encounters with rude tourists flocked to see the famous bits of their city, some for the first time.

36. *Zero Hour!* is the film that formed the basis for *Airplane!* Thus Leslie Nielsen's career-reviving stint as Dr Rumack included a lot of dialogue originally spoken by Geoffrey Toone (9.2, "The Curse of Peladon"; A1, *Doctor Who and the Daleks*) as Dr Baird.

37. We won't mention *Cosby*, the diluted and now unbroadcastable remake of *One Foot*, if you won't. *Father Ted* was shown in New York after 9/11 as a form of therapy, but never went mainstream.

38. The get-rich-quick investment of the 90s, supposedly. Lean, nutritious meat from birds corralled in Belgium. Some people got very rich selling shares in non-existent farms, then went to prison, but as yet the produce has yet to be available even in France.

39. Test Card F, launched with the colour BBC2 service in 1967, took up a lot of screen time in the 1970s. Amid the patterns designed to allow engineers to adjust for coil convergence and contrast was a circular photo of the BBC's chief engineer's daughter, Carole Hersee, losing at noughts and crosses to a stuffed clown. The point is, she's in a red dress on a blue background and with her arms and face to test for reliable skin-tones, and stood in front of a chalk-board with white chalk on a black background with an X at almost dead centre and circles around it. Her half-smile and Alice-band made this child about the most famous "unknown" girl in Britain and Bubbles, the clown-doll, the focus of a generation's nightmares – if you're to believe the kind of comedians who make jokes about Daleks not being able to climb stairs and rude names in *Captain Pugwash*. So using her as the Angel of Death taunting Sam Tyler was an obvious move, and the series ended with her switching off our tellies. Equally obviously, being something supposedly scary to all kids everywhere, she landed up in a Steven Moffat *Doctor Who* episode – X5.2, "The Beast Below" – along-

side a lot of other off-the-shelf dream iconography.

40. Except... they discovered that an administrative error by the vicar meant they weren't legally married after all, hence a whole straight-to-video spin-off where they went to Las Vegas to get hitched. This may explain why they were planning to move to Blackpool when Vera died.

41. Although why English people were talking about *Jeopardy* and "Class One Drugs", why a John Lennon obsessive failed to notice that short-haired Gwyneth had the address "9, Menlove Avenue" and how someone who makes sandwiches for a living can afford to live in that bit of Fulham did exercise many UK filmgoers.

42. If this looks like privileging one iteration of a set-piece plot idea that we've just said was all over the place in the late 90s, consider that the same BBC Wales team had just done an episode of *Torchwood* that was also over-affectionately close to an episode from the same *Buffy* season, only this time it was Tosh getting telepathy for a week: compare Toby Whithouse's "Greeks Bearing Gifts" with *Buffy*: "Earshot" by future *Torchwood: Miracle Day* author Jane Espenson.

43. If you grew up in Britain in the 70s or 80s, the Sheffield Crucible – the appropriately-named theatre in the heart of the most famous steel-manufacturing city in the world (see Series 11) – is almost instinctively linked to televised snooker championships. Snooker was popular with television repairmen and the engineers developing colour transmission as it has spheres of pure colour, especially the difficult-to-get-right yellow, against a green background, slow-moving people and objects and occasional fast-moving balls. BBC2 would devote hours on end to this baffling activity and millions of people would watch, entranced. Nobody is sure why. Some of them even bought the hit single "Snooker Loopy" by equally inexplicably successful duo Chas and Dave. Investigate at your own risk.

45. The BBC hived all their children's output onto two dedicated digital channels, CBBC and CBeebies, the latter for tinies and the former for anyone under 12. This is odd, as the only other age-defined channel was BBC3, for 16-25 year olds, and that went off-air just in time for *Class*.

Officially, the BBC doesn't make anything with 13-15 year olds in mind; conversely, the independent Channel 4 don't seem to make programmes for anyone else these days. The recent moves have meant that *The Sarah Jane Adventures* would never have been commissioned these days. However, Davies has been making *Wizards vs Aliens* for CBBC and *Old Jack's Tales* for CBeebies. Earlier, there was a *Jackanory Juniors* strand launched in early 2007: John Barrowman was one of the storytellers, as were a few other people who'd turn up in *Doctor Who* along the way. As one of the relatively few key players in British television to champion children's output, Davies has been a vocal critic of recent government and BBC decisions, and has been active with Anna Home's Children's Media Foundation.

Links between *Doctor Who* and *Jackanory* are many and peculiar, but the obvious starting-point is that all but two former Doctors read for it before 1995 – Colin Baker and William Hartnell were the exceptions – and Paul McGann did it in 1992, with *The Phantom Tollbooth*. Peter Davison read *The Sheep-Pig* by Dick King-Smith, later filmed as *Babe*. As we mentioned, Tom Baker did *The Iron Man* in 1985, while both Troughton and Pertwee did Scandinavian folk-tales in the early 70s. Sylvester McCoy did two special projects for the series after he'd been the Doctor: one was a spin-off where viewers got to contribute to stories by phone and, for the 25th anniversary, he read *Charlie and the Chocolate Factory*.

46. The trailer for the film has an "in a world..." voice over by none other than Tom Baker. He advertised all sorts of stuff in the late 80s.

47. *EastEnders* has a lot of this – up to and including half of Albert Square going to Cornwall to see the total eclipse of August 1999, or one of the residents being in the Olympic opening ceremony; X2.11, "Fear Her" tried this less well. Most bizarrely, the VE Day anniversary was marked by a flashback episode incorporating scenes supposedly in 1945. They also have kitchen-sink discussions of the deaths at Hillsborough Stadium, or the 2005 bus bombings, grafted in at short notice. Radio 4's *The Archers* has a better track-record on this, being radio and thus quicker to amend when events mess up developing storylines. However, their attempts to weave the Glastonbury Festival into the plots about Tom Archer's organic pig-farm

sausages were less successful. Most alarmingly, they ran their own festival, LoxFest, and braided in stories of made-up acts causing trouble with an episode where the Pet Shop Boys appeared for real. *Coronation Street*'s 40th anniversary was marked by two episodes, one pre-recorded as normal but with Prince Charles visiting the lingerie factory, and then a live one. Ten years later, Phil Collinson, by then producer, pulled a few strings and got The Mill to make a spectacular event – as it turned out, a tram wreck and not the Cyberking trashing Wetherfield. It is perhaps kinder not to dwell on how *Emmerdale* sought to grab headlines.

48. We're saying "British" as if Scotland, Northern Ireland and Wales reliably showed the episodes at the same time as England. For much of the time this was so, but even when they didn't, the smaller national BBC channels showed it at the same time each week. For example, BBC Wales showed Jon Pertwee's last year on Sunday evenings but regularly, to avoid clashing with religious programming and rugby; sorry if this sounds like an ethnic stereotype, but we checked with an old *Radio Times*. Even then, they never showed an episode before it had been seen by the majority English viewers. The BBC2 Sunday repeats that were hoped to stem Series 9's ratings decline weren't shown on the same day in Scotland.

49. Our favourite is the misguided 1975 John Wayne vehicle *Brannigan*, which US audiences thought was over-long, overblown and underwhelming but, to us, looks like the weirdest episode of *The Sweeney* ever – after the mid-way point, where the Duke is in a Ford Capri chasing Tony Robinson on a moped, it just gets sillier. That Wayne, in a series of sweater-vests, looks increasingly like Stephen Fry just adds to the fun.

50. Of course, digital effects from today can also be inserted inside reworked film from way back. The 2|Entertain DVDs of *Doctor Who* offered the option of "improved" effects for old stories but tactfully, and often kitschily "in keeping" (e.g. the hokey 50s-style flying saucer attack in 2.2, "The Dalek Invasion of Earth" to replace the hokier 30-style one of the original broadcast). It's odd how little difference it makes, even with something like 15.2, "The Invisible Enemy".

51. A cumbersome but modish bicycle from early-70s Britain; those who couldn't afford this status-symbol pretended to be really upset. Like the near-contemporary Bond Bug, it tried to look sunshiney and Californian and could thus only be ridden for three weeks in any year.

52. In Britain, especially in the 1970s, calling people "Duckie" was what caricature gay men did, so our take on *Pretty in Pink* – not a title likely to skewer this misconception – was that the irritating lad hanging around Andie was unsure which way he swung, not a trainee serial-killer as Americans all seem to think these days. With John Hughes so keen to strip-mine British pop culture, it would be odd if this detail eluded him. Of late, the US-style Prom has started to catch on in some parts of the UK, a fad mainly promoted by people who rent out stretch limos or, believe it or not, stretch SUVs.

53. In those days, the BBC were obliged by Equity to mention when cast-members of a play or comedy were appearing in the West End. As a number of radio plays featured performers appearing in a farce that ran for 16 years, almost every Radio 4 production seemed to have "_____ is now appearing in *No Sex Please – We're British*", no matter how august the work we had just heard. This is why Fit the Fourth of *The Hitchhiker's Guide to the Galaxy* has John Marsh telling us that "Zaphod Beeblebrox is now appearing in *No Sex Please – We're Amoeboid Zingat-Ularians*" at the Brantisvogan Playhouse".

54. There are reports that, in the mid-90s, there was to have been a stage version of this with six-time *Doctor Who* guest-artist and *Grange Hill* icon Michael Sheard as the Doctor. It couldn't be any more theatrical than the broadcast version, let's be honest. It's also sometimes reported that Milton Subotsky was planning a Marinus-with-Daleks as the third Peter Cushing film, but it's more likely to have been just "The Chase" with some drastic editing and more Mechanoids.

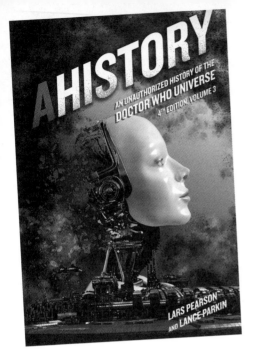

About Time 4
The Unauthorized Guide of Doctor Who (Seasons 12-17) [Second Edition]

Next Time on *About Time*...

Tat Wood and **Dorothy Ail**'s intellectual *tour de force* of *Doctor Who* – examining each story in the social and political context in which it was made, including several madcap theories about it along the way – continues with a re-re-examination of Tom Baker's first six seasons, with benefit of everything that's happened since the first time we looked at this particular patch of ground in (good Lord) 2004. So, before the advent of the BBC Wales series.

As before, some Critiques will be argued by both the Prosecution and the Defence.

New essays in this volume include "What Were the Most Reliable Set-Elements?", "How Did Binro Do It?", "Did *Blakes 7* Wreck Everything?", "What Were the Daftest 'Only' Weaknesses of the Cybermen?", "Has the Time War Started Yet?", and "Did Familiarity Breed Respect and In These Shoes?"

About Time 4: The Unauthorized Guide to Doctor Who (Seasons 12-17) **[Second Edition]**
ISBN: 9781935234258

www.madnorwegian.com

1150 46th Street
Des Moines, Iowa 50311
madnorwegian@gmail.com

who made all this ?

Tat Wood is now really glad his mum moved to Swansea in the 90s.

Recent geopolitical shenanigans have forced him to swap the cosmopolitan lifestyle of Volume 8 for a contemplative, Thoreau-like existence half an hour from Providence. This location may explain why the word "eldritch" keeps cropping up in this book. He's resigned to being the only person in a 50 km radius who shouts ARSENAL! when someone coughs, but can't get used to the bizarre units of measurement. Periodic returns to what he thinks of as normality have allowed him to buy vast amounts of obscure British films and telly on DVD (the Thoreau thing's a work-in-progress) attend an under-the-radar convention in Lyon and experience Jodie Whittaker's *Doctor Who* debut on BBC1 as nature intended. Yes, he had his tea on his lap. No, he doesn't mean a cuppa.

Favourite story in this volume, surprisingly, "Partners in Crime". Least favourite, unsurprisingly, "Planet of the Dead".

Since 2017, **Dorothy Ail** has written several cheerfully unprintable novels as warm-up for the real thing, discovered a fondness for rugby, and developed an unfortunate addiction to the ongoing Brexit soap opera. Since starting work on this volume, she's tried escargot and moules frites (chouette), eel pie (echh), ackees and saltfish (gimme dat) and Dover Sole (*how* much?). She is considering applying for the post of chef for Captain Nemo.

Favourite story from this volume: "The End of Time". Least favourite: "Planet of the Dead".

Lars Pearson has served as publisher and editor-in-chief of Mad Norwegian Press for (gulp) almost 20 years now. The older he gets, the more he realises that kindness begats kindness, and cruelty begats cruelty.

Favourite story from this volume: "Silence in the Library"/"Forest of the Dead". Least favourite: "The Sontaran Stratagem"/"The Poison Sky".

Mad Norwegian Press

Publisher / Editor-in-Chief / About Time Content Editor
Lars Pearson

Senior Editor / Design Manager
Christa Dickson

Associate Editors
Joshua Wilson, Carrie Herndon

Cover
Jim Calafiore (art),
Richard Martinez (colors)

The publisher wishes to thank... Tat and Dorothy, for all the sweat they exude to make this series come to life; Lawrence Miles; Christa Dickson; Carrie Herndon; Jim Calafiore; Richard Martinez; Josh Wilson; Lance Parkin; Paul Kirkley; Robert Smith?; Gary Russell; Shaun Lyon; Jim Boyd; Andrew Cartmel; Emma Wood; Barnaby Edwards (the New York one, not the Dalek one); Shawne Kleckner; Braxton Pulley; Jack Bruner; Heather Reisenberg; Emma Wood; Allison Trebacz and that nice lady who sends me newspaper articles.

The authors wish to thank... Simon Black (our Man in Havana), Daniel O'Mahony (our man in the field) and Giles Sparrow (our man on Mars).

1150 46th Street
Des Moines, Iowa 50311
madnorwegian@gmail.com
www.madnorwegian.com